The National Park Architecture Sourcebook

The National Park Architecture Sourcebook

Harvey H. Kaiser

Princeton Architectural Press
New York

Published by
Princeton Architectural Press
37 East Seventh Street
New York, New York 10003

For a free catalog of books, call 1.800.722.6657.
Visit our web site at www.papress.com.

Editor: Lauren Nelson Packard
Designer: Jan Haux

Special thanks to: Nettie Aljian, Sara Bader, Dorothy Ball, Nicola Bednarek,
Janet Behning, Becca Casbon, Penny (Yuen Pik) Chu, Russell Fernandez,
Pete Fitzpatrick, Wendy Fuller, Clare Jacobson, Nancy Eklund Later, Linda
Lee, Laurie Manfra, Katharine Myers, Jennifer Thompson, Paul Wagner,
Joseph Weston, and Deb Wood of Princeton Architectural Press —Kevin C.
Lippert, publisher

Library of Congress Cataloging-in-Publication Data
Kaiser, Harvey H., 1936-
  The National Park architecture sourcebook / Harvey H. Kaiser. —1st ed.
     p. cm.
  ISBN 978-1-56898-742-2 (alk. paper)
  1. Architecture—United States—Guidebooks. 2. Historic buildings—United
States—Guidebooks. 3. National parks and reserves—United States—
Guidebooks. I. Title.
  NA705.K35 2008
  725.70973—dc22
                    2007044230

Table of Contents

List of Parks

Alabama
Tuskegee Airmen National Historic Site
Tuskegee Institute National Historic Site

Alaska
Klondike Gold Rush National Historic Park
Sitka National Historical Park

Arizona
Casa Grande Ruins National Monument
Chiricahua National Monument
Fort Bowie National Historic Site
Grand Canyon National Park
Hubbell Trading Post National Historic Site
Montezuma Castle National Monument
Petrified Forest National Park
Pipe Spring National Monument
Tumacácori National Historical Park
Tuzigoot National Monument
Wupatki National Monument

Arkansas
Fort Smith National Historic Site
Hot Springs National Park
Pea Ridge National Military Park

California
Cabrillo National Monument
Death Valley National Park
Eugene O'Neill National Historic Site
Fort Point National Historic Site
Golden Gate National Recreation Area
John Muir National Historic Site
Lassen Volcanic National Park
Manzanar National Historic Site
Point Reyes National Seashore
San Francisco Maritime National Historical Park
Sequoia and Kings Canyon National Parks
Yosemite National Park

Colorado
Bent's Old Fort National Historic Site
Dinosaur National Monument
Florissant Fossil Beds National Monument
Hovenweep National Monument
Mesa Verde National Park
Rocky Mountain National Park

Connecticut
Weir Farm National Historic Site

District of Columbia
Ford's Theatre National Historic Site
Frederick Douglass National Historic Site
Lincoln Memorial
Mary McLeod Bethune Council House National Historic Site
National Mall
Rock Creek Park
Sewall-Belmont House National Historic Site
Thomas Jefferson Memorial
Washington Monument
White House (President's Park)

Florida
Biscayne National Park
Castillo de San Marcos National Monument
Dry Tortugas National Park
Fort Caroline National Memorial
Fort Matanzas National Monument
Gulf Islands National Seashore
Timucuan Ecological and Historic Preserve

Georgia
Chickamauga and Chattanooga National Military Park
Fort Pulaski National Monument
Jimmy Carter National Historic Site
Martin Luther King, Jr., National Historic Site

Hawaii
Kalaupapa National Historical Park
Pu'uhonua o Hònaunau National Historical Park
USS *Arizona* Memorial

Idaho
Nez Perce National Historical Park

Illinois
Lincoln Home National Historic Site

Indiana
George Rogers Clark National Historical Park
Indiana Dunes National Lakeshore
Lincoln Boyhood National Memorial

Iowa
Herbert Hoover National Historic Site

Kansas
Brown v. Board of Education National Historic Site
Fort Larned National Historic Site
Fort Scott National Historic Site
Nicodemus National Historic Site
Tallgrass Prairie National Preserve

Kentucky
Abraham Lincoln Birthplace National Historic Site
Cumberland Gap National Historical Park
Mammoth Cave National Park

Louisiana
Cane River Creole National Historical Park
Jean Lafitte National Historical Park and Preserve

Maine
Acadia National Park

Maryland
Antietam National Battlefield
Chesapeake and Ohio Canal National Historical Park
Clara Barton National Historic Site
Fort McHenry National Monument and Historic Shrine
Fort Washington Park
Hampton National Historic Site
Thomas Stone National Historic Site

Massachusetts
Adams National Historical Park
Boston African American National Historic Site
Boston National Historical Park
Cape Cod National Seashore
Frederick Law Olmsted National Historic Site
John Fitzgerald Kennedy National Historic Site
Longfellow National Historic Site
Lowell National Historical Park
Minute Man National Historical Park
New Bedford Whaling National Historical Park
Salem Maritime National Historic Site
Saugus Iron Works National Historic Site
Springfield Armory National Historic Site

Michigan
Father Marquette National Memorial
Isle Royale National Park
Keweenaw National Historical Park
Pictured Rocks National Lakeshore
Sleeping Bear Dunes National Lakeshore

Minnesota
Grand Portage National Monument
Mississippi
Gulf Islands National Seashore
Natchez National Historical Park
Vicksburg National Military Park
Missouri
George Washington Carver National Monument
Harry S. Truman National Historic Site
Jefferson National Expansion Memorial
Ulysses S. Grant National Historic Site
Wilson's Creek National Battlefield
Montana
Glacier National Park
Grant-Kohrs Ranch National Historic Site
Nebraska
Homestead National Monument of America
Scotts Bluff National Monument
Nevada
Lake Mead National Recreation Area
New Hampshire
Saint-Gaudens National Historic Site
New Jersey
Edison National Historic Site
Morristown National Historical Park
New Mexico
Aztec Ruins National Monument
Bandelier National Monument
Chaco Culture National Historical Park
Fort Union National Monument
National Park Service Region III Headquarters Building
Pecos National Historical Park
Salinas Pueblo Missions National Monument
New York
Eleanor Roosevelt National Historic Site
Fire Island National Seashore
Fort Stanwix National Monument
Home of FDR National Historic Site
Martin Van Buren National Historic Site
National Parks of New York Harbor
Castle Clinton National Monument
Federal Hall National Memorial
Gateway National Recreation Area
General Grant National Memorial
Governors Island National Monument
Hamilton Grange National Memorial
Lower East Side Tenement Museum
Saint Paul's Church National Historic Site
Statue of Liberty National Monument
Theodore Roosevelt Birthplace National Historic Site
Sagamore Hill National Historic Site
Saratoga National Historical Park
Theodore Roosevelt Inaugural National Historic Site
Vanderbilt Mansion National Historic Site
Women's Rights National Historical Park
North Carolina
Cape Hatteras National Seashore
Cape Lookout National Seashore
Carl Sandburg Home National Historic Site
Wright Brothers National Memorial
North Dakota
Fort Union Trading Post National Historic Site
Knife River Indian Villages National Historic Site
Theodore Roosevelt National Park
Ohio
Cuyahoga Valley National Park
Dayton Aviation Heritage National Historical Park
First Ladies National Historic Site
James A. Garfield National Historic Site
Perry's Victory and International Peace Memorial
William Howard Taft National Historic Site

Oklahoma
Chickasaw National Recreation Area
Oregon
Crater Lake National Park
Lewis and Clark National Historical Park
Oregon Caves National Monument
Pennsylvania
Edgar Allan Poe National Historic Site
Eisenhower National Historic Site
Fort Necessity National Battlefield
Friendship Hill National Historic Site
Gettysburg National Military Park
Gloria Dei (Old Swedes' Church)
Hopewell Furnace National Historic Site
Independence National Historical Park
Steamtown National Historic Site
Thaddeus Kosciuszko National Memorial
Valley Forge National Historical Park
Rhode Island
Touro Synagogue National Historic Site
South Carolina
Charles Pinckney National Historic Site
Fort Sumter National Monument
South Dakota
Jewel Cave National Monument
Mount Rushmore National Memorial
Wind Cave National Park
Tennessee
Andrew Johnson National Historic Site
Fort Donelson National Battlefield
Great Smoky Mountains National Park
Texas
Fort Davis National Historic Site
Guadalupe Mountains National Park
Lyndon B. Johnson National Historical Park
San Antonio Missions National Historical Park
Utah
Arches National Park
Bryce Canyon National Park
Capitol Reef National Park
Cedar Breaks National Monument
Zion National Park
Vermont
Marsh-Billings-Rockefeller National Historical Park
Virginia
Appomattox Court House National Historical Park
Arlington House, The Robert E. Lee Memorial
Booker T. Washington National Monument
Colonial National Historical Park
Fredericksburg and Spotsylvania County Battlefields
Memorial National Military Park
George Washington Birthplace National Monument
Maggie L. Walker National Historic Site
Manassas National Battlefield Park
Petersburg National Battlefield
Richmond National Battlefield Park
Shenandoah National Park
Wolf Trap Park for the Performing Arts
Washington
Fort Vancouver National Historic Site
Mount Rainier National Park
Olympic National Park
San Juan Island National Historical Park
West Virginia
Harpers Ferry National Historical Park
Wisconsin
Apostle Islands National Lakeshore
Wyoming
Devils Tower National Monument
Fort Laramie National Historic Site
Grand Teton National Park
Yellowstone National Park

Acknowledgments

This book is the culmination of more than twenty years of travel and research on the historical architecture in national parks. My first venture out West in the early 1980s resulted in *Landmarks in the Landscape: Historic Architecture in the National Parks of the West*, published by Chronicle Books in 1997, and supported by a grant from the National Endowment for the Arts. Subsequently, *An Architectural Guidebook to the National Parks: California, Oregon, Washington* and *An Architectural Guidebook to the National Parks: Southwest, Arizona, New Mexico, Texas* (Gibbs Smith Publishers, 2002 and 2003, respectively) produced additional research material. A grant from the Graham Foundation for Advanced Study in the Fine Arts enabled me to study the historical architecture of the Rocky Mountain and Plains states.

This book and the earlier volumes are a tribute to the countless staff and volunteers who contribute to the preservation and interpretation of the precious cultural resources of the National Park System. I always felt relieved during the tens of thousands of miles of travel when I would come within sight of the familiar National Park Service (NPS) white on brown trailblazer signs. The courtesy and interest shown by rangers and volunteers for my challenging project was the difference between discouragement and enlightenment. I wish I had started documenting names early on in my journeys, but unfortunately I did not. To those many NPS staff and volunteers I met along the trail, I owe you a deep-felt appreciation for your dedication and unselfish sharing of information. Interviews were graciously tolerated and access was provided to files that yielded information, often in aged documents and photos not found elsewhere.

In addition to the members of the NPS in the field, there was invaluable assistance from Randy Biallas, Assistant Associate Director, Park Cultural Resources, as well as staff at the NPS Harpers Ferry Design Center in identifying cultural resource locations and refining the list of parks included in this book. I regularly came across research by Laura Harrison Gates and respect her enormous pool of knowledge about the parks and their historic structures, as well as her admirable writing skills.

During the final editing of the manuscript, it was considered prudent to send out individual essays for each of the 216 parks included in the book to park superintendents for review and comments. The complete immersion in the history of a park's cultural resources is nowhere more profound than at the local level and, here, we were made aware of the legacy and myths of sometimes conflicting research and information erroneously carried over from one publication to another. Again, the NPS staff responded, often correcting errors in facts assumed to be accurate and reliable because of their repetition, and providing invaluable observations that were missed while visiting a park.

My son, Robert P. Kaiser ably assisted in the management of the intricate process of distributing the essays, recording their path, and following up on progress.

I am indebted to Clare Jacobson and Kevin Lippert at Princeton Architectural Press for accepting the idea of the book. The editorial work of Lauren Nelson Packard ably guided development of the manuscript. The book's design is due to the creative hand of Jan Haux.

My wife Linda was helpful with her keen sense of the use of language and was tolerant of the endless journeys to distant places, often even sharing in the driving. Her skills at map reading are par excellence, sometimes making the difference between a right or wrong turn and avoiding a day of wasted travel.

Introduction

The historical architecture of the United States National Park System is a vast and varied collection of structures. The cultural resources set amidst the magnificent scenic splendor of the "crown jewels" and urban locations in the nearly 400 parks in the fifty states, Puerto Rico, American Samoa, and Guam are treasures of our nation's heritage. Buildings in this collection include extraordinary icons of patriotic symbolism, grand lodges of the west, forts and fortifications, Spanish missions, mystic abandoned southwest ruins, and both spectacular and prosaic structures commemorating a life or events of historic significance. They appear in the midst of metropolises and small villages, in the Rocky Mountain states, the Southwest, the heartland states, Appalachia, and the shores of the Atlantic and Pacific Oceans, the Gulf of Mexico, and the Great Lakes. They are designated as units of the National Park System because they identify us as a people and memorialize moments of historic importance in our past.

The parks and their buildings described in this book's concise essays represent cultural features that help explain who we are as a nation. John Ruskin, in *The Seven Lamps of Architecture*, aptly framed the notion of preserving and interpreting those features:

> *Speaking of old buildings, they are not just ours. They partly belong to those who built them and partly to all generations of mankind who are to follow us....What other men gave their strength and wealth to accomplish ... belongs to all their successors.*[1]

A minister friend once introduced a talk on the National Park System's historical architecture by saying "the parks contain the God-made and the man-made. We are going to hear about the man-made, and let your imagination fill in the rest." The purpose of presenting the "man-made" in this book is to enlighten and inform travelers to the parks about a rich trove of historic structures in the public domain. Since 1916, the National Park Service Organic Act (16 U.S.C. 1 2 3, and 4), has had the responsibility "to conserve the scenery and the natural and historic objects and the wildlife therein and to provide for the enjoyment of the same in such manner and by such means as will leave them unimpaired for the enjoyment of future generations."

Another important purpose for this sourcebook is to encourage advocacy and to ensure that our historic legacy remains unimpaired for the enjoyment of future generations. Without launching into a diatribe about politics and adequate funding, we must observe that inadequate funding for repair and rehabilitation has created a multibillion dollar backlog of deferred maintenance. This backlog, unless corrected by a partnership of public and private reinvestment threatens the public's future experience for a memorable visit to enjoy sound and safe buildings, roads and bridges, and utilities in good working condition. A diligent public, elected officials, and national park support groups are absolute necessities for stewardship of our National Park System's cultural heritage.

The ambition to write a comprehensive overview of National Park System historical architecture needed the essential ingredient of a publisher who would agree that a wide audience would welcome a single volume with concise and informative essays. I was fortunate that Clare Jacobson and Kevin Lippert at Princeton Architectural Press accepted the idea and helped to shape the book into a sourcebook. Selection of parks and structures for *The National Park Architecture Sourcebook* began in 2002 with a screening process using *A National Park System Map and Guide*, *The National Parks Index* and the National Park Service (NPS) *List of Classified Structures*. Although I had visited many parks in the western and intermountain states to conduct research for previous books, beginning in 1983, and as a casual tourist to parks in the eastern seaboard, a structured process was mandatory for the many visits necessary for onsite observations, photography, interviews, and document review and collection.

After writing several books on the western parks I was familiar with the tasks of mapping out flights, road routes, working around seasonal weather conditions, and planning to reach parks during open hours and finding the right outdoor lighting for photography. Consultation with NPS staff in Washington and the NPS Harpers Ferry Design Center, and superintendents and staff at several parks began to shape a list that hovered around 215 parks. The tentative number of parks spanned a map of the lower forty-eight states from corner to corner, from Florida's Dry Tortugas in the southeast, Maine's Acadia National Park in the northeast, Washington's San Juan Island National Historical Park in the northwest, and California's Cabrillo National Monument in the southwest. Hawaii and Alaska were added to the list to complete the picture of the National Park System in all states, excluding Delaware, which does not have a national park.

A note for the reader about the numerous designations within the National Park System that often confuse visitors may be helpful. These include national park titles, such as national historic site, national historical park, national memorial, national monument, national seashore, national lakeshore, national preserve, and national battlefield park. The names are created in the congressional legislation authorizing the sites or by the president and are generally self-explanatory, while others have been used in many different ways because of the diversity of resources within them. In recent years, both Congress and the NPS have attempted to simplify the nomenclature and to establish basic criteria for the use of the different official titles.

As information on the parks was compiled, the scope of the task that lay ahead became clear. The research and writing of 216 separate essays was formidable. Daunting as a prospective commitment of time and travel, the challenge that it hadn't been tried before, in a single book, was an inspiration that needed structuring. Thus, the reader will find the book is organized into seven regions on a state-by-state basis: Far West and Pacific, Southwest, Rockies and Plains, Midwest, South, Mid-Atlantic, and New England. All states are included with at least one park, with the exception of Delaware, which has no National Park System units.

While not every national park is included, I strove to be as comprehensive as possible. Connecting the dots from park to park became a five-year-long journey that eventually reached around ninety-five percent of the parks contained in this book. I appreciate the NPS staff, especially in those offshore island parks that I was unable to visit, for their information and support in reviewing draft essays. Many long hours on the road to explore parks along the Atlantic, Pacific, Gulf, and Great Lake shores, through the great expanses of the western, intermountain, and Great Plains states on cross-country drives often were ably assisted by my wife Linda, a nonpareil map reader. Although the unrelenting goal was to visit historical structures to experience them for personal observations and photography, we did savor the profound beauty of many of the park's natural features.

The experiences of travels could fill another book, but I only mention a few: falling into the ice-choked Merrimack River to get a closer look at Lowell National Historical Park buildings; a three-day tour of Apostle Islands lighthouses on George and Judy Haecker's boat; Jeanne Adams's tours of Yosemite; the concert by a flock of red-winged blackbirds at a sunrise at Bent's Old Fort; the generosity of Lester and René Crown in assisting in visits to Union Pacific buildings at the Grand Canyon, Bryce, and Zion National Parks; the solitude during a long hike in the searing heat of Chaco Canyon; overcoming severe claustrophobia at the entrance to the "cave" parks; the awe at the Wright Brothers' genius when pacing off the markers of their Kitty Hawk first flights; the spine-tingling booms of the Stars and Stripes at the ramparts of Fort McHenry; and my daughter Christina's guided tour of Yellowstone.

I have made every attempt to include accurate and up-to-date information on the parks and historical architecture. Superintendents and staff at many parks assisted immeasurably in the review of many park essays to correct and update our research as well as material contained in publications and Internet sources. However, changing conditions are inevitable over time for vulnerable buildings from the time of my visit until publication and into the future. I recommend the reader refer to the NPS web site (www.nps.gov) for specific park information when planning a visit.

[1] John Ruskin, *The Seven Lamps of Architecture* (London: E.P. Dutton, 1963).

Far West and Pacific

Alaska

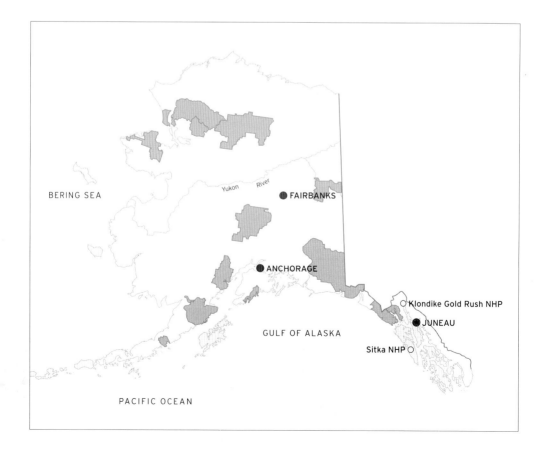

Klondike Gold Rush National Historical Park

Skagway, Alaska

→ www.nps.gov/klgo

→ The park's main unit is located in the Skagway area of the Alaska panhandle. Other Alaska units include the White Pass and the Dyea-Chilkoot Trail, both located nearby. A separate unit is in Seattle. The Skagway unit is eighty miles north of Juneau by air or water and one hundred ten miles south of Whitehorse by road.

Golden North Hotel (courtesy NPS)

The discovery of gold in August of 1896 by Skookum Jim Mason, Dawson Charlie, and George Washington Carmack in a tributary of the Klondike River in Canada's Yukon Territory set off the last of the great gold rushes. The route to the gold-bearing streams near Dawson started six hundred miles away at Skagway and crossed into Canada at the top of either the White Pass Trail or Chilkoot Trail to the Yukon River's headwaters at Bennett. From there the army of gold seekers built boats to haul their year's supply of food—an absolute must—and gear down the Yukon River to the goldfields at Dawson. By 1897–98, Skagway was at its peak population of eight to ten thousand. The previous population of mostly transients staying at Moore's homesteader cabin, built in 1887, and prospector tents quickly grew into a frontier mining town with hotels, saloons, and stores.

Almost as quickly as the town grew, it shrank to a population of fewer than three thousand by 1900 after an 1899 gold discovery across Alaska near more accessible Nome on the Bering Sea. Skagway's decline continued to about five hundred in 1930 and was later revived as a World War II supply base. Revival of the mineral industry in the Yukon in the 1960s, with resources shipped through Skagway and the restored White Pass, allowed the Yukon Route Railroad (a Gold Rush legacy) to reopen by 1988 as a popular tourist attraction. Through all the vicissitudes of time, a core of late 1890s buildings remained intact, many restored by the National Park Service (NPS). The Klondike Gold Rush National Historical Park's thirteen thousand acres authorized in 1976, after more than forty years of efforts, includes the Skagway historic district and portions of Chilkoot and White Pass Trails.

Broadway is at the center of the historic district—two city blocks by six. The architecture is in the vernacular of frontier America—mostly false fronts, an imposing hotel with onion dome (the Golden North, 1898), and a former railroad depot (also 1898) serving as the National Park Service (NPS) visitor center. The architectural legacy is modest. More important than any individual building is the character of the place. Found here, as captured in the words of Robert Service and the twenty-one-year-old Jack London, are the spirit of the Yukon and the experiences of miners on the bone-chilling climbs over the Chilkoot and White Pass Trails.

One gold rusher, Ezra Meeker crossing the Chilkoot Pass in 1898, wrote:

Frequently every step would be full while crowds jostled each other at the foot of the ascent to get into single file, each man carrying one hundred to two hundred pounds on his back....As we looked up that long trough of glistening ice and hard-crusted snow, as steep as the roof of a house, there was not one of us who did not dread the remainder of the day's work.

Meeker made it over the pass to reach Dawson with nine tons of his "outfit." There is no record of his luck at gold mining.

Prominent with its golden dome at Broadway and Third Avenue, the Golden North Hotel, built in 1898, is no longer operating as a hotel. Originally two stories, the building was moved in 1908 by horse and capstan to its present location. A third story and was also added at that time. Purchased privately in 1997, a renovation restored the structure; each of the thirty-one rooms were dedicated to gold rush families and filled with their mementos and antiques. Captured in a display of photographs are memorable views of chains of climbers over the Chilkoot Pass.

The restored old Railroad Depot and General Office Building symbolize Skagway's durability and permanence. Originally two separate buildings, the depot opened in 1898 and the office building was completed in 1900. The buildings were joined to handle the expanding baggage and freight business. The hectic times of 1898 produced a hurriedly constructed depot building. From the second-floor bay windows the dispatcher could see the tracks that once wrapped around the cut-away southwest corner and headed north on Broadway. Unlike the depot, the later office building was carefully designed by an architect, originally with walls and ceilings of plaster on lath. Quality woodwork, stained and varnished, provided a handsome restored interior.

A fascinating architectural curio—and possibly Alaska's most photographed—is the two-story Fraternal Order of the Arctic Brotherhood building. Founded by eleven goldfield-bound travelers en route from Seattle to Skagway, "Camp Skagway No. 1" was erected in 1899. For reasons unknown, the next year, fraternity members created the intricate facade decorated with 8,333 pieces of driftwood.

Today, thousands of tourists arrive by cruise ship or by the long overland highway route to walk the site connected with Alaska's gold rush days. Camera-toting travelers now visit the places where once miners jostled their way over the Chilkoot Trail and White Pass Trail and on to the goldfields. The NPS preservation of the Skagway Historic District and White Pass National Histsoric Landmark and the Chilkoot Trail and Dyea Site National Historic Landmark offer a glimpse into this exciting episode of American history.

Sitka National Historical Park

Sitka, Alaska

→   www.nps.gov/sitk

→   The park is located in Sitka in the southeast Alaska panhandle on Baranof Island (on the outer coast of Alaska's Inside Passage). Access is only by sea and air.

Russian Bishops House (courtesy NPS)

The park preserves and interprets an exotic combination of Russian-American Colonial architecture, the site of a fortification from the 1804 battle between the Russians and Tlingit Indians, a collection of Alaskan totem poles, and a scenic rainforest. The 113-acre park located in and adjacent to Sitka is Alaska's oldest and smallest national park unit (established as a national monument in 1910, and designated a national historical park in 1972).

Russian influence in this part of Alaska originated in 1799 with the establishment of a fur trading post by Aleksandr Baranov, chief manager of the Russian-American Company, at Redoubt Saint Michael located seven miles north of Sitka. In 1802, the native Tlingit Indians moved to end Russian colonization and attacked and wiped out the Russian outpost. Two years later the Russians returned with a force of nearly one thousand Russian and Aleut Indians and defeated the Tlingits at Kiksádi Fort. The new company headquarters in New Archangel (today's Sitka) became the capital for Russian America and the shipping point for the company's trade in furs, fish, ice, and lumber until depletion of the fur seal and sea otter population by the mid-nineteenth century. The United States' 1867 Alaska Purchase ended Russian presence in North America.

One unit of the park located on a heavily forested peninsula projecting into Sitka Sound and divided by the Indian River contains the site of the 1804 Battle of Sitka fort and a self-guided totem pole trail. Fascinating Tlingit and Haida cedar totem poles rise above the grand spruce and hemlock trees along the scenic coastal Totem Trail, leading visitors to the fortification and battle site on the shore of Sitka Sound. Among the poles are originals installed in 1902 and 1906; others are copies by the Civilian Conservation Corps between 1939 and 1942, and others are done more recently.

The park's second unit interprets the National Historic Landmark Russian Bishop's House, one half-mile from the park visitor center. The two-story building, completed in 1843 by the Russian American Company, served as the seminary and offices for the Russian Orthodox Church in Alaska. A National Park Service restoration completed in 1988 returned the building to its 1853 exterior appearance, interior spaces, and furnishings. The house is easily recognizable by its bright yellow paint, evenly spaced white-painted window frames, and red standing-seam metal hip roof. The main section of the sixteen-room building (42 by 63 feet in plan) is a squared-log structure with an unused roof truss system; two attached side galleries of timber frame construction, under sloping shed roofs, have vertical board-and-batten siding. The first floor displays exhibits interpreting the Orthodox Church, the Russian-American colonial period, and the house's history. On the second floor, restored with original and period furnishings, are the bishop's living quarters, and Chapel of the Annunciation, the private worship place of the bishops.

The house is one of only four surviving Russian colonial structures in North America. The others are in Sitka (Building 29/Tilson House); Kodiak, Alaska (Erskine House/Russian-American shop); and California (the Rotchev House at Fort Ross State Historic Park).

Russian Bishops House, Chapel of the Annunciation (courtesy NPS)

The park's visitor center contains interpretive exhibits on Tlingit history and cultural traditions, and houses the Southeast Alaska Indian Cultural Center with artists at work. The visitor should experience other historic structures in Sitka's business district about a half-mile from the main park unit. A replica of onion-domed 1848 Saint Michael's Cathedral, destroyed by fire in 1966, contains a remarkable collection of icons, and the Sheldon-Jackson Museum and Isabel Miller Museum reward the visitor with a view of native Alaskan, Russian, and American cultures.

California

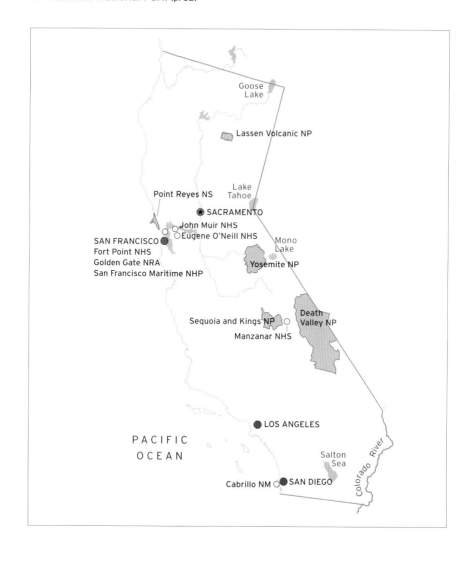

Cabrillo National Monument

San Diego, San Diego County, California

→ www.nps.gov/cabr

→ Cabrillo National Monument is within the city of San Diego at the end of Point Loma. Driving from Interstate 5 or Interstate 8, take the California 209 (Rosecrans Street) Exit; turn right on Cañon Street; turn left onto Catalina Boulevard. Follow signs to the park.

Old Point Loma Lighthouse

San Diego's 160-acre Cabrillo National Monument, established on October 14, 1913, celebrates the first landing of Europeans on what is now the western shore of the United States. Sailing under the Spanish flag, explorer Juan Rodríguez Cabrillo ventured up the West Coast of North America and arrived at San Diego Bay on September 28, 1542. Protecting San Diego Harbor on a headland reaching out into the Pacific Ocean, Point Loma was long occupied by the military and is the site of one of the last of the eight original West Coast lighthouses built in the 1850s.

In the days of intensive whaling (1850s to 1885–86), the lighthouse served as a beacon at the entrance to San Diego Bay, and increasing traffic north up the coast to San Francisco. The site selected by the U.S. Coastal Survey in 1851 as one of a chain of navigational aids along the Pacific shore is 422 feet above sea level, overlooking the bay and the Pacific Ocean. Construction on the lighthouse started in 1854. The lantern containing a Fresnel lens arrived from Paris in August 1855. Although visible for almost thirty miles in clear weather, the location had a serious flaw: coastal fog and low clouds often obscured the beacon. On March 23, 1891, the keeper, Robert Israel, extinguished the lamp for the last time. After thirty-six years, the old lighthouse was abandoned and a new light station went into operation at the bottom of the hill closer to sea level as a beacon for mariners.

The Cape Cod style, two-story, whitewashed sandstone keeper's house (20 by 40 feet), with a brick central lighthouse tower was the typical design for the original West Coast lighthouses. Gable-end chimneys symmetrically frame the dwelling, although only the south chimney contains first- and second–floor fireplaces. The 22-inch-thick sandstone outer walls rise from a basement level containing the 1,240-gallon cistern and the brick base of the 38-foot-high lighthouse tower. The original basement floor tiles may have came from Fort Guijarros.

Emerging from the dwelling on a 10-foot diameter brick cylinder, 6 feet above the roof ridgeline, the glass-and-wood-ribbed lantern rises another 15 feet to the pinnacle. An entrance to the first floor from an exterior porch accesses the first floor living and dining rooms and the tower. A wooden kitchen wing at the building's rear was removed sometime after 1913 and replaced with a stucco exterior lean-to in the mid-1930s. The second floor is divided into two bedrooms and a "watch room" for the keeper and his assistant. Tower access is up a spiral staircase that turns into a metal ladder, which opens onto the lantern floor.

The Point Loma Lighthouse houses a third-order Fresnel lens. Invented by French physicist Augustin-Jean Fresnel in 1822, the U.S. Lighthouse Board resisted using his design until the 1850s. Fresnel lenses are like a glass barrel whose outer surface is made up of prisms and bulls-eyes. They were classified in seven orders; generally, the larger a lens the greater its range. In a revolving or flashing light, the bulls-eyes are surrounded by curved, concentric prisms, concentrating the light of a central lamp into several individual beams, radiating like the spokes of a wheel. In a fixed, or steady light, the bulls-eyes become a continuous "lens belt," with the prisms parallel to it, producing an uninterrupted, horizontal sheet of light.

The Point Loma third-order lens stood over 5 feet high and 3 feet in diameter. In the center, a lamp with three circular wicks, one inside the other, produced a flame of 168 candlepower. The lamp used rapeseed oil (*Brassica napus*) from 1855 to 1867, lard oil from 1867 to 1882, and kerosene from 1882 to 1891. The lens magnified the flame to about 19,000 candlepower and was reported in 1862 as visible in clear weather from a mast height of 20 feet above the sea at a distance of twenty-eight miles.

Disuse of the lighthouse and ravages of time, weather, and vandals brought about a recommendation in 1913 to tear it down. With a change of heart, the army made modest repairs in 1915. In an effort to stabilize the structure, the army encouraged soldiers and their families to live in it. In the 1920s the lighthouse was used briefly as a radio station. Restored in 1935 by the National Park Service and later refurnished as used by the light keeper and his family, the lighthouse is now open to visitors.

Today, the Old Point Loma Lighthouse stands as a symbol of the first successful efforts to obtain aids to navigation for the west coast of the United States. The view from this centerpiece of Cabrillo National Monument is a spectacular seascape of a great harbor. Every January and February the Whale Overlook, one hundred yards south of the Old Point Loma Lighthouse, provides superb views of the whale migration.

Death Valley National Park

Inyo County, California, and Esmerelda and Nye Counties, Nevada

→   www.nps.gov/deva

→   The park is located in southeast California, with a portion in Nevada. US 395 passes west of Death Valley and connects with California 178 and to the park. US 95 passes on the east and connects with Nevada 267, 374, and 373 to the park. Interstate 15 passes southeast through Baker, California, on its way from Los Angeles to Las Vegas. The park is about a two-and-a-half-hour drive from the Las Vegas airport.

Scotty's Castle chimes tower

Death Valley is the hottest, driest, and lowest place in the contiguous United States with fascinating geology, canyons, and salt flats; desert surrounded by mountains; extremes of elevation (Badwater at 282 feet below sea level; and Telescope Peak at 11,049 feet above sea level); and amazingly abundant flora, fauna, and wildlife. The 3.336 million acres of Death Valley National Park, established as a national monument in 1933 and redesignated a national park in 1994, is one and one-third times the size of Delaware.

Within this unique combination of heat, landscape, history, and natural life there are ruins of gold and borate mines, and a remarkable historical structure called Scotty's Castle located in the northern part of the park, three miles northeast of Grapevine

Wildrose Canyon charcoal kilns   Scotty's Castle adobe walls

in Grapevine Canyon, and fifty-three miles north of the Furnace Creek Visitor Center. Some of the sites are identifiable only by markers and accessible only by unpaved roads. The vastness of the park means locating the architectural sites beforehand.

Furnace Creek Visitor Center is a good starting point after entering the park. Along the way there are opportunities to see the remains of once-thriving Wild West mining towns scattered throughout Death Valley National Park or within a few miles of the park's boundaries. Discoveries of silver, gold, lead, and other minerals are memorialized in mines, dumps, tunnels, ruins, cabins, graves, and sometimes only markers within the park at Greenwater, Panamint City, Harrisburg, and Skidoo. A side trip to the ruins at Rhyolite, a mining town of five to ten thousand people during its heyday from 1905 to 1911, is a worthwhile experience. The ruins are located outside the east-side park boundary off Nevada Highway 374, four miles west of Beatty on US Highway 95.

Approaching from Los Angeles, past Wildrose at the end of Wildrose Canyon Road is a picturesque row of ten masonry beehive-shaped charcoal kilns. Built in 1877 to produce charcoal for two silver-lead smelters in the Argus Range, twenty-five miles to the west, the kilns shut down in 1878 when the Argus mines' ore deteriorated in quality. The structures are approximately 25 feet tall and 30 feet in circumference. Each kiln held forty-two cords of pinyon pine logs and would, after burning for a week, produce two thousand bushels of charcoal. The durability of the kilns is attributed to fine workmanship and short duration of use.

Near the visitor center are remnants of the Harmony Borax Works. A historic footnote is the phrase "Twenty Mule Team," coined for the Pacific Coast Borax Company by Stephen T. Mather (later to become the National Park Service's first director) for the teams hauling the 36 half-ton loads of milled ore (borax) 165 miles to Mojave, a one-way trip of ten to twelve days. The Keane Wonder Mine, one of the most productive gold mines in the Death Valley area, is a four-level ruin of buildings, machinery, tanks, piping, and waste tailings north of the visitor center off the Beatty cutoff road, between California Highways 190 and 374.

Death Valley Ranch (Scotty's Castle) rises out of the desert like an apparition of a Spanish Mediterranean hacienda, complete with red tile roof and towers, a chimes tower, and other outbuildings. Through the entrance gate and past the incomplete swimming pool, the visitor arrives at an entry plaza. The main house is to the left, the annex is to the right; the wrought-iron-decorated east gate with intricately stone-carved abutments is aligned with the freestanding clock tower. Built during the 1920s as a vacation retreat by Albert Johnson, a Chicago insurance executive, the multibuilding complex is in good condition and offers living history tours throughout the historic house museum, an additional small museum, which functions as a visitor center, a bookstore, and a snack bar.

Construction of Death Valley Ranch began in 1922. Throughout the ten-year construction period Walter "Scotty" Scott, a friend of Johnson, referred to the building as "my castle," and it soon became known as "Scotty's Castle." In 1926, Los Angeles architect Charles Alexander MacNeilledge was hired to redesign the main house, including many of its furnishings and ornaments. His work continued throughout the construction period. When work ceased in 1931, the complex contained more than 31,000 square feet of floor space, with the castle, swimming pool, and other features left unfinished.

The two-story-high castle buildings are a mix of wood frame, concrete structural tiles, and concrete construction; stucco walls and red Mission-style roof tiles complete

the motif of Spanish Mediterranean exteriors. The castle is adorned with imported handcrafted furniture, European artwork, tile flooring throughout, wrought-iron hardware, and exposed timber structure with hand-adze marking, ceiling planking, and redwood trim. Many of the custom designed furnishings and fixtures crafted in California for the Death Valley Ranch reflect a desert motif by incorporating the images of regional fauna and flora in their design. Ties from an abandoned railroad fueled the fourteen fireplaces. The guesthouse, stable, cookhouse, and the majority of other support buildings maintain the same motif of Spanish Mediterranean character with stucco walls and red Mission-style roofs.

Two-story living hall

The main house contains a two-story living hall with an elegant central chandelier soaring up to the redwood-planked ceiling. At opposite ends of the approximately 32-foot-square room is a fireplace and a grotto fountain framed in decorative tiles, respectively. A second-floor gallery surrounds the room. On the north wall of the living hall, the large door of redwood with elaborate wrought-iron hardware opens onto the 116-foot by 24-foot patio extending the full length of the building. Other rooms on the first floor are Scotty's bedroom, the lower music room, solarium, dining room, kitchen, and porches. The main house's second floor contains the Johnsons' living quarters, a guest suite, a verandah, and stairs to the tower mounted with a mule team weather vane.

The annex's first floor contains Mr. Johnson's office and apartment, Mrs. Johnson's apartment with kitchen, enclosed patio, refrigeration room, and a commissary. The second floor contains two guest bedrooms with random-patterned tile flooring, an upper music room, an "Italian Room" with intricately patterned tile flooring, and a separate open-air lanai. The music room is enriched with a custom-built theater organ, elaborately carved arched redwood roof trusses, and Spanish gothic-inspired woodwork details. An internal spiral staircase provides access to the three-story Moorish tower.

The Johnsons died without heirs in the 1940s and willed the castle to a charitable organization called the Gospel Foundation. The foundation operated the property by providing tours through the castle and renting out some rooms in the castle for overnight accommodations. This foundation also took care of Scotty until his death in 1954, selling the property and donating the historic furnishings to the National Park Service in 1970.

Visitor accommodations and services are available in the park at Furnace Creek Ranch, Furnace Creek Inn, and Stovepipe Wells Village.

Eugene O'Neill National Historic Site

Danville, Contra Costa County, California

→ www.nps.gov/euon

→ The Eugene O'Neill National Historic Site is located in Danville, California, twenty-six miles east of San Francisco in the San Ramon Valley. Visits to the site are by reservation only with the National Park Service.

Nobel Prize and four-time Pulitzer Prize-winning playwright Eugene O'Neill built and lived in Tao House in the hills above Danville, California, from 1937 to 1944. Visitors to the thirteen-acre National Historic Site (also a National Historic Landmark) with a National Park Service (NPS) reservation can view the house and landscaped grounds on a guided tour to learn the story of O'Neill and how he influenced the American theater.

The enormously prolific O'Neill wrote nearly sixty plays in a career spanning three decades, received four Pulitzer Prizes, and is the only Nobel Prize for Literature-winning playwright from the United States. He created exciting plays, often about tortured family relationships and the conflict between idealism and materialism, taxing actors, scenic designers, and audiences with the demands of his imagination. Restless and rootless most of his life, the introspective playwright and his wife, Carlotta, were living in a San Francisco hotel in early 1937: "No roots. No home," she wrote as they searched for a place to live. O'Neill had begun work on a cycle of plays about the history of an Irish American family, planned ultimately as a cycle of eleven plays. The O'Neills sought an isolated place to work so that concentration could be continuous and undisturbed.

The isolated 158-acre ranch in the San Ramon Valley east of San Francisco Bay attracted O'Neill and Carlotta with its privacy and climate. Using the Nobel Prize stipend, in 1937 they purchased the ranch and built the Spanish Mission-style house set against the Las Trampas ridge at an elevation of 700 feet. Here, they planned what O'Neill came to call the Tao House his "final harbor."

Surrounded by extensive landscaped grounds, the two-story structure with white baselite brick walls, verandahs, and a black tile roof reflect the Chinese-influenced interior. O'Neill's interest in Eastern thought and Carlotta's passion for Oriental art and décor inspired the name Tao House. An interior of deep blue ceilings and red doors, terra-cotta tile, and black-stained wood floors, and a collection of fine Chinese furniture create a cool, dark atmosphere. Drawn shades protected Carlotta's sensitivity to light.

A few rooms of Tao House are completely refurnished, and photographs in other rooms show the O'Neills at home. One of the rooms, known as "Rosie's Room," was built especially for the O'Neills' pea-green player piano adorned with painted roses. A glimpse of the intensity of O'Neill's labor can be experienced by a visit to the playwright's second-floor study, which is entered through a sequence of three doors and a closet, sheltered by thick walls, where O'Neill poured out his masterpieces. Carlotta remembered her husband emerging from his study red-eyed and gaunt after working on his "soul-grinding" work. He regarded these plays as his life achievement.

Eugene O'Neill's Tao House

Sheltered by the Tao House solitude, O'Neill produced his final and most successful plays: *The Iceman Cometh, Hughie, A Moon for the Misbegotten*, and his autobiographical *Long Day's Journey into Night*. During his years there he turned his back on the theatrical world, giving himself over to transforming his past into the plays that made him America's most awarded playwright. Wartime unavailability of staff and the inability of either of the O'Neills to drive forced them to leave the sanctuary. Suffering from a rare degenerative disease and unable to write after 1943, Eugene ultimately moved to Boston with his wife where, at age sixty-five, shorn of his writing ability, he died in a hotel room in 1953.

The NPS continues to improve the visitor's experience at the Tao House and grounds through the acquisition of Eugene and Carlotta O'Neill memorabilia and original furnishings or period replicas reflective of the house's character. Seismic ret-

Eugene and Carlotta O'Neill, 1941 (courtesy Bienecke Rare Book and Manuscript Library, Yale University)

rofit in 2001 ensures the stability of the unreinforced masonry walls. O'Neill plays are produced every spring and fall in the restored historic barn, providing a west coast connection with the resurgence of interest in O'Neill's plays on Broadway.

Few visitors can leave this quiet atmosphere without the desire to reach for a volume of O'Neill's plays or seek out listings of active productions. Standing in the isolated second-floor study of the playwright recalls Sinclair Lewis's Nobel Prize lecture (December 12, 1930) about O'Neill, "who has done nothing much in American drama save to transform it utterly, in ten or twelve years, from a false world of neat and competent trickery to a world of splendor and fear and greatness, you would have been reminded that he has done something far worse than scoffing—he has seen life as not to be neatly arranged in the study of a scholar but as a terrifying, magnificent and often quite horrible thing akin to a tornado, earthquake or a devastating fire."

Fort Point National Historic Site

San Francisco, San Francisco County, California

→ www.nps.gov/fopo

→ Fort Point National Historic Site is located beneath the south end of the Golden Gate Bridge in the Presidio of San Francisco. Parking at the fort is limited; driving access is from US 101 northbound before the bridge toll plaza, southbound after the toll plaza, turning left on Lincoln Avenue, and following this road along the shoreline to the fort. San Francisco MUNI buses 28 or 29 or Golden Gate Transit stop at the bridge toll plaza. From there, walk one quarter-mile down the hill to the fort.

Fort Point and the Golden Gate Bridge

Fort Point National Historic Site, beneath the southern anchorage of the Golden Gate Bridge, was built to defend the entrance to San Francisco Bay. The fort, which would have been destroyed in the bridge's original plans, was saved when designer Joseph Strauss reworked the design. The park, established on October 16, 1970 to protect this historic coastal defense fortification, is a fine example of one of about thirty brick and granite forts constructed as part of the "Third System," a national system of coastal defense between the end of the War of 1812 and the end of the Civil War. It was the only one built on the Pacific coast.

Influenced by Simon Barnard, a French engineer brought to the United States, and Joseph Totten, later to become the chief engineer of the United States Army, the Army Corps of Engineers began construction of the fort in 1853. A crew of two hundred laborers, many of them unemployed gold miners, worked on the fort for eight years and rushed completion for the beginning of the Civil War. Designed to mount 141 massive cannons, Fort Point was first garrisoned in February 1861 just in time to resist hopes by Confederate sympathizers to seize Union strongholds. Colonel Albert Sidney Johnston, commander of the department of the Pacific defied the attempt to bring California into the Confederacy. Ironically, the Kentucky-born Johnston later resigned his commission to join the Confederate Army and was killed at the Battle of Shiloh in 1862.

The massive brick structure, trimmed with granite corner quoins and soffit bands, was a fortress and troop garrison. Because the fort was initially designed as a granite structure, stones were imported from as far away as China before engineers gave up on the idea of stone walls. Some eight million bricks to complete construction were made in a brickyard nearby. The fort's plan called for three tiers of arched courtyard-facing casemate openings, a barbette tier with additional guns and a sod roof covering to absorb the impact of enemy fire, around an open-air, irregularly shaped quadrangle. Two water-facing bastions were added to discourage attackers from scaling the fort's walls. Enlisted men's and officers' quarters, mess halls, and offices were located on each of the three tiers. The only entrance was a granite-framed sally port with massive twin-leaved studded doors. The lighthouse—the third built at the site—was used from 1864 until 1934, when the foundation for the Golden Gate Bridge obscured the beacon, rendering it obsolete.

Plans for the massive brick and granite, five-sided structure, with 7-foot-thick walls, placed the lowest tier of artillery near water level so that ricocheting cannon-balls could skip across the water's surface to hit enemy ships at the waterline. Workers blasted the 90-foot cliff down to 15 feet above sea level, requiring a seawall to protect the fort from the San Francisco Bay's surging currents. Completed in 1869, the 1,500-foot wall was constructed of bricks fitted together and sealed with lead strips. After more than one hundred years of being pounded by the powerful waves, it began to give way in 1980. The National Park Service rebuilt the wall and placed boulders at the seawall's base to deflect the force of the waves.

Although occupied by Union forces throughout the Civil War, the fort never fired a shot at an enemy. The introduction of rifled cannon during the Civil War required modifications no sooner than it was completed. In 1892 the army began constructing the new Endicott System concrete fortifications armed with steel breech-loading guns. The fort, moderately damaged in the 1906 earthquake, has survived because of use over the next four decades for barracks, training, and storage. Between 1933 and 1937 the fort was used as Golden Gate Bridge construction headquarters. During World War II, soldiers from the Sixth U.S. Coast Artillery were stationed at the fort to man search-lights and rapid-fire cannons as part of the protection of a submarine net strung across the San Francisco Bay entrance.

A pleasant surprise is in store for the visitor who climbs to the bastion's roof. Braced against the blowing ocean winds, one can see the sweeping panorama unfold:

Fort Point casemates and lighthouse

the Pacific Ocean to the west, the head-lands of Marin County to the north, San Francisco and the bay to the east. Ships and boats are often seen passing beneath the Golden Gate Bridge. The dramatic lo-cation of Fort Point under the Golden Gate Bridge's soaring steel arches attests to the ingenuity of the span's designer. Dem-onstrations by period-uniformed staff and a self-guided tour reveal the massive construction layered tier upon tier. Sepa-rated from the outside world by the sally port and massive walls, the casemate's arched openings and silent cannons echo the hundreds of generations of soldiers who were positioned in this coastal defense garrison.

Golden Gate National Recreation Area

Marin, San Francisco, and San Mateo Counties, California

→   www.nps.gov/goga

→   Golden Gate National Recreation Area is located north and south of the Golden Gate Bridge following the Pacific shoreline, all within an hour's drive from San Francisco.

The Presidio's Coast Guard station

Golden Gate National Recreation Area (GGNRA) is a park of 75,000 acres that spreads across Marin, San Francisco, and San Mateo Counties. Located where the Pacific Ocean meets San Francisco Bay at Golden Gate, it is one of the largest urban parks in the world—two-and-a-half times the area of San Francisco—embracing federal, public lands, including California State Parks managed by the California Department of Parks and Recreation, and private holdings, on both sides of Golden Gate. The Golden Gate Bridge is the link between a spectacular blend of natural beauty, historic features, and urban development. Locations with historic structures are Alcatraz Island, Fort Mason on San Francisco's northern and western edge, the Presidio, and San Francisco Maritime National Historical Park (see page 45).

The GGNRA park headquarters in Building 201 of Fort Mason in north San Francisco provides an orientation and information on features and routes to the various park units. The most popular areas of the San Francisco part of the park are seen on a leisurely scenic walk from park headquarters at the foot of Franklin Street north of Bag Street, and ending at Fort Point and the Golden Gate Bridge.

Notorious in American culture as the legendary U.S. Bureau of Prisons maximum-security facility for hardened criminals from 1934 to 1963, Alcatraz Island, with a long and often turbulent history, dominates the entrance to San Francisco Bay. After California achieved statehood, the island was first the site of Fortress Alcatraz, then in succession became the Pacific Coast's first lighthouse (1854), a Civil War bas-

tion, a military prison that also held Native Americans, and the infamous federal prison. Ten years after the prison closed in 1963 the island was opened to the public as the first unit of the GGNRA.

Visitors can reach the island by daily ferry service from Pier 33 at Bay Street and the Embarcadero in San Francisco. A tour of the architectural sites on the island be-

Alcatraz penitentiary cellhouse

gins at the island dock. The remains of the old military post, military prison, and the civilian prison, blended with ruins of the 1970s Native American occupation, are visible on a self-guided island tour. A switchback road constructed in 1853 leads from the wharf to the top of the island passing fortifications, casements with embrasures, sally port, the guardhouse (1857), and the lighthouse tower (1854) leading to the infamous cellhouse. The San Francisco skyline, the bay, and the headlands spanned by the Golden Gate Bridge are visible from many vantage points.

The next stop on the shoreline walking tour is the Aquatic Park, located in the San Francisco Maritime National Historical Park at the Hyde Street cable car turnaround. This park contains a superb example of streamline moderne-style architecture, the largest collection of historic sailing ships in the United States, and a Works Progress Administration recreational development.

Fort Mason, west of Fisherman's Wharf, Ghirardelli Square, and the San Francisco Maritime National Park, marks the eastern boundary of the GGNRA on San Francisco's northern edge. The site of Spanish earthwork gun batteries built in 1797, the U.S. government established the military reservation of Point San Jose in 1850. The U.S. military occupied the site until 1962. Overlooking the bay, the visitor can experience the military history seen in barracks, officers' quarters, gun batteries, and a parade ground. The great meadow, community gardens, fishing piers, and picnic areas are available for public use. The hospital, built in 1902, now houses the GGNRA headquarters. A former Civil War barracks now serve as the San Francisco International Hostel. The thirteen-acre Fort Mason Center, the former San Francisco Port of Embarkation, has become a national model for the conversion of military facilities to peacetime use. Nearly fifty resident cultural, media, and environmental organizations provide a broad range of activities for all interests.

The 1,480-acre Presidio of San Francisco guarded the entrance to San Francisco Bay for two centuries until closing as a military installation in 1994. The Presidio's historic buildings (469 of 768 on the National Register of Historic Places), and archeological sites are under the joint management of the National Park Service and the Presidio Trust, an executive agency of the U.S. government created in 1996.

Long considered a choice military assignment for its location near downtown San Francisco, spectacular views, beaches, miles of equestrian trails, golf courses, and spacious living quarters, the Presidio contains a rich collection of architectural styles. Building types range from elegant officers' quarters and barracks to large warehouses, administrative headquarters, airplane hangars, and stables. The diversity of structures and architectural styles illustrates specific building campaigns that assisted in the Presidio's growth into a significant western United States Army post. There is a tremendous range of building types and styles at the Presidio. The two most predominant styles from the early twentieth century are Colonial Revival and Mission Revival. By the late 1930s, wood-frame buildings were rapidly constructed to accommodate the pre–World War II mobilization effort. In the early twentieth century the army conducted a large-scale landscaping effort, which included planting tens of thousands of trees to clearly define their property line in an ever-encroaching city and to create the illusion of a larger, more impressive post.

Selected Presidio buildings of interest are the historic Letterman Hospital buildings (1902–30) near the Lombard Gate; two wood-frame cottages behind Presido Building 2 used as temporary relief shacks to house San Francisco citizens after the 1906 earthquake; the Post Chapel; and rows of brick barracks built during the Spanish-American War in 1898. The Officers' Quarters in the east housing area offer a variety of stylistic examples. The Mission revival-style Officer's Club was rebuilt in the 1930s and contains original Spanish and Mexican adobe walls in its foundations. (The Classical Roman rotunda at the Palace of Fine Arts with curved colonnades, built in 1915, near the Lombard Gate was for the Panama Pacific International Exposition on land originally belonging to the Presidio).

Fort Mason, park headquarters   Rodman Common at Fort Mason's Point San Jose

Crissy Field along the bay was filled for the Panama Pacific International Exposition of 1915 and later converted into an airfield whose utilitarian hangars are still prominent. A recent restoration project reclaimed Crissy Field as a shoreline park containing the Golden Gate Promenade. A circular route from Crissy Field leads to the south and west sides of the Presidio, crosses Route 1, and passes other examples of a variety of architectural styles, seen in the Presidio Stables, Cavalry Barracks, and officers' houses in Fort Winfield Scott. At the northwest corner of the post are remnants of the fortifications built to protect the entrance to San Francisco Bay after Fort Point became obsolete. The walkway to Fort Point is accessed through the tunnel under the Golden Gate Bridge toll plaza.

The hardy visitor can include in the San Francisco GGNRA tour a climb up to the Golden Gate Bridge and a walk, bicycle, or drive across this iconic structure one of the world's great water crossings. North of the bridge are the Marin Headlands, Muir Woods National Monument, Olema Valley, and Point Reyes National Seashore (see page 42). Scenic turn-of-the-century Army posts in the Marin Headlands are at Forts Barry and Baker. A rare World War II Mobilization cantonment is at Fort Cronkhite.

John Muir National Historic Site

Martinez, Contra Costa County, California

→ www.nps.gov/jomu

→ The John Muir National Historic Site is located in the San Francisco metropolitan area on the east bay in Martinez at the intersection of John Muir Parkway, Route 4, and Alhambra Avenue. From Berkeley, take Interstate 80 and merge right onto eastbound Route 4.

The John Muir House

The 334-acre John Muir National Historic Site contains the Muir House, orchards, outbuildings, and the two-story, Monterey-style adobe Martinez house and open space. The park, established in 1964, is a remnant of the original Yanacío Martinez 17,000-

acre grant. The historic site's 8.5 acres, a small portion of the Muir family's 2,500 acres of holdings, is where the conservationist lived and worked from 1890 until his death in 1914. The National Park Service (NPS) is the administrator for the Muir and Martinez houses.

Born in Scotland in 1838, the young Muir immigrated with his family to Wisconsin in 1848. After attending the University of Wisconsin he set out on foot to cross the country in his quest for wild nature's meaning. Meeting in 1874, Louisa Strentzel and Muir married and settled in the Alhambra Valley, where he took up the Strentzel family business of fruit ranching. Muir prospered and moved into the family house after the death of Dr. Strentzel in 1890. Financially independent after his ten-year partnership with his father-in-law, Muir ceded the day-to-day management of the fruit ranch to others and devoted the rest of his life to the defense of the environment. Muir returned home periodically from travels around the globe from Alaska to Africa, but predominantly in the nearby Sierras. He was a pioneer spokesperson for the national parks who trekked thousands of miles and publicized little-known wonders. He published prolifically in important American magazines and newspapers to publicize the conservation ethic. Muir was one of the founders of the Sierra Club, and served as its first president until he died in 1914. His books, published in 1894, are republished and excerpted today.

Commemorating Muir's life, writings, and environmental protection efforts the Muir-Strentzel house stands on a rise on the property surrounded by park-like plantings and orchards. Stately Washington palms, the only native species of palm in California, flank the house entrance. The house is a rich expression of the Victorian-era Italianate style with corner quoins, bracketed eaves, and a cupola-topped hip roof; balconies and bay windows offer garden and orchard views. Representing upper middle-class Victorian life, much of the house's exterior was built of redwood, while the floors, of pine and fir, were painted to resemble the period's fashionable light oak.

The generous, 12-foot-high ceiling rooms are furnished in period antiques and a few original family pieces, including an oil painting of Muir by his sister. Heated by seven fireplaces and not electrified until 1914 shortly before Muir's death, the East Parlor contains one of the few Muir modifications to the original house. Following the great earthquake of 1906 that destroyed several chimneys and damaged the East Parlor fireplace, Muir replaced the original marble fireplace with a massive brick Mission style one where he could build a "mountain campfire." He also decided to enlarge the parlor by removing a bathroom, entered by the door that now goes nowhere.

The second floor contains family bedrooms and Muir's study. The hallway was lined with bookshelves full of volumes from his extensive library. The original oak desk in the second floor study is where Muir wrote some of his many books and articles on conservation. From here, he led the cause to create Yosemite National Park (1890); authored articles to protect endangered forest preserves; and influenced President Theodore Roosevelt to greatly increase the amount of protected public land. He called the study his "scribble den" and the desk is characteristically strewn with papers and the floor littered with manuscript pages. It is reported that as Muir finished chapters for a book or an article, he rolled it up and placed it in an orange crate near his desk.

John Muir's "scribble den"

From there, his wife or daughter Helen would then edit and type the manuscript. The metal cup on the desk was a badge of membership in the Sierra Club.

Leaving the house, the Orchard Trail passes the carriage house and windmill in the direction of the Martinez House. Built in 1849 by Yanacío's son Vicente on a portion of the grant given to him by his father, the house passed through several owners before being acquired by Muir's father-in-law, Dr. Strentzel, in 1874. Used as a storeroom and foreman residence by Dr. Strentzel, the two-story structure served as the residence for Muir's eldest daughter, Wanda, and her husband, Thomas Hanna.

The fashionable Italianate John Muir House presents a contrast between the cultivated, domestic grandeur of a fifteen-room mansion and the image of the outdoorsman who reveled in sleeping out of doors, trekking across his beloved Sierra Nevada Mountains, and extolling the virtues of wilderness preservation. Muir devoted the later years of his life at the house in the Alhambra Valley to this pioneering work in the defense of the environment.

Lassen Volcanic National Park

Shasta County, California

→ www.nps.gov/lavo

→ Lassen Volcanic National Park is in the northern part of California at the southern end of the Cascade Range, fifty miles west of Interstate 5 connected by California 44 (forty-eight miles east of Redding) and 36 (fifty-two miles east of Red Bluff) to the thirty-mile-long Lassen Park road (California 89), closed in the winter.

On a still, warm day Lassen Peak's snow-capped crown casts perfect reflections on Manzanita Lake. A far different scene than on June 14, 1914 when two weeks of small eruptions climaxed in a massive blast of smoke, ashes, and flying rocks and began a seven-year cycle of sporadic volcanic outbursts. Until the 1980 eruption of Mount Saint Helens, 10,457-foot-high Lassen Peak, considered the world's largest plug dome volcano, was the only volcano in the forty-eight contiguous United States to erupt in the twentieth century.

A vast landscape of mountains created by the volcanic activity of lava flows, lava peaks, craters, sulfur vents and hot springs, and a plateau of cinder cones and forests cover the park's 106,000 acres. Initially, in 1907 President Theodore Roosevelt proclaimed two national monuments, Lassen Peak and Cinder Cone. Assumed to be extinct, the peak's eruptions starting in 1914 brought national attention and encouraged establishment of the area as Lassen Volcanic National Park in 1916.

A summer day's drive through the western part of the park starting at the south entrance passes through many of the major landscape features—Sulfur Works, Bumpass Hell, Lassen Peak, Emigrant Pass, Chaos Crags, and Manzanita Lake—and historical architectural features. The eastern part of the park, a plateau of cinder cones, hot springs, forests, and rustic buildings, is accessible by some of the park's 150 miles of hiking trails and dead-end unpaved roads.

In the early 1930s the National Park Service (NPS) designed and constructed rustic style buildings and landscaping in the park: a Manzanita Lake entrance administrative complex and a fire lookout tower were of massive lower boulder walls, and shake-shingled roofs; campfire circles at Manzanita Lake campgrounds and Summit Lake formed by full round logs, cut out to provide both seats and backs, and half-round logs; and log ranger residences scattered throughout the park.

NPS buildings at Manzanita Lake, some with alterations from original design and construction, resemble the rustic structures at Crater Lake National Park, without the refinements in scale of boulder walls and finish of workmanship. Consistent in theme, these Manzanita Lake buildings—Park Entrance Station (1930), Ranger Residence (1931), and Comfort Station (1931)—are of cut stone lower walls reducing in size from foundation to roof eave framing, deeply recessed window openings, round log or timber roof framing, and shake-shingled roofs. Roofs are uniformly steeply pitched at forty-five degrees.

The two-story Naturalist's Residence (1933) used construction techniques similar to those employed at Crater Lake National Park to fit the relatively short building sea-

Lassen Peak seen from Reflection Lake

Administration building

son. First-floor masonry walls were laid and then wooden formwork with window openings blocked and concrete placed between the masonry and formwork. Upper walls are wood-frame construction and gable ends covered with board-and-batten siding.

Unique among Lassen Volcanic National Park buildings are the Mae Loomis Museum and Seismograph Station at Manzanita Lake. Benjamin F. Loomis documented the 1914–1915 eruptions through photography and promoted the park's establishment

Loomis Museum   Naturalist's residence

and development. In 1926 he purchased forty acres of privately owned land on Reflection Lake, and in 1927 he and his wife built the Mae Loomis Memorial Museum, named in memory of their daughter.

Both museum and seismograph station have reinforced concrete structural frames and walls clad in gray native volcanic rock of cut face random ashlar masonry and topped by crenellated parapets, stepped in the museum's center front and corners. The museum, with walls 15 feet high, is T-shaped. The rectangular main hall is 25 feet by 60 feet in plan. There are 10-foot by 12-foot wings at the rear of the main section. The main entrance doors are set in an arched opening, wide doors are flanked by sidelight panels with a Palladian window above. A broad terrace edged by low volcanic rock masonry walls surrounds the front and both sides of the building. Six square stones in an arched alignment over the entrance are carved with the word "MUSEUM." Renovated and reopened in 1994, the museum contains a main hall with exhibit space and an auditorium.

The smaller Seismograph Station building is a single-story structure (approximately 10 by 12 feet) designed to contain seismographic instrumentation. An arched band of stone above the entrance door contains the word "SEISMOGRAPH."

The Summit Lake Ranger Station in the center of the park, built in 1934, is representative of original rustic ranger stations with typical NPS rustic design details—log walls corner notched, log sapling chinking, sapling window and door surrounds, exposed log end roof purlins and rafters, and split-shake shingles.

The Mount Harkness Fire Lookout built in 1931 is an example of structures constructed by the NPS in parks throughout the Northwest. Located in the southeast corner of the park, the two-story tower has a stone masonry first floor and a wood-frame second floor. A log frame observation platform and windows on all sides of the 18-foot square plan provides sweeping views from the summit of the 8,048-foot-high peak.

The number and quality of historical structures in Lassen Volcanic National Park are modest in comparison to other "crown jewel" national parks. However, the dramatic landscape with place names like Bumpass Hell will satisfy the visitor traveling through the park from north to south on the thirty-mile-long main park road.

Manzanar National Historic Site
Inyo County, California

→ www.nps.gov/manz

→ Manzanar is located on the west side of US 395, 220 miles north of Los Angeles and 250 miles south of Reno, Nevada; six miles south of Independence, California; and nine miles north of Lone Pine, California.

Dust Storm at the Relocation Center, Dorothea Lange, 1942 (National Archives)

The story of America's World War II confinement camps for Japanese Americans is told at the Manzanar War Relocation Center. Eventually ten thousand persons, having been accused of no crime other than their ancestry nor given any hearing or trial, were herded into barracks located at the foot of the scenic Sierra Nevada range in the Owens Valley of eastern California. Manzanar was closed in 1945. By late 1946 many of the buildings were dismantled and removed from the site. Manzanar was designated a National Historic Landmark in 1985 and established as a National Historic Site in 1992.

The center has a tantalizingly scenic view of the eastern face of the Sierra Nevada range from the Owens Valley. However, the mountain range creates a "rain shadow" for the relocation center in a sandy, extremely arid, wind-blown desert region. Blowing dust was everywhere. The weather was utterly miserable—torrid summer heat and bitter winter cold. Through its strength and resourcefulness, the camp population built a community, beautified by gardens and ponds, to overcome the trauma of evacuation and an uncertain future.

The 6,000-acre facility included an agricultural area, a cemetery, a reservoir, and a

sewage treatment plant, in addition to the barbed wire fence-enclosed 540-acre detention area. The central detention area, laid out on a grid of paved or oiled roads, forms most of the historic site. The area included thirty-six residential blocks containing 576 hastily constructed one-story, 20-foot by 100-foot wood-frame and tar-paper barracks. Initially partitioned into four 20-foot by 25-foot rooms, up to eight people were assigned to each barracks

Manzanar cemetery oblisk

"apartment." Other residential block buildings included a mess hall, a recreation hall, two communal bathhouses, a laundry room, an ironing room, and an oil storage tank. Additional blocks contained an administrative area, warehouse, garage, and hospital blocks. The military police compound was located outside the central detention area immediately south of the barbed wire fence.

With the exception of two sentry posts, virtually all of the buildings were constructed of wood frame, board, and tarpaper. Foundations for the barracks, mess halls, and community buildings were concrete footing blocks set at 10-foot intervals (post and pier). Foundations of the bathhouses, laundry rooms, and ironing rooms were concrete slabs. Although the barracks buildings and block layouts were standardized, the internees personalized their surroundings by adding sidewalks, entries, rock-lined pathways, gardens, and small ponds. Within firebreaks and the cleared area between the internee housing and perimeter fence, there were victory gardens and fruit trees restored from neglect after the pre-war town of Manzanar was abandoned. A five-strand, barbed-wire fence and eight guard towers surrounded the area. Large-scale farming and a chicken farm were located outside the perimeter security fence.

Today the site contains three historic structures: a military police sentry post, an internal police post, and the auditorium/gymnasium. There is a one- to two-hour walking tour of the central detention area and a three-mile self-guided auto tour, both of which allow the visitor to grasp the internees' desolation and distress. More poignant than standing structures are the visible remnants of road grid, foundation slabs, concrete sidewalks and stoops, paved parking areas and gravel walkways, granite and boulder walls, barbed-wire fence posts, broken glass, and the camp cemetery. The barracks area is traced by rows of footing blocks in the brush, sand, and alluvial wash. Remains of the detainee-built gardens, recreation parks, sports facilities, and victory gardens are evidence of valiant efforts to personalize the center with names, initials, and dates inscribed in concrete, stone-lined walks, and garden complexes. An evocative scene is the relocation center cemetery with its large memorial obelisk, constructed in 1943 and inscribed in Japanese translated as "Monument to console the souls of the dead."

Restoration of Manzanar War Relocation Center began with the rebuilding of the perimeter barbed-wire fence enclosing the camp living area. In 2004 the restored auditorium opened as an Interpretive Center (open daily) and park headquarters. A guard tower was reconstructed in 2005 and work continues to stabilize rock gardens, orchards, and other site features. The National Park Service is restoring elements of a single block, beginning with a mess hall in Block 14, located adjacent to the Interpretive Center.

Visitors to Manzanar National Historic Site are reminded not to disturb the existing remains; removal or disturbance of artifacts is illegal.

Point Reyes National Seashore

Point Reyes, Marin County, California

→ www.nps.gov/pore

→ The national seashore is approximately forty-five miles north of San Francisco. The scenic and winding California 101 provides direct access to the park from the north and south. Park headquarters is located at Bear Valley near Olema, eight miles from the southern boundary.

The 71,000-acre Point Reyes National Seashore is a dramatic landscape of forested ridges, tall cliffs, long beaches, lagoons and estuaries, open grasslands, and offshore bird and sea lion colonies. Bisected from the rest of the California mainland by the

Point Reyes Lighthouse

San Andreas Fault, the Point Reyes Peninsula contains more than 140 miles of hiking trails, campgrounds, and beaches. The park was established on September 13, 1962, and designated a biosphere reserve in 1988.

Orientation to the seashore is at the contemporary barn-like Bear Valley Visitor Center near Olema. Other visitor centers are the Kenneth A. Patrick Visitor Center and the Point Reyes Lighthouse Visitor Center. Historical structures are at the Point Reyes Lighthouse district, the Point Reyes Lifesaving Station, the Marconi/RCA receiving and transmitting stations, and the two large historic agricultural districts: the Point Reyes Dairies and Olema Valley Ranches, which comprise over 28,000 acres.

The Point Reyes Lighthouse complex includes a lighthouse, keeper's quarters, and outbuildings located on the westernmost point of the Point Reyes Headlands and is one quarter-mile and three hundred steps below the visitor center. Built in 1870, the beacon revealed the often fog-shrouded peninsula and warned sailors of the treacherous offshore currents at Point Reyes. The view from the lighthouse observation plat-

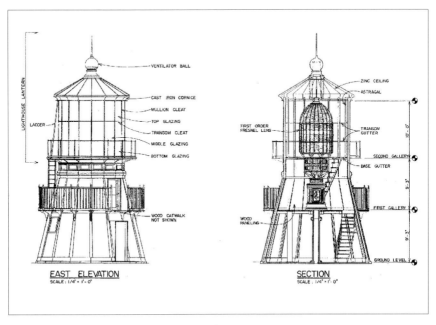

Lighthouse elevation and section (courtesy HABS/HAER)

form is impressive, with sea lions basking on offshore rocks, and opportunities to see migrating gray whales between January and April. The lighthouse survived the 1906 earthquake, shifting 18 feet north in a minute. Retired from service in 1975 when the U.S. Coast Guard installed an automated light, the lighthouse is open to the public, weather permitting.

A standard design of the U.S. Lighthouse Board, the cast-iron light tower approximately 40 feet in height from base to tip of finial is set on 2.5-inch-thick cast-iron plates fixed to the rock of the point's projection into the ocean. Stairs lead from ground level and a bridge spans into the first-gallery level, the location of the clockwork mechanism for rotating the lantern. An internal iron spiral stair provides access to the second (lantern) gallery level. Walkways circle the tower at the first and second galleries. Wood paneling encloses the ground level up to the second-gallery levels. A cast-iron plate roof caps the tower. Height from ground to first-gallery level, and first-gallery to second-gallery level, is 9 feet and 3 inches; the second gallery is 10 feet high to the roof cornice. The restored clockwork on the first-gallery level is visible for inspection. The second gallery cast-iron lantern, still in operation but no longer serving as a warning beacon, is a premade ready-to-assemble design that houses a first-order Fresnel lens, which is the largest size placed in service.

The National Historic Landmark Point Reyes Lifeboat Station, built in 1927 by the U.S. Life-Saving Service to replace an 1890 station, provided a rescue service at the treacherous peninsula. The station includes a two-story framed boathouse, launchway, officer-in-charge's quarters, and support structures. A typical example of a rail-launching station, with launchway and cradle-launched 36-foot-long motor lifeboats, the Point Reyes Lifeboat Station is the only unaltered station of this nationally employed type remaining on the Pacific Coast. Closed in 1969 due to the quick response of larger faster Coast Guard cutters, in its twenty-five years of operation at Point Reyes the service saved many lives and lost four of its own.

Point Reyes lifeboat station

The Marconi/RCA wireless stations are nationally significant for their place in communications history. They were the site of the first transpacific wireless communication in 1913 by the Marconi Company. The discontiguous district is comprised of a receiving station constructed by RCA in 1929 in the north district of the park and a transmitting station constructed by the Marconi Company in 1913 some fifteen miles south in the park near the town of Bolinas. Together with a third site, the Marconi receiving station in the town of Marshall (a California state park), they comprise the only remaining intact Marconi coast wireless station in the U.S. Through the diligent and dedicated efforts of the Maritime Radio Historical Society, transmitters and antennas dating from World War II have been restored to operational condition and used periodically throughout the year.

The agricultural landscapes of Point Reyes are one of the park's most distinctive characteristics. American settlers arriving in the mid-nineteenth century took advantage of the cool, moist Point Reyes climate, a long growing season, and sufficient fresh water supplies provided near-ideal conditions for raising dairy cows. The oldest families still ranching on the Point have been here for over 130 years.

Two districts totaling over 28,000 acres and thirty ranches continue to operate today as they did before the park was established in 1962. The Point Reyes Dairy Ranch district is part of a designed, large-scale agricultural enterprise constructed by the Shafter family in the 1850s and the 1860s and is considered the birthplace of large-scale "industrial" agriculture in California. This system of over thirty tenant dairy "alphabet ranches" delivered butter and cheese products and livestock to the foot of Market Street by way of small schooners, and eventually by rail and ferry. The National Park Service-restored Pierce Point Ranch on Tomales Point, dating back to 1858, is representative of the agricultural heritage of this area. A short, self-guided trail leads visitors through the historic complex including the ranch house, white bunkhouse, and old and new dairy.

The Olema Valley Ranches historic district is a vernacular agricultural district that evloved in a more traditional manner of individually owned properties at about the same time as the alphabet ranches. The Olema Valley is inland from the Shafter ranches and straddles the San Andreas Fault and is easily accessible from State Highway One.

San Francisco Maritime National Historical Park

San Francisco, San Francisco County, California

→ www.nps.gov/safr

→ The park is at the west end of Fisherman's Wharf, at the Hyde Street cable-car terminus; six miles south of Independence, California; and nine miles north of Lone Pine, California.

San Francisco Maritime Museum

The San Francisco Maritime National Historic Park contains a superb example of stream-line moderne architecture, the largest collection of historic sailing ships in the United States, and a Works Progress Administration (WPA) recreational development. Located at the western edge of Fisherman's Wharf and across the street from Ghirardelli Square, the visitor can experience the architecture and site development of the 1930s recreation complex forming a graceful arc projecting into San Francisco Bay.

The National Historic Landmark fifty-acre national historical park, established in 1988, consists of two areas open to the public: the Aquatic Park recreational complex (including the Maritime Museum) and a research center (J. Porter Shaw Library) located in the Fort Mason Center. The museum displays exhibits on the history of West Coast steamers, historic ship models, huge ships' parts, figureheads, and fine arts. The

Maritime Library houses books, periodicals, and oral histories, and provides access to a large collection of photographs, ships' plans, and other historic documents. The park boundary also encompasses the Hyde Street Pier, site of the historic vessels display.

The square-rigged *Balclutha*

The park's historic ships are an eclectic mixture of romantic sailing vessels, military ships, and workhorses of the Bay Area commerce. They include the 1891 scow schooner *Alma*; square-rigged ship 1886 *Balclutha*; the 1895 schooner *C. A. Thayer*; the 1914 river paddlewheel tug *Eppleton Hall*; the 1890 ferry *Eureka*, and the 1907 ocean-going steam tug *Hercules*. All vessels except the *Eppleton Hall* are National Historic Landmarks. Several were spared the scrap yard when acquired by the National Park Service (NPS) and incorporated into this unusual park in the National Park System. The *Hercules* and *Alma* have been restored and periodically steam and sail around the bay. Occasional dry-docking and restoration makes some of the vessels inaccessible at times.

The Aquatic Park's masterful design, proposed for Black Point Cove as early as 1866 by Frederick Law Olmsted and included in Daniel Burnham's 1905 plan for a major redevelopment of San Francisco, was developed between 1936 and 1939 as California's most expensive and ambitious WPA project. In 1939, *Time* magazine declared it "one of the most sophisticated WPA building jobs in the U.S." The group of structures, curved municipal pier, and beach facing the ships of the San Francisco Maritime National Historical Park are an expression of the streamline moderne style. Emulating elements of the clean-lined design of ocean liners, the park has no parallel on the West Coast and, although on a smaller scale, rivals the design quality of Miami Beach's Art Deco buildings. With minor exceptions, the beach, bathhouse, municipal pier, rest rooms, concession stand, stadia, and two speaker towers are essentially unchanged from their appearance when completed in 1939. Before becoming the Maritime Museum and a senior center, the bathhouse served as a casino and barracks for an anti-aircraft battalion during World War II.

The park's centerpiece is the bathhouse, a gleaming white moored ocean liner. Now the Maritime Museum building, the four-story reinforced-concrete structure designed by the William Moosers, Sr. and Jr., is banked into the slope of land as it gradually descends toward the bay. The main entrance is on the second floor at the foot of Polk Street. An oval plan, recessed upper stories, porthole windows, tubular steel railings, air vents shaped like ship's funnels, and historic white color add to the building's illusion as an ocean liner. The nautical theme is carried out in the interiors by murals, statues, and other artwork by artists Hilaire Hiler, Sargent Johnson, Richard

Ayer, John Glut, and Benjamin Bufano. The artwork is significant for its surreal and abstract forms not commonly found in WPA projects. Inside this ship-shaped structure, mast sections, jutting spars, and figureheads are arranged among the colorful fish and gleaming tiles of muralist Hilaire Hiler's expressionist vision of Atlantis. The *Mermaid*, the one-man sailboat that transported a solo adventurer across the Pacific from Japan in ninety-four days, is displayed on the balcony.

The concrete stadia flanking the bathhouse, designed for spectators of athletic events and crowds in the lagoon, is now a setting for outdoor concerts and a resting place for tourists. The concession stand and the men's restroom are west of the bathhouse at the approach to the Municipal Pier. Designed as part of the Aquatic Park complex, the building reflects the streamline moderne character of the bathhouse. The crescent-shaped seawall was built between 1934 and 1938 using granite paving blocks from San Francisco streets.

Sequoia and Kings Canyon National Parks

Fresno and Tulare Counties, California

→   www.nps.gov/seki

→   The parks are due east of Fresno (via California 180) and Visalia (via California 198). Generals Highway connects the roads, making loop trips possible. There is no road access to the parks from the east.

Sequoia and Kings Canyon, the twin national parks at the southern end of California's Sierra Nevada, have as diverse ecosystems as any national park in the country. On a clear day, the snowcapped peaks of the Sierra that bound the parks on the east are visible from Fresno, fifty-five miles to the west. In between are arid foothills, forest belts that include stands of giant sequoia, and alpine terrain. This land so entranced John Muir that he set out countless times to roam among the Sierra heights. He documented the redwood groves ravaged by logging enterprises and the foothill grasslands overgrazed by sheep.

Sequoia National Park was established in 1890, and General Grant National Park (now part of Kings Canyon) in the same year. Only Yellowstone predates Sequoia as a national park. General Grant National Park was incorporated into Kings Canyon National Park in 1940. These two national parks—both designated as biosphere preserves—total nearly 866,000 acres, 737,000 acres of which are wilderness area. Sequoia and Kings Canyon are only accessible to automobiles on the western sides. Within the parks, accessed by Highway 180 from Fresno into Kings Canyon, or by Highway 198 from Visalia into Sequoia, a convenient loop on the Generals Highway exists. The world's premier giant sequoia thoroughfare, it is aptly named after the General Sherman and General Grant trees. Kings Canyon Highway (Highway 180) begins in Fresno and from Grant Grove heads east thirty-six miles through the canyons of the South Fork of the Kings River, terminating at road's end near Copper Creek. Mineral King

Highway, off Highway 198, is a twenty-five-mile route of switchbacks through sublime scenery, ending at the vista of 10,587-foot-high Farewell Gap. Readily accessible historic architecture is found in close proximity to the parks' major automobile routes.

Hand-carved redwood sign at southern entrance   Cabins at Mineral Lakes basin end of Mineral King Highway

Ranger stations on hiking trails present fine examples of National Park Service (NPS) rustic architecture. The adventurous hiker can find the Muir Hut on the John Muir Trail at an elevation of 11,955 feet.

The historical structures in Sequoia and Kings Canyon National Parks are the result of the parks' growth and development over a century and a half of settlement and the NPS stewardship. Generally rustic in character with the use of natural materials, the structures are a subdued contrast with the extraordinary scenery and forests of Sequoia and Kings Canyon, confirming the Grosvenorss' 1916 claim in the pages of *National Geographic*:

> But in that architecture which is voiced in the glorious temples of the Sequoia grove . . . there is a majesty and an appeal that the mere handiwork of man, splendid though it may be, can never rival.

The earliest historic structures at Sequoia and Kings Canyon National Parks are a scattering of nineteenth-century settlers' cabins built out of felled sequoias. Summer colonies on private inholdings at Wilsonia and Silver City also contain small-scale buildings rustic or vernacular in character. These wood-frame cabins, often on post-and-block foundations, suggest impermanence. Although NPS master plans proposed unifying architectural themes for major visitor areas, only the Giant Forest/Lodgepole and Grant Grove areas nestled among the sequoia groves demonstrate a rustic woodsy character. These rustic buildings are modest in scale and were gradually added over the years along simpler architectural themes than those in other national parks.

The Generals Highway climbs to more than 6,000 feet in elevation in the sixteen miles from the Ash Mountain entrance to Giant Forest, site of some of the finest groups of giant sequoia. Once the location of the rustic Camp Kaweah and Giant Forest Village Lodge and guest cabins, the only vestiges remaining are the Giant Forest Market (now the Giant Forest Museum), a ranger residence, and a comfort station. An extensive NPS planning process in the 1990s resulted in the removal of many structures from the Giant Forest area to protect the sequoia groves' fragile environment. The Giant Forest area was restored to as pristine a state as possible, with the removal of almost three hundred shake-exterior cabins, tent cabins, and exterior framing support buildings.

The Giant Forest Market, designed by Gilbert Stanley Underwood and constructed in 1928–29, illustrates NPS plans for Sequoia National Park. The heavy exposed frame, symmetry in the broken masses of the building's wings, heavy wrought-iron hardware, multilight transoms and display windows, paired entrance doors with herringbone patterns, and the exterior dark red-brown color and lichen-green window trim all express a rustic design ethic. The ranger residence (masterfully sited by landscape architect Merel Sager) and comfort station have common features in their granite foundations, exposed structural frames, and cedar-shingled roofs.

Visitors can see early settler shelters from trails in the Giant Forest area. The Squatter's Cabin and Cattle Cabin are preserved examples of frontier log cabins, built of corner-notched peeled logs and gable-end cedar shake roofs. An unusual preserved shelter is Tharp's Log Cabin, combining a downed fire-hollowed giant sequoia with a frame structure complete with granite chimney.

The Generals Highway passes Lodgepole, a mixture of buildings that includes a visitor center, seasonal staff housing, and the Lodgepole Market Center—a mediocre attempt at a modern interpretation of the NPS rustic style. Immediately beyond Lodgepole, hand-cut stone arch bridges at Marble Creek and a half-mile farther at Clover Creek marks the beginning of thick mixed-conifer forests. Similar in design and examples to the NPS integration of site structures with the surroundings are the bridges at Marble Creek (a 45-foot arch span built in 1930–31) and Clover Creek (a 90-foot arch span built in 1931). Spanning granite-walled gorges, the concrete structures are faced with 18- to 24-inch granite masonry walls. The hollow structures formed by the arch and stone walls were filled with dirt and topped with the asphalt roadbed of the Generals Highway.

The Generals Highway continues beyond recent development at Wuksachi Village, Clover Creek and at nearby Dorst Campground is the Cabin Creek Ranger Station and

Dormitory. Further along the Generals Highway, ten miles beyond Clover Creek, a massive, hand-carved redwood sign marks the boundary of the Sequoia National Park and Sequoia National Forest, and ten miles later the road reenters the park. Approaching Grant Grove there is a side trip to Wilsonia, a private community of summer cabins.

Grant Grove Village, once the headquarters of the old General Grant National Park established close to the same time as Sequoia National Park in 1890, contains the visitor center, rustic cabins, staff residences, and support buildings. The former Superintendent's Residence of General Grant National Park is a classic rustic structure of lap siding, alternating shingle patterns in the gable ends, wood-shingle roof, beveled outlookers at the eaves, and a finely constructed granite chimney. Less elegant but retaining rustic features are the other permanent residences in the area. The village cabins, designed by Gilbert Stanley Underwood, are more important as a collection of structures and the sense of place they create than the individual buildings. The cabins are simple frame structures, either duplexes or single cottages, with shake siding, wood-shingle roofs with double coursing every fifth row, six-light casement windows, thick plank doors with wrought-iron hardware, and the traditional dark reddish-brown color with lichen-green trim.

Removed cabin at Giant Forest   Giant Forest Museum, formerly market building

The Gamlin Cabin, near the 267-foot-tall General Grant sequoia, evokes a rugged frontier image with visible broadaxe marks on the building's wood. The size of the logs and planks—massive squared corner-notched logs, three tiers of redwood roof planks, hewn boards set vertically in the gable ends—are in scale with the surrounding landscape.

Leaving Grant Grove, California Highway 180 (Kings Canyon Highway) winds through more than twenty miles of Sequoia National Forest, and reenters Kings Canyon National Park. Historical structures in the canyon area located at Cedar Grove include: the Visitor Center (1930), Naturalist Residence (1935), and Guest Minister Residence (1933), the latter was built by the U.S. Forest Service as a storage shed. Beyond Zumwalt Meadows at road's end are trails leading into mountain canyons with NPS and trappers' log cabins: the Roaring River Snow survey cabin, the Lackey cabin at Scaffold Meadow, Roaring River; and the "Shorty" Lovelace cabins. Joseph Walter "Shorty" Lovelace (1886–1963) trapped throughout Kings Canyon for more than twenty years until the park's creation in 1940 and built one-room log cabins at Vidette Meadow (Bubbs Creek), Gardiner Creek, Woods Creek, Cloud Canyon, Granite Pass, and Sphinx Pass.

At Hammond, located along California Highway 190, about five miles east of Three Rivers Post Office and west of the Sequoia National Park boundary, the narrow, steep, and often tortuously winding Mineral King Highway—with 690 curves—rises in twenty-five miles from an elevation of 1,100 to 7,800 feet at road's end. From two miles east of Hammond to the bridge over the east fork of the Kaweah River (6.5 miles east of Hammond), trestlework is seen attached to the bluffs above the road. This intriguing sculptural form, a wooden "ditch" supported on a timber trestle, is the "Number One Flume" of the Whitney Power Company, part of a flume system in the park completed in 1913, bringing water from the Middle and Marble Forks of the Kaweah River to the powerhouse outside the park near Ash Mountain.

The long, dead-end road enters Sequoia National Park at the Lookout Point entrance and continues past the Atwell Mill Campground and private recreational cabins at Cabin Cove. At twenty miles from Hammond, Silver City is a private community with private cabins, guest cabins, a restaurant, and a small store. Finally, after two hours of arduous driving from Three Rivers, the traveler is rewarded with the site of rustic private cabins in the spectacular setting of Mineral King.

The high country of Sequoia and Kings Canyon National Parks is a vast region of unbroken wilderness, of mountains, canyons, rivers, lakes, and meadows. Ranger stations and hikers' huts are found along some of the most spectacular hiking trails in all of the national parks. Ranger stations are located at South Fork, Quinn Creek, Hockett Meadow, Little Five Lakes, Rowell Meadow, Kern Canyon, Rock Creek, Tyndall Creek, Bearpaw Meadow, Pear Lake, Charlotte Lake, Rae Lakes, LeConte Canyon, and McLure Meadow.

The John Muir Hut at Muir Pass on the John Muir Trail is in the northern corner of Kings Canyon National Park. Emerging from granite mountaintop rubble, the intriguing profile of the native granite structure with course ashlar-pattern walls, on an octagonal base about 20 feet in diameter, is stepped to form a vaulted dome 20 feet high. A stone chimney protrudes from a corner of the dome.

Yosemite National Park

Mariposa County, California

→ www.nps.gov/yose

→ There are four entrances to the park: the south entrance on California 41 north from Fresno, the Arch Rock entrance on Highway 140 west from Merced, the Big Oak Flat entrance on Highway 120 east from Modesto and Manteca, and the Tioga Pass entrance on Highway 120 west from Lee Vining and US 395.

The Ahwahnee hotel

Yosemite National Park's 761,266 acres contain glacial valleys, waterfalls of extraordinary height, giant sequoias, alpine meadows, Sierra peaks, lakes, and streams. This vast place of scenic grandeur has enchanted the imagination of the American public since the 1850s when reports and photographs of it first began to appear. Yosemite's adjective-spilling grandeur is more than just the valley, less than one percent of the park. Away from the concentrated crowds of Yosemite Valley visitors, there is a lifetime of scenic experiences and historical architecture features along the valley's El Portal Road, the east-west Big Oak Flat Road and Tioga Road from the Big Oak Flat entrance to the Tioga Pass entrance, Glacier Point Road, and the Wawona Road (California Highway 41).

A tour of historical architecture in Yosemite Valley follows the one-way road pattern along the path of the meandering Merced River and the head-craning views of 3,000-foot El Capitan. On the right in a grassy meadow, the New England-style, 250-seat Yosemite Valley Chapel was built in 1879, and remodeled and moved in 1901. The building was acquired by the National Park Service (NPS) in 1927 and completely restored in 1982. The original structure consisted of a single room 26 by 50 feet, with a stone foundation, exterior board-and-batten walls painted dark brown with light trim, a shingle roof, bell tower, and steeple.

A half-mile along the Valley road on the right is the LeConte Memorial Lodge. The unusual granite structure, with unique Tudor influences, was built in 1903 by the Sierra Club to serve as a library and club information center. Designed by Mark White and in-

El Capitan

Yosemite Valley Chapel

fluenced by his brother-in-law, Bernard Maybeck, the verticality of the lodge, emphasized by an exaggerated pyramid roof and weathered granite walls, reflects the steep pitches of the granite cliffs surrounding Yosemite Valley. Symmetrically Y-shaped in plan, the building is dominated by the massive wood-shingled roof and gable rough-cut stone end walls. The roof is the lodge's dominant architectural feature; on both the exterior and interior, the steep pitches and shapes of the roof and the parapet walls emphasize the verticality of the structure.

A quarter-mile past the Curry Village, located at the base of Glacier Point at the eastern end of Yosemite Valley, is a camp once of more than four hundred canvas tent cabins (wood platforms and canvas walls and roof) and wooden cabins (some with baths) massed in closely aligned areas. The camp's architectural interest is found primarily in the rustic experience provided for guests and visitors. Although the site contains few structures of architectural significance and some recent additions, Curry Village exhibits a continuity of scale and texture; the remaining tent cabins recall more than a century of traditional rustic camping at Yosemite.

Looping back west, the road reaches Yosemite Village. The Rangers' Club, built in 1920 as an early expression of the fledgling NPS rustic aesthetic, has a distinctive

U-shape plan and steeply pitched shake roofs. Massive peeled logs extending from the ground to the eaves along the exterior walls are shingled and stained dark brown, which, together with the massive granite chimney and multilight windows and doors, afford the building a warm, domestic scale. Also located in the village are concessioner's studios built in 1925, including the Ansel Adams Gallery, base for the world-famous Ansel Adams photography workshops begun in 1940. Beyond the studios is the Park Headquarters complex.

Built in the 1920s, the administration building, visitor center, and museum have a unity in overall form and exterior materials. The three buildings have first-floor bases with battered-stone veneers that give the appearance of structural masonry, and projecting shingled upper stories trimmed with logs. A regular rhythm of window openings recessed into the lower walls conveys the massive nature of the battered-stone wall bases; upper-story windows are spaced and sized to preserve a large, shingled plane. Shallow-pitched, shingled gable roofs reinforce the long, low lines.

Prominent among the architecturally significant Yosemite structures is the dramatically sited Ahwahnee hotel. Set at the end of the valley against the granite cliffs of the Royal Arches, the hotel, opened in 1927, met a need for luxury accommodations that would be unobtrusive and take advantage of the magnificent views. Designer Gilbert Stanley Underwood devised an asymmetrical plan with three wings, each three stories high, radiating out from a six-story central tower. The plan afforded good views of the dramatic scenery from every window. Emphasized by green slate hip roofs, the horizontal sweep of the balconies and terraces at Ahwahnee provides visual interest on the exterior and varied spatial experiences on the interior. Massive granite-boulder piers and chimneys match the cliff walls and soar vertically throughout the complex. Broadened at their bases, the piers cast the first-floor window openings into deep shadow. What appears as rough-cut siding is really board-formed concrete stained the color of redwood.

A rustic atmosphere pervades the hotel interior with Indian artifacts, wrought-iron fittings, kilim rugs, murals, and stained glass windows. Noteworthy public spaces are the 77-foot by 51-foot stately Grand Lounge and 130-foot by 51-foot dining room. One of the grandest rooms in any of the national parks, light pours into the dining room from the 25-foot high south-facing windows and from the alcove at the west end of the room. Triangular wrought-iron chandeliers and wall sconces provide warm light after dark, reflecting off the non-structural timber columns and trusses. Over-scaled Indian patterns on the uppermost wall sections above

Ahwahnee dining room

the wood wainscoting are echoed in the linen curtains and on the china. Granite piers flank the alcove, framing splendid views of the valley and Yosemite Falls.

On the drive through the valley, the visitor should take note of the many bridges spanning the Merced River in a variety of materials (timber, masonry, or concrete) and spans (single or multiple arches). They are typically scaled to meet the expected traffic—foot and horse, and major or minor vehicle use. An aesthetic complement to the environment, the Yosemite bridges represent different eras of bridge builders and purposes.

Leaving the valley, the traveler has the choice of choosing the Tioga Road leading to the park's eastern gateway at Tioga Pass or the Wawona Road to reach Mariposa Grove at the south entrance. Along the Tioga Road are three groups of historical structures, each with a distinctive character. White Wolf Lodge, a complex including a main building with dining room, store, cabins, and tent platforms with canvas tents, is a starting point for hikers or mountaineers going into the high country. Further to the east, in the shadow of dramatic Lembert Dome, Tuolumne Meadows contains a visitor center, rustic ranger station and comfort stations, and Parsons Memorial Lodge. The 1930s NPS buildings carry a consistent rustic theme in the use of heavy ashlar-patterned granite graded in size from foundation to eave, log-roof framing extended at the eaves, and a variety of plank and board-and-batten siding as well as shake-shingled roofs. Constructed in 1915, the rubble granite lodge is a simple building: 1,040 square feet, symmetrical, and rectangular in plan. A summer visit here is deceptive: a rugged, exposed site dictated a solid structure to fit a harsh environment. Thick battered walls contain deeply recessed door and window openings, offset by delicate arched entrance and window frame voussoirs. Note the windows protected by shutters, heavily studded with nails to make them bear-proof.

Moore Cottage, Wawona Hotel

The entrance station at Tioga Pass is a highly refined NPS version of checking stations to control traffic and to portray the unique character of a national park to the traveler. An ensemble effect is created by consistent stone work in the entrance pylons flanking either side of the road and the adjacent compact ranger's house. The house's shallow-pitched roof of shake shingles extends downward to form a porch, supported by peeled-log columns and stone pillars, and the gable-roof pitch parallels the ground and flows into the entrance gate pylon.

The Wawona Road (California Highway 41) leaves Yosemite Valley from the junction near Bridal Veil Falls and climbs to the Wawona Tunnel and Discovery Viewpoint, linking up with the Wawona Road at more than 6,000 feet in elevation, and descends past Wawona, the Yosemite Pioneer History Center, and Mariposa Grove, then exits at the park's south entrance.

The Badger Pass ski area is reached by turning off the Wawona Road at Chinquapin. Architect Eldridge (Ted) Spencer designed the project, which included a lodge and ski lift. The lodge, opened in December 1935, has a simple Swiss-chalet character implied from a shallow-pitched shed roof over the entire building. A wide overhang supported by truss extensions, along with the balcony and terrace, add to the chalet's character. The original furnishings, decorations, and artwork follow Nordic skiing themes.

At Wawona, two attractions for the visitor are the Wawona Hotel and Pioneer Yosemite History Center. The Wawona Hotel is the oldest resort complex in the National Park System; the first building opening in 1876. Today's charming, seven-building complex of two-story white-clapboard clad structures with porches, verandahs, and Victorian trim recall an earlier era of travel that offers a quiet reflective setting after the titanic drama of Yosemite Valley. Constructed over a period of forty years, the architecture is of less interest than the integrity of the whole complex. Unity is achieved through formal placement of the buildings on the rural landscape, by the principal building material of clapboard siding, and by form, massing, and color. The porches and verandahs around all the buildings further unite them and encourage an airy connection with the landscape. The buildings abound with Stick and Eastlake style details. Even Palladian classical elements can be seen, as in the cupola of Moore Cottage.

Adjacent to the hotel is the recently restored studio of painter Thomas Hill. Now in use as a museum, the building, constructed in 1886, shares delicate Eastlake style detailing with the hotel.

The final stop before approaching the Mariposa Grove stand of giant sequoias is the Pioneer Yosemite History Center, a collection of historic buildings, located just over the covered bridge from the hotel. Most of the structures are relocated from their original settings elsewhere in the park and show fine examples of rustic detail.

Hawaii

Far West and Pacific

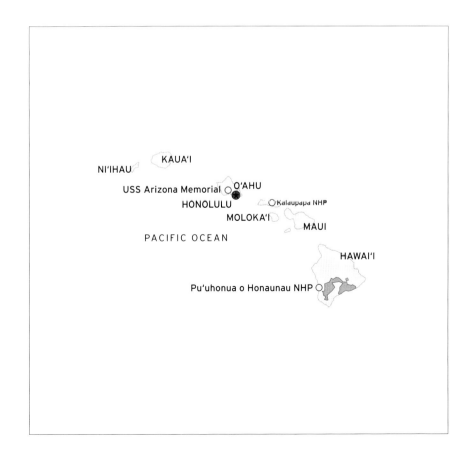

KAUA'I

NI'IHAU

USS Arizona Memorial ○●O'AHU

HONOLULU

MOLOKA'I ○ Kalaupapa NHP

MAUI

PACIFIC OCEAN

HAWAI'I

Pu'uhonua o Honaunau NHP ○

Kalaupapa National Historical Park

Molokai, Hawaii

→   www.nps.gov/kala

→   The park of 10,700 acres is located on the northern coast of Molokai, Hawaii.

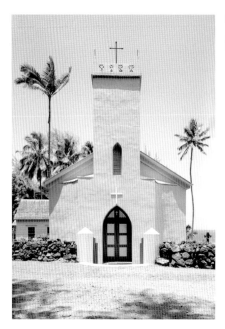 

Saint Philomena Church, exterior   Interior

The park, on an isolated peninsula on the 260 square-mile scenic island of Molokai, is regarded with reverence and compassion for the human stories of the place. Surrounded by ocean on three sides and sheer cliffs on the north, the park's spectacular mountain, valley, and coastal scenery is the site of the dual tragedies of both the removal of indigenous people in the last third of the nineteenth century and the 1866 establishment of the Kalaupapa and Kalawao isolation settlements for people with Hansen's disease (leprosy).

The community of Kalaupapa, on the leeward side of Kalaupapa Peninsula, is still home for many surviving Hansen's disease patients. The communities of traditional Hawaiian plantation-style architecture were organized into housing areas or "homes." The low profile, wood-frame buildings represent a rapidly disappearing vernacular architecture. Bayview is one of the settlement's most elaborate expressions of the plantation style. A complex that originally included patients' housing and a dining hall for the infirm, it now consists of two large detached buildings and three buildings joined by covered porches. A restoration program by the National Park Service (NPS) is preserving and stabilizing the structures.

Among the historic structures of significance are several churches in the Kalawao settlement. On the peninsula's windward side are the Siloama Protestant Church
(1871) and Saint Philomena Roman Catholic Church (1872). The Siloama chapel marks
the site of the original leper colony on Molokai. Set in a lawn surrounded by towering
trees and volcanic rubble walls, the one-story wood-frame gable-roofed structure (20
by 34 feet in plan), completely rebuilt in 1966, has exterior walls sheathed in horizontal
siding, a roof finished with corrugated metal and boxed cornices with return ends,
and a gabled entrance portico. A square tower supports an octagonal louvered lower
section and shingled upper section.

The modest size Saint Philomena Church, associated with Joseph De Veuster (best
known to the world as Father Damien) is striking in its simplicity and architectural na-
ïveté. A 30-foot-tall central bell tower over the entrance portico, capped by a diamond-
pattern railing, is an appealing marker for this white-painted structure of a variety of
materials and forms. The church's historical and cultural significance far outweigh
its architectural significance. Although lacking in architectural continuity, resulting
from two construction stages, the brightly painted white structure is L-shaped in plan
and gabled roofed. The 1888 masonry front section (28 by 60 feet in plan) has 30-inch-
thick walls coated with a plaster finish. Windows and doors of this section have gothic
pointed arches. The attractively restored interior has an ornate chandelier, fluted Corinthian columns with octagonal bases, barrel vaulting, and faux masonry rendered by

painted jointing. Attached at the rear and west side
of the church, a 14- by 18-foot barrel vaulted chapel,
built in 1872, served settlement patients. The wood
structure's exterior is sheathed with shiplap siding.

Be certain to absorb the spectacular scenery
during the journey to the Kalaupapa Leprosy Settlement National Historic Landmark District, which
includes the Molokai Lighthouse. The island is
reached by boat or airplane; the district by hiking
or riding mules down and up the Pali Trail. Lack
of roads in or out of the Kalaupapa Peninsula limit
visitor vehicular access, although cars are present
in the settlements. Overnight stays are limited to
guests of residents. There are no public facilities

Siloama Chapel

(camping, restaurants, stores). Today, the disease is controlled by modern medicine
and is no longer a public threat; regulations continue to be enforced to protect the
privacy and unique lifestyle of the residents.

Pu'uhonua o Hnaunau National Historical Park

Honaunau, Hawaii, Hawaii

→ www.nps.gov/puho

→ The 182-acre Pu'uhonua o Honaunau (Place of Refuge of Honaunau) National Historical Park is located above Kawaihae Bay on the northern coast of Molokai, Hawaii, eighteen miles south of Kaliua-Kona on State Highway 11 and right on Highway 160, four miles to the park entrance.

Hale o Keawe Heiau, protected by watchful *akua ki'i* (god images)

This evocative place of mystic Hawaiian culture is on a low promontory of lava rock on a peninsula jutting into Honaunau Bay. The park is a pu'uhonua (refuge), a sanctuary for those who broke an ancient and sacred taboo (kapu), those defeated in battle, and noncombatants on a losing side. Anyone who reached it by swimming through shark-infested waters received absolution from the priests. Such sanctuaries once existed throughout the islands, sometimes as caves. The Pu'uhonua o Honaunau National Historical Park with its partially restored structures is the best remaining example of a traditional place of refuge.

A great lava stone wall, dating from 1550, separates the park's two sections. The angled wall is approximately 1,000 feet long, 10 feet high, and 17 feet thick at the base and narrowed toward the top. The massive black boulders skillfully fitted in place without mortar, some weighing four to six tons, came from Mauna Loa (the world's largest active volcano) twenty-two miles to the east of the park.

One side of the wall faces the ocean and the other side faces the palace grounds of the Kamehameha dynasty. Within the six-acre refuge compound is the third of three temples (heiau), the reconstructed Hale o Keawe Heiau, which served as the royal mortuary and contains the remains of 'A leale'a Heiau a boulder platform (127 feet by 60 feet and averaging 8 feet in height), the "Old Heiau," and the Hale o Papa (Women's Heiau). The imposing Hale o Keawe Heiau is a National Park Service (NPS) 1966–69 reconstruction. A result of meticulous research, building in this style that was virtually unknown to modern-day Hawaiians, the authentic leaf thatched temple, carved images, and an elevated altar, relied on archeological excavations and sketches of early European visitors. A palisade of sharp-ended poles protects the temple grounds. Standing guard against unwanted intrusions is the collection of wildly grimacing, tall wooden carved effigies *akua ki'i* (translated as "god images").

On the other side of the wall, the site has been restored to a pre-contact state. Six thatched huts stand near the shore a few hundred yards north of the *pu'uhonua*, one left unfinished to demonstrate Polynesian construction. Among the tall coconut palms is a pair of fishponds used as holding ponds for fish caught at sea for royal consumption and a replica outrigger canoe constructed of *koa* wood with coconut fiber lashings. Found in the refuge and the former palace grounds are original flat stones used for an ancient board game (*konane*), similar to checkers and played with black and white pebbles.

An early glimpse of what awaits the visitor to the park was captured by Robert Louis Stevenson in his "Letters from the Sandwich Islands" published in the *Sacramento Daily Union* September 22, 1866:

> At the end of an hour we had made the four miles, and landed on a level point of land, upon which was a wide extent of old ruins, with many a tall cocoanut tree growing among them. Here was the ancient City of Refuge—a vast enclosure....This old sanctuary was sacred to all—even to rebels in arms and invading armies. Once within its walls, and confession made to the priest and absolution obtained, the wretch with a price on his head could go forth without fear or without danger—he was tabu, and to harm him was death. The routed rebels in the lost battle for idolatry fled to this place to claim sanctuary, and many were thus saved....
> The walls of the temple are a study. The same food for speculation that is offered the visitor to the Pyramids of Egypt he will find here—the mystery of how they were constructed by a people unacquainted with science and mechanics. The natives have no invention of their own for hoisting heavy weights, they had no beasts of burden, and they have never even shown any knowledge of the properties of the lever. Yet some of the lava blocks quarried out, brought over rough, broken ground, and built into this wall, six or seven feet from the ground, are of prodigious size and would weigh tons. How did they transport and how raise them?

A rewarding trip for the visitor, Pu'uhonua o Honaunau National Historical Park is a scenic coastal site where the NPS has created an authentic view of vanished Hawaiian culture. The well-designed visitor center is the starting point for self-guided tours of the park and periodic arts and crafts demonstrations.

USS *Arizona* Memorial

Honolulu, Oahu, Hawaii

→   www.nps.gov/usar

→   The 10.5-acre USS *Arizona* Memorial is located in Pearl Harbor on the island of Oahu, two miles west of
Honolulu airport and approximately twenty minutes west of Honolulu on Kamehameha Highway (Highway 90).

USS *Arizona* aerial view (courtesy NPS)

Straddling the mid-portion of the sunken battleship *Arizona*, the gleaming white memorial honors American servicemen and civilians who lost their lives during the attack on Pearl Harbor. The hallowed site is the final resting place for many of the 1,177
crewmen who lost their lives during the Pearl Harbor attack on "the day that will live
in infamy," December 7, 1941.

The launch journey to the memorial, following the orientation film at the visitor
center, provides a pause for reflection and contemplation for a place that literally marks
an underwater grave. Some 1.5 million a year come to one of Hawaii's most visited historic sites with flower wreaths and leis to cast in the water, sometimes spotting irides-
cent slicks of oil that still leak, a drop at a time, from ruptured bunkers after more than
sixty years at the bottom of the sea. Architectural critic Paul Goldberger commented on
the deep, gut-wrenching emotion evoked by the USS *Arizona* memorial at Pearl Harbor
as one of few in the company of "Maya Lin's astonishingly simple Vietnam Veterans Memorial in Washington...and Edwin Lutyens's Memorial to the Missing of the Somme,
in France." The irony of the memorial's symbolism as a dual statement of perfidy and
sacrifice inevitably provokes thoughts of the World Trade Center 9/11 attack.

The focus of the journey across the serene waters of Pearl Harbor is the 184-foot-long memorial structure spanning the mid-portion of the sunken hull 8 feet below the surface, designed to give the appearance of floating gracefully over the shadowy underwater presence of the *Arizona*. The only visible feature of the ship is the barbette to gun turret number three rising above the water; a flag flies from the flagpole attached to the severed mainmast. Two white polygonal grass-roofed concrete blocks alongside the memorial structure depict mooring quays that once secured the great warship in 1941. Arriving at a landing stage, the visitors move up ramps into the first of the memorial's three sections, an entry and assembly room. The next space is the open-air central area designed for ceremonies and a view through side wall portals over the battleship resting on the harbor bottom. The third section is the evocative shrine room, where the names of those sailors and marines who lost their lives on the USS *Arizona* are engraved on the marble wall.

The architect, Alfred Preis, once explained that the sway-back structure with a lattice-like open-air center and rising at the ends, sags in its center but "stands strong and vigorous at its ends," to express "initial defeat and ultimate victory....The overall effect is one of serenity. Overtones of sadness have been omitted to permit the individual to contemplate his own personal responses...his innermost feelings." Pilings

USS *Arizona* water approach

driven deep into the bed of the harbor beyond the sides of the *Arizona*'s hull support the memorial without touching the sunken ship. Two 250-ton steel girders support the structure, 36 feet wide and 21 feet high at the ends, tapering to 27 feet wide and 14 feet high at the center.

The park includes a waterfront visitor center where visitors pick up their free tickets for the USS *Arizona* Memorial tour, a six-minute National Park Service boat ride to the memorial. The USS *Arizona* Memorial was dedicated on Memorial Day 1962 to commemorate the attack on Pearl Harbor and the men who died defending it. In 1989, the USS *Arizona* was designated a National Historic Landmark.

Oregon

Far West and
Pacific

PACIFIC
OCEAN

Lewis and Clark NHP

PORTLAND
SALEM

Columbia   River

Snake River

Crater Lake NP

Oregon Caves NM

Crater Lake National Park

Klamath County, Oregon

→ www.nps.gov/crla

→ The park is located in south central Oregon on Highway 62, sixty miles northwest of Klamath Falls and eighty miles northeast of Medford. The north entrance and thirty-three-mile Rim Drive are closed from mid-October to late June.

Crater Lake

A long drive through the Oregon portion of the Cascade Range offers views of many volcanic peaks—Mounts Hood, Jefferson, Washington, Three Sisters, Bachelor, and McLoughlin. At the south end of the range, a truncated cone (the remains of Mount Mazama) holds a 1,958-foot-deep caldera filled with the waters of a magnificent lake as intensely blue as the Oregon sky on a clear day: Crater Lake.

Two historic districts are noteworthy at the 183,224-acre Crater Lake National Park, established in 1902 as the seventh park in the National Park System. At the Village Historic District overlooking the lake is Crater Lake Lodge, not far from where some of the earliest rustic-style buildings were erected in the Rim Village. As originally executed, the park's Munson Valley Historic District administrative center, located three miles by road from the Rim Village at Munson Valley, is one of the handsomest groups of rustic structures in the entire National Park System.

Crater Lake Lodge has a checkered history of entrepreneurship producing a hurried hotel in 1915 that suffered decades of deterioration before an expensive National Park Service (NPS) supervised rehabilitation. The three-story shingled building now containing seventy-one rooms, some with exquisite lake views, was almost totally dismantled and then reassembled to provide modern accommodations. After a decade of planning and construction, on May 20, 1995, Crater Lake Lodge reopened to the public. The extensive structural rebuilding, replacement of mechanical and electrical systems, installation of new finishes and elevators, and additional exits and safety de-

Crater Lake Lodge

vices make the lodge a safe and attractive accommodation. For the first time since its original opening, Crater Lake Lodge was a project finally completed. The decision to maintain a lodge at the rim of Crater Lake is controversial. However, the efforts made by NPS to retain the building's historic exterior appearance, representative of western national park great lodges, should be appreciated in the context of the safety and comfort provided for guests at this historic cultural resource.

Several Rim Village structures showcase the evolving NPS rustic style. Although not initially planned as a model "village," (its name was coined in 1914, after Crater Lake Lodge started) the buildings are a mixture of concessioner and NPS-built structures unified by the landscape and the limited selection of building materials—stone, wood siding stained dark brown to contrast with white window frames, and steeply pitched shake-shingled roofs—and the promenade that ties the site together. A deliberate decision by the designers was to use local materials, forms, and massing suited to the harsh environment where annual snowfall averages 533 inches at the 7,100-foot elevation.

The Rim Village Visitor Center, built originally in 1921 as a photographer's studio, demonstrates the early use of gable-ended, wood-frame buildings with uncoursed boulder lower walls, horizontal or shingle siding, deeply recessed door and window openings, and steeply pitched shingled roofs. The NPS designed Community House (1924) is a two-story, rectangular wood-frame structure having a massive exterior chimney of uncoursed battered stone. Along with a steep wood-shingle roof, multilight windows with white frames and trim link the building to other structures in the village.

Adjacent to the rim plaza facing the cafeteria, a gable-ended building with a distinctive jerkinhead roof over the entrance wing, is a 1937 comfort station demonstrating NPS skill at refining rustic building designs and use of exterior materials. The modest sized structure built with labor from the Civilian Conservation Corps is an excellent example of the distinctive NPS Crater Lake wall treatment. Exterior battered walls (inclining inward from bottom to top toward the building) are built of massive uncoursed boulders, pyramiding larger stones near the bottom, and become progressively smaller as the masonry walls meet eaves or gables.

The first building to use this wall-building technique was the Sinnott Memorial. Opened in 1931, the unusual irregularly shaped stone-and-concrete structure with a log-framed roof (replaced with steel in 1963) is built into a rock outcrop on the slope of the caldera, about 50 feet below the rim. Building access is from the rim promenade by a moderately steep walkway with steps. Stone parapet 30-inch tall walls that extend out from the exterior walls guards the open elliptically shaped observation platform and also contains exhibit panels. A museum is located along the interior walls. Wall surfaces are uncoursed load-bearing native stone boulders, 3 and 4 feet in height, used to face the structure and make it seem a part of the caldera's inner walls.

A unifying feature of the Rim Village is the 3,450-foot-long promenade wall. The 30-inch-high and 18-inch-thick stone masonry wall minimizes use of mortar for visual interest. Local andesite (a volcanic rock) is placed in an irregular pattern of shapes varying in size and color. Three observation bays of varying configuration along the wall's length focus on prominent lake views.

Muson Valley rustic detail

In the early 1930s, the NPS selected a site for an administrative center in Munson Valley, a glacial trough on Mount Mazama's south slope three miles from the Annie Springs park entrance. Overall, the complex is a rustic jewel integrating an architectural vocabulary with landscaping, all superbly sensitive to the unique mountain location and climate.

NPS landscape architects laid out the administrative, residential, and maintenance facilities and established design guidelines for one of the most comprehensive rustic architectural programs ever undertaken by the NPS. The administrative core included an administration building and a ranger dormitory forming two sides of a plaza. The rustic character of the residential buildings was carried out through a sequence of small stone-and-timber cottages that become progressively larger, culminating in the masterfully executed National Historic

Landmark rustic Superintendent's Residence (1932) on the hill. The residential and maintenance areas are largely tucked out of view in the valley's trees. Buildings are situated at the edge of the meadows and following the contours of the land with building profiles kept horizontal and low.

Munson Valley administration building

The NPS designers were especially conscious of the dramatic setting, over-scaling many architectural features accordingly. They chose massive stone masonry and steeply pitched roofs as the central theme in response to the local climate and geology. Native materials and natural colors were used, and severely straight lines were avoided in order to better imitate nature.

A unique construction method was devised in order to achieve the desired rustic effect for the one-and-a-half-story buildings in Munson Valley in a short building season. The construction sequence started with a heavy wooden formwork framing for the concrete-and-stone foundation walls that outlined the interior surface of the exterior walls. The forms braced the wooden framing of the second floor and roof. Next, massive boulders, 2 to 3 feet in diameter and some as large as 5 feet across, were forced into place as work progressed on the upper wood framing. A space of several inches was left between the masonry and formwork and was later filled with concrete. Finally, as the masonry walls reached the eaves, and after the concrete was sufficiently cured, the formwork was removed and the weight of the second floor was transferred to the masonry walls.

Lauded by the NPS in *Park and Recreation Structures* (1938) for its superb quality of nonintrusive architecture, the complex is constantly under rehabilitation to confront the toll of the harsh environment and adaptive reuse for the structures. Visitors, especially architects and landscape designers, marvel at this extraordinary complex designed and built at the peak of NPS's rustic prowess and the inspiring examples of building in harmony with the environment.

Lewis and Clark National Historical Park

Astoria, Clatsop County, Oregon

→ www.nps.gov/lewi

→ Park visitor centers are located at the mouth of the Columbia River in the northwestern corner of Oregon at Fort Clatsop, five miles south of Astoria, Oregon, off US 101 and in the southwestern corner of Washington at Cape Disappointment in Cape Disappointment State Park, three miles west of Iwalco, Washington, on Washington State Route 100.

The former Fort Clatsop National Memorial, destroyed

The Lewis and Clark expedition of 1804–1806 is celebrated in the National Park System in eleven states. The Lewis and Clark National Historic Trail extends 3,700 miles from the Mississippi River in Illinois to the Pacific Ocean. There are more than one hundred sites, including five National Park Service (NPS) units. One recent addition to the NPS is the Lewis and Clark National Historical Park at the mouth of the Columbia River. The park commemorates the arrival of the Corps of Discovery at the Pacific and includes a combination of twelve state and national historic park sites in Oregon and Washington. The four NPS sites in Oregon are Fort Clatsop (the former Fort Clatsop National Memorial), Fort to Sea Trail, Salt Works, and the Netul Landing. The three NPS sites in Washington are Clark's Dismal Nitch, Station Camp, and the memorial to Thomas Jefferson located within Cape Disappointment State Park.

The NPS parks in Washington (Cape Disappointment State Park and Fort Columbia State Park) and Oregon (Fort Stevens State Park, Sunset Beach State Recreation Area, and Ecola State Park) stretch along forty miles of the Pacific coast from Long Beach, Washington, to Cannon Beach, Oregon, offering an opportunity to explore the expedition's place of arrival at the western end of their 4,000-mile journey. Historical structures include North Head and Cape Disappointment lighthouses in Cape Disappointment State Park.

The Fort Clatsop site includes an exhibit representing the fort where the Corps of Discovery established an encampment from December 1805 to March 1806 and explored the area, interacting with the Clatsop, Nehalem, and Chinook Indians. The full-sized log fort replaces a replica on the site built in 1955 and destroyed by fire in October of 2005. The exhibit was built through the contributions of local companies and community volunteer efforts. The park offers ranger-led programs and period-dressed reenactors to aid the visitor's appreciation of the fort exhibit as a landmark site in the Corps of Discovery's epic march across the continent through uncharted lands. Smoke curling out of the chimneys and the flag at full staff will stir respect for actions of greatness by ordinary men.

Across the mouth of the Columbia River in Washington at Cape Disappointment State Park are two historic lighthouses. The Cape Disappointment Lighthouse, first lit in 1856, is the oldest operating lighthouse on the West Coast. The white-painted plaster brick tower, with attached oil house, stands 53 feet tall with a focal plane 220 feet above sea level. Now lit by a fourth-order Fresnel lens, its black horizontal stripe was added later to distinguish it from North Head Lighthouse located just two miles north. The original first-order Fresnel lens formerly used in both the Cape Disappointment and North Head lighthouses is on display at the Lewis and Clark Interpretive Center.

The North Head Lighthouse now contains an automated light, and the restored tower and keeper's quarters are open to the public. The 65-foot-tall tower is brick masonry, with a white-painted cement plaster overlay, built on a solid basalt foundation, and an attached one-story workroom. The lantern room, reached by a spiral stair with sixty-nine steps, is 194 feet above sea level. The first-order Fresnel lens, which was transferred from Cape Disappointment Lighthouse Center, was lit for the first time in the North Head tower on May 16, 1898. The restored keepers' dwellings, located about a half-mile into the woods from the tower, houses park personnel in one half of the duplex structure; the other half and the single-family dwelling are available for overnight stays.

A unique feature in the park, located at Cape Disappointment State Park, is one of seven art installations of the Confluence Project created by architect Maya Lin, designer of the Vietnam Veterans Memorial. The installations along a 450-mile route that were scenes of meetings between Native Americans and the Lewis and Clark Expedition's westward passage, are inspiring experiences related to the travels of the Corps of Discovery two centuries ago.

Oregon Caves National Monument

Cave Junction, Josephine County, Oregon

→ www.nps.gov/orca

→ Oregon Caves National Monument is fifty miles south of Grants Pass, Oregon, and seventy-six miles northeast of Crescent City, California, via US 199. Oregon 46, an eighteen-mile-long narrow, mountainous highway east of Cave Junction, reaches the park.

The Oregon Caves National Monument is small in size but rich in diversity. The 488-acre park protects caves carved out of limestone formations with all of the earth's six main rock types, diversity of bats, virgin forests of Douglas fir, and exceptional rustic historical architecture in a National Historic District that surrounds the National Historic Landmark Oregon Caves Chateau. The caves are off the well-traveled tourist path in southwestern Oregon's Siskiyou Mountains. The monument was proclaimed in 1909 and transferred to the National Park Service (NPS) from the U.S. Forest Service in 1934.

The Chateau at Oregon Caves National Monument is one of the least-known lodges in the National Park System. Although relatively low in national park lodge visitation (the season is from late April to early October), the Chateau is a tour de force of organic architecture and well worth a visit. This six-story lodge built into a gorge is a strong architectural presence in a rich forest setting among tumbling waterfalls and moss-covered marble ledges.

The Chateau's designer, architect Gust Lium, faced an enormous challenge. An existing roadway and Chalet and employee housing with shaggy cedar-bark siding, long roof shingles, and steeply pitched roofs set a site planning and architectural precedent for the complex. Rather than perching the Chateau on the mountain side of the roadway, similar to the other buildings at the monument, Lium chose to place it across the road and span the small gorge to blend agreeably into the site. He physically brought the outside in and reinforced this interplay with enormous picture windows facing the gorge, ingeniously channeling the cave's stream from the gorge into the Chateau to create an artificial brook through the dining room. Stone retaining walls, two decorative trout pools and a waterfall, a campfire circle, and various walkways by the Civilian Conservation Corps (CCC) embellish the Chateau's integration with the site.

Lium scaled down the perceived mass of the building by constructing the largest volume of the structure inside the gorge. From the "ground" level, where the road curves around the building, the visitor faces an unpretentious two-story structure—something smaller in scale to the surrounding forest, and something that fits with the terrain and rural atmosphere of the development. The full six-story height can be seen looking upward from the rear of the Chateau's lowest level and from a distance across the gorge. Skillfully adapting the floor plan to the site, Lium placed a wedge-shaped central wing on the entrance side 30 feet wide that widens to 48 feet facing the gorge. A pair of rectangular wings approximately 35 feet by 60 feet extend at angles away from the central wing; the long dimension extends into the gorge.

Oregon Caves Chateau, gorge view

A distinctive exterior feature is the shaggy cedar-bark shiplap siding, matching the building to the texture of the surrounding conifer forest. Steeply pitched gable-end main roofs, pierced by shed-roof dormers and further broken by gabled-roof dormers, all with long shake shingles, maintain a scale compatible with the setting. In spite of its formidable mass, the building does not appear to intrude on its setting.

The visitor will find a high integrity of original spaces and furnishings, con-

Chateau, main entrance

ceived by Lium. The dramatic lobby on the fourth floor, accessible from the parking lot, contains a double fireplace. Douglas fir log columns 30 inches in diameter and massive 18- by 24-inch beams felled from surrounding national forests support the timber framing in the lobby and lounge areas. The subtle pale gray wood in the room has a history: construction workers beat sacks of cement against the wooden posts to loosen up the bags' contents. Tiny particles of cement became imbedded in the wood. As the building neared completion, the crew stained wood that had not initially been tinted by the cement to match it.

A handsome rustic staircase of oak, madrona, pine, and fir leads downstairs from the lobby to the dining room and upstairs to the guest rooms. Three-inch thick oak treads rest on a massive pair of stringers. The darker wood of the peeled madrona balusters and the lighter wood of the handrails and newel posts are smooth-finished but retain softened gnarls and knots. Natural light from the large windows overlooking the trout pool highlights the stairwell and creates a pleasing contrast with the darker lobby.

In addition to the majestic Chateau, several other rustic buildings, all built in the same exterior bark treatment and shake-shingle roofs, contribute to the Oregon Caves National Historic District. The Chalet, also a Lium building, was completed in 1934. The three-story structure (the third floor and archway added in 1942) is built on the slope directly across the road from the Chateau. The building mass is diminished in scale by the use of second and third floor dormers projecting from the steep main roof. The upper two floors now serve as dormitory space for seasonal guides. The Ranger Residence (1936), perched on flat ground in the hillside above the cave south of the Chalet, is a one-story structure. A 9-foot-high basement is sheathed in a wall of shaggy bark. A cluster of seven rustic guest cabins were built near the Chalet in 1926 up the slope from the cave entrance and all but one (the ranger residence) were removed in 1988. Two other rustic structures in the historic district are the Guide Dormitory built in 1927 and the Checking and Comfort station, a unique combination of offices and public restrooms, built in 1941 by the CCC.

The visitor will be rewarded by the long drive to this enchanting place of rusticity virtually unchanged from the 1930s. The Chateau and adjacent buildings are superb examples of rustic architecture, a strong presence in harmony with the landscape.

Washington

Far West and Pacific

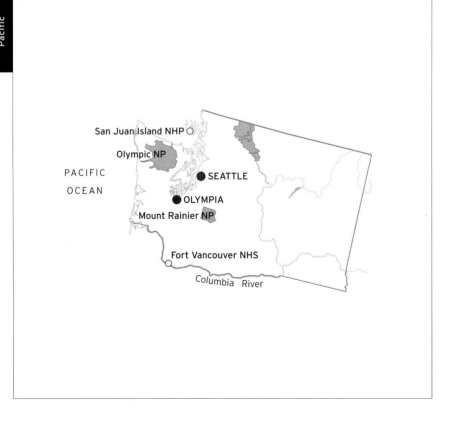

San Juan Island NHP ○

Olympic NP

PACIFIC
OCEAN

● SEATTLE

● OLYMPIA

Mount Rainier NP

Fort Vancouver NHS
○

Columbia River

Fort Vancouver National Historic Site

Vancouver, Clark County, Washington, and Oregon City, Clackamas County, Oregon

→ www.nps.gov/fova

→ Fort Vancouver National Historic Site consists of two units, the reconstructed Fort Vancouver in Vancouver, Washington, and the John McLoughlin House in Oregon City. Fort Vancouver is reached from Interstate 5, take exit on Mill Plain Boulevard and drive east on East Evergreen Boulevard and follow signs to the visitor center. From Interstate 205, exit on Washington 14; go west six miles and take Interstate 5 north, exit on Mill Plain Boulevard and drive east on East Evergreen Boulevard and follow signs to visitor center.

Indian Trade Shop and Dispensary

Main gate

The Fort Vancouver reconstruction of an important trading post in the history of the American Northwest offers a step back in time; try to ignore the intrusive interstate highway bridge from Portland across the Columbia River, the high-powered transmission lines, and the light aircraft from an adjacent airport, and let this recreated British outpost bring to life the era of Northwest trappers and traders. The National Park Service (NPS) has meticulously crafted an experience for visitors that begins with an interpretive center and leads back into history at the palisaded fort. Inside the 15-foot-tall Douglas fir picket walls, surrounding an expansive grassy enclosure, period furnished structures and reenactments by people in period costumes instill the visitor with a sense of Fort Vancouver's history.

The original fort construction by the Hudson Bay Company began in 1829 as a measure to strengthen their position and British claim to the territory. An imposing log palisade enclosed a dozen buildings—dwellings, warehouses, and workshops—

arranged around an interior grassy field. Native Americans went there to trade, trappers and traders took their furs and departed with goods, clerks bustled in and out of the warehouses, and visiting sailors idled between trips. An additional thirty to fifty dwellings were located west and southwest of the stockade walls. John McLoughlin held the position as Chief Factor, directing the Hudson Bay Company's Northwest Department, which encompassed an area larger than New England.

After United States and Great Britain settled the boundary dispute in 1846, the fort became an American possession. Abandoned by the British, the fort's remains burned to the ground in 1866. Columbia Barracks, a U.S. military installation founded nearby in 1849, expanded onto the fort's site. After designation as a National Historic Site in 1961, archeological work and reconstruction began that continues today.

A walk down the rolling surface of the bluff, from the interpretive center past the orchard and garden outside the palisade, provides a gradual transition into the atmosphere of the fort's life in 1844. Entry through the massive wooden gates leads visitors onto the grassy plain of the parallelogram-shaped enclosure. The 15-foot-high Douglas fir log palisade walls over 2,100 feet in length (734 feet across the long dimension and 318 feet across the ends), deceive the eye; the scope here is that of five football fields placed side by side.

An unhurried walk across the enclosure and through the reconstructed buildings reveals the meticulous craftsmanship and typical building techniques completed under NPS supervision. Typical framing methods used throughout the reconstruction are in the Hudson Bay Company's French Canadian post-on-sill style, an assemblage of squared timbers joined by mortise-and-tenon jointing.

A prominent structure is the three-story octagonal bastion at the palisade's northwest corner originally built in the winter of 1844–45. The first two stories of the post-on-sill bastion were 20 feet square and about 20 feet high. Horizontal rifle loopholes were cut in the 12-inch thick log walls. The top floor was octagonal and extended over

Corner bastion

Chief Factor's residence

the base, giving defenders a clear view of the land and a perfect platform from which to protect the fort. Hinged shutters covered three-pound guns mounted on sea carriages and armed for service.

Another important structure is the large white house used as the Chief Factor's residence. Intended to impress the natives and settlers with the power and majesty of the London-based company, construction began in 1829 and took seven years to

John McLoughlin House exterior   Interior

complete. Period furnishings attest to the impressive grandeur of this frontier mansion. Other buildings, free-standing or built onto the enclosure's palisade walls, are the Kitchen/Laundry, Indian Trade Shop and Dispensary, Bakehouse, Washhouse, Fur Warehouse, Carpenter Shop, and Jail.

The best time to see Fort Vancouver is on a foggy weekend morning when the sights and sounds of this century are muted and all that can be seen are the tall fir timbers of the palisade and the outline of its buildings inside. Then, modern intrusions are erased and the scene returns to the timeless quality of the palisade, the river plain, and the Columbia River flowing westward to the Pacific.

Mount Rainier National Park

Ashford, Lewis and Pierce Counties, Washington

→ www.nps.gov/mora

→ Mount Rainier National Park is located in west central Washington within an easy drive from Seattle (ninety-five miles) via Interstate 5 and Highways 512, 7, and 706 or Interstate 5 and Highways 161, 7, and 706, sixty-four miles west of Yakima via US 12 or 410.

Seen from one hundred miles away, snow-capped Mount Rainier floats ethereally in the distance. The peak of the truncated volcanic cone in southwestern Washington State rises in dramatic isolation 8,000 feet higher than the surrounding foothills. Seen from the air, alternating ridges of rock (called "cleavers") and ice radiate out from the peak to the lowlands. The dense snowpack forms a dozen major glaciers at the 7,000-foot level—the largest mass of easily accessible glaciers in the lower forty-eight states. Subalpine meadows are brightened in spring by blossoms that advance behind the melting snow in a stunning array of blue, red, white, pink, and yellow. Dense forests of

Alaskan cedar, Douglas fir, western white pine, and western hemlock splay out along the ridges, girdling the peak in thick stands above the lushly shaded forest floor.

Mount Rainier National Park has a superb collection of historic structures des-

Paradise Inn, exterior   Interior

ignated as National Historic Landmarks and considered one of the finest examples of National Park Service (NPS) master planning in the 1920s and 1930s. The collection of rustic-style structures is lauded as one of the most intact and extensive examples of the NPS master planning process. The buildings at the four historic districts—Nisqually, Longmire, Paradise, and Sunrise—along with remote patrol cabins and bridges, present an appealing and consistent array of rustic park historical architecture.

A two-hour drive from Seattle to Ashford leads to the Nisqually entrance gate, introducing the visitor to the experience that loops over more than forty miles of twisting and turning roads to Sunrise. A massive log archway spanning the road is the visitor's first contact with the park's rustic architecture. The monumental structure of cedar-log columns and beams, completed in time for President Taft's visit to the park in 1911, was replaced in 1973 nearly identical to the original. To the right of the entranceway is the finely crafted Oscar Brown cabin. The structure with a delicate arched gable fan, built in 1908, served originally as park headquarters and an entrance checking station. Just beyond Oscar Brown's cabin is the entrance checking station completed in 1926. These fine examples of early NPS rustic design illustrate the simple forms and carefully executed details devised to fit with a local environment.

The Longmire group of buildings, six miles from the entrance, is significant in the interpretive history of Mount Rainier National Park. Three National Historic Landmark buildings constructed between 1927 and 1929 illustrating the outstanding talents and efforts of the NPS staff are the Administration Building, Community Building, and Service Station. The two-story Administration Building (37 feet by 68 feet in plan) is a careful integration of local stone and log in a highly refined composition of rustic elements. The design and execution of superb field skills and craftsmanship is a suitable candidate as a poster illustration for NPS rustic design at its peak of prowess. The walls up to sill heights are composed of rounded glacial boulders battered to flow upward from the ground in carefully selected graduated sizes, achieving visual stability and emphasizing tapered lower wall windows with deep recesses.

The two-story, T-plan, timber-framed Community Building at Longmire has interesting triple-log column porch supports; the interior main hall is a revelation of timber columns and trusses, log-slab siding, wood floor, and cedar tongue-and-groove ceiling planking—all immersed in light from the ribbons of casement and dormer windows. Note the use of the exterior log column theme repeated inside in the freestanding cedar structural supports for the exposed-log scissor trusses that rise 30 feet above the floor at their peak. The utilitarian Service Station, sited next to the National Park Inn on the approach road to the Administration Building, is so well designed and nestled back into the trees that it is barely noticeable. Even its function does not seem incongruous within the forest setting. Nearby is the Nisqually 180-foot suspension bridge, a timber reconstruction of the original 1924 log bridge.

The road from Longmire to Paradise Valley climbs 2,600 feet in thirteen miles of gentle grades and switchbacks. Along the route, the road crosses Christine Falls Bridge. The 56-foot-long span is one of the finest examples of a necessarily functional design that blends with the natural setting. Another example along the route is the Narada Falls Bridge. As the traveler approaches Paradise, the cloud-wreathed snowcapped peak of Mount Rainier is an ever-expanding presence as the forest thins and alpine meadows with wildflowers come into view. The Cascade Range is arrayed to the south; snowcapped Mount Adams and Mount Hood and the truncated cone of Mount Saint Helens are visible on the horizon.

Administration Building

The National Historic Landmark Paradise Inn, competed in 1917, was built by the concessioner Rainier National Park Company as the park's first hotel lodgings. Using local stone and well-seasoned cedar timbers weathered "on the stump" after an 1885 fire, the soaring, steeply-pitched roof dominates the landscape and fits with the surrounding peaked mountain range. This substantial architectural form makes the Inn—in its isolated setting—seem particularly protective and sheltering. Designers solved the problem of supporting the steeply pitched roof with a fine display of log-working skills used to assemble a pleasing rhythm of posts, beams, and trusses. Dormers pierce the main roofs of the lobby and dining room sections, allowing light to penetrate into the deep interiors. The dramatic lobby (approximately 50 feet by 112 feet) is a masterpiece of rustic framing and spatial architecture that creates a delightful place for skiers, hikers, climbers, and other visitors. Fireplaces with huge stone chimneys, 50 and 60 feet high, warm each end of the lobby. Overflowing the interior are other rustic features, including the unique rustic furniture—piano, a grandfather clock, and probably the woodwork around the registration desk. The Inn closed in 2006 for a two-year rehabilitation project. Near the Inn is a steeply peaked Guide House, a remnant of the park's role as one of the earliest ski resorts in the United States, now serving as the NPS Climbing Information Center and housing for concession employees.

The switchback road from the park's east entrance at White River climbs to Sunrise Village at Yakima Park. The complex at the sub-Alpine 6,400-foot elevation was NPS master-planned and built in the 1930s to provide administrative and visitor services. The cedar-shingle clad Sunrise Lodge is a soaring barn-like structure originally designed as the first wing of a hotel next to a complex of over 200 guest cabins. Never completed, the lodge now serves as a ranger station, snack bar, gift shop, and employee housing; the cabins are since removed.

The centerpiece structures at Sunrise are the National Historic Landmark Yakima Park Stockade group. A fantasy of an imaginary frontier fort, three buildings and a stockade wall were designed as an interpretation of Pacific Northwest frontier architecture. No fort ever existed here; the site was once a summer rendezvous location for the Yakama (the original spelling was reintroduced in 1994 by the tribe) and other tribes, whose ancestors hunted and gathered in the high elevation landscapes like Sunrise for thousands of years. From an approach vista, the buildings blend together into the protective image of a frontier stockade. The three unattached blockhouses enclose a courtyard defined by the forms, textures, and tones of the surrounding walls. There is uniformity between rich textures and the reddish weathering of the buildings' log walls, which contrasts with the random whittled log-end projections. The stone foundations built to windowsill height, the carefully composed placement and proportions of window openings, and the consistent roof height visually unifies the buildings.

The Mount Rainier National Park historic buildings represent public and private efforts to promote, develop, manage, and protect the park's natural and recreational resources. In their natural settings, the group of NPS rustic structures is one of the most extensive and intact examples of a cultural landscape. The Nisqually entrance gate; the rustic structures at Longmire, Paradise, and Sunrise; the bridges and patrol cabins together embody the national park experience of buildings and landscape designed in harmony with the environment.

Olympic National Park

Port Angeles, Clallam, Jefferson, and Mason Counties, Washington

→ www.nps.gov/olym

→ Destinations in the park's two sections, west of Seattle, in the center of the Olympic Peninsula and a strip along the Pacific coast, all can be reached from US 101. No roads cross through the park's interior.

Lake Crescent Lodge

The 922,000-acre park (with almost 877,000 acres in wilderness area) is divided into two parts: a sixty-three-mile strip of coast, and the huge inland block of forest, valley, meadow, and mountain. The biologically diverse World Heritage Site designated park contains distinctly different ecosystems—seashore, rugged glacier-capped mountains, and magnificent stands of old growth and temperate rain forests. The summit of Mount Olympus rises to almost 8,000 feet. Below the jagged peaks and timberline, a network of thirteen rivers threads its way down to sea level. Rain forests, thick stands of conifers, deep-cut rivers, mountain streams pouring through alpine meadows, and lakes and shorelines provide an ecological haven worthy of its designation as a World Biosphere Park.

Discovering the historical structures in Olympic National Park may involve an automobile trip to a specific resort, a long drive to a remote trailhead, or the serendipitous discovery of a shelter, cabin, or chalet along a hiking trail. Because of natural deterioration by the extremely moist climate and park administration decisions to remove specific structures, all the nineteenth-century structures in the park have vanished. The twentieth-century buildings, retaining their integrity in stunning settings, are precious cultural resources. Insights into the park's identity are found at the Humes

Cabin (1900), Storm King Ranger Station (1905), the Park Headquarters (1940), and the buildings that were put up either by early settlers, through recreation development, or by Depression-era relief programs. Backcountry trails and shelters, private chalets,

Rosemary Inn cabin

Rosemary Inn

lakeside and hot springs resorts, housekeeping cabins, and auto campgrounds on lakes and streams—all had their day and left their mark.

Olympic National Park historical structures show a remarkable consistency in materials and design, generally in the vernacular style for privately constructed buildings and rustic for publicly funded structures. Whether this was conscious or accidental, private as well as public buildings were built on a scale and with materials appropriate for their surroundings. Dictated by the availability of local materials and labor, log or drop-channel siding, shingle or shake roofs, and small-pane wood-framed windows prevail. Locations respect rather than dominate sites. Widely differing objectives follow these themes, from cabin to U.S. Forest Service shelter to private resort or chalet.

The Storm King Information Center at Barnes Point on Lake Crescent is one of the few buildings in the park that date from the early days of Federal administration. Built by Chris Morgenroth in 1905, the homesteader and later a Forest Service employee built the structure in traditional notched corner logs, and a steeply pitched cedar-shake-shingle roof.

Resorts of interest are on the north side of the park on Lake Crescent and on the south side's Quinault Lake. Located at Lake Crescent's Barnes Point, Singer's Tavern (now the Lake Crescent Lodge) and Rosemary Inn both opened in 1915. Separated by only a few hundred yards of thick forest, the two resorts—reached originally by ferry—evoke the scale, setting, and landscaping of an earlier era.

The Crescent Lake Lodge two-story shingled, wood-frame main lodge's character remains essentially unchanged, although substantially rehabilitated in the 1980s. The most distinctive feature is the lake front glass-enclosed porch providing superb views of the lake, forests, and ridges. The lobby and main public room's comfortable Arts and Crafts furniture, board-and-batten walls, bric-a-brac, and memorabilia on tables and walls provide a cozy greeting for travelers. A rubble-stone fireplace with a mounted Roosevelt elk head above warms the lodge on chilly days.

In the nearby Rosemary Inn Historic District, Rosemary Inn has a quaint collection of cabins around a main lodge. The real charm of the place is in the randomly sited cabins of either wood-frame or log construction. Much of the delight in Rosemary Inn comes from the almost whimsical mixture of building forms, materials (either wood-frame or log construction), and the sequence of romantically named cabins—Tumble Inn, Cara Mia, Dreamerie, Summerie, Dixie, Alabam, Honeysuckle, Silver Moon, Rock-A-Bye, Dardanella, and Red Wing.

One backcountry structure is the Enchanted Valley Chalet, thirteen miles from the Graves Creek trailhead along the east fork of the Quinault River valley or seventeen-mile trail from the Dosewallips trailhead. The two-story chalet, constructed with locally cut, full-length, squared cedar logs ending in diagonal-cut dovetail joints and other materials hauled to the site by packhorses was built in the early 1930s. Prior to establishment of Olympic National Park in 1938, the chalet was a favorite stopping place for hikers and horse caravans in Enchanted Valley. Today, the chalet, threatened by flooding from the shifting east fork of the Quinault River and in dilapidated condition and closed for visitor use, is under consideration by NPS for future management and protection.

By the mid-1930s, six hundred miles of trails and more than 100 shelters dotted the peninsula's landscape. Built of readily available logs and split-cedar shakes, the simple structures were based on Adirondack shelter design: open on one side with a peeled-pole log frame, a gable shake roof with two unequal pitches, split-shake walls and roofs, and a dirt floor. The shelters were spaced along the trails at reasonable hiking distances and became part of the U.S. Forest Service promotion of recreational opportunities in the reserve. The best examples are found along the Bogachiel River in the Hoh Rainforest subdistrict. Inspired peeled-log structures in the rustic style are the Soleduck Falls Shelter, Elwha Shelter kitchen and Altaire Shelter. Ranger stations at Elwha, Altaire, Elkhorn, North Fork, Quinault, and Staircase are simple designs in "Forest Service Rustic"—functional clapboard siding incorporating the pine tree symbol of both the Forest Service and the Civilian Conservation Corps in the gable end.

The historical architecture in Olympic National Park is a modest collection, subordinate to the natural environment's rich variety. Buildings alongside trails or lakeshores are selective remnants of the park's history and are reminders of the exploration, commercial development, recreation, federal management, and relief programs that have taken place in it. As one discovers a cabin or trailside shelter, a resort hotel or ranger station, the desire to classify a building by its role in interpretive history is lost in the simple act of discovery. After hours of hiking through the wilderness, the sighting of one of these structures is a poignant reminder that in this region weather dominates, and people and buildings are transient.

San Juan Island National Historical Park

Friday Harbor, San Juan County, Washington

→   www.nps.gov/sajh

→   The park is located on an island accessible by Washington State Ferry from Anacortes, Washington, eighty-three miles north of Seattle, or from Sydney, British Columbia, and fifteen miles north of Victoria at Friday Harbor. Park visitor centers are located at American Camp, six miles southeast of Friday Harbor, and English Camp, about nine miles northeast of Friday Harbor.

English Camp

San Juan Island in northwest Washington was at the center of the mid-nineteenth-century American and British dispute over the water boundary between Vancouver Island, British Columbia, and the Oregon Territory. A confrontation in 1859 between the two encampments on San Juan Island almost escalated to a war when an American settler shot a British pig. The ensuing crisis became known as the "Pig War." Cooler heads prevailed and the two nations negotiated a twelve-year joint military occupation. The 1871 Treaty of Washington finally settled the boundary through peaceful arbitration. The 1,751-acre San Juan Island National Historical Park consists of two units protecting the remains of the British and American encampments.

Today, the events of the Pig War may seem like comic opera. At the time, they were deadly serious with more than five hundred U.S. soldiers facing off against three British warships until talk replaced loaded cannons. Captain George E. Pickett (of Gettysburg's Pickett's Charge) and his Company D of the U.S. Ninth Infantry landed on the southeastern tip of the island and established the American Camp. Pickett shipped most of the buildings from Fort Bellingham in 1859–1860. The site covering more than

1,200 acres on the southern end of the island now contains three original buildings: the one-story wood-frame officers' quarters, a laundress' quarters, and the remains of the Redoubt, an earthen gun emplacement. The parade ground is enclosed by a picket fence modeled after an 1868 photograph.

Shortly after Great Britain and the United States confirmed the joint-occupancy agreement, the commander of HMS *Satellite* selected a British site thirteen miles north of the American Camp on Garrison Bay on the island's northwest coast. The Royal Marine Light Infantry contingent landed on March 21, 1860, carrying materials for the commissary. Contemporary photographs and paintings show a compact camp of white-painted, one-story wood-frame buildings on a placid bay. Restored English Camp structures include the barracks building, a two-story waterfront blockhouse, the commissary/storehouse, and hospital. The site also features rock walls and terraces constructed by the Royal Marines on Officers' Hill, as well as numerous chimney ruins scattered about the parade ground. A formal garden duplicating an original planted on the same site in 1867 was recreated in 1972.

Period garrison flags today are flown from 90-foot poles above both parade grounds during summer months. Staff and volunteers conduct historical reenactments in period clothing on Saturday afternoons during the summer months, and an annual encampment with reenactors from throughout the Pacific Northwest and Canada is held the fourth weekend in August.

Southwest

Arizona

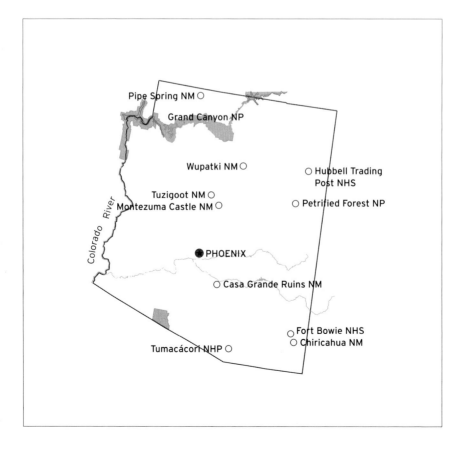

Casa Grande Ruins National Monument

Coolidge, Pinal County, Arizona

→ www.nps.gov/cagr

→ Casa Grande Ruins National Monument is in southern Arizona, halfway between Phoenix and Tucson.
Take Interstate 10 south from Phoenix to Exit 185, then go east on Arizona 387 and 87 for fourteen miles. The
monument is one mile north of Coolidge, Arizona.

Casa Grande ruins and shelter

When Father Kino visited Casa Grande in 1694 he recorded,

> "...the Casa Grande is a four story building, as large as a castle and equal to the largest church
> in these lands of Sonora. Close to this Casa Grande there are thirteen smaller houses, somewhat
> more dilapidated, and the ruins of many others, which make it evident that in ancient times
> there had been a city here."

Today, from a distance, the recognizable feature on the landscape is the massive four-
story *Casa Grande* (Great House), standing under its idiosyncratic protective roof on
four inwardly canted steel columns. In the foreground are the curved adobe walls at
the monument entrance and the Pueblo Revival style visitor center. In addition to the
Great House ruins, the site contains remains of smaller buildings and a compound wall
constructed in the early 1200s and abandoned by the mid-1400s. Recognized for its significance as a prehistoric ruin, the monument was the first archeological site to be preserved (1892) and is the fifth oldest unit in the National Park System.

The enigmatic complex of ruins was the work of the Hohokam people, desert farmers who built the structure in the early 1300s. Sometime between A.D. 1355
and 1450 a slow societal collapse occurred, and the Hohokam culture disappeared.

Archeologists speculate on causes of the disappearance of the Hohokam: failure of the irrigation system; soil depletion from extensive irrigation, along with climatic changes and flooding; raiding by neighboring tribes; or disease. Whatever the reasons, the desert reclaimed the land and erosion began to melt the once-magnificent Great House back into the sand. Without written record of the desert people, speculation has been cast about on the use of the Great House as a defensive watchtower, an observation point for the life-sustaining irrigation canal to the north, a corn storehouse, and a religious center. Archeoastronomers—those who apply the study of celestial events at archeological sites—speculate that the Great House's orientation to the cardinal points and upper-room oval, circular, and rectangular sun or calendar holes were placed for special purposes. Knowing the changing positions of celestial objects guided ceremonial cycles and the planting and harvesting.

The Great House measures approximately 58 by 43 feet in plan. The alignment was almost, but not quite, in line with the cardinal points. The four-story-tall structure is built of the local soil, out of caliche, a concrete-like mixture of sand, clay, and calcium carbonate (limestone). It is estimated that it took three thousand tons to construct the Great House. Caliche mud was piled in successive courses to form walls 4 feet thick at the base tapering to 2 feet thick at the top, in four stories each 30 to 45 feet high. An estimated 640 beams of ponderosa pine, juniper, mesquite, and fir trees were carried or floated down the Gila River to the village. Anchored in the walls, the timbers formed ceiling or floor supports. A lattice of saguaro ribs was placed perpendicular across the beams, covered with bundles of reeds, and topped with a final layer of caliche mud.

Built on 5 feet of fill, the present height of the house closely approximates the original height of four stories. The first story was purposefully filled in during construction; the second and third stories each had five rooms; a single room or tower comprised the fourth floor; and a low parapet may have surrounded the uppermost floor levels. The fourth-story room has a tunnel-like opening in one wall that aligns with the setting sun at summer solstice.

Efforts to stabilize and protect the ruins began in 1890 when a cover was suggested to shield the ruins from the elements; the first cover was erected in 1903. In 1928, Frederick Law Olmsted, Jr., acting in an advisory capacity to the National Park Service (NPS), sketched a design for a new roof with distinctive leaning posts and curved outer truss members finally built in 1932. The most effective wall preservation technique, one probably advocated in 1902, was a light coating of caliche mud. The "magic formula" now in use is called Amended Mud, a mixture of a commercial product and caliche mixed with sand, first tested in 1972. Applied every two years by whisk broom, a coating of this brownish-colored substance allows the capillary moisture in the walls to evaporate.

An NPS museum and a cluster of residential structures existed on the site in the 1920s. The Pueblo Revival style museum/administration structure, built of adobe brick, was constructed in 1932. The visitor center was conceived as a hollow square around an open courtyard, but insufficient funds resulted in completion of only the front part of the square. In 1964, work resumed, and exhibit space was added to create the courtyard, with native plants, a new entrance, and a covered porch along the building's north side.

Casa Grande ruins, visitor center

Additional areas outside the ruins are visible from the observation deck in the picnic area. Although the ruins are open in daylight hours for self-guided tours, an orientation and ranger-conducted tour begins at the interpretive ramada and is recommended for the start of a journey back in time to the enigmatic Great House of the Hohokam.

Chiricahua National Monument

Near Willcox, Cochise County, Arizona

→ www.nps.gov/chir

→ Located in the southeast corner of Arizona, seventy miles east of Tucson on Interstate 10. Take Exit 340 at Willcox, and then go southeast on Route 186 for thirty-five miles. At Route 181, go east approximately four miles to the visitor center.

Deep into the southeast corner of Arizona—fifteen miles west of New Mexico, fifty miles north of the Mexican border, and twenty miles by road from Fort Bowie National Historic Site (see page 93) —is the landscape of the Turkey Creek caldera. Formed by a massive volcanic eruption twenty-seven million years ago, 2,000 feet of ash and pumice fused into a rock called rhyolite tuff and eventually eroded into towering spires, pinnacles, and balanced rocks weighing hundreds of tons that perch delicately on small pedestals. Called the "Land of the Standing-Up Rocks" by Chiricahua Apache and later the

"Wonderland of Rocks" by pioneers, 11,985 acres of this land was set aside as the Chiricahua National Monument in 1924 and transferred from the U.S. Forest Service to the National Park Service (NPS) in 1933. Of historical and architectural interest are

Faraway Ranch

the homesteads of Faraway Ranch, a preserved working cattle ranch and later a guest ranch, and the Stafford Cabin.

The Chiricahua Mountains were the homeland of the central band of Chiricahua Apaches. Led by Cochise and later Geronimo, the Apaches launched attacks from these mountains against the tide of pioneers that began in 1861 with the Bascom Affair. The Apache resistance slowed but did not stop settlement in the area, and

Geronimo's band surrendered in 1886. With the removal of all prisoners of war to distant Fort Pickens in Florida, a new way of life took over.

Ja Hu (Jay Hugh) Stafford arrived in 1880 and built one of the first homestead dwellings in the Chiricahua Mountains. The Stafford Cabin illustrates the techniques and building materials used in one of the oldest surviving log cabins in the region. Built of logs from adjacent forests, the original two-room cabin (approximately 15 feet by 28 feet in plan with later shed and garage additions) has a ridge roof with exposed log purlins and wood-plank ceiling. The simple interiors had pine flooring and a rhyolite fieldstone chimney in the living room. The site surrounding the cabin has evidence of Stafford's early agricultural efforts: an orchard of fruit trees and an irrigation system. In 1924, the Stafford Cabin was remodeled as a guest cabin for the neighboring Faraway Ranch, a commercial guest ranch operated by Lillian and Ed Riggs.

A Swedish emigrant couple, Neil Erickson and his wife Emma, came to homestead in Bonita Canyon seven years after Stafford did. In 1886, then-army sergeant Erickson came upon the canyon while he was pursuing a stolen horse. The couple built a home in the canyon, farmed the land, and raised a family. Erickson, a self-taught carpenter, erected the ranch house in three major stages. The resulting two-story mixture of adobe, wood framing, exterior stucco, and shingle roof stands on the canyon's floor.

By 1917, the homestead was turned into a guest ranch and an Erickson daughter named it Faraway Ranch because it was so "godawful far away from everything." The house is preserved with original furnishings to reflect the 1950s historic period, when it achieved its height of success as a guest ranch. Check with the visitor center for a schedule of tours.

Fort Bowie National Historic Site

Near Willcox and Bowie, Cochise County, Arizona

→ www.nps.gov/fobo

→ Located in southeast Arizona and accessed from Interstate 10, 116 miles east of Tucson and 227 miles from Phoenix. From Willcox, go twenty-five miles on Arizona 186 to the Fort Bowie turnoff, then north on the Apache Pass Road for about nine miles on a graded dirt road to the Fort Bowie trailhead. The fort is reached by following the one and one half-mile sand-and-gravel trail leading from the trailhead.

Fort Bowie adobe walls

Fort Bowie National Historic Site is located near the summit of Apache Pass, between the Chiricahua and Dos Cabezas Mountains in southeastern Arizona. For centuries, Apache Pass was an important Chiricahua Apache campsite and historic American crossing point due to the natural springs there. Troops stationed at Fort Bowie engaged in some of the most hard-fought battles between soldiers and Native Americans in the American Southwest from 1861 to 1886, including battles with Chiricahua Apache leaders, first Cochise and later Geronimo. The 1,000-acre site was established as Fort Bowie National Historic Site in 1972.

When visiting the site, gather your memories of all the great western movies featuring the Apache Wars, tuck a copy of *A Distant Trumpet* by Paul Horgan in your backpack along with water, and take the trail one and one half-miles along the old military road to experience the place. With few visible remains on the site other than the stabilized walls, your experience is to drift back in time to a tumultuous landscape of American legend. Here, Apache leaders and their followers fought long and hard for their homeland. The trail passes by several conflict sites, such as the Battle of Apache Pass, all of which occurred before the fort was established. No battles were fought at Fort Bowie itself; the climate and terrain favored the Native Americans, skilled in hit-and-run guerilla warfare, where the odds were overwhelmingly in their favor. It is all ruins now—the Butterfield Overland Mail Stage Station, the post cemetery, Apache Spring, the site of the first Fort Bowie from 1862, and 1869 fragments of the second fort's ochre-colored eroded adobe walls.

Fort Bowie was a typical southwestern frontier army post: adobe and wood barracks, a row of officers' quarters, storehouses, a schoolhouse, and a hospital soon occupied the four sides of the parade ground. Corrals and stables, a post trader's store, guardhouse, ice machine house, mess hall, and bakery ringed the parade ground buildings. Occupied in 1869, more buildings were added over the years, including a new hospital and an ornate two-story, wood-frame, Victorian-style house, erected in 1884 for the commanding officer. When the fort was abandoned in 1894 there were thirty-eight buildings at the second fort: twenty-nine were of adobe, eight were frame, and one—the magazine—was constructed of stone. Officers' quarters and barracks had long wooden porches facing the parade ground.

Today, Fort Bowie consists of the stone foundations of both forts, and some adobe wall fragments of the second fort. A flagstaff marks the center of the parade ground. The Butterfield Overland Mail Stage Station, abandoned in 1861 when service was discontinued on the eve of the Civil War, is visible in stone foundation ruins. A sturdy material when protected from rain and snow, adobe can last for centuries. Left unsheltered, however, it will melt back into the earth. The preservation of Fort Bowie's adobe wall fragments by lime plaster encapsulation is typical of southwest forts and other adobe National Park Service buildings. It is done conservatively to preserve standing adobe wall for future generations without sacrificing historic fabric.

Grand Canyon National Park

Grand Canyon's 277 miles along the Colorado River are north of Williams and Flagstaff in Coconino County, Arizona

→ www.nps.gov/grca

→ Grand Canyon's South Rim is approached from Flagstaff eighty miles south via US 180 or by US 89 and Arizona 64 (eighty-two miles to Desert View). The North Rim is forty-one miles south of Jacob Lake via Arizona 67.

Grand Canyon of the Colorado River

No matter how well prepared by photographs, videos, or guidebook descriptions, the first-time visitor to the Grand Canyon is always awestruck. The long drive to the North or South Rim crosses distinctly different ecological zones. From the south across the gradually upward sloping Coconino Plateau to the South Rim or the 1,000 feet higher North Rim approach through forests and meadows of the Kaibab Plateau, there is a heightened sense of disbelief; nothing prepares one for the incredible size or dramatic forms of this color-saturated canyon. From the rim down through the depths of the gorge, over two billion years of geological history unfolds. Layers of rock are visible from a vantage place matched nowhere else as deep into the earth's crust and the history of the planet's evolution. John Wesley Powell described it this way: "It has infinite variety, and no part is ever duplicated.... By a year's toil a concept of sublimity can be obtained never again to be equaled on either side of Paradise."

The architects and designers working for the railroads and the National Park Service (NPS) created architectural legacies of outstanding sensitivity in the park. Many buildings are National Historic Landmarks. The North and South Rims—separated by only ten air miles but a circuitous 215 miles by highway—are distinctly different places. The South Rim, closer to population centers, was developed first, and the Santa Fe Railway offered direct service to El Tovar Hotel. The 1923 expansion to Cedar City, Utah, by the Union Pacific Railroad opened the North Rim, with accommodations at Grand Canyon Lodge.

South Rim

The historical architecture attractions of the South Rim extend thirty-two miles along Desert View Drive and Hermit Road. At the center are Grand Canyon Village, the Santa Fe Railway Depot, and El Tovar Hotel. Mary Elizabeth Jane Colter, a brilliant architect employed by the Fred Harvey Company, designed Hermit's Rest, Hopi House, Lookout

Studio, and Bright Angel Lodge, the first three of which are National Historic Landmarks. The NPS built the Operations Building and Power House, excellent examples of the emerging rustic style. Hermit Road ends at Hermit's Rest. The Desert View Watchtow-

El Tovar Hotel

er, also designed by Colter and a National Historic Landmark, and Tusayan Museum, three miles to the west of the Watchtower, are on Desert Rim Drive, which proceeds out of the park as Arizona Highway 64.

The 1909 Santa Fe Railway Depot was conceived as a rustic gateway to welcome travelers to the Grand Canyon and to El Tovar Hotel. The only railroad terminus in a national park (and only structural log depot remaining in the country), the chalet-like two-story structure contained a ground floor waiting room, ticket office, baggage room, and other public spaces. An upper floor provided the station agent's apartment. The central building has a first floor of log construction, and shingled upper floor. The two-bay, log-column-supported waiting platform extends a lowered ridgeline from the main structure. The words "Grand Canyon" in copper letters on the gable facing the tracks and a "Santa Fe" logo greeted travelers. The last passenger train pulled out of the National Historic Landmark station in 1968, and the freight office closed a year later, but in 1989 the line was reopened from Williams to the canyon, restoring the steam locomotives (and sometimes diesel locomotives) that recall the early days of travel to the South Rim.

During the fierce competition for railroad customers at the turn of the century, the Atchison, Topeka, and Santa Fe Railway set out to build a rustic resort that would ful-fill passengers' dreams of the romantic western frontier; they opened El Tovar Hotel in 1905. Here on the edge of a great natural spectacle was a hotel with a western frontier image, and at the same time furnished comfort and elegance for turn-of-the-century romantic tastes. The hotel's location is as dramatic as any in the National Park System. The distinctive silhouette of the 300-foot-long building designed by architect Charles Whittlesey has multiple roof levels, a rooftop turret, finials, chalet-like balconies and terraces, and varied exterior wall treatments. The railroad described El Tovar as "com-bining the proportions of a Swiss chalet and the Norwegian villa."

The hotel's three-story guest wings extending to the north and south from the cen-tral section have a modulated exterior treatment. On the first floor, horizontal courses of rounded log siding with notched corners provide a warm rustic touch at eye level. Using the same log course widths, planks sheath the second floor, and milled lumber was used for window surrounds. The third floor is a shingled mansard with dormers rhythmi-cally punctuating the roofline. Logs stained a weathered brown and a roof shingled with wooden shakes merge the building into the gray-green hues of nearby pinion forests and stone outcroppings. The dark exterior color gives architectural weight to the massive volume and silhouette. The guest room layout assured that each would receive direct sunlight sometime during the day and have a view of some portion of the canyon.

Hopi House

Mary Colter's National Historic Landmark Hopi House, positioned opposite El Tovar Hotel, was initially devoted to the sale of Hopi goods and celebrated the artistry and culture of the Hopi tribe. Instead of bringing the tourist out to the Hopi pueblos, Colter brought the pueblo to the tourists. Hopi House is rectangular in plan, with many stepped terraces reinforcing the Pueblo style. The rough-textured reddish sandstone walls rise to different levels, stone steps and ladders connecting one rooftop with another. Small window openings allow only minimal light into this building. Much of the building's stone and timber came from the area, and Hopi builders did most of the construction. Hopi House was used, in part as an actual dwelling; some of the Hopis who worked in the building lived on the upper floors. Native American artisans were in the workrooms making jewelry, pottery, blankets, and other items that were offered for sale. In the evening, the Hopis sang traditional songs and their dancing on the patio at five o'clock became a daily event.

Colter next designed the National Historic Landmark Lookout Studio. Perched on the edge of the rim west of El Tovar, Lookout Studio is a place where visitors observed the canyon through the Fred Harvey Company's telescopes, with opportunities to take photographs from a cantilevered porch. Inside, a small studio was centered on a fireplace alcove and a display area where postcards, paintings, and photographs were sold. Colter's design took an organic approach, adapting the building to the edge of the canyon, letting the surrounding landscape guide its design. Seen from a distance, Lookout Studio blends into the canyon's walls; when it first opened, the roof itself was covered with sod and native plants, making it even more a part of the landscape. The multilevel structure appears to merge into the natural rock outcroppings, with coursed rubble masonry walls. An uneven roof parapet flows upward into what appear to be random piles of stones, but are in fact a chimney and an observation room. The piles of stones between the chimney and tower were removed when the original roof was replaced.

Seven miles west of Grand Canyon Village, at the end of Hermit Road, is a Colter jewel of ingenious design, uniquely adapted to a special site. The National Historic Landmark Hermit's Rest was built in 1914 to serve as a refreshment stand and rest station. The structure appears to be a random jumble of stones with a chimney spire growing out of it. The canyon side of the structure has a log-frame roof protruding from the stonework, covering a patio that is separated from the rim by a stone wall. The interior is medieval in character, shaped by the rugged stonework and cave-like space, with dramatic changes in volume and light. A huge semi-dome alcove on the southern end of the space shelters an arched stone fireplace.

In 1933, the Fred Harvey Company again called upon Mary Colter, this time to design an economy lodge at Grand Canyon Village. Bright Angel Lodge was designed as a small village of cabins centered on a rustic one-story main lodge with shops, lounges, and dining rooms. The large stone-and-log lodge, under a gable roof and broad overhangs, sets the tone for the collection of buildings, some connected to the main lodge by pergolas and walkways. Small cabins built of stone, logs, and adobe, with three or four guest rooms, extended west across the site to the mule corral. The complex is full of interesting touches that lead the visitor through a rustic complex at a relaxed pace, following the canyon rim to the mule corral, which is at the starting point of the famous trail rides. The rim side of the main lodge is an inviting single-story face of peeled-log walls and paired-log columns supporting a wide overhang. The main lodge lobby is a two-story open space with rough wooden walls, a flagstone floor, and a log ceiling with kerosene lamps hanging from the beams. Colter placed an image of a large thunderbird, the Hopi symbol for the "powers of the air," above the fireplace. For furnishings, Colter collected authentic pioneer furniture, kerosene lamps, glass shades, and bathtubs. Rare finds included a hobbyhorse belonging to the first pioneer child born in Arizona and the lobby's 7-foot-tall Jenny Lind wooden cigar-store figure. The astrological weathervanes of each Bright Angel cabin are interesting finds.

The National Historic Landmark Grand Canyon Powerhouse was designed by a brilliant and anonymous architect capably meeting the challenge to design an industrial building using styling and materials appropriate for a national park. Although removed from the main visitor traffic along the rim, the building is close enough to El Tovar, the Grand Canyon depot, and Bright Angel Lodge to merit attention because of its massive volume and unique design. Put into operation in 1926, clever design techniques managed to combine a straightforward industrial function with the qualities of a Swiss chalet in a delightful artifice of trompe l'oeil. By taking the familiar details of a Swiss chalet and nearly doubling them, the viewer is deceived into believing that the building is half its actual size. Careful adherence to the principle of overscaling reduces the powerful form and large volume to a deceptively modest element in the landscape. The lower two-thirds is stone veneer; the rubble stonework is nearly 1 foot thick and has a deeply raked joint. The upper third combines a sequence of chalet details—an oversized 5-foot-tall fretwork balcony, a deep cornice with brackets, and wood frames around industrial steel sash—making an exposed concrete wall simulating stucco. A gable roof with exaggerated eaves furthers the illusion.

Implementing a 1919 master plan, in 1929 the NPS built a second visitor center (later used as the Ranger Operations building) only a short distance from the "Norwegian-Swiss villa" El Tovar Hotel and the pueblo-inspired Hopi House. Designed in the rustic style, the log-and-stone National Historic Landmark building compares favorably with similarly superb buildings at Mount Rainier and Crater Lake in form, scale, materials, and relationship to the site. Roughly textured stonework recalls the canyon's rock formations, and the paired log columns they support match the diameter of surrounding trees. Even the choice of dark brown paint for logs and siding and green trim for the doors and windows were decisions made with the utmost care to help the building blend into its natural environment. Nearby, the original first visitor center configured an L-shaped, two-story, wood-framed structure that was converted in 1931 into the Superintendent's Residence, and a wing was added in 1938. The final composition appeared as a large-scale residence with many of the elements that would later be refined in other park administration structures at the Grand Canyon and elsewhere in western national parks. The building now serves as administrative office space.

The Yavapai Museum, about one mile east of the Visitor Center on East Rim Drive and perched on the edge of the South Rim, provides spectacular sweeping views of the canyon from an enclosed observation terrace. Designed by architect Herbert Maier as a trailside museum, the recently renovated building (2007) is built of Kaibab sandstone and ponderosa pine logs and displays exhibits on the geological history of the canyon.

The Tusayan Museum and Ruin approximately twenty-two miles east of Grand Canyon Village and four miles west of Desert View on Desert View Drive is an example of early NPS efforts at interpretation. Opened in 1928, the museum is a representation of traditional Kayenta Anasazi buildings. The rectangular structure (with a 1934 addition) of native stone and projecting timber *vigas* offers exhibits as an introduction to the trail leading to the Ancestral Puebloan Village site (dating from approximately 1185), one of the most heavily visited archeological sites in the National Park System.

Desert View Watchtower

Desert View, with its sweeping vista of the canyons, is twenty-five miles east of Grand Canyon Village. To take advantage of the site, Colter conceived a soaring tower 70 feet high in the form of an ancient Puebloan watchtower. For this project Colter chartered a small plane for gathering information on watchtowers of the Four Corners Region, locating ruins, and then traveling overland to sketch and study the forms, construction, and stonework. After six months of research she built a detailed clay model to study the design and how it would fit the terrain. Finally, she built a 70-foot-tall wooden tower on the site to test the form and the views she sought from the promontory overlooking the canyon. Completed in 1933, the watchtower's plan provides for two concentric circles connected by gently arched forms.

The larger circle and arched portions form the ground-floor lounge; the smaller circle is the 30-foot diameter base of the tower. The second floor Hopi Room contains sand paintings as well as murals by Hopi artisan Fred Kabotie, depicting Hopi mythology. These murals were later supplemented by petroglyph representations painted by Fred

North Rim rustic log cabins

Green. Inside the stonework of the tower is a steel framework. This was no random pile of rocks mimicking a ruin; Colter meticulously selected each exterior stone to provide a rich surface texture.

North Rim

Gilbert Stanley Underwood designed the U-shaped log and stone Grand Canyon Lodge, with more than one hundred rustic log cabins, at Bright Angel Point on the North Rim. It is one of the most intact rustic hotel developments remaining in the National Park System from the era of railroad-built "destination resorts." Built in 1927-28, the lodge was rebuilt in 1936-37 after a fire in 1932 that tragically destroyed most of the original lodge and several adjacent deluxe cabins. Unfortunately, the Union Pacific engineers' rebuilding was not as architecturally spectacular as the original. The second story and dramatic observation tower were not replaced, and several flat roofs were modified to pitched surfaces to better shed the heavy snows.

Nevertheless, Underwood's genius is visible in the planning of the classically proportioned entrance side, in contrast with the dramatic organic stonework of the building's canyon elevations. The interior spaces are a marvelous flow leading the visitor down several levels to large expanses of windows facing the canyon. The dining room, one of the grandest rooms in any national park, with its wall of windows overlooking the canyon, is light and airy. Exposed peeled-log roof trusses span the room; large wrought-iron chandeliers and sconces, parchment fixtures, and painted and carved Native American symbols are prominent overhead on the log structural members. At night, the light from the fixtures provides a warm glow against the limestone piers and dark-stained logs.

Underwood assembled the robust detailed rustic deluxe cabins—eighteen duplexes and five quadruplexes—using similar architectural elements, the plans varying in porches, entrances, and interior arrangements. A second complex of modest "standard" cabins in a dense arrangement contain simplified rustic elements. The lodge and cabin are National Historic Landmarks.

The architectural treasures in Grand Canyon National Park are in the contrasting ecological zones of the North and South Rims, focused on the spectacular scenery of the canyon. There is great reward in pausing to visit these historical buildings, which are steeped in the history of the earliest Native American inhabitants, Powell's explorations, the railroaders' developments, and the NPS's struggle to manage legions of summer visitors. The NPS and concessioners have made commitments to conserve and protect the fragile natural and man-made environment, and they have taken valuable strides in the restoration of important structures subject to heavy visitor traffic.

Hubbell Trading Post National Historic Site

Located in northeastern Arizona on the Navajo Nation near Ganado, Apache County, Arizona

→   www.nps.gov/hutr

→   Take Interstate 40 at Chambers, go north twenty-six miles on Arizona 191 to Ganado, then one mile west on Highway 264 to the site. The park is fifty-five miles from Gallup, New Mexico, via Highway 666 north to Highway 264.

Hubbell Trading Post

Hubbell Trading Post at Ganado is a reminder of the days when the reservation trading post was a center for business as well as Navajo social life. Located on the Navajo reservation in northeastern Arizona, the solid stone buildings have changed little since the post's beginnings more than a century ago. The post at Ganado was considered one of the more successful trading posts in the history of Navajo trading and one of the most important in the American Southwest. John Lorenzo Hubbell was one of the first traders on the Navajo reservation, and he influenced the character of trade and traders for more than half a century. The National Historic Landmark structures host a still-operating trading post.

The legacy of relying on traders was a dependency of the Navajos upon traders for supplies in exchange for their wool, sheep, rugs, and jewelry. Born in Pajaritos, New Mexico, in 1853, John Lorenzo Hubbell's relations with the tribe earned him the title

"dean of Navajo traders." Hubbell purchased the trading post in 1878 and traded there
for the rest of his life, at the same time establishing a 160-acre homestead. His success
in maintaining the friendship of the Navajos enabled him to expand his operations to
include twenty-four trading posts; stage and freight lines; a wholesale business in Winslow, Arizona; and other ranch properties and businesses. He died in 1930, and his son
Roman carried on the business until 1957; Roman's wife, Dorothy, ran the store until
1967, when the National Park Service (NPS) purchased the operation.

In Hubbell's time the trading post was a place where the Navajos came for news,
to meet relatives and friends, and to exchange their goods and crafts for food, tobacco,
tools, and cloth. Success as a trader hinged perilously on trust, sustained in great measure by Hubbell. In the 1870s, Hubbell brought Mexican silversmiths to Ganado to teach
the Navajos the craft of making silver jewelry. By the mid-1880s, he was encouraging the
Navajos to discard careless rug weaving practices and improve the quality of their work.
Under his guidance, they used better wool and revived earlier rug designs. The Navajos
recognized the benefits of meeting Hubbell's exacting standards, and he gradually gathered the best of the reservation weavers as his suppliers.

The post's stone-and-adobe buildings began with the main post building sometime in the early 1880s and have remained generally the same since 1900. Minor modifications to the buildings occurred over the years, as doors were added, roofs replaced,
parapets raised, and early chimneys replaced by stovepipes.

Trader's room

The long, stone Trading Post building housed the sales room and storerooms for
trading. Built in four phases (the office and rug room first, the adjoining bull pen storeroom second, the wareroom next, and finally the wareroom extension), the 45-foot by

150-foot rectangular structure is a fine representation of the typical reservation trading post. Walls are made of local sandstone and the roof is supported with ponderosa pine *vigas* and aspen *latillas*. The bull pen with massive counters and grocery-lined shelves still serves the Navajos. The intriguing rug room displays blankets, jewelry, antique firearms, pottery, and small paintings of Navajo rugs that line the walls and were used to show weavers John Lorenzo Hubbell's favorite patterns.

The hacienda, used as the Hubbell family home, was completed around 1900. Until then, the family only summered at the post. At the entrance path to the residence, sandstone pillars support a gate decorated with the wrought-iron initials "JLH." The rambling, adobe brick building was expanded over the years and grew into a complex of spaces filled with Hubbell's personal collection of Indian art and artifacts. The long living room and bedroom walls are enriched with paintings, photographs, and a profusion of Indian artifacts.

To the north of the Hubbell home is a stone hogan built as a guesthouse in the 1930s. A restored barn (1887–1900) and the other residences and utility buildings built of sandstone walls complete the complex. The fire brick bake oven produced nearly four hundred loaves of bread a week and stocked the grocery.

The NPS operates the Trading Post today much as it did in the past. The grocery and hardware sales area serve the descendants of Hubbell's customers and employees across the massive counters where Hubbell himself once did business. Hubbell Trading Post National Historic Site conveys the remarkable nature of the enterprise that bridged two cultures, the type of man who conducted it, the Native Americans who traded there, and the life they led together.

Montezuma Castle National Monument

Located in central Arizona near Camp Verde, Yavapai County, Arizona

→ www.nps.gov/moca

→ Located north of Phoenix ninety miles via Interstate 17 and Arizona 264, three miles north of Camp Verde and fifty-five miles south of Flagstaff.

Montezuma Castle, set into a limestone recess more than 50 feet above the floodplain of Beaver Creek in the Verde Valley, is one of the best-preserved cliff dwellings in North America. The five-story, twenty-room cliff dwelling served as a home for the Sinagua Indians in the twelfth century A.D. With heightened concern over the vandalism of fragile Southwestern prehistoric sites, the government proclaimed Montezuma Castle a national monument and it became a major factor in the nation's historic preservation movement. Montezuma Castle National Monument was established in December of 1906 and is described in the establishment proclamation as "of the greatest ethnological and scientific interest."

Early settlers to the area marveled at the imposing structure, mistakenly assuming that it was associated with the Aztec leader Montezuma. In fact the castle was abandoned almost a century before Montezuma was born. The true builders were farmers of the Sinagua culture, migrating from Arizona's northern high country around 1125. Here in the Verde Valley, they began to build aboveground masonry dwellings in the Ancestral Puebloan style. The Sinagua abandoned the entire valley in the early 1400s. Scholars have long speculated over the fate of the Sinagua: Disease? A growing population stressing the land's carrying capacity? Conflict with the Yavapai, who were living here when the Spanish entered the valley in 1563? Whatever the reason or reasons, the survivors were probably absorbed into pueblos to the northeast.

The visitor can grasp the overall dramatic massing and adaptation to the cliff face from a viewpoint on the paved trail a quarter-mile from the visitor center. Anchored solidly into a deep alcove high in the cliff's curved face, the mud plastered limestone blocks assembled into terraced rooms truly form a castle-like appearance. Looking upward 50 feet to the castle's lowest level from the trail at the base of the cliff wall, you can marvel at the aesthetic of the Sinaguan cliff dwelling. Like many of the cliff dwellings in the Southwest, the location was chosen for practical reasons. The valley's level land could be reserved for farming, and the pueblo built above the flood plain to avoid disaster. The shady, insulated alcove—cool in the summer—reduced the amount of construction by use of the natural surface as a rear wall. Yet it remained warm during the winter months when the low winter sun heated the walls. All told, it was an ingenious "green" design.

Montezuma Castle

Accessible only by ladders, Montezuma Castle is a five-story structure of twenty rooms. The building was fitted into the ledges of the natural cave in such a way that it appears terraced. There are two rooms in the first story, five in the second, eight in the third, three in the fourth, and two in the fifth.

The walls of Montezuma Castle, 2 feet thick at the bottom and a foot thick at the top, are chunks of limestone, usually no larger than two bricks, laid in mud mortar of clay and sand mixed with river water. Building without any metal tools, the builders hewed roof beams from sycamore trees along the river and hauled them up the cliff with ropes twisted from yucca fiber. Inside the pueblo, walls made of rubble, covered with mud plaster divide long narrow rooms. The castle's exterior is punctuated by a few rectangular openings, providing ventilation for the smoke from interior fires as well as a viewshed of the creek below. T-shaped doorways found throughout the castle are a feature derived from Ancestral Puebloans to the north.

Because of the structure's fragility, the Castle is no longer open to visitors. The Montezuma Castle Visitor Center exhibits pottery, textiles, and other artifacts from the site. There is a level paved trail one-third of a mile in length and wayside exhibits along a self-guided trail among sheltering sycamore trees. Under a typical brilliant blue sky, the monument conveys the quiet atmosphere of Sinaguan times in this warm fertile oasis found in a spectacular landscape of forested mountain ranges and high mesas.

Petrified Forest National Park

Located in northeastern Arizona near Holbrook, Apache County, Arizona

→ www.nps.gov/pefo

→ The north entrance of the park straddles Interstate 40 at Exit 311, twenty-five miles east of Holbrook, Arizona and sixty miles from Gallup, New Mexico. The south entrance off US 180 is nineteen miles east of Holbrook.

Painted Desert Inn

Petrified Forest National Park is a marvel of natural wonders forming one of the most unusual landscapes in the United States. It lacks the dramatic features of the crown jewel parks, and Petrified Forest could easily be missed by the traveler hurtling through the desert on Interstate 40. The park is a treasure, though, for those who find it. An entrance from the interstate leads to the nearby Painted Desert Visitor Center and the Painted Desert Inn. From there a twenty-mile-long road loops southward through the unique terrain of petrified logs, prehistoric ruins, badlands eroded by water and wind, and the Rainbow Forest, taking visitors to the Rainbow Forest Museum at the south end of the park at US 100.

Beyond the visitor center, a road curves along a wide mesa and rises over the edge of the Painted Desert. At Kachina Point, the National Park Service (NPS) rebuilt the superb Painted Desert Inn as a fine example of the Pueblo Revival style influenced by Pueblo Indian dwellings and softened by Spanish Colonial decorative touches. This National Historic Landmark's rustic structure is uniquely representative of Southwestern architecture and bureaucratic construction ingenuity.

The inn is a gentle orchestration of building masses set on a flat landscape. From a distance, its earth-colored walls and stepped parapets seem part of the surrounding topography. Stucco-covered stone surfaces simulating adobe take on different color hues, in perfect harmony with the colors of the Painted Desert. In the early morning hours and at twilight, the walls have a pink to orange cast; at midday the sun has bleached them into a flat buff tone. The inn comes into view gradually from the approach road. Its pueblo-like irregular plan, multilevel construction, and massing of individual rooms anchor the inn comfortably to its site. Partial banking into the mesa edge appears to diminish the two-story structure's volume. Terraces on three sides of the building have low walls that define the outdoor spaces, some overlooking the ever-changing colors of the Painted Desert. Exterior walls are pierced by *viga* ends and *canales* (scuppers), which drain the flat roofs, creating a play of light and shadow on the walls.

The fascinating history of the inn begins with the Stone Tree House, a privately owned lodge built over several years in the early 1920s. The lands of the Painted Desert north of the Petrified Forest National Monument, including the original lodge, were

acquired by the NPS in 1936. The structure was constructed of local adobe and petrified logs and, unfortunately, was built on unstable clay soil that damaged the walls. The NPS chose to do a major rebuilding (easier to fund than new construction) following the design by NPS architect Lyle E. Bennett and using Civilian Conservation Corps (CCC) labor. Construction began in the fall of 1937 and, after considerable travail, was finally completed in July 1940.

The inn officially opened in 1940, but its business days were cut short by World War II, after which it no longer offered guest lodging. After the war, the Atchison, Topeka, and Santa Fe Railway's concessioner, the Fred Harvey Company, took over its operation and hired Mary Jane Colter to update the building.

Stucco-covered exterior walls

She changed the interior color scheme and hired Hopi artist Fred Kabotie to paint a series of murals, completed in 1948, incorporating ceremonial and religious symbolism, and some showed scenes from everyday Hopi life. The dining room (no longer serving food) was dedicated as the Kabotie Room in 1976.

When the inn opened, it contained twenty-eight rooms divided between the NPS and concessioner's use. The concessioner's space included a lunchroom, kitchen, dining room, dining porch, six staff sleeping rooms with corner fireplaces, service areas,

Kabotie Room

and the Trading Post Room. The inn closed in 1963, and the building, rehabilitated in 2006, is now operated by the NPS with a ranger information desk, a lower level museum room, sales outlet, and public restrooms. There are no overnight accomodations; a restaurant is open daily.

The most magnificent interior space is the Trading Post Room. An enormous skylight, with multiple panes of translucent glass painted in designs from prehistoric pottery, provides soft illumination over the concessioners' sales items. Six hand-hammered tin Mexican-style chandeliers are suspended from ceiling *vigas*, and the posts supporting the corbels and *vigas* are exposed natural wood. The masterful combination of the skylight, etched floors, and the highly decorative woodwork on posts, corbels, ceilings, and original CCC furnishings makes this building a memorable example of Southwestern design.

Located near the park's south end, Rainbow Forest Museum, built in 1934, has an exhibition room in a skylighted, raised central block building with two symmetrical wings, and beams over the recessed main entrance and windows. The simple block-like forms of the 80-foot-long rough sandstone structure form an interesting merging of styles. In the NPS 1938 *Park and Recreation Structures*, the building is described as "With simple dignity, this building happily succeeds both in capturing the flavor of the architecture of the Old Southwest and in gesturing toward contemporary. This is no mean attainment in itself, and with the added score of an orderly workable plan, it is successful beyond cavil."

Travelers seeking a section of Historic Route 66 will find it in Petrified Forest National Park with a diversion from Interstate 40 to US 180 through the park. Take time to drive the loop tour, pause at the Painted Desert Inn and Rainbow Forest Museum, enjoy overlooks with views sweeping across Painted Desert, and ranger-guided walking tours.

Pipe Spring National Monument

Located in northern Arizona, between Fredonia and Colorado City, in Mohave County, Arizona

→ www.nps.gov/pisp

→ The park is located north of the Colorado River, near the Arizona-Utah border. From Flagstaff, take Route 89 north to Route 89A forty miles to Jacob Lake. Continue north on 89A to Fredonia and take Route 389 west to the site. From the west, take Interstate 15 past St. George, Utah, to Exit 10, on to Highway 9 east to Hurricane, and continue to the monument forty-five miles via Utah 59 and Arizona 389.

Pipe Spring's "Winsor Castle"

The fort complex at Pipe Spring National Monument was built at a time when the Mormons were settling the Dixie Country of southern Utah, and northern Arizona. The red-colored sandstone walls of the fort and outbuildings stand today much as they did when completed in the early 1870s, a reminder of the isolated existence of those pioneers. The preserved Pipe Spring complex is a place of precious water in the vast, thirsty land of the Arizona Strip. Free-flowing water from the sandstone layers to the north provided a cool oasis that attracted Indians, travelers, and settlers for centuries. Mormon Church President Brigham Young personally visited the site in 1879 and directed the building of a fortified ranch house over the main spring for protection from Navajo livestock raids that began in the mid-1860s. Oversight of the construction of the "fort" was assigned to Young's nephews—Joseph W. Young and John R. Young. Anson P. Winsor was assigned as the first Church ranch manager at Pipe Spring, and the main structure became known as "Winsor Castle." With cooling of hostilities with the Navajo, aided by peace negotiations by Jacob Hamblin in late 1870, Winsor Castle was never used for defense purposes.

The restored fort, either from a distance or close-up, gives the clear impression of a complex designed and built with protection in mind. No windows faced toward the outside, and the only openings in the massive, 2-foot-thick walls of random ashlar red sandstone were pairs of wooden gates in the courtyard walls and gaps between the stones for rifle ports—eight in the north building and fifteen in the south. The tapered gun-port openings provided light and served as observation posts as well. Placing the fort on top of Pipe Spring was a safety feature to protect the water supply, and provided cool water indoors for dairy operation and cheese-making. The footings of the north building were built over the mouth of the main spring, and the water was channeled in trenches under the floor of this building into the courtyard and then into a masonry trough or dugout log in the cooler room of the south building and to sandstone masonry-lined pools outside the walls.

The fort's parallel two-story buildings, approximately 18 by 43 feet, are separated by a 30-foot courtyard enclosed by 20- to 30-foot-high end walls. Wagons and teams entered the courtyard at either end through massive 10-foot by 12-foot wooden doors. Sometime after original construction a 2-foot-wide catwalk connected the upper floors on one side of the courtyard. The fort buildings show Greek Revival details that recall the style popular in the 1830s in upstate New York where the Mormon religion and social structure began. White gable and end-return trim, chimneys at the ends of each building, and a wood-frame clapboard observation cupola on the center of the north building's roof ridge suggest the mixed use of residence and fortress. Multilight, double-hung sash windows face the courtyard, and raised-panel doors, doorframe panels, and interior paneling add to the Greek Revival ambience.

The cedar-shingled, shallow-pitched main roof of each building is extended 8 feet to cover second-floor verandahs facing the courtyard. The lower floors are of approximately equal size, divided by a stone-bearing wall. In the north building, first-floor rooms served as the fort's main kitchen and parlor for family gatherings and social events; the upper floor contained a small bedroom and a larger room with a ceiling entry to the rooftop lookout tower. On the south building's ground floor were spaces used as the spring room and cheese room; upstairs were bedrooms, one serving as an office for the Desert Telegraph. The Pipe Spring office of the Mormon Desert Telegraph system was the first telegraph station in the Territory of Arizona and was staffed by young, usually female telegraph operators, such as eighteen-year-old Eliza Louella Stewart, whose photo is still displayed.

Bedroom

Two smaller buildings, located at either end of the fort also exist. The stonewalled one-room structure northeast of the fort, built by the Utah or Mormon militia in 1868, was extended by adding another room and connected by a breezeway apparently to house the John R. Young and Winsor families during the fort's construction. A second stone structure, built west of the fort, served as a bunkhouse for craftsmen assigned to building the fort, ranch hands, and for Major John Wesley Powell's survey crews visiting in 1871. Both were restored by the National Park Service (NPS).

Acquired by the NPS in 1923, Pipe Spring National Monument was the first designated historic national monument in the National Park System and is one of the few places that illustrates the daily life of nineteenth-century ranches. Here, the visitor can learn about the role the Mormons played in opening the West, and interactions with Native American cultures. A visitor center and cultural museum jointly operated with the Kaibab Band of Paiute Indians adds significantly to the visitor experience. New exhibits, completed in 2003, help visitors learn about the history of the Kaibab Paiutes, their interactions with other tribes, the movement of Mormon settlers into the area, and modern day Kaibab Paiute activities. Rooms in the historic structures are furnished with period artifacts. Rangers and guides in period clothing interpret life at Pipe Springs by demonstrating pioneer and American Indian activities and crafts.

Tumacácori National Historical Park

Located in southern Arizona near the Mexican border south of Tubac, Santa Cruz County, Arizona

→   www.nps.gov/tuma

→   The park is located at Exit 29 off Interstate 19, fifty miles south of Tucson and eighteen miles north of the international border with Mexico at Nogales, Arizona/Sonora. Tumacácori includes three Spanish Colonial missions: Tumacácori, Guevaví, and Calabazas. The visitor center is at Tumacácori; the ruins as Guevaví and Calabazas can be visited only on part of a reserved ranger-guided tour.

The white plastered sanctuary dome of the Mission of San José de Tumacácori provides a shimmering landmark at this national historical park in southern Arizona. Established in 1691 by Jesuit priest, Father Eusebio Francisco Kino, the mission has been only partially rebuilt since its abandonment in 1844. The juxtaposition of the mission ruins and the finely crafted Spanish Colonial museum and visitor service buildings, added by the National Park Service (NPS) in 1937–39, provides a unique interpretive perspective on the early settlement of the region.

Construction of the present church at San José de Tumacácori began around 1800, and the church was in use by 1820. After Mexico won independence from Spain in 1821 a systematic expulsion of peninsular-born Spaniards began. Tumacácori's last resident priest was expelled in 1828. Although the native O'odham tribe continued to try and hold the mission together, they gave up and abandoned it in December of 1848. Until its designation as a national monument in 1908, its only protection against weather and vandals was its adobe construction, with walls up to 9 feet thick.

The original mission plan followed the traditional organization of space for spiritual and temporal affairs. A *convento* (church residence), shops, possibly quarters for a military escort, and storerooms all enclosed a patio (courtyard). A mortuary chapel and burial ground (*Campo Santo*) were also part of the plan.

The church construction consisted mainly of sun-dried adobe with some burned bricks. Moorish influences from Spanish mid-sixteenth-century architecture, filtered through Spanish Colonial experiences in Mexico, can be seen in the sanctuary dome and polychrome decoration on the ornate facade. The powerful entrance facade, meant to project over the proposed vault of the nave, unlike those on mission churches farther away from Mexico, was created by modeled plaster decoration over adobe. A twin tracery of projecting adobe brick forms a framework around the edge of the facade, focusing attention on the arched entrance defined by heavily plastered columns and radial arch stones to simulate stonework. The entrance is flanked by a pair of columns—with recesses in between for statuary—that support a beam for the choir loft floor on the interior. The column-and-beam motif repeats on a smaller scale above the beam and supports a pair of engaged columns framing a statuary recess, an architrave, and an oddly proportioned broken pediment.

The church interior is a long rectangular nave with a domed sanctuary that sheltered the main altar and statue of Saint Joseph, patron saint of the church after the mission was moved to the west side of the river, in both Jesuit and Franciscan times. The present flat-roofed nave has an exposed ceiling of *vigas* (beams) and planks, with a procession of altars, pilasters, and niches along the walls leading to the pulpit. In the nave, traces remain of holy-water fonts at each side of the entrance, oval depressions in the walls for

Mission church   Mortuary chapel

Stations of the Cross, and symbolic paintings and designs. The outline on the sanctuary wall marks the location of the altar screen. Small windows above the side altars softly illuminate the nave with morning and afternoon light. A barrel-vaulted sacristy is to the right of the sanctuary. The white plaster dome over the altar, stabilized as part of ongoing preservation work, contrasts with the unfinished bell tower. Appearing hemispherical in shape as it rises, the dome's base is not a true circle. On the interior, the base of the dome still shows its painted classical detail.

Church facade

The uncompleted mortuary chapel behind the church in the *Campo Santo*, the holy ground, was a rotunda designed to carry a dome. The holes around the exterior of the chapel's lime-plastered adobe walls were used to support scaffolding for catwalks used by the builders. The walled enclosure served as the mission cemetery, but after the mission was abandoned, '49ers on their way to California and later cattlemen used the enclosure as a corral. Cows, horses, and other livestock destroyed the original grave markings, and grave looters did additional damage. After the Apache Wars, settlers gradually came back to Tumacácori, and the sanctified grounds were restored to their original use. The last burial in the *Campo Santo* was in 1916, and a floral wreath is placed on the grave on every All Saints Day by the family of the deceased girl.

The ruins of San José de Tumacácori Mission came under federal protection in 1908, but minimal restoration or interpretative efforts ensued. Rather than launching a restoration and reconstruction program based largely on speculation, as the Public Works Administration had done at other mission structures as in San Antonio, officials decided to preserve all the mission structures and focus on interpretation. The NPS design and construction of a combined museum/visitor center began in 1935.

NPS principal designer Scofield DeLong created a structure sympathetic with the mission church using construction materials and decorative elements found in other Sonoran missions. Walls were built of sun-dried adobe bricks, with cornices of fired bricks. The flat-roofed building is surrounded by a parapet with a stepped coping, and is drained by *canales* (channels) cut into the adobe piers of the portals. The scallop-shell motif over the main entrance, symbolizing Santiago de Compostela, patron saint of Spain, was patterned after the church entrance at Cocóspera in northern Sonora, Mexico. A T-shaped plan of 5,500 square feet houses the museum rich with Spanish colonial details and furnishings. Arcades extend from the east wing—one opening into the garden and the other providing views of the church ruins. The patio garden, begun in 1937, contains plantings similar to those grown in the missions of northern Sonora.

Craft demonstrations by Native Americans and Mexicans participating in the park's living history programs capture the Spanish–Native American culture of the old Southwest.

Tuzigoot National Monument

Located in the central part of the state near Clarkdale, Yavapai County, Arizona

→ www.nps.gov/tuzi

→ The park is ninety miles north of Phoenix and fifty-two miles south of Flagstaff, accessible from Interstate 17. Take Exit 287 north to Cottonwood via Arizona 260, continue on US 89A to Clarkdale, and take the access road to the visitor center. An alternate route is from Flagstaff along scenic US 89A through Sedona and to the park.

Tuzigoot Pueblo's hilltop location

The restored and stabilized structures of Tuzigoot (pronounced TOO-zi-goot), crowns the summit of a limestone and sandstone ridge 120 feet above Arizona's Verde River. The site represents the ruins of one of the largest pueblos built by the Sinagua between 1100 and 1450. Taking the name from an Apache word for "crooked water" because of nearby crescent-shaped Peck's Lake, the structures have a commanding view over the landscape.

Gradually deteriorating and under depredations from vandals and looters, the site was excavated as a federal emergency relief project in the 1930s. The unusual nature of the hilltop town's excavated structures and recovered artifacts drew National Park Service interest. The owner of the land, mining company United Verde/Phelps Dodge, transferred the site to the Clarksdale School District who, in turn, sold it to the federal government for the sum of one dollar. In 1939 Tuzigoot and its forty-three surrounding acres were declared a national monument. The park is now 812 acres with 58 in federal ownership.

The pueblo's profile against a brilliant blue sky recalls picturesque hilltop villages in southern Europe: an organic architecture of local building materials in a terraced effect, discernible only by the irregular profile and slight contrast of hue from the ridge. The commanding presence of the pueblo suggests that it may have been built as a fortification, an explanation for many Italian and Spanish hill towns. Further evidence of the defensive nature of the site is the fact that the structure has very few exterior wall openings. However, excavations show no signs of events attributed to conflicts with marauding tribes. The hilltop preserved fertile valley land for farming and provided a center for community life, a tranquil and sociable place evident by the rich treasure of artifacts recovered from the site.

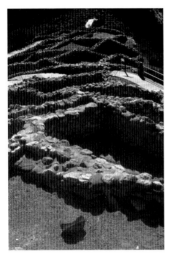

Tuzigoot Pueblo stone walls

Building form and materials at Tuzigoot follow basic shelter patterns in Southwest Ancestral Puebloan structures: simple cubes of space sharing multistoried common walls built of readily available light-colored limestone and sandstone, wood poles for floor and roof construction, and clay-plastered interior walls. Room sizes averaged 7 by 10 feet.

Tuzigoot represents the vestige of one of several pueblo communities in the vicinity. The village began as a cluster of rooms inhabited by about fifty persons for one hundred years. At maximum size the pueblo may have had nearly 110 rooms and housed as many as 300 people. Unplanned as a village, the pueblo grew during four centuries by attached rooms, sometimes built over collapsed earlier structures and gradually extending down the slopes of the ridge.

The Ruins Trail loops around the pueblo and allows visitors to closely view the structures. Remember that the structures are fragile like other stabilized Southwestern sites. Follow the trail and don't sit or climb on walls.

Wupatki National Monument

Located in the north central part of the state, Coconino County, Arizona

→ www.nps.gov/wupi

→ From Flagstaff take US 89 north for twelve miles, turn right at Sunset Crater Volcano-Wupatki National Monuments and proceed twenty-one miles from this junction to the visitor center.

Wupatki National Monument lies atop a windswept mesa northeast of the San Francisco Peaks in northern-central Arizona. Wupatki is the only known location in the Southwest where physical evidence from archeologically separate ancestral Puebloan cultures is found together in more than two thousand Indian ruins built between the years 900 and 1300. Located at the crossroads of Sinagua, Hohokam, Cohonina, and Kayenta Anasazi cultural traditions, the monument integrates traditions from all these cultures. Preserved at the monument are ruins of red sandstone pueblos built by Sinagua and Ancestral Puebloan people. Wupatki, Lomaki, Wukoki, Nalakihu, and Citadel pueblos are short trail walks from the visitor center. Begin an orientation to the park at the renovated visitor center with exhibits including a model of how a Wupatki room was constructed. The Wupatki Pueblo Trail, a half-mile-long self-guided tour of the largest pueblo in the Flagstaff area, starts at the visitor center.

The eruption of Sunset Crater sometime between 1150 and 1300 forced the Ancestral Pueblo and Sinaguan people to flee, but it also improved the farming potential. The volcanic ash, blown by winds over a large area, acted as a water-conserving mulch. Afterward, people moved back to the area and settled twenty miles north of Sunset Crater in Wupatki Basin. The greatest population growth occurred during the years between 1130 and 1160, estimated to reach approximately two thousand people. Occupation of the most well known above-ground pueblo structures dates between 1150 and 1300. Pueblos in the region ranged from one-story, single-family structures to the Wupatki Pueblo. Readily available slabs of sandstone and limestone, chunks of basalt set with a clay-based mortar, and logs from the local forests were ideal for the construction of freestanding masonry dwellings. The distinctive red color comes from the dominant local Moenkopi sandstone.

Ancestral Puebloan structures at Wupatki

Wupatki Pueblo, the largest complex in the monument, was once the home of about three hundred people and contained one hundred rooms. The multistoried structures are situated on the edge of a small plateau and have unobstructed views eastward the Painted Desert and the Little Colorado River. Walls were 2 feet thick, and individual rooms 6 feet high in places. Some walls on the north and west sides extended higher. Roofs, supported by masonry walls and timber posts, were thick assemblages of large beams, cross-laid with smaller beams, bundles of grass, reeds and bark, and overlaid with a mud topping. There were no exterior doorways at ground level, and rooms were entered through openings in the roof and ladders.

Wupatki Pueblo

A nearby oval-shaped, smooth-floored amphitheater, where village meetings and ceremonies may have taken place, lies to one side of Wupatki Pueblo. The masonry ball court at the far end of the village, reconstructed by archeologists from wall remnants, may have been used for games or religious functions. It's one of several found in northern Arizona, probably introduced by the Hohokam culture of the southern deserts. A blowhole, 100 feet east of the ball court, may have had religious importance. This natural surface opening, surrounded by a modern masonry structure, is a vent of unknown depth linked to underground caves that either blows out or sucks in air, depending on the atmospheric pressure.

Wukoki Pueblo is at the end of a two-mile road and is a half-mile round walk from the visitor center. The dramatically sited structure perched on a mesa has a prominent three-story tower and lower walls with six or seven rooms, housing possibly two or three families. An adjacent open area enclosed by a semicircular parapet wall served as a plaza for communal activities. Occupied between approximately 1120 and 1210, Wukoki is one of the best preserved structures at Wupatki National Monument. Reinforcement and stabilization by the NPS, including steel and concrete within the masonry walls, ensures stability of the structure. Lomaki Pueblo, toward the north end of the park road, is another outstanding structure. It is built right on the edge of a little canyon, which was probably formed by faulting or other volcanic activity, and has a good view of the San Francisco Peaks to the west. Box Canyon Pueblo may be visited along the same trail. The other structures are also accessible by short trails.

Ancestral Pueblo petroglyphs are an attraction seen only on ranger-led tours on flat-surfaced basaltic rocks. The petroglyphs depict humans, a variety of birds and insects, and many graphic designs, including large spirals—symbols thought to represent migrations.

Nevada

Southwest

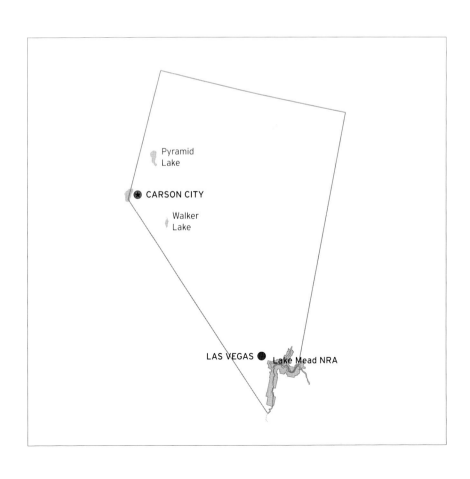

Lake Mead National Recreation Area

Located on the Nevada-Arizona border, Clark County, Nevada, and Mohave County, Arizona

→ www.nps.gov/lame

→ The main visitor center is located about four miles east of Boulder City, Nevada (thirty miles southeast of Las Vegas), at the junction of US 93 and Lakeshore Scenic Drive. Hoover Dam is located seven miles southeast of Boulder City on US 93 at the Nevada-Arizona border.

Hoover Dam

Lake Mead National Recreation Area is a combination of deep, clear water and a desert and mountain landscape stretching for 180 miles in southeast Nevada and northwestern Arizona. The park's severe terrain of 1,500,000 acres contains the improbability of almost 200,000 acres of shimmering blue waters with 850 miles of shoreline at full pool in the fluctuating reservoir. Two lakes on the Colorado River—Lake Mead, formed by Hoover Dam, and Lake Mohave, created by Davis Dam on the Colorado River—compose this first national recreation area established by an act of Congress (October 1964). Nearly eight million visitors a year come year-round to enjoy boating, swimming, sunbathing, and fishing, hiking the desert, and visiting Hoover Dam.

The singular historical architectural attraction in Lake Mead National Recreation Area is the Hoover Dam, the largest dam of its time, which created Lake Mead, the largest reservoir in the United States. Electric transmission towers and a web of high-tension lines extend from the dam hundreds of miles across the desert, supplying Southwestern cities with nearly four billion kilowatt-hours of hydroelectric energy annually. Dubbed one of America's Seven Modern Civil Engineering Wonders by the American Society of Civil Engineers, the setting for the concrete arch-gravity structure is stunning—a precise expression of mathematics in sweeping curves pressed tightly between rock walls. The visitor will be equally impressed by the fluidity of the architecture and engineering frozen in concrete.

Spanning 1,244 feet across the Black Canyon and rising 726 feet above bedrock, the dam was the largest constructed in the world when it was completed in 1935. Weighing in at more than 6.6 million tons, it is 660 feet thick at its base and tapers to 45 feet thick at its crest. There are 4.4 million cubic yards of concrete in the dam, power plant, and related structures. The convex side of the structure toward the lake compresses the concrete, enabling the dam to carry the massive water load by a combination of gravity and horizontal arch action. The functional design by Bureau of Reclamation chief engineer John Lucian Savage was augmented by suggestions from Los Angeles architect Gordon B. Kaufmann who transformed the dam's utilitarian concrete surfaces into modernist Art Deco images.

Because the dam site was so remote, extensive preliminary work was required. Boulder City was constructed to house thousands of government and contract employees and their families; seven miles of highway and nearly thirty-three miles of railway were laid; and a 222-mile-long transmission line was constructed to bring power from San Bernardino, California, to the dam site. At the height of the project, more than 5,200 laborers worked in all-day shifts seven days a week.

Before the dam could be built, the Colorado River was diverted around the construction site through four 50-foot in diameter bypass tunnels—two on each side—through the canyon's rock walls. Two temporary cofferdams—one upstream and another downstream from the work site—were constructed to divert the river into the bypass tunnels and to prevent the river from flowing back into the construction area. Meanwhile, suspended high scalers laboriously chipped and shaved at the rock walls of the canyon, creating a smooth surface to which the dam's walls would adhere. Masses of concrete were poured into forms that created large blocks; these blocks were arranged in rows and columns to build the massive bulk of the dam. The concrete was cooled by pumping refrigerated water through 582 miles of 1-inch pipe that was placed throughout the blocks; these small pipes were later filled with cement grout, making the dam a monolithic structure.

But Hoover is more than just a working dam; its aluminum, steel, and brass features blend with dramatic architectural elements to make it an Art Deco masterpiece. Thirty-foot-tall surrealist winged figures of bronze stand guard over the site. Classical-style bas-relief panels add intricate details to the elevator towers. Ancient Native American designs swirl into colorful terrazzo floors. And under a towering flagpole, a huge map of the cosmos preserves the precise astronomical time of the dam's dedication, demonstrating the ageless fascination for this architectural landmark.

In 1995, a visitor center opened to provide educational exhibits for the nearly one million visitors each year to the site. The center also houses two high-speed elevators that descend fifty-three stories through the canyon wall, bringing visitors to view the turbines, penstocks, and tunnels. The windowless cylinder of apricot-colored concrete and copper-colored windows is incongruous against the color and texture of the dam. A 450-vehicle parking structure tucked into the Nevada canyon wall also incorporates a design of precast concrete colored to mimic the surrounding rock.

New Mexico

Southwest

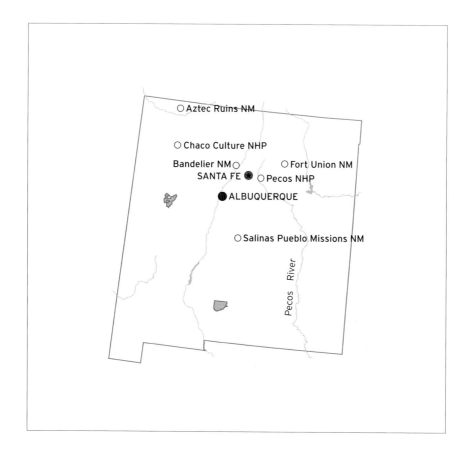

Aztec Ruins National Monument

Aztec, San Juan County, New Mexico

→ www.nps.gov/azru

→ The park is located in the city of Aztec, New Mexico, fifteen miles east of Farmington on US 550. In Aztec, take Ruins Road north of the intersection of US 550 and New Mexico 44 one half-mile to the ruins.

West ruins, kiva in foreground

Early European and Anglo scholars erroneously attributed these substantial ruins to the Aztecs. In fact, the Aztecs of central Mexico lived several centuries after the pueblo was built and occupied from approximately 1100 to 1300 by the Ancestral Puebloan people (formerly known as the Anasazi). The remarkable Aztec Ruins are important as examples of the Chacoan culture's superb ancient pueblo planning and construction in a concentrated area (Chaco Culture National Historical Park is fifty-five miles north, see page 127). Some archeologists think the pueblo was abandoned by the builders around 1150 and occupied by Mesa Verde people and remodeled using construction techniques and building styles characteristic of Mesa Verde (Mesa Verde National Park is forty miles northwest, see page 175). Current interpretations question this scenario and see a longer, more continuous occupation. The occupation lasted for about two centuries, leaving behind the well preserved West Ruin and other significant structures. Excavation and stabilizing of the West Ruin and Hubbard Tri-Wall Site, and examinations of other nearby sites by archeologist Earl Morris began in 1916. Morris established techniques later followed throughout the Southwest.

The Animas River was the center of farming for early settlers on the terraced slope of the ruins. Attracted to the valley by its favorable location and fertile soil, the site is a more amenable place than the desolate Chaco Canyon and fortress-like galleries of the Mesa Verde tableland. Here, the Chacoans' achievement in community planning and sensitivity to design is seen in their pueblo dwellings and ceremonial activities. The visitor can reflect on the cooperative community living in a compact pueblo site, requiring a form of self-government for a division of labor for building, farming, and hunting, as well as leisure time for arts and crafts.

The size, unity, and elegance of design of the West Ruins formed an astonishing planned community built in the shape of a rectangle (approximately 280 by 380 feet) focused on the Great Kiva. The architecture of the early builders of the West Ruins pueblo closely follows the Chacoan practice of building hundreds of rooms (approximately 10 by 12 feet) on multiple levels into "great houses"; kivas for ceremonial purposes are integrated into the room layout and stand separately in a plaza. The rooms were laid out in rows adjoining one another—as one row was finished another was added alongside it. When several rows were completed, second and possibly third stories were added. A fourth story may have been added in some places. The West Ruin's ground level is as much as six rooms deep; interior windowless rooms were used as storage, work rooms, and burial chambers.

Excavated rooms and surface evidence indicate that many more rooms existed than the West Ruin's 352 rooms counted today: 221 first-story rooms, 119 second-story rooms, and at least 12 third-story rooms. The only entrance into the pueblo was along the path by which visitors enter the ruins today. Most plaza level room access was through T-shaped doorways, upper level access was by ladders from the plaza level or through doorways between rooms. Along the northeastern section's second floor are four special doorways, each placed in the corner of a room so it connects with the adjoining diagonal room. One corner doorway, possibly unique in the Southwest, has a second smaller opening beneath it for access into a first-floor room.

In contrast to adobe construction found in other pueblos in the region, this pueblo is Chacoan core-and-veneer masonry, composed of masonry fill and faced with rectangular blocks of fine workmanship. The veneer at Aztec Ruins is alternating courses of large rectangular sandstone blocks from a quarry less than two miles from the site, shaped into rectangles by pecking or grinding with stone hand tools, and fitted with small, tightly wedged rocks between the larger stones. A distinctive feature of the West Ruins is the two very fine bands of green sandstone blocks that extend horizontally along the pueblo's outer west wall and into several interior rooms of the southwest corner. The walls were originally plastered with layers of adobe. Main beams of spruce, fir, pine, or juniper—1 to 1 1/2 feet in diameter and 10 to 12 feet long—roofed the rooms. Laid over these were long poles of various types of wood. Next came a layer of split juniper wood, or sometimes rush or reed matting, and then a layer of dirt and adobe forming the top of the roof or the floor of the room above when there was more than one story.

Toward the end of their occupation of Aztec Ruins, the Chacoans built the Great Kiva in the pueblo plaza. Later generations remodeled it, but it was used only a short time before being abandoned. Descending into the cool underground interior, with its dark red columns and wainscoting lit by daylight from roof and wall openings, reveals a sophisticated structural accomplishment. The 1934 reconstruction has an inner circle of two concentric circles approximately 48 feet in diameter—the kiva proper—and has a floor about 8 feet below the surface. The roof is supported on four columns of alternating courses of masonry and wooden poles, each 3 feet square and an estimated 18 feet high, in turn supporting a grid of log beams and other logs radiating to the periphery. Two concentric benches 3 feet high completely encircle the kiva base. At ground level and surrounding this inner section is an outer circle of fourteen arc-shaped rooms with two doorways—a small one to the interior and one to the outside. For the convenience of visitors, the National Park Service (NPS) has placed modern wooden stairways for access. On the kiva's floor are remains of the central altar or firepit, flanked on either side by two large rectangular stone-lined pits, the bottoms of which are well below the kiva floor. These pits, often referred to as foot drums, may have served at other times as hiding places for the shamans, or medicine men, who performed mystical rites during ceremonies.

The visitor center harbors within its walls the original Morris home. Morris designed and supervised construction of the original house in the Chaco style; it was completed in 1919 and occupied by the archeologist until 1933. Constructed of unplastered masonry

walls out of salvaged stones, beams, and roof poles from the West Ruins to simulate the weathered portion of the ruin, the four-room house with an unfinished exhibit room had a distinctive Southwest pueblo flavor: a living room corner fireplace, tribal rug wall coverings, and cases of pottery and baskets. Several additions and renovations modified the structure to its present appearance.

When Morris first undertook the excavations at Aztec, it was his intention, and that of the American Museum of Natural History, to completely uncover the structures. The massive nature of the undertaking, the intervention of World War I, and a shortage of funds curtailed those ambitious plans. Toward the end of his excavations, Morris realized there was an advantage to leaving parts of any structure unexcavated to benefit from better future archeological techniques. Except for stabilization work, the NPS shares this position, and they are content to leave the partially excavated and stabilized structures as they are seen today.

T-shaped doorways

Bandelier National Monument
Near Los Alamos, Los Alamos and Sandoval Counties, New Mexico

→ www.nps.gov/band

→ The park is forty-seven miles northwest of Santa Fe; travel north on US 84/285 to Pojoaque, then west on New Mexico 502 and south on New Mexico 4 and follow signs to visitor center.

Talus house and cave dwellings

Modern courtyard entry

Located in the dramatic landscape of Pajarito Plateau in north central New Mexico's Jemez Mountains, Bandelier National Monument has the unique distinction of showcasing a combination of Ancestral Puebloan dwellings and a superb National Park Service (NPS) complex—the Bandelier Civilian Conservation Corps (CCC) Historic District—built in the 1930s. The park's fifty square miles contain over three thousand archeological sites, while the Bandelier CCC Historic District, a National Historic Landmark, is a highly refined design of thirty-one Pueblo revival buildings and is noteworthy as the largest unaltered collection of such structures in any national park.

Two huge volcanic eruptions more than a million years ago created the plateau formed by ash flows, later eroded to form steep-sided canyons with colorful pink, beige, and white cliffs of soft rock called tuff. A stream in one of the canyons, El Rito de los Frijoles (Little River of Beans) attracted people to the area thousands of years ago. Early in the twelfth century, the Ancestral Puebloan people settled into the canyon-slashed slopes of the Pajarito Plateau, and for the next four centuries they built villages in the cliffs of the deep gorges and on the valley floors and mesa tops. By the mid-1500s the people left the villages unoccupied, as they stand today. Extending for approximately two miles on the Frijoles Canyon valley floor and carved into cliff walls of compressed volcanic ash are kivas, pueblos, masonry houses, and cave rooms. The monument's Main Loop Trail leads past a Tyuonyi excavated kiva, a large rounded enclosure, canyon-bottom pueblo, and talus villages.

The Bandelier CCC Historic District is described by NPS historian Laura Soullière Gates in a National Historic Landmark Study in the following way:

> The exceptional significance of the Bandelier buildings lies in their impact as a group....Taken individually, each structure was a well-detailed, solid piece of work. Collectively, the development was a masterpiece combining fine architecture, landscape architecture, and arts and crafts. The unity of design threaded through the landscaping to the buildings and their contents...and created a sense of place so strong that it predominates today. The whole is greater than the sum of the parts.

The NPS Branch of Plans and Design shaped a complex located a quarter mile down the canyon from a small dude ranch dating from 1909. Built by the Civilian Conservation Corps (CCC) between 1932 and 1941, the completed facilities provided visitor services, a visitor center and museum, lodging for guests, and office space and residences for employees. The superbly planned complex is a group of single-story, plastered-adobe buildings wrapped around three sides of a central parking plaza. Administrative offices were at one end, the walls of the maintenance yard at the other end, and the buildings of the newer Frijoles Canyon Lodge on a connecting side. Accomodations are no longer available, but a gift shop and snack bar are open year-round. The fourth side is bordered by Frijoles Creek. The two main plaza facades are the lodge lobby and dining room, and the headquarters/museum building; these structures are now the gift shop/snack bar, the administration building, and the visitor center. The individual guest lodges were reached by a series of flagstone pathways that led up from the lodge lobby through small courtyards and patios

Tyuonyi Pueblo   Frijoles Canyon, NPS/CCC development from mesa

that stepped up the hillside on several levels. Outdoor areas were planted with native vegetation. A separate complex of employee residences was placed up the hillside from the bottom end of entrance road, concealed from visitor view by vegetation and the terrain.

Adapting Spanish Colonial and Pueblo Revival themes and using the locally available rhyolite tuff cut into blocks for bricks, with mud plaster, and adobe washed, the complex has an overall unity; landscape design and the existing topography was respect-

Visitor center

ed by constructing buildings on several elevations. Despite strict individual building budget limitations, the architects devised a cohesive and pleasing development by a modular design on a very human scale, connecting small structures with portals, courtyards, and walls. The individual buildings are visually tied together by a series of stone walls, plastered portals, flagstone walkways, and stone-edged planting beds. The interplay of mass and void, as when a solid building face is relieved by a recessed portal, adds spatial diversity.

All interiors and furnishings followed the overall design theme. Wall surfaces were finished with hard plaster, and walls and fireplaces were often painted with Spanish Colonial and Indian motifs. Most ceilings were exposed *vigas* supporting aspen *latillas*, sometimes in herringbone patterns. Many rooms contained traditional corner fireplaces built of tuff and firebrick. Interior woodwork was frequently carved in decorative patterns developed specifically for the project by the designers. Typical floors were flagstone, varnished to a high glossy finish. The additive quality of the Pueblo Revival style was expressed by a one- or two-step change in levels between rooms. Exterior and interior light fixtures, wall switch plates, and mirror frames were cut from tin, scratched, dotted, soldered together, and painted. Federal Arts Project artists Pablita Velarde, Helmut Naumer, Chris Jorgensen, and Raymond Terken all contributed artwork.

The Bandelier CCC Historic District is remarkable for its high-quality craftsmanship. Unskilled CCC enrollees were provided with on-the-job training in using traditional techniques and tools, such as broadaxes and adzes, and produced exemplary work at a master craftsman level. The completed complex shows an architectural unity of theory and style that begins with site and building design and continues inside with fine interior details.

The unusual combination of Ancestral Puebloan structures and the modern CCC-built development can be visited on ranger-led or self-guided tours; self-guiding booklets for each route are available at the visitor center. Here, in Frijoles Canyon, known for its ancient cliff dwellings and cavates, visitors also have the opportunity to view an NPS-designed masterpiece combining fine architecture, landscape architecture, and traditional arts and crafts.

Chaco Culture National Historical Park

Located in northwestern New Mexico, midway between Farmington and Albuquerque and near Nageezi, San Juan County, New Mexico

→ www.nps.gov/chcu

→ Preferred park access is from the north by paved and dirt roads, via US 550 (formerly New Mexico 44). Turn off US 550 three miles southeast of Nageezi onto County Road 7900 (five miles paved) and continue on County Road 7950 (three miles paved and thirteen miles of dirt road) to the visitor center.

Pueblo Bonito

Doorways

Chaco Culture National Historical Park, a World Heritage Site in northwestern New Mexico, preserves one of America's most significant and fascinating cultural and historic areas. From 850 to 1150, Chaco Canyon was the regional center of culture, ceremony, and trade for the Chaco people, an Ancestral Pueblo culture. An elaborate network of roads radiated outward from Chaco Canyon through the present Four Corners area, and linked Chaco to distant communities.

Chaco Canyon seems an unlikely place for a major center of Ancestral Puebloan culture to take root and flourish. This remote and seemingly barren canyon bordered by tall mesa cliffs, fifteen-miles-long and up to a mile wide, appears incapable of sustaining a population that once influenced a vast region. This is high desert country, with long winters, short growing seasons, and marginal rainfall—average annual precipitation at Chaco is only 8 inches. Chaco Wash bisects the canyon. On the canyon's south side, crumbling cliffs spill fans of broken eroded rock onto the canyon bottom. Unlike the canyon's sloping southern side, the northern canyon walls rise smoothly and abruptly, intersected by smaller canyons carrying runoff from the mesa.

In this remote and inhospitable place, the people created an ancient ceremonial center of spectacular public architecture—one that still amazes and inspires us one thousand years later. Chaco is remarkable for its monumental public buildings (great houses) and ceremonial structures standing against the sheer red-and-ocher sandstone canyon walls. This cultural flowering was marked by well-organized planning, design, and construction. The Chacoan people combined architectural designs with consistent use of forms and materials, astronomical alignments, landscaping, irrigation, and engineering.

Today, six Chacoan great houses stand along the Chaco Wash at the bottom of the canyon. Many of the structures have survived the centuries remarkably intact, with original timbers in place. The appearance and condition of most of the park's exposed prehistoric masonry walls are due to the quality of the original construction and to a comprehensive preservation program begun by the National Park Service in the early 1930s. Preservation treatments and maintenance are ongoing.

Just beyond the visitor center, a nine-mile loop drive leads to an unexcavated Chacoan building (Hungo Pavi) before arriving at the impressive pueblo ruins of Chetro Ketl, Pueblo Bonito, Pueblo del Arroyo, Kin Kletso, and Casa Rinconada. The largest and most completely excavated Chacoan structure, Pueblo Bonito, is a vast 3-acre megastructure in a D-shaped plan of more than 600 rooms. The arc-shaped rear wall rises over five stories and is over 800 feet long.

Pueblo Bonito walls

Occupied from the mid-800s to about 1200, construction occurred in stages. The completed complex stepped down to a long, straight row of rooms facing south. Curved upper tiers of terraces focused on a central plaza with thirty-two smaller kivas (10 to 15 feet in diameter) and two great kivas (the larger 52 feet in diameter). Construction methods seen in the ruins reflect stylistic changes through time. Earlier walls were built of simple single course masonry and later ones with an elegant sophisticated technique utilizing an inner core of rubble and outer veneers of shaped and dressed sandstone resembling mosaics. The walls of the second, third, and fourth floors tapered as they rose to distribute the weight. After the walls were built, a plaster coating was applied over most of the walls that concealed this fine stonework, protecting the mud mortar from rain. The many interior plaster-covered walls were decorated with color designs and occasionally turquoise.

Chetro Ketl, one of the largest Chacoan villages, is located about one quarter-mile east of Pueblo Bonito. The building and adjacent villages built along 1,000 feet of the cliff face were constructed in stages from 945 to 1117, determined by tree-ring dating.

Chetro Ketl flourished for about 175 years, and then most building ceased. The great house contains more than five hundred rooms and twenty small and large kivas. Chetro Ketl is distinctive for its two elevated kivas and artificially raised plaza about 12 feet above the surrounding landscape. Chetro Ketl's straight rear wall of three- to four-story terraced rows of room blocks is approximately 500 feet long. Excavations revealed that the courtyard is underlain

Una Vida Pueblo and Fajada Butte in distance

with kivas of all sizes from earlier periods of construction. Some of the lower rooms were filled in or used for storage, while the upper rooms, many of them terraced, may have been living quarters. The thick, core-and-veneer masonry walls were faced with a veneer of Chacoan banded masonry. The veneer consisted of rows of large stone blocks alternating with several rows of smaller stone layers to form banded patterns that varied with each new construction period or remodeling.

Pueblo del Arroyo ("Village by the Wash," in Spanish), located just above the modern channel of the Chaco Wash, was built in stages, from about 1075 to 1105. The D-shaped great house rose three and four stories in the rear, stepping down to one story in front, and had about 280 rooms and more than twenty kivas. An unusual tri-walled structure abuts the rear wall.

Kin Kletso ("Yellow House" in Navajo) is a rectangular, compact pueblo at the foot of the cliff about a half-mile northwest of Pueblo Bonito. This great house had about one hundred rooms and four kivas. The pueblo, which reached at least three stories on the north side, was excavated in the early 1950s.

On the south side of the Chaco Wash is the great kiva known as Casa Rinconada ("Cornered House" or "House Where the Canyons Meet" in Spanish). The kiva, 60 feet in diameter, is the largest in the park and one of the largest in the Southwest. Surrounded by a cluster of excavated villages and almost directly across from Pueblo Bonito, this kiva may have served as a ceremonial center for the community at large. Casa Rinconada is precisely aligned on a north-south axis, established by a line connecting the stairways of the two entrances.

Note that there are no lodgings, gasoline, repair services, or food available in the park. The nearest town in is sixty miles away.

Fort Union National Monument

Located in the northeastern part of the state near Watrous, Mora County, New Mexico

→ www.nps.gov/foun

→ From Albuquerque (156 miles), Santa Fe (ninety-four miles), or Las Vegas, New Mexico (twenty-eight miles) take Interstate 25 north to Exit 366 at Watrous; travel eight miles to the end of New Mexico 161.

Remnants of Fort Union

Fort Union National Monument is located on the barren plains of northeast New Mexico and is crossed by the Santa Fe Trail, the legendary main commercial artery between Santa Fe and Independence, Missouri. For forty-three years, three successive forts at the Santa Fe Trail junction of the Mountain and Cimarron Cutoff Branches protected travelers and local residents from attacks by Native Americans, as well as provided a headquarters for the military department of New Mexico.

The first fort's log buildings, built in 1851 following the 1846–48 Mexican–American War, which won New Mexico for the United States, stood as the guardian of the Santa Fe Trail, acting as a federal presence in the Territory of New Mexico. The second fort was a massive earthwork built in 1861-62 to defend Santa Fe from a threatened Confederate invasion. This fort was abandoned in 1862 after Union soldiers stopped the invading Confederate columns at the battle of Glorietta Pass. The third and final Fort Union, built between 1863 and 1869, whose structures the visitor can see today, functioned as a military garrison, territorial arsenal, and military supply depot for Native American campaigns. All that remains of the third fort are melted adobe walls and a few standing chimneys now preserved as an outdoor museum.

The third fort's buildings were a sharp contrast to its short-lived predecessors. Once the largest frontier fort west of the Mississippi River, the vast Fort Union Post and Fort Union Quartermaster Depot were roughly four large rectangles in plan, two each for the post and depot. Like most

Fort Union masonry chimneys

Southwestern forts, Fort Union was not enclosed by a stockade wall. Built in the Territorial style of architecture that came to be associated with New Mexico, they were simple, functional blocks of adobe, one-story structures adorned with brick copings and white-painted doorways and window openings. Officers' quarters were distinctive, with columned porticos across the front of the building. Materials of local origin were used in stone foundations; walls were of adobe brick, molded from soil dug from the valley north of the fort and coated with plaster fired in limekilns south of the fort. Wall copings and chimneys were made of bricks manufactured in Las Vegas, New Mexico. Some items—tools, nails, window glass, firebricks, and roofing tin—were hauled over the Santa Fe Trail from Fort Leavenworth, Kansas. Water for all three units of the fort came from wells and storage cisterns spotted among the buildings. All the buildings were heated by fireplaces and lighted by spacious windows by day and candles or oil lamps by night.

Although Fort Union continued to grow for another twenty years and to serve as a tactical base and supply depot on the New Mexico frontier, the fort had outlived its usefulness and the Army finally abandoned it in 1891. As elaborate and fine a complex the fort appeared, it's fate was foreordained by its hasty construction. The main trouble lay in faulty roofing, which admitted water to the adobe walls and started an eroding action that made constant repairs necessary. After abandonment, Fort Union fell into ruins. In the late 1950s, the National Park Service stabilized the ruins to prevent further deterioration.

Today, it is difficult to look at the remnants of limestone foundations, adobe walls, and the few chimneys that rise above the serene landscape and realize that this was once a military post with troops serving in operations against hostile native tribes and the principal supply base for the Military Department of New Mexico. A one-and-a-half-mile self-guided tour, that contains exhibits of military life in the fort, starts from the visitor center and leads through the remnants of the third fort and the remains of the second fort erected during the Civil War. In the vicinity of Fort Union are the Santa Fe Trail ruts. During the summer, history talks and demonstrations are offered on weekends.

National Park Service Region III Headquarters Building

Santa Fe, Santa Fe County, New Mexico

→ Southeast of downtown Santa Fe approximately two miles from the Santa Fe Plaza on the Old Santa Fe Trail.

Main entrance

The Old Santa Fe Trail wound its way north from Mexico to the historic center of Santa Fe at Santa Fe Plaza. At a bend on today's paved city street, about two miles southeast of the Plaza, the National Park Service (NPS) selected the site for the Southwest Region III Headquarters in 1937. The completed structure of 24,000 square feet is the largest known adobe building in the United States.

This National Historic Landmark is celebrated as an NPS masterpiece of Spanish Pueblo Revival architecture. Although not a unit of the National Park System, we include the structure as a superb example of NPS 1930s design work sensitive to regional influences.

Designed by NPS regional architect Cecil Doty with landscape design by Harvey Cornell and built by Civilian Conservation Corps (CCC) and Works Progress Administration crews, the building's massing, plan, materials, and construction methods exhibit a mastery of the Pueblo Revival style. The interior details and furnishings incorporate superior workmanship. An outstanding art collection carries out themes of the Spanish Colonial era in the southwest.

The design's focal point is the dominant two-story mass defining the public main entrance, with the lobby and offices of the regional directorate upstairs. The designers created a controlled progression from the parking lot to the building by screening the view of the main entrance behind an adobe wall. A gate in the wall leads to a flagstone path and the entrance doors. Massive buttresses typical of Southwestern mission structures flank the double doors, sandblasted and etched with adze marks to give a primitive appearance.

The building's massing and surface textures are inspired by traditional adobe construction techniques of New Mexico's missions at Santa Fe, Taos, Chimayo, and Las Trampas. The towering main entrance is framed by massive buttresses; an inset, cream-colored two-story-high plastered surface contains recessed, tall, double-leaf, carved doors spanned by a hewn lintel beam. All exterior walls are plastered adobe, typically battered upwards from a 3-foot-wide base to an irregular roofline of parapets. Surfaces are textured with an occasional glint of hay used as a plaster binder. *Viga* ends projecting through the upper wall below parapets sustain the pueblo image of the massive structure.

The building plan maintains the theme of a Spanish Colonial mission compound. At both sides of the entrance are one-story office wings around central patios, a large one to the west and a smaller one to the east. Most of the interconnected offices in the west wing open directly onto the verandah surrounding the patio. The ground-floor conference room and second-floor offices of the regional directorate show careful attention to detail, including *viga-and-latia* ceilings, corner fireplaces, hammered-tin chandeliers, and hand-carved furniture. The irregularity of the overall plan up or down a few steps and the slight changes in building levels demonstrate the informal qualities of Spanish Pueblo Revival architecture.

Courtyard

The building is embellished with fine architectural details, hand-carved furniture, and hammered-tin fixtures designed by Cecil Doty. CCC workers built the mortise-and-tenon furniture. A hand-hammered tin chandelier, massive Spanish Colonial furniture, and a large painting of Stephen Mather fill the lobby space.

The patios are open-air outdoor rooms, with peeled-log columns capped by carved bolsters and *viga* ends around the outside. Water flows into a fountain and a 19-foot-diameter pool that has built-in *bancos* (benches) around it. Plantings add to the serenity of this space, which is favored for work breaks, lunches, and small gatherings.

This tour de force of Spanish Pueblo Revival design serves as a testimony to the talents marshaled by the NPS at the peak of its design prowess. The richness of detailing and outstanding art collection displayed throughout the building are worth the visit to this truly exceptional structure.

Pecos National Historical Park

Located in the north central part of the state near Pecos, San Miguel County, New Mexico

→ www.nps.govpeco

→ The park is located off Interstate 25, twenty-five miles southeast of Santa Fe. From Interstate 25, exit at
Rowe or Pecos interchanges and follow signs to the park.

Modern visitor center

Pecos National Historical Park's more than 6,670 acres at the base of the southern end
of the rugged Sangre de Christo Mountains is a fascinating part of the National Park
System with three areas. The main area includes the ruins of the Pecos Pueblo, the easternmost pueblo visited by Francisco Coronado in 1541, remnants of two missions, and
the attractive Pueblo Revival visitor center containing a fine museum with artifacts from
the site and sections of the Santa Fe Trail. The second area contains Civil War battle sites
at Apache Canyon and Glorieta Pass Battlefield where, on March 26–28, 1862, Union
forces turned back a Confederate invasion attempting to capture military supplies from
Union forts in New Mexico. Although without historical structures, the battle sites are
considered as the "Gettysburg of the West." The third area, where the Confederacy was
forced to abandon attempts to conquer the Southwest, is the 5,500-acre Forked Lightning Ranch with a 1930s Pueblo Revival ranch house.

   The imposing National Historic Landmark Pecos Pueblo ruins of the Franciscan
mission established in the seventeenth-century on a ridge in the Pecos River Valley, set
against the Sangre de Cristo Mountains to the north and Glorieta Mesa to the south, is an
arresting sight of towering adobe walls and arched doorways. Now seen on the horizon
as a reddish-tinted shape with its sloping buttresses emerging from the irregular profile

of the adjacent *convento* (church residence) ruins, Mission Nuestra Señora de los Angeles de Porcíuncula dominates the top of the ridge at Pecos. Alongside the massive mission walls are remnants of a sprawling convento and pueblo ruins. The mission and convento ruins seen today are part of a mystery unraveled by archeological excavations.

Pecos Pueblo mission church

Between 1617 and 1717, the Franciscans built four churches on the site. The standing ruins of the second church, built on the site of a modest size church, have attracted and awed visitors for centuries. The largest Spanish mission church constructed in all of New Spain, covering almost 6,000 square feet of floor space and built of an estimated 300,000 adobe bricks, was finished in 1625 by Fray Andrés Juárez. Thought to be an exaggeration of the church's size from traveler's reports in order to impress the authorities in Mexico and Spain to obtain more money and help for the missions, at its time of completion, the imposing church was 150 feet from the entrance to the altar and 41 feet across at its widest point. Its adobe walls were 8 to 10 feet thick, with great buttresses reinforcing side walls. Six bell towers rose 55 feet above the 40-foot-high main roof. Foundations beneath the one standing wall uncovered by archeologist Jean M. Pinkley in 1967 confirmed the impressive size of the seventeenth-century church. In the Pueblo Revolt of 1680, the enormous building was reduced to a pile of rubble.

After the Spanish reconquered the region in 1692 a temporary chapel was built and then, starting in 1705, the church seen today was built by Fray José de Arranegui and completed in 1717 within the walls of the second church. The nave of this church was 76 feet long, just over half the length of the massive pre-revolt church.

The rebuilt convento, twice the size of the earlier one, contained classrooms, workshops, and living quarters. Built in the ruins of the convento is one of two restored kivas, an underground structure used for religious and community activities. The pueblo ruins are rubble remains of what was once a 666-room pueblo and the partially excavated ruins of a smaller pueblo. Today, a walk through the ruins reveals rough, poorly fitting stones in uneven rows, marking the lower tiers of the two terraced community houses that once towered three to four stories high. After Mexican independence from Spain in 1821, the mission and pueblo fell into ruin.

A mile-and-a-quarter self-guided trail from the visitor center takes visitors to the defensive wall that once surrounded the Native American settlement, the smaller pueblo ruins, two restored kivas, and through the ruins of the mission church and convento. On the first Sunday of August a traditional patron saint mass is held in the ruins of the mission church to commemorate the feast day of Our Lady of the Angels Pecos.

The Forked Lightning Ranch is a significant addition to Pecos National Historical Park (1991), its acreage providing viewshed protection for the Pecos Pueblo and containing a house designed by the distinguished southwest Pueblo Revival architect, John Gaw Meem. Built in 1925 for "Tex"Austin, known as "Daddy of the Rodeo," the adobe house is a traditional New Mexico layout of rooms that enclose a central patio. The house was in the center of a working cattle ranch and Austin promoted it as a dude ranch. In 1941, the house was sold for use as a summer home for oilman and rancher E.E. "Buddy" Fogelson, and his wife, actress Greer Garson. A distinctive feature of the house is a huge, sculpted steer head mounted on the adobe chimney's upper exterior surface. The house can be visited on ranger-led tours.

Included on the ranch are other pueblo ruins, a section of the Santa Fe Trail, and remains of Kozlowski's Stage Station, a tavern and watering stop on the Santa Fe Trail that operated from 1858-1880.

Salinas Pueblo Missions National Monument
The park's three units are located near Mountainair, Torrance County, New Mexico

→   www.nps.gov/sapu

→   The visitor center is one block west of the intersection of US 60 and New Mexico 55. From Mountainair, Abó is nine-and-a-half-miles west of New Mexico 60, Quarai is nine miles north off New Mexico 55, and Gran Quivira is twenty-five miles south on New Mexico 55.

Traveling in central New Mexico between these three ruins of prehistoric Native American pueblos and among the most intact seventeenth-century, Spanish-administered Indian missions in the United States is a remarkable journey into the immenseness of the West. The Salinas Pueblo mission churches and surrounding pueblos are evidence of the struggle between church and state over native labor and taxation that ended with a severe famine that caused the abandonment of the three pueblos eight years before the Pueblo Revolt of 1680. Each of the missions at Abó, Gran Quivira, and Quarai are distinctive. Each setting is striking in a different way, individual in its story depicting Pueblo and Spanish architecture. They portray the struggle between the seventeenth-century Spanish church against civil authorities seeking dominance over the native Pueblo people.

Scenic roads connect the remote sites in the high desert landscape. The Red Abó sandstone of the massive church ruins at Abó and Quarai and the grey limestone of Gran Quivira take on changing hues in sunset or under multi-tiered cumulus clouds.

Although the Abó, Quivira, and Quarai sites are spread over a radius of twenty-five miles from the visitor center, each is worth exploring for its rich history of Spanish New Mexico. The surviving portions of the mission churches have changed very little since their original construction. At all three missions The School of American Archeology (which became The School of American Research and is now known as The School of Advanced Research), the Museum of New Mexico, New Mexico State Monuments, and the National Park Service (NPS) have stabilized the ruins and carried out some limited reconstruction. Most of the material altered or added to by reconstruction is along the tops of the walls. Only in a few places do additions and alterations obscure or change appearance of the surviving structures.

The first Mission of San Gregorio de Abó, begun about 1622 by Fray Francisco Fonte, was constructed as a simple platform of two rectangles consisting of a *convento* (church residence) and a mission church. Surrounding the mission are ruins of a once thriving pueblo. The red sandstone church walls, built of flat stones averaging 1 foot in length and 2 to 3 inches thick, loom as battlements over the rubble of the conventos and pueblos. The original mission church, modified in later years, was simple in plan but approximately 25 feet wide and 83 feet long on the interior, without transepts. Stone buttresses supported relatively thin walls consisting of a rubble core and with stone veneer (small, flat-shaped stones) with an average thickness of about 3 feet along the sides of the nave and 2-3/4 feet along the front and apse ends of the church. The walls stood about 25 feet high to the undersides of the nave roof *vigas*, and 28 feet to the tops of the parapets along the nave. The roof structure was supported on square beams resting on corbels, with a spacing of about two feet between the vigas.

Five years after Fray Francisco Acevedo became Guardian of Abó in 1640, the mission church was renovated, with a nave extending to 132 feet from entrance to rear of apse. A transept changed the floor plan from a simple rectangle to a cruciform plan with a transept approximately 48 feet long by 23 feet wide. The roof was raised to a parapet height of 50 feet and the front bell towers were added. A clerestory window, about 60 feet from the front of the church, was inserted in the 4-foot-high space between the nave roof and higher transept roof to illuminate the altar areas within the transept and apse.

Soon after initial construction started at Abó, Fray Juan Gutiérrez de la Chico arrived at Quarai in 1626 and selected a mound of ruins near the northeast corner of a thriving pueblo of around six hundred people as the site of his church and *convento*. The location on a slight rise of ground in rolling hills sparsely treed with juniper and piñon is dominated by the ruins of the once massive church walls of La Nuestra Señora de Purísima Concepción de Quarai (or Cuarac). The most intact of the three mission sites, the visitor to Quarai can gain an awareness of the vastness of the building shaped by the tall, flat walls and towers and the battlement profile towering over the pueblo ruins.

Red sandstone walls, 4 to 6 feet thick built on foundations 7 feet deep and 6 feet wide, enclosed a nave 104 feet long by 50 feet wide and 26 feet high at the ceiling interior.

The cruciform plan with a 50-foot-wide transept, higher than the nave and apse, permitted a strip of clerestory windows to illuminate the altar. Facade bell towers reached a height of 39 feet, the nave towers 143 feet, and the apse towers 45 feet. Reinforcing

Mission Abó

tower buttresses 10 feet square at principal corners supported the relatively thin 4- to 6-foot-thick walls. *Vigas* spanning the nave and clerestory window were from 37 to 56 feet in length.

As a final touch, Gutiérrez added painted decorations on the white wall plaster. When complete, these consisted of dados along the walls of the church, sacristy, and the choir loft stairwell, and probably painted *retablo* designs behind the main altar, the two side altars, and the sacristy altar. The paintings were executed in red, black, gray, yellow, orange, and probably blue, white, and green. The retablo designs would serve until the new mission could afford to order carved and painted wooden retablos custom-made to fit into the spaces left behind the altars.

The furthest mission site from the Mountainair visitor center, Gran Quivira, is built on a rugged rocky ridge named after the Las Humanas pueblo, the largest of the Salinas pueblos and an important trade center for many years before and after the Spanish *entrada*. Considered an important site because of the large pueblo population and trading routes, Fray Diego de Santandér arrived in 1659 and began the construction of a replacement for the earlier church. The plan for the new church, San Buenaventura, was grand in concept with a large *convento* to serve the Las Humanas villages. Today's ruins are distinctive by blue-gray limestone walls outlining a church built on a platform placed on a mesa, with 6-foot-thick walls enclosing a cruciform plan 128 feet long and a nave 27 feet wide.

Time for the pueblo and the San Buenaventura mission church and convento was running out by 1670, when drought reduced the food supply, and resentment against the Spanish rule and suppression of the native people's beliefs were growing stronger.

Mission Gran Quivira   Mission Quarai

On September 3, 1670, Apaches raided the pueblo and the first Fray Santandér's church was laid waste. Statues and paintings on the altar were destroyed and vestments torn to pieces. Soon after the raid, the Franciscans and those Indians friendly to them moved to other missions and settlements in the Rio Grande Valley. The buildings of Las Humanas—pueblo, churches, and convento—were left to collapse into mounds of rubble, slowly filling with sand and dirt blown in by the wind. Within a century, Las Humanas looked much like it does today.

It is recommended that visitors start the tour of the three Salina Pueblo Missions at the Mountainair visitor center. Exploring the sites is easy on walking trails and paths with self-guided walking tours and a visitor contact station at each site.

Texas

Southwest

Fort Davis National Historic Site

Located in the western part of the state, in Fort Davis, Jeff Davis County, Texas

→ www.nps.gov/foda

→ The fort is located on the north edge of the town of Fort Davis on Highways 17 and 118 and is reached via Interstate 10 from El Paso to the west (about four hours) and San Antonio from the east (about seven hours) and from Alpine to the north by Highway 90.

Officer's Row and Parade Grounds (courtesy NPS)

Fort Davis National Historic Site in west Texas is a long drive west from San Antonio or east from El Paso. Set in the rugged beauty of the Davis Mountains and rising from the flat sun-parched landscape against a backdrop of the 200-foot-high North Ridge rock walls, National Historic Landmark Fort Davis' many buildings—some restored and some in ruins—is considered one of the best remaining examples of any post-Civil War frontier military post in the American Southwest.

From 1854 to 1891, except for the Civil War years, Fort Davis guarded the Trans-Pecos segment of the southern route to California. The fort's strategic location on the San Antonio-El Paso Road protected immigrants, mail coaches, and freight wagons from raids by Mescalero Apaches and Comanches. Troops stationed at Fort Davis, including all-black regiments established after the Civil War—the Buffalo Soldiers—played a major role in the campaigns against Apache leader Victorio, whose death in 1880 largely ended Native American warfare in Texas.

Beginning in 1867, more than sixty stone and adobe buildings were built on the plain at the foot of the mountains to replace the ruined and deserted first fort. In 1891, the fort was abandoned and the 447-acre Fort Davis National Historic Site (later increased to 474 acres) was authorized as a unit of the National Park System in 1961. Visitors to the fort to-day have the opportunity to view twenty-five buildings with restored exteriors, including five with interior restoration work, and the foundation outlines of the first fort. The neatly

Officers' quarters (courtesy NPS)

aligned structures with white-trimmed columned and railed porches reflect the restoration and stabilization program of the National Park Service (NPS) that began in 1963. The visitor center is located in what was originally an enlisted men's barracks. Five of the restored buildings have been refurbished to appear much as they did in the 1880s including a restored enlisted men's barracks that houses cavalry, infantry, artillery, and transportation exhibits, and a furnished squad room and orderly room as it appeared in the summer of 1884 when occupied by Buffalo Soldiers of Troop H, 10th Cavalry. Other buildings have screening over windows and doors for visitors to peer in and view interiors.

Along Officers' Row, two restored and furnished officers' quarters are open for viewing. The thirteen single-story quarters face the parade ground (50 by 20 feet), some with rear extensions, kitchens (one standing), and the foundations of privies. The main structures are uniformly built on tooled stone foundations, with seven officers' quarters constructed of tuff (native rock) and six built with adobe walls, and fireplaces at each end and wood-frame, shingled hip roofs. Tall window openings of double-hung multi-light sashes provided through-ventilation for the dwellings.

The Commanding Officer's Quarters, constructed by 1869, served as the residence for post commanders until 1891. The building is furnished to the period of 1882 to 1885, when Colonel Benjamin H. Grierson, 10th Cavalry, served as post commander. At the south end of the Row is a shared Lieutenants' Quarters refurbished as if a bachelor lieutenant was living on the north side and a married lieutenant occupied the south half. Behind the twelfth officers' quarters is a refurbished two-room Officer's Kitchen and Servant's Quarters. To the rear of Officers' Row is the restored Post Hospital. The one-story structure with a central hospital section (approximately 63 by 48 feet) is connected to two flanking twelve-bed patient wards (approximately 44 by 28 feet) by covered passageways. Wide-columned porches, 10 to 12-foot-high ceilings, and large window openings provided an airy, spacious appearance.

The reward for visitors to the pristine mountain landscape of Fort Davis National Historic Site is the sight of neatly aligned buildings facing the parade grounds and a flag snapping smartly in the prairie wind as it did 125 years ago. During the summer, park rangers and volunteers, dressed in period-type clothing provide living-history demonstrations. It is a worthwhile trip to see one of the most extensive and impressive of any western frontier posts.

Guadalupe Mountains National Park

The park is located in west Texas on the Texas-New Mexico state line, near Pine Springs, Culberson County, Texas.

→ www.nps.gov/gumo

→ The park visitor center at Pine Springs is located on US 62/180, 110 miles east of El Paso via 62 and 180, fifty-five miles southwest of Carlsbad, New Mexico, via 62 and 180, and sixty-five miles north of Van Horn, Texas, via State Highway 54.

Guadalupe Mountains, El Capitan to the right (courtesy NPS)

Texans treasure the Guadalupe Mountains as a well-kept secret, admiring its distinctive majesty towering into the west Texas sky above the Chihuahuan Desert. The National Park Service (NPS) hails the mountains as a place where "a visitor can delight in grand views, diverse landscapes, and small pleasures," according to the NPS *Guadalupe Mountain National Park Official Map and Guide*. Texas geologist Wallace E. Pratt enjoyed the scenic beauty and wanted to share it with the entire country, donating over 5,000 acres and promoting the idea of a park until its establishment in 1972. The 86,416-acre park is a rewarding journey to west Texas to experience the contrasting desert and the mountain range's stunningly beautiful canyons and lushly forested highlands. Like the prow of a great ship rising from the desert floor, El Capitan's steep cliffs are a traveler's landmark.

The park contains portions of the world's most extensive and significant Permian limestone fossil reef, which also shaped Carlsbad Caverns, only forty miles to the north. At one point, the boundaries of the two parks are only five miles apart. Historic structures include stage station ruins, a frontier ranch complex, settler cabin, and Pratt's vacation cabin.

Near the visitor center are the ruins of the Guadalupe Butterfield Overland Mail Line stage station, the Pinery, in service from 1858–59, and located at the 5,534-foot Guadalupe Pass, the highest station on the original 2,795-mile Butterfield Stage Line

Pinery ruins   Frijole Ranch house/museum (courtesy NPS)

route. The fortress-like station formed by a rectangular enclosure of 30-inch-thick and 11-foot-high limestone and adobe walls provided safety and protection from tribal raids. Although short-lived, long after its abandonment the station continued to be a retreat for migrants, freighters, soldiers, outlaws, and drovers. The ruin is fragile; don't climb on the walls.

Only a short distance from the visitor center, accessible by vehicle from US 62 and 180, the Frijoles Ranch Cultural Museum offering a view of frontier life in remote west Texas includes a ranch house, outbuildings, and a school. As the only major building complex in the region for several decades, Frijole Ranch served as a community center for dances and other social gatherings, as well as the region's official post office, from 1916 to 1942. Today's ranch house, renovated by the NPS in 1992, incorporates rooms built in 1876 by cattle ranchers, the Rader brothers. The house was constructed 40 feet from Frijole Spring and had double walls of native stone with a filler of mud between; interior walls were also plastered with mud. In the 1920s, the Smith family expanded the house, adding rooms, a second floor, and a gable shake-shingled roof. The barn and other outbuildings were added and the Frijole Ranch house complex enclosed by a low stone wall. The Smiths also built the red schoolhouse attended by up to eight children from the Smith family and local ranches. The small structure, with vertical wood siding and a low-pitched roof covered with corrugated tin, was later used as a storage shed and bunkhouse and eventually restored by the NPS to its schoolhouse appeance of the 1920s.

The remote Williams Ranch captures the isolation of west Texas ranching operations. An eight-mile-long, four-wheel drive to the western side of the Guadalupe Mountains standing among the rugged foothills 5,000 feet below Guadalupe Peak leads to the house. Approaching the ranch house, well preserved by the dry desert air, a common reaction among visitors is that the steeply gabled structure looks out of place in west Texas. Records are uncertain about the name of the builder and date of construction. Possibly, John Smith of El Paso was recalling wood-frame houses back East when around 1908 he built the house for Henry Belcher and his family. Another version is that the house was built by Henry Belcher's brother for a bride who stayed for only 24 hours before heading for home. After a decade on the ranch, the Belchers left and James Adolphus Williams (known to friends as "Uncle Dolph"), a lone cowman from Louisiana, ranched and farmed the land until his death in 1942. The visitor has to borrow a key at the visitor center to the entrance gates to visit the house.

Along the McKittrick Canyon Trail, approximately seven miles north of the visitor center off US 62 and 180 (2.75 miles from the trailhead), is the stone cabin built by geologist Walter E. Pratt. The McKittrick Canyon attracts thousands of visitors each year to enjoy its hidden beauty and spectacular fall colors. Along the road to the trail is the "Arm Waving Spot," where Pratt's employees noticed that the place "just naturally seemed to make geologists want to wave their arms around." Pratt's "stone cabin," a vacation home designed by Houston architect Joseph Staub and completed in 1932, was built of limestone quarried outside the canyon at the base of the Guadalupe Mountains. An unusual roof of thin limestone "shingles" is supported on heart-of-pine rafters and collar beams shipped in from east Texas. The cabin was furnished with rough plank reclining chairs, four beds and assorted hammocks, and a special table to seat twelve.

Wallace E. Pratt cabin (courtesy NPS)

Two other structures complete the cabin complex: a building that contains a two-car garage and caretaker's quarters, and a pumphouse. Stone fences border the property on the south and west.

Lyndon B. Johnson National Historical Park

The park is located in the Texas Hill Country in Johnson City in Blanco County, and near Stonewall in Gillespie County, Texas.

→ www.nps.gov/lyjo

→ The park has two visitor areas on Highway 290 separated by about fourteen miles: the Johnson City District and the LBJ Ranch District near Stonewall. The park visitor center in Johnson City is fifty miles west of Austin via US 290 and sixty-five miles north of San Antonio on US 281. Tickets for the LBJ Ranch bus tour are purchased at the LBJ State Park and Historic Site Visitor Center.

Lyndon Baines Johnson's boyhood home

The hilly area west of Austin, Texas—the Hill Country—had great meaning to Lyndon Baines Johnson. Here, the thirty-sixth president of the United States developed many of the traits of the southern cowboy that history admired in a great time of national stress. The park traces Johnson's family roots in the Hill Country where he spent his childhood, his reconstructed birthplace, the Texas White House, and the ranching operations that continue today. The park offers a unique perspective into the complete life of an American president.

Lyndon B. Johnson National Historical Park has two sections: the LBJ Boyhood Home and the Johnson Settlement complex in Johnson City, and the LBJ Ranch along the Pedernales River. In Johnson City, from the LBJ Boyhood Home, you can walk to the Johnson Settlement, the family residence from 1865 to 1872. The Settlement's complex of restored historic structures traces the evolution of the Texas Hill Country from the open-range days of Johnson's grandfather, Samuel Ealy Johnson, Sr., to the ranching and farming of more recent times. The LBJ Ranch, north of the president's beloved Pedernales River and maintained by the National Park Service (NPS), contains the rambling ranch house that became the Texas White House, the reconstructed LBJ birthplace, the one-room Junction School attended by the president, and the family cemetery where the president is buried.

The National Historic Landmark LBJ Boyhood Home on Elm Street in Johnson City is where Johnson lived from age five to nineteen. The comfortable, modest-size white one-story house built in 1901 has a folk Victorian spirit with spindle trim boards at the west front porch and distinctive serrated trim board on the ridge of the gable roofs. A hint of Colonial Revival is seen in partial returns at the gable-end walls. The roofs intersect at a central chimney. The house entrance to the east front porch accesses the parlor and a small office. A double-face fireplace opens into the parlor and dining room. The "west wing" of the house (to the left of the central parlor, dining room, and kitchen) contains a small office, the girls' bedroom for LBJ's three sisters (Rebekah, Josefa, and Lucia), and a large sleeping porch at the northwest corner of the house. In the house's "east wing" are the parents' bedroom, the bedroom shared by LBJ with his brother, Sam Houston Johnson, a tub room, and a small porch.

In the Johnson Settlement area, four of the original buildings were still standing when purchased by the NPS with funds donated by the former president soon after he retired from office. In addition to the two-room dogtrot log cabin built in the late 1850s by Samuel Ealy Johnson, Sr., (with later kitchen and bedroom additions), they included two stone barns and a cooler house. The visitor can linger in the Settlement's restored structures arranged around a pasture, usually with a few longhorns on display, to recall the early days of Texas cattle ranching. A chuck wagon near the log house is used for demonstrations of range-style cooking by cowboys in Stetson hats and leather chaps.

The LBJ Ranch House is an imposing two-story structure facing the Pedernales River. The house was purchased by LBJ from a Johnson relative in 1951, and during the Johnson administration it served as the Texas White House. Today's impressive mansion's original section of native limestone fieldstone built in 1894 by a German immigrant, Wilhelm "Polecat" Meier, saw successive additions and renovations throughout the years. Even after many additions and renovations, this original stone section remains the house's defining element.

The current LBJ birthplace home east of the Texas White House is a reconstruction of the original house torn down in 1935. Based on photographs and family recollections, architect J. Roy White of Austin, Texas, designed the house in 1964 to follow the same architectural style as the original house, built in 1889 by the president's grandfather, Samuel Ealy Johnson, Sr.

Near the birthplace home is the Junction School, which served local children from 1910 until 1947. The restored building, with gray pressed-metal exterior walls and wood-

LBJ Ranch House

LBJ's grandparents' cabin

framed windows and doors, was a typical one-room schoolhouse where eight grades were taught simultaneously. The President demonstrated his attachment to the Junction School—the scene of his first formal educational experience at age four— and quality public education for all children by signing the Elementary and Secondary Education Act on April 11, 1965, at a picnic table on the lawn of the Junction School, with Miss Katie Deadrich (his first teacher) at his side.

San Antonio Missions National Historical Park
San Antonio, Bexar County, Texas

→   www.nps.gov/saan

→   A Missions tour starts from the National Park Service Visitor Center adjacent to San José. The four missions of San Antonio Missions National Historical Park–the Alamo is operated separately by the Daughters of the Texas Republic–are all indicated by special signage and distinctive street lighting along the trail from downtown to all sites.

Mission San Juan bell tower

South of the center of metropolitan San Antonio and connected by the Mission Trail leading south from downtown are four Spanish frontier missions. Each mission complex is distinctive for its church and interpretation by the National Park Service (NPS). The park sites, maintained by agreement with several local entities, include the Archdiocese of San Antonio, which maintains active centers of worship at each mission site. The NPS provides preservation of remnants of the mission compounds and visitor information, exhibits, and programs for a special connection to the past. The missions included in the park are the active parish churches of Concepción, San José, San Juan, and Espada, transferred to their present locations from eastern Texas in 1731.

The mission communities flourished between the 1740s and 1780s. The decline of the missions chiefly was due to a reduced native population as a result of epidemics and acculturation. By 1794 four of the missions were partially secularized. At the time, Mission San Antonio de Valero (now known as the Alamo) was fully secularized, and shortly afterward housed additional soldiers and their families sent to help protect the area. By 1824, under the government of the Republic of Mexico, townspeople moved into the abandoned missions, crowding out those small populations of natives that still remained. Auctions were held at each site, and the tracts of now vacant former mission farm lands, empty rooms in the compounds, even the stone rubble of collapsed walls, was sold off. Over the long years of warfare throughout the area that began during Mexico's war for independence from Spain and continued under the Republic of Mexico, and during the brief Republic of Texas, the mission communities along with most of the south central Texas bore the brunt and lay in partial ruin.

Three miles south of downtown San Antonio, Mission Nuestra Señora de la Concepción de Acuña sits back from the road set in an acre of lawn in a quiet, leafy residential area. The facade's twin belfry towers, three-bay division, ornately carved stone columns supporting a steep triangular pediment framing a main entrance door in the central bay, and ocular window are examples of the proportions of Spanish Colonial baroque style. The original effect was much different than what is seen today. In the church's heyday, colorful geometric designs covered its surface, but the patterns have long since faded or worn away. The entire facade originally was plastered and frescoed with yellow and orange squares filled with red and blue quatrefoils and crosses, painted quoins marked the corners, and painted columns flanked each opening in the bell towers.

Started in 1740, the cruciform-plan Concepción church 93 feet long from apse to portal, 53 feet wide at the transepts, with dome at nave and transept crossing rising to an interior height of 44 feet, survived for two centuries due to its wall construction: 45 inches thick constructed of dressed stone facing and rubble and adobe fill. North and east walls were made windowless for defensive purposes. Segments of the *convento* (church residence) walls, workshops, and living quarters at Mission Concepción survive, as well as the Father President's office and the staircase to it that has a Moorish arch. Don't be discouraged by the somber exterior gray walls. The insides of the *convento* refectory are carefully cleaned and the ceiling and wall paintings are preserved. The most intact of the missions and claimed to be the oldest unrestored Mission church in the United States, Concepción is also a National Historic Landmark.

Mission San José

Mission San José y San Miguel de Aguayo, the largest, most impressive, and best preserved of the San Antonio's five missions was founded in 1720. Although extensively restored in the 1930s by the Works Progress Administration and other entities, the mission contains considerable portions of the original church, especially its ornate Spanish Colonial baroque façade, and the sacristy with the famed Rose Window, also a won-

Mission Concepción

Mission San José

derful example of that same architectural style. Alongside the church is the baptistery and behind the sanctuary is the fascinating, long two-story rows of monk cells, now a roofless shell, with arched window openings, Gothic columns, and flying buttresses added by the Benedictines in the 1850s. On the northwest side of the mission grounds is the massive 110-foot-long rubble stone granary with buttresses and barrel-vaulted roof. Outside the walls nearby is the reconstructed Spanish Colonial mill that recently was made operational.

The church is identified by the single bell tower and wide facade, the elaborate Spanish baroque (churrigueresque) carvings at the entrance, attributed as "the finest Spanish Colonial facade in the United States" (Hugh Morrison, Early American Architecture, 1952), and rose window alone are worth the visit. Construction began in 1768 and the original plan for it laid out a long nave, two bell towers, and a transept. Modified during construction, the completed church was shorter and had only one bell tower. Construction on the second was stopped at the church's roofline, and a gun platform was built on top. The transept was never built, and the sacristy with its unique roof and three domes was enlarged on the site of the proposed transept. The church and sacristy were completed in 1782. The 500- by 600-foot surrounding wall enclosed a typical mission complex of church, convento, 18-foot-wide living quarters, and workshops. The church (approximately 33 by 100 feet in plan) has a 62-foot-wide facade, sparkling with decorative detailing. The single bell tower rises to a height of 75 feet.

Originally, the entire San José facade of dressed limestone walls with corner quoins was plastered and frescoed to resemble bright tiles. A small sample of the geometric patterns can be seen near the lower right corner of the tower. The towers, the dome and circular choir stairway collapsed at least once, and all were rebuilt to what may be seen today. Around the church's tower corner is the cylindrical tower leading to the choir loft and bell tower; inside is a remarkable circular stairway of solid local oak built on a central pivot. Further along the walk to the convento is the sacristy wall. Pause to admire the legendary grillwork-covered rose window (La Ventana de Rosa) surrounded by ornately stone-carved scrolls and foliage.

Mission San Juan Capistrano has a smaller-scale church with several buildings, some ruined, with most of the compound wall visible. The mission is in a pastoral setting and is rather humble and muted in appearance. The charm of the mission is its simplicity, created by its buttressed church walls and distinctive silhouette, especially the simple and stark two-tiered pierced espadaña (bell tower). The church and sacristy is rectangular in plan, with overall exterior dimensions of 20 by 110 feet; the sacristy is a room measuring 15 feet square on the interior. The church's plan is unusual for the primary and secondary entrances placed in the east wall of the nave. Construction is random rubble masonry. The interior is a simple space, restored in the 1960s. Lack-

Mission Concepción interior

ing the rich Baroque decorative work of Mission San José, the flat ceiling of exposed beams and latillas rises above the white-painted walls that were once covered with colorful frescoes including musicians playing instruments. A one quarter-mile nature trail beginning across from the entrance gate to the mission compound gives the visitor the opportunity to view the river and vegetation reminiscent of the early colonial landscape.

Mission San Francisco de la Espada is the southernmost church on the Mission Trail, surrounded by woodland in a peaceful rural setting, though just south of busy Interstate 410. It is descended from the oldest mission in Texas, originally situated by the Neches River in 1690. It was moved to its present location in 1731. This small church is notable for its Moorish-arched main entry and two-tiered pierced bell tower, remaining stone compound walls, the convento (closed for use as a refectory), the Native American quarters, and the bastion at the southeast corner built in the 1820s under Mexico and heavily fortified to ward off frequent Apache and Comanche raids. The foundation of a larger church that was started in the 1760s but curtailed due to a dwindling Native American population is seen near the mission church.

Mission San José

Museum Espada

Nearby is the Espada Aqueduct, in use since 1740 and protected as a National Historic Landmark. The massive, arched masonry aqueduct carrying water across the Piedras Creek was part of the acequia system with a network of irrigation ditches serving Mission Espada.

The missions' rescue from ruins is a tribute to the Archdiocese of San Antonio, individuals, local preservation groups, and the federal government. The NPS continues its partnership with the Archdiocese of San Antonio and civic leaders to preserve and interpret this fascinating part of our country's history. Founded when Texas was in the northern reaches of New Spain (Mexico), the missions continue to serve as parish churches. Enjoy the frequent festivals with lots of music, food, and color, sponsored by the local parishes. Religious festivities may include holiday celebrations.

Utah

Southwest

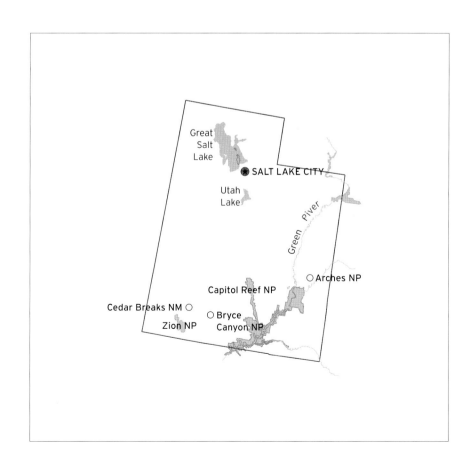

Arches National Park

Moab, Grand County, Utah

→ www.nps.gov/arch

→ The park entrance is on US 191, five miles north of Moab, three miles north of its junction with Utah 128, or twenty-eight miles southeast of Interstate 70.

Double Arch

Arches National Park preserves one of the largest collections of natural sandstone arches in the world. Over twenty-five hundred documented arches and extraordinary geological resources and formations, including windows, spires, pinnacles, pedestals, and balanced rocks, are highlighted by a striking environment of contrasting colors, landforms, and textures. The park's primary historical architecture is the Wolfe Cabin, an abandoned nineteenth-century homestead standing as a prelude to Delicate Arch, the park's signature rock formation.

The Wolfe Ranch is on Salt Wash, at the beginning of the Delicate Arch Trail. The National Park Service (NPS) preserves the cabin, corral, and root cellar as an example of early Western cattle ranching. John Wesley Wolfe, a veteran of the Civil War, came to the area from Ohio with his son Fred and built a homestead around 1898 on the site of what is known as Wolfe Ranch. They selected a 150-acre tract along Salt Wash for their Bar-DX Ranch. Salt Wash provided the water and the surrounding land had enough grass for a few cows. John and Fred lived this solitary life for nearly twenty years. In 1907, John's daughter Flora, her husband Ed Stanley, and their two children moved to the ranch. They built a new cabin and a root cellar, those seen in the park today. John's original cabin was swept away by a flash flood. In 1910, the Wolfe family moved back to Ohio. They sold the ranch to Tommy Larson. Larson sold it to Mary Turnbow in 1914. Emmit Elizondo bought it from Mary's heirs in 1947. The following year he sold it to the federal government. In 1974 the site was designated as the Wolfe Ranch National Historic District. Today the cabin can be viewed from the exterior, and visitors can peer into the sparsely furnished interior.

Edward Abbey, the environmentalist author, spent two summers in the late 1950s as a seasonal ranger in Arches National Park. His *Desert Solitaire: A Season in the Wilderness* (Ballantine Books, 1980) contains a lyrical description of the Wolfe Ranch. Parenthetically stating that "nothing decays here," Abbey goes on to describe the cabin as "a well-preserved ruin made of juniper, pinyon, and cottonwood logs, no two alike in shape or size." He attributed the crude construction of the log walls with remaining adobe chinking and shallow-pitched roof "from the scarcity of wood, not lack of skill." The wall's "morbid greenish hue" is from "dust matching the coloration of the surrounding hills....The cabin has a doorway, but no door, a single window and no glass." The

Wolfe Ranch cabin

Delicate Arch

interior matched the harshness of the crude log walls: "the floor consists of warped, odd-size planks...in the center of the room is a massive post of juniper shoring up the ancient, sagging roof, which is a thatchwork affair of poles, mud and rock, very leaky."

Abbey's final comment on the cabin summarized his respect for the settlers who eked out a living at the ranch, "As shelter, the cabin can not be recommended, except for its shade on a hot day." While today's visitor may peek into the cabin, for safety reasons the cabin is no longer open to public access.

Bryce Canyon National Park

Tropic, Garfield County, Utah

→ www.nps.gov/brca

→ The park is located in southwestern Utah. Access from the west is via US 89; turn east on Utah 12, seven miles south of Panguitch and drive seventeen miles on Utah 63 to the park entrance. From the east travel on Utah 12 and turn south on Utah 63 to the park entrance.

Bryce Canyon is an amphitheater—five miles across and, in places, 800 feet deep—with spires and pinnacles, minarets and domes, windows and arches, and fantastic figures and forms in soft reds, pinks, yellows, oranges, grays, and whites. Bryce's dazzling eroded shale and sandstone landscape was shaped each year by more than two hundred cycles of freeze and thaw. Colors and the changing hues of alternating rock layers dazzle the viewer.

A cluster of outstanding historic structures designed by Gilbert Stanley Underwood for the Union Pacific Railroad's Utah Parks Company and National Park Service (NPS), including the National Historic Landmark Bryce Canyon Lodge and deluxe cabins, are near the visitor center. From here, the magnificent panorama of Bryce Canyon can be seen by short hikes from Sunrise Point, Sunset Point, Inspiration Point, Bryce Point, and

Paria View. The fine collection of rustic structures offers a rewarding counterpoint to the stunning geological panoramas.

Beginning in 1924 the cooperative venture of Underwood, the Utah Parks Company,

Old Administration Building

Bryce Canyon Lodge

and the NPS-constructed buildings of a consistently high quality. The rustic structures reinforced each other with a design continuity expressed in materials, massing, form, and scale. Buildings were of frame, log, and stone construction; stone foundations and fireplaces, and gabled roofs covered in cedar shakes, were typical. Sites were selected to minimize impact on the natural setting, and the use of local materials produced a collection of buildings that mirrored the highest NPS rustic standards. The Utah Park Company's buildings—with an undulating pattern of cedar shingles—is a unique feature repeated in other NPS buildings both in Bryce and other national parks. The integrity of rustic designs at Bryce Canyon represents a peak in the NPS park development program from 1925 to 1940.

The concentration of historic structures are in the Bryce Canyon Historic District: the lodge, cabins, men's dormitory, support buildings, and other NPS buildings. A tour beginning at the lodge explores these features. The overlook at Rainbow Point is the furthest accessible structure.

Bryce Canyon Lodge and the accompanying complex of deluxe cabins are superb architectural creations designed by Underwood. The lodge is a two-story frame structure with first-floor stone masonry walls and a distinctive profile created by a massive hip roof and undulating "hit or miss" shingle pattern. There are references to traditional northern European rustic design in the exaggerated main roof, which rises to 36 feet at the ridge and dominates the finished composition. Here, we can see Underwood's strength in rustic design with the dominance of the massively scaled roof, relieved by long shed dormers to achieve second-story space. A subtle blending of materials and forms in a limited palette of textures and colors satisfied the Union Pacific Railroad's desire for a memorable image of the lodge.

The lodge's first floor contains the lobby, with the registration desk, offices, small post office, dining room and kitchen, gift shop, and auditorium. Underwood established a uniform interior design with milled timbers in the lobby, exposed roof truss-es in the dining room and auditorium, and rough rubble   for the fireplaces. This National Historic Landmark was renovated in the late 1990s to provide modern safety and conveniences, including conversion of a second-floor employee dormitory to guest rooms, while maintaining the character of the 1930s. The building is the only remaining Underwood-designed Union Pacific Railroad Loop Tour lodge.

By 1927, a complex of 67 wood-framed standard and economy cabins and five deluxe log cabins were grouped around the lodge. Ten more deluxe cabins were added in 1929. Pioneer anad frontier cabins were removed in the 1980s and replaced by motel units. The duplex and quadruplex log cabins clustered near the lodge are among Underwood's most exquisite rustic structures. A refinement of his designs at Zion National Park (see page 161), the cabins were masterful creations of rustic forms and materials. The ingenious planning of the cabins with richly detailed interiors created privacy by entrance place-ment. Careful selection and placement of boulders, logs, and hit-or-miss undulating roof shingles artfully solved the problem of combining multiple units within a single structure. Sited in a grove of pines below the lodge, they are small in scale, show adroit use of logs and stone, and have steeply pitched roofs. Rubble-stone foundations, chimneys, and cor-ner piers battered at the base are highly textured with raked joints 3 and 4 inches deep.

Underwood displayed his strengths as a designer in meeting the challenge to add more buildings at Bryce Canyon while maintaining a unified composition for the proj-ect. The dominating massing and larger scale of the lodge is reinforced by the smaller cluster of deluxe cabins. The irregularities of form imitate nature, and the rough stone-work and large logs underscore that connection. The locally quarried stones match the geology, and logs are similar in size to the surrounding pines. Despite the difficulty of designing the Bryce Canyon complex over time, Underwood succeeded in creating a cohesive grouping in the rustic style.

Deluxe cabin by Gilbert Stanley Underwood

Although a difficult challenge for the NPS designers, their buildings at Bryce Can-yon come close to Underwood's high standards. The service structures built in the 1920s adopted Underwood's established forms and details: rectangular plans on a rubble-stone foundation, exposed stud framing over horizontal shiplap siding walls, and cedar-shingle hip roofs. The old Administration Building built in 1932 with additions in 1934 and now used as the High Plateaus Institute is comparable to other prominent NPS rustic design projects of the period such as at Yosemite, Crater Lake, and Mount Rainier.

A visit to Bryce Canyon National Park is a must for the spectacular scenery. Writer Thomas Wolfe effusively described the canyon as "a million wind-blown pinnacles of salmon pink and fiery white all fused together like stick candy—all suggestive of a child's fantasy of heaven." Arriving at the canyon rim the visitor will revel in awe and agree with Ebenezer Bryce, first resident of Bryce Canyon who quipped, "One hell of a place to lose a cow." The tour de force of inspiring rustic historic designs by Gilbert Stanley Underwood and the highly competent NPS-designed structures add to a fulfilling visitor experience.

Capitol Reef National Park

Near Torrey, Wayne County, Utah

→   www.nps.gov/care

→   The park is located in south-central Utah on Utah 24, twelve miles east of Torrey, Utah, and thirty-seven miles west of Hanksville, Utah.

Fruita School House

Capitol Reef National Park preserves the spectacular Waterpocket Fold, a one hundred-mile-long S-shaped warp in the earth's crust. Local Wayne County boosters called it "Wayne Wonderland." The park now comprises 241,000 acres of colorful canyons, ridges, buttes, and monoliths. Located about halfway between Bryce Canyon and Canyonlands National Parks, the Waterpocket Fold divides the south-central part of the state. The park can be experienced from Utah Highway 24—a Utah Scenic Byway—which crosses the park from east to west, on the twenty-five-mile round trip scenic drive from the visitor center and unpaved roads, and many fine hiking trails.

This area of vast natural beauty includes evidence of prehistoric Native American culture and a Mormon pioneer community. Along with the spectacular scenic features, the Fruita Historic District encompasses the remains of Fruita, including fruit orchards, the restored one-room schoolhouse, and a historic homestead, all a short distance from the visitor center.

The one-room Fruita Schoolhouse, completed in 1896, is a 17- by 20-foot rectangular structure; square-cut half-notch log walls with lime log chinking are on a foundation of dressed sandstone blocks. Shallow wood pediments capped pairs of double-hung windows in sidewalls and a south-facing entrance doorway. The original flat roof was covered with bentonite clay; a peaked, shingled roof modification was added in 1917. The ceiling under the peaked roof is beaded planking. The interior walls, originally exposed chinked logs, were plastered in 1935. A woodstove connected to a brick chimney warded off the cold and damp. The log building also served as a community meeting house where dances, elections, church youth activities, box suppers, and celebrations were once held. Desks were not bolted to the floor, so the room could be cleared for different needs.

In the 1960s the National Park Service (NPS) restored the structure to the 1930s period. In 1972, it was listed on the National Register of Historic Places. The school stands alongside Utah Highway 24. Visitors may also peer through the windows into the furnished structure and imagine what school was like, so long ago. Those with a good imagination can still hear the old school bell ringing.

The Gifford Homestead, a mile south of the visitor center on Utah 24, contains the Gifford farmhouse, barn smokehouse, and other outbuildings. The original farmhouse, built in 1908 and slightly modified by a succession of owners until sold to the NPS in 1969 by the Giffords, was a wood-frame structure containing a combined front room/kitchen and two small bedrooms. An outside ladder accessed two small upstairs bedrooms. The Capitol Reef Natural History Association, in cooperation with the NPS, renovated and refurnished the farmhouse and operates a sales outlet in the former kitchen with reproduction Mormon pioneer utensils and tools and local artisans' craft items.

Cedar Breaks National Monument

Near Cedar City, Iron County, Utah

→ www.nps.gov/cebr

→ Visitors traveling south on Interstate 15, exit at Parowan, then take Utah 143 east, to Cedar Breaks National Monument. Traveling north exit Interstate 15 at Cedar City, then take Utah 14 east for eighteen miles, then Utah 148 north four miles. Visitors traveling north/south on US 89 can take either Utah 143 from Panguitch to Cedar Breaks, or Utah 14 west to Utah 148, and north to the visitor center. Heavy snowfall at the 10,400-foot approach road summit closes the road to vehicles between November and April.

Cedar Breaks National Monument is a brilliantly colored amphitheater carved out of the 10,000-foot-high Markagunt Plateau in southern Utah. A product of the same forces and materials that created the spectacular southwest landscapes of the Grand Canyon, Zion Canyon, and the Bryce amphitheater, it is an original work of nature, surrounded by alpine forests and meadows.

In the 1920s the Union Pacific Railroad Company created a "Grand Circle Tour" that allowed tourists to visit several parks in one trip. Tour participants departed from

Cedar City, Utah, on motorbuses and traveled the roads connecting Cedar Breaks, Zion, the North Rim of the Grand Canyon, and Bryce Canyon. A scheduled lunch stop at Cedar Breaks took place in a Gilbert Stanley Underwood lodge, removed in 1972. The National Park Service (NPS) designed and built an administrative complex close to the same location near the South Entrance to the Rim Road.

Today there are two rustic structures near the South Entrance designed by the NPS and built by Civilian Conservation Corps (CCC) crews in 1937. The visitor center and caretaker's cabin are simple in form and share common elements of NPS rustic non-intrusive design and construction. Form and materials minimize the one-story building's impact on the site. Replete with fine details and craftsmanship, with brown painted plaster-chinked peeled-log walls on a stone foundation, saddle-notched corner logs, exposed peeled-log rafters and purlins, and shallow-pitched shake-shingle roofs, the buildings are in the best tradition of the rustic-style principles of architecture.

The visitor center at Point Supreme Overlook is perched on the edge of the amphitheater—a window to the brilliantly colored sandstone formations. The caretaker's cabin is a quarter-mile away, visible from the road and closer to the South Entrance.

The two-room 600-square-foot visitor center has a covered porch on four peeled-log columns. The porch roof is raised slightly at its edge from the main roof as an entrance-defining feature. A 29-foot by 6-foot-6-inch-deep porch with a flagstone floor along the north elevation, added in 1954, provides shelter for viewing the amphitheater. Logs are exposed on the interior walls. Peeled-log beams span from wall-to-wall and short log columns perched on the beams support long logs paralleling the ridge, in turn carrying peeled-log purlins that extend 2 feet beyond the gable end roof edge.

The caretaker's cabin is a one-story, two-room, 600-square-foot rectangular shaped structure. At the building's corners saddle-notched logs step inward from ground to roof purlins and sharpened ends alternate horizontally and vertically, creating a classic NPS image of a random rustic design character to what is a thoughtfully detailed small-scaled structure.

Cedar Breaks caretaker's cabin

Including Cedar Breaks in a tour of the region is a worthwhile venture to reach the six-mile-long rim scenic drive and the revelation of the multicolored scenery below in the amphitheater. The visitor center and caretaker's cabin are superb examples of NPS architecture and CCC construction; nearby is the site of the removed Union Parks Company Cedar Breaks Lodge. There is a small exhibit about the lodge in the visitor center, with a picture of the structure as well as a portion of an oral history from a lodge employee describing what it was like to work there years ago.

Zion National Park

Springdale, Washington County, Utah

→ www.nps.gov/zion

→ The park is located in southwest Utah approximately 150 miles northwest of Las Vegas. Access is from Interstate 15 and Utah 9 to east of Springdale to reach the south entrance. The Kolob Canyons visitor center in the north section of the park can be reached from Interstate 15; take Exit 40 and follow signs to the center.

Ranger dormitory

The magnificent Vermilion Cliffs is part of a 2,000-foot layer of Navajo sandstone in the western region of the Colorado Plateau in southwestern Utah. Unlike the revelation of Cedar Breaks, Bryce Canyon, and the Grand Canyon from a precipitous rim view, Zion unfolds as a canyon; the sheer, vividly colored cliffs tower above the Scenic Drive's 2,000- to 3,000-foot walls of the narrow, deep canyon. The Mount Carmel Highway (Utah Highway 9), approaching the park from US 89 to the east, is an engineering marvel to experience on the journey to Zion Canyon.

When Zion National Monument became part of the fledgling National Park System, in 1916, it had undergone little commercial development. National Park Service (NPS) Director Stephen Mather encouraged the Union Pacific Railroad to develop a Utah Parks Company concession including Zion. A design theme that dominated park architecture during the 1920s and 1930s, NPS rustic was utilized by the concessioner's architect for building designs at the Zion Lodge and the Birch Creek Utility Area, which was used for housing tour buses.

From 1924 to 1934, Underwood designed all of the Utah Parks Company buildings at Zion, including the original Zion Lodge along with the associated cabins, women's

dormitory, swimming pool and bathhouse, bake shop, and cafeteria. The buildings reflect Underwood's skill in adapting to the context of a valley floor, in a dry climate without nearby forests, surrounded by richly colored rock walls. Underwood's design solu-

Men's dormitory

Pine Creek Bridge

tion was to use simple building forms, with exteriors of minimally dressed large blocks
of local red sandstone walls and chimneys laid in irregular courses with wide mortar
joints. He also employed over-scaled sawn wooden timbers and rafters and roof purlins,
studs-out framing over pine plan walls, shallow-pitched roofs, and wide eaves.

The original Zion Lodge design reflected the NPS's strong control over site selection for visitor accommodations and its preference for rustic architecture. The lodge
was tragically destroyed by fire in 1966 and rebuilt that same year on a more modest
scale. In close cooperation with the NPS, the concessioner completed restoration work
in 1992 to bring back some of the character of the original Zion Lodge. The Utah Parks
Company's cabins, support buildings, and the Zion Nature Center (originally the Zion
Inn) remain as part of Underwood's architectural legacy in the canyon. In addition
to the lodge, Underwood designed deluxe and standard cabins similar to the nearby
main lodge in materials and construction. Deluxe cabins contained two or four rooms
that could be combined into suites. The small, rustic structures were placed on rough-
dressed stone foundations made with the same stone that was used in ashlar patterns
for the chimneys. Standard cabins, removed in 1985, exhibited studs-out framing,
similar to the deluxe western cabins but were smaller in scale and the stone chimneys
were omitted.

The NPS built administrative and visitor structures concurrent with Underwood's
Utah Parks Company projects. In the Grotto Picnic Area, stands the oldest structure
in the park—originally a museum built in 1924. The original east and south entrance
pylons and signs, east entrance checking station, and Grotto and south campground
comfort stations were complete by the end of the 1920s. The Temple of Sinawava parking area at the end of the Scenic Drive is a fine example of the simple building forms and
native materials used throughout the Zion National Park. The Oak Creek and Pine Creek
residential areas include early buildings that show a general consistency in materials

and form, although building design and exterior material treatment in the two districts was affected at the end of the 1930s by funding limitations and the use of skilled labor.

The Ranger Dormitory is a solitary departure from early rustic design, built in 1941 in the Oak Creek area. In this two-story structure with Greek Revival detailing, the NPS opted for the local vernacular building style brought to the area in the nineteenth century by Mormon settlers. The Ranger Dormitory is rectangular in plan, with a gable roof and refined masonry work. The smooth-faced sandstone facade is a change from the irregular stone-and-battered walls in Underwood's earlier work. Characteristic Greek Revival details are seen in the wooden cornices under the eaves and returns on the building end walls. Symmetrically placed window openings with double-hung windows and an inset front door with a simple pediment, rectangular transom, and sidelights were typical early-nineteenth-century residential details. Authentic to the last detail, all trim is painted white.

Complementing the attractive rustic buildings are the formidable engineering feats of the Zion-Mount Carmel Tunnel and the Pine Creek and Virgin River bridges to link the Utah Parks Company concessions at Zion, Bryce, Cedar Breaks, and the North Rim of the Grand Canyon in a loop tour. The tunnel, over a mile long, provided access from the east and significantly shortened the Loop Tour. A dramatic series of six switchbacks

Zion Lodge rustic cabins

lined with random ashlar retaining walls lead down to the Virgin River. The Pine Creek Bridge is a single masonry arch of Navajo sandstone-blocks facing with a rubble-stone core; 23 feet above the creek is the massive keystone. The Virgin River Bridge is a 185-foot triple span of steel I-beams carried on massive sandstone piers. The steel is covered with redwood planking.

The pre–World War II buildings in Zion National Park and rebuilt Zion Park Lodge are admirable because of cohesiveness of design, materials, and scale. The same concepts applied to buildings were used on miscellaneous structures throughout the park, resulting in a harmonious collection of bridges, stone curbings, entrance signs, and retaining walls along a curvilinear system of roads and trails. The use of native sandstone and traditions from the local Mormon vernacular architecture resulted in a collection of structures that illustrate the best of the NPS rustic style.

Note that from April through October, the Zion Scenic Drive is accessible by shuttle bus only, departing from Springdale. Check the park web site for schedules as well as vehicle size restrictions for the Zion-Mount Carmel Tunnel.

Rockies and Plains

Colorado

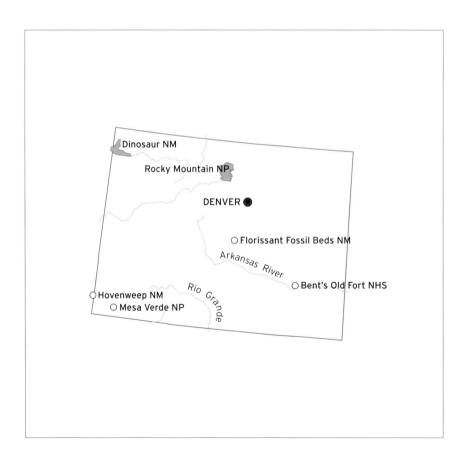

Bent's Old Fort National Historic Site

In southeast Colorado, near La Junta, Bent County, Colorado

→ www.nps.gov/beol

→ The park is eight miles east of La Junta and thirteen miles west of Las Animas on Colorado 194.

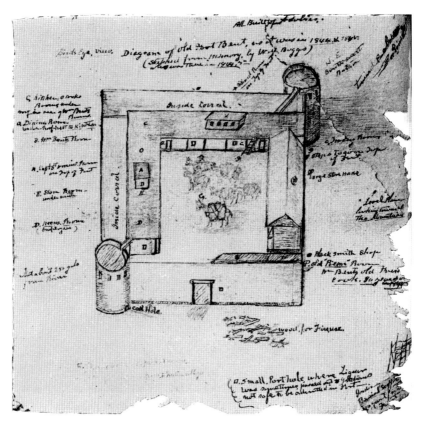

Bent's Old Fort, Lt. James W. Abert sketch, ca. 1845 (courtesy NPS)

Set on a sandy plain on the north bank of the Arkansas River, the reconstructed Bent's Old Fort casts one back to the 1830s and 1840s when Bent, St. Vrain & Company oversaw the largest and most commodious and influential trading post in the Southwest. Tepees and a green freight wagon with bright red wheels now stand in front of the fort's gun-portaled two-story-high adobe walls with bastions and towers facing the open plain; strands of imbedded hay in the adobe glint in the morning sun; the oxen harness clinks at the morning's stirring; a buffalo press stands on a dirt-packed courtyard, and reenactors in period clothing in the central courtyard or period furnished rooms portray the fort's rebuilt image of 1845–46.

Charles and William Bent, and their partner Ceran St. Vrain ran this flourishing trading post on the Santa Fe Trail between Independence, Missouri, and Santa Fe, New

Mexico, for over fifteen years. Abandoned in 1849 and then eventually damaged by fire, local settlers took adobe bricks from the walls for their own use. By the early 1900s little more than wall fragments no more than 8 feet high were visible. For decades, Bent's

Bent's Old Fort

Fort lay largely forgotten with little more than piles of crumbling adobe to mark its former grandeur. When the fort became a National Historic Site in 1960, none of the original structure was visible above ground. Designated a National Historic Landmark, today's reconstruction was built with similar materials and finished in a decades-long campaign completed in 1976 for the nation's bicentennial and Colorado's centennial. The carefully reconstructed structure and landscape closely resembles the original fort. Researchers relied on detailed drawings by visitors, contemporary descriptions, and archeological excavations. The fort is furnished mostly with reproductions.

The plan has the organization of a traditional hacienda; adobe walls and timber and *latia* roof construction reinforce the image of a period Southwest structure. Charles Bent sketched out the plan for a defensive fort and trading post: not quite a rectangle (a trapezoid 178 feet by 137 feet) enclosed by 4-foot-thick, 14- to 15-foot-high walls around a *placita* (central plaza) with an adjacent corral, and rooms around the entire quadrangle facing inward. The post contained about twenty-five rooms, with hard-packed earth floors and plastered walls, averaging about 15 by 20 feet. Just beneath the top of the walls were broad promenades pierced with firing ports for riflemen. Southwest and northeast corner defensive bastions, 30 feet high and 10 feet in diameter, are pierced with loopholes for muskets and an opening for swivel guns for loading with grapeshot.

The fort's main entry facing east is an imposing double-barrier gate with two large iron-sheathed plank doors leading into a passageway between bordering rooms and wide enough to pass freight wagons—9 feet wide by 7 feet high. An inner gate of thick planks sheathed in spiked-iron plating opened into the interior enclosure. A square watchtower manned by sentinels controlled entry to the fort and was fitted with a "first rate spyglass" to scan the horizon for hostile Indians and approaching wagon trains, topped by a belfry and a wooden flagstaff flying the Stars and Stripes. The west, or rear gate opened into the corral enclosed by 6- to 8-foot-high adobe walls, 3 feet thick, and planted thick with cactus to prevent raiders from scaling them. Outside the walls, two hundred yards to the southwest of the fort stood an adobe structure used for storing ice cut from the river in the winter.

A tour of the rooms can be taken at leisure, with an interpretive ranger or volunteer guides. On the ground floor, the council room, dining room, trade rooms, and shops are filled with goods and artifacts from the fort's heyday. On the second floor, the trapper's and hunter's quarters have to be visited with the conjured image of the brief departure from the loneliness and rigors of the trail to the luxury of the fort, including its bar and billiard table in the second floor billiard room. The company's 1839 ledger bears out the diversity of drink—twelve boxes of claret wine, thirty-seven gallons of brandy, and fifty-eight gallons of rum. Susan Magoffin's quarters, named for her twelve-day stay in 1846, was one of the few white women to have seen Bent's Fort.

The National Park Service conducts excellent interpretive activities to help understand life at the fort when it provided explorers, adventurers, and the U.S. Army a place to get needed supplies, wagon repairs, livestock, good food, water and company, rest and protection in this vast "Great American Desert." As you walk through the rooms or look out over the landscape from the second floor promenade, enjoy the fort as it stands today. In the words of a visitor to the fort in 1839, it was "as though an 'air built castle' had dropped to earth . . . in the midst of the desert."

Dinosaur National Monument

The park is in northwest Colorado and northeast Utah, straddling the borders of these states, near Dinosaur, Moffat County, Colorado

→ www.nps.gov/dino

→ Approximately a three-hour drive from Salt Lake City, Utah, and two hours from Grand Junction, Colorado, the Monument Headquarters is two miles east of Dinosaur, Colorado, on US 40. The Dinosaur Quarry Visitor Center is twenty-five miles west of Jensen, Utah, and north seven miles on Utah Route 149.

Dinosaur National Monument is the only park that protects a dinosaur quarry, the Douglass Quarry. Set aside as a small preserve of eighty acres in 1915 to protect fossils from miners and looters, additions to include some of the most scenic canyons in the West increased the park to its present 210,277 acres. Beyond the readily accessible fossil site, considered one of the best places in the world to view Upper Jurassic (150-million-year-old) dinosaurs, the park contains a stunning geological record, settler ranches, and a superb example of National Park Service (NPS) modern architecture at the Dinosaur Quarry Visitor Center rounding out a variety of visitor experiences.

The Visitor Center is a fascinating merging of a dream of paleontologist Earl B. Douglass, the talent of San Francisco architectural firm Anshen + Allen, and a cooperative group of NPS administrators. The building has been recognized for its significant contributions to the broad patterns of American history and its exceptional importance to the evolution of American architecture, particularly American modernism and NPS modern design. It is without a doubt a magnificent structure erected almost literally on a foundation of sand.

Dinosaur Quarry Visitor Center

Spanning a V-shaped cut in rock formations and built onto the tilted 70-degree slope quarry face, the building is an elegant composition of a butterfly roof soaring over the glazed 180-foot south wall and end walls—a ribbon of glass above the quarry face, and a sinuous concrete entrance ramp and cylindrical concrete tower ribbed vertically with glass panels. The short leg of the asymmetrical roof hovering over the quarry face and exhibit galleries extends beyond the south wall as a shading device; the long leg soars upward over the interior spaces of the visitors' gallery and quarry face. Supported on a rigid frame system designed to accommodate the 150-degree temperature range throughout the year, the architect's roof floating over glass walls departed from the traditional park museum model of a fully enclosed, windowless building lit exclusively by artificial light. The building's main area is the visitors' gallery overlooking the fossil exhibit.

Unfortunately, even before completion in 1957, construction problems due to unstable soils began to appear. Over the years, movement within the structure compromised the building's structural integrity and the NPS has conducted major rehabilitation actions. A formal monitoring program that began in May 2006 identified some previously unknown conditions that present serious life, safety, and health hazards. As a result, the building is closed until all alternatives are developed for a long-term sustainable solution. A temporary visitor facility is located adjacent to the closed building in the Outdoor Visitor Center and where ranger-led interpretive programs are conducted and replica fossils are displayed. Scattered throughout the park are homesteaders' ranches and cabins and the Earl Douglass laboratory/workshop. The Earl Douglass house and laboratory/workshop near the quarry face is built of rough-cut sandstone, and a flat roof carried on massive projecting square logs set into the hillside is approached by a stairway of cut stone slabs.

Twenty-five miles north of Monument Headquarters Drive, the unpaved Echo Park Road bisects the historical Chew Ranch. The whitewashed log ranch house, bunkhouse, granary, and enclosed corrals capture the era of homesteader ranching in this isolated location from the early 1900s.

At the end of Cub Creek Road, around eleven miles east of Dinosaur Quarry Visitor Center, is the Josephine Basset Morris Ranch. The cabin was the home of colorful

Josephine Basset Morris from 1924 to 1963. Living a life in solitude, Morris—reputed to be an ex-lover of Butch Cassidy—was well educated and refined and was rumored to resort to stealing from neighbors to augment ranch stock. A visit to the remnant of the Morris Ranch complex is a journey back into frontier western history.

Florissant Fossil Beds National Monument
In central Colorado west of Colorado Springs, Florissant, Teller County, Colorado

→ www.nps.gov/flfo

→ Traveling north-south on Interstate 25 exit at Colorado Springs at US 24 West, drive west thirty-five miles to the town of Florissant, then follow signs two miles south on Teller County Highway 1 to the visitor center.

Adeline Hornbek's homestead cabin

Florissant Fossil Beds National Monument is internationally renowned for its fossil insects and leaves. Set in the great natural beauty of rolling grassy hills and ridges covered by ponderosa pine, Douglas fir, Colorado blue spruce, and aspen is the preserved valley homestead of Adeline Hornbek who settled in the area with her children in 1878.

Adeline Hornbek is the stuff of settler legends and women's fortitude. Her energetic life as a female head-of-household is used for a teaching lesson across the country. In the gold rush days of Colorado, she cut a striking figure at 5 foot 7 inches, tall for a woman in the 1800s, and had a mane of red hair. In her lifetime she had three husbands, four children, and lived between two different Indian tribes.

Today, the Hornbek Homestead is a cluster of restored white-chinked plaster log buildings with split-shake gabled roofs enclosed by a buck-and-rail fence entered by a timber gateway, surrounded by meadows once used for grazing cattle, and forests of ponderosa pine. Farm wagons and implements are placed around the valley site. Adeline's original house stands in the center of the complex; three smaller homesteader

Homestead buildings

Log construction details

cabins moved by the National Park Service (NPS) from Fossil Beds property complete the replica of the Hornbek Homestead.

The grandness of Adeline's house stands in contrast to the relocated homesteader log cabins. The master craftsman she hired to build the one-and-a-half-story, four-bedroom log house cut dozens of ponderosa pines, seasoned, and square cut. Set on a stone foundation, the timbers with dovetailed corners, eleven windows, vertically planked gable ends and split-shake shingled gable roof created an impressive house in the meadow. When completed in 1878 the house, T-shaped in plan, with a one-story well house extension added onto the north side of the house in 1909, was large enough for Saturday night dances in the parlor made special by the sounds of Adeline's foot pump organ and to gather around the wood burning stove.

One of the homestead site's three smaller cabins was redesigned and equipped by the NPS as a carriage house containing a period carriage and blacksmith area. A second cabin functions as a barn. The root cellar, built into a hillside one hundred yards from Adeline's house, has a dovetailed-corner log wall with an entrance door and massive interior timber framing to carry the earth roof. A second interior door helped maintain a year-round 45-degree temperature for storing vegetables and preserves, and ice cut from neighboring ponds to last through the summer.

Interpretive talks by park rangers and demonstrations by volunteers and local crafters dressed in period clothing illustrating life at the homestead are held in the summer when staffing is available and on weekends in July and December. Visitors to the park should be prepared for climate changes at the 8,500-foot altitude. The sun can bake and stiff winds scour the valley on the brightest of summer days. Deep winter snowdrifts at the homestead can offer the same rigors experienced by the Hornbek family. And remember, do not collect or damage any fossil or other natural and historic resource.

Hovenweep National Monument

Located north of the Four Corners, Hovenweep National Monument straddles the Colorado-Utah border west of Cortez, Colorado, in Montezuma County, Colorado, and east of Blanding, San Juan County, Utah.

→ www.nps.gov/hove

→ Travel two miles south from Cortez, Colorado, on US 160/491, then west on County Road G (Airport Road) forty miles to the visitor center; three turns in the last ten miles are all clearly marked. Traveling from Blanding or Bluff, Utah, from US 191 turn east onto Utah Route 262 and then follow the Hovenweep signs thirty miles on unpaved roads to the visitor center. Other outlying park units are within ten miles, but are not marked by signs on the road. Directions and a map should be obtained from a ranger at the visitor center.

Hovenweep castle group

Hovenweep National Monument lies in the rugged canyon country of Cajon Mesa on the Utah-Colorado border north of the San Juan River. The monument consists of six separate prehistoric, late-Pueblo-era units within a twenty-mile drive of each other. Inspiring for their dramatic appearance in a rugged landscape noted for its solitude, clear skies, and undeveloped natural character, these remarkable masonry buildings, constructed in the mid- to late-1200s are still impressive structures. Visitors often remark about their similarity with European medieval fortresses.

A particular feature of Hovenweep is the number of towers—tall, elegant masonry columns perched on canyon rims and rising from detached monoliths on the canyon floor. Unlike their neighbors fifty miles to the east who built in cliff alcoves at what is now Mesa Verde National Park (see page 175), the Hovenweep ancestral people built unique square, oval, and circular towers, along with horseshoe (D-shaped) multiroomed masonry pueblos, in communities clustered at the heads of canyons. Some of the well-preserved masonry walls at Hovenweep reach more than 20 feet in height.

Hovenweep Cutthroat Castle

Towers and other structures dot the landscape while other pueblo walls are now piles of rubble. These can all be "discovered" by visitors in walks along easy slickrock trails clearly marked by rocks. Double-stone walls of precisely shaped Dakota sandstone blocks contain rectangular doorways and small square apertures known as "loopholes." The National Park Service (NPS) has stabilized high-standing walls in many of the Hovenweep ruins by repointing the mortar holding the stones in place.

The six clusters of ruins—four in Colorado and two in Utah—vary in size. The largest unit is the 400-acre Square Tower Group containing nineteen standing structures. The Square Tower and Cajon Units are located in Utah. The units located in Colorado are the Holly Group, Horseshoe and Hackberry Groups, and Cutthroat Castle.

The most accessible site, Square Tower Group, can be seen by following a two-mile loop trail to the head of Little Ruin Canyon starting from the visitor center. It winds around two forks of the canyon, descends 80 feet to the canyon floor, then climbs back up toward the visitor center. The 300-yard section of trail between the visitor center and the first overlook is paved and wheelchair accessible.

The Square Tower Group contains towers, "great houses," unit-type houses, and structures built in alcoves and atop boulders, all grouped around a perennial spring. Typical construction features are compound walls, consisting of outer walls of semi-coursed, loaf-shaped sandstones set in a mud mortar, with rubble infill between the walls. Openings are typically rectangular or T-shaped. The structures are one- and two-stories tall. Roofs and upper floors were constructed of *vigas* (beams) and *latillas* (smaller sticks) covered with mud over bark. Some of the openings appear to be oriented to the semiannual solstices and equinoxes, suggesting a calendrical function.

The Hovenweep Castle ruin, seen prominently on the skyline from the trail, is built on slickrock on the Little Ruin Canyon edge in a small cluster of five structures. A multi-room rectangular dwelling is abutted to a D-shaped tower and other towers. The scene invariably entrances the visitor with marvel and delight. The carefully laid double-stone walls contain doorways and small loopholes that capture the essence of the Hovenweep builder's superb workmanship.

The group's eponymous Square Tower is a tall, elegant column rising from a detached boulder on the canyon floor below Hovenweep Castle. One of several canyon floor towers near permanent springs at Hovenweep Square Tower was constructed with a slight helical twist from top to bottom, which is original.

Staying on designated trails at all times is required. Look but do not touch (oils from your hands permanently stain rock surfaces). Remember that at Hovenweep, and all other federal public lands, the Archeological Resources Protection Act of 1979 protects the site. Any person who excavates, removes, damages, alters, or defaces archeological resources on federal land is subject to arrest and felony prosecution.

Hovenweep National Monument has fewer visitors in a year (30,000) than Yellowstone National Park on a summer weekend. With relatively few visitors, enjoy the solitude and marvel at how once-thriving communities survived on the mesa in a harsh environment.

Mesa Verde National Park

Located in the southwest part of Colorado between Cortez and Durango, Montezuma County, Colorado

→ www.nps.gov/meve

→ The park entrance is eight miles east of Cortez and thirty-six miles west of Durango, Colorado, via US 160. It is fifteen miles from the park entrance to the Far View Visitor Center

Swedish royal couple and Jesse Nusbaum, kneeling, 1926

Mesa Verde National Park is in the southwestern corner of Colorado on a mesa 2,000 feet above the surrounding countryside. Generally hailed as the most notable and best-preserved collection of prehistoric archeology in the United States, the Ancestral Puebloan cliff dwellings were protected with the park's establishment in 1906. Juxtaposed with over four thousand known archeological sites in the park—approximately six hundred of these are cliff dwellings—the Mesa Verde Administrative District core structures including park headquarters, museum, post office, Ranger Club, and subsidiary buildings are a superb collection of National Park Service (NPS) modified Pueblo Revival structures. The combination of the ancient Ancestral Puebloan ruins and NPS buildings, now aging into a century of durability, will reward the visitor with a memorable experience.

The ancestors of the Pueblo Indians (formerly called the Anasazi), settled in the mesa above the Montezuma and Mancos River valleys around sixteen hundred years ago and lived there until their disappearance in the thirteenth century. During their last century, some Pueblo Indians of Mesa Verde left the mesa tops and built their homes in the alcoves that abound in the many canyon walls. The major shift of population from mesa tops took place around 1150–1200, when construction of the large cliff dwellings began. By 1300, the Ancestral Puebloans had moved away.

Cliff Palace

The National Historic Landmark group of twentieth-century Mesa Verde buildings is the work of Jesse Nusbaum, archeologist and superintendent at Mesa Verde, and his wife Aileen. They examined the ethnological roots of the Ancestral Puebloans; together they developed the modified Pueblo Revival style as a suitable interpretation of the archeological sites for functional buildings. The significance of the Nusbaums' work in the context of the emerging NPS log-and-stone rustic style is the establishment of an interpretive alternative suited to local conditions and available materials and craftsmanship. The modified Pueblo Revival style, sometimes with variations, became the standard for the quickly developing Southwestern parks and monuments in the 1930s. The Nusbaums' work at Mesa Verde provided the impetus for a series of culturally related developments at other national parks and monuments.

The park's scenic drive, with steep grades and sharp curves, begins at the park entrance, rising to 8,500 feet in elevation to reach 2,000 feet above surrounding Mancos Valley, Dolores Plateau, and Montezuma Valley. At the Far View Visitor Center (7,500 feet in elevation), visitors may purchase tickets to the ranger-guided tours of the cliff dwellings, then drive on to Chapin Mesa or to Wetherill Mesa to visit additional sites. The NPS headquarters, six miles south of the visitor center on Chapin Mesa, overlooks Spruce Tree House, one of the park's dramatic cliff dwellings built below a ledge above Spruce Tree Canyon.

The modern buildings are Jesse and Aileen Nusbaum's legacy at Mesa Verde, including fourteen Chapin Mesa modified Pueblo Revival style buildings that form the six-building National Historic Landmark NPS Administrative District: Fewkes Cabin Museum (formerly a Superintendent's Residence), Administration Building, Post Office, Mesa Verde Museum, and Ranger Club (now the Research Library). In addition, there is the Aileen Nusbaum Hospital/Spruce Tree Terrace, and NPS staff housing. These are excellent examples of the modified Pueblo Revival style, modified to reflect and enhance the interpretation of the prehistoric structures of the surrounding countryside. The construction and fine details, integrated with landscape features contributing to the ambience of the area, is a casebook of Southwestern design.

A destination alone, these finely crafted buildings enrich the overall Mesa Verde visitor's experience. We recommend a pause on the verandah of the ranger station for a view across the canyon to the Ancestral Puebloan Spruce Tree House. This extraordinary example of a cliff dwelling, tucked under an overhanging mesa ledge, amplifies the mystery of the ancient Puebloans by a dramatic perspective of the overall complex.

The Nusbaum buildings all contain common architectural elements. The principal building material is local sandstone masonry, some stones reused from park prehistoric structures still showing peck marks from shaping the surfaces. Exterior walls averaging 18 inches thick overall have a slight batter, curving inward from the foundation to the parapet. Upper courses are laid with mortar nearly flush with the stone to give the walls a relatively smooth appearance; the mortar was made from local red earth. The load-bearing walls support a roof structure of Douglas fir *vigas* 8- to 12-inches in diameter that project through the masonry to the exterior. Half round *latias* 2 to 3 inches in diameter are laid on top of the vigas, either perpendicularly or in a herringbone pattern. A layer of juniper bark covers the top of the latias for insulation. Wooden decking and the built-up roof of natural materials protect the interior from the elements; latias in these buildings are purely decorative. Parapets surround the flat roofs and are pierced by sheet-metal-lined wooden *canales* (scuppers) projecting from the walls.

Water storage tower

Larger pieces of woodwork on the buildings—columns, lintels, squared beams, doors, and jambs—have adze marks that add texture and a pioneer feeling to the structures. Log columns, often capped by *zapatas* (bolsters) with sawn, serrated Indian patterns, support beams with joints carefully centered over the columns. Adze-marked doors are typically paneled; exterior doors often have openings with narrow wooden bars cut in Indian designs.

Typical interior features of the modified Pueblo Revival style are used throughout the buildings. Interiors have masonry walls plastered with either local red earth or modern plaster, and rounded plastered corner fireplaces typical of the Southwest.

The exposed latia-and-viga ceilings and pierced-tin light fixtures based on Mexican and Spanish Colonial designs contribute to the complementing handcrafted furnishings. Rustic, Franciscan-style *bancos* (built-in benches), tables, chairs, desks, and closets with hand-chiseled textured surfaces were designed by the Nusbaums and fashioned on the site during the long winter months.

Plan for a full day—possibly two—at this extraordinary collection of prehistoric Ancestral Puebloan sites, the Chapin Mesa NPS buildings, and spectacular mesa-top scenery. Enjoy the approach to the park on the Colorado Plateau, and prehistoric sites and modern buildings—what architectural historian Vincent Scully called a "delirium of man-made geometry." Self-guided and guided tours are available to several of the best cliff dwellings. Take advantage of the many interpretive programs and pace yourself on strenuous walks to cliff dwellings in the 6,000- to 8,000-foot altitude. Some NPS advice: Do not enter a cliff dwelling without a park ranger present; Do not leave the trails; Do not climb on the walls; Do not enter any park residential areas—they are private; and Do not deface or remove any object of antiquity from the park (subject to fine of up to $100,000 and imprisonment for up twenty years for violations).

Spruce Tree House   Sun Temple at Far View

Rocky Mountain National Park

Larimer, Boulder, and Grand Counties, Colorado

→ www.nps.gov/romo

→ Visitor centers at the east and west park entrances are connected by Trail Ridge Road (US 34), which crosses the Continental Divide. The main entrance from the east, near Estes Park, is approximately sixty-five miles north of Denver via Interstate 25 and US 36 or south of Fort Collins via US 34. The southwest entrance near Granby is approximately ninety miles west of Denver via Interstate 25 and US 40.

Alpine Visitor Center

Spectacular southern Rocky Mountain scenery of more than one hundred summits higher than 12,000 feet surround the 14,259-foot landmark of Longs Peak, visible at great distances from the plains to the east. The easily accessible park, only two hours from Denver, is besieged by almost 3,000,000 visitors a year, including 600,000 hikers per day. They are drawn to high country glaciers, great rock amphitheaters, and crenellated narrow ridges above the tree line and, below, subalpine meadows, dense woods, serene lakes, rivers, rugged gorges, and parks—level valleys between the mountain ranges, and abundant wildlife.

Historic architecture in the park consists mainly of National Park Service (NPS) structures for visitor services and remnants of the dude ranch and summer home era. Included are two of the finest Mission 66 visitor centers, the Park Headquarters at the East Entrance and the Alpine Visitor Center. Although the park was at one time heavily used by private parties, years of effort have resulted in the NPS acquisition of numerous inholdings and removal of most traces of the park's early history. For many travelers, the current park experience is the two- or three-hour trans-Continental Divide drive on Trail Ridge Road, designed for viewing the magnificent scenic panoramas.

The recently renovated Stanley Hotel, outside the park boundary near the Estes Park entrance, is an elegant complex in the Georgian Revival style. Completed in 1909 by F.O. Stanley—inventor of the Stanley Steamer—the massive, five-story hotel and accompanying Stanley Manor, concert hall, carriage house, and guesthouses are all white-painted clapboard buildings with red-shingled roofs. In its early years, a fleet of eleven-passenger Stanley Steamers conveyed guests to the hotel from nearby railheads.

At the Fall River Entrance on US 34, a three-building complex constructed in 1936 represents the best of NPS rustic design developed in the 1920s. Similar rustic elements of native stone and notched logs, roofs with cedar shingles, and white trim six-light windows were used in ranger stations and patrol cabins scattered throughout the park.

A short distance from the Beaver Meadows entrance station on US 36, the National Historic Landmark Beaver Meadows Visitor Center, designed by Taliesin Associated Architects (successors to Frank Lloyd Wright), shows a successful use of contemporary

Stanley Hotel

Dining room

forms and materials in the rustic style. Completed in 1967, it is one of a few Mission 66 projects to competently interpret a site in a modern design vocabulary, achieving a rustic character using nontraditional materials. The striking building combines use as the park's administrative headquarters with visitor orientation. Clearly Wrightian in inspiration, exterior materials (Cor-ten steel and native stone set in concrete) achieve a design that blends into the surrounding landscape by virtue of a long, low profile set among sheltering pines. The warm reddish-brown oxidizing steel is richly detailed with patterns of mountain profiles. The unusually handsome concrete-and-stone work, both outside and in, is the result of great care taken in the selection and placement of boulders into the concrete masses buttressing the steel. A low-ceilinged entrance opens into the higher ceiling lobby space, emphasized by a pressed steel "cornice" similar to the exterior steel fascia. The two-story plan's organization effectively separates visitors from park staff. Changes in the lobby space and circulation flow from the original plan (and a ten-fold increase in the number of visitors since 1967) results in a usually crowded lobby. An exterior balcony accessible from the lobby around the auditorium end of the building frames a view of the highest mountain in the park—Longs Peak—in a balcony bay.

The Alpine Visitor Center is at an elevation of 11,796 feet on the Fall River Pass at the intersection of Trail Ridge Road and Fall River Pass Road. The sublimely located two-building complex at one of the highest auto-accessible points in the country is open only during summer months. Visitors climb Trail Ridge Road, with switchbacks and overlooks on the country's highest continuous highway, and are suddenly confronted with a modern visitor center in the forbidding alpine tundra landscape. Views sweep out from terraces toward the glacial moraine and tundra landscape, and paths radiate out into the fields of summer wildflowers. Even on the warmest summer days, icy winds sweep across the site and curls of snowpack nest in the moraine.

The visitor center, opened in 1965, contains exhibits interpreting the tundra and a glassed-in viewing area; a second structure built in the 1930s and altered in the 1960s contains a store and dining room. The building conveys a strong sense of shelter, with walls of massive dressed boulders set in concrete and shallow-pitched shingled roofs with wide overhangs. An unusual roof structure is designed to combat two hundred-mile-an-hour winds and heavy snow loads, sandwiching a split-shingle roof between interior timber rafters and an exterior grid of peeled logs. The notched grid of sun-bleached and wind-scoured logs in this position is designed to secure the roof against the fierce winds that sweep the site.

The NPS Utility Area Historic District of more than thirty buildings at the park headquarters area was built between 1923 and 1941 by the NPS and Civilian Conservation Corps (CCC). Although not generally on a park tour, the buildings are significant for their rustic design of uniform construction features. "Logs-out" peeled-log framing braced by corner diagonals, vertical reverse board-and-batten plank walls, and multi-light windows create well-composed exterior elevations. Shingle-covered roofs, extended log purlins and rafters, and brown paint on all exterior walls unify the single-story complex.

There are numerous backcountry buildings scattered throughout the park discovered along some 350 miles of trails and roadsides. Ranger patrol cabins and hiker shelters share the NPS rustic style, although materials vary from stone to log depending on the environment. The Keyhole on Longs Peak (Agnes Vaille Memorial Shelter, 1927) located at an elevation of 13,126 feet—possibly the highest listed on the National Register of Historic Places—is an unusual octagonal shaped stone shelter built into the mountain wall, with a conical stone roof.

An authentic remnant of the dude ranch era is the Holzwarth Historic Site to the north of Grand Lake. This well-preserved example of small-scale log buildings that had

NPS administrative structure

William Allen White house

grown up around ranch homesteads represents the time when enterprising ranchers accommodated the "dudes" seeking a taste of the West and the opportunity to fish in the area's clear lakes, rivers, and streams. A good example of the many lodges once extant throughout the park is the Moraine Park Museum. The single restored building is all that remains of the original cluster of cabins. In 1936, the park completely renovated the building into a museum, which is operated by the Rocky Mountain Nature Association,

Beaver Meadows Visitor Center

serving as the center of the park's environmental education program. The nearby amphitheater built by the CCC in 1936 exemplifies NPS naturalistic design, the landscape architecture counterpart of rustic design.

An example of the summer homes predating the park's founding is seen in William Allen White's five-building complex in Moraine Park. A retreat of the park's prominent vacationers, the buildings are simple and unglamorous of log-and-frame construction, typical of local vernacular building forms and workmanship. An artist-in-residence program is located in the restored retreat.

Idaho

Nez Perce National Historical Park
Located in north central Idaho, Montana, Oregon, and Washington

→ www.nps.gov/nepe

→ This unusual park is located in north central Idaho, Montana, Oregon, and Washington. Park headquarters and visitor center are located in Spalding, Idaho, eleven miles east of Lewiston. An additional visitor center is located at Big Hole National Battlefield, ten miles west of Wisdom, Montana. Access to park headquarters and many of the Idaho units is from Interstate 90 (to the north) and through the park on US 95 and 12 (The Lewis and Clark Highway).

The Nez Perce National Historical Park contains thirty-eight sites, mostly in Idaho, but others that follow a trail from the Wallowa Mountains of Oregon, through central Idaho, Montana, and Washington. Five of the park's sites in Idaho, two in Montana, and one each in Washington and Oregon are administered by the National Park Service (NPS) and the remaining twenty-nine are a mixture of federal, local, and private ownership.

Central to the park experience is an understanding of the native people, the Ni Mii Pu (Ni-MEE-Poo) as Nez Perce tribal members call themselves. It means "we the people" or "the real people." Nez Perce is a misnomer given the tribe through early interactions with fur traders and explorers. The French translated it as "pierced nose." Even though the Nez Perce were never given to the practice of piercing their noses, the name is still used and today is pronounced "Nezz Purse."

The park has many facets commemorating the history and culture of the Nez Perce and their interactions with non-native settlers. Principal historic structures are located near the visitor center at Spalding, Pierce (on Idaho Highway 11), and at Kamiah (on US Highway 12).

The Spalding area, along US Highway 95 approximately ten miles east of Lewiston, Idaho, contains the park headquarters, museum, visitor center, and several historic structures. Today's settlement shows the NPS work in the preservation and interpretation of the Agency Cabin, Agency Residence, and Watson's Store, remaining after removal of old residences and barns in its effort to recreate the historic scene around the Henry and Eliza Spalding mission site. The once lively community of Spalding, busy with stores and other businesses, saloons, hotels, and a railroad station (called "Joseph") began its decline when the Northern Idaho Indian Agency moved to Lapwai, two miles south, the last store finally closing in 1964.

Saint Joseph's Mission (also called Slickpoo Mission) about ten miles south of present-day Lapwai, Idaho, was the first Roman Catholic mission

Saint Joseph's Mission church, Spalding, Idaho

among the Nez Perce. It was dedicated on September 8, 1874, by Father Joseph Cataldo, later moving to Spokane, Washington, where he established Gonzaga University. Surrounded by a rolling landscape and set amidst neatly maintained shade trees, a lawn, ornamental shrubs, and residences, the simple, white-painted clapboard chapel has a bell tower over the entrance inset with a pair of stained glass windows.

The remnants of Fort Lapwai are located near US Highway 95 in Lapwai, Idaho. Fort Lapwai is held in trust by the Bureau of Indian Affairs for the Nez Perce tribe to serve as headquarters for the Northern Idaho Indian Agency, which serves several Idaho tribes. The agency building is owned by the Lapwai School District. The parade ground may still be seen as well as a wood-frame officers' quarters (1883) and the Northern Idaho Indian Agency building (1904). The officers' quarters building at the southwest end of the parade ground has been stabilized and is vacant. The parade ground is also intact, as are some of the stables. Because of the parade ground, the site has a campus-like atmosphere.

Easily passed as an unimposing board-and-batten veneer structure, the two-story Pierce Courthouse was the first public building in Idaho. Located one block off Main Street (Idaho Highway 11) in Pierce where it was built in 1862, the original 20-foot by 40-foot log building sits on a grassy lot surrounded on three sides by residential development. Inside the building that was rehabilitated in 1990 are exhibits about the area's history, including the gold mining era that saw the Nez Perce stripped of most of their land. The building is open on request and on summer weekends.

The McBeth House is located one mile south of Kamiah, Idaho, on US Highway 12. The small frame building is diagonally across the highway from the First Indian Presbyterian Church. Sue McBeth arrived in 1873 as a teacher and her sister Kate joined her in 1879. Contentious among themselves, with federal agents, and tribal members who opposed their strong will and stern Presbyterianism of their native Scotland, they were dedicated missionaries exerting enormous influence on the tribe until the early 1890s. Only with their deaths—Sue dying in 1893 and Kate in 1915—did the zeal and fervor toward extinguishing traditional Indian culture in favor of "civilization" begin to subside.

The park's various sites are separated by great distances and NPS brochures and highway maps of the states of Washington, Oregon, Idaho, and Montana are vital in preparing an itinerary and route for each site. Passage of the Lewis and Clark expedition through the park in 1805–1806 on both westward and homebound journeys has heightened interest in sites along the Lewis and Clark National Historic Trail (portions of US Highway 12). Battlefield and Indian village sites are moving experiences; initial preparation by a visit to the Spalding, Idaho, visitor center museum and bookstore will be helpful to the traveler.

Kansas

Rockies and Plains

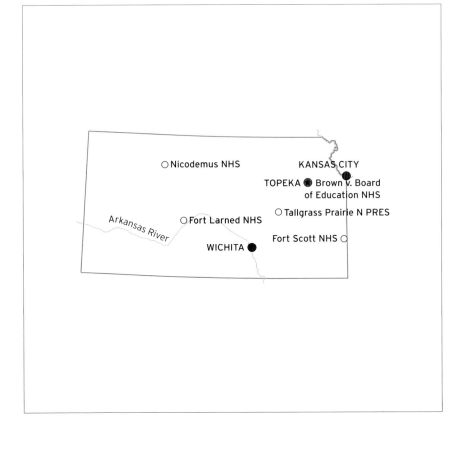

Brown v. Board of Education National Historic Site

Located in Topeka, Shawnee County, Kansas

→ www.nps.gov/brvb

→ Located southeast of downtown Topeka at 1515 Monroe Street at the corner of 15th and Monroe Streets and is accessible from north-south Interstate 75 and east-west Interstate 70 at various exits; follow signs to the site.

Monroe Elementary School

The Monroe Elementary School commemorates the landmark 1954 U.S. Supreme Court decision that declared unconstitutional the country's "separate but equal" policy of segregated facilities for public schools. Rehabilitated and reopened in 2004 by the National Park Service (NPS), this National Historic Landmark offers exhibits and programs throughout the year in the segregated school attended by the lead plaintiff, Linda Brown, in the lawsuit filed originally in 1951.

The Monroe Elementary School is in a neighborhood of mixed use: residential, commercial, and industrial. Long standing as a predominately African-American part of Topeka, there is now a racial and socioeconomic mix living in one- and two-story residential structures of varied maintenance. Small businesses, churches, and light industry buildings dot the neighborhood. To the east of the school, across Monroe Street, is a triangular park.

Designed by Thomas W. Williamson and completed in 1926, the two-story building is the work of an experienced school architect prolific in the Topeka area for more than forty years. The exterior treatment—typical of thousands of elementary schools of the 1920s and 1930s—is nominally an Italian Renaissance Revival design, with a limestone base, dark red common bond brick walls and a projecting entry of contrasting limestone, limestone quoins at the building corners, a cast concrete cornice at the top of the exterior walls under a projecting overhang, and a red clay tile hip roof.

The elevations vary to express interior functions contained in the basic 61-foot by 174-foot central corridor floor plan: the east elevation with projecting elegantly detailed two-story main entry double door with fan window above; north and south elevations, articulated with a door and a window opening above, and pairs of ornamental limestone geometric patterns surrounded by articulated brick trim; and west elevation of a central projecting flat-roofed two-story wing containing a combined auditorium, cafeteria, and gymnasium. Typical windows are tall, paired upper and lower steel casement of four-over-ten lights with a concrete sill and brick soldier course at the window head. Centered on the projecting north two-story wing are three tall Palladian windows. The structural framing system is cast-in-place concrete floor slabs supported by load-bearing exterior masonry walls and corridor walls. Outdoor playground areas were located on the north

Monroe Elementary School

Limestone details

and south ends of the building for younger children and a portion of the park across the street from the main entry served as recreation space for older students.

After closing in 1975 due to declining enrollment, the building went through several owners and alternate uses. When the NPS acquired the building in 1992 it was in sound structural condition, suitable for the handsome rehabilitation to its 1954 appearance. The renovated first floor contains four galleries with exhibits about the Brown v. Board of Education case, the civil rights movement, African-American history, and the continuing struggle for equality. The first floor also houses a bookstore and visitor assistance station. The second floor is closed to the public.

Fort Larned National Historic Site

Located in Larned, Pawnee County, Kansas

→   www.nps.gov/fols

→   The fort is located in western Kansas. Traveling west on Interstate 70, thirty miles west of Salina, take Exit 225 eighty-three miles southwest to the fort on Kansas 156. From Dodge City travel 165 miles northeast on Kansas 56, 183, and 156 and follow signs to the park visitor center.

In 1859, military authorities decided that travelers on the Santa Fe Trail needed protection and established a small detachment of troops at the Pawnee River about five miles from its junction with the Arkansas River. By 1868 Native American resistance in the Fort Larned area had diminished. After completion of the Santa Fe Railroad through Kansas in 1872 the post's necessity declined and, after sale at auction in July 1878, the last contingent of troops departed. Considered one of the nation's best-preserved mid-nineteenth-century frontier military posts, the National Historic Landmark 718-acre Fort Larned National Historic Site was designated a unit of the National Park System in 1964.

Fort Larned National Historic Site's structures of sandstone and elegant porches, arrayed around a parade ground on the open prairie of gradually swelling hills, served from 1859 to 1878 guarding an important post on the central part of the Santa Fe Trail.

Fort Larned, Officers' Row facing the parade ground

Designed for a garrison of four hundred soldiers in four companies of one hundred soldiers per company, more infantry than cavalry served at Fort Larned. Nine stone and timber buildings around the parade ground constructed in 1866–68 replaced a post of uncomfortable adobe and sod buildings built in 1860. Unlike the military defensive positions of the upper Missouri River, Fort Larned was built without an enclosing stockade; the mobile Native Americans preferred to strike soldiers and travelers away from the fort's protection. The commissary, quartermaster structures, and the six-sided stone blockhouse, later converted to a guardhouse and reconstructed by the National Park Service (NPS) in 1988, were originally constructed as defensive structures.

Today's nine restored structures facing the 400-foot-square parade ground are uniform in exterior appearance. The unity of the historic buildings framing the parade ground is established by neatly set sandstone exterior walls surrounded by white mortar, brown wood-shingled roofs, and white painted door and window frames with flat stone sills and heads, and brick chimneys.

The remarkably good condition of the original structures is due to the workmanship and care of civilian owners, despite revisions during eighty years of the fort's private ownership as a ranch. Building designs by the resident quartermaster officer conformed with standard Quartermaster Department regulations with construction adapted to locally available materials. Officers' quarters and barracks are exterior masonry bearing walls and interiors are finished with plaster on lath. Other structures have plaster over stone interior walls and generally wooden floors throughout. Although no construction drawings have been found, a concentrated period of construction—two buildings completed in 1866, six

Barracks/Post Hospital

Quartermaster Storehouse

in 1867, and the last one in 1868 (the original blockhouse was constructed in 1864–65)— contribute to the uniformity of details and overall unity of the historic structures.

A tour of the historical structures begins at the visitor center located in the former West Barracks. Used today as the park visitor center, the barracks contains a museum, bookstore, and visitor services. The T-shaped building was the home of two companies of infantry soldiers, at authorized full strength of one hundred soldiers per company; however, the average was only about seventy per company. The 43- by 150-foot structure facing the parade ground with a rear wing 34 feet square, and 10.5-foot-deep parade ground-facing porch was symmetrical in plan divided in half for each company. The adjacent East Barracks, also housing two companies of soldiers, was identical in plan to the West Barracks, except for a 40- by 60-foot squadroom at the building's north end. Converted into the Post Hospital in 1871, it is restored and furnished to its 1868 appearance.

Officers' Row consisted of three buildings located in a central position on the west side of the parade grounds: the easily distinguished two-story Commanding Officer's Quarters rises between the flanking one-story Company Officer's Quarters (53 by 84 feet, including wings). Identified by the refined stone work, and uniform in overall appearance with railed porches and bracketed columns, dark green shutters, white painted wood trimmed multilight double-hung windows, and roof pitches, the buildings contribute to the overall architectural unity of historic structures in the park. A white-painted picket fence between the Officers' Row structures and a railed boardwalk the length of Officers' Row calls attention to the distinctive structures, tying them together as a unified composition.

Other buildings facing the parade ground are the Quartermaster Storehouse, a long, rectangular building; Old Commissary, a one-story rectangular structure; the hexagonal Blockhouse, designed originally as a a a guardhouse; the new Commissary/Schoolhouse; and Shops Building.

Fort Larned National Historic Site affords possibly the finest experience of a frontier military post. The integrity of the site in the rolling hills of western Kansas is unfettered by any encroaching development. Old Glory flying one hundred feet above the parade ground, long colonnaded porches, and summertime living-history programs will stir the imagined sounds of military commands, of drilling at the infantry garrisoned fort, of harnesses clinking, and a parade of cavalry riding off to guard the Santa Fe Trail.

Fort Scott National Historic Site

Located in Fort Scott, Bourbon County, Kansas

→   www.nps.gov/fosc

→   Fort Scott National Historic Site is located near the intersection of US 69 and 54 in downtown Fort Scott, Kansas, four miles from the Kansas-Missouri border and ninety miles south of Kansas City via US 69, and sixty miles northwest of Joplin, Missouri, via US 54 and 69. Approaches from all directions are well signed.

Well canopy and officers' quarters

A visit to Fort Scott National Historic Site offers a panel of windows each capturing a glimpse into our nation's history. Backwards in time—past the building of railroads in the 1870s, Civil War strife, "Bleeding Kansas," wagon trains heading westward, the Mexican-American War, and the frontier separating Native American and white settlements in the 1830s—the visitor has a unique experience in the thirty-one-year span of history interpreted at Fort Scott National Historic Site. The fort contains superbly restored and reconstructed structures in their 1840s appearance arrayed around a central parade ground.

Established in 1842 as one of a chain of posts for the Army's peacekeeping efforts along the "Permanent Indian Frontier" on the Missouri border south of Fort Leavenworth, the fort was garrisoned by cavalry and infantry soldiers. It eventually was deactivated in

1853. The task of building the post fell on the shoulders of a capable quartermaster officer, Capt. Thomas Swords, an 1829 West Point graduate with previous duties in Florida and Fort Leavenworth. Today, the 16.7-acre site, at the edge of downtown Fort Scott, contains twenty wood-frame and stone structures around a parade ground and a five-acre area of restored tallgrass prairie. The tranquil atmosphere of the fort is achieved by the composition of buildings, with Greek Revival and French Colonial influences. Facing the parade ground centered on a flagpole, the fort displays a Doric-columned well canopy and a similarly proportioned brick-enclosed powder magazine. Enclosing the parade ground are stately two-story structures with consistently applied elements and details of raised first floors on tall ground-floor stone piers, wide single-run stairs to deeply shadowed porches with railings, second floor Doric columns, and white clapboard weather siding.

Post Hospital

Officers' Quarters No. 1

A tour of the buildings begins at the Post Hospital and proceeds clockwise, next to the Infantry Barracks and Post Museum. The Post Hospital, built in 1843, is a dominating two-story building with a wide second-story porch and French colonial influence reflected in the hipped roof. The two-story Infantry Barracks for enlisted men built in 1843 and 1844 (all are reconstructions) are identical structures, similar in exterior appearance to the Officers' Quarters. (Infantry Barracks are located to the left of the Post Hospital, Dragoon Barracks to the right of the Dragoon Stables, and the Infantry Barracks are positioned on the parade ground's south side.) The long, timber fame and clapboard sided one-story Dragoon Stables, built in 1843 and a complete reconstruction, contained over eighty stalls for horses and several rooms for storing feed and tack. The one-story Headquarters Building completing the north side enclosure of the parade ground was home to the commanding officer, adjutant, and the ordnance sergeant. A complete reconstruction, the building contains offices, a court-martial room, an ordnance storeroom, and artillery storage shed.

An early construction project was Officers' Row enclosing the parade ground's east side. The buildings are typical period Army officers' quarters and reflect Swords's experience earlier at Fort Leavenworth. All four originally planned buildings were two-story duplexes built on shallow stone foundations, each with two large rooms on each floor and wide hallways connecting to front and rear exterior staircases. The kitchens are on the ground floor and fireplaces in each room placed back-to-back rise in the pair of brick chimneys in the buildings' center, flanked by dormers. Wide porches across the quarters' front and rear provided some relief from the hot summer sun; tall windows provided cross-ventilation.

Standing at the far east corner of the complex is the Post Bakery. The one-story stone building has a reconstructed bake oven used for demonstrations. The Quartermaster Complex consisted of the Quartermaster Storehouse, the Bakery, and the Quartermaster Quadrangle. The Quartermaster Quadrangle housed blacksmiths, farriers, a carpenter shop, a wheelwright shop, storage bins (corn/grain), quartermaster stables (draft horses/mules), loafing sheds (wheeled vehicles), and a place for storage of raw materials (coal, iron bars, etc.). Buildings are restorations of the original stone or timber framed structures.

The reconstructed one-story stone guardhouse, facing the parade ground and adjacent to the Post Hospital, has a 10-foot-wide porch under an extended roof supported by four stone piers. The interior was partitioned into four rooms, one of which was divided into three cells. These cells were used as solitary confinement cells and included one "dark" cell and two "light" cells. The other rooms were a larger clay cell (for less serious cases), an officer of the day room, and an off-duty room where the guards rested when not on patrol or sentry duty. The original building completed in 1848 survived until 1906 when the city of Fort Scott replaced it with a new jail.

The scale and intimacy of the vast parade ground is modified by the eight-sided well canopy and powder magazine flanking the 65-foot-tall flagpole. The reconstructed well canopy, an open pavilion with a domed roof covering the low stone cylindrical well cap of the 65-foot-deep well, is an elegant Greek Revival structure faithfully reproduced from early photographs. Notice the well is off-centered under the canopy to simplify the drawing of water when soldiers used wagons to haul water barrels. The reconstruction of the original 1848 well canopy is consistent with Swords's theme of Greek Revival details on other principal post buildings. In a sensitive touch of design for the utilitarian Powder

Infantry Barracks and Quartermaster Storehouse

Magazine, Swords repeated the eight-sided well canopy form in a solid structure on a stone masonry base, enclosing brick walls, chamfered smooth limestone columns repeating the well column motif, and limestone beams capping the walls and columns. The shallow roof is clad with tin and the ceiling is an intricate pattern of brick supporting the tin roof.

The site is open daily for self-guided and summer afternoon guided tours. Check for seasonal events with period costume reenactments. Plan on at least a half-day to tour the fine example of frontier fort and the short walking tour through a portion of the prairie.

Nicodemus National Historic Site

Located in Nicodemus, Graham County, Kansas

→ www.nps.gov/nico

→ The park is located in northwest Kansas, approximately fifty miles northwest of Hays on US 24, nineteen miles west of Stockton and thirteen miles east of Hill City.

Nicodemus Township Hall

Nicodemus National Historic Site preserves, protects, and interprets the only remaining western town established by African-Americans during the Reconstruction Period following the Civil War. The Homestead Act of 1862 and the Preemption Act of 1841 allowed the newly freed slaves the opportunities to be landowners. The town of Nicodemus would be established two years prior to the great Black Exodus Movement in 1878. At a time when emancipated Negroes formed a Black Exodus—known as the "Exodusters"—by migrating from the south to western Kansas in 1879 and 1880, the attraction was the promise of freedom, hope, and "forty acres and a mule." There is a great deal of symbolism in this remnant of a period when several all-black towns were founded in this treeless prairie country of rolling hills. Named for a legendary slave and officially founded in 1877 by land speculators, the town grew from its first arrivals to a thriving town within a decade. It quickly started to decline when it was bypassed by railroads.

The Town of Nicodemus, designated a National Historic Landmark in 1976 and National Historic Site in 1996, can be seen by the visitor as it was yesterday, is today, and will be tomorrow.

St. Francis Hotel/Fletcher-Switzer House   District No. 1 Schoolhouse

The town's vibrant history is what it was to hundreds of settlers, faced with a harsh climate and little resources but the promise of a self-governing life free from the shackles of the past. The settlers first lived in dugouts, moved to sod buildings, and then finally into permanent structures in a town with a bank, churches, stores, and hotels for a population of more than five hundred in the late 1880s. A post office, a land company, a society hall, and several general merchandise stores were also in town. By the 1930s the WPA *Kansas: A Guide to the Sunflower State* described an all but abandoned town with dusty streets, electric lights in the churches, and telephones six miles distant in Bogue.

What Nicodemus is today is visible in the town's five historical structures and a scattering of modern buildings and the spirit of Nicodemus in the hearts of the town's descendants who annually return in the last week of July to celebrate "Homecoming." Returnees for the celebration of the legacy of the original settlers find Nicodemus is an active community.

What Nicodemus will be in the future is contained within the plans of the National Park Service (NPS) to restore the historic structures and to interpret the role of African-Americans in the settling of the west.

Nicodemus National Historic Site is a relatively new addition to the national park system, and the NPS is working on plans for the interpretation of the site and restoration of five historic structures, that include the African-American Methodist and Episcopal (A.M.E.) Church, the old First Baptist Church, the Nicodemus District No. 1 Schoolhouse, the St. Francis Hotel/Fletcher-Switzer residence, and the Township Hall. The NPS, and the owner of the A.M.E. Church, are cooperating with descendants of private property owners to preserve this unique town on the western plains of Kansas. The NPS presently leases the Township Hall from the Township Board to house the temporary visitor center. Visitors to the site are encouraged to stop by the visitor center, the only structure accessible to the public to learn more about the site, and to stay on public roads and respect privately owned property as they tour the town. The present conditions of some historic structures pose possible safety hazards.

Tallgrass Prairie National Preserve

Located near Strong City, Chase County, Kansas

→   www.nps.gov/tapr

→   Tallgrass Prairie National Preserve is located in the east-central part of Kansas, midway between Topeka and Wichita connected by Interstate 35. Exit Interstate 35/335 at Emporia and travel seventeen miles west on US 50 passing through Strong City and one half-mile west turn north on Highway 177 (Flint Hills National Scenic Byway) for two miles to the historic ranch headquarters on the west side of Kansas 177.

Limestone barn

The preserve is a 10,894-acre remnant of tallgrass prairie that once covered approximately 170 million acres of the North American continent. Less than four percent of the vast tallgrass ecosystem survives mainly in the Flint Hills of east-central Kansas. The visitor can experience hiking trails and bus tours through the Flint Hills landscape, a trace of the western tallgrass prairie that hosted the cattle industry transition from open range to enclosed stock ranching, a virtually intact nineteenth-century historic ranch headquarters area, and a late-nineteenth-century one-room school house. The Spring Hill Ranch, a National Historic Landmark, is the temporary location of park headquarters and the visitor contact station.

A tour of historic structures begins at the visitor contact station located at the historic former Z Bar/Spring Hill Ranch headquarters. When occupied by the rancher Stephen F.

Jones, the landscape was filled with a panorama of the main house, stone walls, massive barn, and outbuildings unified by rough-faced limestone. The terraced front yard was planted with lilac and rose bushes. A fountain was supplied with water piped from a spring located on the hill.

The imposing Second Empire style eleven-room four-level ranch house completed in 1881 is built on a hillside with a three-level exposure on the upper side and three levels on the downhill facing side. The mansion is replete with mansard roof enclosing the upper story with dormers and projecting mansard gables, cornices, brackets, and stone quoins at the corners of the house. The richness of exterior detailing in coursed limestone and wood is a textbook rendition of the popular Victorian style. The house is built with four levels: a ground floor containing the formal parlors; a second level with the kitchen, root cellar, tunnel, and the spring room; a third level containing Stephen F. Jones's office/bedroom from a later time period, dining room, living room, butler's pantry, and back porch; and fourth level with bedrooms. The interior shows evidence of the fine craftsmanship by local carpenters and some rooms contain period furnishings.

Jones demonstrated his expansive view of suitable ranch buildings by constructing the nearby three-level limestone barn. The imposing structure measures 110 feet wide and 60 feet deep, with 20-inch-thick walls. The bottom level used for stables and a tackroom is built into the side of a south sloping hill, the second level built at grade stored farm equipment and hay, and the third story is connected to ground level by two long ramps on the barn's uphill side. Exterior walls are rubble stone masonry with smooth-faced quoin blocks at the corners. The window openings are rectangular with flat smoothed lintels and sills; barn doors are simple, shallow arched lintels.

Privy

Jones was consistent in adding outbuildings that would be in harmony with the ranch house and barn in the use of limestone. Worth exploring because of unique features are the chicken house and spring house. The privy is a fitting complement to Jones's consistent design and construction for the Spring Hill Ranch complex. The exterior walls are built with block limestone. The keystones have a hammered face with the edges of the stone tooled. The corner stones also have the tooled edges. The interior walls of this three-hole "necessary" are rough-cut ashlar stone, which is dressed at the windows. The outhouse even has curtains in the windows for that added element of privacy.

The Lower Fox Creek Schoolhouse is approximately one half-mile north of Spring Hill Ranch on a rise of land on the west side of Kansas Highway 177. Built in 1882 on land donated by Stephen F. Jones, the one-room schoolhouse—it could be a suitable background for Winslow Homer's renowned painting *Snap the Whip*—is an attractive feature of the cultural landscape of the preserve. The structure's contractor built the Jones's ranch buildings and the schoolhouse using limestone from the same quarry.

Ranch house

Lower Fox Creek Schoolhouse

Walls are rough-faced ashlar course limestone with dressed corner quoins. There are separate boys' and girls' entrances, three tall windows on each side and one at the east (front), with stone sills, arched heads, and smooth-faced stone jambs.

Plan a visit to absorb the cultural landscape by a variety of activities at this unusual partnership between the National Park Trust and the National Park Service. Also available are hiking trails, prairie bus tours, self-guided and ranger-guided ranch headquarters tours, and a summer schedule of weekend cultural events.

Missouri

Rockies and
Plains

George Washington Carver National Monument

Located in southwestern Missouri ten miles southeast of Joplin and approximately two miles west of Diamond, Newton County, Missouri

→ www.nps.gov/gwca

→ Ten miles east of Joplin via Interstate 44, take Exit 11A to US 71 south, take the Diamond Exit four miles east and travel one half-mile south to the park.

Moses Carver House

George Washington Carver National Monument is comprised of 210 acres of the original 240-acre Moses Carver homestead in the rolling hills of southwest Missouri. The birthplace of George Washington Carver—where he was born into slavery in 1864 in a log cabin on the homestead—is in a serene landscape of rolling hills, woodlands, and prairies. The park recaptures the setting that nourished young Carver's wonder of nature throughout the rest of his life as an artist, educator, and humanitarian, as well as his world renowned work as a scientist. Here, freed from many daily chores due to frail health, Carver had time to explore the natural environment.

The park, established as a national monument in 1943, has a self-guided one mile trail beginning from the George Washington Carver bust at the visitor center and winds through the natural setting of Carver's childhood. The trail deftly weaves linked episodes of Carver's early life on the farm: the Carver Birthplace site, the Boy Carver statue, Williams Spring and Pond with its meditative plaques, the relocated 1881 Moses Carver House, and the Carver family cemetery. The National Park Service (NPS) is gradually returning about 140 acres of the park to native tallgrass prairie, an appearance much like the land Moses Carver and other settlers found here early in the nineteenth century.

The Moses Carver House, originally located near the cabin site, was built in 1881

Park entrance sign

after a tornado destroyed the Moses Carver cabin and George's birthplace cabin. The farm's second owner moved the house to the present site in 1916 after Moses Carver died in 1910. Although George never lived in this house, he returned often to visit during his travels. Located on a grassy lawn at the edge of a grove of trees, the white clapboard house is representative of period and area farm homes. The visitor's impression is of the homesteader's solitary life in southwest Missouri connected to George Washington Carver's early life. The original construction and materials are part of ongoing NPS restoration and maintenance.

Simple in plan and form, the one-and-a-half-story house is built on a native rock and mortar foundation with wood-frame construction and white-painted clapboard tongue-in-groove pine siding. An almost 8-foot-deep porch across the front of the building facing east, divided by columns into five bays, was deep in shade by afternoon. The ground floor central portion contains a living room and bedroom separated by a twelve-inch wood partition. A stair leads to an attic bedroom, light and airy with double-hung windows, containing two cord bedsteads.

A casual walk along the trail leaves the visitor impressed with the NPS interpretation of Carver's early years in the Missouri hills. Undisturbed by modern sights and sounds, the visitor reverently experiences Carver's beginnings in a landscape that informs us about the nature of an individual and his eventual greatness.

Harry S. Truman National Historic Site

Located in Independence and Grandview, Jackson County, Missouri

→ www.nps.gov/hstr

→ The park has a Wallace Family Compound unit in Independence, Missouri, and Harry S. Truman Farm Home Unit twenty miles away in Grandview, Missouri. The visitor center is located in Independence at the intersection of Truman Road and Main Street.

The Harry S. Truman National Historic Site is a collection of structures associated with the life of Harry S. Truman, the thirty-third president of the United States. Remarkably complete as a panorama of the president's life, the park's four properties and associated structures at the Wallace Family Compound in Independence and the Truman Farm Home in Grandview, Missouri depict the years Truman, the "most uncommon man from middle America," lived on the farm for eleven years before moving to the white Victorian-era house at 219 North Delaware Avenue after his marriage to Bess Wallace in 1919.

Known as the Summer White House during the Truman administration (1945–1953), the North Delaware Avenue home in Independence was where the Trumans returned after his presidential term ended in 1953 and where they lived until his death in 1972 and Bess's death in 1982. Designated as a National Historic Site in 1983 it was expanded in 1994 to incorporate the Harry S. Truman Farm Home twenty miles south in Grandview, Missouri. Both the Harry S. Truman Historic District in Independence and the farm home in Grandview are National Historic Landmarks.

The Harry S. Truman home at the corner of North Delaware Avenue and Truman Road is an elegant two-and-a-half-story Victorian-era white clapboard structure, with Queen Anne style scrollwork and decorative details, hipped roof, and lower cross gables. The house exterior is a fine representation of a lifestyle at the end of the nineteenth and early twentieth century, seen typically across America as an expression of the emerging middle class. Maintenance work by the National Park Service preserves the rich detailing of Queen Anne scrollwork and Eastlake style touches.

The original 1867 house was expanded in 1885, and with later additions and exte-

Truman House, Independence, Missouri

rior revisions, as it appears today. Construction over a period of years accumulated many of the details and features seen in the style—projecting bay windows, hip roofs, dormers, verandahs, scrollwork at gabled ends, bands of dentil trim, and a rooftop widow's walk. Curbside viewing around the enclosing wrought-iron fence reveals the house's assembly of volumes, porches, and decorative features, all unified into a coherent whole by repetition of detail and white paint over clapboards and trim surfaces.

Truman House living room   Truman Farm Home

A tour of the ground floor rooms shows the unpretentious life of the nation's thirty-third president. The homey furniture and cozy feeling, book-lined library, Margaret Truman's baby grand piano, paintings, and presidential china is a contrast to the trappings of power left behind in Washington.

The unpretentious Farm Home in Grandview, without electricity and indoor plumbing when Harry lived there, is a vivid comparison to the 219 North Delaware Avenue mansion. Built in 1894 by Harry Truman's maternal grandmother Martha Ellen Young, the Farm Home is the centerpiece of a 5.25-acre remnant of the family's former 600-acre farm. President Truman worked on the farm as a young man, from 1906–1917. Today, the restored two-story farmhouse faces the historic gateway posts to the Grandview Farm on the distant Old Grandview Road and the access from Blue Ridge Boulevard. The three-bay, T-shaped vernacular farmhouse has a porch across the front (west) section with parlor and sitting room on the ground floor and two bedrooms on the second floor, a middle section with ground floor dining room and Harry's bedroom on the second floor, and a one-story kitchen at the rear. A porch with a visitor entrance is on the south side of the middle section and a porch is attached to the kitchen.

Visitors are encouraged to begin their tour at the park visitor center in Independence at the corner of Main Street and Truman Road to visit sites of Truman's rural midwestern origins. These sites inspired values he carried throughout his public life, affected by the rich history of the region. Guided tour tickets and information for 219 North Delaware Avenue are issued each day on a first-come, first-served basis; six of the house's fourteen rooms are open to the public. Ranger-guided tours of the Farm Home and self-guided farm tours are available.

Jefferson National Expansion Memorial

Located in St. Louis, Clayton County, Missouri

→   www.nps.gov/jeff

→   The park is located in downtown St. Louis on the Mississippi River. Interstate Routes 44, 55, 64, and 70 converge near the park. Parking is available in the Arch Parking Garage on the north end of the park grounds on Washington Street or at privately run surface lots and garages nearby. The Old Courthouse is located two blocks west of the Gateway Arch and Arch grounds bordered by four streets: 4th Street to the east, Market Street on the south, Broadway on the west, and Chestnut on the north.

Gateway Arch

The centerpiece of the St. Louis riverfront park is the Gateway Arch, a soaring 630-foot stainless steel arch created by the genius of architect Eero Saarinen and a team of gifted engineers and construction experts. Located below the arch is The Museum of Westward Expansion and just two blocks west of the arch, the Old Courthouse is one of the oldest standing buildings in St. Louis, begun in 1839 and completed, finally, in 1862 with construction of the dome. Here, where the countless threads of the story of westward migration occurred, is a fitting Gateway to the West.

The Gateway Arch is one of the most revered and respected structures in America. The highly complex and subtle design, designated a National Historic Landmark, is unique in American architecture and the tallest monument in the United States—taller than the Washington Monument or the Statue of Liberty. The purity of the geometry, span matched by height, base of a triangular cross-section heavier than its apex (thus, the "weighted catenary") dominates the landscape. Symbolic of a gateway to half the nation, the visitor can gain from its genius a fierce pride in the nation's founders.

Architectural historians have sung the arch's praise with unstinting admiration. George E. Kidder-Smith, in his monumental *Sourcebook of American Architecture of the United States* (Princeton Architectural Press, 1996) wrote:

> "Flaming in the sun, disappearing in mists, ghostly by the light of the moon, and, above all, proclaiming that verily here was the country's gateway to the west, the Gateway Arch ranks with the greatest monuments of world architecture....The Saarinen Arch ranks among the

supreme achievements of the United States, a euphoric summation of architecture, engineering, and sculpture working together. It almost seems alive."

Allan Temko in *Eero Saarinen* (George Braziller, 1962) celebrated Saarinen's genius in the creation of a true monument, timeless, as one of "profound expressions of their times that transcend time, lasting as long as things last, as permanent architectural truths." A great arch, "powerful and pure...a spiritual work of art," classic in simplicity of form and geometry to fit Jefferson's soaring mind.

Saarinen conceived the arch in the shape of an inverted weighted catenary curve—the curve formed by a chain or flexible cord hung between two points (the formula is displayed inside the arch). The challenges of structural stability and how to erect the arch without staggering cost shaped the final design. Art, engineering, and technology, nevertheless, produced an audacious structure, satisfying Saarinen with its elegance and tautness thinner at the top than at its bases soaring 630 feet tall and 630 feet wide at its base.

The arch's design solution is integrated with the choice of materials and method of construction. The engineering, led by Fred Severud of Severud, Elstad, Krueger and Associates and Saarinen partner John Dinkeloo, applies in each a cross-section of an equilateral triangle, 54 feet wide at the base tapering to 17 feet at the apex, with a flat side facing out and the point facing in, set on foundations 60 feet deep to withstand earthquakes and high winds. A stressed metal skin, similar to an airplane fuselage and other "shell" structures, forms a composite structure combining to carry the gravity and wind loads to the ground. The outer skin is 866 tons of quarter-inch polished stainless steel; the inner skin is 3/8-inch carbon steel, increased to 1-3/4-inch at the corners. This double wall construction, altering in height of triangular section, spacing of skins, and use of internal reinforcing as it soars, retains its composite structure providing its strength and durability. Walls are 3 feet apart at ground level and 7-3/4-inches apart above the 400-foot level. Up to the 300-foot mark the space between the walls is filled with reinforced concrete laced with a network of horizontal and vertical post-tensioned reinforcing rods. Beyond that point steel stiffeners are used.

Old Courthouse and Arch

Construction of the arch, captured on film viewable at the visitor center and in frames on the National Park Service web site (www.nps.gov/jeff), was solved by placing one triangular section atop another by a traveling 100-ton creeper derrick that climbed simultaneously on the outside of each arch leg. After placement of the top sections with amazing precision, the cranes then went back down each of the respective legs while workmen polished the finished surface, and the temporary tracks were removed. The contractor, MacDonald Construction Company of St. Louis, supervised the care and precision exercised by skilled technicians; the monument was erected on schedule, within the budget, and without loss of life. The Museum of Westward Expansion houses excellent displays and is in the underground visitor center.

Old Courthouse rotunda

The ride to the top of the arch in self-leveling passenger gondolas, attached in trains of eight, each holding five passengers is a highly recommended experience. There are two "trams," one in each leg. The four-minute ride to the observation room takes the visitor to the top of the arch, where, on a clear day, one can look up and down the Mississippi, out over metropolitan St. Louis, and across thirty miles of Illinois and Missouri countryside. An emergency stairway (1,076 steps) descends in each leg from the top to the base.

A fine counterpoint to the Gateway Arch, two blocks to the west, the Greek Revival Old Courthouse, with its towering dome and sumptuous interior of ascending galleries and frescoes, overshadows the surrounding pedestrian "modern" structures. Carefully integrated into Jefferson National Expansion Memorial and aligned with the arch's east–west axis, open space to the west and east through the arch and to the Mississippi riverfront celebrate this structure of both historical and architectural significance.

Ulysses S. Grant National Historic Site

Located in St. Louis, St. Louis County, Missouri

→ www.nps.gov/ulsg

→ The park is located in south St. Louis County, Missouri, on Grant Road, one-third of a mile from State Highway 30 (Gravois Road) and adjacent to the privately-owned and operated Grant's Farm. Access is by Interstate (44, 55, 70, 270), and various state roads. Look for signs to the visitor center.

An inspired National Park Service (NPS) restoration program completed in 2001 attracts the visitor to the park in suburban St. Louis commemorating the life, military career, and presidency of Ulysses S. Grant, as well as his wife Julia Dent Grant. Although Grant and his family owned the property twenty-one years and lived here only five years off and on during the 1850s, the property (also known as White Haven) was a focal point in

Ulysses and Julia's lives for four decades. Intended as a retirement home, circumstances changed and the Grants never returned to live at White Haven.

Grant sold the property in 1884 and around the turn of the twentieth century the then owner began subdividing it. The historic core remained intact until the early 1980s when it was threatened by redevelopment for condominiums. Local residents formed a Save Grant's White Haven in 1985, and their efforts, supported by the State of Missouri, St. Louis County Parks Department, and Jefferson National Expansion Historical Association, resulted in purchase of the property and designation as a National Historic Landmark in 1986. The park was accepted by the NPS and the historic site established in 1989.

Ulysses S. Grant National Historic Site consists of five historic structures (a main house, a stone summer kitchen, a barn, an ice house, and a chicken house) on 9.65 acres of the original 500-acre Grant property. The two-story main house painted in striking Paris Green and other structures are all restored to their 1870s appearance.

The farm originally was owned by Julia Dent Grant's father Colonel Fredrick Dent as part of a 1,000-acre plantation. Ironically, Dent was a slaveholder when the young West Point graduate visiting from Jefferson Barracks courted his daughter in 1843. The couple married in 1848. Throughout a checkered early military career, failures in farming and business, and eventual Civil War success, the Grants continued to think of White Haven as their family home, and it remained the emotional heart of their relationship.

White Haven summer kitchen

The dramatic approach from the visitor center to the imposing two-story main house is along the road first traveled by Grant on horseback for his visit in 1843. Facing southeast on a slight rise of ground, built on a limestone foundation, the two-story main section's colonnaded ground floor piazza and second story balcony under the main roof embody Grant's dream of a retirement home. Limestone chimneys and a one-story wing to the left (west wing) embrace the main section.

White Haven

The present structure originated with the two-story main section built by owner William Lindsay Long around 1818. Modifications by successive owners added the two-room portion to the back of the house (1820), the one-story wing to the left of the main facade and back porch (1840), and other wings and dormers removed during the NPS restoration. Acquiring the house from his father-in-law in 1865, Grant envisioned White Haven as his retirement home, a place for his collection of prized thoroughbreds, with a large barn and ample, fertile farm acreage. Grant had the house's exterior hand-hewn oak or fir lap siding painted Paris Green, a popular Victorian period color. Extensive paint sampling and historical store ledgers confirm that this was indeed the color of Grant's house. Some of the original paint is visible on the back porch, inside the mudroom.

To the rear of the main house is the restored summer kitchen. Reputedly originally slave quarters, the stone masonry structure with oak framing has chimneys set flush in the gable end walls. The restored chicken house and ice house, a gable roof over an underground structure with stone masonry walls are near the main house.

Grant attributed the struggling years spent at White Haven with Julia and her family as helping shape the couple's character for the difficult years of leading the Union Army in the Civil War, as a two-term president of the United States, and through a troubled administration and later personal financial difficulties. A new visitor center (2006) provides an interpretive source for the park and life of the nation's eighteenth president. Free tours of the historic home are offered regularly on a ticketed basis, and interpretive activities are presented by the staff.

Wilson's Creek National Battlefield

Located in southwest Missouri, near Republic, Christian and Greene Counties, Missouri

→ www.nps.gov/wlcr

→ The battlefield is located ten miles southwest of Springfield and three miles east of Republic, Missouri. From Interstate 44, take Exit 70 (Missouri State MM) and continue south to US 60. Proceed through the intersection. MM changes to State Highway M and continues three-quarters of a mile to State Highway ZZ. Turn right on ZZ, continue south 1.5 miles to Farm Road 182 (Elm Street), turn left and the entrance to the battlefield is on the right.

John Ray House, overlooking battlefield

John Ray watched from his front porch as Union and Confederate troops fought in the fields below on August 10, 1861. Cannon shells landed nearby, hitting a chicken coop, while the rest of the family were in the cellar. The battle of Wilson's Creek, the first major struggle west of the Mississippi, was crucial to preserving the strategically important state of Missouri for the Union. In pitched battle with heavy losses on both sides, the Confederates held the field, although unable to pursue the retreating Northerners. The engagement's stalemate at Wilson's Creek and the Union victory at Pea Ridge seven months later secured Missouri as a Union state.

Today, the visitor can take a 4.9-mile self-guided auto tour of the Wilson's Creek Battlefield to all the major historical points. The John Ray House and Spring House are the only surviving structures in the park from the time of the Civil War battle. The rolling countryside of ridges, knolls, and valleys, with the exception of the vegetation, has changed little from its historic setting, enabling visitors to experience the battlefield in near pristine condition. A spectacular battle map display in the visitor center is recommended for an orientation to the battlefield events.

John A. Ray built the simple one-story, wood-frame farmhouse in 1852–53. The Ray Springhouse is the only other period structure on the battlefield. The Ray house served as a field hospital during and after the battle. Shelling around the house was halted

The Soldier in our Civil War, Frank Leslie, 1893   Battlefield cannon

when Southern surgeons raised a yellow flag (recognized on the battlefield as a symbol of a field hospital), and the gunners ceased fire. Confederate Colonel Richard Weightman died in the front room and the body of Union General Nathaniel Lyon was brought here at the end of the fighting and laid out on a bedstead in the east front room.

The house was built facing north by northwest, exposing it to the prevailing southwest wind and provided the Rays with some comfort in the hot summers of southwest Missouri. Archeological excavations under National Park Service supervision indicate that the back room of the house was built first, possibly from remnants of an earlier home on the site, and then the two front rooms were built while the back room was already being occupied.

The house as restored represents the period of the battle in 1861. Built on a stone foundation and with a partial cellar, a wide front porch faces the battlefield and the main roof shadows two front bedrooms. This main rectangle is approximately 36 feet wide facing north of the battlefield, and 26 feet deep with a stone fireplace and chimney on the exterior of the east wall. A rear wing with "middle room" and kitchen completes an L-shaped plan. Exterior walls vary: the south, east, and west are 7-inch lap siding and the tongue-and-groove flush siding is on the north wall.

Montana

Rockies and Plains

Glacier National Park

Located in northwest Montana on the U.S.–Canada border, West Glacier, Glacier and Flathead Counties, Montana

→ www.nps.gov/glac

→ The park's east entrance in St. Mary is thirty-two miles northwest of Browning, Montana via US 89; the west entrance near West Glacier is thirty-one miles northeast of Kalispell, Montana via US 2.

Garden Wall, Glacier National Park

"America's Alps," "An Alpine Paradise," the "Switzerland of America," and "The Crown of the Continent" were the early descriptions extolling the magnificent mountain wilderness of Glacier National Park straddling the Continental Divide and abutting the Canadian border. The spectacular scenery, set between two mountain ranges of the northern Rocky Mountains and divided by glacier-carved valleys, rivals that of any other national park. The park's more than one million acres contain over 200 lakes, waterfalls, glaciers nestled in mountain cirques, a thousand miles of rivers and streams, and abundant wildlife. Dramatic changes in elevation encompass lush, verdant valleys, meadows ablaze with wildflowers, and deep forests reaching upward mountain peaks that rise over 10,000 feet.

The park's abundant richness in historical structures is a legacy of the railroad that arrived and then developed the park for tourists and the National Park Service (NPS) management and interpretation of the park. To attract the public, the Great Northern Railway built a string of hotels and trail chalets in what is likely the largest collection of Swiss chalet-style buildings in America. The NPS erected visitor centers, ranger stations, and backcountry cabins and shelters, and Going-to-the-Sun Highway, one of the most scenic highways in the west. The Great Northern Railway buildings and the high-way are National Historic Landmarks.

Louis Hill's Great Northern Railway ran along the southern boundary of the new

Glacier Park Lodge and "Big Red" coaches Granite Park Chalet

park. Hill knew that a destination resort at "his" park would increase passenger rev-enues along the main railway lines. He wanted what the other railroads had achieved: to build resorts whose architectural styles would create memorable images, buildings that would be noteworthy in their own right. The Great Northern Railway planned two large hotels and an extensive backcountry development of smaller chalets at seven locations in the park. Hill's choice of style and a whole system of lodgings gave an architectural unity to an entire region. His Glacier National Park buildings were complemented by a Great Northern hotel in Canada's Waterton Lakes National Park (the Prince of Wales Hotel), a privately built hotel on Lake McDonald (Lake McDonald Lodge), and many fine examples of NPS rustic style service buildings.

A long journey across the flat landscape in eastern Montana eventually brought the Great Northern traveler to the eastern slope of the Continental Divide. The visitor's ar-rival at East Glacier, just outside the park boundary, was met by a theatrically orches-trated panorama from the railroad station of Glacier Park Lodge across a broad lawn filled with an enclave of Indian tepees.

Hill and his architect, Thomas D. McMahon of St. Paul, Minnesota, appreciated the subtleties of proper building siting. The long three and four-story building mass, under a sheltering gable roof with jerkinheads (clipped gables), extends across a rise of land at a slightly higher elevation than the railroad station and foreground meadow. McMahon set out to recreate the classical volume of the Portland Exposition's Forestry Building in the hotel lobby, and his creation is a marvelous combination of formal and rustic elements. He skillfully expanded the visual appearance of the lobby's interior volume by placing 8-foot-wide balconies for access to guest rooms around the soar-ing atrium behind the columns. Skylights interspersed between the roof structure's kingpost trusses bathe the lobby in natural daylight. At one end of the lobby is the entrance to the dining room, and at the other end a passage leading to the annex. An international atmosphere in the original décor included Japanese lanterns, and the staff dressed in lederhosen and kimonos.

Today's visitor can absorb the lobby's drama from comfortable couches and watch

Many Glacier Lodge

the reactions of other guests as they first enter the huge space and scan with awe along the rows of massive columns and upward to the trusses and skylights. Visitors delight in discovering the lobby's decorative elements, for they enhance rather than diminish the powerful space created by the soaring 3-foot diameter log columns. Tiers of delicate, peeled-log balcony railings are similar in scale to exterior balcony patterns. At the first-floor level, wrought-iron cylindrical lanterns are bracketed onto the face of the columns; three chandeliers suspended from the trusses carry lanterns of the same size and style.

The Two Medicine Dining Hall (now a camp store), the only remaining building from Two Medicine Chalet complex, was built by the Great Northern Railway in 1913 on the shore of Two Medicine Lake to serve horseback riders from Glacier Park Lodge, ten miles to the south. The structure originally housed the dining room and kitchen for the chalet complex. The rectangular building of skilled log craftsmanship has a gable roof with long shed dormers stretching from the roof ridge to the building's outside walls, and a clipped gable end and two-story porch at the entrance.

Many Glacier Hotel was hailed by Louis Hill as the "Showplace of the Rockies." When it opened in 1915, it was the largest hotel in the park and the centerpiece of Hill's resort development for Glacier National Park. Located fifty miles from the railroad station at East Glacier, the site on Swiftcurrent Lake offers an extraordinary natural setting where long, narrow lake basins were scoured out by glaciers. Amidst a landscape of valleys, ridges, and pyramid-shaped peaks, pine forests on the shoulders of the lowest ridges provide a green backdrop for the hotel against the stark gray granite ridge walls. Hill planned a design that would sweep along the lake's edge. Carefully designed for appreciation from a distance across the lake, the hotel is enriched by skillful massing, variations in roof forms, and the contrast of the white trim against a dark brown wood-sided exterior.

Architect McMahon followed the same principles he used at Glacier Park Lodge to assemble long, four-story units into a cohesive image that gives the impression of a series of chalets. The 900-foot-long building mass is disguised by suggestions of smaller chalets at the ends and along the main elevations. Shingled gable roofs with clipped ends, and multiple dormers add interest to the rooflines. The exterior is rich with details. Windows are framed moldings cut into jigsaw designs. The building's multiple balconies have railings with jigsaw patterns. The wilderness setting is balanced by the spaciousness and comforts of the hotel interior. A sky-lit four-story atrium is surrounded by balconies with jigsaw fretwork similar to the one at Glacier Park Lodge. Enormous peeled-log columns topped with log capitals give the space a formal, classical air. A large copper fireplace hood caps an open hearth at one end of the lobby with a painted four-story chimneystack suspended by cables.

On the western side of the park, three miles from the park entrance, Lake McDonald (the park's longest at eleven miles) provided good access to Glacier's interior trails. John Lewis, a hotel owner and fur trader from Columbia Falls, Montana, commissioned the Spokane architectural firm of Kirtland Cutter and Karl Malmgren to design a lodge for it, to be named the Lewis Glacier Hotel. Renamed Lake McDonald Lodge in 1957, Lewis' lodge provided guest accommodations similar to those of Glacier Park Lodge, but more intimate in feeling. Lewis built sixteen guest cabins between 1907 and 1908 and construction began on the forty-one-room main lodge in 1913 and took ten months to complete.

Many Glacier Lodge

Prince of Wales Hotel

Located on a small rise 100 feet from the shoreline, the symmetrical lakeside elevation is rich in chalet details mixed with rustic embellishments. A one-and-a-half-story dining room and kitchen wing are connected to the three-and-a-half-story main lodge and tied to it visually by siding and roofing materials similar to those used on the main building. A stucco ground floor and wood framing above, tempered with natural materials, balconies, shingled gable roofs, jigsaw door and window trim, multilight casement windows, and white trim at each floor level add to the overall chalet character. A framework of unpeeled-log columns, beam, and rafters supports a balcony with a peeled-log railing that runs the length of the first floor; two jerkinhead roofed, three-story elements flank the central section. Brown clapboard siding contrasts with the bands of white trim at the second and third floors in a fretwork frieze. The three-story lobby, richly detailed and furnished is a delightful space.

The Prince of Wales Hotel located in Waterton Lakes National Park is the Canadian component of Louis Hill's Great Northern Railway development. Completed in 1927, the hotel is perched in a barren landscape at the end of the fjord-like Waterton Lake. There are few hotels in North America so dramatically sited and surrounded by such magnificent vistas. Situated on a rise more that 100 feet above the lake, it enjoys unobstructed southern views down the Upper Waterton Lake and along the Continental Divide.

Daunting construction problems—high winds regularly tilted the structural frame—eventually resulted in a seven-story, sixty-five-room hotel. A compact mass verticality emphasized by extensive decorative work, is trimmed with fretwork balcony railings, jigsaw trim, and sculptured columns decorating the hotel's facade. A three-story lobby is framed with squared-timber trusses criss-crossed with wrought-iron strapwork to resist the strong winds. The view of the park framed by the lobby windows at the Prince of Wales Hotel is a memorable experience. In the comfort of one of the hotel club chairs, safe from the high winds buffeting the upper stories, the entire length of Waterton Lakes and Glacier National Park's mountains unfold in the distance. As chandeliers eerily sway overhead and the old hotel begins to creak, one can only say a silent prayer of appreciation to Louis Hill and his determined builders.

Saint Mary ranger stations   Lake McDonald Lodge

Among the many rewards of Glacier's backcountry trails are hikes to the Granite Park and Sperry chalets. These durable stone-and-timber buildings, the two remaining backcountry chalet complexes of the chalet system developed for hikers and horseback trains, have managed to avoid removal either by avalanche, the railway, or the NPS. Granite Park Chalet on the park's west side (the dividing line is the Continental Divide) is a seven-mile walk on the Highline Trail from the Logan Pass Visitor Center, below the

Prince of Wales Hotel overlooking Waterton Lake

dramatic craggy peaks of the Garden Wall and through Swiftcurrent Pass toward Granite Park. Most of the trail remains above the timberline affording unrestricted views. The Sperry Chalet complex is on the park's west side, reached from the Sperry Glacier Trail rising 3,500 feet in elevation from Lake McDonald. The dramatic site welcoming the hiker is surrounded by craggy peaks and cascading waterfalls.

Design of the rustic chalet buildings was based on the simple ideals of a hearty meal and warm bed at the end of a long day's hike or trail ride. Gable-roofed buildings—rectangular in plan and constructed of local stone placed as random rubble, peeled-log timbers, and shake-shingled roofs—are rugged in appearance and fit organically into the mountainside. The interiors restored in the 1990s retain much of their original character and neither site has been electrified.

Located throughout Glacier National Park there are NPS rustic ranger stations, snowshoe cabins, shelters, fire lookouts, and an entrance station. Patrol cabins are strategically located eight to ten miles from a permanent ranger station, so rangers could spend several days on patrol duty without returning to the base station for supplies or shelter. The majority of these structures were built by the NPS in the rustic style during the 1920s and 1930s.

Often asked to name a favorite national park, the author places Glacier high on the list. The spectacular scenery of this World Heritage Site and abundance of historic structures offers a treasure chest of memorable images to be relished long after the visitor returns home.

Grant-Kohrs Ranch National Historic Site
In southwest Montana in Deer Lodge, Powell County, Montana

→   www.nps.gov/grko

→   The park is on the north edge of Deer Lodge, Montana off Interstate 90, forty miles north of Butte and
eighty miles southeast of Missoula. To reach the visitor center, take either Deer Lodge Exit 184 or 187 and follow
signs.

Winter scene at the Grant-Kohrs Ranch

At its peak in the last quarter of the nineteenth century Grant-Kohrs Ranch's 30,000 acres
on the north edge of Deer Lodge, Montana, was one of the largest cattle ranching operations in the country. For four decades it was the center of a 10,000,000-acre operation in
four states and two Canadian provinces controlled by Kohrs through outright ownership
or ownership of water rights. In the 1890s and early 1900s the ranch annually shipped to
Chicago's Union Stock Yards between eight thousand and ten thousand cattle.

The Grant-Kohrs Ranch National Historic Site, once the headquarters of a vast cattle empire, founded in 1853 by Johnny Grant and expanded by Conrad Kohrs, is maintained as a working ranch to interpret the changes from open range cattle ranching to
feed lots. The ranch is unusual in its integrity with most of the nineteenth-century buildings, and successive generations of ranch structures up to the present, intact. The ranch
house has many of its original furnishings, and the jack-leg fenced pastures preserve the
appearance of a century of range cattle operations.

Today, the ninety-three historical structures and features and the other structures
at this National Historic Landmark can be seen on ranger-led tours or self-guided walks
around the ranch headquarters complex. The white-picket fence enclosed ranch house
and thirteen nearby buildings are at the core of the visitor experience on ranch life. A

walking tour can start at the visitor center, then follow a trail leading to the ranch house. Continue on to the buildings to the north and the north corrals and circling around the house to the west corrals and barns south of the ranch house.

Grant-Kohrs Ranch house

The center of the ranch is the thirty-room house that appears much as it did at the height of the Kohrs's residency in the 1890s, resplendent with Victorian furnishings donated by Kohrs family members. The log house of post-on-sill framing and clapboard exterior built by Johnny Grant in 1866 was 60 by 40 feet in plan on a field-stone foundation and two stories high. The brick wing of today's T-plan structure, built by Conrad Kohrs in 1890, added additional rooms, an elegant stick style covered porch and the comforts of lighting, a furnace for central heating, running water piped from a nearby spring, and indoor bathrooms. The addition included the dining room, a larger kitchen, a new bathroom, a basement, and several additional upstairs bedrooms.

Other restored buildings of interest are the Ice House/Tack Room, the 200-foot-long Bunkhouse Row, the log Draft Horse Barn, Garage-Blacksmith Shop, Leeds-Lion Stallion Barn, the buggy sheds, the entire Warren Ranch complex, and the Thoroughbred Barn.

The ranch and ranch life is restored and interpreted by the National Park Service in fine balance between capturing the Kohrs family's lengthy residency—in a home and not a museum frozen in time—and a working ranch. Take time to walk around the range and experience its operations; observe the cattle grazing and draft horses working in the traditions of the ranchers; enjoy the summer living history demonstrations; and admire the landscape threaded by lines of jack-leg fences through the summer pastures or snow cover.

Nebraska

Rockies and
Plains

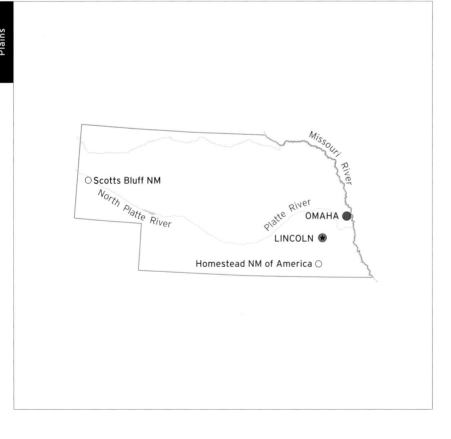

Homestead National Monument of America

Located in the southeastern part of the state near Beatrice, Gage County, Nebraska

→ www.nps.gov/home

→ Homestead National Monument of America is located in southeastern Nebraska, about forty miles south of Lincoln. Visitors traveling north out of Kansas City on Interstate 29 should take US 136 approximately sixty-five miles to the State Highway 4 turnoff.

Homestead Heritage Center (courtesy NPS)

"There was nothing but land; not a country at all, but the material out of which countries are made," recalled Willa Cather in *My Antonia* (Houghton Mifflin Co., 1918). In one of the most significant acts in American history, President Abraham Lincoln signed into law the Homestead Act of 1862. The land was free, up to 160 acres, if you lived on it, cultivated it, and built a dwelling on it within five years from filing a claim. The act partially resolved the dilemma of settling the West; by the 1930s some 1.6 million homestead applications of more than 2 million had been claimed; ultimately about forty percent succeeded.

In 1936 the 243-acre Homestead National Monument of America was designated to memorialize the pioneers who settled the West and the Homestead Act's many impacts on the United States and the world. It was established along the meandering Cub Creek in the Flint Hills of southeast Nebraska on the Daniel and Agnes Freeman homestead, one of the first claims filed under the Homestead Act on January 1, 1863, the first day the act was in effect. Among the park's features are the historic Palmer-Epard frontier log cabin typical of those of eastern Nebraska, the restored Freeman School, and trails that wind through the more than 100 acres of restored tallgrass prairies.

Built in 1867 by George Washington Palmer on a nearby homestead claim, the Palmer-Epard cabin was moved several miles to its present location on a rise near the Education Center. Successive ownerships, including the Lawrence Epard family and

Palmer-Epard cabin exterior   Interior

descendants ended in 1940 with acquisition by the National Park Service (NPS) to recognize this sample of the rough structures built by homesteaders.

The charming diminutive structure, approximately 14 by 16 feet, was restored in 1954 to remove additions and interior changes and continues to receive regular maintenance to preserve the log work. The swayback exterior walls are a composite of log shapes, crooked and twisted, almost no two alike in dimension or shape. While many settlers built sod houses due to lack of timber, Palmer used hardwoods from nearby forests—almost anything he could lay his hands on—white and red oak, hackberry, ash, locust, walnut, and elm. The corner dovetailing is an ingenious fitting with a series of dowels 18 inches long and 1.5-inches in diameter. A steep interior stair reaches the attic. A distinctive feature is the space in the gable ends filled with bricks and vertical wood uprights with windows in each wall above ground floor windows. The cabin contains furnishing, fixtures, and tools of the period.

The one-room red brick Freeman School, added to the Homestead National Monument in 1970, is located a quarter-mile west of the Freeman homestead. The school was built in 1872, operating continuously until 1967, and is restored and furnished to its appearance in the 1870s. Used jointly as a schoolhouse and church in its early years, national attention was drawn to the Freeman School because of a lawsuit filed by Daniel Freeman protesting Bible-based lessons at the school. Freeman was successful in the Nebraska Supreme Court decision to separate church and state before the United States Supreme Court reached the same conclusion.

The building is 20 by 30 feet in plan with a gable roof. A brick chimney rises above the roof ridge on the north wall. The masonry-bearing exterior walls are laid on a shallow fieldstone foundation and are three bricks thick in a common bond. Brick ties to stabilize the walls and limestone sill and decorative head frame double-hung windows, each with pairs of red fixed shutters can be seen from the exterior. Interior flooring consists of rough-cut pine boards and the beaded flat ceiling is 11 feet high. Interior restoration includes gas wall fixtures and fixed-floor desks. The grounds may be visited anytime, but access to the interior of the school is limited to NPS ranger-conducted tours available during normal operating hours.

The new Homestead Heritage Center opened in May 2007 to serve as the monument's main visitor center building. The apex of the dramatically profiled prow-shaped roof, designed to resemble sod pushed up by a plow blade, faces west symbolizing the Homestead Act in America's westward expansion. Trails leading from the center take visitors into 100 acres of restored tallgrass prairie.

Scotts Bluff National Monument

Located in the western part of the state twenty miles east of the Wyoming border on the North Platte River near Gering, Scotts Bluff County, Nebraska

→ www.nps.gov/scbl

→ Visitors traveling east-west on Interstate 80 exit at Kimball, Nebraska, and drive forty-five miles north on Nebraska 71. Follow highway signs; the national monument is located two miles west of Gering, Nebraska. Visitors can also follow the old Oregon Trail along the North Platte River using State Highways 26 or 92 and should follow highway signs.

Scotts Bluff visitor center

The massive castellated Scotts Bluff, rising 800 feet above the high plains of western Nebraska, was a memorable landmark for explorers, traders, trappers, and immigrants traveling the North Platte River valley. Known to the Sioux, Cheyenne, and Arapaho who hunted buffalo here, the weather-sculpted sandstone formation entered American folklore when William Ashley and his trappers encountered Indian hostilities in the Upper Missouri River region in the 1820s and shifted southward to the North Platte route. Named for Hiram Scott, a fur trader believed to have died here in 1828, the bluff marked the Central Overland Route—the Oregon-California Trail.

Scotts Bluff National Monument's 3,003 acres, established in 1919, includes Scotts Bluff, Mitchell Pass, and South Bluff. The park preserves the monument's cultural landscape of the historic Oregon, California, and Mormon Trails and serves as an interpretive center for the Oregon Trail. The park headquarters complex contains the visitor center with the Oregon Trail Museum, exhibiting the human and natural history of the area and also a unique collection of watercolor paintings by the frontier photographer and artist William Henry Jackson. Trails from the visitor center lead to remnants of the Oregon Trail and summit of Scott Bluff, which is also accessible by a 1.6-mile paved road, with its view of Mitchell Pass, South Bluff, and surrounding countryside.

The National Park Service (NPS) park headquarters four-building complex is on Country Road Old Oregon Trail along the corridor of the Oregon Trail through Mitchell Pass. The complex grew from a combined 1935 visitor center/park headquarter/ Oregon Trail Museum designed by the NPS and built by Civilian Conservation Corps (CCC) staff into an expanded complex with an administration building, ranger quarters, and a maintenance building. As seen today, after additions to the original 20-foot by 36-foot administration and museum building, the complex has a uniformity of scale and materials with shallow-pitch gable end roofs and stucco exterior surfaces. The low profile of the structures, unobtrusive in the landscape and marked by a two-story tower, is a suitable gateway to the monument. The style recalls Spanish Colonial Revival influences with a brick-edged segmental arch entrance and high grille windows, somewhat incongruous on the Nebraska prairies.

Unseen to the visitor is the adobe brick construction under a layer of stucco that suggested the prevalent nineteenth-century Nebraska sod structures. The structural frame is essentially post-and-beam with steel or concrete poured-in-place columns infilled with a three-wythe thick wall of adobe bricks (4 by 8 by 16 inches) manufactured on the site by CCC workers. The roof structure of the five-in-twelve pitch roofs is typically wood rafters, except for timber cross-beamed trusses over the exhibit halls now concealed by dropped ceilings. Roof eaves extend uniformly 30 inches around the building, creating a deep shadow line. One distinctive design feature is the deeply recessed windows high on various building elevations, built up of faceted concrete bricks and mortared into a grill pattern.

The number of visitors to Scotts Bluff strains the timeworn visitors center. Planning for expanded visitor services, an exhibit, interpretive and administrative space, along with maintenance work, is underway (2006) to enhance the overall visitor experience.

Oklahoma

→ Chickasaw National Recreation Area

Rockies and Plains

Chickasaw National Recreation Area

The park is located in south central Oklahoma, south of Sulphur, Murray County, Oklahoma.

→ www.nps.gov/chic

→ The park is located on US 177, just south of Sulphur, Oklahoma, east of Interstate 35 approximately ninety miles south of Oklahoma City, Oklahoma, and one hundred-twenty miles north of the Dallas-Fort Worth/Texas area. Exit the Interstate and drive through the towns of Davis (three miles) and Sulphur (ten miles) to the intersection of Highways 7 and 177.

Bromide Springs

Chickasaw National Recreation Area is a prairie oasis in the gently rolling hill country in south central Oklahoma containing a stunningly designed cultural landscape and superb rustic structures. The park, named in honor of the Chickasaw Nation, the land's inhabitants since relocation from the southeast in the 1830s, is in two districts: the 900-acre Platt District (formerly Platt National Park), with freshwater and mineral springs and a distinctive historic landscape, and eight miles to the southwest the 9,000-acre Arbuckle District including the Lake of the Arbuckles. The Platt District contains the designed landscape, primarily the 1933-1940 work of National Park Service (NPS) landscape architects and Civilian Conservation Corps (CCC) crews. Shaped from the natural flow of water through dry, broad prairies and meandering through forests, meadows, and grasslands, reflected in wading and picturesque pools, rippling over rocky streambeds, and flowing over dams, the landscape is enriched by walks and paths, a scenic perimeter drive, and hundreds of historic structures.

The CCC-built Platt District structures are distinguished NPS rustic designs seen in the entrance gates, former park office buildings, Pavilion Springs and Bromide Springs pavilions, comfort stations, stabilized stream banks, dams, and waterfalls. Unity for this picturesque collection of buildings and site work is provided by a consistency of construction and materials throughout the park by the use of large, shaped limestone building bases emerging from the ground to support large, ochre-colored rough-cut blocks of limestone, uniform pitch wood shingle-shake-covered roofs, and massive square-cut timber framing

A favorite scenic spot within the park is the Lincoln Bridge, a gently rising single-arch masonry bridge crossing Travertine Creek. Preceding the depression-era work, the bridge completed in 1909 is approximately 20 feet wide and 100 feet long, with gothic-inspired touches. Four cylindrical crenellated towers form its abutment; the gray-colored limestone masonry used horizontal coursing on the bridge and vertical coursing on the towers. Spiral steps lead up to the towers, each crowned with a flagpole.

On a hill overlooking the confluence of Rock and Travertine Creeks, the picturesque neoclassical Black Sulphur Springs Pavilion entrances the visitor. Distinctive by its overhanging rust-colored metal tile hip roof, the graceful structure was almost abandoned in the 1930s and was restored in the 1990s by the NPS. Built on a concrete slab, the 11-foot by 17-foot structure has an airy, open quality framed by L-shaped stucco corner piers and pairs of Doric columns on the long dimension.

The shelters at Pavilion Springs and Bromide Springs are CCC-built elegant, formal structures. Both pavilions share common features enhanced by superb stonework: integration of terrace walls and structures with the landscape, a wood-shake covered hip roof sheltering an open and airy centrally located fountain pouring out over large stone. The Pavilion Springs structure is set in topography of a shallow oval bowl and the visitor descends several steps to the fountain level with irregular sized stone paving blocks in an enclosure surrounded by stone benches. Bromide Springs Pavilion is along the banks of Rock Creek and is built on a plinth of stone lock flooring extending into a terrace

looking out over a formal pool centered on a fountain. Both structures have massive limestone-coursed boulder corner bases flowing artfully out of the ground to support rough-cut limestone coursed piers and exposed king-post timber trusses supporting the roof. At Bromide Springs and Pavilion Springs the lintels are timber. Stone sills at Pavilion Springs between the piers form seating benches.

Buffalo Springs pool

The comfort stations at Bromide Springs, Flower Park, Central Campground, Cold Springs Campground, Travertine Island, and Buffalo Springs use native materials in simple gable-roof rectangular structures with triple-coursed wood-shingle roofs (modified from original hip to gable roofs) and exposed beam-ends. All the comfort station structures are built of local limestone; plan dimensions range in size and are approximately 20 by 30 feet. Strong corner piers predominate—some with large boulders flared out at the base creating an irregular profile.

Flower Park comfort station

Dark stained wood beams, lintels, and siding are complimented by wood shingles installed with the original sawtooth and double coursing every fifth row, which is reflective of the 1930s design.

Several park administration buildings follow the theme of large limestone block walls, rough-sawn timber roof framing exposed at gable-end shake-covered roofs, and other rustic details. The Ranger Checking Station at Cold Springs Campground is small in scale—approximately 27 by 21 feet in plan, powerful in a well-composed image of flared boulder corners, window openings, and a stone end wall fireplace. Nearby is a former community house (now used as an exercise room) built in 1922 that has an inviting south porch with large timbers. The former park headquarters (now used as a ranger station) is a large hip-roofed structure residential in appearance. A pleasant addition to the park's structures is the Travertine Nature Center, constructed in 1969. The building design is loosely based on the principles of Frank Lloyd Wright. It spans the creek and features banks of windows facing up and down the water, in addition to generous clerestory windows. Building piers, walls, and extended terraces are constructed from brown and tan-colored Arkansas stone, compatible with CCC stonework.

The treatment of site features received the same deft touch as structures in a superb integration of native materials and the natural landscape. The sometimes drought-parched meandering streams integrate seamlessly into man-made stream channels and waterfalls; dams create ponds, swimming holes, and wading pools. Ingenious water crossings—stone block stepping-stones set barely above water level with spaces between for water flow—are almost overlooked until their ingenuity is recognized. Some of these crossings have been bridged over, but many are still visible. A pleasant discovery along the park's many trails is the Buffalo Springs pool. The 40-foot diameter open air stone structure with integrated seating momentarily captures spring flows that bubble from the stream bed.

Other delights enchant the visitor along the meandering trails and roads. Steeper trails are edged with boulders and rock walls. Half a million CCC-planted trees and shrubs are now part of the "naturalized" landscape. Now, more than sixty years after the last CCC camp closed, the Platt District represents one of the nation's finest examples of a historical "designed" landscape.

North Dakota

Rockies and Plains

Fort Union Trading Post National Historic Site

Located in the northwestern corner of North Dakota close to the Montana state line, near Williston, Williams County, North Dakota

→ www.nps.gov/fous

→ The site is located on North Dakota 1804, twenty-five miles southwest of Williston, North Dakota, and twenty-four miles northeast of Sidney, Montana.

Bourgeois House

A couple of decades after Captain Meriwether Lewis stood at the confluence of the Missouri and Yellowstone Rivers, fur trader Kenneth McKenzie established Fort Union Trading Post for the American Fur Company. Opened as Fort Union in 1830, the trading post was built on the north bank of the Missouri River in what is now North Dakota, 500 feet from the Montana line. The location on an expanse of shortgrass prairie has a commanding view of the Missouri River and a receding horizon of rugged buttes, providing ample space for Indian tepee encampments at trading times around the fort.

For the next four decades the imposing timber palisade enclosed fort was considered one of the most important and solidly built trading posts in the country. Built for protection and for the ease of the fur trade, an imposing enclosure was necessary to separate the Northern Plains Indian tepee encampments often surrounding the fort from the American Fur Company traders. Famous travelers—adventurers, scientists, artists, priests—came often and recorded their impressions of this center of a vast trading empire exchanging goods for hides (first beaver and then buffalo). Fort Union was finally abandoned and dismantled in 1867.

When the National Park Service (NPS) acquired the 444-acre site in 1966, grass covered the entire area. Low ridges and mounds defined where the palisade walls and buildings once stood. The NPS reconstructed part of the National Historic Landmark Fort Union Trading Post, including the enclosing palisade walls and two stone bastions, the Bourgeois (manager's) House, Indian trade house, a bell tower, and kitchen between 1985 and 1991. Excavation and reconstruction work continues. The extensive surrounding grasslands preserve an authentic mid-nineteenth-century setting. The Bourgeois House contains a visitor center and museum, with extensive displays of Fort Union and American Fur Company artifacts.

The plan of the reconstructed fort is laid out nearly due north and south, a sturdy 20-foot timber palisade enclosing a quadrangle 220 by 240 feet. Rugged enough to withstand storm or attack, the framework of 12-inch-square hewn timbers, resting on a 12-inch hewn sill placed on a stone foundation and flush exterior surface of stone and timber supports an 8-foot-wide plank gallery. Small huts or houses and stables were built in some places under the gallery.

Freight wagons and the trading tribes and trappers used the main gate facing south and the Missouri River. Inside the main gate a second gate created a reception room for trading without permitting entry to the main enclosure. Another gate on the north side opened to the prairie. Imposing two-story, 24-foot-square, 30-foot-tall whitewashed stone bastions at the northeast and southwest corners of the palisade wall, mounted with cannon and roof level sentry walks, served as watchtowers and defensive positions.

At the north end of the quadrangle stands the impressive, two-story Bourgeois House, white clapboard exterior and red roof proclaiming the center of the American

Outer gate

Fur Company trading empire, and behind it, a bell tower, and kitchen. Wood framed of poplar with exterior plank clapboard and double-hung windows with exterior wood shutters, today's Bourgeois House exterior color scheme is historically accurate: white-painted exterior walls; green shutters; porch and widow's walk columns blue and railings red; picket fence, balcony, and widow's walk spindles white; and red-painted wood shake-shingle roof. The reconstruction represents the house's appearance in 1851 and includes period furniture. Exhibits and an information center are also present.

Other structures included shops for the blacksmith, tinsmith, and carpenters, an icehouse, and enclosures for horses and cattle. The powder magazine protecting the fort's gunpowder supply is 18 by 25 feet in plan, with 4-foot-thick whitewashed limestone walls at the base ascending on the interior to form a semicircular arch, 6 feet thick at the top of the arch covered by an 18-inch layer of stones and gravel. Foundations of two long, low buildings on the west and east sides of the enclosure stood free of the palisades, housing employees, retail store, and storerooms.

During the summer months, reenactors in period clothing interpret the site as employees of the American Fur Trading Company. Every June—usually on Father's Day weekend—the Fort Union Rendezvous once again fills the plain outside the fort with a tepee village and traditionally dressed traders display and trade tools, equipment, and handcrafted items.

Knife River Indian Villages National Historic Site

Located in the central part of the state near Stanton, Mercer County, North Dakota

→ www.nps.gov/knri

→ The park is located one half-mile north of Stanton, North Dakota, on County Road 37, a one hour drive northwest of Bismarck, North Dakota, and one-and-a-half hour's drive southwest of Minot, North Dakota.

Modern visitor center

Tribes of Hidatsa (referred to as the "Minne tarees" by Lewis and Clark and other contemporaries), Mandan, and Arikara Indians settled on terraces above the Missouri and Knife Rivers in what is now western central North Dakota in fortified villages of ingenious, domed timber and earthlodge dwellings. Permanent lodges in the Knife River Indian Villages National Historic Site area are estimated from years 1300 to 1845 when the site was abandoned. Now seen as a series of circular depressions 3 feet deep and 30- to 60-feet in diameter, the remains of three villages are located within the national historic site: Hidatsa Village (Big Hidatsa Site, 110 depressions), just north of a bend in the Knife River; and farther south, along the west bank of the river's meandering course,

Awatixa Village (Sakakawea Site, 31 depressions) and Awatixa Xi'e Village (Lower Hidatsa Site, 51 depressions).

An accurate and full-scale reproduction of an earthlodge with authentic furnish-

Hidatsa Village on the Knife River, George Catlin
(courtesy NPS)

Reconstructed earthlodge

ings is near the visitor center, sympathetic in design to the Hidatsa and Mandan traditions. The three village sites and the prairie grass and woodland surroundings can be experienced along ranger-guided walks in the summer or self-guided hiking trails to the village sites. The Northern Plains Indian Culture Fest in the last weekend of July each year and demonstrations throughout the summer interpret Indian village life.

The Knife River earthlodge is typical of the circular structures built from 30 feet to up to 90 feet in diameter on tamped ground. The interior is a head-swiveling intricate log framework forming the dome-like interior. Structural supports and hanging hides "zone" the interior for a variety of family uses. The major delineator of interior space is a central "cube" outlined by four 18-inch central log columns topped by four 16- to 18-inch beams. The four columns, traditionally representing the four pillars supporting the dome of the sky, compass points or four winds, were believed to be alive and prayed to and decorated with cloth offerings. Smaller diameter log rafters radiate downward from below the central smokehole opening, resting on the beams and a perimeter framework of twelve 6- to 8-inch-diameter log beams and columns. Completing the enclosing framework are split logs slanting from the outer log beams down to the ground. Willow branches are placed on top of the rafters and packed with 5 to 6 inches of sod creating the dome-like effect. A bullboat was left on the roof and propped on a paddle over the smokehole to keep out the rain. The lodge usually lasted eight to twelve years.

The furnished earthlodge is an authentic interior, representing Hidatsa daily life. A partition of upright narrow wooden posts formed a log vestibule. Inside, a buffalo hide kept the elements from entering. Surprisingly bright inside, daylight entering from a central smokehole splashes over the logs, hanging hides, and implements of daily life.

The furnished reproduction Hidatsa earthlodge at Knife River Indian Villages National Historic Site is one of several examples in the area, including those at Fort Abraham Lincoln State Park south of Mandan, across the Missouri from Bismarck, North Dakota.

Theodore Roosevelt National Park

The South Unit and Elkhorn Ranch Site are located in and north of Medora, Billings County, North Dakota. The North Unit is located fifteen miles south of Watford City, McKenzie County, North Dakota.

→   www.nps.gov/thro

→   There are three separate park units (South Unit, Elkhorn Ranch Site, and North Unit). The South Unit entrance and South Unit visitor center are located in Medora, just off Interstate 94 (Exits 23 and 27) and 135 miles west of Bismarck, North Dakota. The Painted Canyon Visitor Center is located seven miles east of Medora just off Interstate 94 at Exit 32. The North Unit entrance is located fifteen miles south of Watford City along US 85. The distance between Medora at the South Unit and the North Unit is seventy miles via Interstate 94 and US 85. The Elkhorn Ranch is thirty-five miles north of Medora via the South Unit Scenic Loop Drive and the dirt East River Road. An alternate forty-five mile route bypasses an occasionally flooded Little Missouri River ford. Check at one of the park visitor centers about road conditions and instructions on how to reach this unit.

Maltese Cross Ranch cabin

Theodore Roosevelt National Park is named for the twenty-sixth president who actively ranched in the Little Missouri River Badlands of western North Dakota in 1884–1887, prior to being elected president. It is the place that transformed him, where he developed conservationist concerns for the land and its wildlife, emerging as a major figure in the conservation of our nation's resources. He wrote: "I would not have been President, had it not been for my experience in North Dakota."

The park contains a variety of badlands landscapes: eroded sedimentary layers of sandstone, sillstone, bentonite clay, and coal in a confusion of weathered landforms carved by wind and rain, their tops level with the surrounding prairies, is exposed in strata—brown, ash gray, yellow, and salmon. There are canyons, caprocks, buttes, and a petrified forest. Abundant wildlife includes feral horses and herds of bison and elk. Bighorn sheep and longhorn steer reside in the North Unit. Historic structures in the South Unit include the Maltese Cross Cabin and three Peaceful Valley Ranch buildings, plus structures built by emergency relief agencies in the 1930s. Civilian Conservation Corps (CCC) structures in the North Unit include stone and log pylons, picnic shelters, and a viewing shelter. The Elkhorn Ranch site is presently undeveloped; neither the ranch house nor any other ranch buildings remain at the site today.

The Maltese Cross Ranch cabin—once the center for Roosevelt's Chimney Butte Ranch (also known as the Maltese Cross Ranch)—has been relocated from its original site in the wooded badlands of the Little Missouri River six miles south of Medora, to a rail fence enclosure adjacent to the South Unit visitor center. Named for the cattle brand of the operation in which Roosevelt bought the major interest on his first trip to Dakota Territory in 1883, this cabin was his home in 1884 and 1885.

North Unit River Bend overlook of Little Missouri River

The simple cabin is a dramatic contrast with the future president's privileged life in Manhattan and the "rough and ready" western lifestyle. More elaborate than the local one-room log buildings, considered somewhat of a "mansion" in its day, with wooden floors and three separate rooms (kitchen, living room, and Roosevelt's bedroom) divided by vertical-board partitions and whitewashed interior. The steeply pitched roof covered with 16-inch-long red cedar shingles, unusual on the northern plains, created an upstairs sleeping loft for the ranch hands. The cabin is approximately 18 by 24 feet in plan and 15 feet at the gabled roof ridge. Corners are saddle notched and chinked with bright white-tinted Portland cement. The cabin's hand-hewn ponderosa pine logs had been cut as ties and pilings for the Northern Pacific Railroad and floated down the Little Missouri River.

A prolific writer, Roosevelt spent many lamp-lit hours laboring at the desk in the living room recording his memoirs and reminiscences of badlands life. He often came home from a long day in the saddle to spend hours at the hutch in the living room that doubled as a library. A foldout writing table is on display that came from the Elkhorn Ranch House. The hutch and writing table represent two of Roosevelt's prime passions—reading and writing. The traditional rocking chair in the living room, in all probability Roosevelt's, was his favorite piece of furniture. A wicker-lined canvas clothing trunk belonging to him sits in the bedroom. Other items not belonging to Roosevelt are from the same time period and would be typical furnishings of the day. The Maltese Cross Ranch Cabin is open for self-guided tours September to May. Ranger-guided tours are offered during the summer months.

Peaceful Valley Ranch in the South Unit is the exception of ranches removed from the park. It was spared to serve as an interpretive site for open range ranching; the surviving ranch buildings today are an ensemble of wood-frame and log buildings used by the NPS and trailride concessioner.

National Park Service (NPS) pylons, picnic shelters, fee station, culverts, and overlook shelters built during the 1930s by CCC crews working from NPS designs can be admired for their ingratiating lack of pretentiousness. Built of local sandstone and timber, the River Bend Overlook Shelter in the North Unit provides dramatic and unparalleled views of the Little Missouri River Badlands landscape.

South Dakota

Rockies and
Plains

★ PIERRE

○ Mount Rushmore N MEM

Jewel Cave NM ○

○ Wind Cave NP

Jewel Cave National Monument

Located in the Black Hills of southwest South Dakota, west of Custer, Custer County, South Dakota

→ www.nps.gov/jeca

→ The main visitor center and cave entrance is thirteen miles west of Custer, South Dakota on US 16, twenty-four miles east of Newcastle, Wyoming, on US 16 and fifty-four miles from Rapid City, South Dakota via US 16 and 16/385.

Ranger cabin

This "gem" of a park, tucked away in the Black Hills in South Dakota's southwest corner boasts over 140 miles of surveyed cave passages, recognized as the second longest in the world with a vast area yet to be explored. Jewel Cave was named for the many jewel-like formations of calcite crystals (called dogwood spar), extraordinary masses of interconnected prisms in a rainbow of colors ranging from black and white to brown, red, orange, yellow, green, and even lavender. Stalagmites reach up from the floor and stalactites hang from the ceilings and a wide variety of speleothems include draperies, frostwork, flowstone, boxwork, and hydromagnesite balloons.

Here, the main attraction is the vast cave complex of shimmering formations. An interesting historic structure in the park is located 0.9 miles west of the main visitor center on a commanding rise of land. A restored Civilian Conservation Corps 1935 cabin built to a National Park Service (NPS) design serves as the center for summer time interpretive programs and the start of the Lantern Tour to the original gated cave entrance. The cabin's design was lauded in the 1938 NPS *Park and Recreation Structures* (Princeton Architectural Press, 1999):

> Being almost a miniature in scale, this cabin is something of a concentrated essence of a log cabin structural technique. Logs are employed for the puncheon floor and steps of the porch,

both details which, in modern log cabins, usually compromise with more modern less sturdy building methods.

The three-room one-story log cabin is modest in size, approximately 34 by 24 feet in a T-plan. The main structure under intersecting gable end roofs contains a living room with finely detailed stone hearth and chimney, a kitchen, and a bedroom. A pair of restrooms executed in the same detailing as the main structure under a lower roof extends from the building's west end. A shallow-pitch gable roof of cedar shakes is capped by a log ridgepole. A shed roof extends from the ridge over a raised porch of half-log flooring. Restored by the NPS, the distinctive white-chinked walls of saddle-notched corners with whittle-ends extending 24 inches rest on a stone foundation. The porch detailing of log columns, railing, and flooring is sympathetic to overall building detail and execution.

Although of secondary interest to Jewel Cave in a park visit, the cabin is a superb example of rustic design and construction. The structure embodies the NPS principles of compatibility with the environment through the use of simple forms and natural materials. Indeed, it forms a stark contrast to the uncertain form and materials of the Mission 66 visitor center design with an array of volumes in polygonal forms and sloped vertical metal siding.

Mount Rushmore National Memorial

Located in the southwest corner of South Dakota, southwest of Rapid City and near Keystone, South Dakota, Pennington County

→   www.nps.gov/moru

→   Visitors traveling on Interstate 90 should exit at Rapid City and follow Highway 16 southwest to Keystone and then Highway 244 to Mount Rushmore. Visitors coming from the south should follow Highway 385 north to Highway 244, which is the road leading to the memorial.

Mount Rushmore is an American icon extolled for its stirring imagery. Created out of a granite outcropping in South Dakota's Black Hills, the four faces of George Washington, Thomas Jefferson, Theodore Roosevelt, and Abraham Lincoln combine art and engineering in a sublime experience, enhanced by extensive new visitor facilities. Sculptor Gutzon Borglum and 400 workers sculpted the 60-foot busts on the 5,725-foot Mount Rushmore between 1927 and 1941 to represent the birth, growth, development, and expansion of the United States. Dedicated as a National Memorial in 1925, the 1,278-acre park joined the National Park System in 1939.

Today's visitor to Mount Rushmore National Monument is greeted by visitors' facilities, completed in 1994, of finely cut granite paving, gateways, exterior building walls, and columns aligned in a processional pathway focused on the monumental faces high on the mountain. Controversial for its formality, in contrast to the rustic arrangement of paths that historically approached the vista indirectly, earlier visitors had a sense of a naturalistic environment without the ostentation of omnipresent granite. This modern version of a formal imperial entrance opened in 1998, moving the more than two million

Mount Rushmore entrance gateway

visitors per year up from below ground parking structures, through the entrance gate with opposing information center and restroom buildings, and onto a wide walkway, past a pair of rectilinear gateways with a bust of Borglum set in a sidewall. To the sides of the gateway are concession buildings containing a restaurant and gift shop.

The Presidential Trail, approximately one mile in total length, makes a loop from the Washington (south) side of the Grand View Terrace to the base of Mount Rushmore and back to the Lincoln (north) side of the Grand View Terrace. From the base of the mountain, stairs take visitors down to the Sculptor's Studio completed in 1940 as the second onsite studio at Mount Rushmore for Gutzon Borglum. The two-story structure, of rectangular plan with a gable roof, had a single purpose for the sculptor: a room with adequate floor space and ceiling height for the working plaster model and a window with an unimpeded view of the faces emerging on the mountain. The upper floor studio, open to knee-braced log roof trusses, log rafters and plank ceiling, has a wide floor to ceiling window facing the monument. The interior walls are vertical wood planking and a wide stone fireplace is set opposite the entrance. The lower floor exterior is a mix of stone and vertical wood planking. Large vertical logs are placed at each exterior corner and systems of smaller vertical logs are placed alongside the windows. The building currently houses Borglum's original plaster model of Mount Rushmore, a model for the Hall of Records, and a plaster mask of Lincoln used for closeup work on the mountain.

Visitors to the memorial come primarily to view the mountain's granite sculpture itself. Admission is always free. The distant view from the Grand View Terrace can be brought into closer focus from the Presidential Trail, circling to the base of the moun-

Gutzon Borglum's Sculptor's Studio   Studio interior

tain and to the Sculptor's Studio built under the direction of the artist. The dramatic story of Borglum and a crew of skilled stone carvers is told by Lincoln Borglum, the sculptor's son, in *Mount Rushmore: The Story Behind the Scenery* (KC Publications, 2005) and *The Carving of Mount Rushmore* by Rex Allen Smith (NY: Abbeville Press, 1985) and well worth reading before a visit.

Wind Cave National Park

Located in the southwestern corner of the state, near Custer, Custer County, South Dakota.

→   www.nps.gov/wica

→   The park entrance and visitor center are sixty miles south of Rapid City via US Route 79, US Route 36, and US Route 87. The park is twenty miles south of Custer and twenty miles west of Newcastle, Wyoming, on US Route 16 and US Route 385.

Wind Cave National Park, in the Black Hills of southwest South Dakota, contains one of the world's longest and most complex caves known for its outstanding display of boxwork, an unusual cave formation composed of thin calcite fins resembling honeycombs. Established as the seventh national park in 1903, the 28,295 acres of mixed-grass prairie and ponderosa pine forest sits over 111.50 miles (2004) of known cave—the sixth largest in the world—in just over one square mile of land, and includes a fine collection of National Park Service (NPS) depression-era historic structures.

The Wind Cave National Park administrative district offers a rich cultural landscape and concentration of buildings dating from the park's establishment in 1903 and NPS structures built by Civilian Conservation Corps (CCC) in the 1930s. Some of the structures have been modified externally and most have had significant modifications made to the interiors, although the 1930s character is retained.

Set in a wooded and landscaped area that absorbs the visual impact of the access road and parking areas for visitors and staff, the complex of wood framed structures has a charming continuity of mass and form suggesting English cottage influences,

Wind Cave visitor center

united by a scale low in height with yellow-tan stucco walls and uniform pitch gable roofs generally flush with the gable ends. Foundation walls, chimneys, and terrace retaining walls are rough cut random ashlar laid sandstone. Rough-hewn timber columns and rafters, eave and window trim, and rough cut lapped board gable ends are stained dark brown. The CCC walkways and trails, retaining walls, signs, and footbridge between the visitor center and elevator entrance building complete the cultural landscape conceived in a 1930s NPS master plan and executed with sensitivity, sympathetic to the natural colors and materials of the site.

The visitor center was designed and built in 1936 to blend in with a stream valley to its rear and to provide the feeling of a natural approach to the cave entrance from the building's lower level. The building is perched on the valley's edge overlooking the walk north to the original "natural cave entrance" at the point of cave discovery and south to the modern elevator entrance building. The building's one-story profile from the visitor entrance level has a pleasant residential scale unobtrusive in the setting. The original structure, H-shaped in plan (approximately 115 by 24 feet), contained wings for administration and concession joined by an open loggia. In 1980, a skillfully designed major addition enclosed the loggia, added space to the building's downhill side, and modified the interior. Infilling of the loggia provided a new entrance to the visitor center. An original covered porch with rough adzed 8-inch by 8-inch timber posts with knee brackets remained after the addition.

Modern access to the caves is by elevators descending 212 feet, housed in the Elevator Building about 225 yards south of the visitor center. Completed in 1938, the structure expresses the basic function of transporting visitors down to the cave with

Superintendent's residence

a three-story central section housing the elevator, and one-story wings containing the transformer room and public areas. A one-story exterior loggia with sandstone terrace and retaining walls, framed by sandstone piers and rough-adzed timbers and knee braces, is a generous space leading to the building entrance.

Approximately 200 yards north of the visitor center, accessible by a footpath from the building's lower level, is the historic cave entrance, discovered in 1881. In the 1890s blasting enlarged the small entrance. A yet newer entrance was constructed in 1936 by the CCC with a gentle grade inlaid with large stones, creating a rock-lined tunnel from the outside to its juncture with the natural rock of the cave. The historic flavor of the 1936 entrance remains, although it is masked by a revolving door installed in 1991 to slow artificial air exchange.

Located on the hillside opposite the visitor center are a row of residences and NPS support buildings, built between 1931 and 1939, all sharing common design elements of yellow-tan stucco and brown trim, random ashlar laid sandstone foundation walls and chimneys, gable ends with plank horizontal siding, and uniform roof pitches. Mature trees and spacious lawns create a pleasant ambiance.

The administrative district structures in this ensemble of rustic architecture include residence and support buildings for NPS staff. Please respect the residents' privacy. Cave tours and tickets for ranger-guided tours varying from one to four hours are conducted year-round, except for Thanksgiving, Christmas, and New Year's Day. Exhibits and orientation programs can be viewed at the visitor center. In addition to the underground experience, the visitor can travel the park's scenic drvies and self-guided hiking trails in the surrounding prairie of rolling hills, grasslands, and forests.

Wyoming

Rockies and Plains

Devils Tower National Monument

Located in northeast Wyoming, twenty-two miles west of Sundance, Crook County, Wyoming

→   www.nps.gov/deto

→   The monument is located in the extreme northeast corner of Wyoming. Visitors traveling east on Interstate 90 take Exit 153 at Moorcroft, Wyoming, and drive thirty-four miles northeast on Wyoming 14 to the park. From west on Interstate 90 take Exit 187 at Sundance, Wyoming, and drive twenty-nine miles northwest to the park. The drive west from Belle Fourche, South Dakota (fifty-two miles on South Dakota 34 and Wyoming 24) is the most scenic with stunning approach views of Devils Tower.

Devils Tower

With an image inspired by the 1977 film *Close Encounters of the Third Kind*, the anticipated first glimpse of the soaring rock formation is rewarding, as it is in the lyric voice of N. Scott Momaday. "A dark mist lay over the black hills, and the land was like iron," he wrote. "At the top of the ridge I caught sight of Devils Tower upthrust against the gray sky as if in the birth of time the core of the earth had broken through its crust and the motion of the world was begun." Located on the northwest fringe of the South Dakota Black Hills, Devils Tower is a geological anomaly of the plains, mysterious and majestic. Geologists generally agree that it formed underground about sixty million years ago in the Tertiary Period, when a mass of molten magma pushed up through sedimentary layers and cooled into a hard, igneous rock called phonolite porphyry.

   Most visitors to the tower come to explore the seemingly extraterrestrial formation and to enjoy activities such as hiking, camping, and observing the wildlife. The prairie dog town near the park entrance is an entrancing sight of the ever-alert creatures, erect until danger is detected and then scurrying into the mounded entrances. Historic structures built in the 1930s by the Civilian Conservation Corps (CCC) are the entrance checking station and the visitors center complex's two buildings. A section of the 1893 tower-scaling ladder is also visible.

The National Park Service's (NPS) rustic Entrance Station, completed in 1939, is a small rectangular one-story log building located just inside the monument boundary. An 8-foot by 14-foot entrance porch over a flagstone entry is set into the building's southeast corner, distinctive by the logs that gracefully step upward and in from the sill log and extend out again at the interior ceiling line. The original structure, designed to double as an entrance station and ranger residence, was modified in 1999 to convert the living room and kitchen into two offices.

The custodian/superintendent's residence and old administration building are located in the Old Headquarters Area Historic District. Built in 1931, the L-plan, former residence/administration building is a log structure appearing as a single story building from the headquarters plaza. Remodeled in the 1990s, the structure now serves as offices for NPS and Natural History Association staff. Today's visitor center, built in 1935 by the CCC as an administration building, served as the park's headquarters and museum until 1959. The main floor now contains visitor services, including an office, small bookstore, and an exhibit area. The exhibit area has exposed log walls with a polished patina; exposed log beams with in-filled ceiling; wrought-iron ceiling and wall light fixtures; and an end wall of Tower-colored stone chimney that narrows from base to top. A large 16-foot floor to ceiling window in the exhibit area provides a view of the Tower.

Certainly qualifying as the most unusual historical structure in the park is the ladder located on the southeast side of Devils Tower first used for the 1893 scaling by local ranchers William Rogers and Willard Ripley. Difficult to spot in photographs and best observed through a telescope, sometime in the 1930s the lower 100 feet was removed for safety reasons (to prevent climbers from using it). The ladder's remaining portion now visible is 170 feet of restored 20 to 30-inch-long wooden pegs driven into a continuous vertical crack between two stone columns, braced at the ends by a plank side rail of 12-foot lengths of 1-inch by 4-inch lumber and attached by nails and/or bailing wire. A restoration by NPS staff in the summer of 1972, a challenge to modern climbers even using professional climbing equipment and rappeling techniques, was a testimony to the challenges facing the two Wyoming ranchers.

Vertical columns of Devils Tower

Fort Laramie National Historic Site

Located in southeast Wyoming, three miles southwest of the town of Fort Laramie, Goshen County, Wyoming

→ www.nps.gov/fola

→ The park is reached from Wyoming 26, twenty-eight miles from Exit 92 on Interstate 25 and twenty-one miles west of Torrington, Wyoming. In the town of Fort Laramie, take Wyoming 160 three miles south to the park entrance.

Fort Laramie Captain's Quarters

Fort Laramie, with nearly a dozen structures restored to their original appearance and other ghost-like standing walls, is legendary in its role in America's movement westward for over five decades as a landmark and way station. Through its gates passed everyone who trekked across the plains: trappers, traders, mountain men, immigrants, missionaries, adventurers, forty-niners, homesteaders, Pony Express riders, and soldiers knew Fort Laramie. The location was an important place for Northern Plains tribes as a trading and annuity site. The short-lived peace treaty of 1868 was signed here. Today's visitor can pause and absorb the rich history of Fort Laramie National Historic Site with its uneven but broad collection of buildings (the majority are of lime grout concrete walls), ranging from accurately restored and furnished military quarters to standing building remnants.

The commonly held image of a western fort is that of an enclosure surrounded by a wall or stockade surmounted by watchtowers. Fort Laramie, however, was typical of the open stockade plains military post, always an open fort that depended upon its location and its garrison of troops for security. The setting today of the sprawling fort looks much as it did over a century and a quarter ago. After the Northern Plains tribes were subdued, the fort was decommissioned in 1890. No town was founded here,

Cavalry Barracks, fourth graders on parade   Old Bedlam

fortuitously leaving an unspoiled setting suitable for the fort's partial preservation by homesteaders purchasing and converting some structures to new uses.

A self-guided walking tour of the structures and standing walls begins at the visitor center in the Commissary Storehouse north of the buildings facing the parade grounds. The tour continues to the adjacent restored Cavalry Barracks, to the Post Trader's Store and Complex, and proceeds to buildings and standing walls facing the parade ground and outlying buildings, including the Old Guardhouse (1866), and Old Bakery (1876) adjacent to the Commissary Storehouse. The tour can continue to the remnants of the Hospital (1874) on a hill to the north.

The Cavalry Barracks was built in 1874 north of the parade ground to meet the need of more housing during the Indian Wars. Fort Laramie's largest building and the fort's earliest lime grout concrete structure, it is the post's only enlisted men's barracks to survive intact. The two-story gabled roof structure is 26 by 270-feet in plan with a 12-foot-wide verandah along the length of the building, added in 1882-83. The barracks provided quarters, kitchens, mess halls, washrooms, reading rooms, and other facilities for two, sixty-man companies of troops. The north end of the barracks building is currently being used adaptively for park support facilities, but the south end is restored and refurnished to the summer of 1876 when it would have housed Company K of the Second Cavalry.

Southwest of the Cavalry Barracks is the Post Trader (Sutler) Store and Complex (the title "Sutler" was used until shortly after the Civil War when it was changed to Post Trader). Built in sections between 1849 and 1883 and restored to its 1876 appearance, the one-and-one-half-story gabled roof complex is a joined pair of structures (approximately 75 feet long and a combined width of 60 feet) built in three sections, an original of adobe brick walls, an addition with stone walls, and another addition in lime grout concrete.

The two-story mansard roofed structure, T-shaped in plan with projecting dormers and lime grout concrete walls known as the Lt. Colonel's House (Burt House) was the last officer's quarters erected at Fort Laramie in 1884. Aside from the commanding officer's house, it is the only single-family dwelling on the post. Most officers and their families lived in duplexes. Although occupied by several officers and their families at various times, it has been restored to 1887–1888 when it was the home of Lt. Colonel Andrew Sheridan Burt, his wife Elizabeth, and their children.

Next in line is the Surgeon's Quarters, an officer's duplex that was constructed in 1875 and refurnished to the years 1880–1882. The Victorian residence has a white sand finish lime plaster covering the T-shaped one-and-one-half story lime grout concrete structure. The parade ground facade, with center dormer, and a six-bay porch was scored originally with half-inch joints painted black to simulate stone coursing.

To many people the symbol of Fort Laramie, "Old Bedlam" (reputedly named after the character of the young officers' parties), was built in 1849 and is the oldest military building in Wyoming. The two-story structure with Greek Revival porch details and symmetrical wings, was originally designed to be a bachelor officers quarters, but served many other purposes during the fort's active years. For several years it was Post Headquarters. The central block, 35 by 56 feet with 9-foot-wide porches facing the parade ground, contains four rooms for bachelor officers' flanked by corridors and stairs on the first floor and the same plan on the second floor. On either side of the central block are two-story wings (16 by 26 feet in plan) covered by a shed roof extending from the main roof. A one-story rear wing with hipped roof contains four rooms with bachelor officers' rooms. Today's impressive structure was near collapse when acquired by the Naitonal Park Service in 1938. The superb restoration completed in 1964 was based on extensive research and even includes use of square-cut nails and oak dowels. Restoration and refurnishing of the first floor right side represents the bachelor officers' quarters in the 1850s

Old Guardhouse

Post Trader's store

and the left side as the Post Headquarters to its appearance in 1863–64.

The attractive, white-painted Captain's Quarters on the south side of the parade ground with three dormers and wrapped on three sides by wide porches was built in

1868–1870 as the Post Commanding Officers' Quarters. Converted into a duplex with two kitchen wings and verandahs for company grade officers, the U-shaped structure is a wood frame filled with adobe bricks and sheathed with vertical board-and-batten, interior wood framing with plaster walls over lath, and multilight double-hung sash windows. The building has been refurnished to its appearance in 1872.

Other restored structures are the Old Guardhouse (1866) on the bank of the Laramie River, a two-story (approximately 20 by 36 feet) gable roofed building with exterior walls of coursed rubble mixed with lime grout concrete; the New Guardhouse (36 by 50 feet in plan with a 20-foot-deep front porch), a one-story structure with lime grout concrete walls at the northeast corner of the parade ground; the one-story Old Bakery (1876) with lime grout concrete walls; and the one-story Commissary Storehouse (32 by 153 feet) built in 1883 with lime grout concrete walls.

The visitor has the opportunity for a glimpse of a bygone military era at Fort Laramie National Historic Site. Ranger-led and self-guided walking tours are available year-round (check for holiday schedules). In summer months period-clothed guides provide living-history reenactments depicting daily life at the fort when you may encounter a mountain man, cavalryman, a surgeon, a laundress, or an officer's wife.

Grand Teton National Park

In northwest Wyoming south of Yellowstone National Park and four miles north of Jackson, Teton County, Wyoming

→ www.nps.gov/grte

→ The Moose entrance station is thirteen miles north of Jackson, Wyoming, on US 26, 89, and 191. The Colter Bay Visitor Center is reached from Yellowstone National Park from the north via John D. Rockefeller, Jr., Memorial Parkway.

Grand Teton National Park is often acclaimed as the most glorious piece of scenery on the continent. The Teton Range completely dominates the landscape. Seen from a distance of one hundred miles or more, the mountain peaks appear as a wisp of clouds on the horizon; up close the dramatic mountain front looms over the valley. The Tetons are spectacularly different from other mountain ranges because they have no foothills, no softening foreground around the forty-mile-long concentration of the tallest peaks. Smaller than most parks but with a memorable landscape, it contains more scenery, more animals, and more recreational opportunities than many areas twice its size. This is a place rich in the historic lore of Native Americans, trappers, settlers, and homesteaders—a witness to the exploration, settlement, and exploitation that characterized the opening of the West.

The controversial and lengthy struggle to establish Grand Teton National Park has left as diverse a collection of buildings as exist in any national park. Overlays of development took place as homesteaders, dude ranchers, and the National Park Service (NPS) played out their roles in the transition from a valley settled under conditions of severe weather and isolation to one catering to tourism. Superimposed on

Chapel of the Transfiguration

the natural evolution of vernacular buildings and architecture are the NPS rustic style and the influence of John D. Rockefeller, Jr. Turn-of-the-century structures, built by homesteaders and ranchers, such as the Moulton barns on Mormon Row and Teton Science Schools (originally the Elbo Ranch) on Antelope Flats Road, or the Cunningham Ranch, were utilitarian log buildings. There is a pleasing uniformity in the prevailing log vernacular, built as an expedient for the homesteaders and ranchers and later adopted by the NPS and Rockefellers for preserving old buildings as well as for new structures. Cross-buck and rail fencing, overcoming the difficulty of digging postholes in the stony Jackson Hole soil, is a constant rustic theme seen throughout the valley.

Clusters of historic structures are seen in the areas of Moose Junction, Jenny Lake Visitor Center, and Jackson Lake Lodge. The new Craig Thomas Discovery and Visitor Center at Moose, which opened in summer 2007, is outside the consideration of a historical structure, however the superb design by Bohlin Cywinski Jackson is an admirable contemporary interpretation of the NPS rustic style.

A short walk from the park headquarters building is the Menor's Ferry Historic District. William D. Menor's homestead, built in 1894, was the first homestead settlement west of the Snake River. The Menor Cabin, smokehouse, and storehouse complex of true log construction is recognizable by the cabin's columned entrance porch and whitewashed walls gleaming in the sunlight. The complex of structures, rebuilt ferry station, and cableworks includes the Maud Noble Cabin outbuildings. The cabin was moved and rebuilt at the site in 1918.

The Murie Ranch Historic District, located in a meadow surrounded by forests on the west side of the Snake River a half-mile from Moose Junction, is a cluster of saddle-notch log buildings built originally as a homesteader's dude ranch and later served as the homes of the Murie families, distinguished contributors to the nation's conservation movement. Designated a National Historic Landmark, the ranch is the home of the Murie Center offering conservation related programs in conjunction with the NPS.

Also near the park headquarters building is the picturesque Chapel of the Trans-figuration three-structure log complex. The assemblage of structures offers a spiritual experience in the sequence of walking past cross-buck and rail fencing to the bell tower "entry arch," then into the modestly scaled chapel. Designed by C.B. Loomis and built by the Episcopal Church in 1927, construction foreshadowed NPS design guidelines; evident are elements of chisel-end saddle-notched logs with sapling exterior chinking repeated in other valley structures. The chapel's worship space is a serene area, T-shaped in plan, with a lower-roofed shed porch entering into the higher roofed main chapel open to a plank ceiling. Side windows, covered by a wood-strip diagonal lattice, light the interior of exposed log walls varnished in a low sheen. Two sidewall stained glass windows splash vibrant color onto rows of wooden benches capped by unpeeled logs. The visitor is induced into a spiritual experience by the view through a picture window behind the altar that frames the Cathedral group of mountains.

Another chapel of more recent origin is the Chapel of the Sacred Heart on Teton Park Road south of Jackson Lake Lodge. The rustic Roman Catholic chapel, built in 1955 and remodeled and expanded in 1969, and recently remodeled, is in the NPS rustic style, constructed of chisel-end logs battered from bottom to top at corners. Distinctive pole chinking is used on exterior walls. The main sanctuary is approxi-

Private ranch on Snake River

Menor's Ferry

mately 45 by 30 feet in plan; overhead are exposed log scissor trusses with wrought iron brackets. A stained glass rose window in the wall behind the altar frames a view of the Teton Range.

The nearby Beaver Creek residential area for NPS staff contains fine examples of the NPS rustic style, including the superintendent's residence. Built by Civilian Conservation Corps workers in 1934, the residence is a cornucopia of finely executed details in the context of a well-proportioned and scaled structure. The two-story L-shaped structure's building mass is visually subdued to one story by use of a dormer and a large gable perpendicular to the main roof. A distinctive feature is the double row of chisel-end logs projecting across the second floor. Please remember to respect the privacy of residents in the Beaver Creek residential area.

Grand Teton Range

The Jenny Lake Visitor Center complex at the south end of a one-way loop contains restored historic structures now used as the visitor center and as a ranger station, and a recently constructed store. The Jenny Lake Visitor Center was built in 1931 for Harrison Crandall's photography business. The restored building combines the original store and a bedroom grocery store addition built in the 1950s. The building is identified by the herringbone-patterned gable end over the front entrance and the log monitor on the roof ridge. The restored Jenny Lake Ranger Station is the former Lee Mangus Cabin built as a homestead sometime prior to 1929. Acquired by the NPS in 1930 and moved from Cottonwood Creek to the present location where it initially served as the Jenny Lake Museum and visitor center. Excellent craftsmanship is shown in the corner saddle-notching, diagonal logs in the gable end, exposed rafters, and roof framing. A simple detail that adds to the continuity of valley architecture is the use of saplings for exterior joint chinking.

Jackson Lake Lodge's location and architecture has stirred controversy since completion in 1955. It is difficult to relate this Gilbert Stanley Underwood design to any of his earlier projects, such as the Ahwahnee Hotel, Bryce and Zion lodges, or Timberline Lodge, which were traditionally in close harmony with the landscape. In contrast, the lodge's design followed architectural trends of the day and the prevailing international style. The starkness of the Bauhaus-inspired lodge's textured and stained wood-formed concrete exteriors and organization of window openings fueled the debate surrounding log-and-stone buildings sympathetic with the landscape versus clear statements of contemporary design made of modern materials. The lodge was designated a National Historic Landmark in 2003.

Today, the lodge's severity is tempered by Underwood's planned landscaping of pines, aspens, and native bushes that surround the building. A porte-cochere entrance leads past ground level business offices through spacious public spaces to the second level lounges, meeting rooms, and dining rooms to accommodate busloads of arriving travelers. There are 348 guest cottage rooms located on either side of the entry spaces and thirty-seven guest rooms in the main lodge building. Arrival at the upper two-story lounge features 60-foot picture windows offering a stunning panorama of the Teton Mountain Range, as well as a collection of Native American artifacts and Western art. Underwood's vocabulary of dramatic structural framing for large spaces is seen in the enormous truss over the upper level lounge; however, it is framed in steel unlike his peeled log examples of twenty-five years earlier.

Author Robert Betts offered a poetic description of the Teton Range "…the Cathedral Group, and it takes only one look to see why it was given this name: Chartres multiplied by six, a choir of shimmering granite spires soaring high above the transept and nave of the valley below." Truly awe-inspiring, Grand Teton National Park offers both an extraordinary scenic outdoor experience and a treasure trove of historic buildings.

Yellowstone National Park

Located primarily in northwest Wyoming with portions in south-central Montana and southeast Idaho, Park and Teton Counties, Wyoming

→ www.nps.gov/yell

→ There are five park entrances. To reach the east entrance, take US 20 from Cody; northeast entrance, take US 212 from Interstate 90 at Billings, Montana or Wyoming 296 from Cody, Wyoming; north entrance, take US 89 from Interstate 90 at Livingston, Montana; west entrance, take US 191 from Bozeman, Montana, or US 20 from Idaho Falls, Idaho; south entrance, take US 89 from Jackson, Wyoming.

Old Faithful Geyser and Old Faithful Inn

Yellowstone National Park is so rich in scenic, geological, and biological attractions that even the most sophisticated traveler is moved by this immense landscape—majestic and diverse—filled with thermal extravagances, mountain ranges that form the Continental

Divide, pristine lakes, impressive canyons and waterfalls, and plentiful game. Established in 1872, the challenge to manage the first national park's vast preserve and provide services for tourists led to the development of a wide assortment of buildings of varying quality and design. Among them are some of the finest examples of National Park Service (NPS) rustic architecture. The U.S. Army left its mark at Fort Yellowstone. Concessioners built grand hotels, several of which survive today, including the iconic Old Faithful Inn, often imitated but never surpassed.

Beginning at Gardiner, Montana, in the north or Grand Teton National Park to the south, major points of interest are linked by a figure-eight loop road joined to outside highways by five entrance roads. A driving tour on the loop road beginning at the North Entrance and ending at the Northeast Entrance takes visitors to Yellowstone's highlights, including the buildings of special architectural interest.

Gardiner Entrance

The park entrance at Gardiner at the beginning of the twentieth century was in a bleak, barren setting, and the impending presidential visit set plans in motion for a gateway structure suitable for the nation's first national park. Robert C. Reamer (designer of Lake Hotel and Old Faithful Inn) developed a monumental design for a 1903 visit of President Theodore Roosevelt that would be tall enough to be seen from the Gardiner railroad depot and wide enough to allow the passage of two stagecoaches. The design called for two soaring massive square columns of roughly dressed, oversized stones set in uniform courses 50 feet high, and 20 feet apart, framing an arch with a crown 30 feet above the ground. Wing walls of the same stone 12 feet high extend from both sides and terminate in columns similar in proportion to the main columns. A concrete tablet above the arch's keystone bears an inscription from the statute establishing the park: "For the Benefit and Enjoyment of the People." The Gardiner area now contains bridges, old rail beds, and other historic structures.

Mammoth Hot Springs and Fort Yellowstone

Further along at the north loop end of the road, the Mammoth Hot Springs area contains a historic hotel and Fort Yellowstone. The sculptured terraces of Mammoth Hot Springs were the earliest attractions at Yellowstone and they became the site of the park's first tourist accommodations. The present Mammoth Hot Springs Hotel and Cabins by Robert C. Reamer drew upon references from contemporary Art Deco style. In 1935 he designed a complex incorporating a wing of the older National Hotel and added a restaurant, recreation hall, and guest cabins. Using classical proportions, simplicity of form, large window openings, and stone-colored stucco walls to contrast with wood trim painted a cream color, the design for the main building's exteriors is held together by rhythms of fluted engaged columns without caps or bases. Dormer windows flush with the restaurant's upper walls recall classical elements, with pediments and fluted columns as window jambs. The restaurant's green-and-white-striped awnings harmonize with the colors, creating a jaunty atmosphere.

Arrival of the U.S. Army in 1886 to guard the park inaugurated thirty years of military control. Selecting Mammoth Hot Springs for park headquarters the Corps of Engineers constructed Fort Yellowstone's roads, sidewalks, and utility systems. Early buildings were utilitarian structures of frame construction with red metal-shingled roofs. Officers' Row had four wood-framed duplexes built in the year of the Army's arrival, which began the distinctive group of buildings facing what was to be a parade ground.

The U.S. Engineer's Office, designed by Reed and Stern of St. Paul and constructed in 1903 was an exotic departure from the usual frame buildings. Cube-shaped, it was called the "Pagoda" because of its bell-cast roof eaves. The battered sandstone walls, tapering from a thickness of 2 feet at the ground to 1 foot at the eaves, the wide overhangs, projecting decorative rafter tails, and hipped green tile roof created an imposing presence at the corner of the parade ground. Built in a Georgian Revival style, the 1905 Post Exchange was a striking departure from the other sandstone buildings with red tiled roofs. The building has a colonnaded entrance portico with four evenly spaced columns on piers, which support a gabled pediment with a circular window. An elegantly arched transom spans the main entrance doors and a pair of sidelights with a fan patterned in leaded mullions.

A surge of construction in 1909 added the seven stone buildings that now dominate Fort Yellowstone. Scottish masons used sandstone quarried nearby for a bachelor officers' quarters (now the Horace N. Albright Visitor Center), a three-story barracks (the NPS Administration Building), two residences, two large cavalry stables, and a combined blacksmith shop and stable. The buildings were symmetrical forms with red clay tile hipped roofs or hipped roofs with monitors. Undressed random ashlar sandstone

Old Faithful Inn

walls were contrasted with dressed stone lintels and sills. The chapel (1913) was the last building constructed by the U.S. Army at Fort Yellowstone. A late Gothic Revival design of coursed ashlar sandstone from a local quarry complements the nearby stone buildings. The steeply pitched slate roof, the stone buttresses, the arched window in the front elevation, the exposed truss system supporting the roof, and the oak furnishings all reflected the popular style.

Other historic structures in the Mammoth area are the Childs House designed by Robert C. Reamer in the prairie style and built in 1908, and the Haynes Picture Shop facing the parade ground, a photographic studio used by the Haynes family.

Old Faithful Area

It is fitting that Yellowstone, the first national park, should contain a tour-de-force icon of rustic design and craftsmanship. Situated in a forest clearing atop a gentle rise overlooking the Firehole River and its namesake, Old Faithful Geyser, Old Faithful Inn is unequivocally tied to its natural surroundings. The Inn's prodigious scale at nearly 700 feet in length, informal massing, and great, pitched gable roof architecturally echoes the shapes of the surrounding mountain peaks. One of the few surviving log hotels in the United States, the National Historic Landmark inn is a masterpiece of stylized design and fine workmanship. The asymmetrical composition and rich detailing defies criticism. Dormers supported by exotically bent log brackets, and unpredictable interior spaces result in an idiosyncratic design. The overall effect is similar to the experience of touring the park—surprises are around every corner. The structure has survived more than one hundred years of use, earthquakes, and forest fires, and has inspired rustic architecture throughout the world.

Seattle architect Robert C. Reamer was twenty-nine years old when the Yellowstone Park Association hired him in 1902 to design a lodge for the Old Faithful area. Construction got under way in 1903 and pushed through the winter for a spring 1904

Old Faithful lobby fireplace   Soaring lobby interior

opening. Key to understanding the inn is Reamer's siting and extravagant use of space and materials. The architect's vision was ingenious. The use of lodgepole pine logs in all their forms is unrestrained: peeled, unpeeled, varnished, and unvarnished. Ninety-two feet from floor to peak the soaring seven-story lobby and its massive stone masonry chimney are unique—an astonishing, cavernous space to be experienced from many levels and vantage points. By day, dormer windows admit shafts of sunlight that play

Old Faithful Lodge Geyser Hall

across the fantasy of beams, columns, and twisted log railings and brackets. Sparkling rings of wrought-iron chandeliers encircle the columns, and wall sconces subtly define the atrium after dark. The room is a spectacle to be slowly absorbed by gazing upward, then by ascending to the upper balconies to explore the mystery of the extraordinary space. The lobby floor and balcony provide ample vantage points for viewing the dazzling log confection overhead and the lobby activity below. An outdoor terrace above the entrance porte cochere is an excellent position for watching Old Faithful Geyser's eruptions.

Old Faithful Lodge, designed by Gilbert Stanley Underwood and built in 1923 with additions through 1927, is at the northern end of the Old Faithful Geyser area. Less heralded than its neighboring Old Faithful Inn, the rambling building's exterior is a mixture of stone, timber, and shingles. The lodge provides cafeteria services and contains an extraordinary recreational hall framed in peeled logs. Approximately 100 by 136 feet in plan and 75 feet high to the plank ceiling's ridge, Geyser Hall is similar in character to the nave in a Gothic cathedral. Side aisles under a lowered shed roof are defined by rows of four-log column clusters. The larger columns in each cluster support the main trusses spanning the "nave" with an array of chords, kingposts, and diagonal bracing joined by large black steel plates with exposed bolts. The Hall's ecclesiastical atmosphere derives from the stately rhythm of columns, the proportion and scale of horizontal log placement, and the clerestory windows in the upper side walls. Unlike the cold interiors of stone cathedrals, the lodge's hall is warmed by the use of wood for all its interior surfaces: plank floors, walls, and ceilings are tied together by a tracery of log columns and truss members. Finely crafted wrought-iron ceiling fixtures light the interior.

The two Hamilton Stores in the Old Faithful area are also of interest. The Upper Store was built by Henry Klamer in 1894 and purchased in 1915 by Charles Hamilton—his first concessioner property in Yellowstone. The wood-frame building has gable roofs distinguished by a fantasy of burled pine logs, with decorative branches on the porches and roof brackets. The Louver Store was built in 1929 and designed to be consistent with the NPS rustic design principles. Three gabled entrance porches supported by dressed stone piers join the long gabled roof of the main sales area. Porch roofs are framed in log trusses with projecting whittled-log rafter and purlin ends. Exterior walls are made of concrete formed to look like hewn logs. The interior of the main sales area is framed by peeled logs: a cluster of three columns placed against the interior walls supports hammer trusses with black connecting plates and exposed bolts.

Lake Village

The Grand Tour circuit in Yellowstone's early days proceeded from Geyser Basin and Old Faithful to the shores of Lake Yellowstone where the destination was Lake Hotel. Construction of this permanent structure to replace a little-used tent camp near the lake's outlet into the Yellowstone River was begun in 1889. In 1903, Robert C. Reamer was hired for remodeling and additions to a rather unpretentious four-story frame building.

He succeeded in transforming a nondescript building into an elegant hotel inspired by the Colonial Revival style. Three gables on the building's lake side were extended and converted into Classical porticos, each with four 50-foot Ionic columns. The dining room was expanded and a porte cochère and lobby sunroom added, along with more guest rooms, bringing the total to almost 200 rooms. Painting the exterior clapboard walls a soft yellow unified the old and new wings. White trim and columns added an elegant air to the long elevation facing the lake. By 1923, Lake Hotel had become an imposing structure of classical beauty extending 900 feet along the lake's shoreline. A complete restoration and new interior furnishings in the 1990s created the gracious landmark we see today.

Lake Hotel

Development around the Lake Hotel added several nearby structures. The NPS built the Lake Ranger Station and Community Center in 1922 to meet the combined uses of management and visitor education programs. An unusual octagonal community room

40 feet across with a central stone fireplace supporting radiating timber beams was joined to a residence wing 26 by 38 feet. A north wing was added in 1930–31. The Lake Ranger Station underwent restoration during the summers of 1985–87. Harrison Goodall directed the exterior work and interior renovations performed by NPS staff. This project is an excellent restoration, serving as a model for national park historic structures.

The Hamilton Store at Yellowstone Lake, a good example of the shingle style, has a well-composed form and distinctive octagonal sales area. Note the octagonal light fixture that adds a touch of rusticity to the store. Cast-iron simulated logs frame translucent glass and are embellished with squirrels, owls, and an acorn-shaped pendant globe.

Fishing Bridge Hatchery Area

The Lake Fish Hatchery had a prominent role in Yellowstone National Park's fishery management program. Constructed for the U.S. Fish and Wildlife Service in the late 1920s and early 1930s, the fish hatchery activities were halted in 1958. The nine-building complex is carefully unified through rustic design elements. Exposed peeled-log framing, with reverse board-and-batten vertical siding inside the framing, includes oversized logs used as corner columns and is sometimes paired along the wall surfaces. Log trusses are exposed on gable ends with arched lintel logs, and a sill rests on concrete foundations. All roofs and column-supported porches have the same pitch, with double-coursed shake shingles. The buildings are further unified by brown paint over all the exterior surfaces and green window trim.

Tower-Roosevelt Area

The northeast corner of Yellowstone National Park is a country of rolling, sage-covered hills, and rivers and streams that drain through pine forests. Tower Junction, near the intersection of the Loop Road and the East Entrance Road, became the site of Roosevelt Lodge to replace a tent camp. Completed in 1920, the lodge served as headquarters for fishing trips and saddle-horse trips, and eventually was surrounded by 110 cabins. The rustic tune of the Roosevelt Lodge complex is sounded loud and clear by the log gateway arch over the entrance road. The one-story log lodge projects a pleasant, welcoming ambience with a wide porch lined with hickory rocking chairs. Cabins surrounding the main lodge (except for a very few that came from other sites in the park, such as Old Faithful Lodge and Mammoth Lodge) are a variety of construction types—logs, board-and-batten, flush plank siding, "logs out," and "studs out." Today's guests use the central lodge building for dining, enjoying the dude-ranch lifestyle of the moderately priced complex, complete with square dancing, cookouts, and stagecoach rides. The lodge was rehabilitated by the NPS in the 1980s, and a kitchen wing was added.

Museums—Norris, Madison, and Fishing Bridge

The National Historic Landmark museums at Norris Geyser Basin, Madison Junction, and Fishing Bridge satisfied the NPS shift from education through the imparting of in-

Norris Museum

Madison Museum

formation to "interpretation." Designed by architect Herbert Maier, they used natural materials, exaggerated architectural features, and organic forms, influencing hundreds built throughout the nation during work relief programs in the 1930s. The Norris and Old Faithful (demolished in the 1970s) museums were associated with thermal geology, Madison Junction with the park's history, and Fishing Bridge with the ecology of the Lake Yellowstone area.

Maier's buildings respond to their sites with pleasingly low profiles and gable or jerkinhead (clipped gable) roofs, bases of massive stone to sill height, and wide shingled-roof overhangs. Interiors stressed simple, natural materials as a background to the exhibits. Observation terraces at least half the size of the interior spaces encouraged visitors to enjoy the local features and reflect upon what they had seen and learned inside the museum. All three remaining Maier-designed museums were stabilized under the direction of Harrison Goodall during the 1980s.

Norris Geyser Basin Museum, built in 1929, is the most architecturally imposing of the three remaining Yellowstone museums. It was conceived as a gateway to the overlooks and trails of the geyser basin, and the building's concept, form, and execution of detail make it a masterpiece of rustic architecture. Site and structure are flawlessly harmonized in the informal building base, native stone masonry, and bold log work. The museum's placement skillfully screens the geyser basin from view until entry into the foyer, which provides access to the flagstone terrace overlooking the thermal springs. The entrance side is a long, low subdued composition of sheltering hip roofs with double-coursed long, wooden shingles on a base of oversized boulders that organically rise from the ground; the overlook side has massive peeled-log brackets to support log lintels and projecting roof rafters. The plan is deceptively simple: exhibition space and a small ranger's apartment are contained in a one-story rectangular plan approximately 94 by 20 feet. A central covered foyer sheltered by a massive jerkinhead roof on trusses of oversized logs rises above the rest of the form. There is a dramatic transition from the shadowed entrance foyer into the naturally lit exhibition rooms. The building's interiors continue the use of natural materials.

Fishing Bridge Museum   Northeast Entrance Station

Madison Museum, also built in 1929, is the smallest of Maier's four museums. Set in a meadow at the point where the Firehole and Gibbon rivers join to form the Madison River, the one-story structure is devoted to the park's history. The design challenge for Maier at Madison Junction was a meadow fringed by lodgepole pines that did not offer contours for blending the structure into the landscape, so the Bungalow-style influence is more evident here. The L-shaped 700-square-foot building contains an exhibition room in the main wing, and ranger-naturalist quarters in a smaller wing.

Fishing Bridge Museum, constructed in 1930–31, is built of native stone and appears to rise out of a rock outcrop. The structure was built to reflect the beauty of nature itself. Approaching from the parking lot, it was designed so that one could see through the building to Yellowstone Lake, hence the notion of focusing on the natural resource that the building was created to interpret. The long, low structure (approximately 120 feet long by 28 feet wide) has a raised roof over the central hall and two lower roofs flanking the exhibition wings. Directly beyond the museum is a stone terrace overlooking Yellowstone Lake. Massive boulders used for the lower walls, some up to 5 feet in diameter, rise to the eaves at the corners. The walls are wood framed and covered with cedar shakes, resting on log sills. The central roof is a simple gable; wing roofs have jerkinhead ends.

Northeast Entrance

Of the various national park building types, the entrance station presented a unique challenge to the talented NPS design staff. It defined a sense of place and identity for the park, serving as a bridge between the outside world and sequestered park environment, established the presence of the NPS for the visitor, and served to collect fees and count visitors. The Northeast Entrance Station is a preeminent example of a rustic architectural solution in the national park system, earning a National Historic Landmark designation.

The one-story log structure, built in 1934–35, has an elegant simplicity. The floor plan (15 by 57 feet overall) is a 20-foot-wide central checking station main office flanked by 12-foot-wide covered roadways and storerooms. The design is unified by the gable roof spanning the entire structure and the intersecting higher central section roof. A rubble masonry foundation over concrete, lodgepole pine log walls, and shingled roofs make up the limited palette of materials used by the designers. Gable ends are finished with vertical channeled siding.

Soldier Stations

The restored Norris Soldier Station (Museum of the National Park Ranger, designed by Robert C. Reamer), is a remnant from the sixteen stations that existed toward the end of the army's administration of the park. Built of logs or wood-frame construction, the stations were for summer detachments of four troopers each, although a few were also used for winter stations. Norris Station was among the longest occupied stations in the park. Constructed in 1897 and converted for ranger use, the building was restored in 1991. The building is T-shaped, with saddle-notched peeled-log walls (73 by 60 feet deep) battened inward from foundation to roof eaves. A distinguishing feature is a pair of lodgepole pine posts with grotesque knots on the entrance porch.

As the world's first national park, Yellowstone stands as an acknowledgment that there are places on earth upon which human beings cannot improve. There is no more fitting place for the ideals of conservation and preservation to be rethought for the continued "benefit and enjoyment of the people."

Old Faithful Geyser

Midwest

Illinois

→ Lincoln Home National Historic Site (p. 123)

LAKE
MICHIGAN

CHICAGO

Mississippi
River

SPRINGFIELD
Lincoln Home NHS

Ohio River

Lincoln Home National Historic Site

→ Located in Springfield, Sangamon County, Illinois

→ www.nps.gov/liho

→ This site is located at South 8th and Jackson Streets in Springfield, accessed via Interstates 55 and 72 to the visitor center with parking at South 7th and Jackson Streets.

Lincoln Home

Abraham Lincoln lived in the house for seventeen years and it is the only home ever owned by the sixteenth president of the United States. Lincoln bought the house two years after he married Mary Todd and they lived there through the birth of three children and the death of a fourth until his election to the presidency in 1860. The National Historic Site includes the two-story Lincoln Home at the corner of South 8th and Jackson Streets and the surrounding four-block neighborhood with fifteen historical buildings.

The original house purchased by Lincoln in 1844 was a small, humble one-and-a-half-story Greek Revival cottage of wood-frame construction. Exterior walls were white-painted horizontal clapboard and a simply detailed recess entrance in the house's center flanked by pairs of multilight windows and shutters. To accommodate a growing family, and to reflect his success as a lawyer, the Lincolns added a downstairs bedroom to the house in 1849. Major changes occurred from 1855 to 1856 with its expansion into a full two-story house. Elegant with Italianate soffit details, the original exterior materials and window opening proportions extended upward to the new floor. An existing one-story T-shaped rear wing was widened and raised to a second floor with a shallow hip roof. The now-grand house befitting one of the state's best courtroom lawyers continued to display the simple nameplate reading "A. Lincoln" on the front door.

The house's interior has a central hallway with a stairway leading to the second floor bedrooms and a rear stairway from kitchen to second floor. To the left of the hallway are front and rear parlors connected by folding doors. A front sitting room, dining room, and kitchen are to the right and behind the central hallway. Upstairs are the Lincolns' bedroom suite, a large bedroom that doubles as a guest room, boys' bedrooms, and a maid's room. A porch with a decorative railing extended along the boys' bedrooms, facing south.

The cherished place held in Lincoln's memory of this Springfield home is captured in his farewell address in 1861 before departing for Washington:

> Here, I have lived a quarter of a century, and have passed from a young to an old man. Here, my children have been born, and one is buried. I now leave, not knowing when, or whether ever, I may return....

The house has been restored and furnished by the National Park Service with original and period pieces to its 1860s appearance and work continues on neighborhood structures, as Lincoln would have remembered them. In addition to the Lincoln Home, open for public tours, two other structures open to the public include the restored Dean House and the Arnold Home featuring exhibits relating to the Lincoln family and neighborhood restoration efforts.

Indiana

Midwest

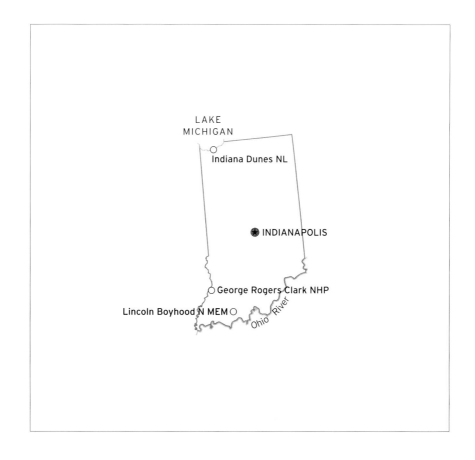

LAKE
MICHIGAN

Indiana Dunes NL

⊛ INDIANAPOLIS

○ George Rogers Clark NHP

Lincoln Boyhood N MEM ○

Ohio River

George Rogers Clark National Historical Park

→ Located in the southwest part of the state in Vincennes, Knox County, Indiana

→ www.nps.gov/gero

→ The twenty-six-acre park is located four blocks west of downtown Vincennes, Indiana. The park entrance on South 2nd Street is reached via the east-west US 50 (6th Street Exit) and north-south US 41 (Willow Street Exit).

George Rogers Clark Memorial

The surrender of Fort Sackville on the east bank of the Wabash River by British forces to those led by Lt. Colonel George Rogers Clark on February 25, 1779 ranks as one of the great military feats of the Revolutionary War. A classical memorial on the fort's site commemorates Clark's leadership in establishing the United States' firm foothold in the frontier region west of the Appalachians, later to become the Old Northwest Territory and eventually the states of Ohio, Indiana, Illinois, Michigan, and Wisconsin.

George Rogers Clark embodied the physical characteristics and personality of Revolutionary leaders such as George Washington and Thomas Jefferson. Youthful at twenty-six, Clark was an imposing physical presence, standing 6-foot-2-inches tall and with auburn hair. A charismatic leader and a persuasive orator, tireless in his leadership of a Kentucky militia and commander of its defenses, a sound strategist with an understanding of Indian customs and habits of thought, Clark led by an extraordinary force of personality. His genius and daring heroic exploits helped win the Revolutionary War.

Enduring privations comparable to George Washington and his troops at Valley Forge, Clark led an army of Virginians and French volunteers to attack the British at Fort Sackville. An eighteen-day mid-winter march across 180 miles of enemy territory swollen by snow and rain, often wading through icy chest-deep water, the army reached Vincennes and surrounded the fort. After a siege of approximately thirty-eight hours and a demonstration of frontier vengeance, the British Colonel Henry Hamilton granted an unconditional surrender.

The approach of the one hundred fiftieth anniversary of the American Revolution during the early 1920s prompted the citizens of Vincennes, Indiana to commemorate the great accomplishments of George Rogers Clark. A competition selected the design of architect Frederick C. Hirons of Hirons & Mellor, New York City. Construction began in 1931 and the memorial was completed in 1933.

The memorial is part of a 26-acre park on the site of old Fort Sackville near downtown Vincennes, Indiana. Set in a pleasantly landscaped formal garden, the Clark Memorial is approached from the visitor center off South 2nd Street. The circular structure clearly derives its inspiration from the classic Greek style and stands more than 82 feet high and 90 feet across the base. A circular 2-foot-thick granite wall, with a green wainscot and red band below the grayish wall, is set 2 feet within a colonnaded peristyle of sixteen Doric columns, 6 feet 4 inches in diameter and 39 feet tall, supporting a frieze, cornice, and massive flat round roof. On the frieze is inscribed, "The Conquest of the West—George Rogers Clark and the Frontiersmen of the American Revolution."

Inside the rotunda is an 8-foot-tall bronze statue of Clark in military uniform as a young man by Hermon Atkins MacNeil. Around the rotunda walls are seven murals, each created on a single piece of Belgian linen 16 feet by 28 feet by Ezra Winter, portraying Clark's winter campaign against the British. The interior is illuminated by a circular skylight made of bronze and carved and colored glass. The remainder of the ceiling and rotunda walls are Indiana limestone. The floor is of Tennessee marble.

A worthwhile experience is the movie shown in the visitor center about Clark and the capture of Fort Sackville. An annual Memorial Day Spirit of Vincennes Rendezvous, weekend patriots in frontier garb, and uniformed British soldiers enrich the experience of learning about an epic period in American history.

Indiana Dunes National Lakeshore

Located in northeast Indiana east of Gary, Indiana, in Lake Porter and LaPorte Counties, Indiana

→   www.nps.gov/indu

→   The park stretches along the southern shore of Lake Michigan between Gary and Michigan City, Indiana and is accessed via Interstate 94, the Indiana Toll Road, Interstate 80/90; US 20, or IN 12 and various state roads.

The 15,067-acre Indiana Dunes National Lakeshore extends nearly twenty-five miles along the southern shore of Lake Michigan. An idea born in the 1910s, more than fifty years of struggle with competing interests for industrial and commercial development resulted in this unique "breathing space" for Metropolitan Chicago and Indiana cities along the lake. Three key individuals helped make Indiana Dunes National Lakeshore a reality: Henry Cowles, a botanist from the University of Chicago; Paul H. Douglas, senator for the State of Illinois; and Dorothy R. Buell, an Ogden Dunes resident and English teacher. They worked to forestall the demise of the dunes by development. The natural and cultural landscape they preserved varies with long stretches of uncrowded beaches, dune ridges paralleling the lake and rising up to 180 feet high, forest covered dunes, bogs, wetlands, and woodland forests. Historical architecture includes the Bailly Homestead, Chellberg Farm, The Century of Progress Architectural District, and Good Fellow Youth Camp.

Trails from the Bailly-Chellberg visitor center west of Porter on US Highway 20 or via Interstate 24, Exit 22 (eastbound) and Exit 26 (westbound), lead to two of the remnants of settlement on this Miami and Potawatomi travel route between the Great Lakes and the Mississippi River and, later, Fort Dearborn (Chicago) and Detroit. Period-clothed volunteers at the Bailly Homestead and Chellberg Farm interpret lives of early settlers in the dunes.

In 1822 Honore Gratien Joseph Bailly de Messein, also known as Joseph Bailly, arrived to establish a trading post. An independent fur trader and one of the earliest settlers in northwestern Indiana, Bailly constructed several log buildings for his business ventures that served as meeting places for Native Americans and whites and a stopping place for travelers and missionaries. Structures on the site evolved over time, including the main house, kitchen/chapel, a two-story cabin, a brick house, and a fur-trading cabin and family cemetery. The imposing National Historic Landmark two-and-a-half-story main house was started by Bailly in 1835, months before his death. The log structure is sheathed in 7-inch-wide unpainted weatherboards beneath the curious assembly of structures restored by the National Park Service (NPS) to its 1917 appearance. The kitchen/chapel, originally kitchen and quarters, was converted to a chapel around 1870. The two-story cabin was built as employee quarters with hand-hewn timbers. The reconstructed log fur-trading cabin represents the original storehouse used by Native American trappers while trapping in local streams and marshland.

The Chellberg Farm represents the flow of Swedish immigrants to the Chicago area in this typical Swedish and northwestern Indiana farmstead. The vernacular brick veneer farmhouse was built in 1885 as a replacement for an earlier wood-framed house that was destroyed by fire in December of 1884. In the 1980s the NPS restored the farmhouse to its turn of the twentieth-century appearance, except for the dining room, which had been modified by the Chellbergs in the 1920s. The large barn was built around 1870.

Anders and Johanna Chellberg (Americanized from Kjellberg), with their young son Charles, made the long journey from Sweden to this country in 1863. Traveling first by boat and then by train, the Chellbergs arrived here four months after their departure from Sweden. After their arrival in northwest Indiana, the Chellbergs became part of a growing Swedish community. They purchased the farm property in 1869 and it was sold to the NPS in 1971.

Located on Lake Front Drive in Beverly Shores near the Dorothy Buell Memorial Visitor Center is an unusual collection of houses brought to the site from the 1933 Chicago World's Fair. Real estate developer Robert Bartlett hoped that the high profile houses would entice buyers to his new resort community of Beverly Shores. The five houses delivered by barge in 1935 are each unique, especially the House of Tomorrow with an airplane hangar integrated into the steel-framed structure. Remarkably, the World's Fair houses have withstood more than seventy years of battering from wind, sand, and surf.

The result of dedicated effort by many individuals, Indiana Dunes National Lakeshore is a treasured recreational place, enjoyed for its dramatic landscape and cultural features.

Lincoln Boyhood National Memorial

Located in Lincoln City, Spencer County, Indiana

→ www.nps.gov/libo

→ The park is located on IN 162. From Interstate 64, exit at US 231, (Exit 57) and travel south through Dale, continue on US 231 to Gentryville, then east on IN 162 for two miles to visitor center.

Reconstructed Lincoln Boyhood cabin   Lincoln Boyhood Memorial

Among the several Lincoln commemorative sites in the National Park System (Birthplace site in Kentucky, Lincoln Home in Springfield, Illinois, and Ford's Theater and the Lincoln Memorial in Washington), the Lincoln Boyhood National Memorial is probably the most poignant. Here, the future sixteenth president of the United States spent fourteen formative years of his life, from seven to twenty-one, and it is where his mother Nancy Hanks Lincoln is buried. Sources of the history of Lincoln's youth on the southern Indiana farm are found here in a Memorial Building set in a formal landscape designed by Frederick Law Olmsted, Jr., the Lincoln Living Historical Farm is a representative pioneer homestead with a reconstructed log cabin, and other structures on a working farm.

The two hundred-acre park incorporated the Nancy Hanks Lincoln State Memorial, donated by the state of Indiana, into the Lincoln Boyhood National Memorial as a unit of the National Park System in 1962. The memorialization of the site actually began as early as 1879 with the placement of the Studebaker stone, a marble monumenet marking Nancy Hanks Lincoln's unknown gravesite surrounded by a wrought-iron fence. The clearing of the post-Lincoln period structures was done by the state in the 1920s and 1930s. No original structures were destroyed for the development; none were in existence by the twentieth century. Based on Frederick Law Olmsted, Jr.'s design, a formal alleé and plaza laid out in a cruciform plan focused on a 120-foot-tall flagpole and with a vista to Nancy Hanks Lincoln's grave in a wooded knoll. The religious symbolism related to Olmsted's concept of a serene setting creating a sanctuary.

A cabin site memorial on the traditional site of a Lincoln cabin consists of a bronze casting of cabin sill logs and fireplace surrounded by a stone retaining wall. The Trail of Twelve Stones, with stones associated with Lincoln's life placed in the park in 1933, added to the site's transition from a shrine dedicated to motherhood to a memorial to Lincoln himself.

Further development of the site occurred with the planning and construction of a Memorial Building designed by National Park Service (NPS) architect Richard Bishop. The classical design of two buildings in Indiana limestone and sandstone, the Nancy Hanks Lincoln Hall (30 feet by 45 feet) and Abraham Lincoln Hall (30 feet by 60 feet), were connected by a semicircular cloister around a Memorial Court with five life-sized demirelief sculptured panels by E. H. Daniels depicting the life of Abraham Lincoln. The building's completion in 1943 finalized the transformation to commemorate Lincoln and his lifetime accomplishments. The park's transfer to NPS in 1963 introduced changes including the relocation of State Highway 162 from the short arms of the cruciform plan to the south several hundred yards, as well as the enclosure of the cloister, and added a wing to the south side of the structure for use as a visitor center.

The Living History Farm was constructed in 1968 using historic agricultural buildings from Spencer and Perry counties and functions as a working pioneer homestead with a cabin, outbuildings, split rail fences, animals, gardens, and field crops. Each building was dismantled and their materials moved to the park for use in the structure seen today. Staff and volunteers, dressed in period clothing, demonstrate the daily activities typical of the 1820s.

The visitor should take time for trail walks along the wooded Lincoln Boyhood Trail to the Nancy Hanks Lincoln gravesite and farm to experience the reverence for Lincoln's boyhood that can be drawn from the serenity of the formal memorial site.

Iowa

→ Herbert Hoover National Historic Site (p. 276)

Herbert Hoover National Historic Site (p. 276)

Midwest

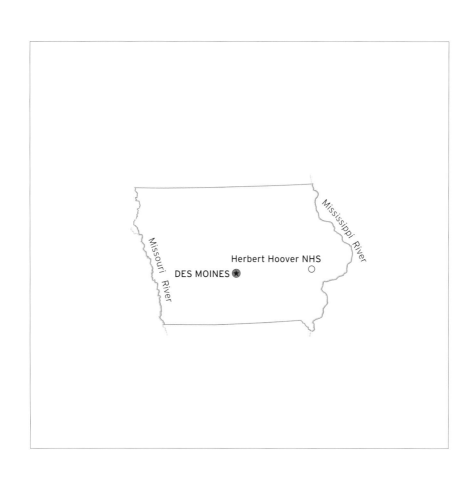

Herbert Hoover National Historic Site

Located in West Branch, Cedar County, Iowa

→ www.nps.gov/heho

→ The park is accessible from Interstate 80 at Exit 254, ten miles east of Iowa City, Iowa, and forty miles west of Davenport, Iowa. The visitor center is a half-mile north of the exit at Main Street and Parkside Drive.

Herbert Hoover birthplace cottage

Herbert Hoover, the thirty-first president of the United States, lived a long and full life filled with tragedies and successes, great public acclaim and rejection, and ultimate recognition as a great humanitarian and statesman. Hoover was born on August 10, 1874 in a tiny cottage fitting in with the small Quaker community of West Branch, Iowa, where his father was village blacksmith. The 187-acre Herbert Hoover National Historic Site includes the president's birthplace cottage, a reconstructed blacksmith shop, a one-room schoolhouse, a Friends Meetinghouse, the Herbert Hoover Presidential Library-Museum, gravesites of President and Mrs. Hoover, and 76-acres of restored Iowa tallgrass prairie on the south and west sides of the park.

The middle of three children, double tragedy struck when Herbert's father died in 1880 and his mother three years later. By age nine the future president and his older brother Tad and younger sister Mary were orphans. The children were dispersed among relatives and, less than two years later, Herbert moved to live with an uncle in Oregon. After graduation from Stanford University, Hoover began a career in mining engineering filled with rapid advancement and financial success in Colorado, Australia, and China.

Hoover served as chairman of World War I and post-war relief commissions, distributing food to war refugees. These posts established his reputation as a humanitarian and skilled and efficient leader. He later served as the secretary of commerce in the Harding and Coolidge administrations. Hoover was elected president in a landslide victory in 1928, which was quickly consumed by the Great Depression that saw the loss of his popularity and, opposing Franklin Delano Roosevelt in 1932, an unsuccessful bid for reelection. Appointed to important government reform commissions by Presidents Truman and Eisenhower, Hoover's work returned him to public service as a respected and effective leader. Herbert Hoover died in 1964.

The centerpiece of the park is the modest three-room board-and-batten wood-frame birthplace cottage built in 1871. The National Historic Landmark is in the style artist Grant Wood used in his Iowa-based painting *American Gothic*. Fitting with the

Quaker community the house was devoid of ostentation: sturdy and functional, containing a small bedroom, a combined dining-living area, and a porch "lean-to" used variously for storage, summer cooking, and occasional guests. The cottage is 14 feet by 20 feet with a 6-foot-deep porch extending along the west side and a shed roof extending over the front door porch. Exterior walls are 1- by 12-inch vertical boards braced by horizontal two-by-fours. Restoration was completed in 1938 with the former president offering advice and recollections. The cottage is furnished with period pieces, including Hoover's childhood cradle.

The blacksmith's shop is a reconstruction similar to one operated by Jesse Hoover from 1871 to 1879. Built across the lane from the Birthplace Cottage, a pair of large hinged barn doors below the vertical "signboard" facade with a simple sign announcing "Jesse Hoover, Blacksmith" faces the cottage.

The white clapboard one-room wood-frame schoolhouse was built in 1853 and served as both the primary school during Hoover's boyhood and the Friends Meetinghouse for worship until a separate meetinghouse was completed in 1857. The building originally stood two blocks away, at the corner of Downey and Main streets, and was moved a number of times until placed in its current location in 1971.

The meetinghouse, built by The Religious Society of Friends, or Quakers, in 1857 is where the Hoover family worshipped. The building has been moved two blocks from its original site.

Near the cottage is a bronze statue of Isis, the ancient Egyptian goddess of life, a gift to Herbert Hoover from the Belgian people for the work he did on their behalf during World War I. Belgian sculptor Auguste Puttemans cast the piece in 1922 where it was located on the campus of Stanford University. President and Mrs. Hoover had it moved in 1939 to overlook the Birthplace Cottage.

The park illuminates Hoover's early years in this small, self-reliant, agricultural community in the gentle rolling prairies of eastern Iowa. There is serenity to the place, minutes from the interstate and a short commute to the University of Iowa in Iowa City. Adjacent to Main Street, with its restored Historic District buildings, tree-shaded lawns and walks, white picket fences, and colorful flowerbeds, the park shares the ambience of the typical Midwestern town that shaped the future president's life. There are blacksmithing demonstrations in the summer; guides are seen often in 1870s period clothes, some dressed in the plain Quaker tradition reminding visitors of the devout Hoover Quaker family.

Schoolhouse

Michigan

Midwest

Father Marquette National Memorial

Located in St. Ignace, Mackinaw County, Michigan

→ www.nps.gov/fama

→ The Father Marquette National Memorial is located near St. Ignace in Straits State Park, just west of Interstate 75 off US 2.

Father Marquette Memorial

Interior

Father Marquette National Memorial is located in Straits State Park at the north end of the five-mile-long Mackinac Bridge in Michigan's Upper Peninsula. The fifty-two-acre memorial is owned and administered by the Michigan Department of Natural Resources and is a National Park Service (NPS) affiliated area. The park commemorates Father Jacques Marquette, a French Jesuit missionary, recognized as one of the great explorers of the North American continent. He established Michigan's earliest European settlements at Sault Ste. Marie and St. Ignace in 1668 and 1671. Marquette lived among the local Native Americans from 1666 to his death in 1675. During these nine years, Father Marquette mastered several native languages and helped Louis Joliet map the Mississippi River.

Departing from the strip of motorist services on US Highway 2 to Boulevard Drive and the Straits State Park entrance leads to an enchanted forest area. A trail through a pine forest passes the memorial pavilion, the site of the museum (destroyed by fire in 2000), an amphitheater, and the overlook facing the Straits of Mackinac and the majestic 3,500 foot-long Mackinac Bridge.

The free-standing pavilion is an example of mid-1960s design with its departure in form and materials from traditional churches and memorials. At Father Marquette National Memorial, the designers created an evocative structure, now somewhat dated, but nevertheless, successful as a memorial and a pleasing experience. The sensitive use of the site and intimacy of the setting in an opening in the pine forest integrates structure and a simple interior partially enclosed by walls standing free of the roof. The visitor is drawn forward on a meandering trail by the symbolic spire reaching skyward above a broad, polygonal low-pitched shingled roof and large-scaled ashlar limestone wing walls. A shadowed interior under the hovering roof is relieved by splashes of daylight filtered through a small roof opening.

The pavilion's soaring spire of laminated arches dramatically emerges through the twelve-sided structure's shingled roof. Partially screened from view by the limestone walls, the roof appears to float on paired 3- by 12-inch columns equally spaced around a 45-foot diameter circle. The columns are spaced 10 feet 6 inches apart and support twelve laminated roof beams, 3- by 24-inches in section. Radiating inward and upward toward the center of the covered space, the beams ascend through an opening; six of the beams spaced inches apart rise approximately 25 feet to form the spire.

At the pavilion entrance, freestanding ashlar limestone walls placed at subtle angles to the trail, sloped at the top and lower than the roof eave line, partially screen the interior from view. Sloped-top limestone walls placed outside the ring of columns provide a partial enclosure 4- to 6-feet high, continuing the visual screening of the interior. Inside this mystical space, benches on the walls between columns face a floor-mounted relief map of Marquette's travels up the Mississippi to St. Ignace centered on the hexagonal limestone floor pavers. Overhead is the precisely spaced columns arching into the exposed wood beam roof structure and supporting the wood plank roof deck. The central opening at the roof's peak for the spire's laminated arches introduces filtered interior daylight, in addition to daylight coming over the limestone walls in changing patterns dappled by the surrounding pine trees. Spaces between columns in the direction of the bridge are open, with the thick surrounding pine forest partially screening the magnificent exterior views.

The visitor's experience at the pavilion is a preparation for the stunning view of the Straits of Mackinac, where once Marquette paddled his canoe, and the majestic Mackinac Bridge.

Mackinac Bridge crossing straits of Mackinac, from Father Marquette National Memorial overlook

Isle Royale National Park

Located in Keweenaw County, Michigan

→ www.nps.gov/isro

→ The park is accessible only by boat and seaplane. Vehicles are not permitted on Isle Royale. Visitors park their cars at the NPS visitor center for ferry rides to the island from Houghton, Michigan (five hours away); Copper Harbor, Michigan (three hours away); or Grand Portage, Minnesota (two to three hours away), or fly with Isle Royale Seaplane Service to the island from Houghton, Michigan (only thirty minutes away).

Visiting Isle Royale National Park for a sight of historical structures (four lighthouses) requires a dedicated travel commitment: up to six hours by National Park Service (NPS) ferry or under an hour by seaplane from Houghton, Michigan. Seen from across the bow from an approaching ferry or below a seaplane wingtip is an island wilderness in the deep waters of Lake Superior. The park encompasses a large island (forty-five miles long by nine miles wide) of ridges, meadows, bays, and forests and extends four-and-a-half miles into Lake Superior from the outermost land areas of the island, and includes four hundred smaller islands. Although one of the least accessible parks—fifteen miles from Canada and fifty miles from Michigan—the untouched character of the island's ninety-nine percent wilderness is an increasing attraction for hikers and backpackers (on 165 miles of trails), boaters, fishermen, and guests at the island's rustic lodge. Set in the largest freshwater lake in the world, Isle Royale's biological and ecological uniqueness was designated an International Biosphere Reserve in 1980.

Navigation around the island's coast of rocky shoreline and shoals resulted in an unusual collection of shipwrecks preserved in the cool, clear water of Lake Superior. Ten major wrecks from 1877 to 1947 include the sinking of the *Algoma* in 1855 with the loss of forty-five lives. Smaller wrecks also dot Isle Royale's bays and harbors. The island's lighthouses probably spared an untold number of ships and lives.

Rock Harbor Lighthouse on the island's northeast corner is one of the oldest extant lighthouses on the Great Lakes. Visible from the NPS Houghton ferry, the lighthouse built in 1855 marked the Middle Islands Passage and harbor entrance for ships reaching copper mines on the island's south shore. A whitewashed 50-foot-tall conical brick tower is attached to a one-and-a-half-story gable-roofed rubble stone and brick keeper's house. The beacon, since removed, was a fourth order Fresnel lens installed in 1875. The light functioned less than ten years as copper mining ebbed and flowed. Starting up in 1855 when the Sault Ste. Marie locks opened—the lighthouse closed in 1858 and started up again in 1859—it was finally closed by the U.S. Lighthouse Board in 1878. Campers used the house and fishermen lived in it until it was again abandoned in 1939. The NPS stabilized the tower that began to lean in the 1950s. The lighthouse now houses a maritime history exhibit.

The still functioning Isle Royale Lighthouse on Menagerie Island off Isle Royale's south shore marks the entrance to Siskiwit Bay. The one-and-a-half-story red rubble sandstone keeper's house with a jerkinhead roof is connected to the tower by a short sandstone enclosed passageway. The octagonal 61-foot-tall sandstone tower was white-washed for improved daytime visibility. The original fourth order Fresnel lens, mounted at 72-feet above lake level was automated in 1941 and is now on display in the Rock Harbor Lighthouse maritime exhibit.

The Passage Island Lighthouse, three miles from the northeast tip of Isle Royale, is the northernmost American lighthouse on the Great Lakes. Castle-like in appearance, the one-and-a-half-story keeper's quarters (40 feet by 27 feet in plan) and tower con-structed in 1882 is built of red rubble sandstone. Surprisingly fine workmanship and details, including arched stone window and door headers, simulated tower buttresses, and brick chimney, is seen in this remote place. An unusual design places the tower into a corner of the keeper's quarters. The 44-foot-tall tower has a square base (8-feet square in plan) changing into an octagonal shaft at the quarter's eaves. The focal plane of the fourth order Fresnel lens, now displayed in the U.S. Coast Guard Station in Portage, Michigan, was 78 feet above lake level. The present automated light is visible up to a distance of twenty-five miles.

The Rock of Ages Lighthouse, five miles offshore from the southwestern end of the island, is one of the tallest and most powerful lights on the Great Lakes. An engineering feat blasted out of a reef and standing on a 56-foot diameter and 30-foot-tall steel crib filled with concrete and containing two basement levels, the cylindrical tower rises 132 feet from water level to the top of the ventilator ball. Completed in 1908 with a distinc-tive spark plug shape, a steel ladder ascends from water level to the top of the tower's foundation deck and the pedimented entrance doorway with decorative molding and pilaster trim. The structure is a steel framework with brick inner and outer walls and an exterior covering of whitewashed concrete parging containing all lighthouse func-tions stacked vertically in the foundation and tower. The two-story, 25-foot diameter cylindrical tower base contains the entry level, fog signal plant, and pillar crane hoisting engine. The four-story section above the base tapering to a 17-foot diameter contains offices, sleeping rooms, and watch room. Ornamental cast iron brackets supporting the exterior gallery and lantern base are all painted black to contrast with the tower. The original second order Fresnel lens, replaced by an automated beacon, is on view at the Windigo Ranger Station.

The park is open from mid-April to the end of October. The island's weather is often rainy and fog-shrouded and is snow-covered six months of the year. Neverthe-less, the journey to Isle Royale is rewarding for the untouched wilderness experience and visits to the surviving lighthouses serving as beacons for Great Lakes traffic.

Keweenaw National Historical Park

Located in Calumet, Houghton County, Michigan

→ www.nps.gov/kewe

→ The Quincy and Calumet Units of the park and eighteen cooperating sites are located on the Keweenaw Peninsula in the Upper Peninsula of Michigan. From the Mackinac Bridge take Interstate 25 north to MI 28 west and US 41 north to Hancock. From Wisconsin take US 2 and MI 28 west to MI 26 north to Hancock.

Calumet and Hecla Mining Company Public Library

Keweenaw (pronounced key-wa-naw) National Historical Park is a rich assemblage of privately owned properties with units in Quincy and Calumet. The park also works in partnership with eighteen Keweenaw Heritage Sites operated independently of the National Park Service (NPS). Each of these sites stretching along the length of the Keweenaw Peninsula, from Copper Harbor to south of Ontonagon contain significant cultural and/or natural resources and make a unique contribution to the Keweenaw Peninsula copper mining story. During the summer and early fall, the NPS operates a visitor information desk at the Quincy Mine Hoist Association Gift Shop located along US Highway 41. Admissions and hours may vary at the sites.

The Keweenaw Peninsula, jutting out into Lake Superior, approximately fifty miles long by fifteen miles wide, is a place of rich copper mining heritage. Some seven thousand years ago Lake Superior peoples developed sophisticated mining techniques. The copper was so pure it could be used straight from the ground to make beads, tools, and ornaments. Copper mining on an industrial scale started in the early 1840s. Hundreds of mining ventures, including companies and individuals, sought and established themselves throughout the region. By the 1860s, the Keweenaw Peninsula was home to the largest copper-producing region in the United States. At one time, the district contained some of the deepest mine shafts in the world, with one shaft reaching 9,200 feet below ground. A continual challenge for the mine owners was the combination of high overhead costs of deep-shaft hard-rock mining, a paternalistic management philosophy, and copper's constantly fluctuating price. As a result of these forces, operations temporarily closed in 1931. By 1968 most mining operations on the peninsula ended.

The copper industry left a cultural impact on the region and a wealth of historical architecture. Eastern investors and immigrants from all over the world poured into the region between 1843 and 1914. At one time, over thirty different ethnic groups called the Keweenaw Peninsula home. Their lives, aspirations, and labor left a legacy that is still visible in the cultural landscapes and built environments of downtown Calumet, areas of company-built housing, and other economically and socially differentiated enclaves.

The National Historic Landmark District Quincy Unit just northeast of Hancock between Portage Lake Road and Quincy Hill contains remnants of the Quincy Mining Company, including the mine shaft, a shaft-rockhouse, hoist houses, several stone ruins, and the only remaining nineteenth-century copper-smelting complex found on the Great Lakes. Located on the west side of US Highway 41, the stately red sandstone Quincy Mining Company Pay Office served as a command center for mining operations between grand homes constructed for former mine managers. The tall brick sandstone chimneys identify the building, bold first floor Richardsonian arches, hipped roof and pedimented dormer, and entrance porch supported by elegant square columns.

The profile of the No. 2 shaft-rockhouse standing 147 feet tall on Quincy Hill looms over the mine works on the east side of US Highway 41. Exploring the surviving

Quincy Mining Company No. 2 Shaft Rockhouse

structures, climbing over ruins, and standing alongside abandoned man-cars and skips (ore cars) is a trek through an industrial archeology open-air museum. Available on the site are surface and underground mine tours. A museum in the old Hoist

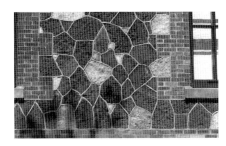

C&H General Office Building detail

House (1894) and the new No. 2 Hoist House (1918–20) invite discovery while a cog rail takes visitors from Quincy Hill to the adit (horizontal mine entrance) where underground mine tours begin.

The 1908 No. 2 shaft-rockhouse, a steel-framed and corrugated sheet metal wrapped structure expressing the functions it performed, was at the center of an integrated operation of raising the ore in cars from within the mine to the shaft-rockhouse. An efficient team of three men and an assortment of crushers and hammers, sorted and processed upwards of 1,000 tons of rock. Ore was sent to the stamp mill, waste or "poor" rock was dumped in huge piles near the shaft-rockhouse, and pure copper was sent to the smelter on Portage Lake opposite the Houghton waterfront. The power sources for the No. 2 shaft-house were the 1882 No. 2 hoist house, the 1894 No. 2 hoist house, and the 1918 No. 2 hoist house. Wheelstands, located between the hoist houses and the shaft-rockhouse, supported cables that connected and transferred power from the hoist to rock ships.

The Nordberg Hoist, the largest steam-powered mine hoist ever manufactured and capable of lifting a ten-ton load of copper from a depth of 6,000 feet at the rate of 3,200 feet per minute is housed in a newer, reinforced concrete building. Highlighting the architectural character of this impressive building is a red brick veneer sandwiched between exterior concrete columns and two-story-tall Palladian windows flooding the column-free interior with daylight and illuminating the gleaming 30-foot diameter hoisting drum. Historically green tile covered the gabled roof rising to a height of 80 feet at the ridge.

The National Historic Landmark District of the Calumet Unit, located about eight miles north of the Quincy Unit, includes the community of Calumet and structures associated with the Calumet and Hecla Copper Mining Company (C&H). C&H was the largest and most successful copper mining company in the Lake Superior region due mainly to its location on the copper-rich Calumet Conglomerate Lode. Several remaining C&H buildings and their associated grounds are part of a larger cultural landscape associated with the mining era. Two impressive C&H buildings that face each other are the General Office Building (1887 and additions) and Public Library (1898), the latter originally housing public baths in the basement. Designed by Shaw and Hunnewell of Boston, the buildings show traces of Queen Anne and H.H. Richardson styles in form and details. Exteriors of the two-story buildings are of carefully selected dark and light-colored mine-waste rock with red brick and sandstone trim. The former C&H General Office Building now serves as headquarters for the Keweenaw National Historical Park while the library houses the Keweenaw History Center.

Quincy Pay Office

Located just outside the C&H industrial operations, the company provided a location for the community of Red Jacket, now known as Calumet, to develop. Included in the commercial district are the Red Jacket Town Hall and Opera House (1886); the Red Jacket Fire Station (1989); Mario Curto's Saloon (1895); and several historic churches including St. Anne's (1900) and St. Paul's (1903).

The Village of Laurium, located east of the C&H Mining Company surface plant, is a residential community with a small commercial district that was home to many of the upper strata of Calumet society. In this area C&H managers and Calumet professionals and merchants built expansive late nineteenth-century and early-twentieth-century residences. The homes are elegant, stylistically diverse, and interspersed among the modest dwellings constructed by the area's middle and working classes.

The visitor reaching the remote Keweenaw Peninsula can enjoy a range of rewarding experiences by exploring this intact cultural landscape comprised of industrial, commercial, and residential areas. Tangible evidence of a past mining era and a thriving community exists and provokes the imagination to recreate the sounds, smells, and sensations of copper mining. Ground once trembled as trains rolled by and charges exploded underground. Machines once operated loudly twenty-four hours a day while workers and families anticipated the bells and whistles that marked the end of a shift or a community or church event.

Pictured Rocks National Lakeshore

Munising, Alger County, Michigan

→   www.nps.gov/piro

→   Located in Michigan's Upper Peninsula, the national lakeshore is between Munising, reached via MI 28 and 94, and Grand Marais reached via MI 77.

The Pictured Rocks National Lakeshore is a vibrantly colored landscape forty miles long and six miles across at its widest point along Lake Superior's south shore. Dramatic cliffs of ochre, tan, and brown sandwiched with layers of white and green and deeply forested are rendered in a rich palette of colors. Created as the country's first National Lakeshore in 1966, the picturesque rocks along a fifteen-mile section at the western end of the park are mineral-stained wave-sculpted sandstone cliffs rising as much as 200 feet above lake level. The picturesque scene conceals a treacherous offshore sandstone reef in places only 6 feet below the surface, extending nearly a mile into Lake Superior. The park also contains lakes, streams, and forests.

Discoveries of copper in the Keweenaw Peninsula and iron near Marquette created a boom in coastal shipping to reach the Sault Ste. Marie Canal opened in 1855. In addition to the shallow reef, thick fogs created a dangerous place that mariners referred to as "shipwreck coast." The site at Au Sable Point was chosen along a dangerous eighty-mile coastline for a light station. Construction began in 1873 and the U.S. Lighthouse Board announced completion of the station with notice of lighting of the "fixed white light on or about August 19, 1874."

The Au Sable Light Station complex—light tower, two dwellings, a fog signal house, and a boat house—built from 1873 to 1910, is reached by a six-mile drive on unpaved Alger County Road H-58 and a one-and-a-half-mile level walk on the North County Trail east from the Hurricane River campground.

The whitewashed round brick lighthouse tower with its distinctive crown of a black painted lens room is 87-feet tall to the top of the ventilator ball. The cliff top location placed the focal plane of the third order Fresnel lens, visible eighteen miles away, at 107 feet above lake level. The tower's walls at the 17-feet diameter base are 4-feet thick and taper to 3 feet at the lower lantern room. The two-story red brick keeper's quarters (originally approximately 27 feet by 31 feet in plan), with jerkinhead gabled roof, is attached to the tower by a 12-foot-long one-story passageway. The quarters built in 1873–84 received an addition for an assistant keeper in 1909. Upon completion of the addition (approximately 12-feet wide) the building contained six-room apartments on the ground and second floor. A one-story porch across the building's front faces the lake. A fog signal building was added in 1897 and another two-story red brick building built in 1909 housed a third keeper. The light was automated in 1957 and a full-time keeper was no longer required to live at the station. Transferred to the National Park Service in 1968, the restoration of the complex is in process.

Au Sable Lighthouse

The climb up the open wrought-iron spiral stair inside the tower to the upper lantern level is a worthwhile experience for the rewarding views. A deck circles the tower and behind the safety of a secure railing there is a 360-degree panorama over Pictured Rocks National Lakeshore and the vast blue waters of Lake Superior.

Sleeping Bear Dunes National Lakeshore
Located in Empire, Leelanau, and Benzie Counties, Michigan

→ www.nps.gov/slbe

→ Park headquarters is in Empire twenty-two miles north of Frankfort via M-22 and twenty-two miles west of Traverse City via M-72.

Sleeping Bear Point Coast Guard Station/
Maritime Museum

Sleeping Bear Dunes National Lakeshore on Lake Michigan's northwest shoreline in Michigan's Lower Peninsula is a year-round recreation haven established primarily for its outstanding natural features, including forests, beaches, dune formations, and bluffs reaching 460 feet high. Offshore are the Manitou Islands. The present day landscape resulted from glacial deposits shaped by winds coming across Lake Michigan that continue to cause migrating dunes of windblown sand. Many of these spectacular views can be seen from the comfort of a vehicle or from one of the many overlooks along the Pierce Stocking Scenic Drive, a former logging road that is now a 7.4 mile self-guided auto tour.

The lakeshore also contains a wide range of cultural attractions depicting the area's rich agricultural and maritime history. The Port Oneida Rural Historic District features rolling fields, and picturesque barns and farmhouses. It is the largest intact agricultural district in the National Park System, and the largest historical district in public ownership in the country. Representative of late-nineteenth and early-twentieth-century farms of the Midwest, it includes eighteen farmsteads with over one hundred historic structures on over 3,400 acres of land. There are also three former U.S. Life-Saving Station/Coast Guard Stations at the Lakeshore. One near the historic village of Glen Haven, is now operated as the Sleeping Bear Point Coast Guard Station/Maritime Museum, and has the reputed largest collection of Great Lakes Maritime history in the world. Another station is located on South Manitou Island near the lighthouse and historic village, and a third is in the historic village on North Manitou Island.

Chartering of the U.S. Life-Saving Service in 1871 inspired the construction of approximately 280 life-saving stations on the east and west coasts and Great Lakes to aid in the rescue of shipwrecked men. (In 1915 the U.S. Life-Saving Service merged with the U.S. Coast Guard.) A typical station complex consisted of living quarters, boathouse, a signal tower, and outbuildings. Assigned to a station were a keeper and crew (called surfmen) selected for their familiarity with local weather conditions and shoreline and the ability to row an open boat in a storm. The station was a base from which to scan the horizon from a rooftop lookout tower for vessels in trouble and signs of impending inclement weather, patrol beaches, and to open beach launch small wooden rowboats to rescue floundering vessels and rescue shipwrecked survivors. One crew on North Carolina's Outer Banks became famous for their assistance to the Wright Brothers flight experiments at Kitty Hawk.

The Sleeping Bear Point Life-Saving Station was established in 1901 with construction of a dwelling (1901), steel signal tower (1914), boathouse and marine railway (1932), and outbuildings. By 1931, shifting sand dunes and shoreline erosion forced the station to move to its current location near the historic village of Glen Haven. The building relocation was by horses, rollers, track, and cable. Deactivated in 1942, the station stood idle until 1971 with temporary use as headquarters for the recently established National Lakeshore. The buildings have been restored to their pre-1931 appearance and are open to visitors.

The simple white clapboard two-story main building with pedimented gable over a front porch housed the keeper and crew. A central hallway and staircase divided the wood-frame structure into equal halves for the lighthouse crew and the keeper and his family. The crew's ground floor contained a living room and kitchen with a bunkroom above. The keeper's ground floor contained combined living room and office and a kitchen with bedrooms above. Today, the building is home to the Sleeping Bear Point Coast Guard Station/Maritime Museum and is refurnished with exhibits on both floors. The Maritime Museum is open seasonally (Memorial Day through Labor Day).

Nearby is the board-and-batten boathouse with large, paired double doors, flared eaves, and a short conical-roof mounted cupola. Along with lifeboat, beach rescue cart, and line-throwing cannon, restored surfboats stand inside the boathouse ready for launching down the double track marine railway. Daily reenactment of the U.S. Life-Saving Service rescue techniques is conducted throughout the summer. In addition to original outbuildings, a steel signal tower built in 1914 stands alongside the boathouse.

A one-and-a-half-hour ferry ride from Leland to South Manitou Island crosses the Manitou Passage. The South Manitou Lighthouse on the southeast tip of the island, a short walk from the National Park Service visitor center near the ferry landing, has become an unofficial symbol of the National Lakeshore. The station was established in 1839, replaced with a 35-foot tower in 1858, and the current tower built in 1871. The 104-foot-tall conical brick tower had a third order Fresnel lens with a focal plane 100 feet above the lake. A 45-foot-long brick enclosed passageway is attached to the two-and-a-half-story gabled dwelling. The painted yellow brick building (30 feet by 32 feet in plan) has ground floor doors and windows with brick soldier course arches. The second floor sidewalls have faux window openings with "1858" set in raised brick in one of the openings. The lighthouse was deactivated in 1958. The exterior of the structure has been preserved.

Minnesota

Midwest

Grand Portage National Monument

Located in Grand Portage, Grand Portage Indian Reservation, Cook County, Minnesota

→ www.nps.gov/grpo

→ Located about 150 miles northeast of Duluth, Minnesota, about one half-mile off Minnesota 61 on Cook County 17 within the village of Grand Portage. The park headquarters complex is part of the new Grand Portage Heritage Center on the national monument property.

Grand Portage Great Hall and Kitchen (courtesy NPS)

Grand Portage National Monument marks the site of a historic fur-trading depot in northeastern Minnesota, halfway between civilization and wilderness, linking Montreal with northwestern Canada. In the late eighteenth century it was the main headquarters for North West Company and other French and English fur-trading businesses employing a cadre of *voyageurs* paddling the lakes and streams of a vast inland water network. Located on the western shore of Lake Superior, the company's post was summer headquarters for the transcontinental trading route. A stretch of nine miles of portage across the "Great Carrying Place" bypassed rapids on the lower Pigeon River, now the U.S. and Canada border, and linked the post to Fort Charlotte to the west.

Today, the National Monument includes the reconstructed fur trade era depot with a stockade, warehouse, kitchen, and Great Hall, and the entire length of the Great Carrying Place. A new Heritage Center opened in July 2007 and includes Ojibwe and French vernacular elements. The monument is enclosed entirely within Grand Portage Indian Reservation, which Anishinaabeg (Ojibwe) families have called home for centuries.

The North West Company's depot construction started in approximately 1778. The post served for a quarter century until abandoned in 1803 when the company moved its trading center north to Fort William in Ontario, Canada, to avoid American duties on all merchandise and furs passing over the portage. Except for the stockade palisade walls, the reconstructed buildings are excellent examples of *poteaux sur sole* (posts on sills) construction using square timbers hewn from logs placed vertically and horizontal planks inserted into grooves in the posts and calked with oakum. Reconstructed buildings are placed over their original archaeological footprints.

Built on level ground on the Lake Superior shoreline, the depot and enclosing walls are set against the background of Mt. Rose. The stockade is an encircling palisade of log pickets 9 to 10 feet tall, tapered to points at the top and braced with horizontal logs. An opening in the palisade accesses the dock extending into the lake. A two-story (13-feet square in plan) lookout tower at the southeast corner stands over the double-leaf door main entrance.

The one-and-a-half-story Great Hall (30 feet by 95 feet in plan) has a porch across the full length of the side facing the lake and contained a main hall with two fireplaces and corner bedrooms used by the partners of the North West Company. The hip roof of cedar shingles has three dormers on north and south to daylight the main hall. Today, the building contains late-eighteenth-century reproduction furnishings and is used for orientation films, exhibits, and a sales area. Trade goods and furs are also on display in the main hall.

The one-and-a-half-story kitchen (35 feet by 27 feet in plan) is connected to the Great Hall by a covered passageway. The gable-ended kitchen has shed roof extensions from the main roof over full-length porches on both sides and is historically furnished based on inventories of the North West Company from 1797. There is a pantry area, a large fireplace in the kitchen, and a Quebec-style bake oven outside behind the kitchen. Both fireplace and oven are used by staff for demonstrations.

The Canoe Warehouse (52 feet by 19 feet in plan) is the third of the park's reconstructed buildings and is located outside the west stockade wall. Definition of its use was inconclusive and it now functions as a canoe shed displaying the park's canoe collection and an exhibit on canoe loads during the fur trade.

A unique experience is in store for the visitor, in addition to viewing exhibits and demonstrations by staff and Ojibwe artisans, during the annual Grand Portage Rendezvous Days and Pow-Wow the second full August weekend every year. At this event period-clothed staff and volunteers present a historic encampment, along with demonstrations and competitive events. Historic buildings are open from mid-May to late October. However, the new Heritage Center with exhibits and interpretive store, is open year-round.

Ohio

Midwest

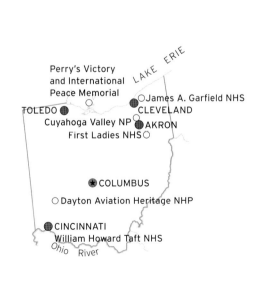

Cuyahoga Valley National Park

Located between Cleveland and Akron in Cuyahoga and Summit Counties, Ohio

→ www.nps.gov/cuva

→ The park is accessible from many different highways, including Interstates 77, 271, 80 (the Ohio Turnpike), and State Route 8. To start a tour at the north end of the park, exit Interstate 77 at Rockside Road then travel east just over one mile, turning right (south) onto Canal Road, and proceeding approximately 1.5 miles to the Canal Visitor Center.

Everett Road covered bridge

Cuyahoga Valley National Park preserves rural landscapes in a pastoral valley along the Cuyahoga River between Cleveland and Akron. A rich collection of historical structures from early settlement in Ohio's Western Reserve, canal and railroad building, and the Civilian Conservation Corps (CCC) offer a natural and cultural landscape throughout the park. The main National Park Service (NPS) visitor center is located at Canal, with a restored canal lock and buildings. Other visitor contact facilities are located at the Frazee House, Boston Store, Hunt Farm, Peninsula Depot, and the Winter Sports Center at Kendall Lake.

The valley's cultural landscape is threaded by the twenty-mile Ohio & Erie Canal Towpath Trail following the historic route of the 1827 canal connecting Cleveland on Lake Erie with Portsmouth, Ohio, on the Ohio River. The heyday of the canal era lasted approximately thirty years. By the 1860s, railroads surpassed the canal as the more efficient way to move goods to market, including between the coalfields of east central Ohio and northern Ohio industrial centers, and connecting Akron and Cleveland. The 308-mile Ohio & Erie Canal waterway ended operations in 1913.

Cultural and recreational attractions abound in the park: the Blossom Music Center, summer home of the Cleveland Orchestra; Porthouse Theater owned by Kent State

University; the Hale Farm & Village, a recreated 1848 Western Reserve village; the Virginia Kendall area; and the Cuyahoga Valley Scenic Railroad running the length of the park with NPS interpreters aboard many trains to enrich the experience of the valley's cultural and natural history.

The Canal Visitor Center is an unusual two-story, twin facade Greek Revival canal-era building facing Ohio & Erie Canal Lock 38. The original building (circa 1830s) was a two-story rectangular, post-and-beam framed of hand-hewn timbers with horizontal clapboard siding, double-hung sash with shutters, and a gable roof. The second adjoining structure is of similar form and materials, constructed of stud framing, with different configuration of windows and a double door, and a frieze board and cornice on the gable end. The one-story porch across the second (south) building was added fifteen or twenty years later. The paired structures served as a residence, tavern, store, and social gathering place for residents and canal boat passengers waiting to pass through the lock. Renovated by the NPS in the 1980s to an appearance of the 1840s, the tavern, for some time, had such a colorful reputation it was called "Hell's Half Acre." Canal lock demonstrations are conducted seasonally on weekends by NPS staff and by volunteers wearing period clothing to give the visitor a full flavor of lock operations.

Near the visitor center (1.5 miles south) is the two-story late Federal-style Stephen Frazee House. Built in 1826 and 1827, the house sits on a hill overlooking the Ohio & Erie Canal. Rectangular in plan (approximately 20 feet by 36 feet) with a one-story L-shaped wing to the rear, the brick wall-bearing exterior and interior wood framing has interesting stepped gable parapets and two corbelled chimney tops at each end of the house. The front facade has a typical five-bay division of the period, with a center entrance flanked by four deeply recessed windows and five windows above.

The Boston Store is located in the village of Boston Mills at a midpoint in the park along the Ohio & Erie Canal Towpath Trail. This handsome, restored two-story structure with white clapboard siding on a smoothly dressed sandstone foundation and a one-

Frazee House   Boston Store

story porch encircling the front and sides originally built in 1836 as the Boston Land and Manufacturing Company Store, illustrates the transition period of the Classic Revival (1780–1830) and Greek Revival (1820–1860), and regional architecture during early settlement of the Western Reserve. The building floor plan is trapezoidal with the long side of the building facing the canal. The early Federal influences are seen in the front pediment containing a lunette located within the pediment, and the small scale of the cornice and rake detail. Superimposed on the Federal style are the Greek Revival Ionic pilasters on the front and east sides of the building. The division of bays on the front elevation is a departure from the typical symmetry of the two revival styles: the second story of four bays and the first story into eight bays, probably related to the building's function.

Located in the southeastern area of the park, the Virginia Kendall State Park was an Akron Metropolitan Park Board development in the 1930s, now incorporated into Cuyahoga National Park. A master plan prepared with the assistance of the NPS and the CCC integrated four "playsteads" into a naturalistic landscape environment and included shelters (Ledges, Octagon, and Lake) and the Happy Days Day Camp surrounded by wooded areas, open meadows, landscaped drives and parking areas, stone guardrails, and a network of trails following the natural terrain. NPS rustic style designs adapted to specific site features, including local quarried sandstone, board-and-batten exterior siding, and wormy chestnut throughout—available by harvesting American chestnut trees which are abundant in the valley and affected by blight.

The Happy Days Day Camp opened in 1939 as a camp for urban children. Now serving as the Happy Days Visitor Center, the structure is in a forest clearing on the crest of a slight hill, surrounded by a play field to the north and west and a parking area to the rear of the building. The long horizontally massed building with board-and-batten vertical siding is set in a corner of a sloping open "playstead" surrounded by trees, creating a visual harmony between building and setting. Connected to the camp by a network of trails are the Octagon Shelter (1937–38), an eight-sided, one-story structure and a one-story covered, open-sided picnic area extension set in a wooded area; the Ledges Shelter (1936), built in a cruciform floor plan combining a two-story caretaker's residence with an enclosed one-story dining room and kitchen and a roofed and open sided picnic area; and Kendall Lake Shelter (1936), a two-story structure set into a hillside and serving as a bathhouse.

The Hunt Farm property is typical of the small family farms that dotted the Cuyahoga Valley in the late nineteenth century. Built in 1880, the one-and-a-half-story farmhouse is 50 feet from the Ohio & Erie Canal. A vernacular example characteristic of farm homes in the valley, the structure is rectangular in plan with a shallow pitched gable roof. The fenestration has plain trim. A one-story porch under a dropped shed roof, supported by turned spindle posts, runs the full length of the double-door entrance facade. A full width addition to the rear creates a "saltbox" appearance as an extension of the main roof. Exterior walls are sheathed in 6-inch-wide weatherboard siding. The NPS restored house now serves as a visitor information center.

West of the Hunt Farm, Hale Farm & Village is a mid-nineteenth-century outdoor living history museum of twenty-one buildings around a village green on 140 acres

operated by the Western Reserve Historical Society. Set in the year 1848, it is populated by period-clothed role players portraying the typical inhabitants of a small town
in northeast Ohio. Buildings were relocated from the Ohio Western Reserve and set

Hunt Farm house   Hadley House

around a village green with period houses, the Hadley House (one of several quite elegant ones), and a New England style Meetinghouse. Restored interiors are furnished
with period pieces.

Two other historic structures of interest are the scenic Everett Road Covered Bridge,
an NPS 1986 reconstruction of a historical bridge on the site, and the Peninsula Depot
Visitor Center, a relocated and restored Baltimore & Ohio "Class A" combination station
that serves as an information and orientation center for people on foot, bike, and rail,
and is a station for Cuyahoga Valley Scenic Railroad (CVSR) excursions between Cleveland and Canton.

The Blossom Music Center opened in 1968 as the summer home of the Cleveland
Symphony Orchestra. Planned and built between 1966 and 1968, an 800-acre site is located in the southeast corner of the park. The Center's signature structure is the Blossom Pavilion. Created by architect Peter van Dijk with Pietro Belluschi serving as consultant to the client, the dramatically soaring and obliquely angled steel arch, spanning
400 feet and rising 200 feet is supported on ten steel columns; trusses carrying the roof
extend outward from the arch, supported on steel columns. A slate-covered conical roof
sweeps outward from the arch in a great arc. Partially open on two sides and fully so that,
at the roof edge, the pavilion has 5,281 seats beneath the roof, an orchestra pit for the
symphony's 110 musicians, and a broad stage for flexible use. Space behind and below
the stage contains offices, green room, dressing rooms, and services. Another 13,500
patrons can be accommodated on the expansive hillside lawn seating area fanning out
from the covered seating. Acoustics and sight lines are superb, even to the far reaches
of the hillside. Structural designer R.M. Gensert Associates capably executed the architectural concept. The acoustician was Heinrich Keilholz, with preliminary acoustical
design by Christopher Jaffe. The center underwent major renovations and reopened in
the spring of 2003.

Dayton Aviation Heritage National Historical Park

Located in and near Dayton, Montgomery and Greene Counties, Ohio

→   www.nps.gov/daav

→   The park's four units are located in and near Dayton in southwestern Ohio. Interstates 70 and 75 intersect at Dayton. The Wright Cycle Company complex and Dunbar House are located in southwest Dayton; Wright Brothers Aviation Center in Dayton History's Carillon Park is in south Dayton; and Huffman Prairie Flying Field is eight miles northeast of Dayton, located on the grounds of Wright-Patterson Air Force Base.

The Wright Cycle Company

Dayton Aviation Heritage National Historic Park consists of four units that are a cooperative effort between the National Park Service (NPS) and its four partners. The sites are The Wright Cycle Company complex (The Wright Cycle Company building and the Wright-Dunbar Interpretive Center and Aviation Trail Visitor Center), containing a historically refurnished Wright brothers' printing office and an original Wright brothers bicycle shop; Huffman Prairie Flying Field and the Huffman Prairie Flying Field Interpretive Center; the John W. Berry, Sr., Wright Brothers Aviation Center, in Dayton History's Carillon Park, housing the Wright brothers' third airplane; and the Dayton History's Dunbar House, Paul Laurence Dunbar's last home. All of these sites are National Historic Landmarks or are listed on the National Register of Historic Places.

The name of this park could be deceiving by suggesting it is only about aviation. Commemorating two of Dayton's distinguished aviation luminaries, Orville and Wilbur Wright, the park also recognizes the life of Paul Laurence Dunbar the first African-American writer to win high distinction in American literature. The Wright brothers' accomplishment—completing the first free, controlled, and sustained flight in a power-driven, heavier-than-air machine—is an incredible tale of inventive genius. Paul Laurence Dunbar, an acquaintance and contemporary of the Wright brothers, in a short life (he died at age thirty-three), fought the bigotries of nineteenth-century America to gain national acclaim for his prolific outpouring of novels, plays, short stories, newspaper articles, essays, and over six hundred poems.

The Wright Cycle Company complex consists of two adjoining buildings located at 16 South Williams Street: the Wright Cycle Company building and the restored Hoover Block. The Wright-Dunbar Interpretive Center is the main visitor center for the park and occupies the Hoover Block. From 1895 until 1897, the Wrights manufactured bicycles on the first floor and operated a printing shop on the second floor of the National Historic Landmark Wright Cycle Company building. The two-story building with a chamfered corner and stone columns and frieze at the entrance is rehabilitated to an approximation of its 1890s appearance. It was here that the brothers developed the technical experience and income to support their subsequent success with gliders and powered flying machines. This was the fourth of five locations for their bicycle business (Henry Ford moved the fifth building to Greenfield Village in Dearborn, Michigan). The Hoover Block on the corner of South Williams and West Third Streets was home to Wright & Wright, job printers from 1890 to 1895. The three-story commercial Hoover Block built in 1890 is where the brothers briefly published the *Dayton Tattler*, the newspaper of Orville's high school classmate Paul Laurence Dunbar.

Paul Laurence Dunbar House at 219 North Paul Laurence Dunbar Street was the modest two-story brick home of Paul Laurence Dunbar during the last years of his life from 1904 to 1906. This first public memorial to an African-American is open to the public.

An unusual National Historic Landmark is the *Wright Flyer III* located in the Wright Brothers Aviation Center in Dayton's Carillon Park (1000 Carillon Boulevard). The privately operated park contains the brother's 1905 airplane restored from 1948 to 1950 with the initial help of Orville Wright before his death in 1948. An estimated sixty to eighty percent of the original plane used to perfect controlled flight remains; an advanced version of the Wrights' first airplane of 1903 is displayed in the Smithsonian Institution's National Air and Space Museum.

Now within Wright-Patterson Air Force Base, the National Historic Landmark Flying Field looks much as it did during the time of the Wrights' use. The site, near active runways, contains replicas of the 1905 hangar and launching catapult. Occasionally, a visitor can watch Galaxy C-5As, the largest American military transport, taking off and landing in the same airspace once occupied by the Wright brothers, and reflect that Orville Wright's historic first flight of 120 feet would fall short of the C-5A's 222-foot wingspan. Prior to visiting the flying field, visitors are encouraged to stop at the Huffman Prairie Flying Field Interpretive Center and Wright Memorial at 2380 Memorial Road.

First Ladies National Historic Site

Located in Canton, Stark County, Ohio

→ www.nps.gov/fila

→ Located in downtown Canton, exit Interstate 77 at Downtown/Tuscarawas Street. Head east on Tuscarawas Street to Market Avenue South, turn right and travel through two stop lights; immediately after the second light is a gated parking lot.

The First Ladies National Historic Site is located at the Ida Saxton McKinley House on the corner of Market Avenue and 4th Street in downtown Canton, Ohio. The renovated seven-story 1895 City National Bank Building serves as the National First Ladies' Library Education and Research Center. The library functions as a national archive of the contributions of America's First Ladies and other notable American women and is open to the public only for guided historical tours and to researcheres by appointment.

Built in 1841 and modified in 1865 the brick Victorian Ida Saxton McKinley House was the Saxton family home and the residence where the twenty-fifth president lived with his wife Ida between 1878–1891 during the period he served in the U.S. House of Representatives. Widowed after the presidential assassination in 1901, Ida lived here until her death in 1907.

The elegant two- and three-story red brick building of irregular massing with Second Empire and Italianate elements has a ground floor wrap-around porch facing Market Street South. The earliest portion is at the rear of the structure and was a two-story gable roofed building. Keystoned arches cap all exterior door and window openings. Undergoing several uses and then restored by a family member with work including removal of a brick facade that covered the entire building, the interior's public rooms are now restored to an opulent splendor, complete with ornate historical wallpaper and period furniture.

Ida Saxton McKinley House

Entering the foyer, visitors are impressed by the introduction to the public rooms with a dazzling array of historically reproduced wallpaper, carpets, and area rugs. Wood trim is polished to a high gloss; the eye is swept upward to the ornate ceiling and the black walnut staircase that wraps up and around all three stories. Tours of the Saxton house by period-dressed docents visit parlor and library, sitting/bedroom, study, and the third-floor ballroom housing a collection of First Ladies' photos. The site is managed by the National Park Service and operated by the National First Ladies' Library by guided tour only. Reservations are highly recommended.

James A. Garfield National Historic Site

Located in Mentor, Lake County, Ohio

→ www.nps.gov/jaga

→ From Interstate 90 (twenty-five miles east of Cleveland) take the State Route 306 Mentor-Kirtland exit. Travel north on State Route 306 for two miles to Mentor Avenue (US 20). Turn right and travel east for two miles. The site is located at 8095 Mentor Avenue, on the north side of the road.

James A. Garfield House facing Mentor Avenue

James A. Garfield National Historic Site encompasses the home of James A. Garfield, the twentieth president of the United States, including an impressive Victorian mansion and the surrounding grounds called Lawnfield. Garfield purchased a run-down one-story farmhouse with outbuildings on 118 acres in 1876, enlarged it to a splendid twenty-room ten-and-a-half-story structure, and increased the farm to 158 acres. The additions included the front porch made famous in his 1880 presidential campaign. Assassinated after only six months in office, the property continued under the ownership of Garfield's widow, Lucretia, who, in 1885, added nine more rooms, including the Memorial Library and vault—setting the precedent for presidential libraries.

In addition to the National Historic Landmark Garfield home, restored to its 1880–1904 appearance, Lawnfield includes the carriage house (rehabilitated into a visitor center), the campaign office, the restored 75-foot-tall windmill, gas holder, granary, barn, chicken coop with run, and a tenant house. The National Park Service (NPS) and the Western Reserve Historical Society jointly operate the James A. Garfield National Historic Site.

The rambling structure resulting from various additions has a variety of roof forms (gable, hip, jerkinhead), slender, tall chimneys at right angles to each other, projecting dormers with Eastlake decorative elements or shingled eaves, and exterior materials (clapboard, stone, and shingle). This potential jumble of forms is rescued as a unified complex by the simple use of color—a medium shade of gray on exterior wood clapboard and shingle surfaces and shutters, red window sashes and dark gray trim, and a red roof. Facing Mentor Avenue (US 20), the strong horizontal line of the one-story 70-foot-long front porch encompasses the full width of the house, with a uniformly spaced rhythm of paired columns, is a building element that further unifies the idiosyncratic elevations. The famous "front porch" campaign originated here where thousands traveled by train to a temporary stop at the back of the property and walked up the narrow lane to the house to hear the candidate speak.

The complete NPS restoration burnished the labyrinth-like interior's oak floors, door and window frames, fireplace surrounds, and paneling to a high gloss. A profusion of Victorian decorative elements are placed throughout the house: furniture, much of it original; stained glass windows; chandeliers and wall sconces; many different bold patterned wall coverings on walls, borders, and ceilings; oriental carpets; and fireplace tiles. The Memorial Library, located off the landing on the second floor is part of Lucretia's addition to the house. The room's elaborately carved white oak panels, shelving, and beamed ceiling and brilliant brass gasoliers provide an elegant setting for the president's extensive personal library, which is still housed on its shelves. The room contains Garfield's congressional desk and a rare Wooton mahogany desk with 122 compartments. Displayed in the study is the specially designed leather chair where Garfield, an insomniac, could read all night with one leg over the left arm.

The carriage house has been converted to the site's visitor center where guided tours of the house originate. Garfield's small campaign office stands in the yard. Commanding the interior of large lawn on the site is the restored water-pumping windmill. Built under Lucretia's direction in 1894, her desire for an "artistic" structure has a rusticated

Victorian details   Visitor Center/Museum (former carriage house)

stone base (approximately 21-feet square in plan) with a tapered eight-sided shingled tower housing a storage tank capped by a shingled conical roof supporting the multi-bladed wind wheel and trailing wind vane.

Perry's Victory and International Peace Memorial

Put-in-Bay, South Bass Island, Ottawa County, Ohio

→   www.nps.gov/pevi

→   The park is located on the east side of Put-in-Bay village on South Bass Island at the western end of Lake Erie. Access is by ferry from Catawba Point (three miles) and Port Clinton (ten miles), eighty-five miles west of Cleveland and fifty miles east of Toledo.

Urn atop Perry Memorial Column

"We have met the enemy and they are ours. Two ships, two brigs, one schooner & one sloop. Yours, with great respect and esteem, O. H. Perry." So wrote Commodore Oliver Hazard Perry to General William Henry Harrison after the stirring American naval victory over the British on Lake Erie on September 10, 1813. Heroism, bravery, and tactical brilliance won the two-hour engagement of equally matched fleets ten miles northeast of Put-in-Bay, Ohio. Costly to both sides in vessels and killed or wounded men, the decisive victory was a turning point in the War of 1812 that ended British control of the Old Northwest Territory, setting the stage for a lasting international peace between the United States and Canada along the 4,000-mile-long border.

The 352-foot-tall Doric column on an isthmus connecting two larger sections of South Bass Island (commonly called Put-in-Bay) is an unusual memorial not only celebrating the American naval triumph, but also a lasting peace reached by arbitration and disarmament. The world's most massive Doric column was the result of a design competition won in 1912 by architects Joseph Freedlander and Alexander Duncan Seymour. Alone as a competition finalist without a museum rotunda at its base, the winning design placed a museum and colonnade dedicated to international peace at either end of a never built 750-foot-wide grand plaza. A cornerstone laying ceremony on the centennial of Perry's victory began construction, directed by nine states and the federal government, and the memorial was completed in 1915.

Today a visitor center with an imposing statue of Perry frames a view of the memorial column. Unimpinged upon by any surrounding structure, a long, curved promenade from the visitor center leads to a raised terraced granite plaza set on a treed berm placed in the broad lawn of the twenty-five-acre park. Rising unadorned from the plaza, the fluted column is topped by a square capital with an observation platform at the 317-foot level, reached by an elevator. On a clear day, from atop the monument, the location of Perry's historic naval victory can be traced on the waters of Lake Erie, along with views of surrounding islands, and the shorelines of Ohio, Michigan, and Canada.

Perry Memorial Column

The logistical challenges of building the column on an island were solved with ingenuity and innovative techniques including climbing interior derricks to lift the eighty-two courses of pink Milford Massachusetts granite in place, topped by a granite capital (abacus and echinus) and a 32-foot-high and 18-foot diameter, eight-legged bronze urn weighing eleven tons. The column shaft, placed on a thick concrete foundation, is 45-feet in diameter at the base and tapers to 35-feet just under the 47-foot square cap (abacus). Wall thicknesses range from 9 feet at the base to 4 feet at the top, incorporating a Classical Greek entasis of 4 inches to counter the optical illusion of the column appearing thinner in the middle. The granite blocks weighing as much as five tons, assembled from a jumble of stones littered around the construction site, arrived on the island, precisely cut and individually crated and marked. The blocks are anchored to a concrete inner lining faced with 4-inch-thick bricks.

A 27-foot-high domed rotunda room with a carved limestone ceiling in the column's base is placed over a crypt containing the remains of three American and British officers killed in this decisive naval battle. The rotunda floor and walls are constructed of Tennessee and Italian marble, Indiana limestone, and granite. Carved on the walls are memorial tablets over decorative garlands. Stairs to a lower elevator landing continue upwards in 427 steps spiraling around the elevator shaft to reach the observation deck. Seen with binoculars from the ground, the details of the observation deck construction show how cleanly the designer concealed an intricate cantilevered concrete structure in the abacus (cylindrical transition from the shaft to the observation deck platform) supporting and counterbalancing the echinus.

A major restoration of the monument is planned to coincide with the bicentennial events surrounding the War of 1812 and the Battle of Lake Erie (2013), and the centennial celebration of the monument's construction (2013–15), as well as the National Park Service (2016).

The visitor arriving in the lakeside resort town of Put-in-Bay has an opportunity for a contemplative experience about war and peace. Set aside aesthetic comparisons of this period piece with the modern Gateway Arch and Vietnam War Memorial. Respect for the remarkable naval tale of valiant American and British seamen almost two centuries ago is balanced by the spirit of the towering memorial structure, unfamiliar to ordinary references, but nevertheless an inspiring work.

William Howard Taft National Historic Site
Located near downtown Cincinnati, Hamilton, County

→   www.nps.gov/wiho

→   The Taft House is at 2038 Auburn Avenue in the Mount Auburn section of Cincinnati. From Interstate 71 north take Exit 2 (Reading Road), make a left onto Dorchester Street, turn right on Auburn Avenue and drive one-and-one-half blocks to the home. From Interstate 71 south take Exit 3 (William Howard Taft Road) to Auburn Avenue, turn left to the home.

William Howard Taft House

The William Howard Taft National Historic Site is the birthplace and boyhood home of the only man to serve as both president (1909 to 1913) and chief justice of the United States Supreme Court (1921 to 1930). Restored to its 1860s appearance, the home contains four rooms furnished with period pieces, representing the lifestyle of Taft and his family, and an exhibit commemorating Taft's life and career.

Taft was born here in 1857. A precocious child, he attended Cincinnati public schools, went on to Yale University graduating second in his class, and then returned to Cincinnati to earn a law degree from the Cincinnati Law School. At age thirty-three he was appointed solicitor general of the United States, then served as governor-general of the Philippines. Anointed by Theodore Roosevelt as his successor as president, Taft ran and was overwhelmingly elected to the office as the twenty-seventh president of the United States. Unsuccessful in his reelection bid in 1912, Taft went on to teach constitutional law at his alma mater, Yale University, and in 1921 was appointed chief justice of the Supreme Court by President Warren G. Harding. Taft served on the court until his death in 1930.

The Greek Revival yellow brick house on the summit of Mount Auburn was a country home in a neighborhood of elegant villas built to escape the conditions of the lower city. Original construction of the two-story house (32 by 41 feet in plan) dates from the 1840s. Shortly after the Tafts moved into the house, a three-story 23- by 40-foot wing to the rear substantially increased the house's size. After a fire in 1877 that destroyed the roof and second floor other major changes were made. Later owners altered features of the house. A historically incorrect restoration in 1964 was undone in a National Park Service restoration completed in 1988, restoring the house to its appearance during the years Taft lived here as a child and young adult.

Today, the approach to the house is from the sidewalk faced by a wrought-iron fence and gate between a pair of limestone piers. Modest in comparison to neighboring rambling Italianate villas, the yellow painted brick exterior walls are embellished by grey window shutters and red sandstone sills, a projecting cornice with scalloped trim, and a 2-foot-tall parapet extended from the lower brick walls. The front section of the house has a hipped roof topped by a rooftop observatory with wrought-iron grille. On the front facade simulated corner piers and a central bay are projected from the brick wall surfaces; a red painted sill course is above the rubble stone foundation wall of the original structure. The simple one-story entrance porch on a two-step platform is supported on chamfered columns, with a scalloped parapet above the flat roof. Brick sidewalks line the site. A latticed two-story porch enclosure is on the rear of the original house and lattice side walls support a metal roof over a basement entrance.

The carefully restored public rooms open for tours on the first and second floors contain some Taft memorabilia and period antique furniture, and reproduction wall paper and fabrics. The adjacent Taft Education Center is the starting point for house tours, an orientation video, and other interpretive exhibits on Taft's life and career.

Wisconsin

LAKE SUPERIOR

Apostle Islands NL

Mississippi River

Lake Winnebago

LAKE MICHIGAN

MILWAUKEE

MADISON

Midwest

Apostle Islands National Lakeshore

Located in Lake Superior near Bayfield, Ashland and Bayfield Counties, Wisconsin

→ www.nps.gov/apis

→ Park headquarters and visitor center is one block off Wisconsin Route 13 in Bayfield in northern Wisconsin, approximately ninety miles east of Duluth, Minnesota via US 53 and WI 13.

Raspberry Island Light Station

Wisconsin's Bayfield Peninsula extends out into Lake Superior as the scenic archipelago of the Apostle Islands. The national lakeshore includes twenty-one islands and twelve miles of mainland Lake Superior shoreline and the largest collection of lighthouses anywhere in the National Park System. Madeline Island, the largest of the Apostle Islands, is not within the park. Access to the islands and visits to the six historical light-houses is by private boat or cruise services from Bayfield. The National Park Service (NPS) conducts ranger-led summer tours at the Raspberry Island Light Station, and generally provides summer volunteer-led tours at the Sand, Michigan, and Devils Island Light Stations. Check with the park web site or visitor enter in Bayfield for details; fees may be charged.

The development of shipping after completion of the canal at Sault Ste. Marie in the mid-nineteenth century necessitated lighthouses to mark the Apostle Islands. Three of the lighthouses—Sand Island, Devils Island, and Outer Island—ring the outer edges of the island group and were built later to guide ships around the archipelago once Duluth and Superior eclipsed the local ports in importance. This fine collection of structures draws lighthouse buffs from all over the world to view the light stations, which remain remarkably intact and complete. Devils Island still has its original Fresnel lens intact, and most have a keepers' residence, fog signal building, and outbuildings. Remarkably, no two are alike. Some are complexes of a freestanding tower separate from a keepers' residence, while others are towers integrated with a keepers' residence. The original Michigan Island Fresnel lens is on display at the park visitor center in Bayfield; the smaller Raspberry Island lens can be viewed at the Madeline Island Historical Museum.

In order, chronologically, dated from original construction, the first Apostle Island's lighthouse was located on Michigan Island. It should have been the second lighthouse, except the contractor decided he preferred Michigan Island to the specified site on Long Island. Only in service briefly between 1857 and 1858, the structure was abandoned and then rebuilt in 1869. Located on a bluff 90 feet above the lake, the visitor can now enjoy two quite dissimilar stations on the same site. The mid-nineteenth-century station of rough stone, its exterior walls stuccoed and whitewashed, combined a small, one-and-a-half-story keeper's dwelling (approximately 30 feet by 24 feet in plan) with a low, conical light tower 57 feet to the top of the lantern. The modern steel frame 112-foot-tall tower perched on a small Greek Revival building has an unusual history. Originally the discontinued 1880 "Schooner's Ledge light" was relocated from Delaware River near Philadelphia. The disassembled tower was brought to Michigan Island in 1919 where it sat on the beach awaiting assembly for ten years until erected in 1929 as the tallest lighthouse in Wisconsin. A tramway, paralleled by a 123-step stair reaches the top of the bluff with a collection of buildings, including a keepers' residence. A turntable at the top of the tramway switches carts that circle the site on rails.

The La Pointe lighthouse on Long Island (1857 and 1895 reconstruction) was built to guide vessels coming from the east into the local Bayfield harbors. The narrow spit of land, now connected to the mainland, was the site of an early wood frame structure with a wooden tower. The new lighthouse, nearly a mile away from the old tower, is a 67-foot-tall pyramidal steel skeleton tower with a central cylindrical shaft containing a spiral stair to the lantern. In 1938 a wood-frame, three-family dwelling was built next to the new lighthouse. There is also a small tower at the very end of Long Island, built in 1897 and restored by the NPS in 2007.

Sand Island light station

Raspberry Island lighthouse was built in 1862 to guide ships into the local harbors. Placed on a cliff 40 feet above the lake and reached by a tramway and stairs, the light station is an elegant white-painted clapboard structure with a central 42-foot-tall tower flanked by symmetrical two-story keeper's residence wings. The red-tiled roof and porches present an attractive 72-foot-long structure facing the lake. A brick fog station building is alongside the handsome proportioned light tower structure, and other frame outbuildings are on the site. A rail tramway line circles the site. The proximity to Bayfield makes Raspberry Island the most visited of the light stations. An NPS ranger is on site to offer interpretive lectures during summer months. The integral light and keeper's quarters were restored to their 1920s heyday by the NPS in 2007.

Outer Island lighthouse stands on a high bluff 90 feet above the lake fully exposed to Lake Superior weather. Built in 1874, the handsome whitewashed brick 90-foot-tall light tower, with a 16-foot-diameter base containing a spiral staircase, is trimmed with Italianate details painted in contrasting black. A two-and-a-half-story keeper's residence is attached to the tower by a one-story enclosed passageway. The red brick structure with white painted wood frames and stone sills has a jerkinhead roof. A brick fog station completes the station.

Westernmost among the Apostle Islands lighthouses, the Sand Island Light Station is the most striking of the grouping. Built on a rocky outcropping in 1881 and serving until 1921, the Norman Gothic structure of locally quarried brown sandstone could be mistaken for a chapel. The picturesque composition has random ashlar walls with segmented stone window arches and sills with green shutters, a hammerhead truss with carved wood trim at the gable ends of the residence, and red tile roof. The light tower

Outer Island Light Station

begins as an 8-foot-square rising from the northwest corner of the dwelling (approximately 45 feet by 28 feet in plan), then gracefully flows into an octagon surmounted by the lantern and walkway. Carved wood trim decorates the steeply sloped gable end of the quarters. When active, a fourth-order Fresnel lens produced a fixed white light from the top of the 44-foot tall tower.

The final lighthouse in the Apostle Islands was built on Devils Island in 1891. A

Michigan Island Light Station

two-story, red brick, Queen Anne style keeper's dwelling and a building for the steam fog signal were completed at this time, but the light was placed in a temporary tower. The tower, made of wooden timbers, held a fourth order, Fresnel lens non-flashing red light. A two-story, brick and shingle house similar in design to the keeper's dwelling was built for the assistant keepers in 1897. Work began on the permanent tower, an 82-foot-tall steel cylinder, that same year. The lighthouse was originally designed as a plain, self-supporting cylinder, but the high winds of its exposed location caused the tower to shake so badly that light keepers complained that the motion sometimes extinguished the lamp. In 1914, external bracing was added for reinforcement, alleviating the problem and giving the tower the appearance we see today.

Devils Island eventually became the last staffed station in the Apostle Islands when replaced by automation in 1978. When the Coast Guard detachment hauled down their flag, it marked the end of over a century of light keepers tending lights in the Apostle Islands. While modern navigational tools decreased the importance of the lights, these lighthouses remind us of the brave men and women who tended these remote outposts to make life safer for sailors navigating the waters of the Apostle Islands.

South

Alabama

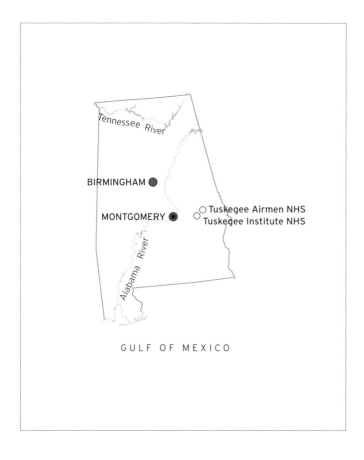

Tennessee River

BIRMINGHAM

MONTGOMERY

○ Tuskegee Airmen NHS
○ Tuskegee Institute NHS

Alabama River

GULF OF MEXICO

Tuskegee Airmen National Historic Site

Near Tuskegee, Macon County, Alabama

→ www.nps.gov/tuai

→ The site is headquartered on the Tuskegee University campus located 1.5 miles northwest of downtown Tuskegee, Alabama, thirty-five miles east of Montgomery, Alabama. From Interstate 85, exit onto AL 81 for six miles and follow signs to the site.

Tuskegee Airmen, 1942, (courtesy NPS)

This recent addition to the National Park System (1998) is under development to celebrate and preserve the memory of African-Americans who, during World War II, overcame racial prejudice and served in the Army Air Corps. The term "Tuskegee Airmen" refers to all who were involved in the so-called "Tuskegee Experiment," the Army Air Corps program to train African-Americans to fly and maintain combat aircraft. The Tuskegee Airmen included pilots, navigators, bombardiers, maintenance and support staff, instructors, and all the personnel who kept the planes in the air.

Tuskegee Airmen National Historic Site includes Moton Field on approximately eighty-seven acres owned by Tuskegee University and the City of Tuskegee, Alabama. Named in honor of Robert Russ Moton, Tuskegee Institute's second president, Moton Field was built from 1940 to 1942 with financial support from the Julius Rosenwald Fund.

A visit to the site and the wartime Moton Field, adjacent to Tuskegee University, and the remaining buildings awaiting rehabilitation requires an imaginary trip back in time—to the days when segregation and Jim Crow ruled the South and a few young black men were told they were not good enough to be a part of the United States Army Air Corps. Only in recent years has the nation become aware of the valuable contributions of the Tuskegee Airmen, exposed through personal memoirs, documentaries, television dramas, and scholarly studies. During the course of World War II and thereafter, the presence of these African-American fighter pilots in the Army Air Corps and their exemplary combat activities went quietly unnoticed by the American public. Indeed, the "Tuskegee Experiment," as one source observed, "was the military's best kept secret" due to the Air Corps' unwillingness to forego its policy of segregation.

Passage of the 1939 Civilian Pilot Training Act (CPT) to provide primary flight training, in case of a national emergency, included provision for training African-Americans and laid the groundwork for enlistment in the segregated Army Air Corps. Tuskegee Institute made a commitment to training black pilots and was one of a very few American institutions (and the only African-American institution) to own, develop, and control facilities for military flight instruction. With the facilities, and engineering and technical instructors, as well as a climate suitable for year round flying, the school was awarded a contract from the military to provide primary flight training. The first CPT program students completed their instruction in May 1940. Despite segregation, the success of the Tuskegee program is recorded in the site's enabling legislation, PL105-355:

> *The Tuskegee Airmen were the first African American soldiers to complete their training successfully and to enter the United States Army Air Corps. Almost one thousand aviators were trained as America's first African American military pilots. In addition, more than ten thousand military and civilian African American men and women served as flight instructors, officers, bombardiers, navigators, radio technicians, mechanics, air traffic controllers, parachute riggers, electrical and communications specialists, medical professionals, laboratory assistants, cooks, musicians, supply, firefighting, and transportation personnel.*

In terms of the site, little change has occurred to the historical scene that existed in the early and mid-1940s. Although a fire consumed Hangar Number Two and a portion of the control tower, original structures such as Hangar Number One, the Locker Building, All Ranks Club, sheds, the entrance gate, and the historic landscape remain very much intact. These remaining buildings, despite their fragile condition, along with the surrounding historic landscape, allow Moton Field to retain its strong place in history, as well as its visual character as an airfield.

As National Park Service and volunteer work on the site progresses, the nation's debt to the pioneering airmen at Tuskegee will be fulfilled to perpetuate the history of African-Americans who participated in air crew, ground crew, and operations support training in the Army Air Corps during WWII.

Tuskegee Institute National Historic Site

Tuskegee, Macon County, Alabama

→   www.nps.gov/tuin

→   The site is on the campus of Tuskegee University located one and one-half miles northwest of downtown Tuskegee, Alabama, thirty-five miles east of Montgomery, Alabama. From Interstate 85, exit onto AL 81, turn right on Franklin Road, and follow signs to the campus.

More than a century and a quarter ago a twenty-six-year-old black educator arrived in Tuskegee, Alabama, to become the first principal of the newly chartered Normal School for Negroes. From 1881 to 1915 Booker T. Washington, later joined by George Washington Carver, pioneered the predominantly black higher education institution, providing practical training for African-Americans and helping them develop economic self-reliance. Both men are indelibly associated with the school that was renamed the Tuskegee Normal and Industrial Institute, adopting the name Tuskegee Institute in 1937 and Tuskegee University in 1985.

Unusual as part of an active private institution, Tuskegee Institute National Historic Site is a fifty-eight-acre district comprised of twenty-two buildings and forms the historic campus nucleus on the original one thousand-acre abandoned plantation purchased by Washington. The district's buildings are owned and operated by Tuskegee University and administered jointly by Tuskegee University and the National Park Service (NPS)

George Washington Carver Laboratory/Museum

from a headquarters building in Tuskegee, Alabama. Three of the site's buildings are owned by the NPS: "The Oaks," the home of Booker T. Washington; George Washington Carver's laboratory (now the George Washington Carver Museum); and "Grey Columns," an antebellum mansion.

Unlike the meager state support for historically back colleges throughout the South and their generally impoverished campus appearance, the persuasive skills of Washington and the Institute's academic success attracted financial support from the likes of John D. Rockefeller, Andrew Carnegie, and Collis P. Huntington. Many of the Institute's buildings, constructed during Washington's tenure, are still standing. Twenty-six of the buildings of classical design were built by the students—including fabrication of the red and brown bricks—designed and supervised by architect Robert R. Taylor, a Tuskegee faculty member and valedictorian and first African-American graduate of the Massachusetts Institute of Technology (1892).

The earliest structures are the Band Cottage (the foundry and blacksmith shop) constructed in 1892, Phelps Hall (the Bible training school) built in 1892, and Thrasher Hall (the science building) built in 1893.

The Oaks, a stately Queen Anne style three-story red brick structure served as Washington's home and the Institute's social center. This is where students received on-the-job experience as part of their vocational training; guests were entertained and faculty and staff frequently visited. Constructed in 1899, and outfitted with steam heat and electricity, the house sat on three acres of gardens, orchards, and pastures. The fine quality of design and workmanship added to the image Washington perpetuated of the Institute's success. Wide porches on three sides, shingled gable ends, soaring fluted chimneys, and arched window openings with soldier course brick embellished the exterior. The interior contained a parlor, library, dining room, den, kitchen, family and guest rooms, breakfast room, and five bathrooms. Restored to its appearance during Washington's life, the house contains many original furnishings.

George Washington Carver was hired in 1896 by Booker T. Washington to teach agriculture at Tuskegee. Arriving as a young teaching assistant, Carver spent over forty years on the Tuskegee campus conducting experiments and developing agricultural extension services for black farmers and homemakers. The attractive two-story red brick George Washington Carver Museum located at the center of the campus was built originally as a central laundry facility and remodeled extensively in 1915 to its present appearance with support from admirer and industrialist Henry Ford. The Institute designated the building as a museum in 1938 and Carver oversaw the conversion to a combined museum and laboratory, until his death in 1943. A pedimented porch with arched brick piers graces the entrance of the 122- by 57-foot structure and three sides of the building have simulated brick columns. The entrance floor is an open airy interior with trusses supporting the hip roof and a skylight.

To the east of the campus toward downtown Tuskegee stands "Grey Columns," an antebellum plantation mansion purchased by the NPS in 1974 as part of the Tuskegee Institute National Historic Site. Constructed between 1854 and 1857 in the Greek Revival style with some Italianate features, the house was the center of William Varner's plantations. The structure is ringed on three sides by a two-story high colonnade of Doric columns and a 10-foot-wide portico. An octagonal cupola crowns the hip roof.

The campus is open for self-guided tours and visitors are requested to respect the Institute's activities and the students' privacy. Although not a historic structure and outside the site itself, the Tuskegee Chapel designed by Paul Rudolph (1969), with its somewhat disjointed exterior, has a superb interior considered one of the most extraordinary religious rooms in the country.

Arkansas

Fort Smith National Historic Site

Located in Fort Smith, Sebastian County, Arkansas

→ www.nps.gov/fosm

→ The park is in downtown Fort Smith, accessible from Interstate 40 east-bound at Exit 326 to downtown
on US 64 and westbound at Exit 8 on Interstate 540, then west on Highway 22 (Garrison Avenue). At Rogers
Avenue turn south at Fourth Street for three blocks and right on Garland Avenue to the entrance of the main
parking lot and a short walk to the visitor center.

Visitor center (barracks/courthouse/jail building)

Fort Smith National Historic Site contains the remnants of two frontier forts and the Federal Court for the Western District of Arkansas. Located on the edge of downtown Fort
Smith on a bluff overlooking the Arkansas River, only vestiges of the first fort founded in
1817 and the second in 1838 mark the site of fortifications once at the western boundary
of the settled United States. The first fort's era lasted from 1817 to 1824 and was a small
(approximately 130 feet square) wooden stockade enclosure intended for peacekeeping on the frontier. The second fort grew out of concerns for settlers' safety, affected
by forced migration of southeastern Native American tribes moving westward on the
Trail of Tears. After serving as the center of the Union regional Civil War operations,
movement of the frontier westward ended the fort's usefulness and it was abandoned in
1871. Establishment on the site of the Federal Court with criminal jurisdiction over the
Indian Territory from 1872 to 1896 provided the courtroom for "Hanging Judge" Isaac C.
Parker. He earned his reputation from sentencing more than eighty men to death.

Today, the visitor will experience an open landscape of level lawn as the setting for the
restored two-story Barracks/Courthouse/Jail Building, the skyline dominated in summer

by a 100-foot-tall flagpole flying a 36-foot by 20-foot, 37-star garrison flag. Other histori-cal structures on the site are the Commissary Storehouse completed in 1846; a reproduc-tion of the 1886 gallows, capable of hanging twelve at a time; and foundations of the first fort. A river trail leads to Belle Point and the Trail of Tears Overlook. Located within the boundary of the site is Frisco Station, acquired by the National Park Service (NPS) in 2003. Plans are to convert the station into the city's last terminal and transfer station.

At the end of the drive on Rogers Avenue, through downtown Fort Smith, the entrance pillars of the second fort's stone walls frame the entrance vista to the site's park-like setting. The visitor center in the barracks/courthouse/jail building, restored accurately to its 1890 appearance, provides an orientation film as an introduction to the park's history. Interpretive exhibits include "Hanging Judge" Isaac C. Parker's Court-room, and the original "Hell on the Border" jail located beneath the courthouse.

The central feature of the park, the two-story red brick barracks/courthouse/jail, is dramatically different in appearance than the barracks completed in 1851. Reconstruct-ed after a fire in 1845 leveled the structure to its stone foundation walls, it was rebuilt in a style repeated in the two two-story officers' quarters and one-story guardhouse.

The 1872 conversion of the barracks to a federal courthouse and jail began the pro-cess of changes in use and renovations and additions represented during its time period, with minor interior changes in the three-year rehabilitation project completed in 2000 that created today's visitor center. Public clamor over the primitive jail conditions, called "Hell on the Border" by prisoners, led to the construction of the new jail in 1888 attached to the former barracks building. Relocation of the courthouse in 1890 to a new building three blocks away resulted in the conversion of the old courthouse to jailer's offices and a hospital; porches were filled in and the roof raised to a second story. The jail addition is on a stone foundation with brick exterior with ornamental brick cornice, roof pitch, and ridgeline closely matching the barracks/courthouse. The building's function is

Commissary Storehouse

recognized by the six tall, jail-like vertical window openings with limestone slab sill and head and quoined jambs. Inside the jail a masonry structure supported three tiers of seventy-two metal-grille-enclosed 5- by 7-foot cells, each tier separated from the exterior walls by an open space 5 feet and 9 inches wide. A portion of this inte-rior jail has been reconstructed. A grav-ity air exhaust system ventilated the cells through a pair of rooftop monitors.

The Commissary Storehouse is the oldest surviving building at Fort Smith. Promi-nent on a slight rise of ground at the second Fort Smith's northernmost corner and origi-nally intended to be a two-story artillery bastion, in 1846 the Commissary was converted into an army commissary storehouse. Trapezoidal in plan, approximately 48 by 50 feet and two stories high, remains of the original stone stockade walls are seen on parts of the exterior walls. The structure expresses its utilitarian function with massive ashlar stone exterior walls punctuated with vertical window openings and sill-high planked doors. Windows typically have limestone sills, arched heads, and a brick header course. Conversions to various use, including an interim courtroom before location in the barracks, modified the exterior and interior, changed window and door openings, removed interior partitions and replaced them with others, and added exterior and interior porches and stairs. The structure has been rehabilitated to its 1850s appearance, the uncluttered exhibit floors show the place ready for storing commissary goods.

The original gallows on the site—not the present 1980s NPS replica—were built in 1873. Judge Parker's first ordered public hanging in 1875 was on a gallows in the southwestern corner of the five-sided fort built against the remains of a blockhouse foundation. Judge Parker had little choice in meting out the death sentence mandated by federal law for the capital offenses of rape and murder. For twenty-three years, the Federal Court for the Western District of Arkansas carried out executions on at least three gallows at Fort Smith. In thirty-nine separate executions, a total of eighty-six men (several women had execution sentences reversed or pardoned) were put to death. More condemned prisoners were put to death by the U.S. government in Fort Smith than in any other place in American history.

Hot Springs National Park

In central Arkansas, west of Little Rock in Hot Springs, Garland County, Arkansas

→   www.nps.gov/hosp

→   To reach Bathhouse Row in downtown Hot Springs on Central Park Avenue (State Highway 7) and the visitor center in Fordyce Bathhouse from Little Rock take Interstate 30 and US 70; from southwest Arkansas take Interstate 30 north to Highway 7; and from Fort Smith take Interstate 40 east to Highway 7 for the scenic drive south through the Ouchita Mountains.

Hot Springs National Park's 5,500 acres blend distinctive resort architecture in downtown Hot Springs with a park system in the surrounding low-lying hills. The eight bathhouses, fountains, Magnolia and Grand promenades, and formal entrance represents the largest remaining collection of early twentieth-century spa structures in the United States. It is a National Historic Landmark District. Remarkable for a small city, an eclectic parade of architectural styles—Italianate, Renaissance Revival, Spanish, and Neoclassical—celebrate a bygone era when the national park was known as "The American Spa."

The hot springs have long attracted health seekers and adventurers. In 1832, Congress formed Hot Springs Reservation to reserve the springs from private ownership, making Hot Springs National Park the oldest of the current national parks—forty years older than Yellowstone National Park. Hot Springs Reservation was placed under the jurisdiction of the National Park Service (NPS) upon the agency's establishment in 1916 and was renamed a national park in 1921. Today Hot Springs National Park includes the hot springs, their watershed, and historic Bathhouse Row. For drinking and bathing, 700,000 gallons of clear, fresh-tasting, odor-free hot water are collected each day from the forty-seven springs flowing from the west slope of Hot Springs Mountain.

The park's twenty-six miles of hiking trails showcase the geology, flora, and fauna of the Ouachita Mountains, and its scenic drives are laced with overlooks, shelters, and picnic areas. At the foot of West Mountain, Whittington Park offers cold spring water, huge trees, and a popular walking trail. Gulpha Gorge Campground provides mountains and a creek to explore, while a 216-foot-high observation tower atop Hot Spring Mountain gives a breathtaking panorama of the city and the national park.

Facing Central Avenue in a north-south alignment, Bathhouse Row is the heart of a unique historic downtown area. Eclectic in architectural style and materials, the eight historic bathhouses achieve unity through similarity of scale, height, and orientation in their park-like setting of gardens, magnolia trees, and grassy spaces. During its heyday, Bathhouse Row had a bathhouse to fit clientele from the wealthy to the indigent, reflected in building form, exterior detailing, interior finishes and services offered beyond the basic theapeutic bath. Fierce competition for the wealthier clientele spurred some bathhouse owners to expand services and space beyond those originally designed, altering exteriors and interiors. All of the designers freely used classical and revival styles—Greek, Roman, Spanish, Italian—to satisfy the bathhouse owners' desire for style and comfort. The result is anything but boring.

Today, only the Buckstaff Bathhouse remains as an operating bathhouse. Quapaw Bathhouse (1922) has recently been leased to a local architectural firm with plans to

Fordyce Bathhouse

National Park Service visitor center/
administration building

turn it into a family spa. The others—Superior (1916), Hale (1892; 1915; 1939), Maurice (1912; 1916), Ozark (1922; 1942), and Lamar (1923)—are being rehabilitated and made available to the private sector for long-term leases to reopen them for public use. The

Fordyce Bathhouse (1915), restored in the late 1980s, serves as the park visitor center and is open for tours. The other historic buildings currently functioning on Bathhouse Row are the comfort stations flanking the Quapaw Bathhouse and the NPS park administration headquarters at the southern corner of Bathhouse Row.

The stately Neo-Classical revival Buckstaff Bathhouse has been in continuous operation since its grand opening on February 1, 1912. It resembles an early-twentieth-century governmental or educational building, softened with blue striped awnings at the front elevation. The three-story building is basically rectangular. A wide spandrel at the second floor with the brass-lettered words "Buckstaff Baths" is centered above the entrance and medallions. Bands of trim finished in white stucco appear at the rusticated base, spandrels, friezes, cornices, and parapet. Exterior walls are a light taupe-colored brick. Engaged columns divide the entrance into seven bays, flanked by pavilions at the north and south ends. First floor windows are arched; second story windows are rectangular, and the small third floor windows are rectangular with classical urns between them and above the cornice that finishes the columns.

Located on the south side of the park's historic Formal Entrance, the impressive three-story Renaissance Revival Fordyce Bathhouse has been rehabilitated to function as a museum and a visitor center. Reminiscent of a Renaissance *palazzo* with its symmetry and three tiers of seven-bay architectural hierarchy, the Fordyce combines Spanish and Italian elements with rich decorative surfaces. The exterior walls of the second and third floors are faced with brick in shades of gold, forming a tapestry design. The first

Quapaw Bathhouse

floor exterior walls are pearl-grey Batesville stone cut into large blocks. The central five-bay portion and its flanking simulated corner towers (with curvilinear parapets of Spanish inspiration) are capped by red mission tile hip roofs. The window surrounds are ivory-glazed, sculpted terra-cotta sporting dolphins and mermaids, with Neptune's face centered atop each of the second floor windows in the front. The current canvas awnings approximate the solid khaki color of the originals, filling the front and corner tower window openings of the upper floors. A parapet of Greek design motifs spans the open entrance porch across the central five bays; its canopy of glass and copper includes a stained glass, lighted marquee. From the exterior of the building front, passersby can look up through French doors into the third floor assembly room where the ceiling's five segmentally arched vaults house curved stained glass skylights with small circular painted glass panels in musical motifs.

Most of the interior rooms have been restored, and the visitor has an opportunity to see refined touches that include American encaustic terra-cotta fountains in the lobby, stained glass windows suggesting the Italian countryside in the women's department, and a massive ocean-themed skylight entitled *Neptune's Daughter* directly above the terra-cotta DeSoto fountain in the men's bath hall. The third floor features a wood paneled gymnasium built to attract famous athletes to Hot Springs—prizefighters like Jack Dempsey and baseball players like Babe Ruth. The most impressive space on the third floor is the assembly or music room with its stained glass ceiling and ceramic tile floor, hand laid in an intricate pattern resembling woven carpeting.

Pea Ridge National Military Park

In northwestern Arkansas, near Pea Ridge, Benton County, Arkansas

→ www.nps.gov/peri

→ The park is approximately thirty-five miles north of Fayetteville, Arkansas. Take Interstate 540 north from Fayetteville to Exit 86 at Rogers, Arkansas, and travel on AR 62 to the visitor center.

Elkhorn Tavern

The 4,300-acre Pea Ridge National Military Park is the site of a decisive Civil War Federal victory, considered as the battle that saved Missouri for the Union. Here, the visitor can experience a battlefield being restored to the 1862 Civil War appearance. The Elkhorn Tavern, the center of bitter fighting on both days, is a National Park Service (NPS) reconstruction on the site of the original structure. The park also includes a 2.5-mile segment of the Trail of Tears National Historic Trail used by the Cherokee between 1838 and 1839 when they were forcibly removed from their homelands in the South to the "Indian Territory" of Oklahoma and Arkansas.

On March 7 and 8 of 1862 nearly 26,000 Federal and Confederate soldiers met on a snow-covered field in the rolling hills of the Boston Mountains in northwestern Arkansas near Pea Ridge to determine whether Missouri would remain under Union control. The border state of Missouri was essential to the Union strategy of dividing the Confederacy by seizing control of the Mississippi River. Fierce attacks and counterattacks took place by both armies during the day of March 7th, but by evening neither side had won a decisive advantage. The fight started anew on the morning of March 8th with a fierce artillery duel. Federal gun placement caught the Confederate batteries in a deadly crossfire and prevented other Confederate guns from moving forward. As the Southern batteries ran out of ammunition and were withdrawn, the Federal guns moved forward and began shelling the infantry hidden at the foot of Big Mountain. The shells exploded in the treetops and among the boulders showering the men with deadly splinters and rocks, causing carnage in the Southern ranks. Around 10 A.M., Federal infantry moved forward. Under pressure and nearly out of ammunition, the Confederate lines started to give way. Seeing the Southerners in retreat, the entire Federal line surged forward routing the Confederates.

The reconstructed Elkhorn Tavern, originally built in 1833 as a rest stop for stagecoaches on Telegraph Road, was the scene of surging battle lines on March 7 and 8 of 1862. The tavern owner's wife Polly Cox (husband Jesse was moving his cattle to Kansas during the battle), members of the Cox family, and five slaves huddled in the cellar under the house for two days while the battle raged outside. Occupied by Union troops, captured by Confederates, and recaptured by Union soldiers, the tavern was hit many times, once by a cannonball striking the upper floor. However, the tavern survived the battle intact. Burned by Confederate guerrillas in early 1863, the Coxes rebuilt a new structure on the site, little resembling the original. When acquired by the NPS in 1960, the rotting building was removed and a third tavern reconstructed, believed to resemble its approximate wartime appearance. Included in the reconstruction is a set of elk horns placed on the ridgepole, which gave the tavern its name.

Today's reconstructed tavern is a two-story clapboard-sided structure (18 feet by 38 feet in plan) built on the original stone foundation. A gable roof projects over the first and second floor porches and runs along the length of the front facade. Square columns support the porches at the corners and center of the porch; another pair of columns frame pairs of doors entering from the porches at each floor. Between the columns and at the porch sides are waist-high railings, except at the ground floor entrance doorsteps. At each end of the tavern are stone chimneys stepped at about 12 feet and rising as rectangular columns above the roof ridge.

A cross-buck and rail fence snakes its way up Telegraph Road (part of the Trail of Tears) past the front of the building. The 6-pound cannons arrayed to the north of the Tavern are positioned where the Union 1st and 3rd Iowa Artillery fired grapeshot and canisters of Minié balls on the 1st Missouri Brigade led by Colonel Henry Little.

A seven mile loop road with twelve stops on a self-guided motor tour mark the battlefield's historic sites.

Florida

South

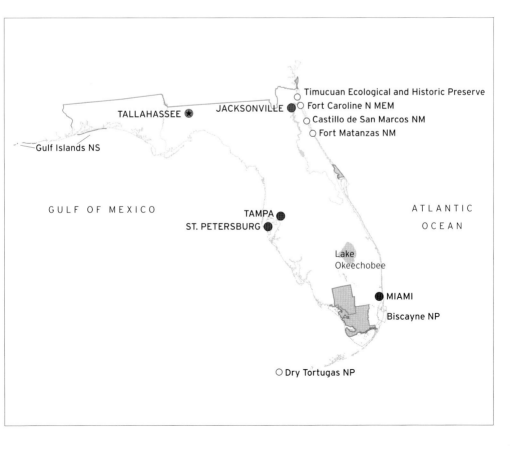

Biscayne National Park

Homestead, Dade County, Florida

→ www.nps.gov/bisc

→ The park is located south of Miami and east of Homestead in southeastern Florida. The Dante Fascell Visitor Center at Convoy Point is reached via North Canal Drive (Southwest 328th Street) nine miles from Homestead and US 1.

Boca Chita Key lighthouse

This unusual national park's major attraction is water—only five percent is land. Subject to hurricanes and changes to surface features, the more than fifty keys stretching twenty-two miles from near Key Biscayne on the north to Key Largo on the south are at the northern end of the ancient coral reefs that form the Florida Keys. The island keys of Biscayne National Park divide the usually placid waters of Biscayne Bay from the coral reefs extending outward into the Atlantic Ocean. A shoreline of miles of thick mangrove forests faces the clear, shallow waters of Biscayne Bay lush with marine life, protected from the ocean by the coral rock keys. An important part of Florida's history of settlement, the park was the site of Native American visits from the mainland, European contact and, a haven for pirates, a treasure ground for shipwreck salvagers, "conch" settlers, pineapple farmers, homesteaders, and resort development. Included in the historical architecture visited by water are structures on Boca Chita Key and the unusual stilt house in "Stiltsville."

The predecessor of today's 172,940-acre national park was established as a national monument in 1968 and redesignated a national park in 1980. Intended to avert the intensive development of the southeast Florida area, the park's enabling legislation declared, "in order to preserve and protect for the education, inspiration, recreation, and enjoyment of present and future generations a rare combination of terrestrial, marine, and amphibious life in a tropical setting of great natural beauty."

Structures on the 32-acre Boca Chita Key forming a historic district at the north end of the island are a remnant of Miami's growth in the early twentieth century when development spread onto the keys in Biscayne Bay. Mark C. Honeywell purchased Boca Chita Key in 1937 and began building a vacation retreat on the island. Today's structures, typically built of Miami oolitic limestone, include the lighthouse, chapel, picnic pavilion, garage, engine house, bridge, canal, cannon, stone walls, retaining walls, and concrete walkways. Other buildings constructed between 1937 and 1939 no longer remain.

The 65-foot-tall lighthouse is at the north of the harbor entrance where yachts belonging to Honeywell and his guests moored during their visits. Designed by the Miami architectural firm of August Geiger, the tapered cylindrical tower is constructed of concrete bricks laid in common bond, with the exterior clad in uncoursed limestone. The base of the tower is approximately 21 feet in diameter and sits on a terrace-like base 28 feet square. An observation deck with painted steel railings projects outward near the top of the tower; the lantern rises from the reinforced concrete deck. The lantern is a dome-shaped steel frame, originally set with glass lights, topped by a small metal finial. Small, deeply inset, rectangular window openings pierce the column of the tower; the doorway has a smooth stone surround that projects slightly from the walls. The interior of the tower houses a circular staircase cantilevered from the walls. Unfortunately for Honeywell, the U.S. Coast Guard rejected the lighthouse as an unchartered navigational aid; it now serves as a boater's landmark. Ranger-provided access to the observation deck offers superb views of the keys, bay, ocean, and Miami and Miami Beach skylines.

The chapel is a 12- by 20-foot structure of concrete block covered with uncoursed stone, with a steeply pitched concave roof covered with asphalt shingles. The building has two symmetrically arranged openings in each wall; doorways are on the north and east walls. A low wall curves out from the southeast corner of the building to flank the south door.

Across the harbor entrance from the lighthouse stands the open-air picnic pavilion. The pavilion's ten squared limestone piers are placed on a concrete slab measuring 15 feet by 52 feet. The piers support a simple classical cornice and frieze, above which rises the hipped asphalt shingle roof. The gabled-roof garage (or barn) (71 by 31 feet in plan) and the engine house or generator building (approximately 16 by 24 feet in plan) are of concrete block with limestone facings.

"Crawfish" Eddie Walker began Stiltsville within sight of downtown Miami and roughly one mile south of Cape Florida at the tip of Key Biscayne in the 1930s. Over the years, a colorful history surrounded the eclectic group of structures that seem to float above Biscayne Bay's shallow seagrass beds, abetted by police raids for suspected illegal alcohol sales and gambling. Built on tall pilings in shallow water, brightly painted and of mixed architectural character, today's collection of seven structures is the remnant of up to twenty-seven structures during Stiltsville's peak in the 1960s. Now owned by the National Park Service (secured with "no trespassing" signs), a non-profit organization called the Stiltsville Trust was established in 2003 to preserve and rehabilitate the buildings to support educational and interpretive services.

An unusual park feature is Biscayne National Park's Maritime Heritage Trail. The underwater archeological "Shipwreck Trail" includes six wrecks spanning a century of maritime history with a wide variety of sizes and vessel types. Viewing from the surface and underwater is an unparalleled experience.

Castillo de San Marcos National Monument
St. Augustine, St. Johns County, Florida

→   www.nps.gov/casa

→   The 20.5-acre Castillo de San Marcos National Monument is located at the northern edge of St. Augustine, Florida overlooking the first permanent European settlement in the continental United States, Matanzas Bay, the barrier island of Anastasia, and the Atlantic Ocean beyond.

Sentry tower

300-year-old battered coquina walls and entry bridge

The impressive fortress of Castillo de San Marcos, built by the Spanish between 1672 and 1695 to defend Spain's North American interests and to protect the sea route for treasure ships returning to Spain, is one of the world's great forts. Visitors will discover an imposing yet welcoming massive fortification, a short walk from the tourist-packed streets of St. Augustine. "The old fort of St. Mark," wrote poet William Cullen Bryant in 1843 about the finest and oldest example of military architecture and engineering in the United States, "is a noble work, frowning over the Matanzas, and it is worth making a long journey to see."

This legacy of Spanish colonization flew the British flag (1763–1784) as Fort St. Marks, then reverted to Spain (1784–1821), and finally ceded to the United States in 1821 (renamed Fort Marion and restored to its original name in 1942). Besieged by the British and colonists in 1702 and 1740, the fort was never conquered in battle.

Beginning in 1565, a series of wooden forts were erected near the present fort. All succumbed to deterioration and one was destroyed by fire in an attack by Sir Francis

Drake in 1586. The star-shaped Castillo designed by Ignacio Daza is an example of European bastion fortifications adapted to the Matanzas River location. The square fort encloses a courtyard with sharply pointed diamond-shaped bastions projecting diagonally at each corner to permit cannons mounted on the roof gun deck (terreplein) to fire in all directions. A 40-foot-wide moat around the entire fortress was normally kept dry; when under attack, floodgates on the outer seawall were opened, filling the moat with sea water. A ravelin, a triangular fortification, detached in front of the bastions shielded the fort's only entrance; today's drawbridges are both working reconstructions.

Constructed of coquina, a stone of compressed seashells quarried on Anastasia Island, the hard material absorbed the impact of cannon balls. Patches of a white coat of plaster, made from burned oyster shells that once covered the fort's walls, are still visible. The outer wall tapers in thickness from 13 feet at the base to nearly 5 feet at the top of the parapet. The dramatic knife-edge taper, most apparent at the bastion corners, was a classic bastion fortification designed to deflect cannon balls upwards. Construction in 1738–1740 increased the wall height to approximately 30 feet above the moat and the gun deck was strengthened on the east side with a 6-inch-thick concrete slab poured over arched bombproof masonry vaults. The iconic domed watchtower on the northeast bastion was added in 1740. Later modernizations vaulted the other three sides (1752–56) and enlarged the *ravelin* (1762).

Spanish mortar

After the British cession of Florida to the United States in 1821 the renamed Fort Marion served as a prison for Osceola, leader of the Seminoles during the Seminole War of 1835–42. Occupied briefly by Confederate troops during the Civil War, Fort Marion also held the chiefs of the Kiowa, Comanche, Cheyenne, Arapaho, and Apache, captured in Western military campaigns. The fort's career as a military prison ended after the Spanish-American War. The fort was established as a national monument in 1924. Preserved and interpreted capably by the National Park Service, this splendid relic of obsolete warfare can be experienced through talks by park rangers, interpretive exhibits on self-guided tours, and periodically presented living-history programs.

Dry Tortugas National Park (Fort Jefferson National Monument)

Garden Key, Dry Tortugas, Monroe County, Florida

→ www.nps.gov/drto

→ The approximately 64,700 square miles of the Dry Tortugas National Park enclosing seven coral reefs and sand islands, shoals and water, is seventy nautical miles west of Key West, Florida.

Fort Jefferson lighthouse

Archways

The ghostly form of the massive redbrick Fort Jefferson on Garden Key, one of the Dry Tortugas National Park's seven islands, is the central feature of perhaps the most unusual national park in the National Park System. Incredibly improbable offshore in the Gulf of Mexico, it is small, remote, and one of the least visited parks in the lower forty-eight states. From aloft through a seaplane window, the hexagonal-shaped classic fortification and interior parade ground, surrounded by a water-filled moat and bordered to the sea by a fringe of beach and docks, is a peculiar geometry in the blue and green water. On a boat ride that can become suddenly treacherous on stormy days, it appears on the horizon, gradually coming into focus with rhythms of wall openings, corner bastions, and a parapet of corbelled brick arches.

Exploring the area west of the Florida Keys in 1513, Ponce de León's crew captured 160 sea turtles in one day, prompting his christening the Keys *Las Tortugas* (the turtles). "Dry" was later added on nautical charts to indicate the absence of fresh water. For three centuries smugglers and pirates used the keys' location on shipping lanes as a base for attacking merchant ships. After acquisition of Florida by the United States in 1821 the U.S. military largely eliminated this activity. In 1825 a lighthouse was built on Garden Key to provide warning to shipping about the dangers of reefs in and around the Tortugas chain. Construction of the Third System of coastal fortification after the War of 1812 from Maine to Texas included the military reservation on Garden Key to control access to the Gulf of Mexico by way of the Straits of Florida. Fort Jefferson was planned as the most extensive and ambitious, representing the apogee of this form of military architecture.

Construction on the fort began in 1846, under the direction of Lieutenant Horatio G. Wright, a twenty-six-year-old 1841 West Point graduate. In 1850 the officers' quarters were completed, and the fort was officially named for Thomas Jefferson. The walls did not reach their final height of 45 feet until 1862. Plans drawn by U.S. Army Corps of Engineers Chief Engineer Joseph C. Totten envisioned a mammoth structure, enclosing 5-foot-thick curtain walls a half-mile in length (long walls are approximately 478 feet in length; short walls are 324 feet long), surrounded by a 70-foot-wide moat partially enclosed by a sea wall. Six tower bastions projected menacingly from the hexagonal plan's corners. A 33-foot-wide roof gun deck (terreplein) held additional gun placements and magazines. An ingenious feature is the remains of "Totten shutters," heavy iron plates covering the gun portals and forced open by discharged gases from firing a millisecond before a cannon ball left the barrel, then slamming shut to protect gunners from enemy fire and flying debris. The hexagonal, 37-foot-tall, three-story lighthouse tower made of boilerplate iron was in place atop Bastion C for its first lighting in 1876.

A complex construction system of arched vaults form an intriguing labyrinth of passageways and chambers throughout the structure. Designed to mount 243 large-caliber guns capable of firing projectiles up to a distance of three miles from two tiers of arched casemates, the elaborate defense was made obsolete, before its walls were finished, by the invention of the rifled gun. Engineers discovered too late that the foundations of the huge structure were settling into the coral reef. Building materials were shipped a fifteen hundred mile passage mainly from New England, as far north as Maine, though until the Civil War the handmade brick came from Pensacola. Construction during the Civil War years went uninterrupted after Florida's secession, an endless supply of materials and labor arriving scrounged from the north. Slave labor under northern masons formed the workforce until Emancipation in 1863, when paid laborers and some military prisoners replaced them. Working conditions were described in a letter from a departing chief engineer to his successor in 1856: "I hope that you are better satisfied at Fort Jefferson than I was, for if not, you must be having a miserable time of it. I offer you very sincere sympathy."

During the Civil War the fort was a Union military prison for captured deserters, also holding four men convicted for complicity in President Lincoln's assassination in

1865. It was abandoned by the military in 1874, returning to service as a quarantine station and later as a coaling station from 1898 until 1908. In 1935 Fort Jefferson National Monument was established to protect the fort. The area was redesignated Dry Tortugas National Park in 1992.

Fort construction dragged on for more than thirty years and was never really finished. The estimated number of bricks finally put in place is sixteen million. In addition to the inconsistency of Congressional funding, the building task was made difficult by the challenges of shipping workers and supplies. Although surviving severe hurricanes for the past 160 years, the fort is now facing compromised integrity and major architectural failures due to sinking of the structure and rotten metal shutters.

Visiting this testimony to military engineering ingenuity in the sometime placid waters off the Florida Keys is a 45-minute flight or a 2.5-hour ferry ride. The hurricane season offers traveling challenges that should be avoided. Take the self-guided tour, enjoy bird watching; the snorkeling, scuba diving, and underwater photography here are excellent. Other than during hurricane months, National Park Service stabilization repair crews often can be seen at work.

Fort Jefferson from air (courtesy NPS)

Fort Caroline National Memorial

Jacksonville, Duval County, Florida

→ www.nps.gov/foca

→ Fort Caroline is located in the Timucuan Ecological and Historic Preserve approximately fourteen miles northeast of downtown Jacksonville, Florida. Access is by various routes from Jacksonville via Monument Road and Fort Caroline Road or Florida Route A1A and the Jacksonville beaches via Mt. Pleasant Street. Follow National Park Service signs to the park entrance.

Moat surrounding Fort Caroline

The reconstructed earth, timber, and sod Fort Caroline is on the site of a 1564 French settlement founded near the mouth of the River of May (now the St. Johns River) in the northeast corner of Florida. The original settlement of three hundred led by René de Goulaine de Laudonnière was an experimental outpost where French Huguenots would be granted religious tolerance. Named La Caroline ("land of Charles"), in honor of the boy king of France Charles IX, the triangular fort lasted only fifteen months.

The Spanish had claimed Florida prior to French expeditions in the area. Uneasy about threat to their sovereignty in the New World, Spain moved to protect its shipping lanes and remove the Protestant heresy by sending a strong message to the French, beginning two centuries of conflict between the two European powers. In 1568 the French revenged a bloody Spanish massacre of the settlers in 1565. The French departed, Spain rebuilt the fort but abandoned it in 1569. Ending their attempt to colonize the American southeast, the French abandoned Fort de la Caroline. The climactic battles fought here between France and Spain marked the first time that European nations fought for control of lands in what is now the United States.

The site was washed away in 1880 after a widening of the Saint John's River channel. In 1953 the 139-acre Fort Caroline National Memorial was established. In 1964 the National Park Service (NPS) constructed a replica of the original fort. The park serves as the principle interpretive center for the vast (46,000 acres) Timucuan Ecological and Historic Preserve (established in 1988).

Arched entryway

The original site of Fort de la Caroline has never been determined and is believed to have been located near the present day replica. The NPS used as sources for the reconstruction a description by Laudonnière and sketch by Jacques le Moyne de Morgues, an artist with the expedition. Laudonnière was wounded in the 1565 attack but escaped to France, where he wrote a history of his colony. According to Laudonnière, the settlers dug a ditch on the landward side of the triangular fort to serve as a moat and built a *gabionade*, a revetment of *gambions* (hollow cylindrical baskets filled with earth or stones). A 9-foot parapet wall protected a raised gun platform facing landward. A palisade of sawed timbers braced by poles protected the side facing the river. Buildings within the fort housed the settlers and supplies. The main fort entrance was an impressive arch topped by a royal shield with the fleur-de-lis.

A drawing by Le Moyne guided the building of today's scaled-down version of the fort. The artist accompanied Laudonnière to paint images of the people, flora and fauna, and geography of this part of the New World. The story of how a complete set of Le Moyne's forty-two engraved plates survived, including one of the fort, is intriguing. The artist was one of the few who escaped from Fort de la Caroline when the Spanish attacked in 1565. He found refuge on a French boat, along with Laudonnière and several others, and returned to Europe. All but one of Le Moyne's original drawings were destroyed in the Spanish attack on Fort Caroline; most images that we now attribute to him are actually engravings created by a Dutch printer/publisher named Theodore DeBry that are based on recreations Le Moyne produced from memory. These reproductions of the engravings, distributed by Le Moyne in printed volumes, are some of the earliest circulated images of European colonization in the New World. The collection is accessible in the University of South Florida Special Collections Department.

Faced by criticism challenging the philosophy of complete recreation of a historical structure, particularly one built on such a slim historical record of the original vanished for three and a half centuries, the NPS unabashedly and yet quite responsibly set out to reestablish and interpret the original's character. The purist can challenge discrepancies in some details seen between Le Moyne/DeBry's engraving and the reconstruction. Not distracting from the visitor experience are differences between the distorted perspective view and the palisade construction and placement of omitted interior structures. While the modern version replicates the elegant entrance arch, the palisade has a delicacy of large matchsticks ready to resist cannon fire. Nevertheless, the recreation of the historical significance of the place is a success. Here, once more the flag with a fleur-de-lis on a deep blue background flies over the fort; the visitor can walk the ramparts, sight down the cannon barrels, and revere in the fortitude of the original French settlers' short-lived experiment in Spanish America.

Fort Matanzas National Monument
St. Augustine, St. John's County, Florida

→ www.nps.gov/foma

→ Fort Matanzas National Monument is approximately fourteen miles southeast of St. Augustine, Florida, via Florida A1A south to the visitor center on Anastasia Island. The fort on Rattlesnake Island is reached by National Park Service ferry.

Fort Matanzas guarding Matanzas Inlet

The rugged, masonry fortification on Rattlesnake Island was built for the specific purpose of defending St. Augustine from a "backdoor" waterborne attack through the Matanzas Inlet and up the Matanzas River beyond the reach of Castillo de San Marco's cannons. The inlet also served as a supply route and possible escape route when St. Augustine, fifteen miles to the north, was under attack. The site also commemorates the place where Admiral Pedro Menéndez de Avilés's bloody *mantazas* (slaughter) of the shipwrecked French from Fort Caroline (see page 335) occurred in 1565. After the unsuccessful British siege of St. Augustine in 1740, the Spanish replaced wood watchtowers on the island by building the fort completed in 1742.

Battered by tropical storms, the masonry fort barely survived under Spanish and British flags. Remaining unoccupied after becoming a United States property in 1821, the fort's condition continued to decline, becoming a mere ghost of its former self, obsolete and in bad repair with its undermined foundation listing and cracked walls overgrown with vegetation. The first flow of Congressional funds for restoration work begun in 1916 arrived almost too late to save the fort. Proclamation as a national monument and transfer from the War Department to the National Park Service (NPS) in 1933 assured the fort's preservation.

Engineer Pedro Ruiz de Olano designed a small fort, simple in plan and impressive in its functional massing of an elevated base for gun deck, a tower for soldiers' quarters, and an observation deck. Built of local coquina stone, on a foundation of close-set pine log cribbing and piling, the sloped base supporting the tabby gun deck (concrete made from oyster shell lime, sand, water, and a shell filler) is approximately 49 feet, 6 inches square and 11 feet above water level. A ladder providing entry to the fort was lowered through an embrasure in the west parapet and raised at night. A timber floor over the gundeck served as a base for five cannon with an effective range of one mile or more set into embrasures in the parapet walls. The two Spanish 8-pounder cannons mounted on the fort in 1793 remain in place today. Through loopholes in the cylindrical domed *garita* (sentry box) at the corner of the gun deck, a sentry could scan the fort's walls to the south and west. Olana solved the source of fresh water in the salty marsh by designing a bottle-shaped, brick-tiled cistern 13 feet tall and 10 feet in diameter set into the base. Filled by drainpipes channeled from the observation deck, the access hatch is located just outside the watchtower entrance door.

The tower rising from the north end of the base housed the six to ten soldiers and their supplies. The enlisted men's quarters on the gun deck level had window and loophole openings and a fireplace at the end of the room. An exterior staircase rose from the gun deck to the second floor commanding officer's quarters under an arched ceiling running east and west. An entrance hole accessed the 4-foot diameter powder magazine set deep in the coquina walls and extending down to the gun deck.

Sentry box

A ladder in the officers' quarters led through a hatchway in the ceiling to the observation deck 30 feet above river level. The tower base was covered inside and out with white lime plaster, and the tower and sharp cordons trimmed in red.

An excursion to picturesque Fort Matanzas is a delightful experience. The striking profile of coquina stone tower rising over the base with replica cannons pointing down the Matanzas River evokes the days of Spanish occupation in the New World.

Gulf Islands National Seashore (Florida)
Gulf Breeze, Escambia County, Florida

→ www.nps.gov/guis

→ Gulf Islands National Seashore is in Florida and Mississippi and both districts are south of Interstate 10. The two districts are about a two-hour drive apart. In Florida, to reach Fort Barrancas, use Exit 12 to Interstate 110, exit at Florida 295 to Barrancas and the Pensacola Naval Air Station main entrance and continue on the Blue Angel Parkway (Florida Route 173). To reach Fort Pickens, located on Santa Rosa Island west of Pensacola Beach, take Interstate 110 to Exit 22 to the Garcon Point Bridge to US 98 and crossing Pensacola Bay to Gulf Breeze, Florida. The damaged Fort Pickens Road currently is closed to vehicles but visitors may currently use it for biking or hiking. Water taxi service is available to the Fort Pickens Area. The Mississippi unit with Fort Massachusetts is discussed in the Mississippi chapter of this book (see page 368).

Fort Pickens, Santa Rosa Island

The Florida section of the Gulf Islands National Seashore contains historical structures including Fort Barrancas, Bateria de San Antonio, and the Advanced Redoubt, located on board the Pensacola Naval Station, and the offshore Fort Pickens on Santa Rosa Island. Managed by the National Park Service (NPS), the Fort Barrancas Area is on Taylor Road approximately one half-mile east from the Museum of Naval Aviation. The half-mile-long Trench Trail connects the Advanced Redoubt to the Fort Barrancas Visitor Center.

The United States began constructing fortifications at Pensacola in the 1820s, when Pensacola Bay was chosen as the site for a navy yard, and as a Gulf of Mexico component of the Third System (1817–67) of coastal fortifications. Defending the navy yard from seaward attack were a triangle of fortifications at the bay's entrance, including Fort Barrancas, Fort Pickens, and Fort McRee, both located on islands at the entrance to the bay (the Third System Fort McRee has been completely destroyed by the shifting location of the barrier island on which it was located).

Fort Barrancas sits on a bluff (*barranca*) overlooking the entrance to Pensacola Bay. The British built an earth and log redoubt here in 1763 and the Spanish built Bateria de San Antonio, a masonry water battery at the foot of the bluff, around 1797. American engineers remodeled the Water Battery in 1840 and built a masonry fort on the bluff between 1839 and 1844, connected by tunnel to the Water Battery to the south. This is the current Fort Barrancas, designed by Colonel William H. Chase of the U.S. Army Corps of Engineers, and restored by the National Park Service (NPS) in 1978–80. To the north, is the Advanced Redoubt, built between 1845 and 1870. The fort saw action in the Civil War, was captured by the Confederates in September of 1861 and was used to bombard the federal garrison at Fort Pickens, and then abandoned to Union troops in May of 1862.

Bateria de San Antonio stands today at the base of the *barranca*, just below Fort Barrancas. The semicircular masonry fortification with white stucco walls and Spanish decorative elements steps down the hill facing Pensacola Bay. A long traverse wall 138 feet long, with an underground postern gate connecting the battery to the fort by passageway, is ringed by a dry moat between the scarp and counterscarp, and a raised firing platform built over vaulted bombproof shelters is level with the top of the traverse wall. A small, lower level parade ground between the platform and a grass-covered terreplein, or gun platform, mounted with granite curbs for gun tracks is set below the grass-covered protective rampart, heavy guns facing seaward and lighter guns were emplaced facing to the northwest.

Approaching the fortification, Fort Barrancas appears as grass-covered slopes (glacis), part of the two long walls of the landward west-facing V-shaped outwork cordon or scarp walls, and a higher grass covered mound in the center of the fort. The sally port main entrance is reached by a sloped ramp down into an arched entryway in the north face of the outworks scarp and crossing a drawbridge over the dry moat between the outworks and the inner scarp wall. A passageway under the rampart leads to a ramp up to the grass-covered central parade ground and terreplein. The outworks counterscarp and scarp walls of the four-sided fortification are constructed of brick four feet thick and twenty feet high. Unusual in its construction, instead of having a hollow central area surrounded by brick scarp walls the central area, dished below the terreplein, is filled with sand and soil and covered with grass. Semicircular granite gun tracks for nineteen cannon were placed on the terreplein above the parade ground level and below the rampart level. Brick barrel vaulted passageways below the parade ground and rampart accessed the embrasures or firing loopholes in the riflemen's gallery and gun casements with firing ports for crossfire to cover the ditch. Additional cannon casemates were located at the ends of the outworks wall facing the bay.

The four-sided Advanced Redoubt is constructed of tall brick scarp and counterscarp walls separated by a grass-covered dry ditch. A drawbridge over the dry ditch accesses the sally port in the east-facing scarp wall. Arched casemate openings face eastward. The earth covered parade ground contained barbette mounts for fifteen 24-pounder cannon.

Fort Pickens, built between 1829–34, was the largest of the Pensacola Harbor fortifications. Designed by French military engineer Simon Bernard, construction was supervised by Colonel William H. Chase of the U.S. Army Corps of Engineers. Ironically, Chase was later appointed by the State of Florida to command its troops and seize for the South the fort he had built. Despite repeated Confederate military threats to it, Fort Pickens remained in Union hands throughout the Civil War. From 1886 to May of 1887, the fort was a tourist attraction drawn by the imprisoned Chiricahua Apache leader Geronimo.

The pentagonal fortification at the western tip of Santa Rosa Island, just offshore from the mainland, is a massive masonry structure built with 21.5 million bricks in its forty-foot-high, twelve-foot-thick walls, with projecting arrow-shaped bastions, and brick arched casemate galleries. The landward side of Fort Pickens has a dry moat, with a counterscarp wall and glacis, which protected the main fort wall from direct cannon fire, and provided another position for infantry to defend the fort. The seaward side of Fort Pickens also had a dry moat, which was filled sometime in the past, with brick arched gun casemates at water level and a barbette level above. Surrounding the interior seven-acre parade ground within the scarp walls is the brick-covered terreplein and rampart, and semicircular granite gun tracks for cannon placed on the terreplein and below the sloped rampart level. The casemate construction, with semicircular granite gun mounts, used an unusual foundation of reverse arches to support the structure on the sand and minimize settling. One of the arches has been excavated to illustrate the principle.

The original Fort Pickens structure and site has changed due to hurricane damage and modifications made for changing weapons technology and coastal defense from the 1890s through the 1940s, including Battery Pensacola, the concrete structure in the middle of the parade ground. In 1899, a magazine explosion destroyed Bastion D exposing the brick arched casemates to view, with bricks landing at Fort Barrancas, more than a mile-and-a-half away.

Today, the round trip to Fort Pickens for a self-guided tour is a fourteen-mile trip from a parking lot and restroom facilities along a marked corridor of pavement and sand. The long, low brick walls with arched gun embrasures, entrance gate flanked by brick piers, and solitary bottle-shaped Rodman cannon are a welcome sight at the end of the trail.

Timucuan Ecological and Historic Preserve
(Kingsley Plantation)
Jacksonville, Duval County, Florida

→   www.nps.gov/timu

→   Timucuan Ecological and Historical Preserve northeast of Jacksonville, Florida contains Kingsley
Plantation, which can be reached from Jacksonville by exiting Interstate 95 at Heckscher Drive (FL 105)
and then driving east for about fifteen miles. After passing the St. Johns River Ferry landing on your right,
turn left at the park sign onto Fort George Island and take the two-mile dirt road to the Kingsley Plantation
parking lot. From Amelia Island travel south on Florida A1A to the plantation.

Kingsley plantation house

The Kingsley Plantation on Fort George Island is a remarkable remnant of the plantation era in Colonial Florida. Preserved
and interpreted by the National Park Service (NPS) as a unit of Timucuan (pronounced ti-moo-kwun) Ecological and
Historical Preserve, the site is in a serene
setting of marshland where the St. John's
River meets the Atlantic Ocean. The visi-
tor can spend the day walking the grounds and absorbing the culture of a 200-year-old
plantation on the 1,000-acre island, isolated from modern encroachments of subdivisions and beachfront condominium towers. The drive down a long sand road through a
maritime forest reverses the centuries, opening to the rare view of the slave tabby houses
then, again, through the forested lane to the barn and beyond to Florida's only surviving
colonial plantation house on the river bank.

The historical structures are contemporary with their times: the plantation house
drawing inspiration from Palladian classical design that inspired Thomas Jefferson;
and the outbuildings, a product of local materials and building skills. The Kingsley
Plantation was operated as a Florida State Park until 1991 when it was brought under the management of Timucuan Ecological and Historical Preserve (established in
1988).

The plantation house, although named for Zephaniah Kingsley, Jr. (third owner of
the cotton-growing plantation), is probably the design of John McQueen, granted the
island by the King of Spain in 1792. Beginning about 1795, it appears that McQueen
drew from the popular literature of the time, the skills of his slave master craftsmen, and
possible inspiration from conversations with Thomas Jefferson in France. Palladian in
its plan and elevation, the two-story structure is framed with locally felled longleaf yellow pine, skillfully mortise-and-tenon joined. The spacious great room (approximately
16 feet by 32 feet), with fireplaces at each end, is divided in half by large, wide-pan-
eled, folding double doors exiting to the north (front) and south (rear) verandahs. The

verandahs connected four identical square one-story pyramidal-roofed corner pavilions. Verandahs on the east and west sides were filled in the additions by later owners. A narrow staircase leads from the second floor to the baluster-enclosed widow's walk used as a lookout for approaching ships.

To the south of the main plantation house, a two-story structure of ground floor tabby (a concrete of lime, sand, water, and oyster shell aggregate) and wood-framed second story served as the kitchen and home for Anna Madgigne Jai Kingsley (known as Ma'am Anna), a Senegalese slave purchased by Kingsley and freed in 1811. The extended shed roof on five tall wood columns with Queen Anne brackets shelters an outdoor patio and exterior stair. The house is connected to the plantation house by a 65-foot-long covered passage.

Approximately two hundred yards south of what may have been Ma'am Anna's house is the two-story L-shaped brick tabby-walled barn and one-story concrete tabby carriage house.

South of the plantation house and barn is an intriguing part of the plantation, a semicircle of thirty-two tabby slave quarters. With the exception of one, all are roofless. Sixteen quarters on either side of the road placed 12 feet apart are flanked at each end by larger quarters assumed to be for the overseers and their families. Possibly built by the Kingsley's slaves and abandoned in the 1890s, the slave quarters began to deteriorate when the cypress shingle roofs rotted and exterior plaster disintegrated, exposing the tabby walls to weather and encroaching vegetation.

Now, the visitor can walk through the one or two room window-shuttered houses with central doorways, tabby chimneys with tabby brick hearths, and tabby floors in various stages of restoration and stabilization. The experience is solemn and sobering, recalling the generations of families once enslaved on this plantation.

Semicircle of slave quarters

Tabby-walled barn and carriage house

At the Kingsley Plantation the visitor can gain an understanding of the early Florida plantation era and examine the fine examples of tabby construction. The NPS requests that visitors respect the fragile remains of the historical structures by not touching, leaning, or sitting on them.

Georgia

South

Chickamauga and Chattanooga National Military Park

Near Chattanooga, Tennessee, in southeastern Tennessee and Fort Oglethorpe in northwestern Georgia

→ www.nps.gov/chch

→ The park has several units prominent in the Battle for Chattanooga in and around the city with visitor centers at the Chickamauga and Lookout Mountain Battlefields. Chickamauga Battlefield is nine miles south of Chattanooga on US 27.

The battles in the thick forests and fields, mountains and ridges, and across streams surrounding present day Chattanooga from September to November 1863 were some of the fiercest clashes of the Civil War. This is where conflicts took place that more than a century and a half later are studied for their tactics, decisive movements, and heroic actions, romanticized as "Rock of Chickamauga," Missionary Ridge, Lookout Mountain, and the Battle Above the Clouds. And this is where a decisive Union victory launched Sherman's move toward Atlanta and the March to the Sea.

The battles' military prize was the strategic rail junction at Chattanooga nicknamed the "Gateway to the Deep South," with tracks leading from Atlanta to Nashville, from Memphis to Charleston, and from Chattanooga through Knoxville to Virginia. A loss would deal a crippling blow to Confederate control of the region; a Union victory would clear an opening for a major thrust into the heart of the South. The numbers engaged were astounding; the losses horrific. The Chickamauga battle engagements on September 18–19, 1863 saw 126,000 armed men facing each other. A resounding rebel victory at Chickamauga drove the retreating Union troops north to Chattanooga. Besieged and then reinforced with ranks swollen by 36,000 reinforcements, Union troops attacked November 23–25, 1863 and drove the Confederates off Missionary Ridge to claim one of the war's most spectacular Union victories. The triumphant Ulysses S. Grant observed, "The battle of Lookout Mountain is one of the romances of the war...it is all poetry." The price was tremendous: 34,624 casualties at Chickamauga and 12,491 casualties in the Battle for Chattanooga. Despite the great Confederate victory at Chickamauga, military fortunes were reversed and the tide that began with Union victories at Gettysburg and Vicksburg surged forward through another year and a half of struggle and eventual Confederate defeat.

A total of 8,000 acres of historic battlefields are in the nation's first national military park (1890). Major units are the Chickamauga Battlefield, Orchard Knob Reservation, Lookout Mountain Battlefield, Point Park, Signal Point, and Missionary Ridge, part of the steep, 20-mile-long ridge east of Chattanooga and 400 feet above the city. The more than 1,400 monuments, markers, and tablets make this one of the nation's best monumented military parks. The National Park Service (NPS) preserves the park as close as possible to its 1863 appearance. In addition to the many monuments, historic structures are located on the various routes and trails in the park.

Beginning at the Chickamauga Visitor Center, a seven-mile seasonally ranger-led or self-guided auto tour reaches major points of interest on the battlefield. The center is a stately, Colonial Revival-style building, built in 1936, with a colonnade front porch across the two-and-a-half-story central block and with one-and-a-half-story symmetrical wings with hipped roofs. The center contains the Fuller Collection of American Military Arms; a recently opened addition provides more exhibition space. Further along the tour is the Kelly House, a 20-foot by 20-foot, single-pen, side-gabled cabin of hewn and notched logs. Less than a mile south is the Brotherton Cabin. The reconstructed 21-foot by 20-foot, single-pen, side-gabled log cabin with half-dovetail notched hewn logs is near the Confederate breakthrough that was the turning point in the Battle of Chickamauga. At the end of the Chickamauga tour at Snodgrass Hill, on the site of the Snodgrass family home, is a 26-foot by 20-foot, single-pen, side-gabled log cabin constructed with hewn, half-dovetail-notched logs using original logs of a larger structure.

A circuitous drive to the Lookout Mountain Visitor Center southwest of downtown Chattanooga is the starting point for a walking tour of major points of Lookout Mountain Battlefield and scenic Point Park at the mountain's tip. The entrance gate to Point Park, built in 1905, may be recognizable to those familiar with the U.S. Army Corps of Engineers insignia. The striking stone masonry structure has castellated walls and two round 33-foot-high observation towers flanking a 12-foot- by 10-foot-high arched opening surmounted by a sculpted eagle. Near the gate is the most dramatic of the many battlefield monuments, the 95-foot-high New York Peace Monument, dedicated in 1910, and topped with bronze figures of Northern and Southern soldiers joining hands in a symbolic display of national reconciliation.

A trail from the visitor center leads to the Adolph S. Ochs Observatory and Museum on the promontory of Lookout Mountain. Named for the owner-publisher of the *New York Times* and *Chattanooga Times* and built in 1939, the two-story, U-shaped building, approximately 15 feet wide is constructed of random course stone. A parapeted balcony and lower viewing platform offers outstanding views of the city and winding Tennessee River below. A downhill walk leads to the Cravens House on the plateau that was the scene of the heaviest fighting during the Battle Above the Clouds. After surviving the battle, the house was destroyed during the winter of 1863 by a group of reporters from *Harper's Weekly* and some Union soldiers who were stationed there, reportedly during a drunken brawl. The rebuilt version after the war on the site of the original house is a one-and-a-half story, side-gabled frame house with wood-shingle roof, a fieldstone basement and foundation, and approximately 56-feet by 26-feet in plan. The house is comprised of one room with seven bays across the front and has a shed-roofed porch wrapping around three sides.

The visitor is encouraged to begin a tour at the visitor center for views of topographic models of the battlefields, to watch the orientation films, and to plan battlefield visits by car or on foot by the many trails in the park.

Fort Pulaski National Monument

Located east of Savannah, Chatham County, Georgia

→ www.nps.gov/fopu

→ The monument is about fifteen miles east of Savannah. From Interstate 95, take Exit 99 for Interstate 16, then onto Interstate 516 to US 80 east, and follow signs for Fort Pulaski, Tybee Island, and beaches.

Fort Pulaski moat, berm *demilune* and southwest bastion

The siege of Fort Pulaski by Federal troops in April 1862 is a testimony to the elusiveness of invincibility. Here, there is a striking example of the conquest of traditional military defenses by new technology. Built on Cockspur Island at the mouth of the Savannah River, the fort was a Third System of fortification introduced along the United States coastlines after the War of 1812. The fort's construction began in 1829 and by 1847 it was substantially complete, although armament was at twenty mounted guns, rather than the intended 146 guns. Built of approximately 25,000,000 bricks, the fort's 7.5-foot-thick walls backed with massive masonry piers were considered impregnable.

Ungarrisoned on the eve of the Civil War, the fort was easily occupied by Georgia militia in January 1864. A Federal strategy to blockade southern ports led to a campaign to recapture southern seacoast fortifications, including Fort Pulaski. General Robert E. Lee, commanding rebel forces in South Carolina, Georgia, and Florida, realized the futility of defending batteries and forts that were isolated on the coastal islands and ordered their abandonment. There were strong opinions about the improbable success of an attack on Fort Pulaski. The U.S. Chief of Engineers, General Totten said,

Damaged east wall, northwest corner

Arched gun galleries

"...you might as well bombard the Rocky Mountains." General Lee, ironically, was involved in the fort's construction three decades earlier. Fort Pulaski was Lee's first military assignment beginning in 1829. Viewing the Federal positions on Tybee Island more than a mile from Fort Pulaski, Lee stood on the fort's parapet in early 1862 and was quoted by Colonel Olmstead in *The Georgia Historical Quarterly* in 1917 as saying, "...they will make it pretty warm for you in here with shells, but they cannot breach your walls at that distance."

The fort's design was a fine example of traditional military architecture and features widespread use of brick arches and galleries. The structure is supported on 70-foot-long pilings driven into the soft mud of Cockspur Island. Surrounded by a wide moat varying in width from 30 feet to 48 feet, and with an average depth of 8 feet and protected by a rear *demilune*, the truncated hexagonal plan enclosing a parade ground about the size of a football field is accessed by two drawbridges. A long, straight rear section called a gorge contains the sally port (the fort's entrance) with double gates, officers' quarters, and barracks rooms. The fort's outward-facing five long walls contain a ground floor of casemate gun galleries, and on the roof an earth-covered terreplein with gun platforms. The Savannah River and wide swampy marshes on all sides completed the fort's defenses.

On February 21, 1862, Federal armament began to arrive on Tybee Island. Working by day and night, eleven batteries with thirty-six mortars, smoothbore, and rifled guns were in place by the morning of April 10, 1862, when Federal troops opened the bombardment on the fort from the northwest shore of Tybee Island. All previous military experience had taught that beyond a distance of 700 yards smoothbore guns and mortars would have little chance of breaking through heavy masonry walls, and beyond 1,000 yards, no chance at all. The rifled guns, unlike smoothbore artillery, had spiraled or rifled grooves inside the barrel that gave improved accuracy, range, and penetrating power.

Pounding away relentlessly, 5,275 shots and shells fired at the fort caused breaches in the brick walls up to 25 inches. The astounding accuracy of three guns—two 84-pounder and one 64-pounder James rifles—struck the walls from a distance of 1,640 yards. The explosive shells passing through the wide gaps and over the walls threatened the main powder magazine. Seeing the hopelessness of the situation and concerned about the lives of the men under his command, the Confederate commander, Colonel Charles H. Olmstead, surrendered only 30 hours after the bombardment began. The death toll was only one soldier on each side. Evidence of the siege gun damage can be seen on the southeast angle facing Tybee Island, where the parapet is reduced 2 to 4 feet in places and repairs made with bright red brick and deep pockmarks are visible. Many of the balls and projectiles are still embedded in the brickwork. Restoration by the National Park Service and Civilian Conservation Corps began in 1933 to stabilize the structure, remove damaged material, and prevent further deterioration.

The drive to the fort though scenic Georgia coastal marshland at the mouth of the Savannah River ends with a return to a relic of military strategy and the site of a siege that caused a drastic revision to meet the threat of a new weapon of war. From the southeast angle parapet, the Cockspur Island Lighthouse, marking the South Channel of the Savannah River, can be seen at the tip of the island. Built in 1856, the small 42-foot-tall conical brick tower was repeatedly damaged by hurricanes and the beacon was extinguished in 1909.

Jimmy Carter National Historic Site

Plains, Sumter County, Georgia

→   www.nps.gov/jica

→   The park is located in Plains, Georgia, ten miles west of Americus, Georgia. From Interstate 75 take Exit 112 toward Vienna on Georgia 27 and continue to Americus and connect with US 280 west to the visitor center/museum in the Plains High School.

The small rural town of Plains was a quiet farming center in southwestern Georgia until the emergence of Jimmy Carter in the presidential race in 1976. Election of the Plains native as the thirty-ninth president of the United States changed the town forever. Deeply immersed in the American consciousness, Plains, Georgia, is identified with its famous native son, long after the crowds drawn to Carter's hometown during the presidential election campaign and term in office were gradually reduced to visitors to the Jimmy Carter National Historic Site.

Born here on October 1, 1924, Carter grew up on a farm a short distance out of town, graduated from Plains High School, and after college and a tour as a Naval officer returned home, after his father's death in 1953, to run the family seed and farm-supply business. A political career beginning with the Georgia state legislature as a state senator and governor, and eventually the presidency, ended with a defeat by Ronald Reagan in 1980. The Carters returned in 1981 to spend a portion of their time in Plains. In 2002 President Carter was the recipient of the Nobel Peace Prize.

A visit to Plains is an exposure to small town, rural South culture that is deeply rooted in agriculture, family, church, and school. These cultural values shaped Jimmy Carter's views on life and established enduring ties to Plains. The Jimmy Carter National Historic Site includes sites associated with the president's life: the Plains railroad depot, Plains High School visitor center/museum, Carter's boyhood farm, and the present Carter residence.

The Plains railroad depot, a simple wood-framed structure with white clapboard siding and green trim, served as the train depot from 1888 to 1951, when passenger service was discontinued. The building was restored and opened in 1976 as Jimmy Carter's Presidential Campaign Headquarters with exhibits focusing on the campaign.

The Plains High School attended by Jimmy and Rosalynn Carter (valedictorian of the class of '44) is typical of many rural American communities with an elementary and high school in the same building. These centers of community life, along with churches, were a source of pride and local identity, and usually were of a classical two-story central section with imposing columns and symmetrical wings, as at Plains. The national trend of regional school district consolidations has either closed or sometimes converted the buildings to lower school levels or non-school uses across the country. The Plains High School, built in 1921, followed in step with this trend and closed in 1979, now serving as the park visitor center/museum.

The Boyhood Home Farm is open for visits; the Carter residence (under Secret Service protection) is not open to the public. The one-story boyhood home where the president lived from age four to just before his eighteenth birthday is on Old Plains Highway two and one half-miles west of downtown Plains. The family moved into the house in 1928 where on the 360-acre farm they grew cotton, peanuts, and corn to sell, and raised vegetables and livestock for their own use. Just east of the house is the old commissary building where Earl Carter sold seeds and supplies to farmworkers and neighbors. The Carter home on Woodland Drive is a one-story ranch house built by the president in 1961 and renovated in 1974 and 1981.

Other sites within the surrounding preservation district are the Marantha Baptist Church where the president occasionally teaches Sunday School; the Lillian G. Carter Nursing Home, formerly a small hospital where the president was born; the Golden Peanut Company, formerly the Carter Warehouse complex; and Billy Carter's service station where the president's younger brother often entertained visitors and members of the news media.

The Jimmy Carter National Historic Site structures can be visited on a self-guided auto tour.

Martin Luther King, Jr., National Historic Site

Atlanta, Fulton County, Georgia

→ www.nps.gov/malu

→ The site is located along Auburn Avenue one and one half-miles east of downtown Atlanta. From Interstate 75/85 take Exit 248C (Freedom Parkway/Carter Center), move to the right lane as soon as possible and at the first traffic light turn right onto Boulevard and follow signs to the National Historic Site parking lot.

Martin Luther King, Jr., birth home

Martin Luther King, Jr., National Historic Site located east of downtown Atlanta is in the heart of Sweet Auburn, a onetime prosperous black community along a corridor between Auburn and Edgewood Avenues. Nicknamed for the opportunities offered blacks, even in the face of Atlanta's segregation laws, the district thrived with black-owned businesses and services, and residences. A stronghold of black Atlanta politics, commerce, spirituality, and social life by 1910, this is where the Nobel Prize-winning minister and a leader in the Civil Rights movement was born, lived, and was laid to rest after his assassination on April 4, 1968. The site, containing the King Birth Home, Ebenezer Baptist Church, and memorial gravesite is joined by the Martin Luther King, Jr., Preservation District on the east, north, and west embracing the larger Auburn Avenue black community by which King was greatly influenced as a youth and as an adult.

Martin Luther King, Jr., was born on January 15, 1929, in an upstairs bedroom of 501 Auburn Avenue. He lived in this house with his mother, father, grandparents, sister, brother, and an occasional boarder until he was twelve years old. King attended public schools nearby and walked to services at Ebenezer Baptist, where his maternal grandfather, father, and brother served as ministers. In 1941, the family moved to another house within the Auburn community. King's emergence as a civil rights leader began after he received his doctorate at Boston University at age twenty-seven and moved to lead the Dexter Avenue Baptist Church in Montgomery, Alabama. His eloquent voice and advocacy for racial justice and human rights was heard beyond Montgomery. In 1960 he resigned his pastorate in Montgomery and moved to Atlanta, and became the president of the Southern Christian Leadership Conference (SCLC). He also served as co-pastor of the Ebenezer Baptist Church and advised the Student

Nonviolent Coordinating Committee (SNCC). His famous "I have a dream" speech, delivered on August 28, 1963 from the steps of the Lincoln Memorial in Washington, D.C. to a crowd of more than 250,000 people electrified the audience.

Today, visitors to the national historic site can begin their tour at the National Park Service (NPS) Visitor Center at the corner of Auburn Avenue and Jackson Street, where park personnel provide information and exhibits and films can be viewed. Across Auburn Avenue is the Ebenezer Baptist Church. The two-story, rectangular, brick, Gothic Revival church with a gable roof and two large towers flanking the main elevation was completed in 1922. The lower level, which contains the meeting hall, is covered with gray stucco and scored to resemble stone. Two-story buttresses divide the side elevations into nine bays containing stained-glass lancet windows. Brick belt courses, panels, corbels, and window hoods ornament the front and side elevations. The church sanctuary is an open, rectangular space, with the pulpit and choir elevated on a platform and a balcony across the rear. The education building was constructed in 1956; in 1971, a new front was placed on it.

Next to the church and located within the boundaries of the Martin Luther King, Jr., National Historic Site is the King Center for Nonviolent Social Change. Nestled in a reflecting pool is a brick island containing the double memorial crypt of Martin Luther King, Jr., and Coretta Scott King.

The historic Fire Station No. 6 at Boulevard that served the Sweet Auburn community is an NPS structure built in 1896. The two-story, brick Romanesque Revival-style building with a shed roof and decorative parapet has a single arched engine bay flanked by pedestrian entrances, windows, and an asymmetrically placed tower with date panel. Elaborate brickwork includes corbels, door and window surrounds, a diamond-patterned frieze, and a machicolated cornice.

Fire Station No. 6

Across Auburn Avenue at 472–488 Auburn Avenue is a row of four identical hip-roofed double shotgun houses with weatherboard siding that have been rehabilitated by the NPS. The Empire Textile Company built the houses in 1905 for mill workers. The houses are so named because, theoretically, a gunshot could be fired down the perfectly aligned doorways, hence the name, "shotgun."

At 501 Auburn Avenue is the two-story, single-family Queen Anne style Martin Luther King, Jr., Birth Home. Built in 1895, the house was restored by the King Center and NPS to its appearance during the years between 1929 and 1941 when his family moved to a house on Boulevard. The irregular massing, a side entrance, a hip roof with lower cross gables, decorative shingles in the gable ends, and a wraparound porch with turned posts, milled brackets, and a plain, openwork balustrade are offset by clapboard and some trim painted mustard brown.

Other buildings within the site and the adjoining historic district include residences and commercial structures worth visiting on a self-guided walking tour to absorb the historic atmosphere of the Sweet Auburn community. The King Birth Home is open for park ranger-led tours on a first-come, first-served basis. It is extremely popular and interested visitors should register at the NPS Visitor Center in person upon arrival at the park.

Kentucky

South

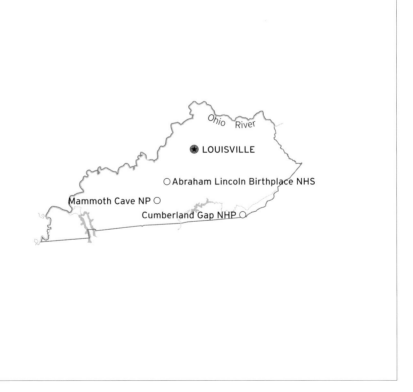

Abraham Lincoln Birthplace National Historic Site

Located in central Kentucky near Hodgenville, LaRue County

→ www.nps.gov/abli

→ Abraham Lincoln Birthplace National Historic Site is in central Kentucky on US 31east, three miles south of Hodgenville, Kentucky. Access via Interstate 65 from the north is at Exit 91 and from the south at Exit 81. The Boyhood Home Unit at Knob Creek (ten miles northeast) is also along US 31east.

Abraham Lincoln Birthplace Memorial Building

The Abraham Lincoln Birthplace National Historic Site south of Louisville, near Hodgenville in the rolling hill country of central Kentucky, contains a neo-classical memorial building housing a symbolic birthplace cabin. In 2001, the park added the Abraham Lincoln Boyhood Home at Knob Creek, the site of Lincoln's home from age two until seven. The park units enshrine Lincoln's towering position in American history and obscure beginnings in backwoods frontier cabins. Travelers should begin a visit to the park's two units at the Birthplace Site's visitor center for an orientation and a self-guided tour and then driving ten miles northeast on US 31east to the Boyhood Home at Knob Creek.

Abraham Lincoln, the sixteenth president of the United States was born on February 12, 1809 on Sinking Spring Farm in a one-room cabin near the limestone spring for which the farm was named. Thomas Lincoln and his wife Nancy Hanks Lincoln moved into the cabin in 1808. Typically, cabins of the frontier era were simple one-room structures of rough-hewn logs, about 18 feet by 16 feet, with a dirt floor, one door, one window, a small fireplace, exposed log purlins and a shingled roof, and a low chimney of hardwood, clay, and straw. Housed within the Memorial Building is a cabin of these characteristics but of doubtful provenance as the authentic Lincoln birthplace cabin. Several moves and disassembly, including storage in the basement of an old mansion in

Reconstructed boyhood cabin at Knob Creek

Long Island, NY, and a lack of documentation caused the National Park Service to cautiously describe the cabin as "symbolic of the one in which Lincoln was born." Nevertheless, placement in the center of the Memorial Building as a jewel within a jewel case enshrines the cabin as part of the Lincoln history.

The centerpiece of the Birthplace National Historic Site is the granite and marble Memorial Building in a formal landscape standing on a knoll surrounded by a grove of trees. Designed by John Russell Pope referencing a mausoleum, the granite and marble Memorial Building of neoclassical design encloses a single exhibition room containing the symbolic cabin and interior circulation space around it. President Theodore Roosevelt laid the cornerstone on the one hundredth anniversary of Lincoln's birth and the dedication by President William Howard Taft occurred two years later.

Symbolism representing Lincoln's life, words, and actions is seen everywhere in a composition that evokes reverence for Lincoln's heroic reputation by the structure's processional approach and classicism. The building's overall dimensions are approximately 50 feet by 36 feet in plan and 35 feet to the top of the common parapet. A tall, one-story south-facing entrance portico of six Doric columns with a coffered ceiling adorns the simple planar wall surface. Placed on a platform ascending fifty-six steps (37-foot-wide steps at the base and narrowing to 30 feet at the summit), one for each year of Lincoln's life, the Stony Creek granite (Milford Pink from Milford, Massachusetts) walls take on different shades of pale color during daylight, ranging from a rosy tint to glaring white. Above the portico columns is an architrave with an inscription that reads "With Malice Toward None, With Charity For All." A band of five windows between each of the portico columns with neoclassical granite grilles are placed above the main entrance double bronze doors. Above the portico is a bold dentil cornice that continues around the building, and a stepped, gabled parapet. The east and west elevations are identical with a four-columned portico composed of engaged Doric columns and tall inset windows. The north elevation is relatively austere with five recessed windows.

The symbolic Lincoln birthplace cabin is in the center of a light, airy exhibition room set on marble flooring surrounded by a herringbone-patterned brick floor. Interior walls are marble with a chair wall wainscoting and plaster walls above. In the center of the ceiling is a skylight with translucent panels concealing fluorescent lighting. Around the panels are sixteen coffers with plaster rosettes based on those found in the Pantheon in

Rome.

The Lincoln family moved to the 228-acre farm at Knob Creek in 1811 after losing Sinking Spring Farm in a title dispute and lived there five years until migrating to Indiana in 1816. The cabin at Knob Creek is a replica built in 1931 possibly from logs taken from the home of Lincoln's boyhood friend Austin Gollaher—reputed to have rescued young Abe from drowning in Knob Creek—a mile away. Appropriately, a split-rail fence encloses the reconstructed one-room cabin of rough-hewn logs with exterior chimney, single door and window, and shingled roof.

The Birthplace Site visitor center contains exhibits and an orientation film. The park hosts an annual ceremony commemorating Lincoln's birthday and summer events, including "A Walk Through Lincoln's Life" each fall with demonstrations of quilting, crafts, rail-splitting, and basket making.

Cumberland Gap National Historical Park

Visitor center in Middlesboro, Kentucky and areas in Virginia and Tennessee

→ www.nps.gov/cuga

→ The park is located at the junction of Kentucky, Virginia, and Tennessee. The park visitor center is in Middlesboro, Kentucky, ninety miles east of Knoxville, Tennessee, reached via US 25east from Kentucky and Tennessee and US 58 from Virginia.

Hensley Settlement cabin

The lure of the bluegrass of what is now Kentucky was blocked to settlers in the American colonies by the Appalachian Mountains extending four hundred miles from Maine to Georgia. Although long known to Native Americans by following buffalo to the Kentucky hunting grounds, American explorers did not discover Cumberland Gap until 1750. In 1775, exploration led by Daniel Boone marked out the Wilderness Trail from the Cumberland Gap into Kentucky. Immigration began immediately and by 1810 an estimated two hundred thousand to three hundred thouand people had crossed the gap heading west. The spirit of the times is captured in the famous George Caleb Bingham's *Daniel Boone Escorting Settlers through the Cumberland Gap* (1851–1852), portraying the intrepid Boone at the head of a party of immigrants.

Modern day travelers can experience the pioneer route in an environment restored by the 1996 rerouting of US 25east through the Cumberland Gap Tunnel. From the visitor center in Middlesboro, Kentucky, there is a four-mile drive on Pinnacle Road past two Civil War earthwork forts to Pinnacle Overlook. The drive is worthwhile for spectacular views of the gap and the rippling Great Smoky Mountains (see page 397) beyond. Most of the 20,450-acre park is accessible only by foot trail. The Iron Furnace is a short trail walk from Cumberland Gap, Tennessee. The restored Hensley Settlement on Ridge Trail is reached by a shuttle ride from the visitor center on ranger-guided tours lasting three-and-a-half hours from mid-May through the end of October.

The Hensley Settlement, more than ten miles along the Ridge Trail from the visitor center, is the once abandoned and now partially restored by the National Park Service (NPS) self-sufficient community that flourished in splendid isolation for nearly fifty years. The settlement's story begins with the purchase of five hundred acres astride Brush Mountain in the Cumberland Mountains in 1903 by Burton Hensley, Sr. He subdivided the land into sixteen parts for his principal heirs, one of whom was his daughter, Nicy Ann. Her husband, Sherman Hensley, taken by Nicy Ann's twenty-one-acre share of the land promptly bought thirty-three acres more and moved his family up Brush Mountain. It was December 1903; Nicy Ann was three months pregnant with her second child. Eventually, Sherman Hensley fathered nineteen children.

Cabin construction at Hensley Settlement

Joined by Willie Gibbons, the isolated community grew to twelve farmsteads with a population of between sixty and one hundred people who made their living farming and from the forests, continuing as a truly rural Appalachian settlement, without roads, electricity, or other modern conveniences. Foot or horseback brought in what was not handmade by the extended family members out and back over steep, narrow mountain trails. In 1951, Sherman Hensley was the last inhabitant to leave; in 1979, he died at the age of ninety-eight.

Since 1965 the NPS has restored three of the farmsteads with their houses, barns, fences, and fields, as well as the schoolhouse and cemetery. The buildings, mostly of hewn chestnut with shake roofs, are being furnished to represent the era when the Hensleys and Gibbons lived there. About 70 acres of the original Hensley settlement have been returned to farming and pasture land.

The park is celebrated for its seventy miles of hiking trails, displays of abundant spring wildflowers, and fall foliage.

Mammoth Cave National Park

In the south central part of the state in Mammoth Cave, Edmonson County, Kentucky

→ www.nps.gov/maca

→ The park is approximately eighty-five miles from Louisville, Kentucky, and Nashville, Tennessee, via Interstate 65. From the north take Exit 53 (Cave City) and from the south Exit 48 (Cave City) and follow signs to the visitor center.

Good Spring United Baptist Church

The dramatically inspiring Mammoth Cave National Park cave network of 367 miles (mapped, so far) is the longest known in the world, appropriately designated a World Heritage Site (1981) and an International Biosphere Reserve (1990). The maze of caves formed by underground streams channeling through the limestone plateau is filled with gypsum formations, stalactites, stalagmites, and columns in bizarre splendor. The whoosh of cool air emerging from underground at the historic entrance begins the descent into a world apart from the rugged, forested hill country and crowds above ground. In a year, more than 2.74 million visitors come to the park, with nearly 358,000 of them taking a ranger-guided cave tour varying in length, some visiting remnants of saltpeter mining, a failed attempt at a tuberculosis sanitarium, and artifacts of prehistoric peoples. Startling sights are of the unusual approximately 130 forms of life, some of which never leave the lightless environment.

From 4,000 to 2,000 years ago early Native Americans ventured into the caves and some traces exist of these first explorers. Mammoth Cave was rediscovered by a bear hunter in the late 1790s and mined for saltpeter, essential for the War of 1812 munitions. In 1816 the first visitors began to arrive and exploration and exploitation as a tourist attraction was under way. Eventually, the cave system dimensions became better known to extend beyond the boundaries of today's 52,830-acre Mammoth Cave National Park.

A park on two levels, above ground the rich cultural history of the farmlands and

Joppa Missionary Baptist Church

forests assembled for the park by the time of its establishment in 1941 is visible in historical structures remaining from those cleared off the land to begin restoration to a natural landscape. Civilian Conservation Corps crews reclaimed thousands of acres of farmland, removed hundreds of structures and miles of fences, constructed cave tour route trails and established surface hiking trails, and improved miles of park roads. Churches and their cemeteries that once were centers of community life still exist within the park boundaries.

Today, Mammoth Cave Baptist Church, established in 1827; Good Spring United Baptist Church, established in 1842; and Joppa Missionary Baptist Church, established in 1862, are still used on occasion by local citizens for celebrations including weddings, funerals, family reunions, and Decoration Day. The churches are seen on drives radiating from the visitor center: Mammoth Cave Baptist Church to the east on Flint Ridge Road; Good Spring Baptist Church to the northwest on Maple Springs Loop off the Green River Ferry Road; and Joppa Missionary Baptist Church to the southwest on Brownsville Road.

The simple, one-story white-painted clapboard structures set in the forested landscape are similar in size, form, and details. Ranging in size from 26-feet wide to 42-feet deep, the wood-framed structures are built on sandstone block piers with gable ends, tin roofs, and without steeples. Two entry doors with either three or four double-hung windows are on each side. The National Park Service and church members maintain all three churches and the cemeteries occasionally are used for burials.

The park contains seventy miles of hiking and bridle-riding trails winding through the dense second-growth forests. Overlooks on paved roads are likely places to spot wildlife and view the seasonal changes in wildflowers and foliage colors. Another perspective of the above ground park is on the Green River cruise.

Louisiana

South

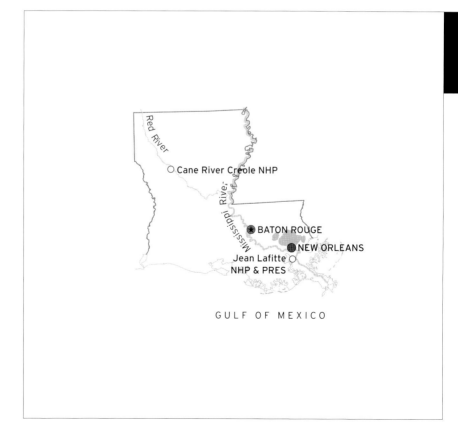

Cane River Creole National Historical Park

Natchitoches, Natchitoches Parish, Louisiana

→ www.nps.gov/cari

→ The park is located in west central Louisiana accessible from Interstate 49 (Exits 119 and 127) and LA 1 and
494. Two park units are Oakland Plantation (twelve miles south of Natchitoches on Highways 1 and 494) and
Magnolia Plantation (twenty-three miles south of Natchitoches on Highways 1 and 494).

Oakland Plantation "Big House"

Cane River Creole National Historical Park is located within the Cane River National Heritage Area of more than 116,000 acres in the Red River corridor between Alexandria (forty-
five miles south) and Shreveport (seventy-five miles north). Natchitoches Parish, located
in the Heritage Area, is the center of the Louisiana Creole plantation culture. The park's
two units at Oakland Plantation and Magnolia Plantation contain remnants of more than
200 years of plantation life in a cultural landscape under restoration, including historical
vernacular structures, in this 1994 addition to the National Park System.

Oakland and Magnolia Plantations have separate histories originating in the creole
settlements from the eighteenth century. Meanings of Creole vary (derived from Portuguese crioulo, meaning "native to this place"). The Creole population in Louisiana originated from people who were born in the New World during French and Spanish colonial
periods and their descendants. Some Creoles are of French or Spanish descent, while
others have a mixed heritage: African, French, Spanish, and/or Native American. Today,
the term is loosely interpreted to distinguish between the region's former colonial residents and incoming Americans. A unifying trait is the French language and the Catholic
religion. Confused with today's Cajuns, they differ from French-speaking people exiled

by the British from Acadian Canada, who arrived in Louisiana years after the Creoles established themselves there.

The historical structures at Oakland and Magnolia Plantations evolved around the years of slaveholding, tenant farmers, and sharecroppers that shifted from early years of growing indigo and tobacco to cotton raising. A variety of structures are intact, including a main house, outbuildings, and an extensive collection of farming tools, equipment, historic furniture, and family personal items left behind by the two to three hundred people who lived at the plantations over time.

Oakland Plantation was established by Jean Pierre Emmanuel Prud'homme, a second-generation native of French descent, on land granted to him by the Spanish crown in 1789. Eight generations of the family lived here on Bermuda Plantation, as it was originally known, on land on the main channel of the Red River, known as *Rivière aux Cannes*, until sale of forty-two acres to the National Park Service (NPS) in 1997. In 1873 two Prud'homme brothers partitioned the plantation, renaming the portion on the west bank Oakland. The intact nature of Oakland Plantation's setting, twenty-four historical structures, and artifacts, almost all dating from the nineteenth century, constitute one of the most complete collections of French Creole buildings in the nation and is representative of plantation life seldom encountered elsewhere in the South.

Oakland's buildings are informally arranged parallel to the Cane River (formerly the Red River) with the main house facing the river and graced by a grove of live oak trees. In front of the house in a short allée of live oaks is a rare surviving example of a bottle garden, a peculiar way of outlining of parterres by pushing bottles into the ground upside down.

Unlike the grandeur of plantation houses such as Louisiana's splendid Greek Revival Shadows-on-the-Teche and Oak Alley, Oakland's "Big House" is typical of the two-story raised French Colonial plantation house adapted to the hot and humid Louisiana climate, with brick ground floor and brick piers, an upper floor of frame and *bousillage* (a wall infill of a mixture of mud, and Spanish moss, straw and/or animal hair), encircling gallery, and a hipped roof. The original main house, completed in 1821, was square in plan and contained four rooms heated by a pair of back-to-back fireplaces. Today's seventeen-room house evolved over a 150-year period with at least seven significant alterations, beginning within a few years of the original construction and the latest in 1964. As NPS restoration and stabilization work continues, the visitor can inspect the cypress timber framing using mortise-and-tenon connections and *bousillage* walls.

Oakland's plantation buildings include two *pigeonniers* of ground floor *bousillage* walls; a one-story raised overseer's house; a massive roofed log corn crib; a carriage house; a mule barn that was originally a smokehouse; a carpenter's shop; a stable; a cotton seed house; storage sheds; and a pair of two-room slave houses (the last of thirty housing 145 slaves), later occupied by share croppers and tenant farmers. An underground brick cistern with a domed top protruding from the ground is located near the main house. The plantation store built after the Civil War became the Bermuda post office and operated until the 1980s.

Magnolia Plantation is the remnant of a large cotton-producing plantation established by Ambrose Lecomte I and Ambrose Lecomte II in the 1830s on a French land
grant that eventually grew in antebellum years to 7,800 acres. This unit of Cane River

Magnolia Plantation cabins

Creole National Historical Park includes
twenty-one historical structures, almost all
built in the nineteenth century. The present French Colonial main house is outside
the park's boundary. Built in 1890, it is a
reconstruction on the site of the original
1850 house, burned by retreating Union
soldiers in 1864. The seven-and-a-half
intact slave cabins are the remnant of an
original twenty-four. The two-room brick
structures housed two families and were
converted after the Civil War into single-family dwellings. The cabin's two interior rooms
built around a central chimney, had front and rear porches, wooden floors and cypress-
shingled roofs and swept yards. The gin house is a massive structure (85 feet by 37 feet)
containing a huge wooden screw cotton press mechanism, probably turned by mule
power, that was used until the 1840s, and a stationary steam engine hydraulically powered cotton gin used until 1939. Other structures include a slave hospital, a *pigeonnier*, a
blacksmith shop, several barns, a stable, and a plantation store.

Preservation and restoration work on these structures and the grounds (beginning
in 2004) for the foreseeable future offer a unique experience to see the work in progress.
Limited services are available to the public. Formal tours of Oakland Plantation are provided daily in afternoons. Self-guided tour maps are available at the Main House.

Jean Lafitte National Historical Park and Preserve

Located in New Orleans and southeastern Louisiana in the Mississippi River Delta region

→   www.nps.gov/jela

→   Six physically separate sites and a park headquarters in New Orleans, Louisiana, stretch 150 miles
between New Orleans and Eunice and are connected by Interstate 10 from New Orleans to Lafayette,
Interstate 49 and Louisiana 190 from Lafayette to Eunice, and LA 90 from New Orleans to Thibodaux and
Lafayette.

Jean Lafitte National Historical Park and Preserve in Louisiana's Mississippi Delta region is
a many-faceted park of six separate units and administrative headquarters in New Orleans
that summons the metaphor of local gumbo soup: ingredients from many cultures. The
unique Acadian (Cajun) culture of the area is seen in park units in Lafayette, Thibodaux,

and Eunice. The Barataria Preserve unit (in Marrero) interprets the natural and cultural Creole history of the region's uplands, swamps, and marshlands. Six miles southeast of New Orleans is the Chalmette unit containing Chalmette Battlefield and Chalmette National Cemetery. The park's headquarters and visitor center for New Orleans is located at 419 Decatur Street in the historic French Quarter (Vieux Carré). Each site has a visitor center and historical structures are located in the New Orleans area, Thibodaux, and Eunice.

The park headquarters/visitor center at 419 Decatur Street, between Conti and St. Louis Streets has a long history typical of Vieux Carré buildings. The three-story facade front building facing the Mississippi River is an assemblage of structures originating at the beginning of the nineteenth century known as the 417–419 Decatur properties. The properties were subject to fires and rebuilds, reused as various commercial enterprises, gussied up with classical cast-iron columns, floors added and removed, decorated with a second floor gallery with wrought-iron balcony extending over the sidewalk, and later joined together for a single use. The facade is typical of many New Orleans warehouses and manufacturing companies in a mixed Italianate and Victorian Neoclassical style, now unified by similarly proportioned second and third floor window openings, and grayish-brown sand plaster coating. Inside there is an assortment of cast-iron and wooden Doric columns inserted to support structural changes, some freestanding and others integrated into walls. The courtyard is a pleasant space and an opportunity to view part of the building's exterior.

Chalmette Battlefield cannon

Chalmette Battlefield is the site of the 1815 Battle of New Orleans. The stunning victory by volunteers and a militia led by Andrew Jackson, including Jean Lafitte's Baratarians, resulted in a British defeat with the 2,000 casualties compared to a reported thirteen by the Americans. Chalmette National Cemetery, established in 1864, is the final resting place for soldiers from the War of 1812, Civil War, Spanish-American War, World Wars I and II, and Vietnam. It is one of fourteen national cemeteries associated with battlefields managed by the National Park Service.

The Chalmette Monument commemorates the victorious two-hour battle by the American side on January 8, 1815. The truncated yellow-grey marble clad obelisk had a fateful beginning when neither Jackson nor the cornerstone appeared at the "cornerstone laying" ceremony on January 8, 1840. Although Jackson visited the site two days later the stone never materialized. A competition design won by Newton Richards followed the proportions seen in the Washington Monument, a 150-foot-tall tapered shaft 14 feet and 2 inches square at the base and mounted on a series of stepped platforms, all resting on a grillage of 8-inch-thick timbers. The ornamentation is found in neo-Egyptian entrance porticos on all four sides, only one of which is functional. A central iron spiral staircase surrounds a brick central support column. And, as with the Washington Monument, construction was delayed for lack of funds until 1855 and stopped at 56 feet in 1859. For nearly half a century the unfinished monument stood on the Chalmette Battlefield until it was ceded to the federal government and work commenced again in 1908, although foundation conditions limited the additional height to a total of 100 feet 2 inches to the pyramidal cap.

The Malus-Beauregard House at the edge of Chalmette Battlefield facing the Mississippi River is a mixture of French-Colonial architectural elements which were modified

Malus-Beauregard House

in 1858 to include Greek Revival features. Never part of a plantation, the house served as a country residence when built about 1833 and named for a succession of owners, one of whom was Judge René Beauregard. The elegantly proportioned two-story house has

Brick-paved gallery

eight full-height Doric columns with an intermediate wood railing at front and rear, a hipped roof with six dormers, and three rooms on each floor. Greek Revival exterior and interior moldings were probably added in the 1850s. The beige stucco-covered brick walls have faux scoring to simulate large stone blocks. The house received substantial damage from Hurricane Katrina in 2005 with the ground floor under 3 feet of water and roofing damaged.

The Liberty Theater in Eunice, although outside the park boundary, is adjacent to the Prairie Acadian Cultural Center, and contributes to an understanding of Cajun culture. The yellow brick 1924 theater, billed as "Southwest Louisiana's Premier Temple of Amusement," could seat one thousand vaudeville and moviegoers. During its hey-days of the 1920s and 1930s, personal appearances were made at the Liberty by Fatty Arbuckle, Tex Ritter, Jimmy Clanton, The Bowery Boys, and Roy Rogers. Restored in 1986, the reconfigured interior is the home of the internationally acclaimed *Rendez Vous des Cajuns* radio and TV show featuring Cajun and zydeco music, local recipes, and Cajun humor. Original murals and contemporary additions grace the interior of this charming anachronism.

The Percy-Lobdell Building in Thibodaux serves as the Acadian Wetlands Cultural Center. Located along Bayou Lafourche, the building constructed by Peter Randolph Percy and John L. Lobdell in 1912, housed a grocery wholesale business in rice, potatoes, and flour. It was typical of late-nineteenth and early-twentieth-century commercial structures in the bayou towns. The St. Mary facade of the 200-foot-long brick structure has a false front, with a narrow central pediment set in a bracketed cornice of pressed metal.

The visitor traveling through the bayou country and New Orleans will find a fascinating journey to the diverse park units in an unusual cultural and natural landscape. The ever-changing Mississippi Delta region is anchored firmly by the historical structures recording three centuries of settlement.

Mississippi

South

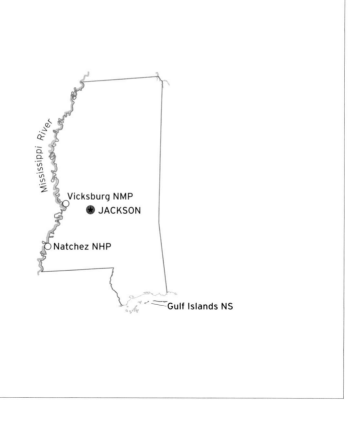

Mississippi River

Vicksburg NMP

⊛ JACKSON

○ Natchez NHP

Gulf Islands NS

Gulf Islands National Seashore (Mississippi)

Ocean Springs, Harrison County, Mississippi

→ www.nps.gov/guis

→ Gulf Islands National Seashore is in Florida and Mississippi and both districts are south of Interstate 10. The two districts are a two-hour drive apart. In Mississippi, to reach Fort Massachusetts offshore on West Ship Island, use Exits 57 or 50 toward US 90 to the visitor center in Ocean Springs. The Florida section is discussed in the Florida chapter of this book (see page 327).

Fort Massachusetts

The barrier islands stretch along 150 miles of the Gulf of Mexico coast from Florida west to West Ship Island, thirteen miles south of Gulfport, Mississippi. The strategic deep-water harbor on the island was used by the British to stage the invasion of New Orleans in the War of 1812. Selected as a site for a Third System coastal defense fortification midway between New Orleans and Mobile, Fort Massachusetts was one of the last forts constructed. West Ship Island became a unit of Gulf Islands National Seashore when the park was established in 1971.

A logistical challenge to construct—including interruption during the Civil War—work started in 1859 and was completed in 1866. At the outbreak of the Civil War the walls stood only 6 to 8 feet high when seized by Confederate troops in early 1861. After Union troops regained control of the fort in September of 1861, construction resumed. West Ship Island was used as the staging area for the Union forces' successful capture of New Orleans in the spring of 1862 and as many as 18,000 United States troops were stationed at the island's harsh environment. The fort was never fully armed, and only manned by caretaker detachments from the end of the Civil War until its abandonment by the army around 1900.

Restoration work by the National Park Service (NPS) through 2001, and United States Army Corps of Engineers dredging to protect the fort's surrounding beach, left the fort in pristine condition. The work was undone by Hurricane Katrina in 2005, when a 35-foot wall of water surged over and through the fort, sweeping away all other man-made structures on the island, removing the berm atop the fort, and knocking the large parapet granite blocks down into the moat. The fort has been reopened to the public and is accessible only by private boat or passenger ferry, March through October, departing from the intersection of Gulfport Yacht Harbor US 90 at Mississippi Highway 49.

Approaching the fort, the compact structure's tall brick walls and the grass-covered rampart above a granite coping seem to emerge directly from the surrounding beach sand. The D-shape (or *demilune*) Fort Massachusetts has a round face oriented toward the deep-water harbor; the flat rear side faces the island. Between the approximately 28-foot-tall brick outer scarp wall, capped by a granite coping, and the 20-foot-high inner scarp wall is the grass-covered rampart and the lower level barbette tier with arced granite curbing to support gun mounts. The hollow core area contains the parade ground. Inner scarp walls are lined with tall, arched casemate openings without interior walls, curving gracefully around the curved exterior surface. The Totten design casemate embrasure openings in the outer scarp wall contain heavy iron shutters to protect the gunners. The sally port entrance is on the flat side of the fort, and is defended by two half bastions to flank the sally port. The half bastions of the fort are located next to the guardrooms, which contain loopholes for the fort defenders to fire through.

The high quality of construction work, despite the difficult wartime working conditions, is seen in the three spiral staircases that lead to the fort's barbette level. Visitors should check with the NPS about access times and site conditions.

Natchez National Historical Park

Natchez, Adams County, Mississippi

→ www.nps.gov/natc

→ Natchez is accessed from both US 61 (from the north and the south) and US 84 from the east and west to Melrose/Montebello Parkway. The park visitor center is located one mile on the right.

Located in the city of Natchez, the 108-acre Natchez Historical Park includes three separate and distinct historical sites: the site of Fort Rosalie, founded by the French in 1716; the antebellum estate Melrose; and the downtown home of a freed black man, William Johnson.

Natchez has a lengthy history based on its prime location on the Mississippi. A flourishing center for the Natchez Indians, the French claiming this region of North America built Fort Rosalie in 1716 on the bluffs overlooking the river. Hostility between the French and Natchez Indians proved fatal to the Natchez Indian culture after devastating attacks by each side in 1729. By 1731 the remaining Indians abandoned the area. Later in the eighteenth century the region changed hands several times, from French to British, to Spanish, and eventually because the Mississippi Territory of the United States, with Natchez as the territorial capital and Fort Rosalie falling into ruins.

By the early decades of the nineteenth century, this southwesterly outpost of the United States began to flourish as the terminus for immigrant travel on the Natchez Trace between Nashville and the Natchez area, and along the Mississippi River. Improvements in cotton growing and production, tied to shipping by the new steamboat traffic on the river (1811), ushered in the era of "King Cotton" and created an economic boom for Natchez. The increasing affluence of plantation owners, planters, and merchants, built by the labor of enslaved people, developed in a small area a fine collection of antebellum houses. During this territorial period a significant number of freed slaves began to emerge, many living in Natchez. Many were the children of white owners who were provided with freedom and often an inheritance.

In the antebellum period, after Mississippi statehood in 1817, the establishment of suburban villas in the Greek Revival style expressed the epitome of the plantation culture, although the estates remained conveniently close to town life in pastoral settings, away from the dirt and noise of the city but free from the isolation of plantation life. By the opening of the Civil War, the location of railroads in Vicksburg caused it to surpass Natchez in commercial importance and the Confederate army decided to fortify the commercially important Vicksburg instead of Natchez. Spared a devastating shelling from Union gunboats, Natchez emerged from the war unscathed, creating today's legacy of superb architecture.

The National Historic Landmark Melrose, designed and built by Jacob Byers for the John T. McMurran family, between in 1841 and 1848, is one of the best preserved and most significant historic house sites in the South—representative of the King Cotton and

NORTHWEST ELEVATION

Melrose house, northwest elevation (courtesy HABS/HAER)

antebellum era, with a full complement of intact outbuildings set in an 80-acre landscaped park and a formal garden. Melrose is exceptional for its ownership by only two families until 1976, uncompromised by additions or alterations, and preserving original interior architectural details, finishes, and furnishings. The context of the main house, dependencies, and outbuildings provide a superb resource for studying plantation life in the antebellum South.

Melrose, southwest elevation   Slave quarters

Typical of the grand Natchez mansion, the main house is nearly square in plan (approximately 67 by 62 feet) with a wide, two-story pedimented entrance portico shading the three-bay center of the five-bay facade crowned by a hipped roof with a square monitor and a glazed and crown-like balustraded belvedere, and spanned across the rear by a giant-order five-bay colonnade. The two pairs of unfluted Doric columns of brick were stuccoed and scored to imitate ashlar masonry. Six tall, stuccoed chimneys rise from the north, south, and east walls; the easternmost chimney on the north wall being "blind" to maintain the balance of the house. The rear of the house has six giant square Doric columns across its width and a deep, airy gallery.

Especially fine is the exterior load-bearing brickwork of pressed brick laid in an all-stretcher bond with narrow, intricately tooled white mortar joints. A number of masonry interior bearing walls run from basement floor to attic level. Although predominantly Greek Revival in character, with some Federal interior details, Melrose incorporated typical Natchez regional architectural features: the raised floor plan, a central hall with lateral stairway—unusual in its widening into a large, central ballroom-sized hall—inclusion of a jib window, the dining room punkah, spacious galleries, high ceilings, and large expanses of windows. The opulent interior is rich with fine details and furnished with many original pieces of furniture.

On the south side of the main house, continuing the symmetry of Melrose is the arrangement of the flanking dependencies, a pair of two-story, side-gable brick buildings containing slave quarters and a kitchen have full height collonaded porches simulating the main house and forming an elegant courtyard. Also built during the nineteenth century, were the one-story brick smokehouse and matching privies, two lattice cistern houses, two slave cabins, a slave privy, stable, and carriage house.

The William Johnson House in downtown Natchez is important for its interpretation of the freed African-American culture in the pre-Civil War Natchez. Born enslaved and freed at the age of twelve, Johnson became a successful barber and entrepreneur. He died at the age of forty-two in 1851, leaving behind a two-thousand-page diary documenting his daily life and offering glimpses of Southern life and relationships between whites, free blacks, and slaves at a time in antebellum Natchez when slavery was common practice.

The three-bay three-story brick house built by Johnson at 210 State Street, recently restored by the National Park Service, is a typical example of a Natchez nineteenth-century middle-class dwelling (approximately 30 feet by 40 feet in plan), with a commercial space on the ground floor and living quarters on the second and third floors. Built between 1840–1841 in the Greek Revival style, the facade is laid in stretcher bond brickwork, with all other elevations featuring courses of common bond. Two tall dormers project from the facade roof and a two-story gallery extends across the rear. A two-story kitchen is at the rear of the property.

Guided tours of the Melrose mansion house are conducted daily. Self-guided tours of the William Johnson House begin at the visitor center in the adjacent restored McCallum House.

Vicksburg National Military Park

Vicksburg, Warren County, Mississippi

→ www.nps.gov/vick

→ The park is to the north and northeast of downtown Vicksburg. The visitor center is near the intersection of Interstate 20 and US 80. Use Exit 4B and follow Clay Street (US 80) west one quarter-mile to the park entrance.

The campaign for Vicksburg memorialized in this 1,800-acre park is the site of an important Union victory on July 4, 1863. The Confederates called the city the "Gibraltar of the Confederacy," named for its strategic position atop the commanding 200-foot-high bluffs over the river. A joint army and navy operation commanded by General Ulysses S. Grant with eventually 71,000 Union troops attacked over land and water, ultimately wresting control of the Mississippi River from Illinois to the Gulf of Mexico. The fourteen-month campaign culminated in a forty-seven-day siege of Vicksburg. The traveler is encouraged to read Ulysses S. Grant's *Personal Memoirs of U.S. Grant* for a chronicling of this important Union victory.

A sixteen-mile interpretive tour explaining the campaign and siege of Vicksburg travels a route encircling the city to the north and east, containing more than 1,300 monuments and markers in possibly the most monumented battlefield in the world with restored earthwork fortifications, trenches, approaches, and parallels; 144 emplaced cannon; as well as Shirley House, an antebellum "witness house." Vicksburg National Cemetery, with over 18,000 interments, contains the remains of Americans of every war from the Mexican War to the Vietnam War, giving it the distinction of having the largest number of Civil War burials of any national cemetery in the United States. Adjacent to the cemetery is the USS *Cairo* (pronounced KAY-row) Gunboat Museum. The park has five detached units: Louisiana Circle, site of a Confederate fortification; South Fort, another Confederate defense work; Navy Circle, the southern anchor of the Union lines; Grant's Canal, across the Mississippi in Louisiana; and the National Historic Landmark Willis-Cowan House in downtown Vicksburg, Confederate General John C. Pemberton's headquarters during the siege.

The state memorials seen in Vicksburg National Military Park are a dizzying array of classical and contemporary designs, the first placed by Massachusetts in 1903 and the most recent by Kentucky in 2001. There are twenty-eight states represented in total—thirteen Confederate and fifteen Union, with two each for Missouri and Kentucky—and a Navy Memorial. Memorials are obelisks and columns, statuary of individual and groups of soldiers and politicians, and colonnaded peristyles. The Illinois Memorial, with a long stairway of forty-seven steps, one for each day of the Siege of Vicksburg, is modeled after the Roman Pantheon. Eagles soar, an allegorical Spirit of the Republic adorns the Missouri Memorial, and a pelican is featured atop the Louisiana Memorial. At 202 feet in height, the Navy Memorial dedicated to the officers and sailors of the U.S. Navy who served in the Vicksburg campaign is the tallest monument in Vicksburg National Military Park.

The Shirley House stood between the Confederate and Union lines. Now directly below the visually overpowering Illinois Memorial on a knoll above the house, the land around the house was once riddled by Union trenches working their way toward Confederate emplacements. Shelled repeatedly during the struggle, the house was restored by the National Park Service to its 1863 appearance. Built in the 1830s, the two-and-a-half-story wood-frame structure has a large central hallway with high-ceilinged rooms to either side and a large dining hall in the basement. The house is easily identified by the three-bay colonnaded entrance porch supporting an upper porch and crowned by a pediment that is actually an elaborate dormer in the center.

The USS *Cairo* Gunboat and Museum is adjacent to Vicksburg National Cemetery at the northwest corner of the park. One of seven ironclad vessels built to wrest control of the Mississippi River from the Confederates and drive a wedge between eastern and western Confederate states, the gunboat's sloping casemate of two-and-a-half-inch-thick charcoal plate iron bristled with thirteen cannon. A 2-foot thickness of white oak timbers backing the plate iron absorbed the shock of impacting shells. The vessel was 175 feet long, 52 feet wide, weighed 880 tons when loaded, and had a 6-foot draft.

On December 12, 1862, while leading a small flotilla up the Yazoo River north of Vicksburg, the *Cairo* struck a pair of mines (referred to as torpedoes at the time) and sunk in 36 feet of water without loss of life. The mines were made from five-gallon glass bottles filled with some 40 pounds of black powder and attached to a wooden float anchored to the bottom of the river. Copper wires led to a galvanic cell on shore where the Confederate volunteers waited to detonate the homemade contraptions. Ignominious in its 12-minute drop to the river bottom, the *Cairo* earned the distinction of becoming the first warship in history to be sunk by an electrically detonated mine. Settling into the river bottom silt and mud, the *Cairo* was discovered in 1956 and raised in 1964. The recovered portion was shipped to the park in 1977 and place on a concrete foundation near Vicksburg National Cemetery. A walking area around the hull brings the visitor in contact with the partially reconstructed interior, where one can walk inside the "ghost framework." The ship is fully covered by a translucent fiberglass tension roof to protect it from weather and sun. The museum contains many artifacts recovered from the ill-fated vessel.

The Willis-Cowan House, commonly known as "Pemberton's Headquarters," is a recent addition (2002) to the park. Confederate General John C. Pemberton chose the handsome Greek Revival-style house on Crawford Street as his headquarters less than a week after the siege began. Built in 1834–36 and expanded in 1850–51, the two-story, masonry, L-shaped house retains much of the 1863 period fabric. The original section is 54 feet by 20 feet. The ell is 32 feet by 22 feet. Perimeter walls and cross walls are handmade brick laid in stretcher course in the original building and common bond in the addition. The side-gabled, symmetrical front facade is five bays wide with an elegantly detailed central entrance and large windows at both levels. The pedimented, three-bay, two-level frame entrance porch is a major architectural feature of the house exterior. With rich detailing and elegant curving, the Greek Revival-style staircase highlights interior public spaces.

The array of earthworks, trenches, and monuments of many different shapes, sizes, and materials, commemorates one of the most decisive battles in the American Civil War. The Vicksburg National Military Park's well-planned and maintained setting is a rewarding destination for the Civil War buff and those generally interested in the strategy and tactics that propelled Ulysses S. Grant to leadership of the Union forces and eventually to the White House.

North Carolina

South

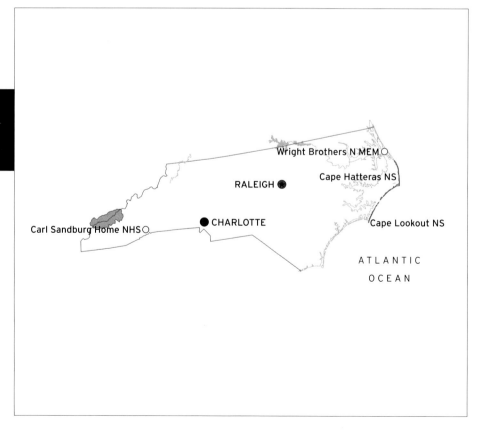

Wright Brothers N MEM○

Cape Hatteras NS

RALEIGH ◉

● CHARLOTTE

Cape Lookout NS

Carl Sandburg Home NHS○

ATLANTIC
OCEAN

Cape Hatteras National Seashore

Buxton, Dare County, North Carolina

→ www.nps.gov/caha

→ The National Seashore's islands of Bodie, Hatteras, and Ocracoke, linked by NC 12 and ferries, are reached from the north via US 17 and 158 or from the west via US 64 and 264. The northern entrance is located at the junction of US 64 and NC 12 south in Nags Head, North Carolina. The Seashore's southern entrance is located on NC 12 just north of Ocracoke, North Carolina (accessible by ferry only).

Cape Hatteras National Seashore is a broken strand of barrier islands projecting into the Atlantic Ocean and forming the Outer Banks of North Carolina. The park's three islands of Bodie, Hatteras, and Ocracoke face the onslaught of nor'easters, hurricanes,

Bodie Lighthouse

and treacherous currents. For centuries, seafarers risked the treacherous Diamond Shoals, a twelve-mile long sandbar projecting twenty-five miles underwater beyond the cape, to take advantage of the north to south flowing currents. Reputed as the Graveyard of the Atlantic, more than six hundred ships were wrecked on the shoals, becoming victims of turbulent water over the shoals, storms, and war. Congress recognized the Outer Banks' dangers to vessels and authorized a lighthouse on Cape Hatteras in 1794. The first lighthouse went into service in 1803.

Today, each island has its own lighthouse, each unique as markers along the dunes and beaches linked by NC Highway 12 and ferries. Cape Hatteras Lighthouse, built in 1870, is at 210 feet the tallest in the United States. Ocracoke Island Lighthouse, built in 1823, is the oldest operating lighthouse in North Carolina. Bodie Island Lighthouse was built in 1872. The Cape Hatteras Lighthouse is open for climbing from mid-April through Columbus Day; the Bodie Island and Ocracoke Island Lighthouses are not open for climbing.

The tall striped tower of Cape Hatteras Lighthouse became a national celebrity in 1999 with an epic journey moving it 2,900 feet to its present location. Facing eventual destruction from beach erosion, the original location 1,500 feet from the shoreline was reduced to a situation of waves washing around the base of the tower. Weighing approximately 2,800 tons and built of approximately 1,250,000 bricks, the tower's move was completed with a relighting ceremony on November 13, 1999.

The black-painted spiral bands on the white brick painted surface creates a striking landmark on the Outer Banks' shifting sands, visible for miles. The conical tower of inner and outer brick walls joined by connecting walls tapers from 32 feet 6 inches at the base to 17 feet 2 inches below the lantern housing a first-order Fresnel lens. Rising from within a one-story octagonal brick base with stone corner quoins and trim and a pedimented doorway on the north elevation, an internal cast iron stairway with treads of

8-inch height following Lighthouse Board specifications spirals upward 268 steps to the watch room balcony level, 160 feet above ground. Three windows aligned vertically in the tower north and south walls at alternating levels illuminate the interior. Exterior cast iron brackets support the tower-encircling watch room balcony. Above this is the lantern gallery, capped by a metal roof and topped by a finial. The

Cape Hatteras Lighthouse stairway

climb to the top brings the visitor to extraordinary 360-degree views of the barrier islands, the Atlantic Ocean, and the mainland.

Near the lighthouse are the double-keeper's (1854, 1892) and principal keeper's (1870) dwellings, typical of such nineteenth-century quarters conveying the lifestyle and history of lighthouse keepers. The double-keeper's dwelling is a two-story wood-framed structure with clapboard siding. Gable roofs with wide overhangs, shutters at all windows, and an eight-bay front porch running the length of the building convey a residential scale and serves as a reference to the majestic height of the lighthouse. The principal keeper's dwelling is a one-and-a-half-story brick structure with a clapboard sided addition. Wide porches, a steep roof, and trim suggest a Gothic Revival cottage.

The Bodie (pronounced "body") Lighthouse stands at 162 feet to the tip of the finial above the first-order Fresnel lens lantern. Lesser known than its legendary spiral-striped Cape Hatteras Lighthouse neighbor almost forty miles to the south, and tucked away in a pine forest and marshlands, nevertheless, the Bodie Lighthouse is a striking landmark with its five alternating approximately 22-foot-wide black and white bands painted over the brick conical tower's surface. Adjacent to the massive load-bearing brick tower's base is a one-story rectangular brick oil house connected by a short covered passageway. The lighthouse tower tapers from a 28-foot diameter at the granite base to 15 feet 3 inches at the balustraded watch room gallery balcony supported by black-painted cast iron brackets. A cast iron stairway ascends internally to the watch room. A historical note is that less than thirty days after the lighting of the station in October 1872 a flock of geese flew into the lamp shattering panes of the .375-inch-thick glass and damaging the lens. Near the tower is a two-story doublekeeper's dwelling with a six-bay porch running the length of the building.

The Ocracoke Island Lighthouse located at the southern tip of Ocracoke Island, marks the inlet providing access to the ports of New Bern, Elizabeth City, and Edenton. The second oldest operating lighthouse in the nation, built in 1823, the 75-foot-tall brick conical tower is stubby in comparison to its neighbors to the north. Painted white, the tower's 12-foot-thick walls at the 25-foot-diameter base taper to 2 feet thick at the 12-foot diameter top capped by an octagonal lantern and fourth-order Fresnel lens.

In addition to the distinctive lighthouses, historic U.S. Life-Saving Service stations are located on Hatteras Island at Rodanthe (Chicamacomico) and Avon (Little Kinnakeet). These building complexes contain lifesaver dwellings with tall watchtowers and boathouses. Reenactments of early rescue drills are performed weekly at the restored Chicamacomico Life-Saving Station during summer months.

Cape Lookout National Seashore

Harkers Island, Carteret County, North Carolina

→ www.nps.gov/calo

→ The Cape Lookout National Lakeshore visitor center on Harkers Island, North Carolina, is reached by car from Beaufort (twenty miles west) via US 70 and Otway, then NC 1332/1335 and follows signs to the visitor center. There are no bridges to the island and privately operated ferries are available from Morehead City, Beaufort, and Harkers Island to the Core Banks.

Cape Lookout Lighthouse

The fifty-six-mile-long Cape Lookout National Seashore is located on a narrow barrier island ribbon of sand on North Carolina's lower Outer Banks. South of Cape Hatteras, the low dunes of undeveloped North Core Banks, South Core Banks, and Shackleford Banks make up the seashore. The historical Cape Lookout Lighthouse and keeper's dwelling are located on South Core Banks Island. A U.S. Life-Saving Station and the abandoned Portsmouth Village are located at the northern tip of the seashore, on North Banks Island.

The dangerous shoals and treacherous currents along the North Carolina coast, mixing with the warm Gulf Stream and cool Labrador Current producing intense fog, resulted in Congressional authorization in 1803 to build lighthouses forty miles apart along the Outer Banks. The particularly treacherous area off Cape Lookout earned a mapmaker's title of *promontorium tremendum* (roughly meaning horrible headland). A Cape Lookout Lighthouse completed in 1812 proved inadequate and was replaced by the present lighthouse first lit in November 1859, providing a model for Outer Banks lighthouse replacements at Cape Hatteras, Bodie Island, and Currituck.

The graceful new 150-foot-tall brick tower rising from a foundation of dressed granite stones was just over 28 feet in diameter at its base with 9-foot-thick brick walls and contains a cast iron spiral stair with 201 wedge-shaped steps leading to the watch room. The spiral stair ends at the doorway into the service room and narrow ladders lead up into the watch room at 156 feet above sea level. A first-order Fresnel lens was visible for nineteen miles. After the outbreak of the Civil War, retreating Confederate troops vandalized the lighthouse by blowing up the internal stairs and damaging the light, darkening the lighthouse for Union shipping. Quickly repaired by Union troops in 1863 with a temporary lens, a permanent first-order Fresnel lens was installed in 1867. Today, the tower is equipped with a radio beacon and automated light installed in 1950.

The strikingly distinctive lighthouse was painted with black and white checkers (often mislabeled as diamond pattern) in 1873, the same year that the Cape Hatteras and Bodie Island lighthouses were painted to provide daymarking for recognition by sailors. The unique Cape Lookout pattern indicates compass direction. A black lighthouse with a white checker pattern meant the ship was sailing east or west facing the deeper waters; a white lighthouse with black checker pattern meant the ship was sailing south or north toward the shallow waters of the shoals and around the headlands.

The adjacent two-story keeper's quarters, with chimneys at gabled ends and shutters at all windows and a porch running the length of the structure, sits on the shoreline against a background of trees and facing a summertime populated beach.

The Cape Lookout Lighthouse is not opened for climbing except during the Open House events held four times a year. Reservations are suggested on the reservation day for the Open House date.

Carl Sandburg Home National Historic Site
Flat Rock, Henderson County, North Carolina

→ www.nps.gov/carl

→ The park is located in western North Carolina three miles south of Hendersonville with access via Interstate 26. Take Exit 53 and follow signs to the visitor center off Little River Road opposite the Flat Rock Playhouse.

The Blue Ridge Mountains of western North Carolina with all its seasonal splendor was a warmer climate than Michigan for Pulitzer Prize-winning author Carl Sandburg. One attraction for the Midwesterner to move south in 1945 was his wife Lilian's herd of champion goats and the appealing Connemara farm, the center of the 263-acre National Historic Site. Suggested as a gentler climate for the goat farm operation by Mrs. Sandburg's brother, photographer Edward Steichen, Carl Sandburg believed they had bought a "village" and Mrs. Sandburg a "million acres of sky." Although Sandburg had established his reputation as a Pulitzer Prize-winning author, biographer, poet, and lecturer, by the time he moved here at age sixty-seven, he continued to produce literary works for the next twenty-two years, including his only novel, *Remembrance Rock* (1948). In 1951, his *Complete Poems* earned him the Pulitzer Prize for poetry. Two years later, his autobiography, *Always the Young Strangers* was published. In 1967, Sandburg died here at age eighty-nine.

The visitor is introduced to the site at an attractive exposed concrete self-serve information station tucked discretely into the forest edge off Little River Road next to the delicate railing of the footbridge over the dam containing Front Lake. A trail one third-mile-long from the entrance parking lot, past the information station, gently winds upward 100 feet to the twenty-two-room white Sandburg Home. Trails continue into the park's rolling pastures past barns, sheds, mountainside woods, walking and hiking trails, two small lakes, ponds, flower and vegetable gardens, and an orchard. The site's large natural area contains Little Glassy Mountain and Big Glassy Mountain.

The Sandburg Home is antebellum in its origins, a contrast to Sandburg's socialist leanings and identification with Abraham Lincoln. Built in 1838 as the summer home of Christopher Gustavus Memminger of Charleston, South Carolina—a lawyer, politician, and soon to be secretary of the Confederate Treasury—named it Rock Hill for the numerous rock formations on the property. He established most of the man-made landmarks that exist today, including the Front Lake. The next owner, Ellison Adger Smyth installed more gardens, added the Side Lake, and renamed the farm Connemara.

The three-story white clapboard main house with gable roof, rooftop dormers, and a pair of brick chimneys is on a gentle rise of land surrounded by lawn. The visitor entrance is a projecting gabled porch supported on four columns and approached by

Carl Sandburg Home

a flight of exterior wooden stairs. From the porch there are sweeping views to thickly forested foothills and the Blue Ridge Mountains. Other one-story porches project from the side and rear of the house, a porte cochere to another side.

The charm of a house tour is the feeling that family just stepped out for a moment and will return. The high, airy first floor rooms contain all of the Sandburg's personal belongings just as he left them before his death. Sandburg's guitar stands next to a baby grand piano, pots and dishes are on the kitchen counters, and more than 12,000 books, magazines, and other personal items are scattered about the comfortably furnished home. Cigars fill the ashtrays, and the dining room table is set for company. The writer's small room on the second floor, with his gray sweater draped over a chair and green eyeshade next to a lamp is utilitarian: walls lined with cubbyholes; papers and books piled on shelves, tables, and the floor, a bulletin board pinned with cryptic notes; and Sandburg's typewriter sitting on a sturdy orange crate.

Near the historic home is the one-and-a-half-story Swedish House distinguished by its steeply pitched gable roof and decorative bargeboards. This is where Sandburg stored his magazines, books, and research material. Further along the trail are the large main goat barn and surrounding outbuildings. A small goatherd of Toggenburgs, Saanens, and Nubians is maintained on the farm. Hiking trails lead to the Little Glassy and Big Glassy Mountains.

Regularly scheduled activities celebrate Sandburg's writing. A Folk Music Festival held in May presents music from *The American Songbag*. Each summer, the home hosts a celebration of the sixteenth president that features Civil War reenactments, poetry readings, and live performances of Sandburg's *Rootabaga Stories* and excerpts from the Broadway play, *The World of Carl Sandburg*, are presented at the park amphitheater.

Wright Brothers National Memorial

Located in Kill Devil Hills on North Carolina's Outer Banks, Dare County, North Carolina

→ www.nps.gov/wrbr

→ The park is fifty miles southeast of Elizabeth City via US 158, about midway between Kitty Hawk and Nags Head. The drive south on US 158 travels south on North Carolina's Outer Banks, past the town of Kitty Hawk, and then four miles south to the Wright Brothers National Memorial.

This historic place is different from Wilbur and Orville Wright's arrival for their first glider flights on September 12, 1900. Kitty Hawk overflows with tourist effluvia; beachfront condos line the highway; summertime traffic clogs the roads; the sand hills are changed by storms and winds and the National Park Service dune stabilization covers the ground with turf. Do not be dismayed to learn that all of the original Wright Brothers structures are replicas of the Wright Brothers' quarters and hangar long since disappeared in the Outer Banks' storms, although faithfully replaced on original sites at the time of the first flight. The flight markers are approximate locations and the Big Kill Devil Hill with its memorial shaft visible for miles is distant from its location when the Wright Brothers soared with their glider testing. Despite the changes, the gulls still careen overhead, soaring and diving over Albemarle Sound to the west and the Atlantic Ocean to the east, as they did in the pioneering seasons of visits by the Wright Brothers from 1900 to 1903, 1905, and a final visit in 1911. The historic stretch of Outer Banks thrills visitors with hushed awe as they peer into the replica quarters, complete with canned goods, books, and burlap-bag bunks, pace off the distances of the historic flights, and climb the now grassy hill to the inspiring Art Deco memorial shaft.

Here is where on December 17, 1903 Orville flew 120 feet for twelve seconds, the first time in the history of the world in which a machine carrying a man had raised itself by its own power into the air in full flight, had sailed forward without reduction of speed, and had finally landed at a point as high as that from which he started. The Wright Brothers never claimed that they were the first to fly. Others had flown in gliders or hung beneath powered hot air or gas-filled balloons. It was Wilbur and Orville, the bicycle mechanics and manufacturers from Dayton, Ohio, untrained scientifically but gifted with a genius that understood the problem of controlled, powered, and sustained flight that earned them their place in history.

When you arrive at the National Monument, leave your car, stopping at the renovated National Historic Landmark visitor center for a brief orientation and a longer visit on this memorable journey, and set out on foot for Big Kill Devil Hill. You cannot miss the 60-foot-high triangular memorial pylon on the crest of the 90-foot-high

Wright Brothers reconstructed sheds

dune. Carved in the Mount Airy granite are bas-relief wings that give the impression of a gigantic bird about to soar into space and at the base is inscribed the testimonial to the brothers' genius: "In Commemoration of the conquest of the air by the brothers

Wilbur and Orville Wright conceived by genius achieved by dauntless resolution and unconquerable faith." Inside the tower are steps to an observation platform where you can scan the 431 acres authorized by Congress in 1927 for the Wright Brothers National Memorial. The actual site of the first four flights is below, including West Hill where the Wrights did much of their gliding from 1900 to 1903, and, beyond, the sound and the ocean.

Descending from the tower, walk around the promenade and scan the site of the flight experiments on the shifting dunes, the barrier island, and surrounding waters. If the wind is what the Wright Brothers experienced in the months of July through late December on their history-making visits, you will understand why they chose this isolated place. Look north, about a half-mile, to the left of the visitor center and the two frame buildings—reconstructed versions of the 1903 hangar and living quarters—for a rough-shaped, head-high stone marker set in place on the approximate site of the takeoff place on the twenty-fifth anniversary of the historic flights, with aviatrix Amelia Earhart standing alongside Orville Wright. As you walk down the grassy slope toward the marker think of the Wright Brothers and their helping hands from the Big Kill Devil Hill's life-saving station carrying the biplane gliders up and down the ankle churning sand. Everything in front of you is either a reconstruction or an addition to the landscape after a century's time. The two-frame wood buildings that formed the camp and the launching rail are at the approximate locations of the originals.

This is where you may begin to shiver at the prospect of a launch in the 605-pound machine (plus Orville's 145 pounds) on wings covered by diaphanous Pride of the West muslin, with Orville surrounded by struts and wire, the four-cylinder engine clattering, and chain-driven 8-foot 6-inch-long hand carved spruce propellers churning the air. All was ready on the brisk morning of December 17, 1903. With winds gusting twenty to twenty-seven miles per hour, a thin layer of ice on puddles, Wilbur's hands on the wingtip poised to run until the machine was airborne, seemingly ready for the moment to be captured on a glass plate with Orville spread-eagled on the lower wing, there was air between the Big Kill Devil Hill's sand and the *Flyer's* skids.

Visitor center by Mitchell and Giurgola

Laid out on the ground next to the granite marker is a replica of the metal-topped two-by-fours the Wrights used as their launching rail. Sweep your view out along the rail and pick out four stone markers receding in the distance with numbers painted in black: 1, 2, 3, and 4; the first at 120 feet marking the release of the *Wright Flyer* from the ground, powered, and under control. Launched at 10:35 A.M. it was a hesitant journey of only twelve seconds, reaching 10 feet above the ground, and ending in "a sudden dart" into the ground. Orville's diary entry is a sparse description, factual and devoid of hyperbole or the excitement of the success. Marker 2 is the landing spot for Wilbur's first try in the air after 11:00 am: 175 feet in twelve seconds, faster in dimin-

Historic first flight

Flight markers

ishing winds: "wind speed not quite as strong," commented Orville in his diary. The third marker is where Orville landed 200 feet from launch after fifteen seconds in the air. Wilbur started the fourth flight at noon ending at Marker 4. After pitching up and down, the flight leveled off and landed, measuring 852 feet over the ground and lasting fifty-nine seconds. More flights were planned after a lunch break but a sudden gust of wind struck the machine, tumbling it several times, and damaging it badly. Testing was finished for the year. Before leaving, Orville's inaccurate telegram, sent to a world that would never be the same, announced that the age of flight had begun on the sands at Big Kill Devil Hill:

> SUCCESS FOUR FLIGHTS THURSDAY MORNING ALL AGAINST TWENTY-
> ONE MILE WIND STARTED FROM LEVEL WITH ENGINE POWER ALONE
> AVERAGE SPEED THROUGH AIR THIRTY-ONE MILES LONGEST 57 [SIC]
> INFORM PRESS HOME CHRISTMAS. OREVELLE [SIC] WRIGHT

South Carolina

South

COLUMBIA

CHARLESTON — Charles Pinckney NHS
Fort Sumter NM

ATLANTIC
OCEAN

Charles Pinckney National Historic Site

Located near Charleston, South Carolina in Mount Pleasant, Charleston County, South Carolina

→ www.nps.gov/chpi

→ The park is six miles north from Charleston on Long Point Road off US 17

Charles Pinckney House at Snee Farm

The Charles Pinckney National Historic Site is the remaining twenty-eight acres of a 715-acre plantation called Snee Farm in the South Carolina Low Country. ("Snee," according to the *Oxford English Dictionary*, means abundant or plentiful.) Located on the Wando Neck, formed by the Wando River on the northwest, the Cooper River estuary on the southwest and the Atlantic Ocean tidal marshes on the southeast, the plantation was one of several in the area that thrived in the late eighteenth and early nineteenth century producing indigo, rice, and, later, cotton. Unlike larger neighbors growing crops for commercial sales, the modest sized Snee Farm primarily served to supply the Pinckney family's principal residence in Charleston with food, firewood, and other farm products. The farm was purchased by Charles Pinckney in 1754 and was inherited by Charles Pinckney III in 1782, known throughout the appellation as "Charles Pinckney." The farm was sold in 1817 to settle debts. Today, Snee Farm is bordered on three sides by subdivision development. The main house was restored after acquisition by the National Park Service (NPS) in 1988.

The National Historic Landmark Snee Farm interprets the distinguished public service career of Charles Pinckney, elected to the state General Assembly at age twenty-two. He served as one of four South Carolina delegates to the Constitutional Convention in Philadelphia, placing him among the Founding Fathers as a signer of the Constitution.

A prominent Federalist, Pinckney served four terms as governor of South Carolina, was ambassador to Spain from 1801 to 1805, and held seats in both state and national legislatures. He died on October 29, 1824, at age sixty-seven.

The Snee Farm cottage was a working farm house. Pinckney's original cottage was replaced by that of William Matthews, the next owner, after destruction by a hurricane in 1828, four years after Pinckney's death. Around 1936, Snee Farm's owner, Thomas Ewing, added two symmetrical wings to the back of the house and constructed a number of outbuildings, including the caretaker's residence.

The central portion of this fine representative example of Lowcountry Coastal Cottages that have largely disappeared from the region is a one-and-a-half-story house with a side-gabled roof, full-width front porch, Georgian plan, and neoclassical ornamentation. Built of local pine and cypress, the house is a vernacular interpretation of the Federal style suited to the local climate. The five-bay structure features two interior chimneys along the ridgeline, three roof dormers, and an engaged full-width porch across the south facade. The house is raised on brick piers to catch breezes and elevate it above dampness, snakes, and insects, and framed with heavy timbers mortised and held in place by pegs. It is clad with beveled wood siding. The ground floor plan, 38 feet in width and 36 feet in depth, has four rooms off a center stair hall on the opening. The second-floor plan follows the first-floor layout with a center hall illuminated by dormers and each of the four rooms is lit by a dormer and a gable-end window. The NPS restoration highlights the neoclassical decorative elements and interior woodwork that dates to the construction of the house and remains largely intact.

Although not a principal Pinckney home, this fine representative of qualities defining Lowcountry Coastal Cottages now serves as the visitor center and the museum and is worth visiting to appreciate Charles Pinckney's public service career, the architectural style, and late-eighteenth- and early-nineteenth-century plantation life. An interpretive trail on the site as well as ranger and volunteer programs add to the visitor experience.

Fort Sumter National Monument

Charleston, Charleston County, South Carolina

→   www.nps.gov/fosu

→   Fort Sumter National Monument includes Fort Sumter and Fort Moultrie. To reach Fort Moultrie on Sullivan's Island from downtown Charleston take US 17 (business) to Mt. Pleasant, turn right on SC 703. At Sullivan's Island turn right on Middle Street and drive 1.5 miles to the fort. Fort Sumter is located in Charleston Harbor and is accessible only by private boat or National Park Service operated tour boats from either downtown in Liberty Square or Patriots Point in Mt. Pleasant.

Appearing as a thin line on the horizon from Charleston's waterfront promenade (the Battery), Fort Sumter National Monument in Charleston Harbor is the site of the eruption of the Civil War, when Confederate artillery opened fire on the Union fortress on

April 12, 1861. On April 13th, Union forces surrendered the fort and evacuated the next day. Confederate forces moved into Fort Sumter and held it until February 1865. Beginning in August 1863, Union forces began bombarding the fort from Morris Island and

Ruins of Fort Sumter's officers' quarters and powder magazine

the shipping channel. The bombardments delivered 3,500 tons of metal and pounded the five-sided bastion into broken brick walls and a pile of debris. A tour boat ride to today's partially reconstructed fort requires a visitor's reversal of time to a century and a half ago when valiant defenders withstood every Union attempt to reclaim the post; screen out modern improvements to recall four years of exchanging cannonades and air and waterborne Union attacks on the then Confederate stronghold.

Fort Sumter, seen today, is a stabilized ruin that still contains elements of its 1861 appearance as one of a chain of U.S. coastal fortifications built after the War of 1812. Construction of a granite base about 5 feet above water level began in 1829. At the outbreak of war in 1861, the fort was about ninety percent complete and by the time of the April 12, 1861 bombardment sixty of its planned 135 cannon had been mounted. The massive 5-foot-thick red brick exterior walls, standing 48 feet above water at low tide, formed a three-tiered symmetrical pentagon enclosing a parade ground. Sides containing casemates were the approximately 190-foot-long left and right faces, the 170-foot-long left and right flanks also containing enlisted men's barracks, and the 317-foot-long gorge with three-story officers' quarters and sally port opening to a wharf.

Union bombardments from Morris Island and ironclad monitor vessels reduced the walls, in the words of Union General Quincy A. Gilmore, to a "shapeless and harmless mass of ruins." The gorge and right flank were bounded into rubble, the left and right faces were seriously damaged, while most of the left flank wall remained at its original height. On the interior the barracks buildings and officers' quarters had been destroyed.

Entering from the wharf, visitors will see the effects of the periodic modernization of the fort for coastal defense, and the National Park Service (NPS) stabilization of the ruins. A climb up the outdoor stairs to the top of the right flank offers views over the harbor; brick-vaulted casemates in the right face and left flank can be explored; and representative cannon inspected. A bewildering site is the massive Battery Huger built across the parade ground during the Spanish-American War, now containing a museum with a splendid model of the Civil War fort.

Fort Moultrie on Sullivan's Island, a unit of Fort Sumter National Monument administered by the NPS, is accessible by car. The first fort built on the site in 1776, replaced by a second fort in 1798, and today's third fort completed in 1809 and continually modified through World War II, finally ended service in 1947. It was this fort that was involved in the start of the Civil War, guarding the main channel to Charleston and standing over one mile east of Fort Sumter. The NPS stabilized and retained surviving elements of the 1809 fort through its World War II service; interpretive signage and visitor center exhibits address the first and second forts.

Fort Sumter 100-pounder Parrott rifles on original carriages (courtesy NPS)

The approach to Fort Moultrie suggests a typical brick-walled fort with projecting sloped bastion corners flanking a new limestone-framed sally port (1875). The earth-filled 15-foot-high brick walls enclose one-and-a-half acres and a parade ground. Arrays of gun emplacements were mounted on earth-filled platforms. The Confederate occupiers converted the fort into a massive earthwork, burying the masonry walls to protect against the deadly, new Union rifled cannons. Entering Fort Moultrie today the visitor is

Fort Moultrie Endicott batteries

confronted with swelling grassy mounds covering underground structures and a panorama of the changing complexities of harbor defense from the War of 1812 through World War II. The third Fort Moultrie's major remains are the northwest bastion to the right of the sally port mounted with period cannon, and containing the yellow brick, gable roof 1809 powder magazine.

The Fort Sumter National Monument Visitor Center is located opposite Fort Moultrie on Sullivan's Island. Ranger- and self-guided tours are available.

Tennessee

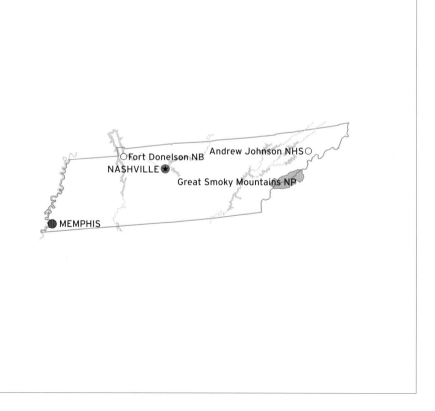

South

Andrew Johnson National Historic Site

Greeneville, Greene County, Tennessee

→ www.nps.gov/anjo

→ The park's three units are located in the eastern part of Tennessee seventy miles northeast of Knoxville in downtown Greeneville. From Interstate 10 take Exit 36 to Route 172 south to Greeneville and from Interstate 81north take US 11east (business) Exit 23 south and follow the signs to the visitor center at the corner of College and Depot Streets.

Andrew Johnson homestead

Andrew Johnson, the seventeenth president of the United States (1865–1869), is a historical figure mainly known for succeeding Abraham Lincoln and in 1868 successfully withstanding impeachment proceedings. His adult life, spent mostly in Greeneville, Tennessee, is an inspiring story captured evocatively in the three units of the Andrew Johnson National Historic Site. Across from each other in downtown Greeneville are the visitor center, housing Johnson's Tailor Shop, and the earlier of two homes where the Johnson family lived from the 1830s until 1851. Two-and-a-half-blocks away is the second unit, the Homestead, which was the Johnson family home from 1851 until the president's death in 1875. Approximately one-half-mile south of the visitor center is the third unit, the national cemetery and gravesite of Andrew and Eliza Johnson.

Carried by his oratorical and keen legislative skills, Johnson overcame his humble beginnings to rise through elected offices that eventually led to the White House. Born in Raleigh, North Carolina on December 29, 1808, he was apprenticed to a tailor as a child and ran off at age fifteen, traveling through the Carolinas and Tennessee and settling in the quiet Scots-Irish town of Greeneville where, in 1826, he established a tailor's shop. Although never attending school a day in his life, Johnson hired readers, and his wife

Eliza improved his basic reading and writing skills. He also attended lectures at Tusculum Academy (now Tusculum College). At age twenty-five, Johnson was elected the town's mayor, then served as representative and senator in the Tennessee state legislature. At age thirty-four he began the first of five terms in the U.S. House of Representatives followed with election to the U.S. Senate, and in 1864 as Lincoln's vice president.

Johnson's tailor shop

The stately Georgian visitor center within a red brick Flemish bond similar to the Homestead is the starting point for ranger- and self-guided park tours. Upon entering the visitor center, visitors are given a replica of the 1868 ticket of admission to Johnson's impeachment trial and can cast a vote for guilt or acquittal. Inside the building is the authentic Tailor Shop of weatherboard siding with a simple wooden slab over the entrance inscribed "A. Johnson Tailor." This modest building was a center for political debates and where Johnson launched his public service career.

Across the street from the visitor center is the Early Home purchased in 1831. Restored meticulously by the National Park Service (NPS), the two-story red brick house has a classical entrance door with sidelights and arched fan above, and is flanked by a pair of tall double-hung windows with shutters. The basement and first level exhibits are open to the public.

The Homestead, built approximately in the year before Johnson's purchase in 1851, is a two-story red brick wall-bearing masonry structure with exterior chimneys at gable ends and Flemish bond and penciled joint exterior walls. The front facade facing the street, flush with narrow brick walk, has a classical doorway with pilasters and entablature and top and side lights, flanked by a pair of shuttered windows with classical scrolls above, and three evenly spaced second floor windows with the same details. A two-story brick ell at the rear appears as three stories above the exposed basement level. The ten-room structure's main block is approximately 40 feet by 20 feet in plan; first and second floors are divided into pairs or rooms by central halls. Each floor of the approximately 30-foot by 20-foot ell contains two rooms, one behind the other separated by a chimney wall, and opening onto verandahs overlooking gardens.

The Johnsons were forced to leave the house during the Civil War, not returning until his presidential term ended in 1869. Occupation by Union and Confederate forces left the house in a shambles, and a collection of graffiti on the walls is exposed for visitor viewing. Repaired and lived in by Johnson until his death in 1875, the house underwent considerable alterations throughout the years, including an extensive remodeling in the Victorian style in 1884–85. A fine restoration by the NPS preserves and interprets the house in its

1869–1875 appearance. Park-guided tours visit ten rooms, furnished with original family furniture and possessions as well as period furniture, and richly decorated with Victorian wallpaper reproductions in the formal rooms, the bedrooms, and the central hall.

Andrew Johnson early home

Though his life is often a footnote to history because of the impeachment proceeding, the significance of Andrew Johnson National Historic Site is the inspiring story of Johnson's humble beginnings and rise in politics in nineteenth-century America when fiery speechmaking established reputations. It is a worthwhile visit only forty miles from Great Smoky Mountains National Park (see page 397)

Fort Donelson National Battlefield

Dover, Stewart County, Tennessee

→ www.nps.gov/fodo

→ The park is located in north central Tennessee, northwest of Nashville. From Nashville, take Interstate 24 west to Clarksville (Exit 4) and continue on US 79 thirty-five miles to the visitor center.

In early 1862, Union forces endured a string of losses on the battlefield to Confederate armies. Seeking a way to pierce the Confederate defensive line stretching westward, Union General Henry W. Halleck chose to strike toward Nashville from a base in Paducah, Kentucky. The natural avenue of attack was along the Cumberland River. Batteries of cannon at the earthwork Fort Donelson, west of the village of Dover, commanded the river with a stronghold that garrisoned fifteen thousand soldiers. On February 14, 1862 a Union force led by Brigadier General Ulysses S. Grant, equal in number to the Confederate forces, moved against the fort, first with a gunboat attack that proved ineffective, and then with a charge against the fort. Escape by the Confederates was blocked and Brigadier General Simon Buckner, seeing the hopelessness of the situation, requested surrender terms. Grant's famous response was "No terms except an unconditional and immediate surrender can be accepted." It was the famous epigram christening the Union general as "Unconditional Surrender" Grant. Buckner answered the same day "the overwhelming force under your command compel me, notwithstanding the brilliant success of the Confederate arms yesterday, to accept the ungenerous and unchivalrous terms which you propose."

Dover House

Confederate capitulation and the capture of Fort Donelson with approximately thirteen thousand soldiers delivered a devastating blow to the Confederacy. The defeat set the stage for the Union's invasion of the Deep South. The victory propelled Grant into national prominence and eventual command of the Union Army.

From the visitor center off US 79, a self-guided tour circulates through the 551.7-acre Fort Donelson National Battlefield. The terrain is relatively untouched since the days of battle. A drive along the park's roads takes the visitor to several battery locations aimed menacingly downriver, and the fifteen-acre earthwork fort with 10-foot-high walls enclosed on the landward side by almost three miles of rifle pits. Inside the fort are several reconstructed log huts used as Confederate soldier winter quarters.

Located in the center of the village of Dover less than two miles from the visitor center is the park's Dover House. Built between 1851 and 1853 at a riverfront location to serve riverboat travelers, the two-story frame structure with wide ground and second floor porches, was Confederate headquarters during the battle, the site where Buckner surrendered to Grant and Buckner, and a Union hospital after the surrender. A footnote to the surrender is that the first Union general to reach Dover House after Buckner's acceptance of the surrender was Lew Wallace, later to become famous as the author of *Ben Hur*. After surviving a wartime fire that devastated the town, the Dover House continued in business as a lodging until the 1930s. Reconstructed through the efforts of the Fort Donelson House Historical Association and the National Park Service (NPS), the exterior's appearance dates to the time of the surrender.

While the battlefield illustrates Grant's tactical prowess in the Union's first important victory, the significance of Dover House is its historical role as a "witness structure" to an important event in the Union's change in battlefield fortunes. Recognized as the "Surrender House," it may not be as impressive or as historically eventful as Grant's final surrender site at Appomattox Court House (see page 402). However, this modest structure is the place where Grant and the Union armies began the inexorable march toward victory ending the nation-wrenching conflict.

Great Smoky Mountains National Park

Located along the Tennessee-North Carolina border, near Gatlinburg, Sevier County, Tennessee, and Cherokee, Jackson County, North Carolina

→   www.nps.gov/grsm

→   The park has three main entrances (Gatlinburg, Tennessee; Townsend, Tennessee; and Cherokee, North Carolina) and connects with Newfound Gap Road (US 441) that bisects the park. The park is fifty miles south of Knoxville, Tennessee, and sixty miles north of Asheville, North Carolina.

Gregg-Cable House and sorghum mill (foreground), Cades Cove

The 520,000 acres of Great Smoky Mountains National Park is a cherished respite for travelers fascinated by the blue haze often seen during summer months softening forested mountains and ridges. The park is the place of blue smoke, called *shaconage* by the Cherokee. The park's many attractions, straddling the Tennessee-North Carolina border at the southern end of the Appalachian Mountains, makes it the most visited of any of the fifty-seven national parks: nine million recreational visits annually, more than double the next most visited national park. Attractions are great; natural beauty is dramatized by a collage of thickly forested valleys and ridges and sixteen mountains over 6,000 feet in elevation. Diversity of plant and animal life—earning designation as a Biosphere Reserve

(1976) and World Heritage Site (1983)—and remnants of Southern Appalachian mountain culture can be seen in several historic districts and surviving settler buildings.

The natural beauty and solitude of the park is regarded as a hiker's paradise with

Caldwell House, Cataloochee Valley

over eight hundred miles of maintained trails, ranging from short, self-guided trails to the Appalachian Trail traversing the length of the park. Trekking across the valleys and ridges in spring is a revelation of botanical delights from early May to fall. Not to be outdone is the spectacular autumn foliage display. After leaving the tawdry tourist gateways at Gatlinburg, Tennessee, and Cherokee, North Carolina, the traveler can find an orientation to historic places and structures at the National Park Service (NPS) visitor centers at Oconaluftee and Sugarlands. The visitor centers, open all year, are located inside the park entrances at ends of Newfound Gap Road (US 441) that bisects the park.

The process of land assembly for the park beginning in the mid-1920s required purchasing sixty-six hundred tracts owned by timber and pulpwood companies, twelve hundred farms, and more than five thousand lots and summer homes; seventy-three hundred people lived in the park. Now, sixty years after the park's establishment, the park is almost whole and wilderness is in the ascendancy. From this patchwork of parcels Great Smoky Mountains National Park retains a sampling of historical structures representing Appalachian country life, including one of the best collections of log buildings in the eastern United States. The cabins, ranging from crude one-room affairs to elegant two-story buildings show hewn log dovetailing details that have withstood the test of time. Nearly one hundred historical structures—houses, barns, outbuildings, churches, schools, and gristmills—have been preserved or rehabilitated in the park. The best places to see them are at Cades Cove, Cataloochee, the Mountain Farm Museum near the Oconaluftee visitor center, and along the Roaring Fork Motor Nature Trail.

Cades Cove is a broad, six-mile long valley at the end of Little River Road, fifty-seven miles from Cherokee, twenty-seven miles from Gatlinburg, and nine miles from Townsend. The bucolic scene in an unspoiled atmosphere preserves the early settler's self-sufficient lifestyle in the Smokies. First settled in 1818, scattered throughout the cove are log homes and outbuildings, a working grist mill, a variety of barns including the unusual cantilever form, and three churches dating back to the late nineteenth and early twentieth centuries. Some of the buildings were brought into the cove from other areas by the NPS. The nearby Cable Mill area includes a visitor center, the working John Cable Mill and adjacent Gregg-Cable House, a cantilever barn, and typical outbuildings. An eleven-mile one-way loop road takes one by many buildings and farm groups, some requiring a short trail hike.

The Cataloochee Valley, at the eastern edge of the park is accessed from Exit 20 on Interstate 40 and long winding gravel roads. The isolated valley, surrounded by 6,000-foot peaks, was the largest and most prosperous settlement in what is now the Great Smoky Mountains National Park. Peaking in 1910 at around twelve hundred people, historical buildings in this picturesque setting, accessible by motor vehicle, include the handsome 1906 Caldwell House, Palmer Chapel, built in 1898, and several other historical structures. In nearby Little Cataloochee Valley, accessed by hiking the Little Cataloochee Trail, are the 1864 Hannah Cabin and the Little Cataloochee Baptist Church, with multi-gabled belfry tower, jigsawn bargeboard, scalloped shingles, and stark white-painted interior, typical of churches built in isolated valleys.

At the southern end of Newfound Gap Road is Oconaluftee, settled around 1800. Adjacent to the visitor center is the Mountain Farm Museum, a unique collection of historic log farm buildings gathered by the NPS from throughout the park and preserved on a single site. Most of the structures were built in the late nineteenth century and were moved here in the 1950s. Buildings include the two-story Davis House, unique in its log construction of chestnut wood, the large drover's barn, an apple house of stone lower walls and log upper walls, a spring house, and a smoke house. A half-mile north of the Oconaluftee Visitor Center is Mingus Mill, located at its original site. Built in 1886, this historic restored two-story gristmill is powered by a metal water turbine rather than a waterwheel.

Palmer Chapel interior, Chataloochee Valley

Other historical structures are seen along the Roaring Fork Motor Nature Trail from a one-way loop near the Sugarlands Visitor Center at the Gatlinburg entrance, including a number of well-preserved log cabins, grist mills, and other historical buildings.

Certainly revered as the travel destination for hikers enjoying the many scenic trails, Great Smoky Mountains National Park offers many opportunities for surprise arrivals at a single building or collection of remnants of rural Appalachia. Living history demonstrations are held year-round at many sites.

Virginia

Wolf Trap Park for
the Performing Arts ○ ○ Arlington House, The Robert E. Lee Memorial
Shenandoah NP   ○ Manassas NBP
Fredericksburg and Spotsylvania ○   ○ George Washington Birthplace NM
County Battlefields Memorial NMP   Richmond NBP
                    RICHMOND ✸ Maggie L. Walker NHS   ATLANTIC
Appomattox Court House NHP○   ○ Colonial NHP   OCEAN
                            ○   ● NORFOLK
Booker T. Washington NMO○   Petersburg NB

South

Appomattox Court House National Historical Park

Appomattox, Appomattox County, Virginia

→ www.nps.gov/apco

→ The site is located ninety-two miles west of Richmond, twenty miles east of Lynchburg, and two miles
northeast of the town of Appomattox on VA 24.

Tavern Guest House (right), Tavern Dining Room (center), and Clover Hill Tavern (left)

The historic surrender by General Robert E. Lee to Lieutenant General Ulysses S. Grant,
effectively ending the Civil War, occurred in the small village of Appomattox Court
House in south-central Virginia on Palm Sunday April 9, 1865. On that crisp, cool spring
day, as memorialized in many paintings and lithographs, the generals met at the house
of Wilmer McLean to sign surrender documents. In his characteristic direct language,
Grant later informed Secretary of War Edwin M. Stanton of the day's events:

> General Lee surrendered the Army of Northern Virginia this afternoon on terms proposed by
> myself. The accompanying additional correspondence will show the conditions fully.

Again, in a sparse description of the historic event, Grant in his *Personal Memoirs*
(Charles L. Webster & Company, 1886) provides a memorable description of the contrasting appearance between victor and the vanquished, sixteen years apart in age:

> General Lee was dressed in a full uniform which was entirely new, and was wearing a sword of
> considerable value, very likely the sword which had been presented by the State of Virginia; at
> all events, it was an entirely different sword from the one that would ordinarily be worn in the
> field. In my rough traveling suit, the uniform of a private with the straps of a lieutenant-gen-
> eral, I must have contrasted very strangely with a man so handsomely dressed, six feet high and
> of faultless form. But this was not a matter that I thought of until afterwards.

The McLean House stood in the small settlement of Appomattox Court House, the county seat of a rural, agricultural area. The town grew around the Clover Hill Tavern, a stopping-off point on the Richmond-Lynchburg Stage Road, and after the county court-house was built in 1846 slowly developed into a village of homes, stores, and lawyer's offices. Two battles were fought here on the evening of April 8th and the morning of April 9th. Three monuments and markers commemorate the actions of the North Carolina troops during the battle of Appomattox Court House on April 9th, 1865. The Confeder-ate Cemetery, where some of the last fatalities are buried, is also on the grounds west of the village.

Today, the visitor can walk along the tranquil country roads and lanes of Appomat-tox Court House, distant in miles and signs of tourism from the more heavily visited bat-tlefield parks at Gettysburg, Richmond, Fredericksburg, or Manassas (Bull Run). The entire village of restored and reconstructed structures, appearing as it did in April 1865, is within the 1,774 acres of Appomattox Court House National Historical Park. Thirteen of the buildings that existed at the time of the surrender remain in the village today, while nine other structures, including the McLean House, have been reconstructed on the original sites.

The park extends outside the historic village center to include other places asso-ciated with the events of April 1865. The acreage surrounding the village straddling both sides of State Highway 24 provides a buffer from any visual encroachments on the park.

The first stop on a visit to the park is the visitor center located in the reconstructed Appomattox Court House. The original structure, built in 1846, was destroyed by fire in 1892 and prompted the county seat's relocation to Appomattox Station, now the pres-ent-day town of Appomattox, a five-minute drive to the southwest. No surrender events took place in the original courthouse. Adjacent to the courthouse is a cluster of build-ings that formed the village's core, and the Appomattox County Jail. The brick three-

McLean House

Appomattox County Jail (left), Bocock-Isbell House (right)

story austere-looking county jail was completed in 1870 and is an original building. The visitor can wander at leisure to the Clover Hill Tavern, completed about 1820 and the oldest building in the village—and where the parole passes for the Confederate soldiers were printed—and the Tavern Kitchen, now serving as a bookstore. The nearby Wood-son Law Office and Plunkett-Meeks Store are both original structures.

The pristine McLean House is a couple of hundred yards west of the visitor center. The three-story brick house, built in 1848, has a wide five-bay porch running across the full length of the front facade. The porch is raised on brick piers that add dignity to the structure, and has wide, central stairs and a latticework porch railing. A running bond brick course is used on all elevations of the gable-ended structure, with chimneys flush in each gable end wall. Within the approximately 30-foot by 22-foot floor plan, a central hall with staircase on the first floor is flanked by the parlor, where the surrender took place, and a master bedroom. Two children's bedrooms are on the second floor and a warming kitchen and dining room on the ground floor. Furnishings in the house are typical of those owned by the McLeans; some are originals and others reproductions of original pieces. The house was reconstructed based on meticulous National Park Service (NPS) research and dedicated in 1950. Behind the house are the reconstructed slave quarters and a log kitchen. In the front yard, surrounded by a white picket fence, is a lattice-covered gazebo enclosing the well.

Leaving the McLean House, the visitor can return eastward at a leisurely pace along the road past the courthouse and visit several of the park's original buildings: the modest-size Jones Law Office stands in a white-picket fence enclosure; the substantial two-story white clapboard Bocock-Isbell house and its outbuildings; the Mariah Wright House built in the mid-1820s; and the two-story clapboard Peers House. Approximately six thousand Union soldiers lined both sides of the Richmond-Lynchburg Road, from a point just east of the Peers House to the McLean House, on the morning of April 12, 1865 to receive the surrender of the Confederate Army of Northern Virginia.

The park extends outside the historic village center to include other places associated with surrender events. A five-mile walking trail connects the sites of Grant's headquarters and Lee's headquarters. Along the trail is the Sweeney Prizery (tobacco leaf packing), near Grant's headquarters and built between 1790 and 1799, cannon symbolizing emplacements during the historic final days of the Confederate Army of Northern Virginia, a Confederate cemetery, and monuments.

Appomattox County Court House

Park rangers lead tours through the village and a self-guided brochure is available at the visitor center. Living history programs with employees in period clothing portraying soldiers and civilians from the 1860s are offered daily during the summer months, and occasionally on weekends in the spring and fall.

Arlington House, The Robert E. Lee Memorial
Arlington, Alexandria County, Virginia

→ www.nps.gov/arho

→ The memorial is located in northern Virginia, within Arlington National Cemetery across the Memorial Bridge from Washington, D.C. Parking is available at the Arlington Cemetery Visitor Center. The visitor may walk to the house from the parking lot or ride the concessioner-operated Tourmobile.

Arlington House portico facing Washington, D.C.

Arlington House, also known as the Custis-Lee Mansion, is magnificently sited with a commanding panorama of Washington and, in turn, impressively viewed from the city. The hilltop site displays the boldly scaled portico seen from across the Potomac River. Celebrated for its historical associations and sublime architecture, it is considered one of the nation's finest examples of the Greek Revival style. The primitive Greek temple facade (suggested by the Temple of Poseidon at Paestum, 460 B.C.) with a prominent hexastyle portico of Doric columns stands in front of two lateral wings in the Federal style. Construction of architect George Hadfield's design took place in three distinct building periods that began in 1802 with the construction of the wings and the two-story central block completed in 1818.

The Arlington House's historical associations are with the families of Washington, Custis, and Lee. The house was built by George Washington Parke Custis, grandson of Martha Washington, as a monument to his adoptive father George Washington, and as the center of a 1,100-acre plantation estate. Custis' daughter, Mary Anna Randolph Custis, married Robert E. Lee, who shared the house while on military assignments, in 1831 and the Arlington estate was home to the Lees for thirty years. Mary inherited the house when George Washington Park Custis died in 1857. Robert E. Lee left Arlington at the outbreak of the Civil War to accept command of the Confederate Army of Northern Virginia and the Lees never returned.

Occupancy by Union troops and confiscation of the property in 1864 included the setting aside of a military cemetery, the beginning of today's Arlington National Cemetery. In 1882 a family lawsuit to recover the property ended successfully but by then the hundreds of graves covered the hills of Arlington, and the property was sold to the federal government. Restoration of the house began in 1925 and continued under National Park Service supervision from 1933 to the present time.

Family Dining Room (courtesy NPS)

Typical of plantation house building at the time, construction began with the wings to provide modest living quarters. One-story high, over a basement, the approximately 50-foot by 40-foot hipped roof wings with Palladian windows in arched recesses stood approximately 56 feet apart, and were completed in 1804. Completion of the temple-like two-story central block towering over the wings followed fourteen years later, its imposing columns and pedimented gable facing the capital city. The building is of brick masonry bearing construction and exterior surfaces are stuccoed and marbleized with paint over a buff-colored surface, including the hollow brick columns.

Today's visitors enter the house through the ground floor portico and into the approximately 10-foot-wide center hall running from front to back through the house. The ceilings are a gracious 14 feet high. To the left is the White Parlor, left unfinished for thirty-seven years, and beyond are the Morning Room, the Conservatory, and Office and Studio. To the right of the central hall are the Family Parlor, Family Dining Room, guest chambers, and the School and Sewing Room. Formal and service stairs at the rear of the central hall lead to the second floor with four bedrooms, two on either side of the central hall, along with several smaller rooms. Interiors are in restoration to the antebellum Custis-Lee Period. Original family furnishings are mixed with period reproductions.

West of the main house, accessible from the west circular drive is the summer kitchen and a pair of slaves' quarters. The approximately 40-foot by 21-foot in plan buildings are one-story gable-ended, brick masonry over a fieldstone exterior basement. The floors are divided into three bays. Exteriors are covered with stucco in a pebble finish and Doric columns recessed in arches are on the elevations facing the main house.

To the north of the main house is a potting shed built by the U.S. Army Corps of Engineers in 1880 to supply the cemetery grounds. Rectangular in plan (approximately

32 feet by 22 feet), the two-story hipped-roof building was constructed of brick masonry with a crenellated soffit below the roofline.

Arlington House is set in the quiet repose of Arlington National Cemetery, with its revered memorials and gravesites. The house's superb architecture and historical associations qualify it as an accomplished structure, well worth a visit.

Booker T. Washington National Monument

Hardy, Franklin County, Virginia

→ www.nps.gov/bowa

→ The park is in southwestern Virginia, sixteen miles northeast of Rocky Mount, Virginia via VA 40E and VA 122N; twenty-five miles southeast of Roanoke, Virginia, via US 220S, VA 40E, and VA 122N; and fifty miles southwest of Lynchburg, Virginia, via US 460W and VA 122S.

Reconstructed Burroughs farm buildings

This park is the place where the famous African-American educator, orator, and presidential adviser, Booker T. Washington, was born into slavery, reared, and emancipated. A small 207-acre plantation formerly owned by James Burroughs presents a microcosm of the antebellum life of middle-class farmers and enslaved people. Located in the rolling landscape of the Virginia Piedmont, about half of the Burroughs farm was cultivated; the rest was a self-sufficient farm with a cash crop of tobacco (earning the title of "plantation") to support the owner and his slaves. Today, the visitor will find a preserved landscape of original regional agricultural life in the rapidly developing corridor along Virginia Highway 122 (Booker T. Washington Highway), prompted by development on one of Virginia's largest lakes, the man-made Smith Mountain Lake.

It was on this farm, as restored by the National Park Service (NPS), that Booker T. Washington began his journey to seek an education and ascend to heights from a place he once described as "about as near to nowhere as any locality gets to be." Born to a slave mother and neighboring white farmer on April 5, 1856, Washington lived in a small one-room cabin with his mother and two half siblings. His search for an education led him to Hampton Institute where he excelled. At age twenty-five he was appointed to develop a new school in Alabama—the Tuskegee Normal and Industrial Institute (which later became Tuskegee University). Recognition as the nation's foremost black educator, and controversial in some of his views, during his lifetime he was arguably the single most influential American in the areas of race relations and black education. Washington died at age fifty-nine in 1915. He is best remembered for his personal achievement of over-coming near-impossible barriers and providing a strong beacon to help black Americans overcome economic slavery long after emancipation as free citizens.

The former Burroughs farm, expanded to 239 acres, is the center of the Booker T. Washington National Monument. From the visitor center, a one-quarter-mile Planta-tion Trail loops through the historical section restored by the NPS to its general mid-nineteenth century appearance. Most buildings are reconstructions, and design and location are replicas based on anecdotal evidence and local reminisces, including those of Booker T. Washington when he visited the site in 1908.

The replica of the simple, one-story 12-foot by 16-foot hewn log birthplace and kitchen cabin where Washington was born contains an interior re-creation according to the description in his autobiography, *Up from Slavery*. The dirt floor, log walls, and rough furnishings all illustrate the difficult early years of the future educator. Other replica buildings include the adjacent smokehouse, the horse barn, blacksmith shed, chicken lot, and the original 1890s tobacco barn. Based on a 1998 archeological excava-tion, the main plantation house foundation has been outlined in stone. The original house burned down in 1950. A zigzag, split-rail fence indicates the farm area improved for crops and animal grazing.

In addition to the quarter-mile Plantation Trail, the Jack-O-Lantern Trail is a one-and-a-half-mile walk winding through fields and woodlands of the original Burroughs property. A picnic area is available. Exhibits, film, guided tours, and special events are available at the visitor center. A casual and unhurried visit is recommended to absorb an experience similar to the George Washington Carver National Monument (see page 200) in rural southwest Missouri. Both of these National Park System parks are ideal for meditative visits to understand the less-than-grand farm life outside the glamorous plantations experienced by American blacks prior to emancipation.

Colonial National Historical Park

Located near Williamsburg in southeastern Virginia, the Jamestown unit is in James City County and the Yorktown unit in York County, Virginia. A third unit is Cape Henry Memorial in Virginia Beach, Virginia

→ www.nps.gov/colo

→ Access to the park is by Interstate 64 Exit 242B (southbound) and Exit 250B (northbound); follow signs to Colonial Parkway and units in Jamestown, Yorktown, and Lynchburg, Virginia, via US 460W and VA 122S.

Restored Yorktown Main Street house

The twenty-three-mile drive along Colonial National Historical Park's Colonial Parkway in southeastern Virginia links two historic sites that were the beginning and end of British colonial America. The park includes a unit at Jamestown, site of the first permanent English settlement in America; a unit at Yorktown, site of the last major battle of the American Revolution; the scenic Colonial Parkway that connects the two; and Cape Henry Memorial at the Fort Story military reservation in Virginia Beach, the site where settlers first came ashore in North America. The "Historic Triangle" of colonial sites includes the restored Colonial Williamsburg, not part of the National Park System. At the entrance to Jamestown Island and adjacent to the National Park Service (NPS) Jamestown unit is the Commonwealth of Virginia-administered Jamestown Settlement, a living history site with replicas of the three ships (*Susan Constant, Godspeed, and Discovery*) that arrived from England in 1607, and recreations of the colonists' fort and a Powhatan village. The Yorktown Victory Center, administered by the Commonwealth of Virginia, is off the parkway on the approach to Yorktown and features a museum dedicated to the American Revolution and a recreated Continental army encampment.

Jamestown Island, the landing place of 104 men and boys on May 13, 1607, is where the Virginia Company of London established the Colony of Virginia. The story of the original town site, woven into the American mythology by the legend of John Smith and Pocahontas, was renewed in the nation's consciousness by celebration of the four hundredth anniversary. The colony established on the neck of land on the James River is now seen as reconstructed brick outlines of original building foundations; the only remaining above ground seventeenth-century structure is the Old Church Tower, believed to be built around 1680. Statues and monuments commemorating people and events can be seen on a walking tour of the site. A heroic statue of John Smith facing the river with Pocahontas bracket the church. Near the entrance to the Jamestown unit is the reconstructed Glasshouse, where costumed craftsmen demonstrate seventeenth-century glassmaking, one of America's first industries. The NPS and the APVA Preservation Virginia jointly manage Jamestown. The site now features a new Visitor Center, wayside exhibits, and the Archaearium, a museum that focuses on the archeology of James Fort.

The importance of the Battle of Yorktown and the British surrender to American forces on October 19, 1781, is succinct: it was the last major battle of the American revolution, virtually assuring American independence, and significantly changing the course of world history. The engagement's strategy and tactics placed British General Charles, Lord Cornwallis moving his army into Virginia from North Carolina attempting to subdue Virginia and leverage a victory to return the southern states to British allegiance. Cornwallis was ordered to establish a base for operation, and unwisely chose Yorktown

on the York River where it empties into Chesapeake Bay. The alliance with France that provided much needed supplies and troops under the command of Rochambeau enabled George Washington and the Continental army to launch a daring plan to secure a major vicotry. With the cooperation of French naval forces delivering siege guns to Washington's army and blockading a sea escape by the British, the allied forces began the siege on September 28. After weeks of continuous bombardment with no chance of escape, Cornwallis agreed to surrender.

Today, the active community of Yorktown, smaller than it was during colonial times and a must visit for history buffs, functions within the NPS Yorktown unit that encompasses the battlefield extending outwards in all directions approximately two miles from

Yorktown Victory Monument

the center of town. Walking the streets of this small village and touring the battle site is the best way to understand the importance of Yorktown. Several historic houses and other structures from the colonial period retain the early character of the town. Dominating the landscape is the imposing 98-foot-high Yorktown Victory Monument, built in 1881, and standing near the east end of Main Street. Some of the original and restored houses are closed to visitors: the Dudley Digges House (1760), the Sessions House (1693), the Smith House (1750), and the Ballard House (1720). Open to the public are: the Somerwell House (restored), Pate House (early 1700s), Poor Potter archeological ruins (1720), the Swan Tavern (reconstructed), Medical Shop (reconstructed), Customhouse (1721), and the Thomas Nelson House (1730).

Pocahontas statue, Old Church Tower, and Memorial Church

The Nelson House, at the southwest corner of Main and Nelson Streets is considered one of the finest examples of early Georgian architecture in Virginia. Thomas Nelson, Jr., was an ardent patriot who signed the Declaration of Independence and commanded the Virginia militia at the siege of Yorktown. The restored two-story brick house in Flemish bond is richly detailed with stone corner quoins, bold keystones over the windows in the five-bay facade, a heavily dentiled cornice, pedimented gable, and five hipped dormers. The interior contains several fine paneled rooms, including the outstanding dining room. The house was shelled during the Yorktown siege (a lodged cannon ball is visible in an upper wall) and again during the Civil War, but escaped serious damage.

A self-guided auto tour of the battlefield and allied encampments, begins at the visitor center and leads to various points of interest, including Surrender Field and the Moore House British Siegeworks behind the visitor center. Park rangers conduct tours of the siege lines and town. Reconstructed earthwork redoubts, siege lines, and battery emplacements are viewed from the exhibit panels, an audio program, and the Surrender Field overlook, an intriguing cylindrical open-air structure with an elevated platform, and a collection of artillery pieces captured at Yorktown.

The Augustine Moore House, also known as Surrender House, is where officers from both sides met to negotiate terms of Cornwallis's surrender. The wood-framed house, severely damaged in the 1862 Civil War Peninsula Campaign, was completely restored from 1931 to 1934, one of the first of its kind by the NPS. The gambrel roofed, one-and-a half-story clapboard sided structure (approximately 46 feet by 32 feet in plan) with tall brick chimneys at each end, surrounded by grounds and outbuildings restored to the time of plantation days, contains the surrender room with period furnishings.

Visitors to these sites can enjoy the drive on the gracefully designed Colonial Parkway, which is listed on the National Register of Historic Places, through typical Tidewater countryside. Annual celebrations are held at both sites with period-clothed reenactors. A Historic Triangle shuttle from Williamsburg provides summer service between Jamestown and Yorktown.

Fredericksburg and Spotsylvania County Battlefields Memorial National Military Park
Located in eastern Virginia, in the Fredericksburg area

→   www.nps.gov/frsp

→   Fredericksburg is fifty miles south of Washington, D.C., and fifty miles north of Richmond, Virginia, and three miles east of Interstate 95. Fredericksburg Battlefield Visitor Center is located at 1013 Lafayette Boulevard (US 1 Business). Chancellorsville Battlefield Visitor Center is approximately seven miles west of Interstate 95, located on the north side of Route 3. Heed a caution that traffic can be extremely congested in the area.

Ellwood Manor, Wilderness Battlefield

Here, between 1862 and 1864, within a radius of seventeen miles, over 100,000 men became casualties in four major Civil War battles scattered over the city of Fredericksburg, Virginia, and four counties. Robert E. Lee and the Confederate Army of Northern Virginia defeated the Union Army of the Potomac in the battles of Fredericksburg (December 11–13, 1862) and Chancellorsville (May 1–4, 1863). In the Battle of the Wilderness (May 5–6, 1864) and at Spotsylvania Court House (May 8–21, 1864) the armies fought to a bloody draw. The 1864 battles were confrontations between Lee and Ulysses S. Grant that changed the course of the war as the armies began the road to Lee's surrender at Appomattox Court House (see page 402).

Recorded by contemporary photographers and artists, and in first person accounts, the vivid scenes of unprecedented carnage present a grim arithmetic. One observer described the action "a cataclysm like pieces of meat pushed into a grinder." Casualties were horrific: at Fredericksburg 18,000; Chancellorville's totaled 30,000; the Wilderness cost 25,000 killed or wounded; and the toll at Spotsylvania was 32,000. Included in the 8,374-acre park is Fredericksburg National Cemetery.

A visit to this multi-unit battlefields park can take two full days, although a concentration on one may take up to a full day. It is best to start a visit at a park visitor center, either on the Fredericksburg Battlefield or on the Chancellorsville Battlefield, for an orientation and maps to prepare the visitor for navigating through the city of Fredericksburg and suburban residential areas to selected destinations. In addition to the battlefield, there are also four historical buildings that are open—Chatham Manor, Salem Church, Ellwood Manor, and Stonewall Jackson Shrine. Of these, only Chatham Manor is open daily. The others are open less often depending on the season of the year and day of the week.

Chatham Manor is located on Stafford Heights at 120 Chatham Lane across the Rappahannock River from Fredericksburg. The well-proportioned Georgian mansion dates from 1768 to 1771, built by William Fitzhugh as the center of a large, thriving plantation. The seven-bay two-story central block, with raised first floor and lunette entrance, and flanked by hyphens and dependencies has an imposing total 185-foot-long facade. A large central hall runs from front to back through the house and several rooms have fine detailing. During the Battle of Fredericksburg the house served as headquarters, field hospital, and artillery and communications center. Five of the ten rooms contain exhibits and the rest of the building, as well as the outbuildings, serve as park offices.

Old Salem Church, located approximately three miles west of Fredericksburg on Virginia Highway 3 was built by the Spotsylvania County Baptists in 1844. The simple brick building, approximately 42 feet by 38 feet in plan, has a large open sanctuary with two facing balconies. The pulpit under a single window in the rear wall is the only decorative element in the austere interior. Openings in the entrance facade are a pair of doorways; gable ends are broken pediments with a clapboard infill. Rows of three lower and upper side wall windows admit light to the sanctuary floor and balcony. Today, the church, now in a heavily trafficked area of shopping centers, was the scene of a swirling engagement during the Battle of Chancellorsville. Confederate sharpshooters were posted in the upper gallery of the church on the north side. Federal soldiers aimed at the upper windows where the sharpshooters were; the pockmarks from their bullets are still visible. Other bullets ripped through the galleries. The church was used as a field hospital by both sides and was also a civilian refugee center during the Battle of Fredericksburg.

Ellwood Manor (Lacy House) was part of an agricultural operation perched on a knoll overlooking Wilderness Run, fifteen miles east of Fredericksburg. The center of the original 642-acre estate, purchased in 1788, at one time was over 5,000 acres. Around the house are spread a group of outbuildings: stables, barns, slave cabins, and a kitchen. The five-bay clapboard house on a brick foundation has austere Georgian lines more representative of a prosperous farmhouse than a plantation house. During the battle of the Wilderness, Ellwood and its surrounding fields teemed with Union artillery and soldiers as they prepared for, or recovered from, intense fighting a mile to the west. The house served as a hospital by the Confederates during the fighting at Chancellorsville and by the Union during the Wilderness Campaign. General "Stonewall" Jackson's arm is buried in the family cemetery. Today, a visit to Ellwood in its rural setting is a relief from the heavy traffic and suburban development around other areas of the battlefield parks.

The final historic structure on a tour of the park units is the Stonewall Jackson Shrine where Confederate General Thomas "Stonewall" Jackson died on May 10, 1863. After being mistakenly wounded by one of his own men at Chancellorsville on May 2, Jackson was transported to Fairfield Plantation at Guinea Station to await the repair of the railroad that would send him to a hospital in Richmond. Jackson contracted pneumonia and, with his wife and baby daughter in attendance, he died. The shrine is a woodframed structure that served as an outbuilding on Fairfield Plantation. The structure was restored in the 1920s and 1960s. The National Park Service has augmented some of the items used during Jackson's stay with other pieces from the era, along with a few reproductions, to recreate the scene of those tragic last days of his life. The room he died in contains the original bed frame, blanket, and clock.

George Washington Birthplace National Monument

Near Colonial Beach on the Potomac River, Westmoreland County, Virginia

→   www.nps.gov/gewa

→   The park is located on the northern neck of Virginia, thirty-eight miles east of Fredericksburg, Virginia. From Fredericksburg take Virginia Routes 3 and 204 and follow signs to the park.

Reconstructed George Washington birthplace

George Washington Birthplace National Monument commemorates the birth of George Washington on a recreated eighteenth-century Tidewater tobacco farm on Popes Creek, where George Washington was born on February 22, 1732. The site is one of three plantations where Washington spent his formative years, moving at age three-and-a-half to Little Hunting Creek Plantation, better known today as Mount Vernon, and three years later to the Ferry Farm in Fredericksburg, known at the time as Washington Farm, all within three days' ride of each other. During his adolescence he returned for long periods of time to Popes Creek, inherited by his half brother, Augustine, Jr., and Little Hunting Creek, where he learned the culture of the Virginia aristocracy and gained an understanding of the ideals of honor, dignity, and especially public service that guided him through his lifetime.

Today's visitor can experience a working eighteenth-century living farm in a sublime pastoral setting on the Potomac River with a Colonial Revival-era Memorial House, plantation outbuildings, demonstration plots of tobacco and flax, gardens, livestock, and a scenic natural landscape from open farmland to upland forests to beaches. Freeman Tilden wrote of visiting the scene of Washington's birthplace on Pope's Creek in tidewater Virginia, "The house he enters is not the house where George Washington was born, but the spirit of our great whole man is there; and in these lovely and provoking surroundings, the staunch character of our hero comes to the imagination."

The Memorial House constructed in 1930–31 by the Wakefield National Memorial Association to commemorate the bicentennial of Washington's birth borrows from the design of Gunston Hall (home of George Mason) and Twiford (childhood home of Josephine Wheelwright-Rust, founder and first president of the Wakefield National Memorial Association). There are no known plans, drawings or written descriptions of the original birthplace, believed to be a timber-frame, U-shaped brick house that burned on Christmas Day in 1779. The original birth home of 1732 was never rebuilt.

Designed by architect Edward W. Donn, Jr., a consummate colonial revivalist, the Memorial House represents a middling (middle-class) Virginia plantation house of the period. The Georgian style one-and-a-half-story, seven-bay brick structure with large exterior chimneys and dormers has a central hallway and four rooms on each floor. Rooms are furnished and decorated in the period 1730–1750. A tea table is believed to be from the original house and most furnishings are more than two hundred years old.

The Memorial Shaft at the park entrance is a one-tenth replica of the Washington Monument in the nation's capital. The walkway from the visitor center takes the visitors past gardens and fields to the recreated Memorial House. The house stands about 80 feet from the birthplace house. Extensive excavations located the foundations of the original house, now marked by an oyster shell outline. A colonial style kitchen on the site is furnished in the 1730–1750 period style with cooking utensils and equipment. Other furnished outbuildings include the Weaving Room, Farm Workshop, and Barn. A mile from the entrance is the Burial Ground surrounded by a modern brick wall. Generations of Washingtons are buried here, including George Washington's father, grandfather, and great-grandfather, marked by tombs, headstones, and memorial tablets.

Ranger-led tours are offered daily and period-clothed interpreters demonstrate colonial farm activities during special events.

Maggie L. Walker National Historic Site

Richmond City, Virginia

→   www.nps.gov/mawa

→   The site is located in downtown Richmond, Virginia. Access is from Interstate 95 at Exit 75A or 75B.
Follow signs to the visitor center at 600 North Second. Street parking is available.

Distinguished as a civic leader and gaining national prominence, Maggie Lena Walker moved into the townhouse at 110 1/2 East Leigh Street on Quality Row in the Jackson Ward Historic District in 1904. She lived here with her extended family in this prosperous black enclave until her death in 1934. The Walker family owned the home until 1979, when it and all the contents were purchased by the National Park Service (NPS).

Born in 1860s into poverty, Maggie Walker achieved a position of leadership for the rights of black Americans and women, notably for her belief in economic empowerment. She shared the dedication and genius for good works of the other African-Americans who overcame personal hardship and tragedy and are now represented by NPS units: George Washington Carver (see page 200), Booker T. Washington (see page 407), Frederick Douglass (see page 437), Mary McLeod Bethune (see page 441), and Martin Luther King, Jr. (see page 351).

At age fourteen Walker joined the local Independent Order of St. Luke, a benevolent society aiding African-Americans in sickness and providing a proper burial at death. After Normal School graduation and a brief teaching career she focused her energies on strengthening the society and in 1899 rose to the position of right worthy secretary-treasurer. Under her management and genius for public relations a financially sound and profitable organization prospered with a newspaper, department store, and bank. In an address to the 34th Annual Session of the Right Worthy Grand Council of Virginia, she urged, "Let us put our money out as usury among ourselves and reap the benefit ourselves. Let us have a bank that will take the nickels and turn them into dollars." Two years later the St. Luke Penny Savings Bank opened with Walker as president, the first American woman to found and be president of a chartered bank. Today the bank is known as the Consolidated Bank and Trust Company, and is the oldest continually operated African-American bank in the United States.

William Boyd, a local African-American builder, built the two-story red brick Victorian house with Italianate detailing in the 1880s. The Walkers purchased the house in 1904 and soon began making changes, introducing electricity and central heating. Over the years, the nine-room house grew to a complex of twenty-eight rooms, including the two-story front porch, twelve rooms, and an elevator in the rear of the house to provide Mrs. Walker access to the second floor. As spaces were added for Mrs. Walker and four generations of her family, the complex eventually covered almost all the 30-foot by 139-foot lot.

A visit to the Maggie L. Walker House invites a walk along East Leigh Street to view the elegant restored houses on Quality Row. The Jackson Ward National Historic Landmark District containing turn-of-the-twentieth-century Greek Revival and Italianate houses, now being revitalized, was at the center of a prosperous black community. A tour of the house, now owned by the NPS, begins at 600 North Second Street, just around the corner from her residence and then proceeds through the house restored to its 1930s appearance using original Walker family furnishings. Italianate style residences at 116 and 118 East Leigh Street, also owned by the NPS, have been restored and contain exhibits on Mrs. Walker's life and the Jackson Ward community and are open to the public.

Manassas National Battlefield Park

Manassas, Prince William and Fairfax Counties, Virginia

→   www.nps.gov/mana

→   The park is twenty-six miles west of Washington. Henry Hill Visitor Center is one mile north of Interstate 66 via Exit 47B, Route 234 north (Sudley Road). Proceed through the first traffic light. The entrance to the Henry Hill Visitor Center is on the right.

Henry House (during reconstruction)

Union and Confederate armies met twice in the open fields and rolling hills of northern Virginia just outside the railroad junction known as Manassas Junction and along the banks of a creek called Bull Run. Known in the North as First and Second Bull Run while the South called it First and Second Manassas, the battlefield park is designated as Manassas in recognition of the Confederate victories here. A third "battle" of national historical preservation importance occurred here and continues with the ongoing struggle to retain the integrity of the park against encroaching urban development. Expanded from the original park of approximately 1,600 acres formed in 1940, the park's 5,073 acres includes major features of the battlefield and several historic buildings.

On July 21, 1861, troops met here in the first major battle of the Civil War. Festive crowds ventured from Washington to watch the conflict and retreated in panic as the Confederates routed the Union army. Both sides suffered a loss of innocence and experienced casualties that were modest compared to later Civil War battles: nearly 2,000 Confederate and more than 3,000 Union soldiers were killed, wounded, and missing. Thirteen months later, on August 28th, 29th, and 30th of 1862, a second and much larger battle took place between the more experienced armies. Again it was a victory for the South with the Union army retreating from the field. Both sides suffered heavy losses, five times greater than for First Manassas: 29,474 Confederate soldiers were killed, wounded, captured, or missing; Union losses were 14,462.

Stone House

The distractions of encroaching suburban development and sometime heavy local traffic is erased by beginning a visit to the battlefields and original "witness" historic structures at the Henry Hill Visitor Center. The building with museum exhibits is strategically located in the historical area overlooking the settings of critical fighting in First Manassas. A one-mile-long Henry Hill foot trail loops around key points of the battlefield and includes the Henry House; the grave of Mrs. Judith Henry, an eighty-four-year-old invalid who was the battle's only civilian fatality; an equestrian statue of General Thomas J. "Stonewall" Jackson; and Union artillery positions seized by the Confederates.

The Henry Hill Visitor Center is a National Park Service (NPS) designed structure built in 1942, with later additions. The massive two-story central block of the original structure in native brownstone rather than brick has a massive and primitive Doric columned portico reminiscent of Arlington House (see page 405), the Robert E. Lee home in Arlington National Cemetery. One-story wings extending to each side amend the antebellum period design.

About 650 feet northwest of the visitor center stands the Henry House that was erected shortly after the war on the site of the famous original structure. Fighting seesawed around the hill in both battles. During the first battle, the original little house was caught in the line of cross artillery fire and badly damaged. By March 1862 the house was a complete ruin. Rebuilt in 1870 and later restored by the NPS, the two-story wood-frame vernacular dwelling (approximately 40 feet by 16 feet in plan) is built partially overlapping the original house site.

A twelve-mile-long driving tour covers sites prominent in the Second Battle of Manassas. On the corner of US 29 (Lee Highway) and Virginia Route 234 (Sudley Road) intersecting in the middle of the battlefield stands the Stone House; the best-preserved and most conspicuous landmark on the battlefields was restored by the NPS in the 1960s. The house was built in 1848 and was used as an ordinary, or tavern, into the 1850s. A solidly constructed two-and-a-half-story structure (approximately 40 feet by 24 feet in plan) of one-and-a-half-foot-thick reddish brown native stone walls with a gabled roof, the house has chimneys at each end and deeply recessed window openings on the north and south elevations. In both Manassas battles, it served as a Union military field hospital. During the fighting on August 30, 1862 Union General Pope made his headquarters directly behind this house. Artillery shells embedded in the stone walls by a post-war owner are still visible today.

At the intersection of the Groveton-Sudley Road (Route 622) and Lee Highway, is located the Dogan House, one of the main landmarks of the second battle and one of the three remaining original structures in the park. It was in the center of the battle, with assaults moving back and forth on August 29, 1862 and was the house remaining in the line of heavy artillery and infantry fire the next day. The small, one-story house of weatherboarded logs originally served as the overseer's house on the Dogan farm. The Dogan family occupied it after their main house was burned in 1860.

The third "battle" of Manassas has great significance for historical preservation in the nation, especially for sites engulfed by urban sprawl. The construction booms that northern Virginia and the town of Manassas experienced beginning in the late 1940s demonstrated that historically significant lands excluded from the initial park boundaries were threatened. Subsequent Manassas National Battlefield Park land acquisitions prevented mushrooming development from overwhelming the park's integrity. A citizen coalition marshaled against proposed shopping centers and theme parks precipitated national headlines and congressional actions that focused attention on the development of lands adjacent to national parks. One episode required purchase of 550 acres of adjacent Manassas land at a cost of $134 million (1988). As Manassas and other vulnerable sites are threatened by the next development proposal, the NPS and preservation advocates stand between protecting lands of the national heritage while also respecting the political and economic choices of local communities.

Petersburg National Battlefield

Battlefield units are located in and around Petersburg, Prince George, and Dinwiddie Counties, Virginia

→ www.nps.gov/pete

→ The park's units are the Eastern Front Visitor Center and battlefield located 2.5 miles northeast of downtown Petersburg, Virginia, via Interstate 95 and State Route 36; the western front which includes the siege lines around the south side of the city; Five Forks twenty-five miles southwest of the city via Interstate 95 and State Route 627; and Grant's headquarters at City Point in Hopewell, Virginia, eight miles northeast of the city via State Route 36. Petersburg is twenty-five miles south of Richmond, Virginia.

Appomattox Manor, Epps family home at City Point

The battle at Petersburg was an important link in the Civil War chain of events that led to General Robert E. Lee's surrender at Appomattox. A series of Northern maneuvers in 1864, at the Wilderness, Spotslyvania, North Anna, and Cold Harbor, was drawing the noose tighter on the Confederate Army of Northern Virginia. Grant, intent on destroying Lee's army, moved his much

larger, stronger, and better supplied Union Army of the Potomac relentlessly south toward the strategic railroad center of Petersburg supplying the Confederate capital at
Richmond twenty-five miles to the north. Union control of Petersburg would force Lee
to leave both cities.

Grant Cabin at City Point

Despite an overwhelming force of 120,000 men (Lee had about 60,000 men at the
siege's beginning), the Union Army of the Potomac stalled in attempts to take Petersburg.
Between June 15, 1864 and April 2, 1865, a ten-month siege grinded away at the Confederates, the Union army encircling Petersburg and cutting Lee's supply lines from the
south. At one point, Lee's line stretched out thirty-seven miles. A precursor of World War
I trench warfare developed here, with continuous Union Army of the Potomac pressure
by shelling, small arms fire, and small skirmishes during the rainy, cold, and miserable
winter. Seeing his position becoming untenable, Lee gambled on a breakout, March
25, 1865 at Fort Stedman, and after an initial victory was defeated by a Union counterat-
tack. On April 2, 1865, after a victory the evening before at Five Forks, a tide of 60,000
Union soldiers swept over Confederate lines, diminished to 46,000 men by casualties
and defections. Lee's last major offensive of the Civil War was over. The Confederate
Army of Northern Virginia withdrew west to Appomattox Court House and, within a
week, surrendered.

The Eastern Front unit of the park is seen on a four-mile Battlefield Tour east of the
city. Although the daring attempt to pierce Confederate lines by tunneling at the Crater
is partially grown over and filled in somewhat, evidence of the work of Pennsylvania coal
miners is still visible. The sixteen-mile Western Front Tour contains park areas south
and west of Petersburg. Traces of entrenchments can be seen in the midst of modern

developments. Grant's Headquarters at City Point unit in Hopewell village contains the historic Appomattox Plantation (Eppes House) and Grant's Headquarters Cabin.

The full strength of the Union Army of the Potomac was displayed at City Point, the confluence of the James and Appomattox Rivers northeast of Petersburg. It is difficult to believe that this now peaceful, residential neighborhood of Hopewell in the once sleepy village of City Point, with less than one hundred inhabitants mushroomed to a vast supply center for the Union army. Grant's headquarters were here and, by April of 1865, 280 buildings of all descriptions covered the site, a mile of wharves lined the shore, and eighteen trains a day ran from the depot to the front lines. The encampment covered almost all the land of the 531-acre Appomattox Plantation owned by Dr. Richard Eppes. Grant set up his headquarters on the front lawn of the main dwelling. A lone cabin remaining on the site is Grant's headquarters, built in November 1864. Reclaimed by the Eppes family after the war, the site was cleared of soldier's huts and sheds and the building and grounds were restored.

The sprawling wood-frame house of the Eppes family, a typical Tidewater plantation, is the result of several enlargements made to the original 1763 dwelling. A central hallway was flanked by rooms on either side of the original seven bay fronted, one-and-a-half-story house. The house was expanded in 1840, 1850, and 1913 to today's U-shaped plan, with pedimented projecting dormers, projecting pavilions and porches on the south and east sides. An eighteenth-century kitchen and other dependencies were constructed in the nineteenth century. The National Park Service (NPS) restored house with period furnishings is open for ranger-guided tours.

The only visible reminder of the Union army's occupation of City Point is the cabin occupied by Grant. For several months during the Petersburg campaign Grant directed army affairs across the country from here. The T-shaped cabin built of vertically placed logs had two rooms separated by two sliding wooden doors, an office (14 feet square) that faced the James River and a sleeping area (25 feet by 9 feet). Disassembled and reconstructed in Philadelphia's Fairmount Park in 1865, the cabin was returned to its original site and reassembled by the NPS in 1983. The cabin is furnished with reproductions of items known to have been in the cabin between 1864 and 1865, from painted window shades to irons made from rifle barrels, and boxes of cigars.

The park's units scattered around Petersburg can be absorbed by starting with a visit to the Eastern Front Visitor Center and taking the four-mile drive, followed by the Western Front Tour. There is a large supply of information on the battle illustrated with contemporary photographs, sketches, and journals for the visitor to gain an understanding of this key Civil War campaign. During summer months regularly scheduled walking and driving tours are conducted, including those held in downtown Petersburg at the park's new Home Front unit. Refer to the park's website for times and locations.

Richmond National Battlefield Park

The park includes thirteen separate sites with three visitor centers along an eighty-mile tour. A fourth visitor center, the Chimborazo Medical Museum on the city's east side, is also operated by the National Park Service. Battlefield sites and visitor centers are located in Richmond City, and Henrico, Hanover, and Chesterfield Counties.

→ www.nps.gov/rich

→ The Tredegar Civil War Visitor Center at 490 Tredegar Street is in downtown Richmond on the James River. Access is via Interstate 95/64 at Exit 75 (Southbound) or Exit 74C (Northbound). Follow signs to the visitor center.

Civil War Visitor Center at Tredegar Iron Works

Richmond was the industrial and political capital of the Confederacy. Its capture represented a strategic and psychological objective of the Union armies in the eastern part of the country. Seizing the city with its factories and arsenals would cripple the South's war machine and be a shattering blow to Confederate morale. Union forces mounted seven major campaigns to take Richmond between 1862 and 1864. Two of those campaigns—the Peninsula Campaign (Seven Days' Battles) in June and July of 1862 and Grant's Campaign (Battle of Cold Harbor in May and June of 1864)—resulted in battles that were visible from the city.

Richmond defied seizure despite horrendous Confederate casualties in suicidal charges in both campaigns. At the Malvern Hill battle on July 1, 1862, at the last of seven days of confrontation, rebel soldiers marched uphill against dozens of Union cannons on the crest of the hill; the ensuing slaughter cost five thousand men in casualties. "It was not war," said Confederate General Ambrose P. Hill, "it was murder." But the Confederates tenaciously held Richmond. Two years later, at Cold Harbor on June 3, 1864, sixty thousand Federal troops surged toward the Confederate lines and in less than a few hours six thousand men were killed or wounded. Although the Confederate capital withstood repeated attacks, Grant's Army of the Potomac victory at Petersburg on April 2, 1865 sealed Richmond's fate and forced its evacuation.

The National Park Service (NPS) recommends a full day to experience the entire battlefield park; an abbreviated tour includes the historic structures at Tredegar Iron Works, Cold Harbor and Gaines Mill, and the Chimborazo Medical Center. Among the battlefields, the well-preserved Cold Harbor and Malvern Hill are worthwhile visits to fully comprehend the vast number of soldiers involved in Civil War engagements and the horrific carnage that often occurred.

The Tredegar Iron Works at Fifth and Tredegar Streets on the Richmond Canal Walk opened in the year 2000 as the Richmond National Battlefield Park's main visitor center. The creative and skillfully done reuse of original, fire damaged, and dilapidated build-ings—the three-story brick Pattern Shop serves as the NPS visitor center—integrates the surviving antebellum buildings with ruins, industrial machinery, and the redeveloped waterfront. The Iron Works, named for an iron works in Wales, covered nearly five acres during the Civil War, operating day and night with a work force of twenty-five hundred at its peak to produce artillery and munitions, rails, and steam locomotives. Almost 1,100 cannon, roughly one-half of the guns made in the South during the war, and the 2-inch-thick plating for the Confederate ironclad ships were produced here. Exhibits in the Pattern Shop orient the visitor to the battlefields, and living-history demonstrations and ranger-led interpretive tours are regularly scheduled during summer months.

At Gaines Mill, one of the Seven Days' Battles, Lee defeated the larger Federal forc-es. A "witness" building to the engagements fought here is the Watt House. Built in about 1820, the unpretentious one-and-a-half-story farmhouse (approximately 31 feet by 28 feet in plan), is on a raised brick basement with weatherboard exterior, a gable-end roof with dormers, and a pair of stepped chimneys on the east end wall. In 1957 the NPS restored the house to its original ap-pearance. It is closed to the public. Union General Fitz-John Porter used the house as headquarters during the Battle of Gaines' Mill fought on June 27, 1862. A short walk from the Watt House is today's vivid scene of artillery batteries and split-rail fences zig-zagging across the landscape where both armies suffered more than fifteen thousand casualties in one day's battle.

Garthright House, Cold Harbor

The restored Garthright House at Cold Harbor was used as a field hospital by the Union Army after the Battle of Cold Harbor in June 1864. Portions of the two-story house date to the 1700s and the major extension can be detected from the mixing of brick and weatherboard on the exterior. The gable-ended house has a shake-shingle roof and an exterior brick chimney on one end and another flush with the opposite end wall. The interior is closed to the public. Near the house, in Hanover County's Cold Harbor Park, a walking trail passes a line of well-preserved trenches and Union artillery batteries.

Tredegar Iron Works

Not yet open regularly to the public is the 1725 Shelton House on the Totopotomoy Creek battlefield, which was the site of a May 30, 1864, fight just before the Battle of Cold Harbor. The 5-bay, 1-story, gambrel roof, brick house sits on an English basement with a classic water table. The brickwork is Flemish bond with glazed headers. Some original interior woodwork is evident, including a remarkable staircase. No outbuildings or cemeteries remain.

The Confederates used Chimborazo Hospital (now destroyed) as a central collection point for battle casualties. The site on a hill overlooking the James River and Kanawha Canal was convenient for several reasons: supplies could reach the site by water; ample underground springs were available; and steep slopes on three sides of the hill afforded good drainage. Opened in 1861, the hospital grew to a complex covering forty acres and operated between seventy-five and eighty wards, with capacity for thirty-two patients in each ward, grouped in five separate divisions, and treated more than 76,000 Confederate sick and wounded. Under the astute medical direction of Dr. James McCaw the hospital mortality rate was twenty percent, high by today's standards but remarkably low for nineteenth-century medicine. The NPS operates the Chimborazo Medical Museum on the site in a 1909 former Weather Bureau building.

Shenandoah National Park

The seventy-five-mile-long park is along the Blue Ridge Mountains in northern Virginia.

→ www.nps.gov/shen

→ The 105-mile Skyline Drive extends the length of the park. Entrances are located at Front Royal (North), Interstate 66 and US 340 and Virginia 55; Thornton Gap at Mile 31.5 on Skyline Drive, US 211; Swift Run Gap at Mile 65.7, US 33; and Rockfish Gap (South), Interstate 64 and US 250. Dickey Ridge (Mile 4.6) and Byrd (Mile 51) visitor centers and the Loft Mountain Information Center (Mile 79.5) are open April to November.

Shenandoah National Park is a blanket of green, one to thirteen miles wide, astride the crest of the Blue Ridge Mountains in northern Virginia from Front Royal to Waynesboro. Views from seventy-five overlooks and pullouts along Skyline Drive running the length of the park provide sublime vistas eastward of Piedmont country rolling farmland and westward to the Shenandoah River Valley between the Blue Ridge and Allegheny Mountains. The entire Skyline Drive and developed areas are listed on the National Register of Historic Places.

The visitor will discover seasonal majesty throughout the year. Conditions in this magnificent woodland of ridges and valleys, hills and hollows, and streams and waterfalls have continuously improved after establishment of the park in 1935. Superb experiences are found that are grander today than those poetically described in the Works Progress Administration's *Virginia: A Guide to the Old Dominion* in 1940:

> Each season brings its own beauty to this wild, elevated world. The winter-dark forest is brightened in spring by dogwood breaking into bloom everywhere, like thin puffs of steam. Later azalea, and mountain laurel flood the sheltered hillsides with pink and white. Summer pours warm sunlight from clear skies onto the peaks and into the valleys, where streams splash down over rocky beds and falls, and often, especially in the early morning, onto clouds covering the lowlands far below. Autumn tints the leaves of every tree but the evergreen and intensifies the blue haze ever-present along the ridge. The clear air of Indian summer becomes even clearer with winter, and then snow blankets the upper slopes intermittently until another late spring.

The traveler on foot can climb peaks or hike along the ninety-five miles of the Appalachian Trail within the park to appreciate the splendor of Shenandoah National Park.

Dickey Ridge Visitor Center

The park's original settlers left behind cabins seen along the trails. Historical structures are also accessed from Skyline Drive at Skyland Resort (Mile 42), Big Meadows (Mile 51), Rapidan Camp (Mile 52.8,) and Lewis Mountain (Mile 57.5).

Skyland Resort, founded in the 1880s by a failed copper mining company, was developed with the construction of rustic cabins. A later owner (1906) was George Freeman Pollock, son of an investor in the company. Acquisition and condemnation was by the Commonwealth of Virginia, which transferred it to the federal government in 1935. The Civilian Conservation Corps altered the original layout and cabins, including replacing rough-bark siding with weatherboard siding, between 1933 and 1942. Concessionners added cabins and other buildings to the resort, relocating some from Dickey Ridge to the site in 1951 and 1952. Newer style motel accommodations were added between 1960 and 1980 and the resort with lodge and other visitor services is operated by a concessioner. The recently restored Massanutten Lodge, constructed in 1911, illustrates early privately built rustic cabins at Skyland. Twenty-one buildings and over fifty structures at Skyland are listed on the National Register of Historic Places.

Big Meadows has historically been an open space, and is the largest open meadow within the boundary of Shenandoah National Park. Mixed in with nondescript modern buildings are early National Park Service designed and built rustic cabins.

Historical structures at Lewis Mountain, six miles south of Big Meadows, have a place in the dismal history of segregation in the United States. The ten historic rustic cabins built in the 1930s, along with several moved from Dickey Ridge, were controversial in the segregated society of the time. Popular with African-Americans, the Department of the Interior acknowledged the need for accommodations by opening the Lewis Mountain as a campground with the conspicuous sign, "Lewis Mountain Negro Area," at the entrance. The campground was finally integrated in 1950. The interested reader can learn more about the history of segregation at Lewis Mountain campground at Shenandoah National Park's Web site.

The Hoover Camp, built in 1929 as Rapidan Camp, was a summer White House for President Herbert Hoover and his wife Lou Henry Hoover on land they owned now within the boundaries of the park. The president described it as a means to escape "the pneumatic hammer of public life." The National Historic Landmark camp contains three restored rustic cabins of the original thirteen. The camp was the precursor of the current presidential retreat, Camp David, which is located in the Catoctin Mountain area of Frederick County, Maryland. The Rapidan Camp is accessible by a 4.1-mile round-trip hike on Mill Prong Trail, which begins on the Skyline Drive at Milam Gap (Mile 52.8). The NPS also offers guided van trips that leave from the Harry F. Byrd Visitor Center at Big Meadows by reservation only.

Wolf Trap National Park for the Performing Arts

Vienna, Fairfax County, Virginia

→ www.nps.gov/wotr

→ The park is located fifteen miles west of Washington, D.C., and is accessed via the Capital Beltway (Interstate 495, Exit 45), Interstate 66 at Exit Route 267, and local roads. Exits and local roads are clearly marked Wolf Trap National Park for the Performing Arts.

Filene Center

The rolling hills and woods of northern Virginia west of Washington, D.C., are rapidly being eradicated by an increasingly urbanized countryside. Wolf Trap National Park for the Performing Arts, located in a natural enclave of rolling hills and woodland in the midst of this sprawling development, is the nation's only national park dedicated to the performing arts. Within the park's 130 acres—less than half developed—are four performance venues: The Filene Center, a summer amphitheater with a total maximum capacity of 7,024 (3,874 seats under cover and 3,150 on the sloping lawn); the Theater-in-the-Woods, an outdoor theater in a rustic natural setting seating approximately 750; the Meadow Pavilion, a stage used for special events and programs; and The Barns of Wolf Trap, a 352-seat indoor theater in two faux eighteenth-century barns just outside the park boundary and owned and operated by the Wolf Park Foundation. The venues are superb sites for diverse entertainment, replete with often-elegant dinners on the lawn before Filene Center performances.

The farm and the original Filene Center were the very generous gift of Catherine Filene Shouse. Purchase of land for construction of the Dulles Access Road in the late 1950s divided her farm property. Mrs. Shouse donated the remaining land to the

National Park Service (NPS) and additions brought the park to its current acreage. In 1982, the center burned to the ground and the rebuilt Filene Center II designed by Dewberry & Davis, John MacFadyen, and Joseph Boggs opened in 1984. Lev Zetlin and Associates were the structural engineers; Paul Veneklasen, acoustic consultant; and Clarke & Rapuano, landscape architects.

Filene Center interior

The Filene Center is the focal point of the park, the most visible structure over 110 feet to the top of the boxy stage house sheathed in Douglas fir. By day it is intriguingly angled, while at night it reveals a dramatic vitality. The roof enclosing the covered orchestra and balcony splays down and outward, hovering as a surprisingly airy structure. The undercover balcony seats are entered near the top grade level by two dramatic gangplanks. The column-free interior and only two columns at the roof's outside edge provide virtually unimpaired sightlines from the lawn seating area. The angled sides of the theater are open but the spaces between slender, wood-sheathed piers at the sides placed perpendicular to the interior offers views out to the surroundings and lets breezes filter in during summer evening performances; top-seated awnings can be closed for inclement weather. Interior surfaces are warmed by soft tones of the yellow pine ceiling, and huge laminated Douglas fir beams. The uncluttered interior focuses on the 70-foot-wide by 45-foot-high proscenium, and a stage 116 feet wide by 65 feet deep to the back wall.

Wolf Trap National Park for the Performing Arts is administered by the NPS, including technical and operational responsibilities for the Filene Center. The nonprofit Wolf Trap Foundation is responsible for performance programming, publicity and marketing, and operating the box office for the performance venues. The Filene Center season usually runs from the end of May to the end of September with an average of ninety-five performances a year. From October to early May, The Barns at Wolf Trap, continues to present a diverse line-up of artists in a casual and more intimate atmosphere. The Barns are also the summer home to the Wolf Trap Opera Company.

Filene Center from the amphitheater lawn

West Virginia

→ Harpers Ferry National Historical Park (p. 430)

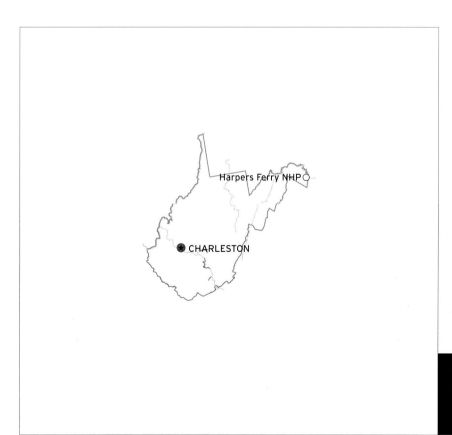

Harpers Ferry NHP○

● CHARLESTON

Harpers Ferry National Historical Park
Harpers Ferry, West Virginia, Virginia, and Maryland

→   www.nps.gov/hafe

→   The park is primarily in the eastern panhandle of West Virginia, with sections in Virginia and Maryland, approximately sixty-five miles northwest of Washington, D.C., and twenty miles southwest of Frederick, Maryland, via US 340. Follow signs to the visitor center.

Wilson Stagecoach Inn

The town of Harpers Ferry, at the confluence of the Shenandoah and Potomac Rivers and the junction of West Virginia, Virginia, and Maryland, is notorious in history as the scene of John Brown's raid on the U.S. Armory in October of 1859. More than this single event, the town has many layers of history interpreted by six National Park Service (NPS) themes: the natural environment, industry, transportation, the John Brown raid, the Civil War, and African-American history. Always present is the stunning natural beauty with rivers carved through the mountains that Thomas Jefferson declared "The passage of the Patowmac through the Blue Ridge is perhaps one of the most stupendous scenes in Nature....This scene is worth a voyage across the Atlantic." Carl Sandburg described Harpers Ferry as "a meeting place of winds and water, rocks and ranges."

The town is there because of its mountain gap location and as a natural point of crossing the rivers from a bench of land, first by ferry and later by bridges to carry railroads to the town's rapidly developing industries. Readily available waterpower inspired the first industry, a gristmill built by the eponymous Robert Harper in 1747. George Washington, familiar with the area from surveying work, spurred the town's growth by recommending to Congress in 1796 the building of a federal armory and arsenal. A turnpike company built a toll road in the early 1830s from Frederick, Maryland that connected the town with points eastward. But the major impetus for the town's growth was the arrival of the Baltimore and Ohio Railroad, the Winchester and Potomac Railroad, and the Chesapeake & Ohio Canal (Chesapeake and Ohio National Historical Park, see page 459) in the mid-1830s. By 1859 the town had swelled to a population of nearly three thousand with four hundred employed at the armory producing muskets, rifles, and pistols. Trapped between the North and South, the town's strategic location made it a Civil War battleground changing hands eight times. Until the 1950s, Harpers Ferry was the site of Storer College founded in 1867, an integrated normal school for freed blacks. Harpers Ferry never recovered from the war's devastation and ruinous floods in the late nineteenth and early twentieth century.

Designation as Harpers Ferry National Historical Park began a lengthy process by the NPS of restoring buildings and the environment to Harpers Ferry's nineteenth-century appearance. Two-and-a-half and three-story buildings lining Lower Town streets typically were built of Harpers shale blasted from the hills and placed as rubble masonry and covered with plaster. Federal government buildings are distinguished by red brick construction. Although the individual buildings are not of outstanding design, the collection portrays the town's mid-nineteenth-century character. Restored buildings include a working blacksmith shop, a dry-goods store stocked with typical provisions (including souvenir bits of the rope supposedly used to hang John Brown), and a tavern. The old Winchester and Potomac Railroad trestle between the Shenandoah River and Shenandoah Street is a reminder of the railroads' importance in Harpers Ferry's burgeoning growth as an industrial center. Cafes, restaurants, and craft and souvenir shops are on the side streets adjoining the park.

The John G. Wilson Building, now housing an NPS bookstore and information center, is a good example of regional architecture. Built in 1826 by John G. Wilson, with additions in 1843, the two-and-a-half-story structure originally contained ground floor commercial space and two floors of living quarters above. The load-bearing masonry five-bay by two-bay building (approximately 50 feet by 35 feet in plan), with a two-story porch across the front and four dormers projecting from the shake-shingle gabled roof, was converted to a hotel in 1830. Adjacent houses were built in 1845.

The Master Armor's House down the street, built in 1858 as the home for the armory's chief gunsmith, contains an information center and orientation exhibits about the park. Further down the street is John Brown's Fort. Originally built in 1848 as the Armory Fire Engine House, the structure was relocated several times and placed in 1968 at its present location. The one-story brick bearing masonry building (approximately 22 feet by 34 feet in plan) has three 8-foot-wide arched openings with soldier courses, wooden roof trusses supporting a gabled slate roof and an open-air wooden cupola. End walls have arched recesses and a crenellated roofline. Brown's raid was centered here and it is where the wounded Brown was captured by U.S. Marines.

On the hillside stands the Harper House, the oldest surviving structure in Lower Town, built from 1775 to 1782 and extensively remodeled in the 1830s when it became part of the adjacent Wager House. The narrow two-and-a-half-story structure (approximately 23 feet wide and 34 feet deep), with shuttered windows and a pair of rooftop dormers, was built of exposed 18-inch-thick rubble stone bearing walls and covered with many coats of plaster.

In addition to the buildings of Lower Town, other vernacular structures within the park are seen on the hillsides on Camp Hill and Bolivar Heights. The magnificent landscape is too often overlooked by a hurried visit to see the places identified with John Brown and a meander along Lower Town streets. The visitor center at the main entrance to the park is the place to begin an understanding of Harpers Ferry and the role this town played in our nation's history. The visitor will miss the experience of the place without the NPS orientation, the ranger-led tours, and taking advantage of the park's living-history program, museums, exhibits, and trails; the Appalachian Trail crosses through the town and over the Potomac River by footbridge.

Mid-Atlantic

District of Columbia

Ford's Theatre National Historic Site

511 10th Street NW, Washington, District of Columbia

→ www.nps.gov/foth

→ The theater is in downtown Washington at 511 10th Street NW, between E and F Streets. The house where Lincoln died is at 516 10th Street. The nearest Metro stop is Metro Center at 11th and G Streets.

Ford's Theatre

Presidential Box

Ford's Theatre, remembered forever as the place where Abraham Lincoln was assassinated on April 14, 1865, and the Petersen House directly across the street where the president died the following morning, is a national historic site, restored and interpreted by the National Park Service (NPS). The story is well known of the moment Lincoln was enjoying a performance of *Our American Cousin* when the assassin John Wilkes Booth entered the Presidential Box, fired the fatal shot, leaped to the stage shouting, "Sic semper tyrannis," and fled the building.

Crowds of nearly one million visitors annually come for a tour of the building and to view the faithful restoration of the Presidential Box to its appearance on that fateful night in 1865, festooned with bunting and an original engraving of George Washington, and a reproduction of the rocking chair in which the president sat that evening. The theater's basement contains a museum with interpretive exhibits on the events of assassination and Lincoln's life, as well as a bookstore. Ford's Theatre is also an active theater, producing a full schedule of plays distinguished for their American cultural and ethnic diversity through partnership with the Ford's Theatre Society.

Across the street from the theater at 516 Tenth Street is the Petersen House where the stricken president was carried for treatment. Built in 1849 by William A. Petersen, a tailor, the three-story three-bay-wide narrow brick residence on a raised basement (approximately 22 feet wide and 38 feet deep), with a Federal style entrance at the top of a curved stairway, was purchased by the U.S. governmment in 1896 and transferred to the NPS in 1926. Known as "The House Where Lincoln Died," the house's interior and exterior restoration to the appearance at the time of Lincoln's death includes the front parlor where Mary Todd Lincoln and her son Robert waited through the night of April 14th; the back parlor where Secretary of War Edwin M. Stanton began his investigation by interviewing witnesses; and the back bedroom where the unconscious president lay and finally expired on the morning of April 15th.

The origins of today's theater began in 1861 when theatrical entrepreneur John T. Ford leased the First Baptist Church originally built in 1833 and converted it into a music hall. Successfully reviewed productions came to an abrupt end when fire destroyed the building in December of 1862. The intrepid Ford began construction of a new theater on the site in February of 1863 and the first of 495 performances took place in August of 1863. One of the few new buildings constructed in wartime Washington, the new theater was lauded in the local press for its fine quality. Closed by the federal government during the assassination investigation, after sentencing and hanging of the accused, Ford reopened the theater only to close it upon threats that the building would be burned down. In August 1865 the War Department started leasing the building from Ford and began conversion into a three-story office building. After a collapse of interior floors in 1893 the theater was closed and eventually restored by the NPS to its former glory in the early 1960s and opened to the public in 1968 as a museum and working theater.

The theater is rectangular in plan, approximately 110 by 72 feet, with a four-story brick wing at the northeast corner providing an office and dressing rooms, and a slate-roofed three-story brick wing flush to the street facade, with a wood-paneled ground floor originally housing a saloon and lounges. The west, or street facade is in a five-part design defined by engaged brick piers above a white-plastered first floor base containing five arched doorway openings; above the first floor are two floors of windows centered on the doorways and capped by arched Victorian detailed stone headers, and a horizontal brick cornice supporting a pediment in an outline of the truss-supported main roof. Three large, wood-frame louvered ventilators, and ten rooftop hatches provided ventilation lauded in contemporary accounts of the theater.

The theater interior was a grand space with three tiers of seating for a reputed audience of 2,700. Entered from a narrow lobby directly from the street, the first floor contained the orchestra and parquet. All seats were movable wooden chairs with cane bottoms. Boxes were arranged stage right and left. Pairs of lower boxes are below stage level and the more elegant and spacious pairs of upper boxes, including numbers 7 and

8 when combined to serve as the Presidential Box, gave an excellent and unobstructed view of both stage and audience. The horseshoe-shaped, steeply pitched dress circle contained about 422 movable wooden chairs, similar in design to the orchestra and parquet seating. The topmost upper circle, with decorative plaster appliqué, had a separate lobby for the 600 wooden bench seats. Above the auditorium was an elaborately painted and decorated, inverted, saucer-shaped domed ceiling.

The stage was ample for a variety of performances, 43 feet deep and about 62 feet wide. The stage house was 44 feet high and the proscenium opening 36 feet wide by 38 feet deep. The drop curtain was painted with a landscape scene and a bust of William Shakespeare. An orchestra pit, set about 18 inches below the orchestra floor, was bow-shaped and was about 4 feet wide at stage center.

NPS ranger-conducted interpretive talks are held regularly from the stage, and visitors are free to roam the orchestra and peer into the Presidential Box. Note the theater is not open to the public during rehearsals and matinee performances, although the Lincoln Museum in the basement and The House Where Lincoln Died remain open.

Frederick Douglass National Historic Site

1411 W Street SE, Washington, District of Columbia

→ www.nps.gov/frdo

→ From the Mall, by car travel south on 9th Street to Interstate 395 north. Exit onto Interstate 295 south and cross the 11th Street Bridge. Exit onto Martin Luther King, Jr. Avenue. Turn left on W Street SE. Proceed three blocks to visitor center parking lot on the right. From Interstate 495/95 Beltway, take Exit 3 north onto Indian Head Highway (Maryland 210), which becomes South Capitol Street. Bear right onto Martin Luther King, Jr. Avenue. Turn right on W Street to visitor center parking lot on the right.

Frederick Douglass House

Frederick Douglass distinguished himself as the nation's leading nineteenth-century African-American spokesman. Freeing himself from slavery, he established his abolitionist views in his book *Narrative of the Life of Frederick Douglass: An American Slave*. Also a newspaper publisher, orator, women's rights activist, and statesman (ambassador to Haiti), he spent his final years at Cedar Hill in the Anacostia district of Washington, D.C. The Victorian house overlooking the Washington skyline to the north, with the Washington Monument and the Capitol Building prominent in the distance, was his home from 1878 until his death in 1895. Here, Douglass took respite from forty years of activism and led a warm family life, visited by the influential people of the era, and surrounded by mementos of his distinguished career.

The L-shaped house on 8.5 acres is a spacious wooded estate and includes Douglass's retreat, the small stone Growlery. Douglass purchased the modest two-story brick house (built originally around 1855) in 1877, and expanded it from fourteen to twenty-one rooms. The original three rooms on the first floor were extended with a two-story library wing, and the two-story kitchen wing to the south.

The house plan and main facade (43 feet wide) facing north has the characteristics of a modest mid-nineteenth century romantic cottage following principles of Andrew Jackson Downing. A central axis of interior room arrangements is expressed on the exterior by a decorative front door and a gable intersecting the main roof in the central bay. A second-floor bay window—along with those added later on the first floor, and floor-to-ceiling first-floor windows—introduces volumes of light to the house's interior and provides broad views of the surrounding countryside and the national capital land-

Front porch

marks. The front porch, with delicate upper trellis work supported by Doric columns, extends the interior to the outdoors. Many visitors could cherish the memory of gathering on the porch and Douglass raising his violin to entertain with tunes ranging from the melancholy to the rollicking.

Upon Douglass's death his widow, Helen, vigorously preserved Cedar Hill as his memorial. Unfortunately, by the early 1960s, lack of funds caused the house to slip into a deteriorated state, although all the abolitionist's memorabilia was intact. The National Park Service acquired the property in 1964 and undertook a major stabilization and restoration. The property underwent another restoration program and reopened to the public in February of 2007.

Today, visitors can tour Cedar Hill and view the well-furnished rooms as they were during Douglass's lifetime. Each room is filled with items from his public life. Approximately ninety percent of the furnishings are original to the house: Abraham Lincoln's cane given by Mrs. Lincoln after the assassination; a leather rocking chair from the people of Haiti; a hand carved German clock; and Douglass's most treasured possessions, his library of books. Prominently displayed throughout the house are paintings, lithographs, unique photographs, and several portraits of Douglass.

A short distance from the house is the reconstructed "Growlery." Borrowing from Dickens's *Bleak House* ("This, you must know, is the growlery. When I am out of humour, I come and growl here."), Douglass used the small stone building with a gable roof as his "lion's lair," a retreat for study and writing.

The visitor center, discretely tucked into a hillside a short distance from the main house, contains interpretive exhibits about Douglass's life and people who influenced his philosophy.

Lincoln Memorial
Located on the National Mall, Washington, District of Columbia

→ www.nps.gov/linc

→ The memorial is located at 23rd Street and west end of the National Mall.

Lincoln Memorial

The Lincoln Memorial, standing on a mound of land at the western end of the National Mall, is an iconic memorial to the sixteenth president of the United States and a symbol of dreams and hopes for many people. A visit to the serene site to see the contemplative statue of the seated Lincoln portrayed in a heroic scale by sculptor Daniel Chester French is infused by a perfect balance of the temple-like structure among elements of architecture, the landscape, sculpture, and the written word, all culminated in the sensitive design by Henry Bacon, completed in 1922. A combination of grandeur and simplicity, the classical design is dominated by the majestic seated Lincoln gazing from the memorial's interior toward the rising sun from an acropolis on the two-mile-long axis of the reflecting pool, the Washington Monument, and the U.S. Capitol.

Bacon designed the building with layers of symbolism. The architect saw the build-ing as a logical conclusion to the historical development of the National Mall, a sym-bol of democracy, and American institutions: government symbolized by the Capitol, the Washington Monument dedicated to that government's founder, and the Lincoln Memorial to its savior. The building is enhanced by its physical isolation and elevated position on land filled in on the Potomac's tidal flats forming West Potomac Park from 17th Street to beyond 25th Street, placement designed to reflect Lincoln's character, con-sidered above petty politics.

The experience of approaching from the National Mall was conceived so that viewers first encounter the gleaming white building at the end of the reflecting pool, then approach it from an off-axis diagonal, finally arriving at the broad plaza and steps ascending to the terrace 256.9 feet long by 187 feet wide. The progressive experience culminates by mounting the broad steps and entering the lofty, uncluttered interior generously accommodating the 19-foot-high Lincoln in a monumental chair, its carved twenty-eight blocks of white Georgia marble appearing flawlessly monolithic. Skylights above introduce subdued lighting through a ceiling of thin slabs of Alabama marble made translucent with beeswax; artificial light accentuates the statue.

The harmony and design of Bacon's inventive approach modified the Greek pro-totype. The box-like structure (188 feet long, 118 feet wide, and 74 feet high) is oriented with its entry on the long side, unlike the Parthenon that is entered at the narrow end, and has a flat roof rather than a sloping one. The refined treatment of the thirty-six Doric Colorado Yule marble columns on the periphery (44 feet high, 8 on the short sides and 12 on the long) against the white interior walls makes the building appear perfectly rectilinear and symmetrical. The entasis of the fluted drums and a slight tilt inward skill-fully follow classical precedent. In addition, the spacing between end columns is closer than the others, while nearly square (44 by 45 feet) at the center entry, and the outer wall has a slight inward tilt. The frieze above the columns carries the names of the thirty-six states along with their dates of admission existing at the time of Lincoln's death. In the recessed attic above, a frieze contains the names of the forty-eight states of the Union existing when the memorial was completed in 1922. A large stone bearing inscriptions for Alaska and Hawaii was added near the foot of the approach stairs in 1985.

On either side of the central chamber (60 by 74 feet) are smaller chambers defined by screens composed of 60-foot-tall Ionic columns; all interior chambers are made up of Indiana limestone walls and pink Tennessee marble floors. On the south wall, there is an inscription of the Gettysburg Address and on the north wall is that of Lincoln's second inaugural address. Above each engraved speech are Jules Guerin's 60-foot-long allegorical paintings on canvas.

Some critics, unmoved by the cold stone walls and realistically rendered statue, are refuted by the memorial's more than four million annual visitors wrapped up in the symbolism and vital creation of Henry Bacon, Daniel Chester French, and Jules Guerin. An ideal time to visit the site is at night, when the crowds are smaller, and the stone walls and columns glow under spotlights. From the memorial, there is a stirring view east toward the reflecting pool and floodlit buildings lining the National Mall, the Washington Monument and the U.S. Capitol, or west across the Potomac River to the Virginia skyline.

Mary McLeod Bethune Council House National Historic Site

Located at 1318 Vermont Avenue NW, Washington, District of Columbia

→ www.nps.gov/mamc

→ Located in the Logan Circle area at 1318 Vermont Avenue NW. The nearest Metro stations are McPherson Square (Blue and Orange lines) and U Street/African American Civil War Memorial/Cardozo (Green and yellow line).

Mary McLeod Bethune Council House

The Victorian row house at 1318 Vermont Street NW was the home of Mary McLeod Bethune from 1943 to 1949 and served as the first headquarters of the National Council of Negro Women founded by Bethune. Today, the Council House is a historic house museum and archival center for the collection, preservation, and interpretation of African-American women's history with an active year-round program of speakers and events.

Mary McLeod Bethune was born in 1876 the fifteenth of seventeen children of former slaves in Mayesville, South Carolina, and rose to national prominence as an educator, presidential advisor, and political activist. Education at Scotia Seminary in Concord, North Carolina and Moody Bible Institute in Chicago, and then disappointment as a missionary candidate, led to teaching school in Daytona, Florida. With unshakable faith, in 1904, she founded the Daytona Normal and Industrial Institute for Negro Girls, with five girls, her son, and one dollar and fifty cents. A gifted speaker and astute fundraiser, she expanded the school for African-American girls to a high school, then a junior college, and in 1923 merged with Cookman Institute in Jacksonville, Florida. Bethune served as president of the new coeducational Bethune-Cookman College from 1904 to 1942 and from 1946 to 1947. The College currently enrolls over 3,500 students.

Bethune went on to become a leader in the black women's club movement while continuing to direct the college, and served as president of the National Association of Colored Women. At the national political level, she served on the National Child Welfare Commission under presidents Calvin Coolidge and Herbert Hoover and was appointed by Franklin Delano Roosevelt as director of negro affairs in the National Youth Administration from 1936 to 1944. Bethune died in 1955 at the age of 79.

Within the context of similar houses on tree-lined Vermont Street in the Logan Circle Historic District, the large sign attached to a wrought-iron fence distinguishes the Council House from its neighbors. Built in 1875, the Second-Empire-style elements are prominent on the ornately detailed street facade: a large ground floor bay window with a railing suggesting a second story porch; elegant header and jambs framing the main doorway and second floor windows; an elaborate frieze at the third floor; and a slate mansard roof with projecting window frames.

Set on a 23-foot-wide lot, the building maximizes the use of the site by a three-story, 34-foot-deep main block facing the street and a rear three-story ell, also 34 feet deep. A small courtyard is between the rear ell carriage house at the back of the property. The interior of the house is bathed in natural daylight through its large windows on the street facade, including the projecting bay, and the ell side and rear walls. The ground floor, with a generous 12-foot-high ceiling, contains a large paneled front parlor and rear room for meetings, receptions, and exhibits. The second floor contains additional exhibition and meeting space and the third floor contains office space. Original furniture from the National Council of Negro Women, photographs, and facsimiles of historic documents are displayed throughout the house. The Carriage House at the property's rear houses the Bethune Archives featuring materials documenting the political activity and accomplishments of African-American women.

Visitors are welcome to tour the house daily from 10 A.M. to 4:00 P.M. and attend special events. Note that parking is extremely limited in the area.

National Mall and Memorial Parks
Washington, District of Columbia

→ www.nps.gov/nama

→ In Washington, District of Columbia

The National Mall is more than merely a landscaped park at the heart of the nation's capital. The swath of green, tree-shaded and bordered by a host of imposing museums and anchored with powerful monuments and memorials, is a remarkable urban space, perpetually green and continuously evolving. Vistas—"democratic vistas," Walt Whitman called them—from varied locations, by day or night, offer dramatically different perspectives of the axial composition from the U.S. Capitol to the Lincoln Memorial and beyond to the Potomac River. An aerial view through an airplane window, or from the Washington Monument observation windows, portrays the full panorama of this pastoral place among the beacons of the Capitol, Washington Monument, Lincoln Memorial, other memorials, and museums. The distant perspective from Arlington House (see page 405) across the Potomac River, or at closer proximity from the steps of the Capitol or Lincoln Memorial, offers a timeless experience of twenty-first-century life in the nation's capital.

Reflecting Pool and Washington Monument

Technically, this sublime achievement of urban planning and design stretches from 1st to 14th Streets between Independence and Constitution Avenues (146.5 acres), with separate parks to the west for the Washington Monument Grounds and West Potomac Park, totaling 545 acres in the center of Washington. Oblivious to this fine point of legislative delineations, today's visitor can appreciate the vision of many individuals who established and sustained for more than two centuries this place of contemplation, repose, recreation, and national gatherings. Beginning with Thomas Jefferson, then Pierre-Charles L'Enfant, and followed by a succession of America's leading architects and landscape architects, the concept of an axial composition running east to west from Capitol to Potomac prevailed.

The current composition, destined to be the most enduring, is the work of the Senate Park Commission Plan of 1901–1902, often known as the MacMillan Commission Plan for the Michigan Chairman of the Senate Committee on the District of Columbia. Among other important land and water features, the plan reinforced the city's axial composition created by L'Enfant, and established the sites for museums along the Mall and near the Lincoln Memorial (see page 439) and Jefferson Memorial (see page 449).

The National Mall, the vibrant center of the nation's capital, is the framework for many historical structures and memorials on its borders, including the President's Park (the White House, see page 452), U.S. Botanic Gardens Conservatory, and the Smithsonian Institution museums: the Smithsonian Institution building (known as the Castle), the National Museum of African Art, the Arts and Industries Building, the Hirshhorn Museum and Sculpture Garden, the National Air and Space Museum, The National Museum of the American Indian, the National Gallery of Art, National Museum of Natural History, the National Museum of American History, the Freer Gallery of Art, and the Arthur M. Sackler Gallery.

Certainly, the most emotionally charged of the many modern memorials on the Mall is the Vietnam Veterans Memorial. This bold slash in the ground with two 247-foot-long polished black granite walls, one end pointing at the Lincoln Memorial and the other at the Washington Monument, designed by twenty-one-year-old architectural student Maya Ying Lin, is vivid testimony to those who gave the ultimate sacrifice to their country.

The Mall is the frequent scene of festivals. On the Fourth of July a free concert by the National Symphony Orchestra on the Capitol grounds is closed by a spectacular display of fireworks over the Mall.

Rock Creek Park

Washington, District of Columbia

→ www.nps.gov/rocr

→ The park is located in northwest Washington along Rock Creek, from the outlet into the Potomac River to the District of Columbia boundary, with many access points, including Rock Creek Parkway between the Potomac River and the Maryland border.

Old Stone House, Georgetown

Rock Creek Park is a diverse swath of green winding its way through northwest Washington, following Rock Creek from the District of Columbia boundary to the creek's mouth as it empties into the Potomac River. The park's main section of 1,754 acres between the National Zoo and the boundary contains picturesque gorge-like scenery, a one-mile stretch of rapids and a rocky stream bed immediately south of Military Road, forested valley slopes, grassy meadows, intensive recreational facilities, Civil War earthworks, bridges, and several historical structures. Additional park components are parkland on other nearby tributaries flowing into the Potomac River and the Old Stone House in

Georgetown. Opportunities for recreation and exploring nature in this urban woodland retreat include picnicking, hiking, biking, rollerblading, playing tennis, kite flying, fishing, horseback riding, listening to a concert, or attending programs with a park ranger. Children can participate in a wide range of special programs, including planetarium shows, animal talks, exploratory hikes, crafts, and junior ranger programs.

The Rock Creek Parkway connects the main section of the park south to the Potomac River and links with Beach Drive north of Military Road to form a twelve-mile long commuter-filled, low-speed drive from the Maryland suburbs to Georgetown and the city center. The pleasure for the driver—bisecting the capital, only aware of the sinuous valley, rocks, and forested slopes—is an unusual urban experience of context even more than content.

The park is one of the oldest in the National Park System, established in 1890. Unlike contemporary great nineteenth-century American parks, such at Central Park in New York (1856), Golden Gate Park in San Francisco (1870), or the Boston Metropolitan Park System (1878–95), natural forces created Rock Creek Park. Fortunately, planners and builders have respected the natural environment, even carefully placing roadways and parking lots to minimize intrusions.

Park origins are rooted in a Senate committee search beginning in 1866 for a healthier location for a presidential mansion outside of swampy downtown Washington. The 1867 report by army engineer Nathaniel Michler described the inherent values of Rock Creek valley:

> All the elements which constitute a public resort of the kind can be found in this wild and romantic tract of country. With its charming drives and walks, its hills and dales, its pleasant valleys and deep ravines, its primeval forests and cultivated fields, its running waters, its rocks clothed with rich fern and mosses, its repose and tranquility, its light and shade, its ever-varying shrubbery, its beautiful and extensive views, the locality is already possessed with all the features necessary for the object in view. There you can find nature diversified in almost every hue and form.

Although the proposal for a new president's house was dismissed, the park proposal gained support and, finally, approval as a federal resource to be preserved in its natural state, following the topography and the narrow creek bed in its lower third near the Maryland border and sloping hills, broad meadows, and woods near the National Zoo. The first construction work within Rock Creek Park got underway in 1897.

Highly visible from Beach Drive, around a mile north of the National Zoo and accessed from Tilden Drive is Peirce Mill, a three-and-a-half-story structure of irregularly coursed blue and brown granite. Massive in construction with 2-foot-thick perimeter walls of the 40- by 50-foot plan, braced by stout wooden joists, windows were located on each elevation, on each floor. A waterwheel powered by water flow fed by a tailrace from Rock Creek drove wooden shafts and gears that turned massive millstones.

Built in the 1820s by Isaac Peirce, along with the adjoining barn and other outbuildings, the mill operated commercially until 1897 when the wooden machinery failed and it was no longer economically feasible to produce flour on Rock Creek. A depression-era Works Progress Administration project, directed by restoration architect Thomas T. Waterman, using authentic wooden machinery from old mills in Pennsylvania and Maryland restored the mill in 1935–36. Flour produced in the mill was used in government cafeterias during the 1930s and 1940s. In April 1993, the wooden waterwheel shaft failed and the machinery has been still since then. Now undergoing restoration, the mill is open to the public periodically. Directly west of the mill is one of several barns built by Peirce. Predating the mill and now referred to as the Peirce Barn, it has a woodframe front and sides of blue granite. A blue granite springhouse, built in 1801, is now straddled by the divided lanes of Tilden Street.

Less visible is the imposing Peirce-Klingle House (also known as Linnean Hill or Klingle Mansion), named in honor of the Swedish botanist Carolus Linnaeus. Located on Williamsburg Lane (not accessed from main park drives) above the west bank of Rock Creek and less than half a mile below Peirce Mill, the house was built in 1823 by Joshua Peirce, a son of the mill builder. The three-story house is built of 2-foot-thick walls of blue and gray granite fieldstone and, following the Georgian style, is five bays wide with end wall chimneys and gable roof. A gabled two-story entrance wing is on axis with a central hall plan; a parlor and dining room flank a hall with stairs to bedchambers on the second and attic floors. The house was enlarged by a kitchen wing addition on the west side twenty years later. An unusual feature is the elaborate two-story cast-iron verandah on the south elevation. The house now serves as park headquarters.

The log Joaquin Miller Cabin built in 1883 by the American poet is a unique rustic structure in Rock Creek Park located west of Beach Drive and approximately one half-mile north of Military Road NW at the north end of a picnic grove. Born Cincinnatus H. Miller (1838–1913) and known as the "Poet of the Sierras," the one-and-one-half story, L-shaped cabin of saddle-notched logs and a steeply pitched cross-gabled roof covered by shingles was originally constructed at a nearby site. The cabin was disassembled and relocated to its present location in 1911–12. Although some of the original fabric was lost in the move, the cabin was replicated authentically as a memorial to the poet.

The Park Police Rock Creek Station, located approximately one quarter-mile south of Military Road on Rock Creek Parkway is a fine example of NPS rustic architecture of the 1930s, designed to blend a modern facility into its environment. Completed in 1936, the symmetrical one-and-one-half story Colonial Revival style building has a simple rectangular three-part plan of a center block and two subordinate wings. Walls are rough-cut ashlar stone walls laid in irregular courses. The central block has a gable roof and balanced projecting clapboard sided hipped dormers. The one story wings are hip roofed. Doors and windows of the central block have segmented arches. Originally, the south wing was designed as a comfort station and the north wing as a garage.

The Old Stone House located at 3051 M Street NW in Georgetown, built in 1765, is one of the oldest surviving buildings on its original lot in the Federal City, predating the creation of the District of Columbia. Daily, countless numbers of people walk past this modestly scaled blue-granite house with brick east gable and chimney, and peculiar run of wooden stairs and wooden porch reaching the main floor entry, and miss the opportunity for a brief respite from the hectic pace of Georgetown. The house's colonial furnished interiors and English garden can be toured daily during normal work hours.

The front room of the house standing today was built by Christopher Layman, a cabinetmaker by trade, as both a residence and a shop. Layman died shortly after constructing the house and different sections were completed by others. The street-facing two-and-a-half-story main block, 30 feet wide and less than 20 feet deep, has a 20-foot-deep ell attached to the rear. The irregular coursed whitewashed rubble granite walls and building form recalls the Pennsylvania Dutch origins of the builder.

Sewall-Belmont House National Historic Site

Washington, NE, District of Columbia

→ www.nps.gov/sebe

→ The house is located in Capitol Hill at 144 Constitution Avenue at the corner of 2nd Street and Constitution Avenue, next to the Hart Senate Office Building. Nearest Metro stations are Union Station (Red Line) and Capitol South (Blue and Orange Lines). Street parking is metered and difficult to find.

Sewall-Belmont House

The prominent location of this modified Federal style brick house was eminently suited for lobbying Congress for women's rights when acquired by the National Women's Party in 1929. Today, even though overwhelmed in scale by adjacent innocuous government office buildings, the National Historic Landmark has evidence of its lineage from the eighteenth century as a surviving example of the residential neoclassical style in the Capitol Hill neighborhood. Regularly festooned by symbolic purple, gold, and white suffrage banners once worn by women demonstrating for the right to vote, the free-standing structure surrounded by a black cast-iron fence is an active lobbying center for political actions against sex discrimination. The site is an affiliated area of the National Park System and is operated by the Sewall-Belmont House and Museum in cooperation with the National Park Service.

Built in the late 1790s by Robert Sewall incorporating an existing brick structure from 1750, the Sewall family retained the house for 123 years for occasional use as a town house. A distinguished tenant from 1801 to 1813 was Albert Gallatin, secretary of the Treasury. The house was partially burned by the British in 1814 during the War of 1812. In later years the house was used as a full-time family residence and then fell into disrepair after a period of vacancy in the early 1900s, to be sold and restored in the 1920s, and then sold again to the Women's Rights Party and named after the party's benefactor, Mrs. Alva Belmont. Closely identified with the house is Alice Paul, a suffragist leader and lifelong activist for women's rights. From the Sewall-Belmont House, Paul led the movement that helped Congress in 1920 to finally pass the nineteenth amendment to the Constitution, granting women the right to vote.

Rebuilt, restored, and modified over the years, the two-and-a-half-stories over a raised basement retains Federal style articulation with the balanced three-bay facade, original Flemish bond brick walls, and flat window lintels with sunken bull's-eye corner blocks. Late-nineteenth- and early-twentieth-century additions include a peacock fanlight entrance under a molded arch with keystone and sidelights, the exterior double staircase, and mansard roof with three dormer windows. Interior alterations modified the house to accommodate various living arrangements.

The main block with a center hall Georgian plan is approximately 40 feet deep and 30 feet wide across the Constitution Avenue facade. The elegant stained glass entrance fanlight and sidelights flood the paneled hallway's dark wood walls with a daylight rainbow of colors. Attached to the main block is the kitchen wing with bedrooms above and to the side of an exterior terrace (40 by 13 feet), and the one-story library (48 by 16 feet in plan) extending to the rear of the property, a total of approximately 131 feet facing 2nd Avenue.

The house offers public programs and docent-led tours that interpret memorabilia from the suffragist movement, including busts and portraits of the pioneers of the women's rights movement, suffrage parade banners, Susan B. Anthony and Alice Paul's desks, political cartoons, and historic photographs. The Florence Bayard Hilles Library has an extensive microfilm collection and published material related to the suffrage campaign.

Thomas Jefferson Memorial

Washington, NW, District of Columbia

→ www.nps.gov/thje

→ Thomas Jefferson Memorial is located on the south bank of the Tidal Basin near downtown Washington, D.C. It is open daily from 8:00 A.M. until 11:45 P.M. every day except Christmas Day.

Thomas Jefferson Memorial

The challenge architect John Russell Pope faced in designing a suitable memorial to Thomas Jefferson was formidable: a prominent site near the center of the national capital on a north-south axis opposite the White House and forming a giant cross in plan with the east-west axis of the National Mall (see page 442). The U.S. Senate Park Commission (the MacMillan Report of 1902) selected the general site at the Tidal Basin in West Potomac Park. Architect John Russell Pope chose a daring scheme inspired by the third president of the United States' fondness for classical design expressed in his taste for Monticello, his home, and the University of Virginia Rotunda in nearby Charlottesville, Virginia. Thus, Pope decided that the memorial would stand as a symbol and as a reminder of the very things that Jefferson wanted for this country: equality, education, liberty, freedom, and independence.

Controversial in its concept, opposing camps of classicists argued with modernists that the solution was an orthodox example of Beaux-Arts design versus an uproar over "applied archeology." The classicists prevailed after Pope's design and redesign were pushed forward over the objections of the U.S. Commission of Fine Arts. After Pope's death, the partnership of Otto R. Eggers and Daniel P. Higgins, his firm's successors, completed the design and the memorial was dedicated in 1943 on the two hundredth anniversary of Jefferson's birth.

The finished structure soon became and remains one of Washington's most picturesque landmarks. Varied vantage points reveal the brilliant setting edged by the waters of the Tidal Basin; a stunning glory in a backdrop of early evening light when the Vermont Imperial Danby marble exterior walls turn a warm pink and a glow of artificial light bathes the rotunda interior and Jefferson's towering bronze statue (19 feet tall on a 6-foot pedestal), seen in silhouette through careful placement of walls and columns. Indeed, the perfectly proportioned merging of Roman Pantheon and Greek portico is sublime architectural sculpture seen from across the Tidal Basin, its refined landscape evoking traditional garden pavilions. The glorious early April display of flowering cherry blossoms on trees ringing the Tidal Basin is one of America's most memorable sights.

There is legerdemain in the subtlety contrived here by Pope to engage the visitor by using the finest traditions of the Beaux-Arts repertoire. Within the classical context of a rotunda married to a portico, he placed the memorial on a stylobate with an overall diameter of 183.9 feet. Thus, by isolating the central form from its surroundings, an acceptable modification to the model of an enclosed Pantheon is achieved by placement of twenty-six Ionic columns (41 feet tall) around the rotunda perimeter as a colonnade, rather than within it, with an octastyle pedimented portico facing the basin. The unusual device of inverting the enclosing walls to inside the colonnade sustains Pope's treatment of allowing for the interpenetration of space by creating white interior Georgia marble walls in quadrants (86 feet in diameter), separated at four cardinal points by a 30-foot-wide opening measured on the interior wall's surface, so that there is fluid visual movement from the rotunda interior to the outdoors and the reverse from the outdoor promenade.

The sense of enclosure is replaced by one of shelter—the interior extending to views of the basin, trees, and even the distant Washington Monument. In turn, exterior views of the Jefferson statue are seen as vignettes through the spaces between interior walls. The smooth surfaced interior walls under the soaring coffered ceiling of Indiana limestone, almost 92 feet above the Tennessee marble floor, create a spacious ambulatory around the sculptor Rudolph Evans's standing figure of Jefferson.

There are interior and exterior panels with inscriptions of quotations from Jefferson's writings. These serve to ground the visitor in Jefferson's genius and the greatest of his accomplishments, as recognized by President John F. Kennedy when he told a 1962 gathering of American Nobel Prize winners that they were the greatest assemblage of talent in the White House since Thomas Jefferson dined there alone.

Washington Monument
Washington, NW, District of Columbia

→ www.nps.gov/wamo

→ The monument is located on the National Mall at Constitution Avenue and 15th Street NW.

Washington Monument

The 555-foot and 5.125-inch-high marble-clad Washington Monument obelisk on the National Mall honoring the Father of the Country is the tallest free-standing stone structure in the world. Probably the least contentious monument in a city of memorials, it is rivaled nationally only by Eero Saarinen's soaring Jefferson National Expansion Memorial Arch in St. Louis (see page 204) for simplicity, purity of form, and gracefulness. Located near the intersection of the powerful axes formed by Pierre-Charles L'Enfant's plan for the national capital, one extending south from the White House and the other extending from the Capitol, unsatisfactory soil conditions required a move to a site 371 feet east and 123 feet south of its intended position.

The purity of today's striking landmark differs from the Robert Mills winning competition entry of 1833, which called for a 600-foot-tall obelisk rising from a classical colonnaded temple at its base, 100 feet high and 250 feet in diameter. Construction on the Egyptian obelisk portion began in 1848 and continued fitfully over the next six years. Work was suspended after 1854, following the theft of a stone donated by the Vatican, leaving an unfinished stump at a height of 156 feet standing through and after the Civil War. "It has the aspect of a factory chimney with the top broken off," observed Mark Twain. The change in color at the demarcation of old and resumed work, approximately one-third up from the base, is due to a change in the exterior marble's source.

Construction resumed in 1878 under the direction of Lieutenant Colonel Thomas L. Casey of the U.S. Army Corps of Engineers. Various solutions for completion were proposed but the idea of a simple, unadorned obelisk prevailed. Casey found that the obelisk was out of plumb and shored it up with a 13-foot-thick pad of Portland cement. At the same time, the American minister to Italy, George Perkins Marsh, determined that the correct relationship of the base to the shaft, based on classical Egyptian proportions, was a ratio of one to ten times its baseline. The angle of the pyramidion seldom varied from seventy-three degrees and the obelisk walls tapered at about a quarter-inch per foot. Casey transposed the geometry to the incomplete shaft with the baseline of 55-feet and 5.5 inches setting the height at 555-feet and 5.125 inches. Completion of the monument on December 6, 1884 after placement of the marble capstone (34 feet and 6 inches square at the base) and a 100-ounce cast aluminum pyramid. Visibility from the observation level of the monument extends beyond forty miles in clear weather.

The walls of the monument range in thickness from 15 feet thick at the base to 18 inches at the upper shaft. They are composed of white marble from Maryland and Massachusetts, underlain by blue gneiss on the lower portion and Maine granite above. The interior walls contain 195 carved commemorative stones presented by individuals, societies, cities, states, and nations of the world.

Throughout 1999, scaffolding around the entire structure for the Washington Monument Restoration Project allowed sealing of exterior and interior stone cracks, pointing of exterior and interior joints, cleaning interior wall surfaces, sealing eight observation windows and eight aircraft warning lights, and repairing chipped stone. Simultaneously, interior work included cleaning wall surfaces and restoring the 195 interior commemorative stones.

Note that tickets are required for admission to the monument and can be purchased in advance for a fee over the internet at http://reservation.gov. Free tickets can be obtained for same-day visits from the Monument Lodge at 15th Street and are distributed on a first-come first-served basis. Tickets run out early; one person can obtain up to six tickets.

White House (President's Park)
Washington, District of Columbia

→ www.nps.gov/whho

→ The White House is located at 1600 Pennsylvania Avenue, NW.

The White House, or the President's House as it was once called, is arguably the most famous address in the United States. Here, all presidents but George Washington resided and conducted the business of the nation's executive branch of government. For over two hundred years the original structure grew from some thirty rooms to now about 132 rooms. It was rebuilt from the ruinous burning by the British in 1814 and rescued from structural collapse by Harry S. Truman's interventioin. Altered, adapted, and extended, the white painted Aquia Creek light gray sandstone walls (first whitewashed in 1797 and later painted to cover the 1814 fire damage) were extracted from a Virginia quarry downriver from Mount Vernon and the original interior configuration is the same as what greeted the first tenants, John and Abigail Adams on November 1, 1800. The house was not quite finished when the second president moved in. His wife Abigail is reported to have used the East Room to dry the family wash. Abigail wrote her sister that the building was "twice as large as our meeting house" in Massachusetts, and was "built for ages to come."

On June 28, 1791, George Washington and Pierre-Charles L'Enfant selected the location for the President's House. A competition proposal written by Thomas Jefferson, and corrected by George Washington, was announced in March of 1782. On July 17, 1792, Irish born architect James Hoban's competition proposal was selected and he was awarded the commission with a prize of $500 or a medal (he chose the medal). The cornerstone was laid on October 13, 1792. Recalling elements from an English or perhaps Anglo-Irish type country house (neoclassical style Leinster House in Dublin is frequently cited as an influence on Hoban's design), the building the Adams moved into underwent several major changes from Hoban's competition design: a raised basement was cut down in height, a complete third story and a full-width south porch were deleted, and it was greatly enriched with stone carving.

The result seen today is an elongated rectangle, approximately 168 by 85 feet in plan, eleven bays wide, and two stories over a raised basement with colonnades extending to the West and East Wings. Benjamin Henry Latrobe designed the north and south porticos made of Seneca sandstone from Maryland; James Hoban supervised the construction. The south portico (61 feet wide), semicircular and colonnaded with six Ionic columns and sweeping curved stairways from the lawn was completed in 1824; the pedimented north portico (51 feet wide) on four Ionic columns, also serving as a

White House, south portico

porte cochere, was completed in 1829. The East and West Terraces, designed by Thomas Jefferson and Latrobe, were originally built in 1805 (the East Terrace was rebuilt and expanded in 1902).

The interior, rebuilt after the 1814 fire with Latrobe's design and supervised by Hoban, called for a large, rectangular Entrance Hall on the north axis with a perpendicular Cross Hall and an oval room (Blue Room), resulting in the bowed south portico. On

North portico

The Red Room

either side of the Blue Room are rectangular shaped parlors (Red Room on the west and Green Room on the east). Traversing the entire east side was a large reception room (East Room). The west side contained the large State Dining Room to serve as the banquet room (enlarged to its present size in 1902); the smaller Family Dining Room; and a pantry next to the dining room dating from after the 1817 reconstruction. Prominent ground floor spaces reconfigured under varioius administrations include the oval Diplomatic Reception Room and Grand Staircase (T. Roosevelt), China Room (Wilson), Library (F. D. Roosevelt), Map Room (Nixon), and Vermeil Room (Eisenhower).

The Truman renovation (1948–52) rectified the extent of damage and structural problems sustained during two centuries of the building's life. Many interior changes had weakened the structure to the point where serious concerns were raised for occupant safety. In a major rebuilding, the house was gutted to its exterior walls, a new basement was excavated, new foundations were laid, and a load-bearing structural steel and concrete frame inserted within. Only the original south front, central portion of the north face, basement walls, the third floor, and the roof were retained. Architect Lorenzo Winslow supervised the removing and reinstalling of the interiors, retaining the general arrangement of rooms in the reconstruction, with many architectural modifications and changes of materials.

Figuratively and symbolically the White House endures: as the home of the president, and as a place that has witnessed great national joy and sorrow, episodes of pride and shame, and, inevitably, the enduring triumph of the Republic.

Post September 11, 2001 security concerns are now relaxed to enable public tours of the White House once again. Tours are scheduled Tuesday through Saturday from 7:30 A.M. to 12:30 P.M. (except for federal holidays). Admission is free and requests must be submitted through a member of Congress and are accepted up to six months in advance.

Maryland

Clara Barton NHS

Antietam NB

Hampton NHS

Chesapeake and
Ohio Canal NHP

BALTIMORE

ANNAPOLIS

Fort Washington Park

Fort McHenry NM
and Historic Shrine

Thomas Stone NHS

ATLANTIC

OCEAN

Antietam National Battlefield

In the northwest part of the state, seventy miles west of Washington near Sharpsburg, Washington County, Maryland

→ www.nps.gov/anti

→ Take Interstate 70 to Exit 29 onto MD 65 South toward Sharpsburg. Travel about ten miles south to the park visitor center entrance one mile north of Sharpsburg.

Antietam Battlefield, "Bloody Lane" (sunken road)

Today's peaceful countryside of Antietam National Battlefield and its surroundings belie the awful carnage that overwhelmed the place on September 17, 1862. The once wartime-blasted landscape is now a placid scene of rolling hills, ridges, woodlots, and fields between Antietam Creek and the Potomac River. Here, General Robert E. Lee leading the Confederate Army of Northern Virginia, met the Federal army on his first invasion of the North, following the Battle of South Mountain, moved Confederate troops in a wide arc to the west of Washington, and across the Potomac River into Maryland. And here took place the bloodiest day in American history.

On a foggy and gray morning turning into a golden, warm September afternoon, the 41,000 soldiers under Lee faced 87,000 Union Army of the Potomac troops led by General George B. McClellan. The killing-field at Antietam, where soldiers were "mowed down like grass before a scythe," is the site where battles raged over a 12-square-mile area along Hagerstown Turnpike, in the cornfield north of Sharpsburg, and at crossings of Antietam Creek. After twelve hours of continuous struggle, day's end left an estimated 12,400 Federals and 10,320 Confederates killed, wounded, or captured; one out of every four combatants was killed or wounded. American casualties on June 6, 1944—D-day, the famous "longest day" of World War II—were about one-quarter as great. Indeed, the total casualties on D-day, Allied and Axis, did not exceed three-quarters of the Antietam toll.

The engagement was a tactical draw; Lee's advance was halted and he then withdrew the Army of Northern Virginia southwards. Historian James M. McPherson in *Crossroads of Freedom: Antietam* (Oxford University Press, 2002) defined the Battle of Antietam as changing the course of the war.

> The Union victory, limited though it was, arrested Southern military momentum, reversed a disastrous decline in the morale of Northern soldiers and civilians, and offered Lincoln the opportunity to issue a proclamation of emancipation. . . . Foreign powers backed away from intervention and recognition, and never came close to considering them.

A self-guided nine-mile battlefield auto tour highlights main points of interest. The "witness" buildings of historical interest remaining after the battle's devastation are the Dunker Church and farmhouses and barns. Markers record sites of other farmhouses destroyed during the battle.

The Dunker Church (Church of the Brethren, or Dunkard) ranks as perhaps one of the most famous battlefield churches in American military history. Hundreds of men on both sides died as fighting swirled around this humble house of worship. Built in 1852 by local farmers, the congregation consisted of about half a dozen farm families from the local area. The structure is whitewashed brick of stark exterior with gable roof and plain windows, and interior simplicity (approximately 38 feet square in plan) with crude wooden benches arranged around a pot-bellied stove and reader's table. The church was heavily battle scarred with hundreds of bullet marks in its exterior walls and roof and walls damaged by artillery rounds. By 1864 the Church was repaired, rededicated, and regular services were held there until the turn of the twentieth century. The building was destroyed in a windstorm in 1921 and rebuilt by the National Park Service (NPS) in 1961 on the original foundations. Portions of original woodwork, pews, and bricks were incorporated into the construction.

Dunker Church

The Philip Pry House, built in 1844 on a knoll with commanding views of the area, served as the headquarters of General George B. McClellan. The design is typical of many Maryland vernacular Greek Revival two-and-a-half-story farmhouses with a central hall and a single room on either side with fireplaces. The main block of the L-plan red brick structure (40 by 28 feet in plan) with headers every sixth course on the front facade and common bond elsewhere, has a five-bay facade raised on a limestone foundation wall, with stone window sills and headers, shuttered windows, a restrained classical Greek Revival porch, and a gable roof and twin chimneys. The ell to the rear (40 by 28 feet in plan) has a two-story porch. The bank barn on the property (approximately 102 by 42 feet) with wagon shed extension, has a fieldstone ground floor at grade and wooden plank upper floor reached by ramp. Today, the restored Pry House contains exhibits sponsored by the National Museum of Civil War Medicine.

The Observation Tower built by the War Department in 1896 was part of early development efforts to create an open-air classroom at the battlefield. The 67-foot-tall cut limestone tower with observation platform under a wide-eaved pyramidal roof is located at a corner of "Bloody Lane" and is open except during inclement weather.

There are many interpretive markers and tablets in one of the best-preserved battlefields in the nation. There are ninety-six monuments at Antietam, the majority of which are Union. An intriguing sight is the mortuary cannon, barrels mounted on their muzzles in blocks of stone that mark the names and locations where generals were

Observation Tower   Maryland Monument

killed or mortally wounded during the battle. There are three for Confederate generals (Starke, Anderson, Branch) and three for Union generals (Mansfield, Richardson, and Rodman). Scattered around the park are over 500 cannons, possibly including some that participated in the battle, firing over 50,000 rounds of ammunition in cannonades so severe that Confederate artillery commander Colonel S.D. Lee described the battle as "artillery hell." The NPS is restoring elements of the battlefield, including post and rail and split rail fences, orchards, and trees that existed at the time of the battle.

Visitors to Antietam National Battlefield should begin a tour of the park at the Mission 66 Visitor Center, designed by William Cramp Scheetz, Jr., of Philadelphia and the Eastern Office of Design and Construction, (1961–62). An excellent orientation film, *Antietam Visit*, can be followed by a ranger talk, and the self-guided 8.5-mile driving tour with eleven stops beginning at the Dunker Church. Allow two to four hours for the tour and check at the visitor center for ranger talks and walks of the battlefield.

Chesapeake and Ohio Canal National Historical Park

The 184.5-mile-long park parallels the Potomac River between Washington, D.C. and Cumberland, Maryland.

→ www.nps.gov/choh

→ Visitor centers are located in Georgetown (Washington, D.C.) and Great Falls Tavern, Brunswick, Williamsport, Hancock, and Cumberland, Maryland.

The nation's outstanding preservation of the Chesapeake and Ohio Canal overcame a long period of neglect and several destructive floods—as recent as 1996—that now provides a recreational, historical, and natural pathway from tidewater at Georgetown in Washington, D.C., to Cumberland, Maryland on the Allegheny Plateau. Once an ambitiously conceived link between the eastern seaboard and the trans-Allegheny crossing beyond the original thirteen colonies, the canal thrived for a short period before becoming obsolete.

Great Falls Tavern

The original canal, now in various stages of restoration, consisted of seventy-four locks to raise it more than 600 feet at Cumberland, Maryland, winding its way through the Piedmont, past the dramatic Great Falls of the Potomac, and then through the ridges and valleys of the Appalachian Mountains. Today, the legacy of a bold scheme, one of many nationally in the first half of the nineteenth century, contains sections with quiet waters for canoeists, boaters, and anglers, and mule-drawn replica canal boat rides at Georgetown and Great Falls, Maryland. The towpath provides an almost level route for hiking, bicycling, boating, and horseback riding. The route is replete with an array of canal-related structures, including locks and lockhouses, aqueducts, dams, culverts, and the 3,118-foot-long Paw Paw Tunnel near Milepost 155.

The Chesapeake and Ohio Canal had its beginning on July 4, 1828. The grand scheme was to stretch from Georgetown to Pittsburgh, Pennsylvania, a 460-mile-long canal connecting the Chesapeake Bay and the Ohio River. Prophetically, the rival Baltimore and Ohio Railroad began construction on the same day as the canal. By the time canal construction was completed in 1850 at Cumberland, Maryland far short of the goal of Pittsburgh, the railroad had arrived there eight years earlier. Generally 50 to 60 feet at the 12-foot-wide towpath level, a minimum of 6 feet deep, and locks 15 feet wide and 100 feet long, the canal was obsolete by the time it was finished. The Civil War disrupted operations and major flooding in 1889 caused further costly damage. Finally, severe flooding in 1924 drove the canal company into bankruptcy, ending operations and drawing to a close a way of life for those dependent on the canal.

A famous episode in the canal's protection and revitalization is the eight-day hike of the entire canal led by Supreme Court Justice William O. Douglas in March of 1954. Prompted by the threat to a favorite hiking route by paving over to create a parkway, Douglas challenged a *Washington Post* editor to join him on a hike from Georgetown to Cumberland. The hike, with thirty-seven other people, led to a public outpouring of support for protecting the canal.

A visible reminder of the canal's active days is the historical lockhouses seen today at some of the locks. Construction on a total of fifty-seven lockhouses began soon after the canal company started work in the summer of 1828. Along the canal's earliest section the houses were built of stone, a standard one-and-a-half-stories, and approximately 18 by 30 feet in plan; above the Monocacy Aqueduct the company ran into dwindling supplies of quality stone and construction money and shifted lockhouse construction to brick, wood-frame, and logs. Not all locks had houses for the lockkeepers; several locations with multiple locks in succession had a single lockkeeper's house.

Lockhouse No. 2

The structures now discovered along the towpath are in various states of repair and with non-historical additions, some sites are marked only by rubble and foundation stones, and other houses are no longer visible. Today, there is evidence of fifty-two houses and only twenty-six of those are standing. The largest number of houses, some restored or stabilized by the National Park Service (NPS) and through local partnerships, such as the Potomac Conservancy, is in the section between Lock 5 and Lock 28, and accessed from MacArthur Boulevard or River Road.

A prominent example, although atypical of the standard design, is the Great Falls Tavern at Lock 20 now serving as a visitor center (temporarily closed to 2008). The elegant Federal style whitewashed brick structure, opened in 1831, and enlarged as a

Lockhouse No. 75

Paw Paw Tunnel

hotel for canal travelers, became the social center for a small community. A visit to the tavern's park-like setting, functioning locks, mule-drawn canal boat rides, and the short walk to the Great Falls of the Potomac overlook is an attractive outing when in the capital area.

A fine example of a restored stone lockhouse is at Lock 8, across Seven Locks Road near Cabin John, Maryland. The whitewashed structure with a basement, first floor divided by a large fireplace into a living room and kitchen, and a second floor divided into two large bedrooms stands alongside the towpath. Wooden front and back porches were added in the early 1900s. Other stone lockhouses in good condition are at Locks 6, 10, 11, 21 (Swain's Lock), 22 (Pennyfield), and 24 (Riley's Lock). The Lockhouse at Lock 10 is used as private residences and the residents' privacy should be respected. Further north are examples of restored brick lockhouses at Locks 25 (Edwards Ferry) and 29 (Lander) used seasonally for educational and interpretive programs. A good example of wood-frame structures is the whitewashed Lockhouse No. 44 at Williamsport, built as a division superintendent's house. At the northern end of the canal at Lock 75 is an NPS reconstructed log lockhouse.

The final link between Georgetown and Cumberland was the Paw Paw Tunnel designed to by-pass a winding six-mile stretch of the Potomac River known as the Paw Paw Bends. Dug 3,118 feet through troublesome hard loose shale, the tunnel's original contract was for a two-year project. Eventually, construction of the brick-lined narrow one-lane channel took fourteen years to complete. Today, a 20-minute walk takes the visitor through the arched interior of the canal's largest and most impressive structure.

Clara Barton National Historic Site

Glen Echo, Montgomery County, Maryland

→ www.nps.gov/clba

→ The park is located in Glen Echo, Maryland, three miles north of the District of Columbia. Adjacent to Glen Echo Park, access is via MacArthur Boulevard and Oxford Road or from Interstate 495/Beltway Exit 43 at Cabin John to the Clara Barton Parkway; follow signs to the parking lot.

Clara Barton House

Clara Barton, founder of the American Red Cross, lived in this unusual yellow house on a bluff overlooking the Potomac River for fifteen years until her death at age ninety in 1912. The famous humanitarian was a controversial figure, a mixture of selfless devotion tempered by self-doubt and an irrepressible fear of delegating authority. Her singular activities close to the battle lines in the Civil War at Second Bull Run, Antietam (see page 456), and Fredericksburg and Spotsylvania County (see page 412); the Franco-Prussian War; in national natural disasters; and during the Spanish-American War, were part of the legend embellished by the struggle to successfully establish the American Red Cross in 1881. Although she always managed her relief activities in a highly personal style, Barton's reputation as "Angel of the Battlefield" and resourcefulness is unchallenged among historic American women.

A Matthew Brady photograph of Miss Barton taken in 1866 captures a straightforward confrontation with the camera, an attractive woman in her mid-forties standing erect with one hand firmly grasping a chair and her other hand with finger pointing downward as though poised to be raised to give directions. Her chin is proudly held square with the camera; piercing dark eyes veil the experienced horrors of the battlefield; and softening her countenance is a controlled smile that would have been a welcome sight to the wounded and dying.

The National Park Service (NPS) official National Park Handbook to this site, *Clara Barton*, describes the character of this extraordinary person photographed by Brady:

> She was a remarkable woman. She was neither the Christ-like figure Dr. Hubbell idolized, nor the grasping Red Cross potentate that others saw. She was an individual capable of firm action, strong beliefs, and an ability to see a need clearly and fulfill it. To everything she did—schoolteaching, Civil War aid, and Red Cross relief—she brought strong idealism and unfailing energy. She was truly exceptional.

The Clara Barton House on its 8.6-acre site has an intriguing exterior and an equally curious arrangement of interior space. The evolution of the three-story wood-frame house, dating from 1891, originated with the dismantling of a warehouse used as an emergency relief building for the Johnstown Flood in 1889 and its lumber shipped to Glen Echo, Maryland. The offer by Brothers Edward and Edwin Baltzley, founders of a combined large suburban development and educational center (a Chautauqua Assembly) at Glen Echo Park, was a dual gift of a parcel of land for Miss Barton to build construction of any structure of her choice, in exchange for permission to use her name and the name of the Red Cross in the advertising for the Glen Echo Chautauqua. The offer fitted Barton's desire to build a new headquarters for the Red Cross.

A design by Miss Barton's chief field agent and an amateur architect, Dr. Julian B. Hubbell, created a warehouse with living quarters and an elaborate 48 feet wide Potomac granite facade with a central door flanked by narrow windows to harmonize with planned Chautauqua buildings. The second story also had narrow windows and a red brick cross set within an arched wall and a third floor "lantern" room was added. In this manner, the footprint of the approximately 89- by 49-foot structure and framing system was established. Although Barton temporarily moved into the house in the summer of 1891, commuting to and from Washington was too taxing and the house at Glen Echo was used primarily as a warehouse.

Extension of electric trolley lines to Glen Echo in 1897 improved access and extensive remodeling created today's National Historic Landmark structure. Much of the stone facade was removed, a wooden one built in its place and windows, and the red cross windows on the third floor were installed. The cellar was excavated to a more substantial size (using the dismantled stone facade as material for the foundation walls) and the third-floor 18-foot-wide gallery of rooms running the length of the house was suspended from the roof rafters. The clapboard exterior was painted a warm yellow; window, doorframes, and decorative woodwork were painted white; and a white-trimmed porch was added to the front. When completed, it was a three-and-a-half story frame structure with twin tin-capped granite towers and a false gable in the front. Interior partitions are built of wooden bead board, simple vertical planks, and board-and-batten walls, with a variety of molding styles. Floors are random width pine boards, and ceilings are covered with cotton muslin, painted and unpainted, or plaster. Cupboards lining the first floor hall were used for storing Red Cross supplies.

The Glen Echo House served as the American Red Cross headquarters from 1897 until Miss Barton's resignation as president in 1904 at age eighty-three. The history of the house from this time is muddied by criticism over her management of the American Red Cross. Passed on through a succession of owners, the effects of the conversion to apartments prior to acquisition by the NPS in 1979 is gradually being undone. Original furniture and Miss Barton's memorabilia are seen throughout the house during guided tours.

A short walk from the Clara Barton House is Glen Echo Park, also a unit of the National Park System, and not treated separately in this book. A popular recreation place for generations of Washingtonians, remaining elements of the 1890s amusement park in use into the early 1960s managed in cooperation with Montgomery County now serve as a revitalized community resource and include the Chautauqua Stone Tower, the Yellow Barn, the Dentzel Carousel (summertime operations), the Bumper Car Pavilion, the Spanish Ballroom, the Arcade complex, the Cuddle Up, the remnants of the Crystal Pool, and the Picnic Grove.

Fort McHenry National Monument and Historic Shrine

Baltimore City, Maryland

→   www.nps.gov/fomc

→   The fort is two miles from downtown Baltimore via Light Street, Key Highway, Lawrence Street, and East Fort Avenue. For access from Interstate 95, take Exit 55 and take Key Highway, Lawrence Street, or East Fort Avenue to reach the visitor center parking lot.

Stars and Stripes over Fort McHenry ramparts

Fort McHenry is probably one of the best-known forts in the United States. It was here that the thirty-five-year-old lawyer from Washington, Francis Scott Key, came on a mission to release a hostage held on a British warship at the mouth of Baltimore harbor and witnessed the fort's bombardment. From aboard ship he watched a relentless, twenty-five-hour bombardment pounding on the fort. Guns and mortars thundered, traceries of shells and terrifying Congreve rockets glowed against the underside of low rain clouds and, yet, the fort's thick brick walls remained standing.

At dawn, Key trained a spyglass on the fort and saw that the Stars and Stripes—an intentionally oversized 42- by 30-foot flag with fifteen stars and stripes—was still flying over the battlements. Overjoyed at the sight, Key jotted down a few poetic lines describing his excitement over the glorious triumph of the fort's defense, which he later incorporated into a full-length poem published a few days later as *The Defense of Fort M'Henry*—sung to the tune, *To Anachreon in Heaven*. Renamed *The Star Spangled Banner* and reprinted in newspapers from Maine to Georgia, the song continued to grow in popularity.

One cannot help but be stirred when standing at the fort's parapet, on a day when the fifteen stars-and-stripes flag is snapping in a seaborne breeze, looking down the Patapsco River at the anchorage site of the bombarding British fleet. There are many other forts in the National Park System of historic significance, but Fort McHenry provides a unique visitor experience enhanced by a lack of any encroaching modern features, the respectful distance of parking lots and restrained visitor center, and the manicured grounds surrounding the sloped walls of the brick-faced fort. A superb restoration by the National Park Service (NPS) and ongoing maintenance retains the character of the more than two-centuries-old fortification of classic star-shaped plan with projecting bastions.

French engineer Jean Foncin designed the fort as an improvement on incomplete earlier designs to defend Baltimore. Construction began in 1799 with federal funds approved by the eponymous Secretary of War James McHenry and was completed by 1802 and retained the same appearance until after the battle of September 13–14, 1814, during the War of 1812.

A pentagon in plan with five bastions for overlapping fire, and surrounded by a moat 35 to 55 feet wide, brick walls (scarp) covering earth fill averaged 12 feet in height. Walls between the bastions are approximately 120 feet long; bastion side walls 40 feet long, and the bastions front and leading edges 75 feet long. Stone quoins at bastion corners provided a decorative touch. A grass covered parapet and bastions (planked in 1814) at the rampart level enclosed an interior parade ground. The flagpole was located on the parade ground to one side of the sally port entrance. Interior garrison buildings included Commanding Officer's Office and Quarters, Powder Magazine (taking a direct hit by an unexploding British mortar bomb), Officers' Quarters, and Number 1 and 2 Soldiers' Barracks. The freestanding triangular *ravelin* protecting the fort's entrance was added a year before the battle. Post-bombardment additions include the sally port, casemates (internal bomb proof chambers), and guardrooms.

Significant as an American high point in the War of 1812, the failed attack on Baltimore saved the city from the fate of burned out Washington, D.C. Summertime activities include cannon-firing demonstrations, volunteer Fort McHenry Guard living-history reenactments and special Flag Day (June 14) celebrations. Defender's Day (September 8) marks the anniversary of the battle and is commemorated with a symbolic ship-to-shore bombardment, a concert of patriotic music, and fireworks show.

Fort Washington Park

Fort Washington, Prince George's County, Maryland

→ www.nps.gov/fowa

→ From Washington, D.C., the park may be reached via Capital Beltway (Interstate 495) to Exit 3 (Indian
Head Highway or Maryland 210); at traffic light at end of exit turn left (Maryland 210 South) continue for
approximately four miles to Fort Washington Road, turn right, follow to the park entrance.

Fort Washington Park (courtesy HABS/HAER)

The 341-acre Fort Washington Park is a superb open space on the Maryland side of the
Potomac River six miles south of Washington, D.C. This prime location for the defense
of the capital reputedly selected by George Washington in 1794 and, coincidentally,
across the Potomac from Mount Vernon, is on a bluff commanding approaches up and
downriver. A many-layered, two-century history of coastal defense driven by new strategies and technology is visible in this outstanding example of early-nineteenth-century
fortifications amidst well-groomed park grounds in a superb restoration by the National
Park Service (NPS).

   The first redoubt on the site was Fort Warburton, built in 1809 as part of the young
country's effort to defend its ports and harbors. During the War of 1812 the fort was
abandoned upon the attack and subsequent capture of the City of Washington, and the
fort blown up to prevent falling into the hands of the British. Within a month, work
began under the direction of acting Secretary of War James Monroe, who commissioned
the temperamental designer Pierre-Charles L'Enfant to design a new and more robust
fortification to be named Fort Washington. L'Enfant, the celebrated creator of the plan
for Washington, D.C., adopted a star-shaped plan following classic French fortification

design pioneered by Sèbastien Le Preste de Vauban. Disagreement between Monroe and L'Enfant about costs and design and the latter's replacement in 1815 by Colonel W. K. Armistead, and then a lessening concern about the defense of Washington, slowed construction until finally declared complete in October 1824. About twenty years later, the fort was strengthened structurally and by the placement of eighty-eight gun platforms.

During the early years of the Civil War the fort was the only river defense for the capital; however, despite the massive brick walls and commanding position high above the river introduction of rifled cannon forced the fortress into obsolescence and by 1872 it was abandoned. Coastal defense fortifications never left the strategies for protecting America's ports and rivers, and armaments were added at Fort Washington through the Spanish-American War. Various uses for training in World War II, garrisoning Washington area troops, Veterans Administration use of part of the buildings and other buildings as public housing ended in 1946 with transfer to the Department of the Interior.

Today, the fort's apparent isolation as seen from Mount Vernon across the Potomac or from the river is deceptive. The area was rural until about 1960 when suburban development began and continues, adding many oversized luxury riverfront homes near the fort. Still, the formidable brick bastion walls with stone corner quoins and gun embrasures, some 70 feet above the Potomac and 7 feet thick, are sheltered from surrounding development by parkland and provide a moving experience.

The yellow stuccoed two-story visitor center rises upward to a swell of land and a view of the brick walls of the Northwest and Northeast Bastions and the main gate, a resplendent towering Roman-inspired stone structure with central entrance arch, engaged Doric columns, and flanking stone walls. A dry moat protects the outer walls from the river, a drawbridge spanning through the main gate and onto the parade ground.

L'Enfant's plan adapted the customary star-like, five-sided fortification design to the river site. Here, a four-bastion scheme places the Northwest and Northeast Bastions prominently facing north, the subordinate Northeast and Southeast Bastions providing additional protection from land or water. The Northwest and Northeast Bastions are unusual by projecting beyond the river-facing curtain wall and forming a deep open space between the parade ground edge and the bastion gun platform level.

Tucked into the corners of the parade ground near the Northeast and Southeast (landward) Bastions, respectively, are the well-designed and restored Officers' Quarters and Soldiers' Barracks. These two-story brick structures have elegant porches with white-painted columns and railings on front and rear elevations. A guided tour of these structures, along the bastion promenades, gun platforms, and casemates illustrates the various periods of defense strategies and subsequent modifications to the fort.

Fort Washington has an extensive living-history program with period-clothed reenactors and regularly scheduled firing demonstrations. This is a dual attraction for the historical fortifications and a recreational facility for the greater Washington area. Picknicking and hiking on the grounds is encouraged.

Hampton National Historic Site

Towson, Baltimore County, Maryland

→   www.nps.gov/hamp

→   The site is located ten miles north of downtown Baltimore and accessible from 695, Interstate 70, and Interstate 95. From the Baltimore Beltway (Interstate 695) take Exit 27-B, Dulaney Valley Road northbound toward Towson, Maryland, turn right on Hampton Lane and proceed to the parking area.

Hampton Mansion cupola

Acclaimed as one of America's great houses, the elegant mansion at Hampton National Historic Site is an exuberant display of eighteenth-century Georgian Colonial architecture. Once the center of a vast agricultural and commercial estate, the setting on a hilltop surrounded by more than sixty acres of manicured grounds and nearby farm buildings, now amidst suburban Towson, Maryland, is a delightful discovery for the traveler in the Baltimore area.

Built between 1783 and 1790 by Charles Ridgely and owned by the family for more than 150 years, the house is notable for its tremendous scale and conformity to the Georgian formula for classical detail and balanced effect: rigid symmetry, a five-part composition, axial entrances, pedimented gable ends, and sash windows. Add to this pedimented two-story porticos front and back, dormers and urns on each side of the pediments, coupled chimneys at the ends, and a giant ornate cupola atop the ridge. Two-story dependencies, laterally, with the one-story hyphens, extend the overall length to 175 feet. The overall impression of the mansion when first completed, prominent on the hill and before extensive plantings were put in place in the nineteenth century, was a spectacular sight.

No architect is recorded as the house designer. A talented master carpenter, Jehu Howell, guided the owner in the design, influenced by examples in the colonies and England, and probably an extensive collection of reference books.

Today's visitor should approach the building by walking around the exterior and begin to taste its opulent delights, savoring the building and terraced formal and herb gardens like a fine meal. The simple basic volume is built of local stone quarried on Ridgely property and is stuccoed in a terra-cotta pink color derived from the iron bearing sand used in the stucco, unlike typical Maryland Georgian houses with brick exteriors. Note the richness of details that may escape the eye at first viewing: Palladian windows and doors at the entrances; portico gables, and dormers; exterior windows set in classical elements of architraves, friezes, and cornices; massively proportioned dormers buttressed by decorative scrolls; elaborate faux windows applied on the chimneys as a trompe l'oeil effect; decorative urns over-scaled to appear as crowning finials; second-story portico Chippendale railings; and the massively proportioned cupola containing a large chamber for views over Hampton lands in all directions.

The vastly scaled interior matches the exuberance of the exterior. The central pavilion has large public rooms. The central hall, 22 feet wide, 53 feet long, and more than 13 feet high, was designed for entertaining, served as a banquet hall (seating fifty), a ballroom, and art gallery. The main staircase, unlike a central placement typical of five-part Georgian houses, was located between two parlors and left the central hall unencumbered. A music room and drawing room completed the four formal ground floor parlors. Walls and ceilings throughout the house are plastered with richly detailed carved or molded wood cornices, chairrails, wainscoting, and baseboards. First floor flooring is precisely cut and placed pine boards. The second floor, originally with six large bedchambers, has a central passage with amazingly rich architectural details of fluted columns and doors crowned with broken pediments. Four storage closets facing

Slave quarters

the hall, once used for guest's clothing, are now exhibit cases. The one-story hyphens, to the east and west of the central pavilion, contained, respectively, the kitchen and reception room.

Much of the furniture is original, the house remaining in the Ridgely family's six-generation ownership until acquired by the Avalon Foundation and transferred to the National Park Service (NPS) in 1948. The superb Baltimore dining room furniture, and the many fine Ridgely family paintings exemplify the house's museum quality collection. The house was completely restored by the NPS and furnishings meticulously placed according to original house inventories. Docent-led tours are recommended to

learn about the owners and the house collections, as well as the labor force and economic system that made this lifestyle possible. The east wing now serves as a gift shop to
browse before setting out to view the ground's many specimen trees, and the parterres

Log farm building

Ridgely Farm House

below the Great Terrace gardens. Note the earth-covered, 34-foot-deep domed icehouse
and reconstructed orangerie to the west and north of the mansion.

Across Hampton Lane is the farm area, once part of the thousands of acres of Ridgely farmland. The Farm House (Lower House), occupied by the Ridgelys in the eighteenth
century, was altered several times, including an addition made when the sixth genera-
tion owners moved from the mansion to the farm in 1948 where they remained until
1978. Three late antebellum slave quarters, two of stone and the third of logs, represent
housing for the plantation's enslaved workers who numbered up to 200 in the 1800s and
functioned in a variety of agricultural, domestic, and industrial capacities. The two-story
Long House Granary of exposed local stone was rebuilt in the nineteenth century. Other
historic structures on site include a dairy, mule barn, two stables, greenhouses, a garden
maintenance building, a caretaker's cottage, and a variety of small domestic structures.

Thomas Stone National Historic Site

Near La Plata, Charles County, Maryland

→   www.nps.gov/thst

→   Located in southern Maryland about thirty-five miles south of Washington, D.C., between the Potomac
and Chesapeake Rivers. From US 301 at La Plata, take Maryland 6 west three miles and turn north on Rose
Hill Road for one mile to the visitor center.

Thomas Stone, born in 1743, was a prosperous Maryland landowner and moderately successful lawyer when passion against the Crown began to sweep the colonies in 1775. Stone
literally wrote himself into history as a Founding Father, one of four Maryland Declaration
of Independence signers whose patriotism exceeded concern for his plantation, Haberde-
venture (alternatively in the French, *Habre-de-Ventre*, "dwelling place in the winds").

A fine example of colonial Maryland architecture, Stone's National Historic Land-mark house is modest in comparison to some Tidewater plantations. Stone purchased the property in 1770 as a home for his young family. Although there is an uncertain

Thomas Stone House, south elevation

history of construction, probably beginning around 1771 and completed in stages, an unusual feature is the arc formed by the handsome assemblage of a five-part Georgian design with wings and connecting hyphens built at angles to the central block, forming a forecourt facing to the south.

Considered a deliberate person in thought and action, in 1774 Stone was elected a member of the Charles County Committee of Correspondence, charged with keeping in touch with the other colonies as tensions mounted against Great Britain. Beginning in 1775 he was chosen to serve in the Continental Congress and, although little is known of his service, he was a member of the committee that framed the Articles of Confed-eration. Originally a "moderate" opposed to war, he became convinced to stand with the rebels and voted for and signed the Declaration of Independence. He served as a Continental Congress delegate until 1778 and again in 1783–84. Stone moved with his terminally ill wife, Margaret, and family to Annapolis in 1783. His death followed his wife's by four months, in 1787, at age forty-four.

Today, the plantation house's north elevation is first seen poised on a slight rise, at the end of a long entrance drive and then from the visitor center discretely screened by a line of trees. The modest two-story brick central block, defined by a gambrel roof with three dormers in the shingle-shake roof, a one-story porch across the full 46-foot length, and tall gable-end engaged chimneys, is flanked by hyphens connecting differ-ent sized wings. The total length from end-to-end is approximately 140 feet. A similar approximately 10-foot-wide one-story porch on brick piers is on the south elevation. The gambrel roof, uncommon in Tidewater plantation houses, was common to smaller farm homes in the area.

One-story hyphens connected at the central block south corners vary in length and width. The smaller east hyphen is a false passageway that conceals the entrance to a crawl space and visually connects the original farm house (east wing) on the property to the home's central block. Stone added the west hyphen for additional living quarters and used the west wing as a kitchen. The two-story wing (approximately 32 by 18 feet) has a gable shake-shingled roof, brick gable ends, and white clapboard sidewalls. This was a later addition to the home and dates from the 1840s following a kitchen fire that destroyed the original west wing.

The woodwork in the original handsomely paneled ground floor parlor was removed from the house and installed in the Baltimore Museum of Art in 1928. In 1977 the central block and west hyphen and wing was severely damaged by a fire. The National Park Service, acquiring the property after the fire in 1981, restored the damaged portions and reopened the Thomas Stone National Historic Site to the public in 1997. The site contains barns and outbuildings, pleasant walking trails, and the Stone family cemetery.

New Jersey

Mid-Atlantic

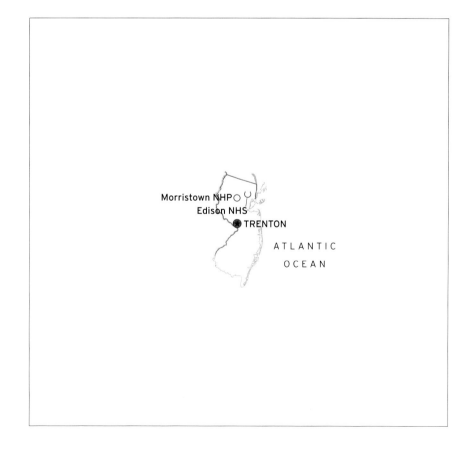

Morristown NHP ○
Edison NHS
● TRENTON

ATLANTIC
OCEAN

Edison National Historic Site

West Orange, New Jersey, Essex County

→ www.nps.gov/edis

→ Located in northeastern New Jersey fifteen miles west of New York City. The site is accessed via the Garden State Parkway (Exit 145), New Jersey Turnpike (Interstate 95, Exit 15W), and Interstate 280 (Exit 9 Eastbound, Exit 10 Westbound) to Main Street and follow signs to visitor center.

Glenmont, the Thomas Edison estate

Born in Milan, Ohio in 1847, Thomas Alva Edison's life is the stuff of an American legend. One of the most famous and prolific inventors of all time, he exerted a tremendous influence on modern life, contributing inventions such as the incandescent light bulb, the phonograph, and the motion picture camera, as well as improving the telegraph and telephone. An eccentric genius, Edison used the laboratories he built to manufacture his inventions, generating funds to sponsor his inventing. In his eighty-four years he created 1,097 U.S. patents—the record still stands for an individual—but along the way he invented the modern research and development laboratory, set up with the specific purpose of producing constant technological innovation and improvement.

The Edison National Historic Site includes the impressive Edison estate, Glenmont, on a ridge less than one mile from the red brick laboratory complex including a chemistry lab, machine shop, library, and a replica of the world's first motion picture studio building.

Edison attended school for only a short time and his mother withdrew him from school and taught him at home. At an early age, he showed a fascination for mechanical things and for chemical experiments. He was independent at age twelve, working on railroads where he learned telegraphy and experimented to improve the equipment's performance. After moving to Boston in 1868 he became a full-time inventor. His first invention to receive a patent was the electric vote recorder, in June of 1869. Daunted by politicians' reluctance to use the machine, he decided that in the future he would not waste time inventing things that no one wanted. Edison moved to New York City in the middle of 1869 and then into his first laboratory in Newark, New Jersey, in 1870. At age twenty-nine he built his second laboratory in Menlo Park, New Jersey, considered to be the first private research and development laboratory in the world. There, invention of a telephone transmitter, the phonograph, the first practical incandescent lamp, and the power system to illuminate it earned him the nickname of "Wizard of Menlo Park."

Edison moved into the West Orange mansion in 1886 and the laboratory complex was finished a year later. The twenty-nine-room Glenmont was built in 1880 on a four-teen-acre estate by Henry Peder and designed by Henry Hudson Holly. A widowed Edison purchased it soon after marrying his second wife Mina Miller. The house is an epic version of the suburban mansion of the 1880s in the Queen Anne style, devoid of some of the excesses of Victorian-era turrets and stylistic elements. The three-story house, with an attic and basement, has an irregular L-shaped plan with many projections and indentations. A dizzying array of intersecting gables (some shingled), porches, balconies, tall brick chimneys with corbelled tops, and terra-cotta decorations, are bound together by a ground-level base of bluestone foundation wall, slate roof, and a deep rose toned first floor with pressed brick walls and mortar joints, and wood-frame upper floor exterior walls.

The first floor entrance leads to a large foyer with fireplace and wide staircase. Rooms are generously proportioned, well-lit by tall windows, and typically with elaborate carved wood paneling. Frescoed ceilings, large chandeliers, and stained glass windows appear in many first and second floor rooms. The tastes of the day are made evident by many of the original furnishings in place, including animal rugs, damask-covered furniture, statuary, paintings, and gifts from around the world. The expansive grounds with greenhouses, barns, stables, and garage completed the country estate.

Main laboratory building

Today, the West Orange laboratory is an enclave of industrial brick buildings in the midst of a busy urban area. The original five, one-story brick buildings were Edison's "Invention Factory," bringing together in one complex the literature, machinery, materials, instruments, and talents to conduct systematic research. The buildings housed a machine shop, experiment rooms, library, and individual chemistry, physics, and metallurgy labs. The style of the three-story main building is an understated Renaissance Revival appearance, noticeable by the tall arched windows, pilastered chimneys, and free-standing brick smokestack. The library located in the east wing of the main laboratory building is a three-story hall with a thirty-foot ceiling and two tiers of galleries rising from its main floor. Filled with a valuable collection of working experiments, artifacts, and archives of such great volume that it presents a challenge for the National Park Service (NPS) staff to catalogue and control.

Restoration of the laboratory buildings is an ongoing process that includes the artifact cataloguing and preservation process. Building 11, a small wood-frame building unlike others in the complex, is one aspect of the restoration. Built in 1899, the structure was used by Edison for metallurgical experiments and later adapted for other uses. Building 11 was disassembled in 1940 and shipped to the Henry Ford Museum in Michigan, where it languished unused until recently returned to the NPS and placed near its original location.

The recently restored mansion and part of the laboratories are open to public tours. An attraction always drawing attentive visitors is the Black Maria, a replica of the world's first motion picture studio in use from 1893 to 1903. It was built on a turntable so the window could rotate toward the sun throughout the day, supplying natural light for hundreds of Edison movie productions over its eight-year life.

Morristown National Historical Park

Morristown, Morris County, New Jersey

→ www.nps.gov/morr

→ The park's four units located in and near Morristown in north central New Jersey are accessed via Interstate 287; Washington's Headquarters and Museum in Morristown from Exit 36 (Morris Avenue) and the visitor center at Jockey Hollow from Exit 30B (Bernardsville).

During two critical winters of the Revolutionary War, the Continental Army struggled to survive in the countryside in and around the quiet village of Morristown, New Jersey. After the triumphs at Trenton and Princeton, George Washington led the army to the strategically located village, west of the Watchung Mountains, into winter encampment. From January to May 1777, protected from the British Army split between New Brunswick and New York City, thirty miles away, the army prepared to take the field again. In 1779–80 Washington and the army returned to Morristown and endured the region's severest winter of the eighteenth century. Here, the inadequately clothed soldiers faced bitter cold, hunger, hardship, and disease, and Washington and his officers led the army through a time of one of its severest trials. Although two more winters were to pass before the Revolution's end, Morristown's major role in the war had concluded.

During the second encampment ten thousand soldiers built more than a thousand log huts for their barracks area called Jockey Hollow, a few miles southwest of Morristown.

Washington's headquarters in Morristown was located at the Ford Mansion, a large house near what was then the edge of town. The other senior commanders and officers lodged in private homes in and around the village.

Washington's Headquarters and Museum   Ford Mansion

Today, a visit to Morristown National Historical Park (the first National Historical Park, designated in 1933) begins at the visitor center at the Jockey Hollow unit. Roads loop through this area of the park with sites at Henry Wick's farmhouse that served as headquarters for General Arthur St. Clair; the Pennsylvania Brigade encampment with a representative cluster of restored log huts; and the Grand Parade used for ceremonies, training, and discipline. From the Jockey Hollow unit, part of Patriots Path leads southwestward to the New Jersey Brigade encampment site. To the northeast of Jockey Hollow, Western Avenue leads to the Fort Nonsense unit, a crest of land fortified with earthworks to protect the town. An unlikely legend says that Washington set his men to fortify the hill simply as a way of keeping troops busy, but its purpose is clear by original designation as the Upper Redoubt. From Fort Nonsense, visitors may drive to Washington's Headquarters (Ford Mansion) and Museum unit approximately one mile east of Morristown Green in the center of town. (All routes between the park units are well marked.)

Reconstructed examples of the hastily erected log structures built in the winter of 1779–80 are seen on the Pennsylvania Line overlooking Jockey Hollow. The Pennsylvania Brigade encampment huts are 14 by 16 feet in plan and intended to house twelve men.

Near the visitor center is the restored Wick House, a comfortable farmhouse built circa 1750. The Cape Cod style, probably adopted by Wick from his New England origins, a one-and-a-half-story wood-frame structure (approximately 40 by 30 feet in plan), was slightly larger than the average local farmhouse of the area at the time of the Revolutionary War. The front elevation is shingled, side and rear walls clapboard and the roof shake shingled with a center chimney. Period-clothed reenactors interpret the colonial atmosphere of the farm itself, as reflected in the nearby garden, barnyard, orchard, and open fields. Wood shingled walls and a shake-shingle roof with center chimney were typical of vernacular buildings of the region and the period.

Morristown's finest house was built by Colonel Jacob Ford, Jr., an influential local citizen who died on January 10, 1777. His widow and four children offered the hospitality of her home to General and Mrs. Washington for use as a residence and headquarters

Pennsylvania Line Soldier Huts

Wick House

in early December 1779. Known as the Ford Mansion, or more properly Washington's Headquarters, the house is an excellent example of late colonial architecture in wood. The five-bay center hall plan has a Palladian entry beneath a Palladian window and bold cornice above, the more pronounced as set against the front facade's flush siding. The house's other sides are sheathed in clapboard siding. The symmetry of the two-story house, emphasized by the hip roof and pair of chimneys projecting above the roof ridgeline, is relatively undisturbed by the recessed kitchen wing. The first floor rooms in the main section of the house on the west side were converted into an office, meeting rooms, and dining space for Washington and his staff. A complete restoration and refurnishing by the National Park Service (NPS) is in the time of the Washingtons' use of the house.

Housed in a separate building to the rear of the Ford Mansion is a Historical Museum designed by architect John Russell Pope in collaboration with NPS Branch of Plans and Designs and built between 1935 and 1937. A slightly scaled-down interpretation of Mount Vernon, General Washington's home in Virginia, the one-story hip-roofed structure with light yellow colored stucco walls, standing seam copper roof, and cupola has a diminuitive charm with its interplay of classical elements on the exterior walls. The museum contains exhibition rooms displaying collections associated with the Revolutionary War period in Morristown.

The hardy traveler is encouraged to experience the park, often when there are Jockey Hollow encampment reenactments with period-clothed interpreters. Driving the two-mile loop road tour offers opportunities for making stops and reflecting on the times when hardy patriots and their leaders persevered to return to the battlefield and gain the country's independence.

New York

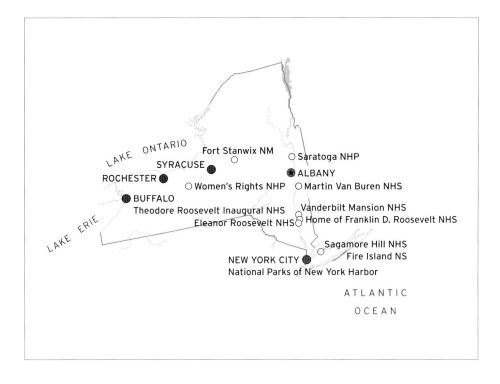

Eleanor Roosevelt National Historic Site

Hyde Park, Dutchess County, New York

→ www.nps.gov/elro

→ This site is located on the east side of the Hudson River about six miles north of Poughkeepsie, New York, and south of the village of Hyde Park, on New York 9G.

Val-Kill pond and cottage

Val-Kill's picturesque bridge and dam on the Fall Kill was originally a favorite picnic spot of Eleanor Roosevelt and her family and friends. In 1924, Franklin Roosevelt suggested that his wife build a cottage on this part of the Roosevelt estate to enjoy year-round with her friends Nancy Cook and Marion Dickerman. The spot is two miles from Springwood (see page 486), the imposing Roosesvelt country home near Hyde Park, New York. FDR described his wife's ambition for a cottage on land he offered the women for their life-time use:

> My Missus and some of her female political friends want to build a shack on a stream in the back woods and want, instead of a beautiful marble bath, to have the stream dug out so as to form an old-fashioned swimming hole.

In 1925, architect Henry Toombs of the firm of McKim, Mead & White designed a small fieldstone cottage near the stream on the property the Roosevelts named Val-Kill, a combination of the Dutch word for "stream" (Kill) and its English translation (valley stream). The cottage, built of local fieldstone and designed with the close supervision of FDR, is typical of Hudson River Valley early farmhouses. The simple, vernacular building included an enclosesd porch facing the Val-Kill Pond and a swimming pool, and was later expanded to include additional first floor living space and a rear laundry.

In the next year, Mrs. Roosevelt built a second, larger building on the site to house Val-Kill Industries, an experimental business to train farm youth in the art of cabinet making in an effort to supplement their farming incomes. The business produced high quality replicas of Early American furniture, pewter, and weavings. When the factory closed in 1936 Mrs. Roosevelt remodeled the building as a residence. To her, "the cottage was an adjunct to our lives at Hyde Park, but it was mine and I felt freer there than in the big house."

Val-Kill became Mrs. Roosevelt's primary home after her husband's death in 1945, and was treasured by her as a sanctuary until her death in 1962. The rambling structure, comprised of twenty rooms, provided apartments for herself and her secretary, Malvina "Tommy" Thompson, a dining room, seven bedrooms, a dormitory for young people, two large porches downstairs, and a sleeping porch upstairs.

The furnished cottage resembles its original appearance when Eleanor Roosevelt occupied it, and reflects the comfortable, cozy atmosphere she cherished. Seen throughout the cottage are personal memorabilia and furniture produced by Val-Kill Industries. The decor includes many personal photographs of family, political associates, foreign heads of state, and guests from around the United States and the world. Adjacent exhibit spaces and a shop have recently been refurbished by the National Park Service.

During her residence at Val-Kill, Mrs. Roosevelt served as a U.S. delegate to the United Nations General Assembly where she chaired the Human Rights Commission (1946–52), and continued to be a powerful force in the Democratic Party. She produced her daily "My Day" newspaper column begun in 1936 until shortly before her death, she lectured at Brandeis University, discussed crucial issues on numerous radio and television programs, wrote books, and traveled widely. The significance of Eleanor Roosevelt's human rights work and her political prominence are evident in the candid photographs with Adlai Stevenson, labor leader Walter Reuther, and John F. Kennedy, who sought her support for his 1960 presidential campaign.

The Stone Cottage

The site's other, earlier cottage now houses the offices of the Eleanor Roosevelt Center at Val-Kill (ERVK), a non-profit organization devoted to promoting economic and social justice, the need for civic involvement in a democratic society, and the empowerment of women.

The Val-Kill property comprised of 180 acres of woods, fields, marshes, and ponds is open for public use year-round, and is linked to both Springwood and Top Cottage by public woodland trails.

Fire Island National Seashore

Patchogue, Suffolk County, New York

→ www.nps.gov/fiis

→ Fire Island is located on the south shore of Long Island, New York, with driving access from the west via Interstate 495 or NY 28 via Robert Moses Parkway, and from the east via William Floyd Parkway. Ferry access is from the south shore of Long Island from Bay Shore, Sayville, and Patchogu.

Fire Island Lighthouse

Fire Island National Seashore's thirty-two-mile-long barrier island beaches on Great South Bay are a long-time recreational attraction for metropolitan New Yorkers. This splendid strip of sand, two hundred yards to one-half-mile wide, contains guarded swimming areas, marinas, visitor facilities, patches of pine and holly forests, seaside plants, hardwood groves, salt marshes, and a wide variety of wildlife. More than a dozen communities of summer homes are scattered the length of the island, many accessible by ferry directly from Long Island. The historical Fire Island Lighthouse is located at the western end of the National Seashore, and the William Floyd Estate is a detached unit on the mainland on Washington Avenue in Mastic Beach.

Located just east of Robert Moses State Park and accessible by a walk of six-tenths of a mile, the Fire Island Lighthouse is a 168-foot tower with an adjacent lighthouse keeper's quarters. Replacing an earlier tower built in 1826, the current brick tower of alternating black and white bands was lit for the first time on November 1, 1858. The original light was a first-order Fresnel lens, currently in storage. Decommissioned in 1974, the Fire Island Lighthouse was restored with funds raised by the Fire Island Lighthouse Preservation Society, including repairing damage caused by covering the tower's brickwork with a cement coating, and converting the two-story stone double keeper's dwelling into a museum and gift shop. Built in 1858 along with the tower, both buildings were placed on a flagstone terrace built of stones from the 1826 lighthouse. The 1858 tower now serves as a private aid to navigation and is open to the public.

The National Historic Landmark 613-acre William Floyd Estate is in the town of Mastic Beach east of Fire Island National Seashore and facing Moriches Bay. The rambling, twenty-five-room Old Mastic House mansion was built around 1718 and managed by eight generations of Floyds until finally serving as a summer house, and donated to the NPS in 1965. The estate also includes the family cemetery and a cluster of outbuildings interpreted for rural farm life in the late eighteenth century.

William Floyd, a Revolutionary War general and a Founding Father, was born in the house in 1734. Expanded with wings and porches over three centuries, the original two-story main block (approximately 60 by 30 feet in plan) represents William Floyd's stature as a successful farm owner, merchant, and major local political figure. Although not distinctive in decorative detail, the house is a pleasing composition and orderly in plan. As a member of the Second Continental Congress in 1774–76, forty-one-year-old William Floyd was the first of the New York delegates to sign the Declaration of Independence on August 2, 1776. In 1789 he was elected to the U.S. Congress under the new Constitution. He returned to the New York State Senate in 1808.

There are no roads on the island except entrance drives to the Wilderness visitor center (formerly Smith Point West) and from the Robert Moses State Park. Check for seasonal ferry schedules and operating hours for the Fire Island Lighthouse and William Floyd Estate.

Fort Stanwix National Monument

Rome, Oneida County, New York

→ www.nps.gov/fost

→ The monument is located in downtown Rome, New York, forty-five miles east of Syracuse and ten miles west of Utica, New York, at the convergence of NY 69, 49, 46, and 26. Access via Interstate 90 (New York State Thruway) is from Exits 31, 32, or 33 and then follow signs to the fort and nearby parking.

Fort Stanwix, southeast bastion and projecting fraise logs

Fort Stanwix National Monument is a reconstructed Revolutionary War fort in downtown Rome, New York. Designated a National Historic Landmark for historical associations connected with the site, this well-crafted portrayal of an eighteenth-century colonial fort, based on thorough archeological excavations and research, authentically captures the turbulent times of the Revolutionary War and a significant victory in defense of the young country.

The British built a fort here in 1758, named for its builder, General John Stanwix, to protect a strategic portage on the Mohawk River (the Oneida Carry) along the waterborne gateway for settlers to the vast territory north and west of the Susquehanna River. Abandoned after the British conquest of Canada in 1763, the fort was rebuilt by the Americans in the Revolutionary War and played a key role in defeating the British Campaign of 1777 strategy to divide the colonies along the New York waterways of the Hudson-Champlain river valleys. In Indian affairs, Fort Stanwix played a significant role in the history of Native American treaties. Seven treaties and land transactions beginning in 1768 were signed here formally ending Six Iroquoian Nations' rough hegemony over large portions of territory east and later west of the Ohio River and aided in the Westward expansion of the United States. The last four treaties and land transactions were acknowledged and made binding by the federal government when included in the 1794 Treaty of Canandaigua.

The British Campaign of 1777 was a planned three-pronged movement with General John Burgoyne advancing south from Canada to Lake Champlain, capturing Fort Ticonderoga, and then continuing on down the Hudson River. Joining Burgoyne would be General Sir William Howe and his army marching north from New York City, already under British control. However, Howe became engaged in a campaign to capture the national capitol in Philadelphia and would never reach Albany. Colonel Barry St. Leger

Gateway

would come as a third force, advancing west along the Mohawk River Valley as a diversion to draw Continental and militia troops away from the Hudson River Valley. Departing from Fort Oswego on Lake Ontario on July 26, St. Leger's army of 1,700 British, German, Loyalist, and American and Canadian Indians began the seige of Fort Stanwix on August 3rd. Three days later he met and severely defeated General Nicholas Herkimer (where he received a fatal wound) and his militia at Oriskany in one of the most desperate and bloody battles of the Revolution. Deceived by reports that Fort Stanwix was poorly constructed and garrisoned, St. Leger came with inadequate cannon; a clever ruse by the colonial forces caused the withdrawal of St. Leger's Indian allies, and later Loyalists, to reduce his army to one-third in size. Troops garrisoned at the fort under Colonel Peter Gansevoort withstood the twenty-one-day siege, causing St. Leger to withdraw to Canada, thus preventing reinforcements from reaching General John Burgoyne at Saratoga. The ill-fated British campaign ended with the defeat and surrender of Burgoyne at Saratoga in October 1777. Fort Stanwix was garrisoned until 1781 when it was damaged by fire.

In the early 1960s, economic conditions in Rome, New York, prompted urban renewal projects that included a 1967 master plan for

15.5 acres dedicated to the site of a reconstructed fort. The City of Rome boldly chose to demolish its downtown and bank its future on urban renewal, heritage tourism, and Fort Stanwix. Although the ruins lay below downtown Rome without any visible above ground remains, work by NPS archeologists Lee Hanson and Richard Hsu determined the locations of the fort's major structural features. The final design is the result of the archeological findings and extensive research into other colonial era forts consolidated by architect Orville Carroll. Construction began in 1974 and was partially complete in time for the bicentennial. Further work was done in 1977–78.

Soldiers on fort wall

The reconstructed fort is encircled on the north, west, and south sides with an outer defense of a grass-covered glacis surmounted by a palisade fence. A ditch formed by the glacis' counterscarp and the upward sloping grass-covered scarp wall. Omitted in the reconstruction is the traditional defensive *ravelin*—arrow-pointed outward to protect the drawbridge over the ditch—and approaching visitors immediately see the log-faced fort's south walls. The scarp and four prominent bastions, built of horizontally placed yellow pine logs on a reinforced concrete structure, have log-faced curtain walls pierced by embrasures for reproduction cannons mounted on plank platforms. Around the entire permiter, the curtain walls bristle with a mid-wall high *fraise* of sharpened logs. Corner sentry boxes are positioned at each bastion apex. A mighty hewn-log drawbridge of square mortise-and-tenoned logs leads into a covered entranceway under projecting *fraise* logs. The fort's rectangular interior is faced with log-walled casemates and contains the freestanding log one-story Store House and East and West Barracks buildings with brick fireplaces and chimneys. Some other unreconstructed typical colonial fort features are the sally port, headquarters building, guardhouse, and necessary.

The fort is enlivened regularly by period-clothed reenactors—the Fort Stanwix Garrison wearing uniforms of the Third New York Regiment, militias, and Native Americans—and is often the site of encampments replete with a tent colony outside the fort. The annual Honor America Day is a moving event on the last Saturday of July with a grand illumination concluded by Syracuse Symphony Orchestra playing Tschaikovsky's 1812 *Overture* accompanied by live church bells, cannon firing, fireworks display, and John Philip Sousa's *Stars and Stripes Forever*.

Home of Franklin D. Roosevelt National Historic Site

Hyde Park, Dutchess County, New York

→ www.nps.gov/hofr

→ The Home of Franklin D. Roosevelt is located on Route 9 in Hyde Park, New York, about eighty miles north of New York City and six miles from Poughkeepsie, on the east side of the Hudson River. Access via Interstate 87 (New York State Thruway): take Exit 18, New Paltz, and follow signs to the Mid-Hudson Bridge and continue north on New York Route 9 about five miles to the park.

Springwood, Home of Franklin Delano Roosevelt

Franklin Delano Roosevelt (known as FDR), the thirty-second president of the United States, was born (January 30, 1882) and spent his childhood years on this family estate in Hyde Park, New York. He returned routinely throughout his life and was buried here after his death in office on April 1945. The 719-acre site overlooks the bluffs of the Hudson River, only a two hour drive north of New York City. The centerpiece of the estate is Springwood, the rambling stucco and fieldstone Roosevelt mansion. Adjacent to the home and original buildings and outbuildings, the park also includes the Henry A. Wallace Visitor and Education Center and the Franklin D. Roosevelt Library and Museum. Nearby is the FDR retreat at Top Cottage.

Franklin Delano Roosevelt was descended from an aristocratic Knickerbocker family with long ties to the Hudson River Valley dating back to the seventeenth century. A cousin of President Theodore Roosevelt, on whom he patterned his political career, FDR had already served as a New York state senator and had been appointed assistant secretary of the Navy when, in 1921, he fell victim to polio. Although restricted in physical activities, Roosevelt reentered public life and was twice elected governor of New York before becoming president of the United States in 1932. He was elected an unprecedented four times and served twelve years until his death in 1945, leading the nation through two of its greatest crises, the Great Depression and World War II.

FDR's father, James Roosevelt, was trained in law, worked as director of the Delaware and Hudson Railroad, and was active in Hyde Park town politics. In 1866 he purchased the 110-acre riverfront property with a seventeen-room farmhouse and named it Springwood. At Springwood he lived the life of a gentleman farmer. James converted the house into a Hudson River bracketed villa in the Italianate style with a three-story tower, a full-length porch to the front and rear, additional bedrooms, and an enlarged servants' wing. James also built the handsome large carriage house (1886) for his driving horses and finest carriages.

In 1915, another major expansion of Springwood was undertaken by FDR and his mother, Sara, along with the architectural firm Hopping & Kohn. FDR's influence upon the changes is evident in the presence of Dutch Colonial stylistic elements within the comfortable mixture of styles. The old clapboard exterior was replaced by stucco, the pitched roof was raised to create a hip-roofed third story, the piazza was removed except for a small portion near the dining room, and at each end large, two-story fieldstone wings were added. In the front, a semicircular Doric portico and a fieldstone terrace with balustrade were complimented by Georgian decorative elements of finials, swags, and tablets. The visually pleasing result, seen today, is an elegant Georgian Revival mansion befitting FDR's Hudson River lineage and his presidential aspiration.

Today the house interior retains much of the old family home's charm and grace. On National Park Service guided tours visitors can see rooms furnished as they were during the president's occupancy. The spacious main hall contains FDR's boyhood collection of stuffed birds. Formal entertaining took place in the dining room and Dresden Room facing the Hudson River. The south fieldstone wing addition contained the living room-library. Upstairs is the room where FDR was born, and his boyhood bedroom, later used by each of his sons in turn. Prime Minister Winston Churchill, King George VI and Queen Elizabeth II, and other distinguished visitors stayed in bedrooms off the

House and stable

same hall. The servants' wing housed the resident staff, ranging from six to ten.

Visits to the estate begin at the Henry A. Wallace Visitor and Education Center, where tickets are available for the tour of the Home of FDR. The center, named in honor of the man who served as secretary of Agriculture (1933–40) and vice president during FDR's third term, was designed by architects R.M. Kliment & Frances Halsband. It is a superb introduction to the life of FDR, and can serve as a model for unpretentious

Garden house

The Roosevelts (and friend) at Wallace Visitor and Education Center

visitor centers based on a skillful interpretation of regional architecture. Facilities include ticketing, orientation exhibits, and a film. The building also includes conference and education spaces, an auditorium, bookstore, and Mrs. Nesbitt's Cafe, named for Roosevelt's housekeeper.

A tour of the estate includes a visit to the Roosevelt Presidential Library and Museum, America's first presidential library, operated by the National Archives and Records Administration. The library was designed by President Roosevelt and is built of local fieldstone in a style reminiscent of local colonial architecture. The building was opened to the public in 1941 and in 1972 two wings were added to the original structure. The library's archival holdings include the president's personal and family papers, papers covering his public career, Eleanor Roosevelt's papers, as well as those of many of their associates in public and private life. The museum's exhibits explore the lives and times of the Roosevelts, the New Deal, and World War II.

Between the library and museum and the Roosevelt Home is the tranquil hedge-bordered Rose Garden containing the gravesite of FDR and Eleanor. A block of white marble, 8 feet long, 4 feet wide, and 3 feet high is unadorned except for the couples' names and years of birth and death.

Tickets are available for tours of Top Cottage, built by FDR as a personal retreat atop nearby Dutchess Hill with sweeping views of the Catskill and Shawangunk Mountains to the west. The fully accessible National Historic Landmark structure, completed in 1939, once again reflects his love for Hudson River Valley Dutch Colonial architecture. Top Cottage became part of the national historic site in May 2001.

Martin Van Buren National Historic Site

Kinderhook, Columbia County, New York

→ www.nps.gov/mava

→ The park is located approximately twenty miles southeast of Albany, New York, just south of the village of Kinderhook on Old Post Road (New York Route 9H). Follow signs to the park.

Lindenwald, Martin Van Buren House

The Hudson River Valley's east bank was a storied land of vast land holdings originating in patroonships doled out by the Dutch West India Company. Washington Irving's tales of the Dutch settlers in the valley resound of an Old World farming culture settling into the New World. Supposedly named by Henry Hudson, Kinderhook (Children's Corner) was the village where Martin Van Buren, the eighth president of the United States was born in 1782. Van Buren's parents kept a tavern and made a moderate living farming amidst the rolling hills and streams. The Martin Van Buren National Historic Site, the Lindenwald estate, is within two miles south of the village.

The precocious and ambitious Van Buren began law studies at fourteen and practiced in Albany and Kinderhook. He rapidly developed political skills and earned the reputation of a skilled politician, a behind-the-scenes operator with the nickname "Red Fox." During a lifetime in public office Van Buren served as state senator, U.S. senator, U.S. secretary of state, ambassador to the Court of St. James, vice president, and was elected to the presidency in 1837. He suffered a political fate similar to Herbert Hoover when, within a year after election, the Panic of 1837 created a major national depression. Never recovering his popularity, Van Buren was defeated for reelection in 1840 by William Henry Harrison, but his career as a leader of northern antebellum Democrats continued. He ran for the presidency twice more from Lindenwald, nearly regaining the Democratic nomination in 1844, only to lose the convention on the ninth ballot to James K. Polk. As the issue of slavery became more contentious, he was persuaded to run for president in 1848 on the "Free Soil" ticket.

Martin Van Buren purchased Lindenwald (named for the linden trees on the property that extended to Kinderhook Creek), the Federal style mansion (built in 1797) once owned by the father of his boyhood friend William Van Ness. Rundown and neglected when acquired in 1839, Van Buren set about restoring the fields for farming, making interior improvements, and elegantly furnishing the house. An interior hallway was altered to create a grand dining hall that Van Buren embellished with fifty-one vividly colored wallpaper panels imported from France (an 1831 *Passage à Chasse*, "Landscape of the Hunt," manufactured in Alsatia by Jean Zuber).

In 1849 Smith Thompson Van Buren, the president's son, engaged the eminent Gothic Revivalist architect Richard Upjohn to design modifications to the original house (the working drawings are at Columbia University's Avery Library). Tolerantly accepting his son's preferences with good grace and humor, Van Buren saw the disappearance of the house's simple massing and plan into a two-family house with Italianate and Gothic features. Within this hybrid of styles, in 1849–50 Smith added the south and west wings,

Lindenwald tower

dormers, a Victorian Gothic central gable, a four-story Italianate tower, new entrance porch, and Renaissance-looking bay windows. After Van Buren's death at Lindenwald in 1862 the property changed hands many times.

The thirty-six-room mansion seen today, containing original wallpaper, furnishings, and exact reproductions has been restored to the Van Buren period of ownership by the National Park Service (NPS) after acquisition in 1976. Among the many fine pieces of

art work and furniture is a circa 1860 piano belonging to Jenny Jerome, mother of Winston Churchill and daughter of Leonard Jerome, an owner of the property (1864–66). NPS work must be admired for the exacting restoration standards, including four years of painstaking work to restore the magnificent central hallway wallpaper panels.

Although the estate was a working farm under Van Buren's direction that grew to 226 acres, the current national historic site encompasses only forty acres. However, much of the land surrounding Lindenwald is under conservation protection for a visitor experience in the agricultural setting as it was in Van Buren's time.

Architect Richard Upjohn's front porch

A visit to Hudson River Valley estate in the Martin Van Buren National Historic Site offers a rare opportunity for insights into the nation's history through the long life of the one-term, mid-nineteenth-century eighth president of the United States. Born into the Revolutionary War's last year and dying in the Civil War's second year, his lifetime spanned the gaining of independence, stabilizing into a democratic nation, emerging as an international power, and entering the throes of a civil war.

National Parks of New York Harbor

New York, New York

→ www.nps.gov/npnh

The New York City area contains a diverse number of park units, some instantly recognizable as national icons, such as the Statue of Liberty, Ellis Island, and the General
Grant National Memorial, and others lesser known but of national significance. Several
parks are clustered around lower Manhattan and others are spread around the metropolitan area. Many parks can be reached by public transportation. A tour of the parks
can be a planned itinerary or one taken casually as opportunities arise in travels around
the city. For travel planning, check www.nps.gov/npnh for directions and seasonal
schedules when open to the public.

Castle Clinton National Monument

Battery Park, Lower Manhattan

→ www.nps.gov/cacl

Castle Clinton

Located at the southernmost tip of Manhattan Island in Battery Park, Castle Clinton is at one of the most scenic spots in
America. A sweeping panoramic view of
New York City Harbor unfolds from here,
to the south beyond the Statue of Liberty
and Ellis Island, Governors Island, and
the harbor's enfolding arms extending
from Staten Island and Long Island. To the
north are the towers of Manhattan. Tour-
ists and daily ferry commuters to Staten Island and the Statue of Liberty easily overlook
the unusual circular, squat fortress's sandstone wall with an austere gateway and deeply
recessed cannon embrasures.

Built between 1807 and 1811 as a fortification to defend the city, and originally called
the South-West Battery, complementing East Battery (Fort Williams) on Governors Island,
the end of hostilities with the British relieved the city's need for protection from seaborne
attack. The fort, vacated by the army in 1821, was renamed in honor of Mayor DeWitt Clinton, later governor of New York. The structure was deeded to New York City in 1823, renamed Castle Garden in 1824, and converted into the city's premier cultural center.

By 1855, the structure built on rocks in 35 feet of water and connected to land by a
200-foot-long bridge, was part of an enlarged Battery Park created by successive land-
fills. In that year, the structure opened as America's first immigrant receiving center,
welcoming over eight million people before it was succeeded by Ellis Island in 1890. In

1896, the Castle was transformed into the New York Aquarium, one of the nation's first public aquariums, until it closed in 1941.

Saved from demolition in 1946, the Castle was restored to its ground story fortification walls with only two octagonal kiosks in the courtyard remaining of the many layers of structures once standing here. Today, the historical structure serves not only as a museum, but as a Statue of Liberty and Ellis Island ferry ticket office.

Federal Hall National Memorial

24 Wall Street, Manhattan

→ www.nps.gov/feha

Federal Hall

The corner of Nassau Street and 26 Wall Street in the middle of lower Manhattan's financial district is the site of layers of history and where now stands the Federal Hall National Memorial. A 1703 City Hall stood here, then later expanded to house Congress in the interim capital city's (1785–90) Federal Hall. Here, too, George Washington was inaugurated in 1789, the Bill of Rights was written, the principle of freedom of the press established in the 1735 Peter Zenger trial, and a wood-frame Customs House stood until replaced by the current building. The structure was known as the Sub-Treasury Building for its many years of service in that function (until 1920 it was a repository for seventy percent of the nation's money supply).

Designed by eminent Greek Revival architects Ithiel Town and Andrew Jackson Davis, and substantially influenced by John Frazee, the superb Parthenon-inspired U.S. Customs House was constructed from 1835 to 1842. Except for sculpture in the tympanum and metopes, the building is a slightly smaller scale version of the Parthenon in proportion of eleven to twelve. The Doric temple, with fifteen 32-foot-high columns on the long sides and eight on the ends, has solid marble blocks laid without mortar. The facade, often strikingly bathed in sunlight despite the surrounding skyscrapers, rests on a plinth to adjust to the drop in grade from back to front. The happy result is the steep flight of entry steps containing a podium with a heroic bronze statue of George Washington by John Quincy Adams Ward.

The perfection of Greek Revival form and detailing surviving in this environment of real estate speculation is a pleasant interruption in the bustle of the financial district (the New York Stock Exchange is only a few yards away). Taking time for a tour of the interior—probably unknown to the district's denizens—provides a surprise because of the shallow Roman dome ringed by columns. The incongruous dome in the front chamber of the building rises to a rooftop monitor introducing shafts of light onto the marble floor. The basement and sub-basement, arch-supported by brick vaults, is worth visiting.

The building now serves as a memorial to our first president and the beginnings of the United States of America, the New York Harbor Visitor Information Center, and a museum with changing exhibits.

Gateway National Recreation Area

Brooklyn, Queens, Staten Island, and Monmouth County, New Jersey

→ www.nps.gov/gate

Sandy Hook Lighthouse

Gateway National Recreation Area is an unusual urban park comprising more than 26,000 acres of marshland, wildlife sanctuaries, recreational facilities, miles of sandy beaches, old military installations, historical structures, and open water in New York and New Jersey. The park's four units are the Jamaica Bay Unit, Breezy Point Unit, Sandy Hook Unit, and Staten Island Unit.

The majority of the more than 9,000-acre Jamaica Bay Unit, extending from Plum Beach to Kennedy International Airport includes the historic former Floyd Bennett Field, New York City's first municipal airport and a site associated with many famous record-breaking flights and fliers, including Amelia Earhart, Howard Hughes, Roscoe Turner, Douglas "Wrong Way" Corrigan, and John Glenn, Jr. The field includes a mile-long runway, Art Deco administration building, and hangars housing vintage aircraft.

The Breezy Point Unit is located on Rockaway Island. The barrier island contains miles of public beach, Jacob Riis Park, and Fort Tilden. Riis Park, built in the 1930s on the site of Rockaway Naval Air Station (the departure point of the 1919 first transatlantic flight), was the novel approach by city-builder Robert Moses of an automobile oriented destination in a city accustomed to public transportation access to recreation. Fort Tilden, established in 1917, served as a coastal artillery installation and was established as a fort about the time of American involvement in World War I in 1917 and was decommissioned in 1974.

The Staten Island Unit is located on the south shore of Staten Island within Lower New York Bay. It includes Fort Wadsworth, a historic collection of granite-walled masonry fortifications on the site of much earlier fortifications. The fort, the site of a Dutch blockhouse in 1663, was the longest continually manned military installation in the United States until decommissioning in 1994. Divided into several smaller units, including Fort Tompkins and Fort Richmond, historic structures include Battery Weed, directly on the harbor, and Fort Tompkins on the bluff above. Both were built in the mid-nineteenth century and are open to the public on guided tours only.

The Sandy Hook Unit is a 2,044-acre barrier beach peninsula at the northern tip of New Jersey. The park includes miles of ocean beaches and salt marshes. Historic architectural sites are the decommissioned Fort Hancock (a ghost-like collection of abandoned structures can be seen in the back dunes) and the National Historic Landmark Sandy Hook Lighthouse, the oldest working lighthouse in the United States (1764). Originally called the New York Lighthouse, the octagonal whitewashed brick structure (29 feet in diameter at the base and 103 feet from ground to tip of finial) is lit by a third-order Fresnel lens installed in 1856 and remains in use. Originally standing 500 feet from the tip of the hook, Sandy Hook Lighthouse is now over a mile and a half away. Attached is the lighthouse keeper's quarters.

General Grant National Memorial

Riverside Drive and 122nd Street, Manhattan

→ www.nps.gov/gegr

General Grant Memorial

This startling eclectic structure, popularly known as Grant's Tomb—the burial place of the eighteenth president of the United States, Ulysses S. Grant—is passed by tens of thousands of motorists daily on the Henry Hudson Parkway in Manhattan's Upper West Side. The location is a scenic overlook perched on a bluff above the Hudson River at Riverside Drive and 122nd Street. There was extraordinary public interest in this mausoleum during the design competitions (1888 and 1890), construction, and dedication and final entombment in 1897. Considered one of the world's most impressive mausoleums and the largest in the country, the site in four-mile-long Riverside Park designed by Frederick Law Olmsted and Calvert Vaux is enjoyed by joggers, walkers, rollerbladers, and dog owners. Although routinely bypassed by tourists, the General Grant National Memorial should be experienced for its extraordinary design honoring Grant's life and accomplishments.

The imposing 150-foot-high granite structure is the design of architect John Duncan. The three-part composition of 90-foot-square base, drum, and pyramidal cap combines elements from the tomb of King Mausolus at Halicarnassus in present-day Turkey, the tomb of Roman Emperor Hadrian, Napoleon's Tomb de Invalides, and the Garfield Memorial in Cleveland, Ohio. A colonnaded portico faces south; above are two recumbent figures, interpreted as personifying Victory and Peace, supporting Grant's epitaph: "LET US HAVE PEACE." The ground floor interior contains busts of Grant's favorite Civil War generals (William T. Sherman, Philip H. Sheridan, George H. Thomas, James B. McPherson, and Edward O. C. Ord). In the interior, a crescendo of columns and arches soar upward 107 feet to the top of a coffered dome containing allegorical reliefs on the vaulting designed by J. Massey Rhind depicting Grant's life. A balustraded circular opening overlooks the ground level with identical 8.5-ton polished red granite sarcophagi containing the bodies of Grant and his wife, Julia. Daily ranger-guided tours are available. Check the park's Web site for hours and tour schedules.

Governors Island National Monument

New York Harbor

→   www.nps.gov/gois

Castle Williams

In an historic event, in January of 2003 the federal government transferred Governors Island in New York Harbor to the City and State of New York. Located on the 172-acre island one half-mile south of the tip of Manhattan and a short ferry ride away is the 22-acre Governors Island National Monument. After being off-limits to the public since the colonial era, the monument became part of the National Park Service (NPS) in 2001, providing future public access to the historical fortifications of Fort Jay and Castle Williams.

Steeped in history, Governors Island played important roles as a bulwark in the city's defenses for two centuries. When the Revolutionary War broke out, the colonists fortified the island with an earthenwork fort and used it as a deterrent against a British landing on Manhattan. In 1800, New York transferred the island to the United States government. Between 1806 and 1809 the latter constructed star-shaped Fort Jay with four-bastions on an earth rampart; interior barracks at the island's northern end on a rocky outcropping facing the harbor; and the three-tiered, circular, red sandstone casemated Castle Williams. In addition to the fortifications, the park contains the 1930 Liggett Hall, a regiment-sized barracks designed by McKim, Mead & White, and officers' quarters. From the 1820s to the 1960s the United States Army occupied the island and in 1966 it was transferred to the U.S. Coast Guard and served as the largest coast guard base in the world until it was decommissioned in 1996. Physically, the island changed dramatically in the twentieth century with the southern part's addition of 103-acres created by fill from construction of the Lexington Avenue subway and construction of a mix of residential, recreational, educational, and support structures.

Access by the public to this location—long treasured by the military as a favorable posting for the impressive views of the lower Manhattan skyline, the Statue of Liberty, and New York Harbor—is eagerly anticipated as the NPS develops restoration and interpretive plans. Coupled with the potential for development of the rest of the island by a city-state agency, this important place in New York Harbor will begin an exciting chapter in its history.

Hamilton Grange National Memorial

287 Convent Avenue, Manhattan

→   www.nps.gov/hagr

"The Grange," named after his grandfather's estate in Scotland was the home of Founding Father Alexander Hamilton, statesman, and first secretary of the Treasury. The National Historic Landmark Federal style two-story frame mansion at 287 Convent Avenue in Harlem in upper Manhattan (between West 141st Street and West 142nd Street) was completed in 1802 from designs by New York architect John McComb, Jr. Hamilton enjoyed it only a few short years before his fatal duel with Aaron Burr in July of 1804. The house was relocated in 1889 from its site on the original 32-acre estate at 237 West 141st Street to its present location four blocks away. The original porches, entrance, balustrade, and other details were lost at that time.

In May of 2006 the Grange was closed to the public for architectural and structural investigations as part of a long-term plan for relocating the house to a site overlooking St. Nicholas Park, coincidentally within the boundary of land once owned by Hamilton. The new location will allow for features lost in the 1889 move to be reconstructed, as well as provide a more appropriate open setting for the Grange.

Lower East Side Tenement Museum

108 Orchard Street, Manhattan

→   www.nps.gov/loea

The founder of the Lower East Side Tenement Museum, Ruth Abrams, sought to promote greater social tolerance from a historical perspective by interpreting the urban immigrant experience. The site selected in 1988 to achieve this ambitious goal was a six-story brick building at 97 Orchard Street (approximately 25 by 69 feet in plan). Built in 1863, the building has the correct credentials to qualify as a tenement typical of the thousands of apartment buildings that sprouted up on the Lower East Side during the nineteenth century: a six-floor walk-up with cold-water flats (defined as no elevator or gas for heat and light), containing twenty-two, three-room apartments and two ground floor stores, and lacking indoor toilets and running water. Romanticizing the hardships of life for the estimated seven thousand people who lived here from 1863 to 1935 is avoided by the museum—just off Delancey Street, South of Houston Street five blocks from the Bowery—by stepping back in time to candidly portray living conditions for recently arrived immigrant working-class people. The museum does a facile job of bringing the people who lived here to life, telling their stories and the legacies of the early years of hardship.

A revision in housing laws in 1867 began changes to improve tenement conditions and eventually produce the treasure discovered by Abrams. Landlords installed gas lines, running water and interior flush toilets, dressed up the interiors, and cut windows into apartment walls to provide air and light in the apartments. In 1935, rather than continue to modify the building, the residents were evicted and the building was boarded up and sealed, leaving only the storefronts open for business. Thus, what opened as the museum in a tiny storefront in 1988, today, conveys a vivid sense of the deplorable living conditions experienced by its tenants, especially the top two floors that contain rooms, wallpaper, plumbing, and paper preserved as they were found.

Lower East Side Tenement Museum

Designated a National Historic Landmark in 1994, and in 1998 an Affiliated Area of the National Park Service, the museum is located in three buildings, with 97 Orchard Street as the core. The Tenement Museum entrance is at 90 Orchard Street, at the corner of Broome, and tours begin at the Tenement's visitor center at 108 Orchard Street, between Delancey and Broome, near Delancey. Viewed only by guided tours of one to three hours, restored and furnished apartments can be seen along with untouched boarded-up space.

Saint Paul's Church National Historic Site

897 South Columbus Avenue, Mount Vernon, Wstchester County, New York, Manhattan

→ www.nps.gov/sapa

Saint Paul's Church at 897 South Columbus Avenue in Mount Vernon, New York is just north of the Bronx, New York. Three-and-a-half centuries ago this was in the Town of Eastchester, a leafy countryside where Saint Paul's parish was founded in 1665. Today's Saint Paul's Church National Historic Site is comprised of the fine example of early colonial church architecture, a museum located in a restored storage shed, and grounds including a remnant of the historic Village Green and six acres of historic cemetery.

The site is noteworthy—in addition to the superb example of a Georgian Revival church—for its association with issues of freedom of religion and the press. Events took place here that led to the famous trial in 1735 of John Peter Zenger and his acquittal in a case that was a landmark decision providing the basis for the guarantee of freedom of the press. The Zenger trial stemmed from an account he wrote about voting procedures that began with placing a notice of an election on the church door without a specified date and the denial of voting rights to Quakers for their refusal to swear on the Bible that they owned land, which was contrary to their beliefs. The British royal governor favored a Loyalist candidate and the Eastchester citizens had their own candidate who was successful after the votes were counted. Zenger, a former newspaper apprentice, covered the story and published the truth in the first edition of his *New York Weekly Journal*. He was jailed and tried on the charge of libel. His acquittal was cited in support of fundamental press freedom in the Bill of Rights' First Amendment.

Another historical association of the church is its use as a hospital following the important Revolutionary War battle at Pell's Point in 1776, fought less than a mile from the church. After the battle, sick and wounded Hessian mercenaries were housed here. The cemetary contains remains of buried Hessian soldiers and several American soldiers moved here in the early twentieth century. Hundreds of soldiers died and were buried in a mass grave that was later discovered.

Today's church, completed in 1787, replacing an earlier wood structure built in 1695, is built of local fieldstone, brick, and timber. The main block of the church (approximately 55 by 38 feet in plan) was extended to the rear by an addition (1853) of the vestry. The present stone belfry was added in 1886, and stained glass windows in the 1880s. The church's tower contains an 1,800-pound bell that was cast in 1758 at Whitechapel Foundry in London, the same foundry where the Liberty Bell was cast five years earlier. The bell still hangs in the tower today. The organ, built in 1830 by Henry Erben & Sons, is one of the oldest American-made organs still in use.

The changed neighborhood character around Saint Paul's Church in the early twentieth century led to the decline of the parish. In 1942, as part of an effort to revitalize the congregation and draw attention to the site's historical significance, the interior of the church was restored to its eighteenth-century appearance, based on the original pew plan of 1787. A committee chaired by Sara Delano Roosevelt, mother of President Franklin Delano Roosevelt, raised funds for the project. The congregation began to decline and by the 1970s the parish had dwindled to only a handful of worshippers. The last Sunday service held at Saint Paul's took place in May 1977. In 1980, the site was transferred from the Episcopal Diocese of New York to the National Park Service. The site opened to the public in 1984 and is operated under a cooperative agreement with the Society of the National Shrine of the Bill of Rights at Saint Paul's Church, Eastchester.

Guided tours through the church and the newly established Bill of Rights Museum interpret the rich history of the site and the importance of the Zenger trial. Colonial fairs, military encampments, and candlelight tours with period-clothed demonstrators all help recreate the past for visitors of all ages. Check in advance of a visit for seasonal schedules when open to the public and for special events.

Statue of Liberty National Monument

Liberty Island, New York Harbor

→   www.nps.gov/stli

Statue of Liberty

Liberty. Freedom. Opportunity. The famous 151-foot-tall copper-clad statue, poised majestically on her 154-foot-high pedestal in New York Harbor, is an emotionally charged symbol for millions of people from around the world. "A mighty woman with a torch," as Emma Lazarus called it in her celebrated poem, "The New Colossus," is the country's most enduring symbol and most visited monument. She has evolved into much more than her creators imagined, and has come to have many different meanings to our citizens and to people elsewhere in the world. The Statue of Liberty is an inspiring reminder of the millions who passed by her into a new world of hope, and a proud symbol of the freedom and privileges our society enjoys.

The statue's story began just after the end of the Civil War, when French scholar Edouard de Laboulaye proposed a monument as a gift to the United States to commemorate the continuing friendship between the two countries and the end of slavery in America. He invited sculptor Frédéric-Auguste Bartholdi to join him in the project. By 1871, Laboulaye sent Bartholdi to the United States "to find a happy idea, a plan that will excite public enthusiasm." Laboulaye and Bartholdi selected the symbolic form the statue would take—ancient Rome's goddess of liberty—and in 1875 Laboulaye launched a fundraising campaign in France to support the project. Bartholdi, on a visit to the United States in 1876, secured the support of Congress and members of New York's elite Union League Club, and the American fundraising campaign to finance the construction of a pedestal worthy of the magnificent statue was launched. Bartholdi collaborated with engineers Eugéne Emmanuel Viollet-le-Duc and Alexandre-Gustave Eiffel to design a support structure. The statue was finally completed in Paris in 1885.

The star-shaped Fort Wood on Bedloe's Island (now Liberty Island), which had been guarding New York Harbor since 1811, was selected as the location to build the statue. The American architect Richard Morris Hunt designed the granite-faced pedestal and General Charles P. Stone supervised construction of the foundation and pedestal inside the fortress walls. Meanwhile, in Paris, the statue was taken apart piece by piece (350 individual pieces packed in 214 heavy cases) and shipped to New York on board the French warship Isere. The arrival of the statue in June 1885 was an exciting moment but also an embarrassing one since the pedestal was not finished. Finally, on October 28th, 1886, after the completion of the pedestal and the erection of the statue above it, *Liberty Enlightening the World* was formally dedicated and accepted by President Grover Cleveland.

Nearly a century later, President Reagan launched the statue's restoration by appointing Lee A. Iacocca to lead a national fundraising campaign. The restoration resulted in a superb revitalization of the statue and pedestal, while a permanent Statue of Liberty exhibit was installed in the base. The monument's restoration included replacing the greater part of the Liberty's internal support structure, removing badly corroded sections of the statue's copper skin, and installing a completely new torch and flame. In 1984 UNESCO designated the Statue of Liberty as a World Heritage Site. The newly restored statue opened to the public on July 5, 19986.

The inspiring companion to the Statue of Liberty is the nearby Ellis Island. Opened on January 1, 1892 as the nation's primary federal immigrant inspection station, the small island off the New Jersey coast was enlarged from its original 3.3 acres to 27.5 acres by landfill. The original wooden immigration hall caught fire in 1897 and burned to the ground. The current French Renaissance brick-and-limestone Main Building, with its four ornamental turrets, deeply recessed arched ground floor and rectangular clerestory windows, was designed by architects Boring and Tilton and was opened on December 17, 1900. To accommodate a greater than anticipated influx of new immigrants, new structures were added to the island including medical buildings, dormitories, contagious disease wards, and kitchens.

On the immigration station's opening day in 1892, the first immigrant to be inspected was the fifteen-year-old Irish girl Annie Moore, accompanied by her two younger brothers. As a remembrance of the occasion, the immigration commissioner gave her a ten dollar gold coin. Over the next sixty-two years, approximately twelve million immigrants followed in her footsteps. It is estimated that some 140 million Americans—over forty percent of America's population—can trace their ancestry through Ellis Island.

Ellis Island Immigration Museum

In 1954 the operations on Ellis Island ceased. After thirty years of abandonment and seven years of laborious rehabilitation, the Main Building opened as the Ellis Island Immigration Museum on September 10, 1990. The National Park Service (NPS) chose the years 1918–22 as the historic period to guide the rehabilitation of the 220,000-square-foot Main Building; it was believed at the time to be the largest project of its kind ever undertaken in the United States. The Registry Room in the Main

Building, where immigrants were questioned before being allowed to enter the United States, is a spectacular space with a vaulted ceiling of glazed tile, known as "Guastavino tile" after the inventor of the structural system. The American Family Immigration History Center, established and operated by the Statue of Liberty–Ellis Island Foundation, an NPS partner organization, is located on the ground floor of the museum and is a popular place for tracing ancestors that came through the port of New York between 1892 and 1924.

In April 2007 the NPS, with the assistance of another partner, Save Ellis Island, Inc., opened the restored Ferry Building to the public, the first such project since the 1990 opening. The 1934 Art Deco Public Works Administration Building was the departure point, immediate entry, or detention for further evaluation. It is a spectacular space with a white glazed tile vaulted ceiling and red tile floor. Facilities for tracing ancestry are a popular attraction at the museum. This is the first of around thirty buildings on the south end of the island, closest to Liberty Island, left untouched until the U.S. Supreme Court decided in 1998 that New Jersey and not New York controlled the island.

The Statue of Liberty on Liberty Island and the Ellis Island Immigration Museum on Ellis Island are accessible by ferry service only. Ferries are operated by Circle Line-Statue of Liberty Ferry, Inc. in lower Manhattan (Castle Clinton) and Jersey City, New Jersey (Central Railroad Terminal Building and Museum in Liberty State Park). One round-trip ferry ticket includes visits to both islands. The docking of private vessels is strictly prohibited. Don't be daunted by the security screening system that is in place. It is very similar to airport security procedures.

Theodore Roosevelt Birthplace National Historic Site

28 East 20th Street, Manhattan

→ www.nps.gov/thrb

The reconstructed brownstone on a Manhattan side street where the twenty-sixth president lived until he was fourteen was once in the center of New York's most fashionable residential district on a quiet, tree-lined street. Born on October 27, 1858, this was Theodore Roosevelt's home until the fall of 1872 when the family left for Europe and returned a year later to their new house at 6 West 57th Street. Although the original Theodore Roosevelt birthplace was demolished in 1916 to make way for a commercial building, after his death in 1919 the site was purchased and the house reconstructed by the Women's Roosevelt Memorial Association. Constructed at the same time on the adjoining lot were museum galleries and other facilities.

A visit to this inconspicuous four-story brownstone, marked by a plaque on the wall and an American flag flying out front, is a journey back in time to the Gilded Age,

Theodore Roosevelt birthplace house

as seen in the painstakingly accurate reconstruction and superbly furnished period rooms. Open to the public are the master bedroom, library, Rococo Revival parlor, formal dining room, nursery, the "Lion's Room," and Lower Museum exhibit rooms. Restored to their appearance between 1865 and 1872, five rooms contain forty percent of the birthplace's original furnishings. Another twenty percent came from the president's widow, Edith, and sisters; the rest of the house's contents are period pieces. Roosevelt family members provided advice on color schemes, layouts, and other details.

There are ranger-guided tours; schedules can be checked at the site's web page.

Sagamore Hill National Historic Site

Oyster Bay, Nassau County, New York

→ www.nps.gov/sahi

→ The site is located near the village of Oyster Bay, New York about thirty-five miles from New York City. By car, take either Exit 35N from the Northern State Parkway or Exit 41N from the Long Island Expressway (Interstate 495) to Route 106 north for four miles toward Oyster Bay and follow signs to the park. Taxis to the site meet Long Island Railroad trains at Oyster Bay or Syosset.

Sagamore Hill was the home of Theodore Roosevelt, the twenty-sixth president of the United States, from 1886 until his death in 1919. The main attraction of Sagamore Hill National Historic Site is TR's (TR, as Roosevelt preferred to be called by the public and "Theodore" to his friends and family; he didn't like being called "Teddy") superb twenty-five-room Queen Anne shingle style mansion. Also on the hilly, wooded 83-acre park between Sagamore Hill Road and Cold Spring Harbor is the Old Orchard Museum, the family home of the president's oldest son, Brigadier General Theodore Roosevelt, Jr., a reconstructed windmill, an historic barn and other farm buildings, paths, and a nature trail. The Old Orchard Museum, located at a corner of an orchard, contains exhibits about TR's early and public life.

TR was a larger-than-life personality, insatiably interested in everything around him. He was a cowboy, scientist, historian, a prolific writer, skillful politician, statesman, explorer, big-game hunter, and dedicated family man. He was a public servant for most of his life, and served largely as an elected or appointed official, including: New York state assemblyman, U.S. Civil Service commissioner, New York City police commissioner, assistant secretary of the U.S. Navy, an officer in the U.S. Army, governor of New York State, vice president, and president of the United States (1901–1909). An ardent conservationist, he used the Antiquities Act of 1906 to establish the first eighteen national monuments and fifty-one bird refuges. TR won the Nobel Peace Prize (1906) for his efforts in negotiating

Sagamore Hill

the peace that ended the Russo-Japanese War. In 2001, he posthumously was awarded the Congressional Medal of Honor, an honor shared by Brigadier General Theodore Roosevelt, Jr., his eldest son for his actions at D-Day (also posthumously in July of 1944).

While walking from the visitor center to the sprawling mansion, the visitor can reflect on the times when, here, the energetic president and his family of six children practiced his philosophy of the "strenuous life," even while he found time to pen some of the thirty books written over his lifetime. Woodland now obscures some of the views of the surrounding area, but the spirit of the place that once served as the summer "White House" is appreciated in the well-tended buildings and lawns.

Although a native of New York City, Theodore Roosevelt spent summer vacations as a boy with his family in the Oyster Bay area. In 1880, when he was twenty-two and engaged to Anna Hathaway Lee he purchased 155 acres of farmland on Cove Neck, a small peninsula around two miles northeast of the village of Oyster Bay. In 1884 he hired the New York architectural firm Lamb & Rich to design a house for the property. Tragically, his wife died forty-eight hours after giving birth to their first child, Alice, and his mother died the same day. Two years later he married Edith Kermit Carow and moved into the house constructed in 1884–85. Sagamore Hill, as TR named it after Indian chief Sagamore Mohannis who sold the land, and its surrounding farmland became the primary residence of Theodore and Edith Roosevelt for the rest of their lives. Roosevelt lived here for thirty-five years until dying in his sleep in January of 1919. Edith Roosevelt continued to occupy the property until her death, nearly three decades later, in September of 1948.

The three-story house is remarkable for its adherence to Queen Anne stylistic elements and its condition is free of alterations or additions with the exception of a 30- by 40-foot North Room built in 1905. In addition to the house's outstanding architectural qualities, the Roosevelt family's house was acquired by the Theodore Roosevelt Association in 1948 and opened to the public in 1953. The house was left virtually intact to reflect the president's and his family's public and private life. The house is filled with more than ninety percent of the original furnishings, including the souvenirs and memorabilia collected by TR as president.

The plan of the wood-frame structure is roughly cruciform, with longer east and west wings. The exterior, expressing the shingle style, has a raised basement on a stone foundation, prominent gables, dormers, verandahs and porte cochere, red painted flush-pointed brick walls with terra-cotta medallions in a sunflower motif, decorative wooden "fish-scale" shingles, and massive rusticated brick chimneys. A spacious raised porch shaded by green and white striped awnings surrounds the house.

The first floor contains the large central front hall, library, which served as the president's private office, dining room, kitchen, and drawing room. The second floor contains the bedrooms, nursery, guest rooms, and the room with the great porcelain tub. The third floor contains the gun room, which housed TR's large gun collection and served as a den, and family and servants' bedrooms, and has sweeping views of the bay and Connecticut shoreline. Interiors, filled with memorabilia and trophies, contain elaborate paneling and a variety of hardwoods with natural finish for doorways and window architraves exhibiting heavily molded profiles.

Sagamore Hill is open to the public seasonally by guided tour, and also hosts special events and programs throughout the year.

Saratoga National Historical Park

Stillwater, Saratoga County, New York

→   www.nps.gov/sara

→   The park's main unit, the Saratoga Battlefield, is located forty miles north of Albany and fifteen miles southeast of Saratoga Springs on Route 4 and Route 32. From Interstate 87 (Northway), take Exit 12 (if heading north) or Exit 14 (if heading south) and follow signs to visitor center off Route 32 approximately three miles north of Stillwater. The Philip Schuyler House and Saratoga monument units are located near Schuylerville, New York. These sites are reached from the battlefield by US 4, a twenty minute drive.

The 3,400-acre Saratoga Battlefield is the largest of three sites making up Saratoga National Historical Park. On this scenic location overlooking the Hudson River Valley, in the fall of 1777, American forces met, defeated, and forced a British army flush from its capture of Fort Ticonderoga to surrender. This crucial American victory was the turning

point in the Revolutionary War, renewing patriots' hopes for independence, and secur-
ing essential foreign recognition and support. The American success at Saratoga is
considered one of history's most decisive battles. Two other sites that are part of the

Neilson farmhouse

park, the Saratoga Monument, and the Schuyler House are located eight miles north in
Schuylerville.

In two days of fierce battles the American forces commanded by General Horatio
Gates defeated the British army of General John Burgoyne. Here, the Americans check-
mated the British Campaign of 1777 designed to sever the north and south colonies
by a thrust along the Hudson-Champlain Valley. General Burgoyne's slow southward
advance from Canada enabled the "rabble in arms" to organize themselves into an effective army. Other elements of the three-pronged attack failed to materialize with St.
Leger turned back in the west at Fort Stanwix (see page 483), and General Henry Howe
engaged in an advance on Philadelphia. Starting in September the 8,500-man American
army built a long, L-shaped defensive line armed with twenty-two cannons on Bemis
Heights, a bluff overlooking Howe's line of march on the river road along the Hudson
River. On September 19, 1777 the Americans attacked the British army depleted to 6,800
men at Freeman's farm on Bemis Heights and, although suffering heavy losses, the British held the battlefield. On October 7, 1777, in a hotly contested three-hour battle, the
Americans attacked the British in a clearing near the Barber farm and forced them to
retreat north. Burgoyne, as slow in his retreat as in his southward advance, was surrounded at Schuylerville and forced to surrender.

The attractive visitor center boasts an impressive scenic overlook of the battlefield,
exhibits, and bookstore. The scene of the battles looks as much today as it did during the

three weeks in 1777, with heavy tree growth, hills, and ravines overlooking the Hudson River Valley. The National Park Service (NPS) has restored the landscape to enable the visitor to travel an auto tour of nine miles with ten stops (open April 1 to November 30 as weather permits). The tour bears evidence to the American strategy of combining terrain and defensive structures on Bemis Heights overlooking both the Hudson River and the River Road (now US Highway 4) to block British movement southward.

Along the tour are seen authentic and reproduction cannons on red field carriages and collapsed wooden "snake" fences zig-zagging across the open fields appearing very similar to the time of the battles. Locations of redoubts made up of earthen walls fortified by log walls are marked today with white wooden marker posts. American lines on the battlefield are indicated with blue-topped posts. British lines, seen later on the tour, have red tops.

The NPS-restored Neilson red farmhouse on Bemis Heights, with a nearly 360-degree panoramic view of the area, was built by John and Lydia Neilson in 1775 or 1776. It is the only standing building on the battlefield from the time of the Battles of Saratoga. Situated within the American entrenchments it served as the headquarters for Generals Enoch Poor and Benedict Arnold during the Saratoga campaign. The one-story timber frame and brick nogging structure with attached lean-to on a fieldstone foundation, approximately 18 by 24 feet in plan) has a 7-foot-wide porch across the front and is furnished as when it was occupied by the American officers.

Saratoga Monument

The restored summer house of American General Philip Schuyler, second of three sites making up Saratoga National Historical Park, is located approximately seven miles north of the battlefield south of Schuylerville on US 4. The two-and-a-half-story wood-frame house was built after 1777, taking the place of the original burned by Burgoyne. The house was visited by Washington, Hamilton, and Lafayette.

Saratoga Monument, the third of three sites making up Saratoga National Historical Park, is located approximately eight miles north of the battlefield in Victory, on Burgoyne Street west of Schuylerville. Standing 154 feet and 6 inches high, the renovated granite obelisk completed in 1883 is on the site of Burgoyne's camp during the final days of the campaign. Designed by architect Jared Markham, the shaft of hybrid Gothic and Egyptian elements rises from a 38-foot-square granite plinth and tapers from 20 to 10 feet. Uppermost windows offer magnificent views of the Hudson River Valley, the Berkshire and Green

Mountains to the east, and the Adirondacks to the west. On the exterior are four niches, three containing statues of Generals Schuyler and Gates and Colonel Morgan, and the fourth empty symbolizing the place American General Benedict Arnold would have occupied if he had not turned traitor after a heroic role in the Battles of Saratoga.

The visitor to the park should not confuse this Saratoga with the more familiar City of Saratoga Springs fifteen miles to the northwest. The city, famous for its spas and racetrack, was formed from the Town of Saratoga. The original settlement of Schuylerville, dating from 1689, and known as Saratoga, was destroyed by the Native Americans in 1745. The village was incorporated under the name of the illustrious patron, General Philip Schuyler in 1831.

The battlefield site of Saratoga National Historical Park, today with its calm and peaceful scenery, belies the fierce battle fought with roaring artillery cannonades, withering musket fire, and bayonet charges over two centuries ago. The park, rich in natural beauty and wildlife is a pleasant outing for hikers and bikers. NPS guides provide tours and period-clothed reenactors recall colonial times in the area and battlefield events. A wide range of special events and activities are held throughout the year at all three sites.

Theodore Roosevelt Inaugural National Historic Site

Buffalo, Erie County, New York

→ www.nps.gov/thri

→ The park is located at 641 Delaware Avenue one mile north of downtown Buffalo. The house is near the intersection of Delaware Avenue and North Street. Free parking is available to the rear of the building accessed from Franklin Street. Avoid some confusing one-way streets by following brown and white National Park Service signs.

The Ansley Wilcox House in Buffalo, New York is the private residence where, in its library on September 14, 1901, Theodore Roosevelt was sworn into office as the twenty-sixth president of the United States.

Fateful events drew president William McKinley to the Pan-American Exposition in Buffalo where, on September 5, 1901, he was critically wounded by bullets shot by anarchist Leon Czolgosz. Vice-President Roosevelt was in Vermont on a speaking engagement when attending surgeons operated and declared excellent chances for the president's recovery. Roosevelt arrived in Buffalo September 7th and stayed as an overnight guest at Ansley Wilcox's house. Assured by McKinley's improving condition, Roosevelt left for a family vacation in the Adirondack Mountains of upstate New York. Two days later, while on a mountain trail hike, he learned of McKinley's worsening condition. After a frantic nighttime carriage dash Roosevelt arrived at a waiting special railroad train at North Creek, New York. There he learned that the president was dead. The future president reached the Wilcox House on the afternoon of September 14 where, changing from his mountain outfit into borrowed formal wear, he stood before Judge John R. Hazel of the U.S. District Court and took the oath of office.

The Wilcox House, as seen today, is a superbly restored Greek Revival–style mansion with a fascinating history of changes and historical connections. The house was constructed immediately following the Canadian 1837 Patriot's War as part of a defense against possible conflict with the Canadians. Most frequently referred to as the Buffalo Barracks, the new facility was also occasionally known as the Poinsett Barracks after Secretary of War Joel Poinsett. The majority of the buildings surrounded a rectangular parade ground on the northern end of the post. The building, which was to later become the Theodore Roosevelt Inaugural National Historic Site, was most likely not erected until mid-1840. Intended as senior officers' housing, it was much smaller than its present size, comprising the present-day library, exhibit room, and the second floor above. Completion of nearby Fort Porter had rendered the temporary barracks redundant, and in September of 1845 the army formally abandoned it. Over the following year most of the fort's buildings were dismantled and removed. The house that became the inaugural site is the only known remnant of Buffalo Barracks structures to survive to the present day.

After several owners, in 1883 the house came into the possession of Ansley Wilcox. During the 1890s, he retained architect George Cary for major changes to the struc-

Ansley Wilcox House, site of Theodore Roosevelt's inauguration

ture. The building was tripled in size by a 60-foot extension of two floors and an attic, although the original Buffalo Barracks part of the house was left intact. In the most dramatic change, the two-story portico on the east side of the house facing the Buffalo

Barracks Parade Grounds was moved to the west side facing Delaware Avenue, prominently taking a place along Buffalo's "Millionaires Row." The stately house (approximately 43 by 115 feet in plan, with several projections and bays) is readily recognized by the Delaware Avenue five-bay facade with a deep two-story portico supported by smooth Doric columns, and pedimented gable containing a Palladian window set in the gable's flat tympanum, and tall arched entrance doorway.

Drastic changes to convert the house to a restaurant in 1938 were all removed or restored by the National Park Service in the 1960s. A guided house tour visits four furnished period rooms and an exhibit area, and several rooms containing elegant restored Victorian fireplaces. The Wilcox Library is the primary focus of the tour. Meticulously restored to its 1901 appearance and containing the most original furniture, the library was the scene of Theodore Roosevelt's inauguration. The Greek/Georgian Revival style Dining Room, the most architecturally elegant room in the house, is where Theodore Roosevelt dined during his visit. The Morning Room was used as a temporary office and was the scene of Roosevelt's first official act as president. The second floor Victorian Lady's Bedroom is furnished as representative of the era and contains a few pieces of the Wilcox's furniture.

In addition to house tours, there is an excellent herb garden on the property. Scheduled events are held regularly, including an inauguration reenactment on September 14, celebration of a Victorian Christmas, and an annual Teddy Bear Picnic in August.

Vanderbilt Mansion National Historic Site
Hyde Park, Dutchess County, New York

→ www.nps.gov/vama

→ The site is located along the Hudson River at 4097 Albany Post Road (US Route 9) around a two-hour drive north of New York City and eight miles north of Poughkeepsie, New York. Access is by Interstate 87 (New York State Thruway) from Exit 18 (New Paltz) take New York 299 east to Route 9W south, follow signs to Mid-Hudson Bridge, cross bridge to US Route 9, and drive seven miles north to park.

The opulent Vanderbilt Estate in Hyde Park, New York, is an extraordinary site, one of America's finest examples of the height of the Gilded Age because so few examples survive in the twenty-first century. The architecture, interiors, road systems, and landscape built by Frederick William Vanderbilt is a country estate modeled on the English country house. The 211-acre Vanderbilt Mansion National Historic Site, skillfully masked by trees from US Route 9 at its doorstep, contains the more than fifty-room mansion, Upper and Lower Gate lodges, the Pavilion, Coach House, centuries old tree plantings, the elegant formal gardens, and stunning Hudson River and Catskill Mountain views.

The picturesque countryside along the Hudson River captivated the turn-of-the-century new American aristocracy founded on vast fortunes from finance and industry.

In September of 1895, while yachting up the Hudson River, Vanderbilt was captivated by the sight of a magnificent plateau 300 feet above the river dominated by splendid-sized trees. Learning it was for sale, he happily purchased the property that included a run-down mansion and an untended landscape. "Frederick William Vanderbilt," reported the *New York Times* in 1895, "who has recently joined the little colony of millionaires up the river, is getting ready to make extensive improvements on his house and grounds... said by some to be the finest place on the Hudson between New York and Albany."

Commissioned by Vanderbilt to add wings to the existing mansion, architect Charles Follin McKim of McKim, Mead & White discovered the house structurally unsound and proposed a new house on the site. Modeled after the original house, the design would be an eclectic rendition of the Beaux Arts style, with exterior walls of Indiana limestone around a brick core, modified interior layout, extensive use of plaster and marble, and a structure virtually fireproof and rotproof. Although disappointed by the need for a completely new house, the Vanderbilts moved forward and in 1898 the mansion was completed. Thus, this splendid faux Renaissance palace was designed and built with no expense spared. The mansion was to remain in the Vanderbilt family for over four decades as their center for entertaining for a few weeks in the spring and fall and occasional winter weekends. The cost of construction and furnishings was more than two million dollars.

The imposing South Gate lodge serving as a gatehouse at the park entrance off busy US Route 9 is a prelude to the grounds with the glimmering walls of the mansion seen

Vanderbilt Mansion

in the distance across a pond and the White Bridge; in some seasons, an early morning mist shrouds the building and elements of the boxy three-story facade, imposing two-story portico, and balustraded cornice can be traced in the verdant landscape. The gatehouse and the companion gate lodge at the property's southwest corner, both designed by mansion architects McKim, Mead & White, are of Indiana limestone capped with copper roofs, and were occupied by the Vanderbilt staff.

Mansion details

The three-story mansion over a raised basement is derived from the Italian Rennaisance style, expressing severe classicism, perfect balance, and heavy ornamentation. The composition is faithful to the highest examples of the style with a colonnaded portico with fluted columns topped by Corinthian order column capitals at the central entrance and porticos extending the full width of each side elevation and rising to a second floor cornice. A cornice and balustrade caps the third floor. Rectangular window openings are framed by pilasters and projecting cornices at the first and second floors. A three-bay-wide two-story-high semicircular colonnade portico faces the river. Decorative escutcheons are located in frieze courses and projecting, and flat, engaged fluted columns with Corinthian capitals are at the corners and sides of the entrance portico.

Today's visitor can experience the mansion with interiors and furnishings intact as when Vanderbilt died here in 1938 and, later, when his niece Louise gave the property to the federal government in 1940. The principal rooms of the first floor were the work of Stanford White, McKim's flamboyant partner. The carved dining room ceiling, along with rugs, chimneybreasts, marble columns, and tapestries were purchases White made on travels abroad. In contrast to the imported European artifacts, are the effects introduced by decorations and furnishings by designers Ogden Codman and Georges A. Glaezner. Hushed awe fills crowds guided through the house by park rangers and volunteers upon entrance to each differently styled room. The vast enterprise of mansion and grounds required over sixty full-time employees, seventeen in the house, two in the Pavilion, and forty-four on the grounds and farms.

Now serving as a visitor center, the porticoed Greek Revival Pavilion was built in 1895 and served as the Vanderbilt's living quarters while the mansion was being built. The sixteen-room Pavilion contained kitchen and dining facilities. It became a guest house for men after the Vanderbilts moved into the mansion. Single ladies could join the married couples as guests in the mansion.

The well-tended grounds reflect the naturalistic design of Belgian landscape architect André Parmentier in the 1830s. Vanderbilt, a graduate in horticulture from the Sheffield Scientific School at Yale, diligently supervised the ground's improvements throughout his lifetime. To the south of the mansion are the restored Italian gardens with an elegant tile-roofed, triple-arched gazebo, fountains and statuary. Much of the garden as it appears today, laid out along the natural terraces of the terrain, was the work of James Greenleaf, founder of the American Society of Landscape Architects and preeminient practitioner of "Country Place" era landscape design. Nearby are the Coach House and Stable designed by architect Robert Henderson Robertson, a combination of Renaissance and Tudor elements, originally used as a horse stable and altered in 1910 for automobiles, contained seven double stalls, many work rooms, and seven bedrooms for staff.

In addition to tours of the historic house, the estate grounds are open daily from dawn to dusk. Visitors may hike carriage trails, picnic at the Overlook, or access the Hudson River at Bard Rock.

Women's Rights National Historical Park

Seneca Falls and Waterloo, Seneca County, New York

→ www.nps.gov/wori

→ The park is located midway between Rochester and Syracuse, New York. The park's visitor center at 136 Fall Street in Seneca Falls for units in Seneca Falls and Waterloo is reached via Interstate 90 (New York State Thruway). Take Exit 41 and go south three miles on New York Route 414 and left (east) two miles on US Route 20 to the visitor center.

Wesleyan Chapel, Seneca Falls

The long struggle for women's suffrage was secured in 1920 through the nineteenth amendment to the U.S. Constitution. The long journey of seventy-two years to obtain the franchise for all Americans, regardless of gender, gathered momentum in the small villages of Seneca Falls and Waterloo in central New York in the 1830s and 1840s. The region was known as "The Burned-Over District," because of the popularity of religious revivals and new religious sects that "spread like wildfire." Abolitionist fervor was strong and the Underground Railroad flourished here.

The Women's Rights National Historical Park was authorized in 1980 with locations in Seneca Falls and Waterloo, New York, to celebrate the birthplace of the women's rights movement. It was at the Waterloo home of Jane and Richard Hunt at an early July 1848 tea party that Elizabeth Cady Stanton voiced her frustration with domestic life to Jane Hunt, Lucretia Mott, Martha Wright (Lucretia's sister), and Mary Ann M'Clintock. Drawing inspiration from each other, a week later the group met to draft a *Declaration of*

Sentiments denouncing inequities in property rights, education, employment, religion, marriage and family, and suffrage.

The First Women's Rights Convention was convened on July 19 and 20, 1848 at the Wesleyan Methodist Society Chapel in Seneca Falls to discuss expanding the role of women in America. Three hundred attendees joined this first meeting to be held for the purpose of discussing the "social, civil, and religious conditions and the rights of woman." Frederick Douglass (see page 437), a former slave and prominent abolitionist, publicly seconded Elizabeth Cady Stanton's highly controversial motion for the right of women to vote. At the end of the two days, one hundred people made a public commitment to work together to improve women's quality of life. It was the beginning of the women's rights movement in the United States. Twelve days later a second convention was held in Rochester. The long march for the convention's radical demands—led by the active mind and writing of Stanton and strengthened in 1851 by the dedicated women's rights campaigner Susan B. Anthony—was launched.

The park's historical structures include the remains of the Wesleyan Chapel and homes of the women involved in the movement's earliest days. Today's visitor to the Women's Rights National Historical Park should begin at the visitor center at 136 Fall Street (US Route 20) in the center of Seneca Falls. In addition to exhibits, an orientation film, and publications, the visitor center lobby contains sculptor Lloyd Lily's *The First Wave*, vivid life-size bronze statues of the five women who organized the First Women's Rights Convention, and a few of the men who came in support of social, political, and religious equality for women.

The centerpiece of the park, next to the visitor center, is the preserved remains of the Wesleyan Chapel—the site of the First Women's Rights Convention. A brick wall encloses the chapel's stabilized side walls and roof beams under a protective roof, with adjacent outdoor tiered seating, a small lawn—Declaration Park—and a commemorative

Elizabeth Cady Stanton House

Hunt House (M'Clintock)

waterwall symbolizing the original Seneca Falls inscribed with the words of the Declaration of Sentiments and the document's one hundred signers. The chapel, built in 1843, was a local haven for antislavery activity, political rallies, and free speech events. Altered by time and neglect, after purchase in 1985 by the National Park Service (NPS), there was very little original fabric left to work with. Using great restraint and avoiding a replica building, the NPS placed under a modern metal roof the original roof beams and the

two partial multicolored brick side walls, which were stabilized by interspersed solid blonde-colored brick and reinforced with steel bracing. A tall and dressed sandstone wall creates an entrance gateway facing Fall Street and continues around the corner on Mynderse Street. A low wall of the same stone is extended from the entrance wall toward the visitor center.

When Anthony Met Stanton, A.E. Ted Aub

The Elizabeth Cady Stanton House at 32 Washington Street, Seneca Falls, is where the suffrage leader lived from 1846 to 1862 with her husband and seven children before moving to New York City. The house seen today, restored and furnished by the NPS, has undergone additions and removals of wings to the 1830s original one-story section. During the Stanton's occupancy the house was nearly twice the size it is now, with a mirror image of the one-story wing with a front porch on the other side of the two-story section (approximately 18 by 28 feet in plan). Only two of the four portions of the house have been preserved.

Located east of Waterloo on East Main Street (US Route 20), the white-columned, two-story red brick Georgian Colonial style Hunt House is where the five women met on Sunday, July 9, 1848 and ended their day deciding to call the first-ever women's rights convention. The house is not open to the public.

Two-story, red-brick Federal style M'Clintock House between Virginia and Church Streets also in Waterloo, New York, is where the *Declaration of Sentiments* was drafted on July 16, 1848. Richard Hunt built the two story red-brick house at 14 East Williams Street in 1836, but never lived there. Rented in 1836 by the M'Clintock family, Quakers with strong anti-slavery and temperance beliefs, the house was used as a station for fugitive slaves on the Underground Railroad.

The Villages of Seneca Falls and Waterloo are now quiet, former industrial towns with modest downtowns overshadowed by regional malls. The towns are connected by road and water with the Cayuga and Seneca Canal flowing through the historic districts in the center of each town. Seneca Falls has a network of parks and pleasant walks connecting sites related to women's rights and is enlivened regularly by events of local, regional, and national stature.

Pennsylvania

Mid-Atlantic

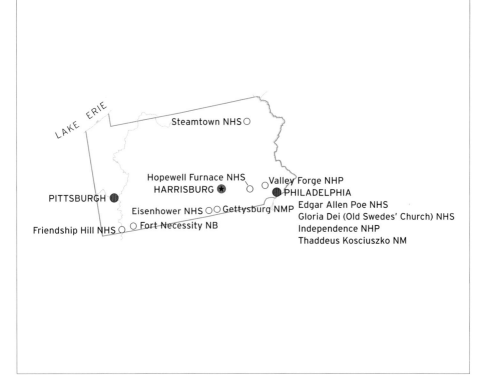

Edgar Allan Poe National Historic Site

Philadelphia, Pennsylvania

→   www.nps.gov/edal

→   Located at 530 North Seventh Street, Philadelphia, Edgar Allan Poe house is in close proximity to Interstate 95 and 276 highway exits and five blocks north of Center City. On-street parking is usually available near the site.

Poe's Raven at 530 North Street

The spirit of Edgar Allan Poe, distinguished as an American literary genius for his invention of several forms of fiction and for his critical acumen, reverberates through this three-story brick townhouse in the center of Philadelphia. With so little known about his personal life and contents during Poe's occupancy, the National Park Service (NPS) has taken a minimalist approach to furnishing the house. In contrast to the typical writer's historical site with the usual trappings seen as though he would return momentarily to his cluttered desk to take up his pen and cigar, the interpretive comments of ranger guides inspire a hushed awe and visitors can use their imagination to probe Poe's literary meanings and sources.

Poe, born in Boston 1809 to itinerant actors and orphaned at age two, endured a life of struggle and poverty. He attained his greatest successes as an editor and critic in the six years (1838–44) he lived in several Philadelphia houses. This National Historic Landmark house on North Seventh Street, which he moved into sometime between the fall of 1842 and June of 1843 and left in April 1844, is the only Poe residence that survives and serves as a link between the famous writer and his productive years in Philadelphia. Poe left the house for New York City with his ailing wife, mother-in-law (and aunt), and $4.50 in his pocket and quicly sunk into despair over health and finances. After his wife Virginia Clemm Poe's death there in 1847 of tuberculosis, his physical and mental health declined and he died in Baltimore in 1849.

A visit to the Edgar Allan Poe National Historic Site helps refresh familiar tales of mystery and horror and, especially for those unacquainted with Poe's career, to understand his impact on American letters. The breadth of Poe's literary accomplishments, including tales ranging from the masterful to the ludicrous, is overshadowed by his popular recognition as the inventor of the modern detective story. Indeed, his process of "ratiocination"—a process of exact rational thinking—first appearing in 1841 in *The Murders in the Rue Morgue*, established the genre. Besides his experiments with science fiction in *The Unparalleled Adventure of One Hans Pfaal* and his tales of terror, such as *The Pit and the Pendulum,* his articles and essays critically assessed modern poetry and formulated the concept of the short story.

The park consists of a complex of three buildings, two facing 530 North Seventh Street that serve as a visitor center, and the Poe residence to the rear. Buildings have been removed from the south side of the house to suggest the Spring Garden district in the early to mid-nineteenth century. A wrought-iron fence and gate blocks access from North Seventh Street. Behind the fence is a brick walkway and atop a tall, black pylon is a striking raven with wings outstretched, a reminder of Poe's famous poem:

> *Once upon a midnight dreary, while I pondered, weak and weary*
> *Over many a quaint and curious volume of forgotten lore,*
> *While I nodded, nearly napping, suddenly there came a tapping,*
> *As of some one gently rapping.*

Eisenhower National Historic Site

Near Gettysburg, Adams County, Pennsylvania

→   www.nps.gov/eise

→   Due to a lack of on-site parking and space limitations in the Eisenhower home, visits can only be made by a shuttle bus leaving from the Gettysburg National Military Park Visitor Center located at 1195 Baltimore Street (State Route 97), Gettysburg, Pennsylvania. Once at the farm you can stay for as long as you like, catching any of the returning shuttle buses back to the visitor center every thirty minutes in summer and on fall and spring weekends, and once an hour during the week.

Eisenhower home

The rolling hills of south central Pennsylvania is a bucolic area selected by Dwight David Eisenhower as a retreat and eventual retirement home. Following World War II and while serving as the president of Columbia University, Eisenhower and his wife Mamie purchased a farm adjoining Gettysburg National Military Park. The thirty-fourth president of the United States used the original 189-acre farm to escape the pressures of office during his two terms (1953–61), recuperate from a heart attack (1955), and after leaving the presidency lived there until he died in 1969. Mamie continued to live there until her death in 1979. The pleasure the Eisenhowers enjoyed on the farm as the only home they ever owned is evident in the charm and grace of the elegant yet comfortable modified Georgian house.

In his autobiography, Ike (a childhood nickname) called the farm home "an escape from concrete to the countryside." Mamie Eisenhower, experiencing at least thirty-seven other residences worldwide, including the White House, explained why the property was so important to the couple, "we had only one home—our farm." After conferences at nearby Camp David (named after grandson, David Eisenhower), Ike received distinguished guests to the farm, such as French President Charles De Gaulle, Soviet Premier Nikita Khrushchev, and British Prime Minister Winston Churchill. Retirement life included working at his office at Gettysburg College writing his presidential memoirs and autobiography, and touring the battlefield—imagine the interpretation from the supreme allied commander!.

Born in 1890, the future five-star general and president of the United States lived his early years in Abilene, Kansas. The ambition to receive a college education—and a free one at the U. S. Military Academy—for the third of six sons brought Ike to West Point in 1911. Eisenhower first came to the Gettysburg area in 1915 as a young cadet on a West Point field trip and began living there in 1918 as commander at Camp Colt, the Army Tank Corps training center. Eisenhower quickly became attached to this area in the Appalachian foothills, about fifty miles south of where his ancestors had settled in the 1700s.

In 1950, the Eisenhowers, looking forward to retirement, purchased the Allen Redding farm and red brick farmhouse adjoining Gettysburg National Military Park. Although in disrepair, remodeling proceeded to uncover within the brick veneer a deteriorating 200-year-old log cabin threatening to collapse. Disappointed that the Redding house could not be completely saved, but undaunted, Mamie had chief architect Milton Osborne of the Pennsylvania State University work with the contractors to salvage what was possible from the dismantled structure and build a new house, incorporating the den floorboards, wainscoting, and ceiling beams from the old house. Construction and landscaping for the National Historic Landmark house were completed in 1955.

The finished house, without the pretensions of a grand Georgian estate, has a two-story white-painted brick main block, an L-wing and a one-story fieldstone dormered wing. Next to the smaller wing built of salvaged material from the Redding farm is the windmill used to pump water to the original house on the site. Inside are eight bedrooms, nine bathrooms, a stately living room, a formal dining room, a large kitchen and butler's pantry, an attic studio, and the family's favorite room, a large enclosed porch facing Seminary Ridge on the Gettysburg battlefield. The house contains nearly all the original furnishings, including the collection of many years accumulation of furniture, decorative objects, housewarming gifts, and the president's paintings displayed by the proud Mrs. Eisenhower.

Adjacent to the farmhouse is a small brick guest house; the well-constructed large "bank" barn, a typical central Pennsylvania structure with the cattle on the lower level and hay and straw on the upper level; tea house; and greenhouse. A path leads from the Eisenhower Farm to 285-acre adjoining Farm 2, the site of the Angus cattle operation.

Fort Necessity National Battlefield

Located in southwestern Pennsylvania near Uniontown, Fayette County

→   www.nps.gov/fone

→   The park is in three units: the main unit comprised of the Fort Necessity battlefield and Mount Washington Tavern is on US Route 40, eleven miles east of Uniontown, Pennsylvania; the Braddock Grave unit approximately one-and-a-half miles west of the main unit; and the Jumonville Glen unit is approximately seven miles northwest of the main unit.

Fort Necessity's log palisade walls

The wooded mountains and river valleys of southwestern Pennsylvania is the scene of the opening battle of the French and Indian War in 1754. Here, west of the Allegheny Mountains far from British colonial settled areas along the Atlantic seaboard and inland French settlements, a battle that ignited hostilities between the two worldwide powers known as the Seven Years' War ended in 1763 when control of the North American continent was resolved in favor of the British. As British statesman Horace Walpole put it: "A volley fired by a young Virginian in the backwoods of America set the world on fire." The young Virginian was George Washington, leader of the Virginia regiment sent to participate in the eviction of the French from western Pennsylvania. The action at Fort Necessity was the first major event in the military career of George Washington. It was the only time he ever surrendered to an enemy.

Fort Necessity National Battlefield, its preserved landscape, a reconstructed log stockade, and nearby early-nineteenth-century George Washington Tavern, is a remnant of this important military action and along with Fort Stanwix National Monument (see page 483) the only National Park System units representing the French and Indian War.

The events leading up to the engagement where Washington, a twenty-two-year-old lieutenant colonel sent west by Governor Robert Dinwiddie of Virginia, was part of the struggle in North America between the British and French for control of the lands west of the Alleghenies. The Ohio River Valley between the Appalachian Mountains and the Mississippi was crucial to control of the region. The British were eager to obtain the land for westward expansion of the colonies, while the French were seeking a strong link between New France (Canada) and Louisiana.

Visitors to the Great Meadows, the place Washington selected to build defensive fortifications, should not be disappointed by the small scale of the circular log-palisaded stockade, seemingly diminished in size by the surrounding open land. The modest size fort looms large in the sweep of historic events that took place here. The exhibits at the visitor center, a short, discrete distance away and unimpinging on the scene of the conflict, and ranger-guided tours provide an informative introduction to the historic engagement.

Washington had previously visited the area while doing surveying work when he was eighteen and later, during the winter of 1753–54, when he delivered a notice of trespass to the French building forts on or above the Allegheny River. Sent by the governor to lead a road-building team and then proceed to help defend an English fort at the fork of the Ohio River in the spring of 1754, he was thorough in reporting the expedition's events. An excellent historical record exists documenting the newly commissioned officer's thoughts and observations. In a letter to Governor Dinwiddie (May 27, 1754), Washington described the Great Meadows:

> I thereupon hurried to this place as a convenient spott…and by clearing the Bushes out of these Meadows prepar'd a charming field for an Encounter.

But it was not a good place; an outnumbered Washington commanded and bad weather dominated as events unfolded. Today, you can trace the natural entrenchments

Stockade log store house

Mount Washington Tavern

at the junction of Indian Run and Great Meadows Run, to which Washington refers in one of his communications. By June 3, Washington's soldiers completed a stockade of logs, 9 to 10 inches in diameter, 10 feet long and split lengthwise, and sunk into a

2.5-foot-deep entrenchment flat side facing out, tops axed to a point. Inside, the logs forming a circle with a diameter of about 53 feet were placed between smaller unsplit logs about 7 feet long to close the gaps and serve as gun rests. A 3.5-foot-wide gate, facing west, was hung between two upright timbers. At the center of the stockade was a small log storehouse about 14 feet square, the pitched roof of which was covered with bark and hides. The present reconstructed stockade, with its swivel gun mounted outside the entrance, was completed in the spring of 1954 in the exact location of the original stockade posts, based on extensive archeological excavations and research.

Mount Washington Tavern

The eight-hour battle was fought in a torrential downpour; the low ground Washington chose was poorly suited under the conditions, and worsened by the stockade's placement within sixty yards of protective woods on the southeastern side of the fort. But Washington had said he intended to avoid a battle at the temporary works at Great Meadows and build a real bastion some miles away. Obvious to Washington that defeat was inevitable, he surrendered for the first and last time in his long military career.

On the crest of the hill north of the park entrance, on what is now US Route 40 and was once the National Road, stands a handsome Federal-style two-story brick house overlooking Great Meadows. As the National Road built by the federal government was developed from Cumberland, Maryland, and eventually into Indiana and Illinois, around 1827 Judge Nathaniel Ewing of Fayette County, then owner of the Great Meadows tract, erected a large house on a crest of the new road near land formerly owned by George Washington. Converted into Mount Washington Tavern and operated by James and Rebecca Sampey, the imposing two-story red brick house served as one of many stagecoach stops on the National Road. The five-bay Federal-style house with a Palladian entrance facing the road, end chimneys, and attic dormers is restored as a museum with period furnishings, relics of the Washington and Braddock campaigns and exhibits of the National Road era.

The visitor center, a short discrete distance by paved path from the fort and un-impinging on the scene of the conflict, provides an informative introduction to the historic engagement more than two-and-a-half centuries ago. Ranger-led tours, talks, and historic weapons demonstrations are offered during summer months. The Fort Necessity park grounds are open daily from sunrise to sunset, year-round.

Friendship Hill National Historic Site

Located in southwestern Pennsylvania midway between Uniontown, Pennsylvania, and Morgantown, West Virginia, in Fayette County, Pennsylvania

→ www.nps.gov/frhi

→ Access is from PA 116. From Point Marion or Smithfield, Pennsylvania, follow signs to the site.

Friendship Hill Mansion

This rambling mansion on a hill overlooking the Monongahela River in the southwestern corner of Pennsylvania was the home of Albert Gallatin for almost forty years. The young Swiss-born emigré arrived in America in 1780 and rose to become an influential figure in the early years of the new republic. He chose western Pennsylvania as an area of opportunity for land speculation. Arriving in the area in 1784, he purchased Friendship Hill as the site for his home in 1788.

Gallatin entered politics and rapidly rose to elected office, serving in the U.S. House of Representatives from 1795 to 1801. His greatest distinction came through his service to Presidents Jefferson and Madison as secretary of the Treasury (1801–14), guiding the young nation to fiscal accountability by structuring national finances. Gallatin later served in the diplomatic role of negotiator of the Treaty of Ghent, ending the War of 1812 with Great Britain, and as U.S. minister to France (1816–23) and to Great Britain (1826–27). Gallatin's career in finance, politics, diplomacy, and scholarship often took him away from Friendship Hill for long periods. In his absence, the mansion was expanded, and finally sold in 1832 when the family permanently left western Pennsylvania. Gallatin died in 1849 at age eighty-eight.

A visit to today's Friendship Hill is a pleasant experience of a short uphill walk from the site's parking lot, past a full size statue of Albert Gallatin peering through a surveyor's transit, to reach the hilltop restored mansion. The mansion is set in manicured grounds, gradually revealed as a composition of varied architectural styles and materials, including post-Gallatin additions. The L-shaped composition includes the core elements built during Gallatin's ownership: the 1789 Brick House, the 1798 Frame House, 1823 Stone House, and 1824 Stone Kitchen. Remaining intact are the stuccoed 1895 State Dining Room, inserted between the Frame House and Stone House, and the 1895 Servants' Quarters connected to the Stone Kitchen by a porte cochere.

Construction on the two-story Brick House was underway in 1789. Approximately 26 by 29 feet in plan, the first floor built on an exposed stone foundation contained a parlor, library, and sitting room; two bedrooms were on the second floor. Designed in the Federal style, exterior brick walls were in Flemish bond; first and second story porches on the front, facing the Monongahela River, and a balcony on the rear side. The two-and-a-half-story 1798 Frame House, approximately 20-foot-square, was built for Gallatin's growing family including his second wife, Hannah, and children. Wall construction was half-timbered framing members with brick infill, originally covered by clapboard siding and later stuccoed.

The most imposing element of Friendship Hill, the two-and-one-half-story Stone House has a curious combination of styles; Gallatin preferred Greek Revival, his Irish carpenter creating a disorder described by Gallatin as "Hyberno-Teutonic." The exterior is built of ochre-colored sandstone walls, and has a slate roof with pairs of dormers on north and south elevations, and an 8-foot-wide one-story porch wrapping north and east sides. Completed with two first-floor parlors, two second-floor bedrooms, and four third-floor rooms, the house was richly ornamented with marble fireplaces and mantel pieces, and classical door and window trim.

Albert Gallatin surveying

The 1895 State Dining Room, although not part of Gallatin's Friendship Hill years, was retained during restoration to serve as a visitor center to avoid intrusion on the historic scene.

Gettysburg National Military Park

Gettysburg, Adams County, Pennsylvania

→ www.nps.gov/gett

→ The nearly 6,000-acre park surrounds the Borough of Gettysburg in south-central Pennsylvania, three miles west of US 15 near the Maryland border.

The Gettysburg National Military Park is hallowed ground, reverberating through American history with place names such as Cemetery Ridge, Little Round Top, Devil's Den, the Wheatfield, the Peach Orchard, and the desperate final Pickett's Charge. Abraham Lincoln came here on November 19, 1863 to dedicate the new cemetery to the Union soldiers who fell in the bloodiest struggle ever fought on the North American continent. He was mistaken when he modestly assumed "the world will little note, nor long remember, what we say here, but it can never forget what they did here." The world has remembered and millions of people have come to reverently walk the town and sites of the bloody battle fought between July 1 and 3, 1863.

The bold move by Robert E. Lee to invade the north, conceived to counter the successes of Ulysses S. Grant in the lower Mississippi River Valley, had great strategic implications for the South. Marching north through the Shenandoah Valley and screened from Federal forces by the Blue Ridge Mountains, Lee's army crossed the Potomac River at Williamsport, Maryland, and Stephenstown, West Virginia, and moved into southern Pennsylvania. By destroying a railroad bridge at Harrisburg, a major link between the Eastern Seaboard and the Midwest, in his own words Robert E. Lee opened the tantalizing possibilities to then "turn my attention to Philadelphia, Baltimore, or Washington as may seem best for our interest."

On the gently rolling farmland surrounding Gettysburg, the titanic struggle between 75,000 Confederates and 97,000 Union troops raged about the town and left 51,000 casualties in its wake. The disaster of the famed Confederate assault on July 3, which has become known throughout the world as Pickett's Charge, ended those dreams, Lee ordering a retreat south for his battered army on July 4. The escape succeeded and the Gettysburg Campaign was over, marking the beginning of a gradual decline in Southern military power.

The main attraction for the nearly two million annual visitors to the park is to understand the events that took place here on the three days in July of 1863, within the context of American history. The resources of primary concern are the natural features of the 6,000-acre battlefield and the sites of engagements, as well as 1,320 monuments and memorials; 410 cannon; Soldiers National Cemetery with 7,000 interments; twenty-six miles of historic avenues, seven miles of historic paved roads, and eight miles of unpaved historic lanes. There are historical "witness" buildings in the park—farm complexes existing in 1863 that have undergone changes for continued use.

The visitor center designed by Richard Neutra and completed in 1962, containing the Cyclorama—a cylindrical drum housing the famous *Battle of Gettysburg*, a 360-degree circular oil-on-canvas painting by the French artist Paul Philippoteaux that depicts Pickett's Charge, completed and exhibited in 1884—is destined for removal and replacement by the new Gettysburg Museum and Visitor Center. A lengthy and sometimes contentious national debate about removal of the Neutra building involved a highly consultative public process. The issue was resolved with a determination by the President's Advisory Commission on Historic Preservation that preservation of the battlefield historic landscape and Cyclorama painting took precedence over preservation of the Cyclorama building.

The new museum and visitor center is adjacent to the battlefield, but sited at a low point in the terrain so it will not be visible from the major interpretive points. Located near the intersection of Hunt Avenue and Baltimore Pike, a short distance from the current visitor center, the new facility is on ground that saw no major battle action. Funded through donations coordinated by the Gettysburg Foundation, and designed by Cooper Robertson & Partners with architect of record LSC Design of York, Pennsylvania, the facility housing the restored Philippoteaux painting is scheduled to open in 2008.

There are a number of ways to tour the battlefield beginning at the visitor center. From mid-June through mid-August park rangers provide a series of free tours and programs on the battlefield. A self-guided eighteen-mile auto tour taking two to three hours is available, and licensed battlefield guides are available for private tours. Audio tours can be downloaded as podcasts, or rented or purchased at the visitor center. The best way to understand what happened here, and why, is to walk the battlefield on the mile-long High Water Mark Trail, short paths leading to prominent sites, the three and one half-mile Johnny Reb trail, or the longer nine-mile Billy Yank Trail.

Gloria Dei (Old Swedes' Church)

Philadelphia, Pennsylvania

→   www.nps.gov/glde

→   The church is located in South Philadelphia at Delaware Avenue and Christian Street, approximately one half-mile south of Penn's Landing. Access is from Interstate 95 at Exit 16 (Columbus Boulevard/Washington Boulevard) and follow signs to church. Enter the church parking lot from Christian Street.

This striking red brick church constructed of Flemish bond and glazed black header brick south of central Philadelphia is the oldest church still standing in the state of Pennsylvania. Consecrated to the Glory of God (*Gloria Dei*) on July 2, 1700, the structure tranquilly sits behind its high brick churchyard walls separated from an interstate highway on one side and the surrounding industrial Delaware River waterfront. Swedish emigrants settled New Sweden in the Delaware Valley in 1643. Although the colony did not flourish, the Swedish churches survived. After serving as the Swedish Lutheran Church for almost 150 years, Gloria Dei joined the Diocese of the Episcopal Church of Pennsylvania. The Gloria Dei congregation owns and maintains the church, rectory,

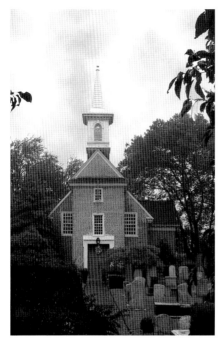

Gloria Dei (Old Swedes' Church)   Interior

parish house, sexton's house, the grounds, and cemetery. Additional land provided by the National Park Service within the enclosing walls creates a park-like setting in the midst of an industrial area.

The church built for the Swedish Lutheran congregation at Wicaco, then distant from the Quaker town, and ultimately as part of the Borough of Southwark incorporated into the city of Philadelphia, used vernacular forms common in William Penn's colony. The symmetrical composition, steeply pitched roofs, and the strong cornice line are characteristic of the period. Although the congregation emigrated from Sweden, there lacks any connections to traditional Swedish construction materials and methods because the church was designed and built by Philadelphia builders trained in the English craft guild tradition, including some of the carpenters and bricklayers who had built the new church at Fort Christiana (Wilmington, Delaware).

Over the years, the simple church form (approximately 34 feet wide and 65 feet deep from entry to east end semicircular apse) was modified with transept-like wings and tower additions, and interior changes to the original building. The plan provided for a tower, but the tower was not completed until 1703. Although the walls were quite thick, they began to bow outward in 1704 under the weight of the steep sloping roof. To arrest this process and preserve the building, a sacristy was built onto the north side of the church and a vestibule was built onto the south side. These acted as buttresses and gave the building a cruciform footprint. By the 1840s a growing congregation required more worship space. A renovation completed after 1845 raised the floor, added balconies, and a center pulpit and the stained glass window. The building was restored in 1999 but remains essentially unchanged since 1846.

The church interior is a simple, open space with a plastered, vaulted ceiling shaped to a half-dome over the pulpit, and paneled wainscoting. It contains many items from the original log church built in 1643 by the New Sweden settlement at Tinicum, including the baptismal font, paintings, biblical quotations on the wall, and the bronze church bell clapper. In front, suspended from the ceiling are models of the ships *Fogel Grip* and *Kalmar Nyckel*—ships that brought the Swedish settlers to this country in 1638. Tall, multilight windows flood the interior with daylight; the stained glass window behind the pulpit sparkles in the morning light. A Swedish and American flag flank either side of the pulpit.

The cemetery and grounds contain, among others, graves of Revolutionary War soldiers and a black granite memorial to John Hanson who served as the first elected president of the Continental Congress, arguably, the first president of our country. The church continues many Swedish traditions including the popular Feast of Santa Lucia, on the weekend near December 13 and a Christmas Day Swedish service called *Julotta*.

Hopewell Furnace National Historic Site

Located in Elverson, Chester County, Pennsylvania

→ www.nps.gov/hofu

→ The park is in southeastern Pennsylvania forty-five miles northwest of Philadelphia. It is located within French Creek State Park about five miles south of Birdsboro on Route 345 and ten miles northeast of Exit 298 (Morgantown) on the Pennsylvania Turnpike (Interstate 76) via Route 23 West to Route 345 North.

The Hopewell Furnace National Historic Site restored iron-making village captures the time in the late eighteenth and early nineteenth century when the waters of French Creek churned the massive wooden waterwheel feeding the blast furnace at Mark Bird's iron works. Nearby were the basic ingredients for iron production: reliable water power, deposits of iron ore, limestone (to reduce impurities in the ore during smelting), and hardwood forests for creating charcoal. The National Park Service (NPS) recreated a setting for the years 1820–40 to depict the iron-making production process—the massive 30-foot-diameter water wheel still churns, the blast furnace glows, and the blacksmith's hammer shapes iron products—and the community, including the ironmaster's mansion, workers' homes, schoolhouse, and company store.

Hopewell Furnace National Historic Site depicts early iron-making technology and an industry that drove the colonies into ascendancy as a republic and a leading world center of iron goods production. Here, one can walk the grounds of the 848-acre park and peer into the cast house that surrounded the furnace stack, the very heart of the entire community. When the stack glowed day and night there was prosperity; when

Cast house, tunnel head to rear

it cooled down there were hard times. Supporting operations, seen in the charcoal hearths, charcoal house, connecting shed and bridge house, and blacksmith shop are all of modest building size and small in scale. The assemblage of structures predate the steel-making technology that eventually drove the obsolete Hopewell Furnace to make its final blast in 1883. There are contrasting housing types distinguishing a hierarchy of social positions and skills, almost feudal in character—the ironmaster's mansion, tenant dwellings, and boarding house. The office store, schoolhouse, springhouse and smokehouse, and barns complete the community as it was in its peak years.

Hopewell Furnace—"Iron Plantations" as they were called in colonial times—was founded by ironmaster Mark Bird in 1771 to take advantage of the locally abundant raw materials and the relatively simple blast furnace process of converting iron to ore. Although England prohibited the manufacture of finished iron products by the colonies, Americans defied the law. Bird immediately began casting stove plates, and produced Revolutionary War cannon and ammunition. During peacetime, the furnace prospered with a wide variety of iron products, including the popular Hopewell stove. Although demand in the Civil War caused a temporary resurgence of operations at Hopewell, the peak production of the 1830s could not be repeated. The new technology of large-scale Bessemer steel production in urban-based steam-powered and hot-blast coke and Pennsylvania anthracite-fueled furnaces replaced the rural charcoal-fired and water-powered furnaces.

The restoration of the core fourteen Hopewell Furnace buildings began with a deserted village, many of the buildings badly deteriorated. Interest in the site by the federal government in the early 1930s led to purchasing the lands, not for historic preservation but for use in the New Deal conservation program. Works Progress Administration investigative work and Civilian Conservation Corps members laid the groundwork for the NPS restoration that began in earnest in the 1950s. With buildings restored and operational—the waterwheel and blast machinery were almost completely rebuilt and were in operation in 1952—work continues on the restoration of the rural-industrial landscape.

Ironmaster's mansion

In summer, the living-history programs with period-clothed interpreters demonstrate metal casting, blacksmithing, charcoal-making, and other traditional iron-making skills and tasks. Whistles blow, the furnace's blast of hot air pumps from bellows driven by the waterwheel, the anvils clang, the waterwheel and blast machinery toil away, livestock graze in the meadows, and wagons are on the move with goods and material. The visitor can take a self-guided tour or join the park ranger guides and volunteers for informative talks on nineteenth-century life at Hopewell.

Independence National Historical Park
Philadelphia, Philadelphia County, Pennsylvania

→   www.nps.gov/inde

→   The 45-acre park is in downtown Philadelphia with a Visitor Center at Sixth and Market Streets and a parking garage is underneath, accessible from either Fifth or Sixth Streets. Access to the park is via Interstate 676 connecting Interstate 76 and Interstate 95. Follow signs to visitor center and parking garage.

Independence National Historical Park is a national and international symbol of freedom. Here the nation's founders drafted both the Declaration of Independence and the United States Constitution, and preserved here are many American landmarks in one of the most popular historic areas in the country and destinations in the National Park System. Many of the meticulously restored buildings retaining the flavor of colonial America are within walking distance of the visitor center. The National Park Service (NPS) recommends at least a day, and longer if possible, to visit and absorb this place where the United States was founded.

Buildings suggested by the NPS in a one- to two-day visit are: Visitor Center, Liberty Bell Center, Independence Hall, Great Essentials exhibit, Congress Hall, Old City Hall,

Portrait Gallery in the Second Bank of the United States, Franklin Court, Carpenters' Hall, New Hall Military Museum, Bishop White House, Declaration House, Thaddeus Kosciuszko National Memorial (see page 537), Edgar Allan Poe National Historic Site

Independence Hall, north elevation

(see page 517), Deshler-Morris House, and City Tavern. To that list we add other buildings open to the public: Philadelphia Exchange, Christ Church, Gloria Dei (Old Swedes' Church; see page 526), and the Market Street Houses. The visitor should begin at the Visitor Center for an orientation and to plan a tour that will require some driving outside downtown Philadelphia to the Poe, Kosciuszko, Deshler-Morris, and Gloria Dei parks/sites.

The Liberty Bell Center (by Bohlin Cywinski Jackson) is a striking building exquisitely designed as a frame of reference to display the Liberty Bell. In a sequence of rooms and vistas that culminate in the bell, the final chamber places the bell seen at first in silhouette against a stunning backdrop of Independence Hall, then experienced in the round.

Independence Hall, designated a World Heritage Site in 1979, is the park's focus. The splendid creation of master carpenter Edmund Wooley and amateur architect, Andrew Hamilton, was built between 1732 and 1756 as the Pennsylvania State House. Most widely known for the events in the Assembly Room where the Declaration of Independence was signed (1776), the Articles of Confederation ratified (1781), and the United States Constitution drafted and signed (1787). The two-story, nine-bay main block (approximately 106 feet long and 44 feet wide) Palladian inspired Georgian Colonial architecture exterior is red brick laid in Flemish bond, and is embellished with marble panels, belt courses, and molded cornice,; quadruple chimneys at either end serve as terminals

for a balustraded roof deck. Seen from Independence Square to the south, the building is dominated by the Wren-influenced tower, with the Palladian window in its base.
Viewed from Independence Mall to the north, the tower inspires an ecclesiastic appearance, although placed in the center of the long side, rather than at the end.

Soon after construction of the main block started, the flanking symmetrical three-
bay arcades and two-story-high six-bay wings were added. Until the addition of the
tower, a merely competent version of the prevailing fine Georgian mansion with balanced hip-roofed dependencies was in place. On the first floor the Assembly Room and
Supreme Court Room extended to either side of a wide hallway; a "Long Room" above
ran the full length of the building. The dependencies served as office space. Interiors are
splendid both in scale and detailing of woodwork. The external tower, conceived "as a
place to hang a bell," grew to the magnificent steeple reaching 170 feet from ground to
tip of weathervane. Today's elaborated version of the 1781 original, restored in 1828 by
architect William Strickland, is approximately 31 feet square, almost dividing the Independence Square-facing facade of the main block into equal thirds. With the tower and
steeple in place, the competent building was converted, at least from the south, from its
horizontal prominence to the drama of vertical emphasis, flowing upward to the steeple
weathervane with impeccable Georgian details.

Flanking Independence Hall is the Old City Hall, second home to the U.S. Supreme
Court (until 1800), and Congress Hall (the County Courthouse), where Congress met
from 1790 to 1800. The south elevation of the complex faces Independence Square, where
on July 8, 1776 the Declaration of Independence was
first read in public. To the right of the Square (to the
east) a brick walkway leads to the National Historic
Landmark American Philosophical Society Hall, a
two-story late-Georgian red brick building constructed in 1789 to house one of the nation's oldest
and most honorable learned societies.

The building immediately to the east is Library
Hall, a reconstruction housing the Philosophical Society library. The home of the oldest learned society
in America, founded by Benjamin Franklin in 1743,
the original building designed by William Thornton
(the original architect of the U.S. Capitol) stood on
the site from 1789 to 1888. The recreated building
was constructed in the mid-1950s. And further to
the east is the National Historic Landmark Second

Carpenters' Hall

Bank of the United States. Awarded in a design competition to architect William Strickland and modeled on the Parthenon (sans sculpture), it is one of the finest examples
of Greek Revival architecture in the country and was completed in 1824. The struc-

ture, with octastyle Doric porches on each end, is significant for its influence on public architecture in the first half of the nineteenth century. On the side are arched windows and the inside is a Roman rotunda, and the main banking room occupying the entire

Christ Church interior

Second Bank of the United States

center of the building—a handsome space with freestanding Ionic columns supporting a vaulted ceiling. The building was remodeled for the nation's bicentennial to serve as a portrait gallery featuring important early Americans, including a superb collection of portraits by artist Charles Willson Peale.

Following along the walkway east from Independence Hall and across Fourth Street is Carpenters' Hall, a National Historic Landmark built between 1770 and 1774 by the Carpenters' Company of Philadelphia, the oldest trade organization in the country. Designed by Robert Smith, this fine example of Georgian public architecture is a tour-de-force demonstration by Philadelphia's master carpenters and contractors building skills. Although modest in size, Greek cross in plan and 50 feet wide and deep, a raised basement, pedimented gables on all sides, and a central cupola enhance the impressive craftsmanship to the viewer. The facade embellishments of wood details—cornices, string courses, framing for arched windows, each with a section of balustrade underneath, and shutters—lend elegance to this marvelously restored building.

Along Walnut Street, to the south of Independence Square, are rows of restored brick houses and gardens, typical of the colonial period. East of Third Street at the northeast corner of Walnut Street is the Merchant's Exchange, built for the Philadelphia Exchange company, the acknowledged Greek Revival masterpiece of architect William Strickland built between 1832 and 1834. The three-story structure is an eclectic design in its use of classical elements adopted for a commercial purpose and manipulated on a moderately sloping triangular site. A rectangular main block is merged with a semicircular rotunda, raised over a high base and surrounded by a Corinthian octastyle portico, at the site's east end to house the exchange room. A cupola with a lantern lighting the exchange floor is set over the imaginary temple.

East of Dock Street at Walnut and Second Streets is City Tavern, a reconstruction of a fine Revolutionary-era tavern, open to the public for lunch and dinner in an authentic eighteenth-century atmosphere. Located on Market Street between Third and Fourth Streets, is Franklin Court, the site of Benjamin Franklin's house. The site contains restored brick rowhouses built by Franklin and the creative steel frame "ghost structures" designed by architects Venturi and Rauch outlining his original house and his 1786 print shop. There is an underground museum and post office commemorating Franklin's position as the first U.S. postmaster on the site.

North of Market Street on Second Street is the National Historic Landmark Christ Church, considered the most elegant colonial church in America. The western portion was first completed in 1731, the eastern end completed prior to 1744, and the tower and steeple in 1755. This Anglican city church, inspired by the Georgian style seen in contemporary London's finest examples (St. Martin-in-the-Fields, 1721–26), prospered greatly and by mid-eighteenth century was the most fashionable in Philadelphia. It was here that the Protestant Episcopal Church in the United States was born, severing ties with the Church of England. The 62- by 87-foot in plan church is richly embellished in Georgian style exuberances with accents of stone trim on its red brick exterior walls, projecting chancel, with an enormous Palladian window (in 1954 the Victorian-era stained glass was restored to original clear glass), and parapet with balustrade and urn. The design device of the end (east) wall containing the Palladian window carried above the balustrade and beyond the entablature into an attic and crowning pediment emphasizes the tall nave of the interior. A ground-based tower with spire reaching to 209 feet is well integrated into the overall exterior design. The richness of the exterior is reflected in the interior with axial emphasis created by tall Tuscan columns, with impost blocks, parading down nave and lateral balconies recessed behind the columns. Elliptical arches spring from the columns and carry the vaulted ceiling and pendant chandeliers.

Although distant from central Philadelphia in Germantown at 5442 Germantown Avenue, a visit to the restored Deshler-Morris House, where the Cabinet moved in 1793 during the yellow fever epidemic, and later as a country retreat for the first family in 1794 is worth the side trip. The restored two-story colonial house contains a bedroom where George and Martha Washington slept.

The visitor should check all building open days and hours at the visitor center before starting off for tours. Visitation in the park is heavy during the day, especially school holidays and summer. A good time to see the most popular sites is either early in the morning or late afternoon. Traffic in the area is heavy, and parking space is limited.

Steamtown National Historic Site

Scranton, Lackawanna County, Pennsylvania

→ www.nps.gov/stea

→ Located in downtown Scranton, Pennsylvania, accessible via Interstate 81, Interstate 84, Interstate 380, and Interstate 80. Take Interstate 81 to Exit 53 (Central Scranton Expressway) and follow signs to the park.

The days of the mighty steam locomotive and railroading's powerful effect on the transition of an agricultural to industrial nation is interpreted here in the former switching yards of the Delaware, Lackawanna, and Western Railroad. The fifty-acre site is a pilgrimage for the steam railroad buff. Captured in permanent and changing exhibits and once proud rolling stock restored to superb condition, the switchyard is alive again with the unmistakable smells and sounds of coal-fueled locomotives spewing clouds of smoke from their smokestacks.

Located in the center of Scranton in northeastern Pennsylvania, the Steamtown National Historic Site is a composite of restored 1902 and 1937 roundhouse sections and successfully blends with new infill structures. The designers wisely chose to adopt a

Steamtown turntable and switch yard

simple industrial building character and used exposed materials of brick and structural steel for visitor center and exhibit spaces. The utilitarian design is arranged in a circle around the switchyard and a restored switching turntable that is regularly in use.

The walk from the parking lot to the visitor center, a spacious new facility located in the circular complex enclosing the switchyard is filled with distractions of locomotives and rolling stock on the railroad tracks parallel to the site. The roundhouse entrance is along the path of a railroad track that passes through an open-air section of the building to reach the switchyard and turntable. Once in the visitor center the complex unfolds, moving clockwise to a theater for an orientation film, the Museum of the History of

Railroading, the thirteen stall roundhouse section (1902 and 1937) displaying engines from the Steamtown collection, the three stall section (1902) with restoration and repair shops, and the Technology Museum presenting changes and advances in railroads through the years. Standing separately outside the circular structure is the restored oil house, now serving as a bookstore. In addition to visitor facilities, the site contains locomotive repair shops.

Locomotive shop

The Steamtown collection is comprised of more than twenty locomotives, and seventy-five passenger cars, freight cars, and maintenance—equipment is the main attraction for many visitors. At least three of the locomotives are in running condition and steam along the tracks outside the roundhouse. The locomotives range in size from a tiny industrial switcher engine built in 1937 to one of the biggest steam locomotives ever built, a 4-8-8-4 Union Pacific Big Boy (the numbers refer to the way the wheels are arranged). Nearly 133 feet long, it carried twenty-eight tons of coal and could run at more than eighty-miles-per-hour.

When first proposed, the Steamtown National Historic Site was derided as pork-barrel legislation at its worst. Attached to a funding bill by a local congressman, it was pilloried by the press as a "boondoggle," a weak excuse for an urban redevelopment project, and by historians and museum curators as a second-rate collection of trains on a third-rate site. The success of Steamtown disputes those early charges; the site has proven popular, informative, and is a pleasant visitors' experience. Reliving the end of the steam locomotive, enriched by the restoration work of dedicated and skilled volunteers, is a fun and informative day for young and old. The cadre of park rangers are enthusiastic and instill their knowledge on guided tours to both the initiates to railroading and the seasoned railroad buff, often with tape recorders in hand to catch the sounds of a restored piece of history.

On certain seasons and days of the year trolleys and trains run (approximately late April through Thanksgiving), including a short ride to the nearby historic Scranton Iron Furnaces or longer excursions to destinations such as Moscow and Tobyhanna, Pennsylvania. Check the park Web site for excursion schedules and programs.

Thaddeus Kosciuszko National Memorial

Philadelphia, Philadelphia County, Pennsylvania

→ www.nps.gov/thko

→ The memorial is located at 301 Pine Street, three blocks from the Independence Square in Independence National Historical Park.

Kosciuszko's lodgings

Thaddeus Kosciuszko (pronounced KOS-CHOOS-KO) was one of a cohort of idealistic foreign volunteers to enlist in the cause of the American Revolution. While some proved to be adventurers with little skills, the Polish-born Kosciuszko was one of the important contributors to the struggle for American independence.

Arriving in Philadelphia just weeks after adoption of the Declaration of Independence, the thirty-year-old Polish native applied to the Continental Congress for a commission, although he had no previous military experience. Educated in Warsaw and Paris where he studied military engineering and attained a broad academic background, Kosciuszko received an appointment as an engineer in the Continental army. Among many accomplishments during the next six years, his most notable successes were designing fortifications at Saratoga and West Point. The Americans' ability to hold fortifications near Saratoga (see page 505) and defeat troops under General John Burgoyne in 1777 is considered to be a turning point in the Revolutionary War. Ending his American service in 1783 as a Brigadier General, in the next year he returned to Poland.

The site of the National Memorial was the Polish patriot's residence during his brief return to the United States from August 1797 to May 1798. By then a respected international hero for his fight for Poland's freedom from the Russians, but exiled from his homeland and suffering from wounds that left him partially paralyzed, Kosciuszko rented rooms in Mrs. Ann Reif's boarding house at 301 Pine Street. The three-and-a-half-story house, built in 1775, is the smallest unit in the National Park System. An extraordinary National Park Service restoration rescued the building from a disfigured shambles to today's elegant late-eighteenth-century Philadelphia row house. The Flemish bond red brick exterior walls, with a pedimented gable surrounded by a cornice, have glazed black headers, a water table, and belt courses at second and third floors. Refined pedimented doorways with classical door jambs and headers are on the Third and Pine Streets facades. Entrance to the building is from Third Street.

The house contains exhibits and a bookstore on the ground floor. The focus of the memorial to Kosciuszko is his modestly furnished personal rooms on the second floor. The appearance of the Polish patriot's residence is as it was when he was recuperating from his severe wounds and welcoming guests. A floral patterned wallpaper and checkered drapes, oriental rugs, and blanket on the rope bed warm the rented quarters. A crutch is propped next to a divan with a pillow for resting or reading and a gaming table with paper and quill pen and a chess set is ready for passing time with guests. Young women seeking portraits frequently visited the room. Thomas Jefferson came often to discuss shared Republican ideas.

Although modest in size, this memorial to a hero of the American Revolution and ideals of freedom is worthy of a visit. The exterior and Kosciuszko's bedroom are superb restorations.

Valley Forge National Historical Park

Valley Forge, Chester and Montgomery Counties, Pennsylvania

→ www.nps.gov/vafo

→ The park is located twenty miles west of Philadelphia at the intersection of Pennsylvania Route 23 and North Gulph Road. Access is via Interstate 76 (Pennsylvania Turnpike) at Exit 326 and follow signs to the park.

George Washington's Headquarters

The saga of the Continental army at Valley Forge during the winter of 1777–78 echoes through the annals of American history as an inspiration derived from hardship, perseverance, and eventual triumph. On April 21, 1778, George Washington recorded his emotions about the twelve thousand troops who had followed him here five months earlier:

To see men without clothes to cover their nakedness, without blankets to lie upon, without shoes ... without a house or hut to cover them until those could be built, and submitting without a murmur, is a proof of patience and obedience which, in my opinion, can scarcely be paralleled.

Washington's Headquarters

Interiors

Named for an old iron forge on Valley Creek, Valley Forge was chosen as winter quarters because of its proximity to the British occupying Philadelphia and the ability to monitor their raiding and foraging parties in the countryside, and far enough away to avoid surprise attacks. The Schuylkill River to the north, combined with the high ground of Mount Joy and Mount Misery, made the area naturally defensible. No battle was fought here, no sabers rattled in the face of the enemy or cannon fired, but around two thousand men died from shortage of supplies and disease during the winter ordeal. On June 19, 1778, six months to the day after its arrival, the Continental army left the winter encampment miraculously shaped into an effective fighting force and with a sense of purpose, carrying the "Spirit of Valley Forge" with them to eventual victory six years later.

Valley Forge National Historical Park's nearly 3,500 acres (all of which are designated as a National Historic Landmark) provides ample separation from surrounding suburban encroachments to preserve the landscape's historical character. National Park Service (NPS) ownership of the land on the north side of the Schuylkill River is an important contributor to the protected viewsheds from park's core.

Visitors touring the park can find an introduction to the 1777–78 encampment in the attractive glass-walled welcome center designed by Walter Ogg of the Philadelphia firm of Eshbach, Glass, Kale, and Associates. The building serves as a museum, viewing place for an interpretive film, and bookstore. From the welcome center a self-guided driving tour (or seasonal bus touring the site) circles the park, on a one-way drive along outer Line Drive, leading to a cluster of replica log huts at the site of General Peter Muhlenberg's Brigade along the Outer Line defenses. Representing the more than one thousand log huts built by the ragged army, the 16- by 14-foot huts of hewn logs with shake-shingle roofs, stood 6.5 feet tall to the eaves, had a chimney at one end, and slept twelve men. The small log huts built as winter shelter are replicated in several locations, and along with other historical structures are reference points around the Grand Parade where troops gathered for drilling by the charismatic Prussian drillmaster Friedrich Von Steuben, and gained training and the will to fight again in the spring. Other huts not

reconstructed were larger ones for officers (typically 18 by 16 feet with chimneys at both ends), hospitals, and commissaries.

The impressive National Memorial Arch west of Muhlenberg's Brigade cabins on Outer Line at the intersection with Gulph Road is the park's tallest structure at 61 feet above grade. Placed on a prominent rise of ground in an austere landscape,

Muhlenberg's Brigade cabins

architect Paul Cret's design is a contemporary, Beaux-Arts interpretation of the Roman Arch of Titus. A reinforced concrete structural system substituting for a load-bearing arch supports the sheathing of pink Milford granite.

The tour then reaches the western end of the drive to Valley Creek Road (Pennsylvania Route 252) with several large residential structures, including the rambling, colonial Philander Chase Knox Library, a research library open to the public by appointment, and turns north along a winding stretch of Valley Creek.

Continuing along Valley Creek Road and crossing north of Gulph Road is George Washington's Headquarters, known as the Isaac Potts House. A National Historic Landmark, the sturdy stone house next to the Schuylkill River was built around 1750 by Potts. The two-story main block (approximately 30 by 25 feet in plan), with pedimented entrance, gable ends, and a single chimney, is on a raised basement. A 24-foot-long one-story kitchen wing is attached to the north end of the house. Exterior walls are local stone roughly squared and layered in courses on the main building and random sized on the kitchen block. The house has an elaborate Georgian interior and is furnished to the period of Washington's occupancy. In a field across the creek from the Potts House are several replica log huts on the site of the Commander-in-Chief's Guard's encampment.

From Washington's Headquarters, the one-way Inner Line Drive leaves Route 23 eastbound, climbs Mount Joy, and passes sites of redoubts, the Inner Line defenses, and the artillery park with a collection of authentic cannon. Returning to Route 23 eastbound, a two-story vernacular stone farmhouse that served as General James Varnum's Quarters overlooks the Grand Parade. The NPS restored structure has an unusual shingled projection the length of the house at the second floor, which serves as a canopy for front and rear entrances. The restored interior represents furnishings during Varnum's occupancy.

Across the road from Varnum's Quarters to the east and built on private property inside the park is the Washington Memorial Chapel. Architect Milton B. Medary, Jr., composed the two elements of the chapel and the National Patriots Bell Tower and Carillon in perpendicular Gothic. The chapel was completed in 1917 and the fifty-eight-bell tower in 1953. Both are staggeringly laden with symbolism that will delight the visitor to the chapel interior and entertain as the bells ring in the tower. For example, the tower contains a national birthday bell, a bell for each of the fifty states, Washington, D.C., Puerto Rico, Guam, American Samoa, the Virgin Islands, Midway, and Wake Islands. The population of the states, territories, and the District of Columbia determined the size of each bell. The interior is profuse with sparkling light from thirteen stained-glass windows and a ceiling decorated with hand-carved seals of all the states. Note especially the solid oak 19.5-foot-tall choir stalls carved in Belgium, each stall with a carved statue of a member of the Commander-in-Chief's Guard and hand painted in the correct colors of their uniforms.

Next to the chapel, and also on private property, is the Valley Forge Society Museum. The museum's collection in the American Revolution Center includes the most stirring portrait connected with the winter of 1777–78, *The March to Valley Forge* by William B. T. Trego. The monumental canvas painted in 1883 portrays General George Washington sitting astride his white horse as snow falls around him, a central figure in a tableau of the ragtag procession of dispirited soldiers headed for Valley Forge.

New England

Connecticut

→ Weir Farm National Historic Site

★ HARTFORD

○ Weir Farm NHS

ATLANTIC
OCEAN

Weir Farm National Historic Site

Located in southwestern Connecticut between Ridgefield and Wilton, Fairfield County, Connecticut

→ www.nps.gov/wefa

→ The park is at 735 Nod Hill Road reached from the south via Interstate 95 and the Merritt Parkway or Interstate 84 from the north. Exit at US 7 then to Connecticut Route 102 west onto Old Branchville Road and follow signs to the visitor center.

Weir House

American Impressionist painter, J. (for Julian) Alden Weir (1852–1919) chose this quintessential Connecticut farmland of rolling hills, woodlots, rock outcroppings and boulders, wildflowers, and stone walls as a summer retreat from his New York City studio in 1882. Purchasing the 153-acre farm three miles from the eighteenth-century village of Ridgefield, reputedly in exchange for ten dollars and an oil painting worth $560, for thirty-seven summers, he called the Branchville land ("The Great Good Place") home. Weir built a studio, twice enlarged the main farmhouse, and acquired more land in 1907. The general character of the southwestern Connecticut landscape familiar to Weir is preserved by an additional 110 acres of contiguous open space called the Weir Preserve and managed by the Weir Farm Art Center. The sixty-acre Weir Farm National Historic Site is the only National Park Service unit devoted to American painting.

The significance of the Weir Farm is captured eloquently in Connecticut Senator Joseph Lieberman's testimony in 1990 supporting the park as a National Park Service Site:

> Weir Farm provides us a rare opportunity to commemorate the quiet marriage of art and the tended landscape that so clearly defined the American Impressionist movement.

The landscape of Weir Farm National Historic Site has been a source of continuous inspiration for artists for more than 125 years. Three artists, Julian Alden Weir followed by sculptor Mahonri Young and painter Sperry Andrews, made the farm their home from 1882 to 2005. In 1931, Weir's daughter Dorothy married sculptor Mahonri Young, and the couple spent a good deal of time at the farm. In 1932 Young built a studio suitable for large pieces of sculpture adjacent to Weir's studio. After Young's death in 1957, Doris and Andrew Sperry, fellow artists and friends of Mahonri Young, purchased the farm.

Weir began painting as a boy under the guidance of his father, a drawing instructor at West Point, and studied at the National Academy of Design in New York City and later at the École des Beaux-Arts in Paris. He became a late convert to impressionism, repulsed by the style in his first encounter in Paris in 1877, but by 1891 he adopted it as his own. Through the remainder of the 1890s and 1900s, inspired by his Connecticut farm and Branchville's surrounding landscape, Weir painted impressionist landscapes and figurative works. The landscape of Weir Farm National Historic Site has been captured in many of his paintings and sketches, with around 450 in private and museum collections. His style varied from traditional, vibrant impressionism to a more subdued and shadowy tonalism. He also became skilled at etching.

By the turn of the twentieth century Weir became a leading figure in American art. He was a founding member in 1897 of the Ten American Painters along with his friends Childe Hassam and John Twachtman, the group that became the core of American Impressionism. He served as president of the Society of American Artists, the National Academy of Design, and the Association of American Painters and Sculptors. Weir would later sit on the board of directors at the Metropolitan Museum of Art.

Today, Weir Farm National Historic Site preserves sixteen historical structures, including the red painted clapboard, white-trimmed homes, studios and barns of the

J. Alden Weir studio

farm, and also the rolling hills, fields, and distinctive stone walls. (Note the gilded plaster stars Weir fixed to his studio's ceiling.) The visitor center is located in the Burlingham House, the eighteenth-century farmhouse on the property occupied by Weir's third daughter, Cora Weir Burlingham. Ranger-guided tours are conducted of the studio and grounds. The "Weir Farm Historic Painting Sites Trail Guide" features a self-guided tour of twelve sites at the farm and compares reproduction paintings to the actual landscape views that inspired them.

Maine

Acadia National Park

Located near Bar Harbor on the southeast coast of Maine, Hancock County, Maine

→ www.nps.gov/acad

→ The park's three units—Mount Desert Island, Isle au Haut, and Schoodic Peninsula—are two-thirds of the way up the Maine coast, forty-eight miles southeast of Bangor. From Boston, take Interstate 95 north to Augusta, Maine, then Maine Route 3 east to Ellsworth and on to Mount Desert Island. For an alternate route, continue on Interstate 95 north to Bangor, Maine, then take Route 1A east to Ellsworth. In Ellsworth, take Maine Route 3 to Mount Desert Island.

Bar Harbor Head lighthouse

Acadia National Park's magnificent glacial landscape of granite mainland and islands, towering mountains (Cadillac Mountain is the tallest on the U.S. Atlantic coast), shimmering lakes, thick forests, and shoreline is one of the nation's most scenic places. The nearly 48,000 acres has miles of trails and carriage roads passing through spectacular scenery, with fabled resort towns of Bar Harbor, Seal Harbor, Northeast Harbor, and Southwest Harbor outside the park on Mount Desert Island.

At the end of the nineteenth century the park came about because of concern by summer cottagers that over development and logging would spoil a summer haven. Gradually, The Hancock County Trustees of Public Reservations expanded small gifts of land at key locations by a donation of 5,000 acres on Mount Desert Island. This gift in 1914 formed the basis of a national monument, established in 1916 that became Lafayette National Park in 1919 and renamed Acadia National Park in 1929. A gift of 11,000 acres by John D. Rockefeller, Jr., a summer resident, encouraged the establishment of Acadia National Park as the first national park east of the Mississippi.

One treasure of Acadia National Park is the forty-five miles of rustic carriage roads, the gift of John D. Rockefeller, Jr., and family, that weave through Mount Desert Island's mountains and valleys. Rockefeller's desire to travel his estate by horse and carriage on motor-free routes resulted in the construction from 1913 to 1940 of a splendid system of broken-stone roads (using three layers of finely graded stones) with gentle grades and stone-faced arched bridges separating traffic. Road stones and bridge facing came from island granite quarries. Eventually, seventeen stone-faced bridges, each unique in design, spanned streams, waterfalls, public roads, and cliffsides, fifteen of which are located within Acadia National Park. Although the bridges are faced with rusticated granite, they are reinforced concrete structures.

Two carriage system gate lodges, one at Jordan Pond and the other near Northeast Harbor, built by Rockefeller, are among the most unique structures on Mount Desert Island. Built where the carriage roads intersected public highways, these gateways permitted Rockefeller and his friends access to the public roads while deterring motorists from entering his carriage road system. Rockefeller retained architect Grosvenor Atterbury to design the picturesque complexes reminiscent of the provincial architecture of the Le Puis district in France. After their completion in 1932, Rockefeller donated both gatehouses to the park.

Buildings at both locations use similar features of form and materials, although distinct in layout. The Brown Mountain Gate Lodge, the larger of the two complexes, located just north of Northeast Harbor near Lower Hadlock Pond, has three elements of a central two-story house, a garage, and the monumental gate towers providing access to the carriage road. The high masonry wall bordering the front of the structure, as well as the positioning of the entrance and garage behind it, result in a nearly unbroken 257-foot-long facade intended to draw the visitor's attention to the gate. The Jordan Pond Gate Lodge, built in the vicinity of the popular Jordan Pond Teahouse, includes a main house, garage, and carriage road gate all connected by a high masonry wall. In contrast to the dramatic layout of Brown Mountain Gate Lodge, the one near Jordan Pond emphasizes the house and garage rather than the gate itself.

The main structures in both complexes have steeply-pitched, side-gabled roofs and are covered with shingle tiles and feature matching terra-cotta chimney pots. Upper walls are half-timbered and lower masonry walls are banded in the Le Puis district style of alternating layers of brick and granite.

The cliffside Bass Harbor Head Light marking the entrance to Bass Harbor is located on the southwestern side of Mount Desert Island. The cylindrical, white brick

Carriage road bridge   Jordan Pond Gate Lodge

tower is 32 feet tall. Perched on a bluff overlooking the harbor, the fourth-order Fresnel lens light is 56 feet above mean high water level. The site is a small area notched into the pink granite outcroppings. A two-story keeper's dwelling (40 by 20 feet in plan) connected to the tower by a covered 21-foot wooden walkway is part of a white-painted clapboard complex that includes a nearby tall, pyramidal bell tower with a 1,500 pound bronze bell for fog warnings, a brick oil house, and barn.

Certainly, the extraordinary scenic marvels of the rockbound Maine coast, the glacial landscape, and forests—especially the stunning fall foliage colors—are the major attractions of Acadia National Park. There are splendors to see beyond Bar Harbor and the twenty-mile park loop road, too often missed by the visitor. Fare-free Island Explorer buses operate on various routes to extend the visit to Schoodic Peninsula. Historical structures and features are unique to the park and worth discovering.

Massachusetts

New England

ATLANTIC

OCEAN

Saugus Iron Works NHS
Longfellow NHS
Salem Maritime NHS
Lowell NHP
BOSTON Boston African American NHS/Boston NHP
Minute Man NHP
Cape Cod NS
Springfield Armory NHS
Frederick Law Olmsted NHS
New Bedford
John Fitzgerald Kennedy NHS
Whaling NHP
Adams NHP

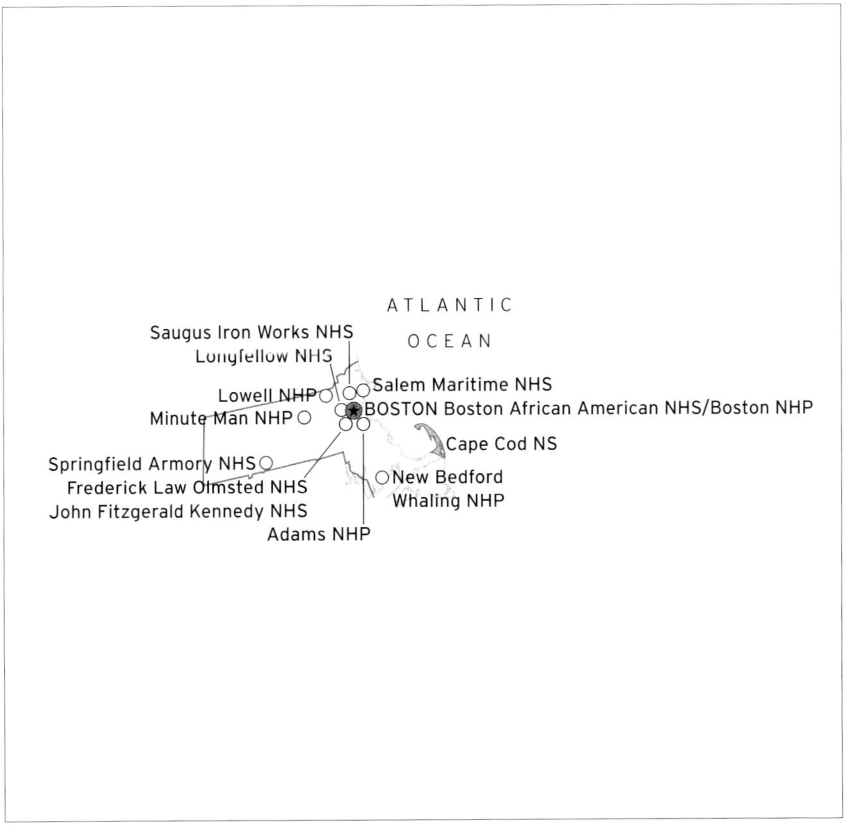

Adams National Historical Park

Located in the City of Quincy, Norfolk County, Massachusetts

→ www.nps.gov/adam

→ The park is located in the center of Quincy, Massachusetts, approximately ten miles southeast of Boston. The park's visitor center is at 1250 Hancock Street in the Presidents Place Galleria, accessed from the MBTA ("T") Red Line train to Quincy Center Station and by car from Interstate 93 to Route 3 South to Exit 18. Follow signs to the National Park Service Visitor Center.

United First Parish Church of Quincy

The Adams National Historical Park in Quincy, Massachusetts, tells the story of four generations of the distinguished Adams family members dedicated to the development and service of the United States. An intriguing day can be spent learning about the lives of two presidents (second president John Adams and sixth president John Quincy Adams) their celebrated First Ladies, three U.S. ministers of Foreign Affairs, historians, writers, and other family members. A tour begins at the visitor center located in Presidents Place Galleria at 1250 Hancock Street, and then continues via trolley to the main historic sites: two National Historic Landmark birthplace houses of the two presidents; the Old House occupied by four generations of the Adams family; and the National Historic Landmark United First Parish Church of Quincy, the burial place of the presidents and their wives.

The small, late-seventeenth-century two-story saltbox houses, unique as the oldest still-standing presidential birthplaces in the United States and only 75 feet apart on a lot at the corner of Franklin Street and President's Avenue, were once farmhouses in a rural landscape on the Boston-Plymouth Highway. John Adams lived in this house with weathered clapboard siding, built in 1681, from his birth in 1735 until his marriage to Abigail Adams in 1764. John Quincy Adams was born in 1767 in the adjacent house built in 1663. One room of the house was used as a law office for several years. Many of Abigail's letters to John while he served at the Continental Congress and as ambassador to France were written from here (see David McCullough's Pulitzer Prize-winning *John Adams*, Simon & Schuster, 2001).

Both wood-frame clapboard houses are remarkably similar in form, plan, and details, except for the lean-to addition to John Adams's birthplace house. Modest in size (38 by 31 feet), the houses have a finely detailed Greek Revival–style doorway centered in a three-bay facade entering into a small hallway with steep winding stairs to the second floor. The John Quincy Adams birthplace house with gray clapboard siding contains hand-hewn ceiling beams and a large fireplace and central chimney.

Peacefield, as John Adams called the property about a mile north of the birthplace houses, including the Old House, originally was a small structure built in 1731 by Leonard Vassall, a West Indian sugar planter. Adams bought the house of seven rooms at 135 Adams Street off Burgin Parkway in 1787 and expanded it to twenty rooms. The spacious clapboard mansion served as the Adams's family residence for four generations until 1927. It was home to Presidents John Adams and John Quincy Adams while they were in office, First Ladies Abigail and Louisa Catherine Adams, Civil War Minister to Great Britain Charles Francis Adams, and literary historians Henry and Brooks Adams. John Adams died here on July 4, 1826.

The three-and-a-half-story house, set in attractive historic gardens, is U-shaped in plan, 80 feet across the front elevation with eight shuttered windows and five dormers under a central portion gambrel roof. The five-columned porch was added in 1800. The gable-roof west ell extends approximately 70 feet from front to rear and the west ell approximately 31 feet. The main rooms on the ground floor all had impressive fireplaces. The Long Room in the west ell is where distinguished guests were entertained and contains the formal Louis XV furniture Adams purchased in 1780 for the first U.S. embassy abroad in the Netherlands. The spacious dining room to the left of the entrance and the mahogany paneled room to the right are steeped in history by hosting famous guests. The second floor Long Hall and Study contains the elaborately inlaid escritoire where John Adams signed the Treaty of Paris, thus creating the new nation. The continuous family occupancy by one of the country's most distinguished families left a rich trove of original furniture, paintings, and decorative objects collected by the family and represents one of the best maintained historic houses in the country.

Adjacent to the mansion is the Stone Library, built in 1870, and containing more

John Adams birthplace

John Quincy Adams birthplace

than 14,000 books that belonged to the Adams. The unusual structure with a foreboding granite exterior, designed by Edward Cabot, is a departure from the colonial architecture of the first two generations. The interior space is a pleasant surprise, a two-story volume is filled with floor-to-ceiling shelves and a steep wooden ladder leads to an intermediate level balcony. The large central table was used by generations of Adamses for editing volumes of family papers and writing original works.

After completing a guided house tour, the visitor should stroll the Old House grounds transformed by John Quincy's son, Charles Francis and his wife, Abigail Brown, from a working farm to a country estate formal garden featuring thousands of annual and perennial flowers and a historic orchard.

In the center of the city of Quincy is the United First Parish Church (1306 Hancock Street). John Quincy Adams was instrumental in its construction; he donated the land, and bore most of the costs. This imposing church of local Quincy granite illustrates a transition in style from Georgian and Federal to Greek Revival. A Greek Revival facade containing a four-columned, broadly pedimented Doric portico was designed by Alexander Parris and built in 1827 and 1828. Behind and above the portico, a square tower base containing a clock on each facade is topped by an open, circular cupola with a dome. Arched windows in the north and south side walls reflect earlier Georgian and Federal architectural traditions. Galleries extend around the north, south, and west sides of the main worship area and a plaster dome adorns the ceiling. This fine example of New England church architecture is also known as the "Stone Temple" and "Church of the Presidents."

Boston African American National Historic Site

Boston, Suffolk County, Massachusetts

→ www.nps.gov/boaf

→ The park is located in Boston's Beacon Hill neighborhood. The National Park Service (NPS) Visitor Information Center on 15 State Street in Boston Common can provide directions to the Black Heritage Trail, a 1.6-mile walking tour linking fourteen sites. Ranger-guided tours begin at the Memorial to Colonel Robert Gould Shaw and the 54th Massachusets Regiment at the corner of Beacon and Park Street, facing the State House across the street is available year-round by appointment. Public transportation is recommended. Take the MBTA Red or Green Line and exit at Park Street Station. Many of the sites are privately owned and not open to the public. The Museum of African American History, located in the Abiel Smith School and African Meeting House at 46 Joy Street, Boston, is open Monday through Saturday, 10A.M. to 4P.M.

The Boston African American National Historic Site links fourteen buildings and sites in Boston's Beacon Hill neighborhood and comprises the largest concentration of pre-Civil War African American historic sites in the United States. It is identified by signs, takes about two hours, and includes a couple of steep hills. Brochures for a self-guided tour are available at the Museum of African American History. Ranger-guided tours start at the African Meeting House at 8 Smith Court. While most of the buildings are private residences and not open to the public, the African Meeting House and the Abiel Smith School are open to the public.

The Memorial to Colonel Robert Gould Shaw and 54th Massachusetts Regiment monument was dedicated in a ceremony on Boston Common in 1897 in honor of the Massachusetts 54th Regiment, the first African-American regiment recruited in the North to fight for the Union army during the Civil War. The memorial is located at the corner of Beacon and Park Streets on a plaza facing the State House and over-looking Boston Common. Acclaimed as the greatest American sculpture of the nine-teenth-century, the bronze relief by Augustus Saint-Gaudens, in a setting designed by Charles F. McKim, combines the real and allegorical, balancing restraint with vitality. The relief depicts the regiment's farewell march down Beacon Street, past the Shaw family residence at 44 Beacon Street. Colonel Shaw was only twenty-six years old when he died with scores of other men in a valiant attack on Fort Wagner, South Carolina, on July 18, 1863. (Shaw's and the regiment's story are told in the movie Glory.)

At the intersection of Joy Street and Smith Court are five residences represen-tative of eighteenth-century black Bostonian homes, and the former Abiel Smith School. The brick school building located at 46 Joy Street, open to the public, was constructed in 1834, and, in 1835, became the first schoolhouse in America built to educate black school children. The Smith School closed after the desegregation of Boston's public schools in 1855. It reopened in 1887 as headquarters for black veterans of the Civil War. The school was fully renovated in 2000 and is now part of the Museum of African American History containing exhibit space with a gallery, classroom, and museum store.

The last stop on the Black Heritage Trail is the African Meeting House, a Na-tional Historic Landmark. Built in 1806 to house the First African Baptist Church of Boston, it is now the oldest extant black church building in America. The red brick Federal style facade is an adaptation of a townhouse design published by Boston

architect Asher Benjamin. It was a reli-gious center as well as a school and a hall for meetings and lectures. Here, in 1832, William Lloyd Garrison founded the New England Antislavery Society, and many leading abolitionists, including Frederick Douglass and Maria Stewart, spoke from the pulpit. During the Civil War, members of the Massachusetts 54th Infantry enlisted at the Meeting House. By the end of the nineteenth century the

Robert Gould Shaw and 54th Massachusetts
Regiment Memorial

building was sold to a Jewish congregation. It served as a synagogue until it was acquired by the Museum of African American History in 1972 and since restored to its mid-1850s appearance.

The common starting point for the Boston African American National Historic Site and Boston National Historical Park (next section) at the NPS kiosk on Tremont Street in Boston Common allows visitors to plan joint Freedom Trail and Black Heritage Trail visits for a couple of days, or more.

Boston National Historical Park

Boston, Suffolk County, Massachusetts

→   www.nps.gov/bost

→   Many of the sites of Boston National Historical Park are located along the 2.5-mile Freedom Trail from Boston Common across the Charles River to Bunker Hill and to the Charlestown Navy Yard. The trail is best experienced on foot. Maps and information about Boston and the park can be found at Boston National Historical Park Visitor Center at 15 State Street, Bunker Hill Pavilion at 55 Constitution Road, and Charlestown Navy Yard.

The State House

The city of Boston is a museum of early American history. Boston National Historical Park is a distinctive group of public and private sites linked by the 2.5-mile-long Freedom Trail, wending its way back into history. The trail begins on the Boston Common, and leads through historic landscapes and buildings in the downtown area past government buildings, steepled churches, meeting halls, and across the Charles River to the Charlestown Navy Yard. The visitor should wear comfortable walking shoes to set out on a journey that 1.5 million people take annually to discover colonial and Revolutionary America.

For years after it was completed in 1798, Charles Bulfinch's superb Federal style Massachusetts State House (Beacon Street at Park Street) crowning Beacon Hill was one of the most important public buildings in the United States. The National Historic

Landmark was directly responsible for America's first native-born professional architect's appointment as architect of the Capitol in Washington, D.C. Clearly inspired by British interpretations of Andrea Palladio, Bulfinch's bold structure topped by a dazzlingly gilded dome (originally shingled and whitewashed, then sheathed in copper by Paul Revere in 1802, and covered with gold leaf in 1874) has housed the Massachusetts state government for over two centuries.

Additions have been made to the rear (1889–95) and sides (added in 1917) but the mostly original facade, dominated by the dome is one of Boston's most familiar architectural images. The assemblage of elements in the "Bulfinch Front" is a study in subtlety. Across the front is a classical portico in a projected central block flanked by two Federal wings and topped by a continuous balustraded cornice. The seven arches of the ground level loggia are more widely spaced at the two ends than in the center, coordinated with the pairing of wooden Corinthian columns for the end bays of the upper porch. On either side of the porch recessed, arched windows, the central ones Palladian, tie in with the arches below, unifying the 172-foot-long facade. The dome and splendid cupola, perched on a pediment upper portion, with its distended verticality hover upwards into the sky, contribute to the soaring brilliance of Bulfinch's classicism.

The interior is a succession of elegant public rooms: the second floor Doric Hall with ten Doric columns and Hall of Flags; and the third floor semicircular House of Representatives, gold-domed Senate Chamber (approximately 55 feet square) and the barrel vaulted Senate Reception Room, supported by four Ionic columns, located in the Bulfinch front.

Park Street Church (Park Street and Tremont Street), built in 1809 and designed by British architect Peter Banner, is both an architectural and historic landmark. The brick Georgian structure with a soaring 217-foot steeple and spire was inspired by the latest Christopher Wren London architecture. An unusual feature is the use of semicircular porches between the tower base and the body of the main building. The engaged square tower base rises in a wedding cake profusion of four tiers with louvered and glazed Palladian window openings, pediments, urns and finials, and ogee windows to support the needle-like spire, for many years the highest building in Boston.

King's Chapel

Located on the corner of Tremont and School Streets, King's Chapel (a National Historic Landmark) was built between 1749 and 1754 and is distinct by the establishment of two faiths in America: as the first Church of England in New England and the first Unitarian church in America (1789). Services are still held today—its own Anglican/Unitarian hybrid liturgy.

The design of architect Peter Harrison, a student of Sir John Vanbrugh and a younger contemporary of Sir Christopher Wren, reflects the British influence in one of the most important surviving examples of ecclesiastical Georgian architecture in the nation. The church's 4-foot-thick granite walls were built around a small, deteriorating church on the site. After completion the old church was dismantled and then pieces removed through the windows. It was the first major building in British America to be built of stone, using Quincy granite. A bell forged in England was hung in 1772. It cracked in 1814 and was recast by Paul Revere and rehung in 1816.

Architecturally, King's Chapel is similar to a coin with one side tarnished and the other brightly polished. The rectangular building, surmounted by a hipped roof, has two stories of arched windows on the north and south and Palladian windows on the east. The colonnade of wooden Ionic columns was added in 1785–87. The church's form—with a squat base for a steeple that was never built due to lack of funds—lacks the warmth and drama of other colonial Boston churches inspired by Wren and his followers, attractive with their red brick exteriors, tall, multilight Palladian windows, and soaring needle-like spires. Indeed, when absorbing the skies of Boston's drearier days the granite exterior shapes a cold and dark foreboding pile of stone. In contrast, the magnificent light-filled sanctuary is perhaps the finest colonial church interior extant. The cream-colored walls glow in a lustrous light. It is stately in the Palladian proportions, use of Corinthian columns, placement and size of Palladian windows, red damask-lined box pews, the old church's altar (presented to the congregation by William and Mary in 1696), fine canopied pulpit (pulpit 1717, canopy later), and other elegant details.

The Old Corner Bookstore, located on the corner of School and Washington Streets, is a three-story rose red brick, gambrel-roofed structure built by Thomas Crease around 1718 for his apothecary shop and residence. When Ticknor and Fields Publishing House located here from 1832 to 1865, it became known as the Old Corner Bookstore. During the nineteenth century, this building became the center of literary Boston when such noted authors as Nathaniel Hawthorne, Ralph Waldo Emerson, Henry Wadsworth Longfellow, Henry David Thoreau, Harriet Beecher Stowe, as well as Charles Dickens, and Oliver Wendell Holmes would gather here and chat.

When the Old South Meeting House (corner of Milk and Washington Streets) was built in 1729, its Puritan congregation merged a traditional church hall with Georgian architectural styling into the largest capacity of any public building in Boston. The building (approximately 93 by 66 feet in plan) in simple massing, with severely plain brick exterior laid in Flemish bond, and brick tower surmounted by a handsome wooden spire, is turned on its long axis to create a wide hall with two balconies on sides and rear, focusing on an arched recess behind the pulpit. This arrangement made it a useful forum for the fervent oratory of Revolutionary days. It was from here on the night of December 16, 1773 that Samuel Adams's fiery harangue before an audience of 5,000 about the tea tax sent a secret signal to a hundred men to dump 342 chests of tea into the harbor.

The National Historic Landmark building, designed by Robert Twelve and built under the supervision of master builder Joshua Blanchard, has a 180-foot steeple and a double row of Palladian windows around the exterior. The interior is done in spartan Georgian detailing. Turned into a riding stable by the British during the Revolutionary War, in March 1783, after sustaining enormous damage, Old South was restored by the congregation as a place of worship. Today, the completely restored Old South Meeting House, managed by the Old South Association, is open daily as a museum and continues to provide a place for people to meet, discuss, and act on important issues of the day.

Located on the corner of State and Washington Streets, the Old State House, built in 1712–13, is Boston's oldest public building and a fine example of early Georgian design in the country. The National Historic Landmark served as the seat of the British government in Boston (attested by the reproduction British lion and unicorn on the east facade) and Commonwealth government after the Revolution, until the new State House was ready in 1798, as well as a merchants' exchange. A cobblestone circle beneath its balcony marks the site of the 1770 Boston Massacre when British soldiers fired into a crowd of Bostonians. Fugitive slave Crispus Attucks was among the five victims who died that day.

The Old State House is a two-and-a-half-story structure, approximately 144 by 37 feet in plan. The load-bearing brick construction is an English bond exterior, alternating rows of headers and stretchers, and contains details of molded brick water table, and wide belt courses around the entire exterior. Its steeply pitched gambrel roof with stepped and pedimented gable ends, and its tower with gracefully telescoped members finished by a three-tiered cupola rising from the middle of the building, are enhanced by the building's separation from towering office building neighbors in the center of a heavily trafficked area. High on corners of the State Street facade are the British lion and unicorn. The second floor balcony below the symbols of the crown is where the

Old State House

Declaration of Independence was first read to Bostonians on July 18, 1776. Classic details in doors, windows, and cupola were a new note in Boston at the time of the building's construction. The interior of the ground floor was one large room that served as a mercantile exchange. The second and third floor contained council and court chambers, and offices and committee rooms.

The famous building, whose architect's identity is a mystery, had a significant influence on the architecture of its time. Today, the Bostonian Society maintains the building as a museum of Boston history, as well as Revolutionary and maritime history.

For over 250 years, National Historic Landmark Faneuil Hall (locally pronounced "Fan'l") has been at the center of Boston's commercial district. Faneuil Hall is now part of a larger festival marketplace named Faneuil Hall Marketplace, which includes

three long granite buildings called North Market, Quincy Market, and South Market, daily surrounded by thousands of tourists and workers from the nearby office buildings flowing around Quincy Market. This is the third building on the site. Boston's wealthiest merchant, Peter Faneuil, gave the first building to the city in 1742. Completed from the plans of colonial portrait painter John Smibert, its market and meeting hall served as a focal point of colonial protest against British rule. Because of the protests against the British taxation policies voiced here during the 1760s, the meeting hall is dubbed the "Cradle of Liberty."

Faneuil Hall

The second hall on the site evolved when fire destroyed the original building in 1762. It was promptly rebuilt on the original plan. In 1805–06, the hall was greatly expanded by Charles Bulfinch, doubling its height and width and adding a third floor. Four new bays were added, to make seven in all, the ground floor open arcades were enclosed, and the cupola was moved to the Dock Square gable end of the building. Original bricks were large, laid in Flemish bond with dark headers; later brickwork is smoother and lighter in color. The three floors and gable end are demarcated by cornices between each floor and squared brick pilasters between each window (two at the ends) appear to support the cornices. Bulfinch applied Doric brick pilasters to the lower two floors, with Ionic pilasters on the third floor. This renovation added galleries around the assembly hall and increased its height. All door and window openings have rounded arched tops with a stone keystone.

In 1898–99 the City of Boston rebuilt the building using noncombustible materials, and the ground floor and basement were altered in 1979. It was again restored in 1992. Throughout all these changes the building's functions remained faithful to the original: ground floor market stalls service shoppers much as they did in Paul Revere's day; the second floor holds the historic meeting hall; and the third floor houses the armory of the Ancient and Honorable Artillery Company Museum, the nation's oldest military group founded in 1638. In addition, the familiar Boston landmark—the 4-foot-long grasshopper weathervane of gilded copper—remains in place.

The National Historic Landmark Paul Revere House at 19 North Square in Boston's North End is a rarity—a wood-frame house surviving from the seventeenth century in the fire-prone city's oldest residential neighborhood. It is now the oldest remaining house in downtown Boston. Built after the devastating Boston fire of 1676, in about 1678–1680, Paul Revere owned and occupied the house most of the time from 1770 to 1800. It was from here that the patriot set out on his fabled (but ill-fated) midnight ride in 1775 to warn his friends-in-arms that the British were coming.

Paul Revere House

The compact North Street–facing facade with its overhanging second floor, dark-stained clapboard walls, and small diamond-shaped window panes is architecturally typical of Massachusetts Bay Colony seventeenth-century homes. The L-plan house, as originally built, was one unit in a two-story steeply pitched, gable-roofed row. The main part of the house, four bays wide, contained one room on each floor (approximately 30 by 18 feet in plan), and an ell (approximately 16 square feet). The low-ceilinged rooms have small leaded windows providing light and view. The interior court side of the ell has an uncoordinated group of window openings, in contrast to the well-organized street facade. The Revere House has changed greatly from its original appearance due to a variety of uses, including a cigar factory and bank appearance, and the infusion of Colonial Revival romanticism by architect Joseph E. Chandler in a 1907–1908 restoration. Today it is operated, along with the neighboring Pierce-Hitchborn House, as a house museum by the Paul Revere Memorial Association.

Old North Church interior

Built from 1723 to 1740, Old North Church at 193 Salem Street (officially Christ Church) was Boston's second Anglican church and is a superb example of Colonial Georgian architecture. It is Boston's oldest church building and still an active Episcopal Church. Located in the densely developed North End, the well-tended Wellington Garden to one side and Revere Mall across the street gives the building some relief from its neighbors. The design of William Price, a Boston print-seller and draftsman who, while in London, made a study of Sir Christopher Wren churches, produced a typical British model of brick with square tower base and steeple attached to a plan measuring 70 by 51 feet. The interior is a simple, U-plan with balconies and high-walled box pews. In the approved Church of England manner the pulpit is at the left—rather than the center according to Puritan tradition—its height enabling both those in the balconies and in the pews to see the minister, and vice versa.

It was from the handsome three tier, 175-foot wooden steeple of Christ Church on April 18, 1775, that Paul Revere's friend church sexton Robert Newman hung two lanterns that signaled that the British troops were arriving "by sea," thereby sending Paul Revere on his famous "midnight ride" to Lexington and Concord to warn Samuel Adams and John Hancock that the British were coming. Henry Wadsworth Longfellow's account in his poem, *The Midnight Ride of Paul Revere*, memorialized Old North's role at the start of the Revolutionary War.

Old North Church's steeple has been replaced twice since the display of the signal lanterns. During a violent gale in 1804 the steeple was blown down and replaced in 1808 following a design by Charles Bulfinch, lower in height by 16 feet. Destroyed by Hurricane Carol in 1954, the present steeple dates from 1955. The National Historic Landmark is Boston's oldest church building and still an active Episcopal church.

The battle popularly known as the Battle of Bunker Hill, although most of the fighting actually took place on nearby Breed's Hill, is the site of the Bunker Hill Monument and exhibit lodge. Located on the north side of the Charles River, the 221-foot-high granite obelisk marks the approximate center of a redoubt occupied by American forces. On June 17, 1775 a hard-fought bloody action with British regulars proved to be the bloodiest single battle of the Revolutionary War. After an intense two-hour hand-to-hand fight the Americans fell back to Bunker Hill. Although the Americans were defeated, the British took terrible losses and realized they were going to face a more difficult time with the rebels than expected.

Bunker Hill Monument

The National Historic Landmark monument of unprecedented height is the design of Solomon Willard and is constructed of grey Quincy granite 30 feet wide at the base and tapering to 15 feet near the apex. A railroad was created from the quarry in Quincy to move the slabs to Charlestown. Inside, visitors may climb 294 steps to an observation platform. Lafayette laid the cornerstone in 1825, and it was dedicated in 1843 by President John Tyler accompanied by Daniel Webster's stirring oration. At the base of the monument is a statue of the commander of the Charlestown forces Colonel William Prescott—he cautioned to withhold fighting with, "Don't fire [some accounts say 'shoot'] until you see the whites of their eyes"—in a spirited pose, by sculptor William Wetmore Story. The Greek Revival style Bunker Hill Lodge near the base replaced an earlier structure and was completed in 1903. The building houses the statue of General Joseph Warren who was mortally wounded on the field. Across the street at 43 Monument Square is the Bunker Hill Museum with exhibits and portraits of other key battle figures, battle memorabilia, and a 360-degree cyclorama mural depicting the battle.

Serving the nation from 1800 to 1974, Charlestown Navy Yard played an important role in the development and support of the U.S. Navy. After nearly 175 years of serving the fleet, 30 acres became part of Boston National Historical Park. The NPS visitor center orientation is in Building 5 and is the starting point for tours of the historic structures including the Commandant's House, USS *Constitution* Museum, the Old Paint Shop, Shipyard Gallery, and Dry Dock 1. The Commandant's House, the Muster House, and Ropewalk are closed to the public.

The USS *Constitution* is the black-painted oak hulled frigate that was considered the strongest, heaviest, and fastest ship of the day, and is dramatically afloat at pierside. Also known as "Old Ironsides," the forty-four-gun warship was launched in Boston on October 21, 1797. Today, standing aboard the deck of the oldest commissioned warship afloat in the world recalls days of the crew of 450 men on the fearsome vessel heeling to the wind with rigging towering 220 feet from keel to truck, overhead thirty-six sails carrying almost an acre of canvas on three masts, and the gun deck's thirty, 24-pound long gun cannons loaded for action.

Legend has it that during the War of 1812, while withstanding the brutal bombardment of the HMS *Guerriere* off Nova Scotia the British captain declared, "Huzzah, her sides are made of iron." The *Constitution* bore down on the *Guerriere* and after a pounding of massive broadsides took less than an hour for a stunning victory over the British ship. The venerable ship fought in over forty engagements, never beaten or boarded by an enemy. Major preservation work was completed for the bicentennial. The U.S. Navy conducts tours, and a stirring sight is the annual Turnaround Cruise on the Fourth of July.

"Old Ironsides," USS *Constitution*

The USS *Cassin Young* represents the type of ship built in the yard during World War II. The 2,050-ton, 376-foot-long Fletcher-class destroyer commissioned on December 31, 1943 was one of seventy-five built and decommissioned in 1960. She saw distinguished action in the Pacific Ocean during World War II and survived kamikaze attacks in the Battle of Okinawa.

Cape Cod National Seashore

Wellfleet, Barnstable County, Massachusetts

→ www.nps.gov/caco

→ The park is located on outer Cape Cod peninsula in southeastern Massachusetts. Reached via US Route 3 south from Boston via Sagamore Bridge in Bourne then along US Route 6 to Eastham and Provincetown, or from Providence, Rhode Island, via Interstate 95 north to Interstate 195, then to US Route 6, as above. The Salt Pond Visitor Center is located at Eastham; the Province Lands Visitor Center is located on Race Road, off Route 6, at the northern end of the park.

Highland Light (Cape Cod Light)

Cape Cod National Seashore, on a map of Massachusetts, is that familiar flexed forearm extending into the Atlantic Ocean and enclosing Cape Cod Bay. Before European contact, tribes of the Wampanoag people were here, and recorded by Giovanni di Verranazzo who sailed the area in 1524. Later explorers—the Englishman Bartholomew Goswold and Frenchman Samuel de Champlain—anchored at the Cape. The peninsula's prominence as a landfall attracted the Pilgrims' first landing in 1620 before going on to Plymouth. Later, settlers, whalers, and then generations of vacationers came for relief from eastern seaboard summer heat to the small colonial settlements, pristine beaches, grassy, shifting dunes, and mesmerizing ocean views. The Cape—as it is universally known in the east—stretching eastward toward Europe attracted Guglielmo Marconi to establish his wireless station at Wellfleet in 1903 and also was chosen as the place for submerged underwater cables to and from Europe.

Today, more than five million people annually come to the forty-mile sandy stretch of shoreline from Chatham to Provincetown containing 27,700 acres of land area (43,604 acres, including the offshore land within its boundaries) that includes beaches, scenic overlooks, ponds, trails, and historic towns and structures. Established in 1966 by Congress, the park was created through acquisition of state and town land, in addition to private properties. Development within the national park's boundaries was essentially frozen at 1959 levels. The National Park Service (NPS) oversees natural resources, historic homes, and a number of dune shacks within the seashore's boundaries, as well as eight lighthouses: Highland Light, Nauset Light, and the Three Sisters (owned and operated by the Coast Guard), and Long Point, Wood End, and Race Point (owned by the NPS).

Two of the eight lighthouses within Cape Cod National Seashore, Highland Light and Nauset Light, were relocated in 1996 back from the eroding cliffs of the Outer Cape. In both cases grassroots organizations alarmed by the proximity of the coastal bank to their beloved lights spurred governmental action to save the lights beginning in the early 1990s. Each lighthouse stood at a location served by two earlier generations of light towers, towers that had either been replaced over time or lost to the encroaching sea.

Traveling north on Route 6, the Highland Light is 3.3 miles north of Truro Center. Also known as Cape Cod Light, the original Highland Light built in the 1790s on a cliff 183 feet above sea level was the first lighthouse on the Cape. The present 66-foot brick tower with a first-order Fresnel lens replaced the deteriorating short-lived second lighthouse in 1857. By 1990, Highland Light's original distance of 500 feet from the shoreline was shortened by erosion to 100 feet. To protect the lighthouse, in a span of eighteen days in July of 1996, the lighthouse was moved to a new position 570 feet from the cliff. The Queen Anne style keeper's quarters was moved at the same time. The base of the lighthouse is open to the public daily during the summer (visitors over 51 inches tall can climb to the top of the light), and a concessioner offers tours from May to October.

Nauset Light

The nearby Highland House in North Truro, acquired by Cape Cod National Seashore in 1964, is home to the Truro Historical Society Museum, which houses a collection of items relating to Truro's history, including flotsam and jetsam from numerous shipwrecks. The present Highland House, built in 1907, replaced the original Highland House, a two-story clapboard farmhouse, built in 1835.

The Nauset Light, located one mile north of Coast Guard Beach on Ocean View Drive in Eastham, was one of two built in 1877 and moved from Chatham to Eastham

in 1923. The 48-foot cast iron, brick-lined tower is painted a distinctive red on the upper part and the lower part is white, with a black lantern. When threatened by shoreline erosion, in 1996 the lighthouse and keeper's quarters were settled onto the new

Race Point Light

Three Sisters Light

foundation 300 feet to the west via flatbed truck in a mere three days. The original
fourth-order Fresnel lens is now on display at the Salt Pond Visitor Center in Eastham.
The keeper's house is a private residence.

In 1838, three brick towers were built in a row on the cliffs of what is now the
Nauset Light Beach. Known as the Three Sisters, the towers fell victim to erosion in
1892. Although the only station in the United States designated by three towers, the
original configuration was replaced with three movable 29-foot-tall wooden towers.
Two of the towers were discontinued as beacons in 1918, sold, moved, and lanterns
discarded. This peculiar pilgrimage ended in 1983 when the three towers were moved
into their original configuration—150 feet apart and approximately 8.5 degrees off
north—and later restored at a site near Nauset Beach about a quarter mile from their
original location.

At the very tip of Cape Cod, on the west shore are three additional lighthouses.
Race Point Light is located approximately 2.5 miles from Provincetown at the northwestern tip of the Cape. Built in 1876, the 45-foot cast-iron tower lined with a brick interior is painted white with a black lantern. The adjacent two-story Victorian keeper's
residence, restored in 1998 along with the whistle house, is available for overnight
guests. Long Point Light is situated at the very tip of Cape Cod. In 1875, the original
structure was replaced with a new keeper's house and 38-foot brick tower painted
white. Only the tower and oil house remain. Nearby is the Pilgrim's monument marking first landfall. Wood End Light, built in 1872, is between Race Point and Long
Point, at the elbow of the sandbar that surrounds Provincetown harbor. The light
was designed as an exact replica of Long Point Light, the oilhouse is the remaining
support building.

Old Harbor Life-Saving Station, built around 1897, is the remaining bastion of
Cape Cod's U.S. Life-Saving Service. The design by architect George R. Tolman used

the same plans for at least twenty-seven other lifesaving stations. The rectangular plan is divided into two sections, one side as living space, and the other as a one-story, two-bay boat room. Decommissioned in 1944, the station was acquired by the NPS in 1973. Threatened by coastal erosion in its original location at Nauset (North) Beach in Chatham, the structure was floated by barge to its present location at Race Point in Provincetown in 1977. The station is open during the summer afternoons and historical reenactments of "Beach Apparatus Drill" rescues are performed weekly.

The Atwood-Higgins House in Wellfleet is an example of the quintessential Cape Cod house. The modest one-and-a-half-story wood-frame house (approximately 36 by 30 feet in plan) with a steeply pitched roof and a clapboard front with shingled sides was built in 1752. The restored interior contains a massive chimney centrally located in line with the front entrance. The door opens onto a tiny entrance hall, then immediately into parlors to either side. A narrow, winding stair leads to the second floor.

Captain Edward Penniman built his opulent French Second Empire style house on the west side of Town Cove in the Fort Hill section of Eastham in 1868. The entrance to the house's walkway is marked by a set of whale jaws, announcing Penniman's occupation as captain of a whaling ship. Although the architect is unknown, the imposing two-and-a-half-story, wood-frame structure is symmetrical in design with a characteristic mansard roof. The exterior is covered with clapboards and millwork trim painted in their circa 1890 colors: yellow clapboards, white trim, black window sashes, green window blinds, and brown and red roof shingles. The house interior is also symmetrical with two rooms on each side of a central hall. The restored interior is unchanged in plan as it was 1868 and most of the interior woodwork and hardware, the wall and ceiling coverings, and the "grained" finish on some of the woodwork are original.

The Cape Cod National Seashore dune shacks are among the most unusual historic structures in the National Park System. Located on the "Backshore" near Provincetown, amidst dunes reaching 80 feet high facing the ocean from Race Point to High Head, the remaining nineteen (2007) colorful small, weathered, and rustic-looking shacks range from one-room structures to multiroom cottages. Built originally on log skids that can be jacked up or moved to adapt to the shifting landscape, they now rest on pilings. The earliest shacks were built to shelter families of coast guardsmen stationed nearby. Sturdier replacements were discovered in the 1930s by many artists and writers who used them as retreats for inspiration, including poet e.e. cummings, painter Jackson Pollock, and writers Eugene O'Neill, Jack Kerouac, and Norman Mailer. Today, all but one is NPS owned. Eligibility for listing on the National Register of Historic Places contributes to a protected future for these unique structures and their associated landscapes. Nonprofit groups currently operate three of the shacks to provide "artist-in-residence" experiences. Other shacks are used by private individuals leased from the NPS. A ranger-led hike in summer visits one of the artists in residence.

Frederick Law Olmsted National Historic Site

Brookline, Norfolk County, Massachusetts

→ www.nps.gov/frla

→ From Boston, follow Route 9, Boylston Street, west to third stoplight past Brookline Village. Turn left (south)
on Warren Street to intersection with Dudley. Olmsted NHS is on right-hand corner with National Park Service
(NPS) sign and distinctive archway at house front. (Note that the park is closed for rehabilitation until 2010.)

Fairsted, Frederick Law Olmsted house (HABS/HAER)

The Frederick Law Olmsted National Historic Site at 99 Warren Street in Brookline,
Massachusetts, preserves the National Historic Landmark home and office where the
distinguished landscape architect and environmentalist lived and worked from 1883
until his death in 1903. Located in a leafy suburb of Boston, in the small estate Olmsted
(1822–1903) named "Fairsted," are the carefully restored National Park Service (NPS)
grounds Olmsted used as a laboratory to illustrate his principles for suburban living.
It was here that Olmsted established the world's first full-scale office for the practice of
landscape architecture in the country. The site is identified from the street by a spruce
log fence and arched gateway, a gently curving driveway revealing the "Olmsted" red
painted house through the dense plantings.

We spare the reader a lengthy treatment of Olmsted's extraordinarily adventurous
life and career that is well covered by biographers. A brief list of highlights range from
his early literary career to his design of New York City's Central Park, in association with
architect Calvert Vaux, and extends to a vast list of urban, city, state, and national parks;
educational and hospital campuses; zoos; residential subdivisions; and private estates.
The impact across the nation of Olmsted, his sons John Charles (1852–1920) and Freder-

ick, Jr., (1870–1957), and successors' philosophies and projects is described by the NPS:

> Perhaps more than any other person, Frederick Law Olmsted affected the way America looks. He is best known as the creator of major urban parks, but across the nation, from the green spaces that help define our towns and cities, to suburban life, to protected wilderness areas, he left the imprint of his fertile mind and boundless energy. Out of his deep love for the land and his social commitment he fathered the profession of landscape architecture in America....In what he created and what he preserved for the future, Olmsted's legacy is incalculable. The informal setting he made popular characterizes the American landscape....From the broadest concepts to the smallest details of his profession, the sign of Olmsted's hand is everywhere in our lives.

After managing Central Park's construction Olmsted moved to Brookline in 1881 and two years later purchased the two-and-a-half-story farmhouse, originally constructed in 1810. It served as both an office for his busy firm and as a home base for his extended family. Today's historical house resulted from the expanding needs of the world's first professional landscape architecture office.

The original farmhouse was extensively remodeled between 1883 and 1930 during the Olmsted family occupancy, with wings added, roofs raised for inserted upper floors, and the barn relocated and connected to the expanded residence. The house was both a family residence and the location of Frederick Law Olmsted's principal office and sole workspace of the firm prior to construction of the office complex, which be-

Fairsted, Frederick Law Olmsted house (HABS/HAER)

gan in 1889. A total of twenty-two rooms in four interconnected, two-story structures built between 1889 and 1925, all unified by the "Olmsted" red painted siding and dark green trim and shutters, served as the primary working office of the Olmsted design firm for nearly a century. A turn-of-the-century atmosphere prevails in the office and drafting room, with dark woodwork, antique drafting tables, and printing equipment. The plans vault, added in 1901, contains some documents of over 5,000 landscape design projects undertaken by the Olmsted firm from the 1860s to 1980.

The barn originally stood diagonally across from the house but was moved to its present location soon after 1883. Added to and extensively remodeled for office use by the Olmsteds, the barn functioned variously after 1914 as a model shop, photographic darkroom, soil-testing laboratory, and storage area. Upon completion, the 2007–2009 barn rehabilitation will provide space for education programs, public meetings, and exhibitions.

The fewer than two acres of Fairsted gardens were the Olmsteds' living laboratory to test design principles and concepts. In the woods, a hollow, a rock garden, and lawns are incorporated design techniques of perspective, vistas, and obscuring backgrounds. Deftly displayed here are recurrent themes in Olmsted designed parks: subtleties of the picturesque (the dramatic use of shadow and light) and pastoral (the use of greenery to soothe the spirit). An additional 5.35 acres of woodland was added to the site in 1998.

Thousands of visitors and researchers on a pilgrimage for inspiration come to the site each year; however, during an NPS major rehabilitation program the site is closed to visitors until 2010. Access during construction to the Olmsted Archives, preserving an extraordinary collection of Olmsted drawings and records of project documents, is available by appointment.

John Fitzgerald Kennedy National Historic Site
Brookline, Norfolk County, Massachusetts

→   www.nps.gov/jofi

→   The park is accessible by car and MBTA ("T"). Direct access from downtown Boston is via Beacon Street, turn right onto Harvard Street, and proceed for about one mile. Turn left onto Beals Street and continue to #83. The MBTA service to Brookline is along two routes of the Green Line. Take the "C" Cleveland Circle trolley to Coolidge Corner; walk four blocks north along Harvard Street, turn right onto Beals Street, and continue to #83. Or, take the "B" Boston College trolley to Babcock Street; walk four blocks south along Babcock Street, turn right onto Manchester Street, turn left onto Stedman Street, take the right fork onto Beals Street and continue to #83.

John Fitzgerald Kennedy birthplace house

The National Historic Landmark birthplace of President John Fitzgerald Kennedy was repurchased, restored, and given to the National Park Service (NPS) by the president's mother, Rose Kennedy, in 1969. The two-and-a-half-story Colonial Revival style house was five years old when the newly wedded Joseph and Rose Kennedy purchased and moved into the house at 83 Beals Street in Brookline, Massachusetts, in 1914. The future president was the second son born here, in a second floor bedroom on May 29, 1917. In 1920, the family now grown to four children moved to a larger house in the same neighborhood.

Kennedy, the thirty-fifth president of the United States, until in his early teens, walked and played, and went to school and church in this quiet suburb of Boston. It was a privileged life in a family that lived the American dream of prosperity and power in a few generations. The tragic end to his life on November 22, 1963 stilled the country, leaving a destiny unfulfilled. The promise of greatness lost—for the person and the nation—saddened a shocked and mournful world from the moment of the announcement of the assassination.

The meticulously restored house is noticeable along the row of homes by the American flag at the sidewalk's edge and a pristine exterior. Shingled walls painted in a pleasant shade of dark green, the wide porch and balustraded second floor balcony and window trim painted a yellow color, green shutters, and front gable dormers distinguish the house from its neighbors. Rose Kennedy personally supervised the restoration to the appearance at the time of the president's birth in 1917, with the assistance of Robert Luddington, a decorator with the prestigious Jordan Marsh retail store.

The compact house, a rectangular floor plan approximately 34 by 26 feet, was completely filled by the family with four children living active lives and two servants living on the third floor. Many objects throughout the house—first floor living room, dining room, and kitchen, and second floor bedrooms and study—were used by the Kennedy family from 1914 to 1920 and placed through the remembrances of Rose Kennedy. The house is filled with many significant mementos. The master bedroom, in which John F. Kennedy was born, is arranged in much the same way as it was on the day of his birth. Much of the furniture, photographs, and decorative pieces in the room belonged to the family during the president's years in the house. Other highlights of the collection include the bassinette that cradled him during his first nights in the nursery, the silver porringer bearing his initials, and the piano on which he later took lessons.

National Park Service ranger-guided tours lead small groups through the principal rooms of the birthplace. On self-guided tours, visitors can follow a multilingual audio tour with Mrs. Kennedy's recorded nostalgic personal reminiscences of family life in the house. The NPS makes several cautions to the visitor. First, the house is open seasonally and tour tickets are obtained in the basement level visitor center. Second, street parking in this neighborhood is limited to two hours. The NPS strongly recommends public transportation or a taxi to the site. And, finally, a minimal encroachment on the house for visitor facilities restricts the restroom facilities to one single-use room in the basement. Heed the caution; this is a residential community and there are no other public restrooms or vendors located in the immediate vicinity. The site currently is not accessible to wheelchairs. However, visitors with mobility impairments may request a "virtual" tour of the house.

Longfellow National Historic Site

Cambridge, Middlesex County, Massachusetts

→ www.nps.gov/long

→ The park is located at 105 Brattle Street in Cambridge, about one half-mile from Harvard Square. On-street parking is very limited in the neighborhood and public transportation is encouraged. From downtown Boston by MBTA ("T") take Red Line (Alewife) train outbound to the Harvard Square Exit and follow signs out of the station for Church Street. At intersection of Church and Brattle Streets, turn right onto Brattle and walk for 7-10 minutes. Longfellow NHS is on right-hand side of Brattle Street at #105.

Henry Wadsworth Longfellow House

Longfellow National Historic Site preserves the home of Henry Wadsworth Longfellow, one of the world's foremost nineteenth-century poets. The stately, pre-Revolutionary mansion (also known as the Vassall-Craigie-Longfellow House) located at 105 Brattle Street in Cambridge, Massachusetts, served as the headquarters for General George Washington during the Siege of Boston, July 1775 to April 1776. The National Historic Landmark house was occupied by Longfellow and his family for more than a century and is operated today by the National Park Service (NPS).

The magnificently Georgian Colonial–style Vassall-Craigie-Longfellow House is easy to spot on the tree-shaded street with its light yellow clapboards, white trimmed columns, pediment, dormers, and rooftop balustrade. Partially screened from the street by plantings, the brick walls, and a Chippendale fence, the gate at the sidewalk opens to a wide path; the broad lawn sweeps slightly upward to the main entrance. Surrounding the two-and-a-half-story mansion are elegant grounds containing a formal garden with heirloom plants and a pergola. This property is one of the remnants of the fine Loyalist (Tory) country estates along the Kings Highway from Boston to Watertown that once lined the street. Across the street is Longfellow Park, which preserved an unimpeded view of the Charles River from the house.

John Vassall, Sr., a wealthy merchant, purchased the property in 1746. His son, Colonel John Vassall, Jr., built the mansion in 1759 with many features typical of Georgian architecture, most notably its symmetry of the plan and facade, axial entrances, central hallway, and low-hipped roof. Four decorative, non-structural Ionic pilasters on the facade enhance the prominence of the house, as do the two man-made terraces, which raise the house approximately 4 feet and are surmounted by three short flights of sandstone steps. Other architectural features, such as a projecting central pavilion and a balustrade atop a hip roof, further enhance the prominent character of the house.

Abandoned by Vassall in 1774, the house was confiscated by the Continental Congress and eventually purchased by Dr. Andrew Craigie in 1792. He lavishly improved the mansion and grounds earning it the common reference of "Castle Craigie." Craigie also substantially increased the size of the house by relocating the north wall further north, adding a new hallway and enlarging the northeast parlor (now library), a two-story ell north of the hallway for a new kitchen and bedrooms, and one-story piazzas to the sides and rear. Craigie's additions were executed in Georgian Colonial and Federal-style details and totally compatible with the original structure.

After Craigie's death in 1819, his widow, Elizabeth, struggled with massive debts and rented rooms, often to Harvard students and faculty. Upon Longfellow's arrival in Cambridge to take the position as Smith Professor of Modern Languages at Harvard, he visited a friend at the Craigie house. In August 1837, he persuaded Mrs. Craigie to rent him rooms. A pleasure and inspiration to him, the house and grounds were a wedding gift to Longfellow and his wife Fanny from father-in-law Nathan Appleton in 1843. Longfellow cherished the house and improved the gardens. Here, for forty-five years, the poet entertained people from around the world and wrote his most popular works and translations, including *Evangeline* (1847), *The Song of Hiawatha* (1855), and *The Courtship of Miles Standish* (1858). In a tragic accident in the house in 1861, Fanny Longfellow's dress caught fire. Despite Longfellow's attempts to extinguish the flames, Fanny died the next day. Longfellow continued to live in the house until his death in 1882. The house remained in the Longfellow family until 1972, when it was acquired by the NPS. The house is open seasonally for NPS-guided tours.

A rehabilitation of the romantic Persian-pattern garden, and addition of the plantings, the trellises, and, especially, the magnificent pergola, was begun in 1904 by landscape architect Martha Brookes Hutcheson.

The Longfellow family filled the mansion with objects reflecting their interest in other cultures. European and Asian artwork, furniture, decorative objects, and books are found throughout the house. The Longfellow National Historic Site remains home to large archival and museum collections dating from the late seventeenth to the mid-twentieth centuries. The Longfellow family library contains 14,000 volumes. On exhibit or in storage are 35,000 items of historic furnishings and decorative arts, rare documents, letters, and family journals, as well as 12,000 photographs.

The Longfellow House is an example of dedicated private financial support, which supplements federal funding to preserve and maintain a heritage property. The tradition of preservation by private philanthropy began with the Longfellow Memorial Association shortly after Longfellow's death in 1882. It continues today through the Friends of the Longfellow House, established in 1994, who raise private funds and volunteer time to contribute to the preservation of the mansion, its gardens, and outdoor structures.

Lowell National Historical Park
Lowell, Middlesex County, Massachusetts

→   www.nps.gov/lowe

→   The park is located in the city of Lowell, Massachusetts, around thirty miles northwest of Boston. Take the Lowell Connector from either Interstate 93 or Interstate 495, exit at Thorndike Street north (Exit 35C). Drive about one half-mile to Dutton Street and follow signs to the Market Mills Visitor Center and adjacent parking lot at the corner of Market and Dutton Streets.

Mill on the Merrimack River

Lowell National Historical Park in the midst of the city offers an ambitious program to interpret a slice of the American Industrial Revolution. Founded as one of the first cities in America to be developed entirely as an industrial community, waterpower from the 32-foot drop in the Merrimack River controlled by an intricate system of canals and locks fueled the building of massive textile manufacturing mills. Although several of the major mills were either demolished completely or in part or converted to other uses, the remaining restored mills illustrate the transition from

farm to factory, replacing hand-assembled goods by integrated technology and the turning of raw materials into finished products in one building. The National Park Service (NPS) has joined in a rejuvenation of the city that was for years the nation's center of cotton manufacturing.

Today, the park preserves and interprets the city's virtually unaltered National Historic Landmark 5.6 miles of the canal and lock system, historic nineteenth-century cotton textile mills, machinery, and mill worker housing. Most informative for the visitor are the stories of the people who came to the mills for opportunities to better their lives, the history of immigrant labor and the subsequent diverse cultural identity of the city, and the stress of manufacturing moving elsewhere.

Eastern Canal, Boott Cotton Mills Museum

The eponymous Francis Cabot Lowell led a group of Boston investors in establishing the town in 1826. Reacting to the industrial slums of England, an employee structure was created using local farm girls during the mills' first two decades of operation. The paternalistic mill owners developed a benevolent society by building boarding houses—substantial three-and-a-half-story brick dwellings—for the women who worked seventy hours a week (at half the wages of men), and spent their "spare" time at company-sponsored classes and lectures. The Lowell Mills drew the industrialized world's attention to the city's utopian character and the apparent contentment of the workers.

By the middle of the nineteenth century Lowell's growth to one of the biggest textile-manufacturing centers in the world required more and more labor. Strife began over wages and work demands and a wave of immigrants—Irish, French Canadians, Poles, Greeks, and other Eastern Europeans—flocked to the mills, creating today's cultural diversity. By the end of the nineteenth century the utopia days had ended and Lowell struggled with the same problems of other American industrialized cities with aging equipment, fierce competition with Southern mills and, finally, the Depression. By the 1960s, Lowell's appearance was typical of the Northeast's other industrial cities with blight and decay, vacant storefronts, and empty lofts. In the 1970s and 1980s a partnership of a spirited local group and the NPS focused on the city's ethnic and industrial heritage by rehabilitating historic downtown buildings, the mills, and canals.

There are several ways to tour the park, starting at the restored Market Mills Visitor Center for an orientation and where reservations can be made for several tours of the city, including the seasonal two-and-a-half-hour canal boat Mill and Canal Tour, by trolley, and on foot. The NPS Visitor Center is illustrative of the integration of city building rehabilitation and NPS structures in the park with rental housing in upper floors, and mixed-use ground floor retail space. Spanning the street opposite the visitor center is a massive brick vault, once the foundation of the Boston and Lowell Railroad Depot, and a restored Boston & Maine locomotive and rail car. Highlights of the walking, canal, or trolley tours are the buildings and locks along the Merrimack Canal, Eastern Canal, and canyon of red brick walls of some of Lowell's oldest mills on the lower Pawtucket Canal. Also seen along the tours are the Suffolk Mills with a turbine exhibit (two blocks west on Father Morissette Boulevard), and the Boott Cotton Mills boardinghouse and mill building.

Boott Cotton Mills clock tower

The Lowell boardinghouse system was based on company-built housing, typically, three-and-a-half-story brick structures housing twenty to forty people and containing a kitchen, a dining room and parlor, a keeper's quarters, and up to ten bedrooms. The majority of the residents were single females, known as "mill girls." The company boardinghouses were closely supervised and extended to the moral guardianship and physical care of the young factory women. One example of the system is the restored Boott Cotton Mills boardinghouse, the last of eight rows built in the Georgian style between 1835 and 1838 (approximately 150 feet long and 36 feet wide). Unseen now is the Boott Corporation's chilling effect on the workers living in an orderly and rigidly disciplined society in this parade of buildings with gable-roofed dormers, tall chimneys, and symmetrically placed windows. The boardinghouse, with an outdoor theater in Boarding House Park, is the summertime site for concerts, plays, and festivals, contains the Mogan Cultural Center with "mill girl" exhibits. The building also houses the Center for Lowell History of the University of Massachusetts Lowell.

The Boott Cotton Mills is one of the oldest surviving textile mill complexes in the country and considered the best example of mill architecture in Lowell. Sensitively rehabilitated by a private developer in 1989–90 for use as office and technology space, the building retains many of its original architectural and working loom floors. The square bell tower, a distinctive Lowell landmark, is around 125 feet from ground to the tip of the finial. The tower is composed of a six-story brick base, then a 50-foot-tall clock and bell cupola, and topped by a golden shuttle. The massive six-story mill building (five floors above grade) is flooded by daylight from the almost floor to ceiling multilight windows. The approximately 45-foot interior width of the loom floors with one row of central columns amply housed at the mill's peak in 1890 more than 2,000

Boott Cotton Mills boardinghouse

Weave room at the Boott Cotton Mills Museum

workers operating over 4,000 looms and other textile machines. On the ground floor the visitor can walk on the creaking wood board floors and hear the roar of a mere eighty-eight operating power looms. Upstairs are excellent exhibits about the Industrial Revolution, and the history of Lowell's mill era.

Minute Man National Historical Park
Lexington, Lincoln, and Concord, Middlesex County, Massachusetts

→ www.nps.gov/mima

→ The park is located twenty-two miles northwest of Boston along State Highway 2A between the towns of Concord and Lexington. Minute Man Visitor Center is on Route 2A in Lexington, less than one mile west of the intersection of Routes 2A and I-95/Route 128 (Exit 30B).

Concord's North Bridge

Minute Man National Historical Park preserves and interprets the sites, structures, and landscapes connected with the opening battle of the Revolutionary War on April 19, 1775 at Lexington and Concord. The clash of colonial minute men and British soldiers on this twenty-mile winding, hilly route is the scene of the events known to history as "the shot heard round the world." A five-mile stretch of restored Battle Road Trail is walked and biked by some one million visitors a year to view the beautiful New England scenery of restored historic buildings, rolling hills, farmlands, marshes, wetlands, streams, and cemeteries.

Begin your visit at the Minute Man Visitor Center for an orientation at the attractive structure near the park's eastern entrance. Starting at the visitor center, the Battle Field Trail traverses farm fields, wetlands, and forests and connects historic "witness"

Minute Man statue

houses and landscapes from Meriam's Corner in Concord to the eastern boundary of the park in Lexington. After park authorization in 1959, the National Park Service (NPS) purchased more than 300 land parcels between Fisk Hill and Meriam's Corner to create the trail and restore the historic landscape to the eighteenth-century appearance. Hiking or biking the trail is strongly recommended. Driving and stopping at parking lots along Route 2A to visit structures and places of significant events is also an alternative.

Continuing west towards Concord, the restored Samuel Brooks House was built in 1753 in an area that was farmed by the Brooks family as early as 1652. Samuel Brooks, a member of the Continental army, lived in the house on April 19, 1775 at the time of the Concord and Lexington battle. The two-story house's central portion (40 by 30 feet in plan), is a side-gable, wood post and girt framed structure with a central brick chimney, set on a fieldstone foundation. Nearby are three houses (not open to the public) associated with members of the Brooks family: Noah Brooks, Job Brooks, and Joshua Brooks.

Around 0.75 miles west, at Meriam's Corner where the brown clapboard Meriam House was already seventy years old in 1775, sporadic fire between the darting and weaving militiamen and the British grew intense, and continued as the British marched east along the Battle Road. The NPS purchased the Corner and the two-story, five-bay "witness" house with a large central chimney and brightly painted red door. Author Henry David Thoreau was born near here and was inspired by the landscape.

The next stop along the park tour westward is The Wayside, a National Historic Landmark house associated with the Revolutionary War and nineteenth century writers. Built around 1700, The Wayside was the home of Samuel Whitney, muster master of the Concord Minute Men. The house is easily identified from the highway by its brightly painted yellow siding and white trim, and tall brick chimneys. Over the years, alterations and extensions to a typical two-story post-and-girt framed structure on a granite stone foundation resulted in a sprawling mansion with the additions of two-story wings, Victorian trim, a three-story vaulted tower, and piazzas. During the literary renaissance of the nineteenth century it was home to famous authors. Louisa May Alcott lived here from 1845 to 1848 where she wrote her first published novel (*Little*

Hartwell Tavern

The Wayside

Women); Nathaniel Hawthorne owned it from 1852 to 1868; Harriett Lothrop, using the pen name "Margaret Sidney" wrote the Five Little Peppers series at this "Home of Authors." The house is open for guided tours and the interior is preserved to the time of Lothrop's death in 1924.

New Bedford Whaling National Historical Park

New Bedford, Bristol County, Massachusetts

→ www.nps.gov/nebe

→ The park is in the city of New Bedford in southeast Massachusetts fifty miles south of Boston via Interstate 93 to Massachusetts Routes 24 and 140 and thirty miles east of Providence, Rhode Island, via Interstate 195.

Visitor Center, former New Bedford Institution for Savings

New Bedford, Massachusetts, is a contrast of remnants of a great whaling port filled with historic structures and a modern working port, home to hundreds of commercial fishing vessels. Within a thirteen-block National Historic Landmark District, New Bedford Whaling National Historical Park recalls the days when the city was the nineteenth century world's center of whaling and one of the nation's wealthiest cities. The drive of about one hour from Boston, and less from Providence, Rhode Island, rewards the visitor with a comfortable walking district of cobblestone streets, including a working waterfront, that contains a visitor center in a restored historic structure and a collection of privately owned and operated properties. The visitor should plan on a full day to walk the district lined with stately buildings, banks, storehouses, and residences from the days that Herman Melville, in *Moby-Dick*, asserted "The town itself is perhaps the dearest place to live in, in all New England."

The visitor should begin a walking tour of the historic district at the National Park Service (NPS) Visitor Center at 33 William Street. Ranger-led guided tours start from the center. This rare example of Italian Renaissance style in an era of Greek Revival style monumental banks was built in 1854 for the New Bedford Institution for Savings. The ornate facade of the two-story structure in smooth brown sandstone is on a granite base with a low enclosing granite wall open at the center for steps to the main entrance. In addition to serving as a bank, the building was a courthouse, auto parts store, antique mart, and a bank again before restoration by the NPS.

Diagonally across the street from the visitor center at the corner of William and North Second Street is the oldest continuously operating U.S. Custom House. The austere Greek Revival–style building, designed by Robert Mills, architect of the Washington Monument, was built in 1836. A 10-foot-deep portico with four Doric unfluted columns and pediment projects from the main two-story building mass (approximately 53 by 51 feet in plan). Exterior walls are rough faced granite ashlar. A peculiar, tall cupola with four corner chimneys was added to the building in the 1860s. The interior is arranged around an east-west central hall. Here, captains came to clear cargos through customs and seamen registered, like Herman Melville who sailed from New Bedford on a four-year whaling voyage on the *Acushnet* in January of 1841.

Seamen's Bethel

Prominent at 15 Johnny Cake Hill is the Seamen's Bethel, a landmark in New Bedford's waterfront area from completion in 1832 and known as the Whalemen's Chapel in Melville's *Moby-Dick*. Built by New Bedford citizens concerned with the moral welfare of thousands of seamen, the Bethel was intended as a moral oasis in the waterfront area. The building is a simple New England meeting house form (approximately 43 feet wide by 56 feet deep) with ship-lapped siding and shingled side and rear walls. A tall tower with chamfered corners projects from the front facade and contains the ground floor main entrance, with a large window above it. The building is especially memorable for the inspirational interior. Walls are lined with thirty-one black marble cenotaphs inscribed with names of sailors lost at sea and box pews and side galleries focus on the unusual bow-shaped pulpit. Although Melville described such a pulpit, it was, at the time, a product of his imagination. The popularity of the John Huston-directed 1950s film version of *Moby Dick*, staring Gregory Peck, drew many visitors to the Bethel. The current pulpit was built in 1961 to fill that void. The Bethel is open to the public Memorial Day through Columbus Day.

Seamen's Bethel interior

Mariners' Home

The Mariners' Home next to the Seamen's Bethel has provided lodgings for transient seamen for more than 140 years. The large but unpretentious Federal-style mansion was originally the home of William Rotch, Jr., the grandson of Joseph Rotch, an early leader of New Bedford's whaling industry. It was built in 1787 on the corner of William and North Water Streets and, after donation to the New Bedford Port Society in 1851, moved in the late 1850s 200 feet from its original location to Johnny Cake Hill. East and west walls are yellow narrow clapboard siding; north and south walls are in Flemish bond brick with stringcourses at each floor. The five-bay front has a central, pedimented entrance. The three-story building (approximately 51 feet wide and 44 feet deep) stands on a 5-foot-high dressed granite base. The Mariners' Home is not open to the general public.

Across the street from the Bethel and Mariners' Home at 18 Johnny Cake Hill is the New Bedford Whaling Museum. Heralded as the world's preeminent whaling museum, the complex of historic and modern structures occupies an entire city block and is a must during a visit to the New Bedford Whaling National Historical Park. There is a large collection of scrimshaw, figureheads, marine paintings, and tools of the whaler's trade, rare whale skeletons, and an enormous painting of a whaling voyage. The museum's pride is a half-scale replica of a full-rigged whaling bark, the *Lagoda*; at 89 feet it is the largest ship model in the world.

A walk toward the waterfront passes two important buildings connected to the whaling era. The Double Bank Building at 56–62 North Water Street on New Bedford's "Wall Street" once housed two banks, the Merchants Bank and the Mechanics Bank. Designed by architect Russell Warren and built in the mid-1830s, each owner employed a different builder on the two-story smooth granite ashlar Greek Revival structure. A projecting portico with eight wooden Doric columns and Ionic entablature above uses a unique interpretation of column entasis for each tenant. The Rodman Candleworks building on Water Street is typical of structures in the waterfront district. Built for production of spermaceti candles, the structure was built in 1810 of granite rubble covered with stucco and then scored to look like a block of granite. The candleworks closed in 1890 and the building is now occupied by a popular restaurant and professional offices.

The thriving nineteenth-century waterfront, once the scene of maritime-related businesses and wharves, was reduced by 1960s and 1970s urban renewal and road-building to the current preserved structures and port. A self-guided walking tour passes several historic structures. Local historic preservation efforts preserved the Sundial Building, an 1820 brick-and-stone identified by the eponymous vertical sundial on the Union Street facade. The building now houses the New Bedford Whaling Museum administrative offices. The Wharfinger Building, formerly the offices of the city port manager, was the site of the city's seafood auction from 1947 to 1985, and now serves as the city-operated Waterfront Visitor Center. The original Works Progress Administration 1934 Dutch Colonial brick building has a one-story modern addition that houses an NPS exhibit on the contemporary working waterfront.

The two-masted 156-foot schooner *Ernestina* was launched as the Grand Banks fishing vessel *Effie M. Morrisey* in 1894. After multiple ownerships with careers exploring the arctic and as a packet, carrying immigrants and goods between the Cape Verde Islands and the United States, in 1982 the Republic of Cape Verde donated the restored vessel to the people of the United States, where additional restoration retained the schooner's exceptional integrity. Now docked at the New Bedford State Pier, the black-hulled National Historic Landmark vessel sails regularly with passengers during summer months as the official vessel of the Commonwealth of Massachusetts.

Around a ten-minute walk from the visitor center on a full city block of gardens, the stately Rotch-Jones-Duff House and Garden Museum was built for whaling merchant William Rotch, Jr., in 1834 and designed by Richard Upjohn. The National Historic Landmark is a fine surviving example of a New Bedford Greek Revival mansion, as described in *Moby-Dick* "...nowhere in all America will you find more patrician-like houses; parks and gardens more opulent, than in New Bedford...all these brave houses and flowery gardens...." Furnished period rooms display the decorative arts, furniture, and belongings of the families and time frame. The museum offers permanent and changing exhibits, lecture series, and community and educational programs.

Salem Maritime National Historic Site

Salem, Essex County, Massachusetts

→ www.nps.gov/sama

→ The site is on Derby Street in Salem a forty-five minute drive north of Boston via Route 1 to Exit 45 and then Route 128 North to Route 114. Follow signs to the Salem Visitor Center (near a pay-parking garage) and a five-minute walk to the site's NPS Orientation Center on Derby Street.

East Indiaman *Friendship*

During the Great Age of Sail, when Salem's wharves were lined with ships returning from global voyages to Africa, India, and the Far East, great fortunes flowed into this waterfront New England settlement. Today, Salem can be easily traversed by foot and visitors can admire nearly four centuries of distinctive architecture, enjoy numerous visitor attractions, and learn about a rich maritime heritage. On the city's waterfront, Salem Maritime National Historic Site contains ten historic structures and three historic wharves that interpret this rich maritime history.

Starting points for a visit to the National Historic Site are the Salem Visitor Center, operated by the National Park Service (NPS), and the NPS Orientation Center on Derby Street. The visitor center on New Liberty Street, across from the municipal parking garage and next to the Peabody Essex Museum, is five blocks from the waterfront in a building that was once the Salem Armory. The orientation center is housed in a late eighteenth century warehouse and is typical of the type of structure that once lined Salem's many wharves. The building was originally located on Front Street in downtown Salem and was moved to its present site in 1977. Most of the original materials of the building have been replaced over time, with the exception of the frame, which can be seen in the buildings's interior.

The imposing red brick Federal style Custom House, surmounted by a gilded eagle clutching arrows and a shield was built in 1819 to house offices for the U.S. Customs Service, as well as the attached Public Stores warehouse. Outstanding architectural

Custom House

Derby House

features include the Palladian window above the composite order, balustraded portico; the round-headed first floor windows; main entrance with fanlights and sidelights; and octagonal cupola. The front block of the T-plan structure is the two-story Custom House (approximately 48 by 40 feet) on a raised granite-walled basement; the attached rear three-story warehouse is approximately 70 by 28 feet in plan. Fine original woodwork is seen in the interior with the preserved office and desk where Salem native son Nathaniel Hawthorne worked from 1846 to 1849. He described the Custom House in the opening pages of The Scarlet Letter. Behind the Custom House is the one-story Scale House. The red brick, single-room structure with a slate-shingle gable roof still houses the nineteenth-century Customs Service scales used for weighing cargo on board ships. Facing the Custom House are three wharves remaining in Salem from the more than fifty extending into Salem Harbor—Central Wharf, Hatch's Wharf, and Derby Wharf. Reaching nearly a half-mile into the harbor, Derby Wharf was the longest wharf constructed in Salem. Built by Elias Derby from 1764 to 1771 and completed at its present length in 1806, the wharf was lined with warehouses that were the hub of Derby's trade empire.

Anchored at Derby Wharf is a full-size replica of the three-master, square-rigged 342-ton East Indiaman Friendship. The original ship, completed in 1797 across the river from Salem Maritime National Historic Site, was authentically reproduced in the Scarano Shipyard in Albany, New York, from detailed documentation in 1996 to 1998. The ship is open for tours and sails only with NPS staff and volunteer crew. At the end of Derby Wharf is the white-painted brick lighthouse, 12 feet square and 14 feet tall, with a black lantern completed in 1871. Restored by Friends of Salem Maritime in the early 1980s, the light was relit by the U.S. Coast Guard in 1983.

The Hawkes House is a fine example of the large late Georgian style homes built throughout Salem in the late eighteenth and early nineteenth centuries for wealthy shipping merchants. Construction on this three-story, five-bay hip-roofed house, designed by famous Salem architect Samuel McIntire whose houses line the streets of Salem, was started for Elias Derby in 1780. Derby, however, never completed the house, and the unfinished building was purchased and completed around the year 1800 by Benjamin Hawkes, who owned a shipyard next to Derby Wharf. Today, the bright yellow-painted clapboard Hawkes House contains the administrative offices for Salem Maritime National Historic Site.

The Derby House, built in 1762, is prominent in the waterfront grouping of buildings and faces Derby Wharf. Built by Captain Richard Derby in 1762 as a wedding gift for his son, Elias Derby, this fine example of Georgian style architecture was the home of Salem's most prominent and successful merchant for twenty years. The central hall floor plan of the five-bay facade is T-shaped with an original two-and-a-half-story front block (approximately 44 by 28 feet) and a kitchen ell (approximately 24 by 22 feet) added in 1811. Pairs of chimneys flush with exterior walls are on the east and west ends. The use of brick on this gambrel-roof house, rather than the more commonly used timber, reflects the owner's wealth. The oldest brick house remaining in Salem, the restored structure is furnished with period pieces and has outstanding interior details, including the intricately hand-carved main stair, paneling, and fireplace mantels.

In the block to the rear of the Hawkes House is the gray-painted clapboarded Narbonne House. The high peaked, gable-roofed portion was built by butcher Thomas Ives in 1675, with a gambrel-roofed addition built in 1740. The house is a remarkable example of a Salem middle-class home of the seventeenth and eighteenth centuries.

The West India Goods Store, built circa 1800 by merchant Henry Prince, was originally a warehouse, and later became a shop selling imported goods, as connoted in the name. Moved twice and restored by the NPS, the shop sells spices and other trade goods, just as it did nearly two centuries ago.

At the east end of the site is St. Joseph Hall, built by St. Joseph's Polish Roman Catholic Society. The building initially served as the religious, social, and political center for Polish immigrants. In 1988, the NPS purchased the property and it is used for multiple purposes.

Saugus Iron Works National Historic Site

Saugus, Essex County, Massachusetts

→   www.nps.gov/sair

→   Saugus is ten miles northeast of Boston. From Route 1 northbound take the Main Street Saugus Exit and
follow the National Park Service signs east through Saugus Center to the iron works. From Route 1 southbound
take the Walnut Street Exit (East) and follow the National Park Service signs 1.5 miles to the iron works.

Reconstructed forge

The once rural, agricultural area on the edge of the wilderness north of Boston along
the Saugus River was chosen by Richard Leader, successor to the founder of the Company of Undertakers of the Iron Works in New England and John Winthrop, Jr., son of
the governor of the Massachusetts Bay Colony, as the site of an integrated iron works
where raw materials would be converted into finished products in a single place. Today, the Saugus Iron Works National Historic Site, a National Historic Landmark,
contains the reconstructed blast furnace, a forge, a rolling mill, a blacksmith shop,
the restored seventeenth century Ironworks House, a museum, and a National Park
Service (NPS) Visitor Center.

The site of Leader's venture had vast holdings of forests and iron ore providing
abundant raw materials. The settlement known as Hammersmith, built around one
of the most advanced iron mills of its time, flourished for a brief period. Production
began in 1646 and closed in 1668, ended by high production costs, low capital, mis-
management, and lack of skilled labor. During operations, finished products loaded
at the dock on the tidal Saugus River onto shallow draft boats were brought to Boston where they were transferred onto ships for shipping elsewhere. The Saugus Iron

Works helped lay the foundation for the nation's future iron and steel industry and workers and technicians who trained here went on to establish new mills and manage existing ones.

The reconstruction of the iron works, financed by the American Iron and Steel Institute, began with meticulous archeological excavations under the supervision of Roland Wells Robbins in 1948. Led by Conover Fitch of the architectural firm of Perry, Shaw, Hepburn, Kehoe, and Dean, and supported by a team of technical consultants and the archeological findings, the extensive research produced a fascinating recreation of the seventeenth-century iron works. After six years the iron works opened to the public in 1954 to the acclamation of preservationists for its authenticity and depiction of early industrial America.

When in operation, the iron works was a din of noise and smoke; the blast process would run continuously for thirty to forty hours, waterwheels churning away, and smoke curling upward from chimneys at the forge and rolling and slitting mill. Today, the iron works' reconstructed buildings are the massive rubble stone-sided blast furnace with a bridge for trundling material into the furnace's charge hole, where the huge waterwheel powered bellows at the hearth and melted bog iron ore was tapped and hardened into "sows"; the forge, operated by waterwheels raising and dropping a 500-pound hammer to form the iron "sows" into wrought-iron "merchant bars"; and the rolling and slitting mill producing pieces of flat bar for shipment and slit rods later cut into nails. A blacksmith worked in a small shop producing finished products for the ironmaking plant. Today, NPS blacksmiths make tools for demonstration purposes. The small warehouse building next to the dock held products ready for shipping.

The Iron Works House was probably built by Samuel Appleton, Jr., a grandson of the last owner-operator of the iron works. The house, one of the remaining First Period seventeenth-century homes in New England, has steep gables, diamond-paned leaded casement windows, batten doors, an immense central chimney, and ornamental drops suspended from the second floor overhang. In the interior are the approximately 2-foot-square original exposed ornamentally carved timbers of native oak. The 9-foot-wide fireplace in the parlor contains pot hooks and cranes cast at the iron works' furnace in 1646; the ones featured in upstairs rooms are reproductions. Altered from its original condition over the years, the Iron Works House was restored by Wallace Nutting in 1915.

To the side of the Iron Works House is a small NPS Visitor Center, and to the rear is a museum containing artifacts found at the iron works. The site is open from April 1 to October 31 and contains a half-mile nature trail through woodlands and tallgrass marsh. It is a delight to visit the picturesque site, especially when groups of school-children, some dressed as colonials, watch the waterwheel operating twin 18-foot bellows, learn about the iron working process, and observe a blacksmith demonstration, just as it was when in operation 350 years ago.

Springfield Armory National Historic Site

Springfield, Hampden County, Massachusetts

→ www.nps.gov/spar

→ The park is located in the city of Springfield, Massachusetts, and accessed by Interstates 91 and 90 (Massachusetts Turnpike). From Interstate 91 southbound take Exit 5 (Broad Street) or northbound Exit 4 (Broad Street) and follow city signs to the park and Springfield Technical Community College sharing the site bounded by Federal, State, Byers, and Pearl Streets. The entrance is from Federal Street and parking is available next to the Armory Museum.

Main Arsenal/Museum

The hilltop location of the Springfield Armory National Historic Site overlooking the Connecticut River in Springfield, Massachusetts, is the site of the building complex that played an important role in American military and industrial history. The original Armory stretched over two city blocks where the National Historic Landmark is now co-administered by the National Park Service (NPS) with Springfield Technical Community College (STCC) that occupies most of the twenty-two original buildings in a creative adaptation of historic structures. The 55-acre Springfield Armory National Historic Site portion of original armory property includes the Main Arsenal, Master Armorer's House, Commanding Officer's Quarters, and open land. The integration of the historic site with the community college presents a mixture of early-nineteenth-century brick buildings, some renovated for college use, and contemporary educational buildings. Deactivated as a military installation in 1968, the Main Arsenal Building operated by the NPS is open to the public by appointment or for scheduled tours and contains a superb museum of firearms.

The Armory evolved from its origins as a Revolutionary War arsenal for ammunition and weapons storage in 1777 into the site selected by George Washington as an armory (a second one was at Harpers Ferry) for weapons manufacturing. Over the next 174 years the Armory served as a center for production and research and development of shoulder arms, and innovative manufacturing techniques. The military's fascination with interchangeable parts led to the pioneering introduction of mass production. Most United States armed service small arms were developed in the laboratories at Springfield Armory by inventors who increased the Armory's fame through their innovations. Here, in 1819 Thomas Blanchard developed a special lathe to turn out identical shapes; Eskine S. Allin converted the muzzle-loading Civil War rifle-muskets into breech-loading rifles; the 1903 Springfield Rifle and 1917 Enfield Rifle were designed and manufactured; and John Garand invented the famous M1 Garand rifle, a World War II staple weapon. The greatest number of employees, mostly civilians, was in World War II from 1941 to 1945 when over 14,000 men and women worked around the clock fabricating over 4.5 million M1 Garand rifles.

The entrance to the site from Federal Street passes the historic fence, a curtain of steel 9-foot palings, alternating as pikes and spearheads, set into a red Longmeadow sandstone base. The steel was cast from melted cannons. A historic brick gatehouse completed in 1876 (12 by 14 feet in plan), and symmetrical in exterior appearance with a hip roof extending over corner columns), and then the long three-story structure, now the STCC Administration Building, screens the large open green space of Armory Square. The spacious square was created as a grand design by commanding officers Roswell Lee and James W. Ripley in the 1840s, arraying two and three-story brick buildings around a treed lawn.

Main Arsenal interior

A one-way drive passes the rear of historic structures on the south side of the square, some dating from the early 1800s and leads to parking in front of the Main Arsenal Building, now the Armory Museum. Completed in 1850, the structure—purportedly partially copied from the design of the East India House in London—provides a visual terminus of the west end of the square, its tower reflecting that of the administration building at the opposite end of Armory Square. The imposing scale of the massive brick building (approximately 89 feet wide and 189 feet long) represents the structure's function: storage of arms. The proportions, symmetry, and fenestration suggest a classic Renaissance Revival influence. The long facade's three tiers of windows (arched ground floor and rectangular upper openings) and a regularity of brick pilasters and windows express interior structural bays. The cornice is at a height of 50 feet and the clock/bell tower projecting from the center of the east facade (approximately 26 feet square) reaches 84 feet and 6 inches to the tower roof. The gable-roof pavilion on the west facade's center is 69 feet wide and projects 12 feet. A principal interior feature is the tower's spiral stairway set in a circular well. The second floor museum contains a large collection of standard and experimental small

Commandant House

Commanding Officer's Quarters

arms, interpreting the history of small arms design and production.

Located northwest of the Main Arsenal, the Commanding Officer's Quarters is a large imposing Greek Revival–style house completed in 1847 and now houses administrative offices for the Springfield Armory National Historic Site. The two-story symmetrical main section (approximately 48 by 45 feet in plan) with a front porch, a Victorian addition of cast-iron columns and decorative panels running the length of the building, has a two-story wing 35 feet wide and 56 feet long. The hip-roofed building has an encircling cornice and railing and is topped by a square cupola with four corner chimneys. The center hall plan has double parlors to one side and a library and dining room on the other side.

At the east end of Armory Square is Building 16, now serving as the Community College main administration building. Three two-story buildings erected on this site between 1817 and 1824 were connected and unified by a third floor during the Civil War. The tower was added to balance the tower of the Main Arsenal at the opposite end of the green.

To the rear of the college buildings lining the north side of the Armory Square are several examples of red brick Greek Revival style. The Master Armorer's House (Building 10) was moved to its present location in 1895 and reduced in size by partial demolitions. The officer's quarters and Building 19 were completed during the Civil War. The long, two-story structure with tall arched ground floor doorways was built originally as a storehouse for wood used in gun stocks; it has also been known as a casern, a combination stable/barracks for cavalry, and may be one of the best remaining examples of this type of facility in the United States. In 1863, when the foundations were being dug, the remains of twelve soldiers buried in full regimentals were found, presumably soldiers quartered here during the War of 1812.

Before visiting check for dates and times for museum tours, live firing demonstrations, seasonal encampments, and outdoor concerts.

New Hampshire

Saint-Gaudens NHS

● CONCORD

ATLANTIC

OCEAN

Saint-Gaudens National Historic Site

Located in western New Hampshire in Cornish, Sullivan County, New Hampshire

→ www.nps.gov/saga

→ The site is located just off NH 12A in Cornish, New Hampshire. The park can be reached via Interstate 89 (Exit 20, West Lebanon); take US 5 north to Windsor and cross the covered bridge to NH 12A, or Interstate 91 (Exit 8, Ascutney) and drive twelve miles south on NH 12A.

Little Studio (foreground), Aspet (rear)

Augustus Saint-Gaudens, one of America's foremost sculptors, came to the rolling New Hampshire hills overlooking the Connecticut River in 1885 to find a summer retreat from New York City. He rented a former country inn (called Huggins Folly) and a few years later bought the Federal-style structure and transformed it into an elegant mansion, converted a hay barn into a studio, and began landscaping the grounds. Today, the approximately 150-acre former Saint-Gaudens estate, contains the Saint-Gaudens house (Aspet) furnished with family possessions, studios, stable and ice house, galleries, and carefully crafted gardens with over one hundred of the artists' works.

Brought to America in 1848 at the age of six months by his French father and Irish mother, Saint-Gaudens grew up in New York City and was apprenticed as a cameo cutter and attended art classes. After study at the École des Beaux-Arts and in Rome, he returned to New York and won his first major commission in 1876: a monument to Civil War Admiral David Glasgow Farragut. Tremendously successful, the work led to other public commissions, including *Diana* for the original Madison Square Garden (now at the Philadelphia Museum of Art), the Memorial to Colonel Robert Gould Shaw and the 54th Massachusetts Regiment in Boston (see page 554), and the Adams Memorial in

Washington, D.C.'s Rock Creek Church Cemetery. Bronze casts of these sculptures can be seen at the historic site. Saint-Gaudens also completed other public statues, reliefs, plaques, and medallions and coins.

The Aspet mansion was built around 1800 as an inn. At first unimpressed on a dreary April 1885 visit, Mrs. Saint-Gaudens persuaded the sculptor to rent the house as a relief from New York City summer weather. Saint-Gaudens came to appreciate the setting with a spectacular view of Mount Ascutney. He engaged architect George Fletcher Babb to extensively remodel the late Georgian style house's interior, including the graceful, curving stairway, and add elegant porches and a wide terrace encircled by an ornate fence around three sides of the house. Later work added electricity, changed the brick gable ends to a stepped parapet, painted the red brick exterior white, and added the second floor sun room. The attractive front entrance and tall brick chimneys were retained. The barn was suitable for a makeshift studio and Saint-Gaudens soon became highly productive and enchanted by the life and scenery. Renaming the property Aspet, after Saint-Gaudens's father's birthplace in the south of France, the family spent summers there from 1885 to 1900 (he purchased the inn in 1891), except for three years in Paris. From 1900 to the time of his death in 1907, Saint-Gaudens lived there year-round.

Other well-known artists followed the sculptor's arrival in Cornish. Aspet became the center for the "Cornish Colony" of painters, architects, musicians, actors, and writers. In 1905, members of the art colony produced a play at the site to honor Saint-Gaudens's twentieth year at Cornish. The Greek temple stage set was later redone in marble and now holds the remains of the Saint-Gaudens family.

Also on the site is the converted barn, the Little Studio, with a long pergola and containing a large sky-lit open sculpting space with a version of the statue of Diana; the stable and ice house containing an exhibit of horse-drawn vehicles; the Ravine Studio used by the sculptor-in-residence; and the Picture and New Gallery Buildings with changing exhibits of Saint-Gaudens's and other artists' work.

Little studio interior

A delight in visiting the attractive Saint-Gaudens National Historic Site countryside setting is the superbly maintained flower and cutting gardens, spacious lawns, the quarter-mile Ravine Trail, and scenic two-mile trail through the unspoiled Blow-Me-Down woodlands. Check for seasonal openings of the buildings for ranger-led tours, summer concerts, and sculpture workshops. The grounds are open year-round.

Rhode Island

→ Touro Synagogue National Historic Site (p. 545)

PROVIDENCE
Touro Synagogue NHS

ATLANTIC
OCEAN

Touro Synagogue National Historic Site

Newport, Newport County, Rhode Island

→ www.nps.gov/tosy

→ The site is located in downtown Newport at 85 Touro Street one block north of Washington Square near the intersection with Spring Street.

Touro Synagogue interior

Touro Synagogue is the oldest synagogue in the United States and the only one that survives from the colonial era. Sephardic members of Rhode Island's first Jewish community founded the congregation Yeshuat Israel in 1658 with assurances by Roger Williams that all who came within the borders of the Colony of Rhode Island and the Providence Plantations were free to practice their religion. A century later, under the leadership of Reverend Isaac Touro, ground was broken for the synagogue on August 1, 1759 and dedicated December 2, 1763. This National Parks System area is under the supervision of the Touro Synagogue Foundation. The National Historic Site is home to an active congregation preserving and enriching this extraordinarily fine American religious building.

Peter Harrison, who by then was considered the colonies' most distinguished Georgian-style architect after completing King's Chapel in Boston and Christ Church in Cambridge, designed Touro Synagogue, considered his finest work. Although it presents a humble buff colored brick exterior to the street, the interior is one of the most accomplished rooms in the American colonies. The interior treatment, including carved wooden furnishings and galleries, is a rich, sophisticated work characteristic of late-eighteenth-century English and Continental design. Most of the architectural elements are Harrison's interpretation of the Palladian Revival, freely adopted from details inspired by James Gibbs, but they were incorporated with an emphasis on space and detail. Some authorities believe that Bevis Marks, the Spanish and Portuguese synagogue (1701) on Hencage Lane in London—the oldest in England—was influential in the Newport building, particularly for its centralized, two-aisled temple interior. The Sephardic Synagogue in Amsterdam is also seen by some as a model for the Touro structure.

The Touro Synagogue, set in a spacious lawn and separated from the sidewalk by a wrought-iron fence with intermediate Egyptian Revival stone piers and an arched gateway with a pedimented cap, is turned at an acute angle from the street in order for the Ark of the Covenant to face east toward Jerusalem. A square Ionic columned portico painted brown with a sanded finish shelters the main entrance. A molded doorway topped by a molded triangular pediment with dentils frames the women's entrance in the north wing. All windows in the synagogue are round-headed with finely molded frames and a double-hung sash stopped by a glazed fan. The overall dimensions of the main two-story structure are approximately 45 by 39 feet with a two-story north wing (approximately 28 by 16 feet). A brown sandstone belt course is set into the brickwork at the second floor line. A steep hipped roof on the main portion is covered with slate shingles.

The subdued plain exterior is contrasted with the richness of the temple's dramatic interior, a two-story rectangular volume (approximately 40 by 30 feet). The modest sized space is impacted on three sides by women's balconies, and by the bema (central reading desk) and sanctuary for the ark (an ornately carved cupboard for storing the Torah), occupying much of the central floor space. Twelve columns signifying the twelve tribes of ancient Israel, Ionic below and Corinthian above, support the galleries. Each column is carved from a single tree. Details and carvings on columns, balustrade with turned and tapered balusters, molded railings, and entablature are executed with fine precision, the balusters around the bema and sanctuary repeating those defining the galleries. The lofty coved ceiling, rising to 32 feet above the floor, has a rectangular inset panel framed by a carved molding with a running neoclassical guilloche design. A massive twelve-branch candelabrum is suspended from the center of the ceiling; four smaller brass candelabra hang from the ceiling corners. Above the ark is a representation of the Ten Commandments in Hebrew, painted by the Newport artist, Benjamin Howland.

During the Revolutionary War the synagogue experienced difficulties from English occupation (as did Newport) and almost the entire congregation dispersed to New York. One of the few public buildings in Newport to survive the Revolution undamaged, the synagogue served as the meeting place for the Rhode Island General Assembly and for sessions of the Supreme Court of Rhode Island (1781–84). On a 1790 visit George Washington was presented with an address by Moses Seixas, warden of the synagogue. Washington replied in a letter to "The Hebrew Congregation in Newport," paraphrasing the address:

> For happily the government of the United States, which gives to bigotry no sanction, to persecution no assistance, requires only that they who live under its protection should demean themselves as good citizens, in giving it on all occasions their effectual support.

For much of the nineteenth century the synagogue was closed. The generosity of the sons of the first spiritual leader, Isaac Touro, and the funds' management by their sister ensured the synagogue's preservation. Permanently reopened in 1883, as the Congregation Jeshuat Israel—a different spelling but still meaning the Salvation of Israel—Touro Synagogue is an active house of worship with a thriving congregation. This inspiring building is open for daily tours (call in advance for hours and tours) in the summer months except Thursdays, Saturdays, and Jewish holidays.

Vermont

New England

BURLINGTON

★ MONTPELIER

Marsh-Billings- ○
Rockefeller NHP

Marsh-Billings-Rockefeller National Historical Park

Woodstock, Windsor County, Vermont

→ www.nps.gov/mabi

→ The park is located off VT 12 in Woodstock, Vermont, and reached via Interstate 89 from Concord, New Hampshire, and Boston, Massachusetts; Interstate 91 from Hartford, Connecticut; and Interstate 87 (New York State Northway) from Albany, New York. From Interstate 89 take Exit 1 (US 4) west thirteen miles to Woodstock and follow signs to the visitor center parking lot.

Marsh mansion

Nestled among Vermont's Green Mountains with their winding valleys, small farms, and picturesque villages, the Marsh-Billings-Rockefeller National Historical Park focuses on conservation history and land stewardship in America. Located in Woodstock, Vermont, a charming village on the banks of the Ottauquechee River, the park is named for three families influential in conservation history. The park was the boyhood home of George Perkins Marsh, pioneering conservationist, and later the home of Frederick Billings who developed a model farm and forest. His legacy was continued by his granddaughter Mary French Rockefeller and her husband Laurance S. Rockefeller. Visitors can begin their visit at the Carriage Barn, tour the Mansion (furnished and containing a splendid art collection) and grounds, and walk the twenty miles of trails and carriage roads in the 643-acre park's forest. Across Vermont Highway 12, adjacent to the visitor parking, is the Billings Farm & Museum, a working dairy farm and museum of agricultural life operated in a partnership between the National Parks Service (NPS) and The Woodstock Foundation.

George Perkins Marsh was born in Woodstock, in 1801, educated at Dartmouth College in Hanover, New Hampshire, and taught briefly before becoming a lawyer and moving to Burlington, Vermont. He subsequently became a member of the U.S. House of Representatives. On his trips home to Vermont, Marsh was profoundly disturbed by the changes he observed in the countryside, plagued by loss of population, overgrazing, and economic decline. Later, while serving as ambassador to the Kingdom of Italy, Marsh saw the devastation caused by deforestation in Europe, and observed Europeans devising land management plans to remedy the damage. In 1864, his vision of how man could control his imprint on the natural world appeared in his book *Man and Nature*, considered a seminal text in the founding of the conservationist and environmental movements.

In 1807, George's father, Charles Marsh, Sr., built a large brick house with Federal-style detailing and proportions on the Woodstock property, placing it on a bridge over the Ottauquechee River on the village's grandest residential street, Elm Street. In 1869, Frederick Billings, a Vermont native who made his fortune as an attorney and real estate developer during the California Gold Rush, bought the farm and house from the Marsh family. He retained architect William Ralph Emerson of Boston to renovate the house, and began buying up additional land. The dramatically changed three-and-a-half-story mansion (approximately 78 by 129 feet, overall, excluding porches) bore little resemblance to the old Marsh house, although the exterior brick walls and some of the window and door openings were retained. Entrances were revised, and additions included a new brick englargement of the rear service wing, a full third floor, tall chimneys with ornamental brickwork, a mansard roof, a wrap-around verandah, gables, bay windows, and porches trimmed with lattice and spindle work. Stick style ornamentation prevailed in 1885–86.

Mary French Rockefeller, granddaughter of Frederick Billings, and her husband Laurance S. Rockefeller, inherited the estate in 1951. They remodeled the Mansion and its adjacent outbuildings, and modernized the Billings Farm. While the Rockefellers made modest changes, including removing the two second- and third–floor balcony porches; stripping paint off the exterior red brick walls and painting the trim white; updating electricity and plumbing; and replacing many wallpapers, paints, and upholsteries, nonetheless most of the original lighting fixtures, furnishings, and works of art were retained, and the Billings Mansion remained largely unchanged from its appearance circa 1886. In 1967 the mansion was declared a National Historic Landmark. In 1992, the Rockefellers donated the residential property, along with 555 acres of Mount Tom forestland, to the NPS. The Marsh-Billings-Rockefeller National Historical Park opened on June 5, 1998.

The mansion interiors, which date from 1869 exhibit fine craftsmanship. The reception room is finished in mahogany; the dining room has a richly carved oak fireplace, a built-in sideboard, and elaborate parquet flooring; the central hall has an oak-paneled ceiling and stairway with fine spindle and dado work; and the library is finished in walnut with burled veneers. The parlor has two fireplaces with Tiffany tiling and heavily embossed and gilded wallpaper of the period. There are excellent Tiffany stained glass windows in the parlor and library.

A highlight of the daily tour is a stroll through the grounds and gardens, designed initially by landscape architect Robert Morris Copeland for Frederick Billings. The large glass greenhouses that originally adjoined the gardens were designed by the New York architect Detlef Lienau. The garden plantings were enhanced for Billings's daughters in the early twentieth century by Ellen Shipman and Martha Hutchinson, two important early female landscape architects working in the Colonial Revival style. By the 1930s, the greenhouses had been mostly demolished. The Rockefellers refreshed the formal gardens in the 1960s, with the help of landscape architect Zenon Schreiber. The Belvedere, a two-story building in the Swiss Chalet style, can also be seen from the gardens. It was originally a recreation building and annex to the greenhouses, and contains a modernized bowling alley.

Today, visitors to the Marsh-Billings-Rockefeller National Historical Park can learn about conservation stewardship as they explore the interconnected stories of the mansion with its landscape art, the formal gardens and grounds; the managed woodlands climbing the slopes of Mount Tom; and the Billings Farm, where sustainable agriculture is practiced on the 200-acre working farm.